The International Economics of
WINE

World Scientific Studies in International Economics
(ISSN: 1793-3641)

Series Editor   Keith Maskus, *University of Colorado, Boulder, USA*
Editorial Board Vinod K. Aggarwal, *University of California-Berkeley, USA*
    Alan Deardorff, *University of Michigan, USA*
    Paul De Grauwe, *London School of Economics, UK*
    Barry Eichengreen, *University of California-Berkeley, USA*
    Mitsuhiro Fukao, *Keio University, Tokyo, Japan*
    Robert L. Howse, *New York University, USA*
    Keith E. Maskus, *University of Colorado, USA*
    Arvind Panagariya, *Columbia University, USA*

World Scientific Studies in International Economics includes works dealing with the theory, empirical analysis, and evaluation of international economic policies and institutions, with topics covering international macroeconomics and finance, international trade theory and policy, as well as international legal and political economy. Monographs and edited volumes will comprise the core of the publications.

Vol. 73   *The International Economics of Wine*
    edited by Kym Anderson (University of Adelaide, Australia &
    Australian National University, Australia)

Vol. 72   *Foreign Direct Investment*
    by Bruce A Blonigen (University of Oregon, USA & National Bureau of
    Economic Research, USA)

Vol. 71   *Offshoring: Causes and Consequences at the Firm and Worker Level*
    edited by Holger Görg (Kiel Institute for the World Economy, Germany) &
    Aoife Hanley (Kiel Institute for the World Economy, Germany)

Vol. 70   *Policy Externalities and International Trade Agreements*
    by Nuno Limão (University of Maryland, USA)

Vol. 69   *Economic Analysis of the Rules and Regulations of the World Trade Organization*
    edited by Kamal Saggi (Vanderbilt University, USA)

Vol. 68   *International Trade, Capital Flows and Economic Development*
    edited by Francisco L. Rivera-Batiz (Columbia University, USA) &
    Luis A. Rivera-Batiz (University of Puerto Rico, USA)

Vol. 67   *Megaregionalism 2.0: Trade and Innovation within Global Networks*
    edited by Dieter Ernst (East-West Center, USA &
    The Centre for International Governance Innovation/CIGI, Canada) &
    Michael G. Plummer (The Johns Hopkins University, SAIS, Italy)

Vol. 66   *International and Interregional Migration: Theory and Evidence*
    edited by Francisco L. Rivera-Batiz (Columbia University, USA)

Vol. 65   *International Trade Theory and Competitive Models:*
    Features, Values, and Criticisms
    by Ronald W. Jones (University of Rochester, USA)

The complete list of the published volumes in the series can be found at
https://www.worldscientific.com/series/wssie

73 World Scientific Studies in International Economics

The International Economics of
WINE

Editor
Kym Anderson
University of Adelaide and
Australian National University, Australia

NEW JERSEY · LONDON · SINGAPORE · BEIJING · SHANGHAI · HONG KONG · TAIPEI · CHENNAI · TOKYO

Published by

World Scientific Publishing Co. Pte. Ltd.
5 Toh Tuck Link, Singapore 596224
USA office: 27 Warren Street, Suite 401-402, Hackensack, NJ 07601
UK office: 57 Shelton Street, Covent Garden, London WC2H 9HE

Library of Congress Cataloging-in-Publication Data
Names: Anderson, Kym, author.
Title: The international economics of wine / Kym Anderson.
Other titles: World Scientific studies in international economics.
Description: Hackensack, NJ : World Scientific, 2019. | Series: World Scientific studies in international economics | Includes bibliographical references.
Identifiers: LCCN 2019008587 | ISBN 9789811202087 (hardcover)
Subjects: LCSH: Wine industry. | Wine--Economic aspects.
Classification: LCC HD9370.5 .A53 2019 | DDC 338.4/76632--dc23
LC record available at https://lccn.loc.gov/2019008587

British Library Cataloguing-in-Publication Data
A catalogue record for this book is available from the British Library.

Copyright © 2020 by World Scientific Publishing Co. Pte. Ltd.

All rights reserved. This book, or parts thereof, may not be reproduced in any form or by any means, electronic or mechanical, including photocopying, recording or any information storage and retrieval system now known or to be invented, without written permission from the publisher.

For photocopying of material in this volume, please pay a copying fee through the Copyright Clearance Center, Inc., 222 Rosewood Drive, Danvers, MA 01923, USA. In this case permission to photocopy is not required from the publisher.

For any available supplementary material, please visit
https://www.worldscientific.com/worldscibooks/10.1142/11327#t=suppl

Desk Editor: Yulin Jiang

Typeset by Stallion Press
Email: enquiries@stallionpress.com

Preface and Acknowledgements

I am indebted to my co-authors, and to the original publishers, of the articles included in this volume (both listed below), for their permission to reprint them. I am also grateful for the financial support provided for the research underlying them, especially by Wine Australia and its part-predecessor, Australia's Grape and Wine Research and Development Corporation, as well as the Australian Research Council, the Winemakers Federation of Australia, and the Faculty of the Professions at the University of Adelaide. All research funders are acknowledged in the first footnote of each article.

My co-authors of the included articles, in alphabetical order with their affiliation at the time the research was undertaken, are Julian Alston (University of California, Davis), Nick Berger (University of Adelaide), Joseph Francois (University of Berne), Kimie Harada (Chuo University and Australian National University), Alexander Holmes (University of Adelaide), Hans G. Jensen (University of Copenhagen), Giulia Meloni (Catholic University of Leuven), Douglas Nelson (University of Tulane), David Norman (University of Adelaide), Olena Sambucci (University of California, Davis), Guenter Schamel (University of Bolzano), Johan Swinnen (Catholic University of Leuven), Ernesto Valenzuela (University of Adelaide), Glyn Wittwer (Monash University), Danielle Wood (University of Adelaide) and Xueyan Zhao (Monash University).

The publishers with current copyright of the included papers, who have kindly given permission to reprint these articles, in alphabetical order are Annual Reviews Inc. (Article 26), Cambridge University Press

(Articles 3, 6, 11, 13, 15, 21, 22, 23 and 25), Elsevier (Articles 1, 5 and 14), Taylor & Francis (Article 24), Wiley-Blackwell Publishing (Articles 2, 4, 7, 8, 9, 10, 12, 17, 18 and 20), and Winetitles (Articles 16 and 19).

Kym Anderson
Adelaide, Australia
July 2019

Contents

Preface and Acknowledgements   v
Introduction   xi
    Kym Anderson

A.   Globalization of Wine   1

Chapter 1   A Model of the World's Wine Markets   3
Glyn Wittwer, Nick Berger and Kym Anderson

Chapter 2   Globalisation of the World's Wine Markets   27
Kym Anderson, David Norman and Glyn Wittwer

Chapter 3   Modeling Global Wine Markets to 2018: Exchange Rates, Taste Changes, and China's Import Growth   51
Kym Anderson and Glyn Wittwer

Chapter 4   Intra-Industry Trade in a Rapidly Globalizing Industry: The Case of Wine   91
Kym Anderson, Joseph Francois, Douglas Nelson and Glyn Wittwer

Chapter 5   How Might Climate Changes and Preference Changes Affect the Competitiveness of the World's Wine Regions?   115
Kym Anderson

| Chapter 6 | U.K. and Global Wine Markets by 2025, and Implications of Brexit | 131 |

Kym Anderson and Glyn Wittwer

| Chapter 7 | Cumulative Effects of Brexit and Other UK and EU-27 Bilateral Free-Trade Agreements on the World's Wine Markets | 147 |

Kym Anderson and Glyn Wittwer

B. Australia's Wine Internationalization — **167**

| Chapter 8 | Accounting for Growth in the Australian Wine Industry, 1987 to 2003 | 169 |

Glyn Wittwer and Kym Anderson

| Chapter 9 | Who Gains from Australian Generic Wine Promotion and R&D? | 189 |

Xueyan Zhao, Kym Anderson and Glyn Wittwer

| Chapter 10 | Wine Quality and Varietal, Regional and Winery Reputations: Hedonic Prices for Australia and New Zealand | 225 |

Günter Schamel and Kym Anderson

| Chapter 11 | What Determines the Future Value of an Icon Wine? New Evidence from Australia | 255 |

Danielle Wood and Kym Anderson

| Chapter 12 | Australian Wine Industry Competitiveness: Why so Slow to Emerge? | 283 |

Kym Anderson

C. Market Developments in Caucasia and Asia — **309**

| Chapter 13 | Is Georgia the Next "New" Wine-Exporting Country? | 311 |

Kym Anderson

| Chapter 14 | Asia's Evolving Role in Global Wine Markets | 347 |

Kym Anderson and Glyn Wittwer

Chapter 15	How Much Wine Is *Really* Produced and Consumed in China, Hong Kong, and Japan?	379
	Kym Anderson and Kimie Harada	

D. Distortions to Wine Producer Incentives and Consumer Prices — **405**

Chapter 16	On the Impact of the Canada-United States Free Trade Agreement on U.S. Wine Exports	407
	Kym Anderson	
Chapter 17	Impact of the GST and Wine Tax Reform on Australia's Wine Industry: A CGE Analysis	415
	Glyn Wittwer and Kym Anderson	
Chapter 18	Excise and Import Taxes on Wine Versus Beer and Spirits: An International Comparison	437
	Kym Anderson	
Chapter 19	Excise Taxes on Wines, Beers and Spirits: An Updated International Comparison	461
	Kym Anderson (with the assistance of Nanda Aryal)	
Chapter 20	Wine Export Shocks and Wine Tax Reform in Australia: Regional Consequences Using an Economy-Wide Approach	479
	Kym Anderson, Ernesto Valenzuela and Glyn Wittwer	
Chapter 21	How Much Government Assistance Do European Wine Producers Receive?	505
	Kym Anderson and Hans G. Jensen	

E. Internationalization of Winegrape Varietal Choices — **527**

Chapter 22	Changing Varietal Distinctiveness of the World's Wine Regions: Evidence from a New Global Database	529
	Kym Anderson	

Chapter 23 Drifting Towards Bordeaux? The Evolving Varietal
          Emphasis of U.S. Wine Regions   559
          Julian M. Alston, Kym Anderson and Olena Sambucci

Chapter 24 Evolving Varietal and Quality Distinctiveness
          of Australia's Wine Regions   599
          Kym Anderson

F. Convergence in National Alcohol Consumption Patterns   629

Chapter 25 Convergence in National Alcohol Consumption
          Patterns: New Global Indicators   631
          Alexander J. Holmes and Kym Anderson

Chapter 26 Global Alcohol Markets: Evolving Consumption
          Patterns, Regulations, and Industrial Organizations   671
          Kym Anderson, Giulia Meloni and Johan Swinnen

Introduction

Kym Anderson

A few years ago, World Scientific kindly invited me to put together a collection of my writings on *Trade, Development and Agriculture: Essays in Economic Policy Analysis* (Volume 20 in this series of World Scientific Studies in International Economics, 2013). In doing so, I chose to leave out my writings on wine economics, since wine was of minor importance to all but a handful of developing countries and not a large part of almost any country's foreign trade or its agricultural sector.

For those same reasons wine economics has been — until recently — a tiny field of economic scholarship. In addition to being a small contributor to global gross domestic product (GDP), the wine industry has not been growing in *volume terms*: world production in the 1950s was barely double that of the 1860s, and that volume is no higher now than it was in the 1960s.

However, wine sales have begun growing in *value terms*, with global consumer expenditure doubling in nominal US dollars since the start of this millennium. This suggests a dramatic rise in the quality of wine consumed. Indeed prices of the finest wines from the best regions now can be thousands of dollars per bottle. Those prices can vary substantially from year to year though, according to perceptions of buyers as to how weather during the growing season will affect the future price of each wine (bearing in mind that, being an experience good, its quality cannot be ascertained prior to consumption). As well, climate change is increasing the frequency and magnitude of extreme weather events at the same time as altering the mean and variance of key climate indicators such as annual temperature and rainfall. This is increasing the uncertainty associated with investments by both producers (in vineyards and terroir-based brand development) and consumers (in storing fine wines for future consumption or subsequent resale).

Alongside those changes have been large increases over the past quarter-century in:

- the number of countries in which wine is a sizable share of national alcohol consumption,
- in particular the emergence of East Asia, and especially China and Hong Kong, as an important wine-importing region,
- the share of global wine production volume that is exported, which has risen from an average of 10% during 1860–1990 to 40% during 2012–17, and
- the quality of wine exports, with the unit value of global wine exports trebling in nominal US dollars between the 1980s and 2013–17 despite the huge increase in the volume of exports.[1]

The unique features of wine, the spreading of wine culture, and the expansion of wine expenditure and international trade and foreign direct and portfolio investment have led to a huge increase in economic analyses of wine production, investment, consumption and trade. That in turn has prompted the creation of two new economics journals (the *Journal of Wine Economics* by Cambridge University Press, and *Wine Economics and Policy* by Elsevier), the publication of at least two large handbooks, namely the *Handbook of the Economics of Wine* (Ashenfelter *et al.* 2018) and *The Palgrave Handbook of Wine Industry Economics* (Alonso Ugaglia, Cardebat and Corsi 2019), and the expansion of the Annual Conference of the American Association of Wine Economists to more than 150 paper presenters each year.

---

[1] Unless otherwise indicated, data quoted in this Introduction are from Anderson and Pinilla (2017) or, in the case of consumer expenditure, from Holmes and Anderson (2017).

New World countries were major contributors to the massive growth in wine exports after the 1980s, led initially by Australia. In seeking to understand this development, Australia's role in it, and the implications for various wine-producing and -consuming countries, a wine economics research program was launched at the University of Adelaide in the late 1990s. Initially it was a program of research within the University's globally focused Centre for International Economic Studies, but it grew enough to become its own Wine Economics Research Centre from 2010 (see www.adelaide.edu.au/wine-econ).

This volume brings together a subset of papers from that research program that were first published in academic and industry journals between 2001 and 2018 and that relate to the internationalization of this fascinating product.

The volume is divided into six sections, and articles are presented within each section in chronological order according to their original publication date. Those sections are: globalization of wine, Australia's wine internationalization, market developments in Caucasia and Asia, distortions to wine producer incentives and consumer prices, internationalization of winegrape varietal choices, and convergence in national alcohol consumption patterns in both wine-exporting and wine-importing countries.

The rest of this chapter provides a brief guide to those articles, but that is preceded by outlining two preparatory steps that were necessary for this research program to progress: compiling national and global annual time series data, and building economic models of national and global wine markets.

First preparatory step: Compiling data

Before beginning empirical analysis of trends, cycles and shocks to national and international wine markets, it was necessary to first assemble annual time series data. A beginning was made for Australia by Osmond and Anderson (1998). Their data stretch back to 1850, which put Australia's boom in vine plantings during the 1990s into *historical perspective*. That compilation was subsequently updated and greatly expanded by Anderson (2015) so as to include also regional and winegrape varietal data. Those data reveal that the country had four previous booms in vine area and wine production, each followed by a long plateau or slump; but in none of those previous booms did Australia become very export focused or a significant player in global wine markets.

Also necessary were global annual data, so that each country's wine production, consumption and trade developments could be seen in *international perspective*. To that end, two statistical compendia were generated in the late 1990s (Anderson, Berger and Stringer 1998; Anderson, Berger and Spanhi 1999), which were subsequently blended and updated regularly, including by Anderson and Norman (2003) and Anderson and Nelgen (2011). As well, global databases were compiled on changes in the bearing area of winegrapes by variety and region (Anderson 2013) and on changes in the volume and value of wine and other beverage consumption (Holmes and Anderson 2017). Those data only illuminated the most-recent globalization wave, however. To be able to compare and contrast developments in that era with those in the first globalization wave a hundred years before, the national and global market data were pushed back to 1860 (and forward to 2016) by Anderson, Nelgen and Pinilla (2017), and even earlier for some countries by Anderson and Pinilla (2017). That was possible thanks to the willing cooperation of two dozen colleagues from around the world as a stepping stone to preparing national chapters for a volume on wine's globalization over the past two centuries (Anderson and Pinilla 2018).

Second preparatory step: Building economic models

Once comprehensive national and global wine production, consumption and bilateral trade data were compiled in the late 1980s, it made sense to build a model that captured those national components of global wine markets. A prototype was built by Berger (2000) and fine-tuned by Wittwer, Berger and Anderson (2003 — Article 1).[2] The model has been expanded and updated several times. Its most-recent version, which distinguishes four wine types, is detailed in the Appendix to Anderson and

---

[2] Articles reprinted in this volume are cited in this chapter by their author and original year of publication and then 'Article x', where x refers to the number of the article listed in the table of contents.

Wittwer (2017 — Article 6), pending a further expansion in 2019–20 to include beer and spirits, the other key alcoholic beverages.

In parallel with that, a computable general equilibrium model of the Australian economy (Dixon *et al.* 1982) was adapted to simulate the effects of shocks at home and abroad on the grape and wine industry by region. The first version simply divided the nation into South Australia (responsible for the majority of the country's wine production and exports) and the rest of Australia (Wittwer 2000). It has since been updated and disaggregated into 30 wine regions and six residual regions, and the same four wine types as in the global wine model so that domestic regional impacts on Australia's wine trade from shocks to global wine markets can be simulated (see http://www.monash.edu.au/policy/oranig.htm and Anderson, Valenzuela and Wittwer 2011 — Article 20). This national model is being further improved and updated during 2019–20.

Globalization of wine and Australia's wine internationalization

Globalization of the wine industry had been slowly progressing for eight millennia, but with very little product trade. The cultivation of *Vitis vinifera* grapes (by far the most suitable for winemaking) began around 6000BC in or near the Caucasus region. It spread west to the eastern Mediterranean from 2500BC, and spread north into much of Europe by 400AD. It then took another 1100 years before spreading to Latin America from the 1520s, South Africa by 1655, Australia by 1788 and California and New Zealand by 1820 (Unwin 1991). But it involved mostly the transfer of vine cuttings and grape and wine production knowhow rather than trade in wine, since wine deteriorated quickly prior to the use of corked bottles which only began to be used from the 1700s (Johnson 1989, pp. 195–98).

Nor did the first globalization wave that ended at the outbreak of World War I affect global wine markets much except in one important respect, namely, the transfer of the tiny phylloxera insect from the United States to Europe. That insect devastated the majority of Europe's vineyards. It led to French vignerons investing hugely in nearby Algeria, whose share of global wine markets rose from 0.1% in 1870 to 8% of production and more than 40% of exports by 1910. But if colonial Algeria is thought of as part of France (as the French Government did), then the share of global wine production that was exported was no higher at the end of the first globalization wave — nor indeed in 1960 — than it was in 1860, at around 5%. By contrast, exports as a share of global wine production grew from 5% to 15% during 1960–90, and then to 40% by 2012. In the past half-century (the second globalization wave), wine has switched from being one of the world's least-traded agricultural products to one of the most traded internationally. This has been an unprecedented boom for consumers everywhere. There have been huge improvements in the quality and diversity of wines available to middle-income consumers in an ever-expanding number of countries, at very affordable prices.

Not all winegrowers have benefitted though. The rapid expansion in wine exports from the Southern Hemisphere since 1990 put additional pressure on European producers who, since the early 1960s, had been facing declining demand in their domestic markets (Anderson, Norman and Wittwer 2003 — Article 2). More recently, winegrowers in some newly exporting countries have been struggling to retain competitiveness too, while others (e.g., in New Zealand and the United States) have been enjoying high wine and hence grape prices.

Why did it take until quite recently for temperate New World countries with ideal winegrape growing conditions to develop a comparative advantage in wine? Most were net importers of wine prior to 1900, despite Europe's phylloxera epidemic devastating traditional supplies from Europe. To shed light on this, a group of economists from both Europe and the New World recently analyzed developments in all key countries and regions (Anderson and Pinilla 2018). That multi-authored volume examines each national wine market in the lead up to and during the first and second globalization waves and in the decades between them. It also looks at how the timing, length and amplitude of each country's wine cycles compare with those in other countries, and how its wine market developments affected other countries. In doing so, those case studies focus on the roles of new technologies, and of policies, institutions, real exchange rate movements, beverage preference changes, and international market developments. That new volume is thus a major advance over the studies brought together in Anderson (2004), which focused mainly on the New World takeoff in wine exports from the late 1980s to the early 2000s. It also enabled a more-complete analysis than in Anderson (2015) of Australia's dramatic rise from the late 1980s, relative decline in the decade to 2016, and then turnaround in its international competitiveness in wine (Anderson 2018 — Article 12).

To get a sense of the relative importance of different forces that have or could have an impact on wine's globalization and on national markets, a series of model simulation studies have been published over the past two decades. An early one looked at the sources of growth in Australia's wine industry in the 1990s (Wittwer and Anderson 2001 — Article 8). Productivity growth is shown to be one of the important contributors. Who along the supply chain gains most from research and development (R&D) investments aimed at boosting productivity, as compared with investments in generic wine promotion at home and abroad, is explored by Zhao, Wittwer and Anderson (2003 — Article 9). That study shows that foreign consumers of Australian wine enjoy a significant share of the global economic benefits from Australian grape and wine R&D investment. It also shows that producers get a far larger share of the benefit from export promotion than from domestic promotion. Promotion can affect prices of wines in various ways though. Schamel and Anderson (2003 — Article 10) show the extent to which regional generic promotion, as distinct from winery brand promotion (and winegrape variety), influences prices paid for individual wines. When it comes to the most iconic of Australia's fine red wines, though, their secondary market price variation across different vintages is shown by Wood and Anderson (2006 — Article 11) to be largely determined by a small number of weather variables in the grape growing season — information that is freely available to buyers at the time of harvesting (as first found for the best of Bordeaux wines by Ashenfelter, Ashmore and Lalonde 1995).

The emergence of New World wine exporters added to rather than displaced European wine exporters, with both contributing to the rapid rise in the share of global wine production that crosses national borders. But a further contributor has been the expanding complexity of demands for wines as incomes have grown. This is leading to many wine-exporting countries also importing more wine (Anderson *et al.* 2016 — Article 4). Another reason for that expansion in so-called intra-industry international trade has been the emergence of winegrape growing in cool-climate regions of the world where consumers were previously reliant mostly on imported wines (Anderson 2017 — Article 5).

Yet another contributor to intra-industry trade in wine, in addition to income growth and accompanying taste changes, has been a series of shocks to real exchange rates (Anderson and Wittwer 2013 — Article 3). The country most affected by that over the past 15 years has been Australia, thanks to a huge growth and then slump in demand for exports from its mining sector.

Free trade agreements (FTAs) and customs unions also have affected bilateral wine trades. They can (but do not always) expand trade, including intra-industry trade, but they also can cause trade diversion (replacing one country's wines with those of another partner country). A good example of a very positive influence of an FTA on wine is the Canada-United States FTA that preceded the North American Free Trade Agreement (NAFTA): it was expected to decimate Canada's fledgling wine industry, but instead it stimulated producers in that country to specialize in what it was best able to do with its cool climate (Anderson 2001 — Article 16). By contrast, the potential withdrawal of the United Kingdom from the European Union (EU28) is projected to have a negative effect on the world's wine markets, which subsequent bilateral FTAs by both the UK and a shrunken EU27 will only partly offset (Anderson and Wittwer 2018 — Article 7).

Market developments in Caucasia and Asia

The United States and New World countries in the Southern Hemisphere are not the only ones to have become prominent as wine exporters over the past quarter-century. Especially notable in the Old World has been the re-emergence of Georgia, which considers itself the cradle of wine. Having been hit by the Soviet Union's anti-globalization push in the 1980s, and then the disruptions and income declines following the collapse of that Union and subsequent squirmishes with Russia, Georgia's wine industry has been modernizing and re-postioning itself over the past two decades (Anderson 2013 — Article 13). Other Caucasian and Central

Asian countries also have been striving to re-build their wine industries, but so far none have shown the export promise of Georgia.

In East Asia, meanwhile, there is a steadily growing demand for wine imports. In the more-advanced of those economies the quality of those wine imports is very high, with average prices more than double the rest of the world's. The most dramatic development of the past decade or so is in China: despite a very substantial rise in domestic wine production, China's wine import growth rate has been spectacular, and that trade is expected to continue growing for the foreseeable future (Anderson and Wittwer 2013 and 2015 — Articles 3 and 14; Anderson 2019). Certainly, there are some doubts about the statistics on levels of wine production and consumption in northeast Asia, but if anything those doubts give further reason to be bullish about import growth projections for the region (Anderson and Harada 2018 — Article 15).

Distortions to producer incentives and consumer prices

Trade in wine, and in other alcoholic beverages, is affected also by policies that directly distort producer and consumer prices within each country. Consumer (excise) taxes are the most severe but, for some countries that do not produce wine, high import taxes serve as a proxy consumer tax. Wine consumer taxes vary from zero in the key wine-producing countries of Europe to moderate in Australia and very high in wine-importing Northwest Europe, Southeast Asia and South Asia (Anderson 2010 and 2014 — Articles 18 and 19).

It matters also how wine is taxed: alcohol consumption is discouraged more, per dollar of tax revenue, if the tax is based on the volume of alcohol rather than on the price of the product. Australia is one of the few countries that chose to use the latter (*ad valorem*) tax instrument when it introduced a tax on wine consumption in the 1980s and again when it altered taxes at the time of introducing a goods-and-services tax (GST) at the turn of this century. That measure was an additional stimulus for Australian wineries to look to export markets rather than the domestic market as they expanded (Wittwer and Anderson 2002 — Article 17).

Most wine-producing countries provide at least some types of direct support to their grapegrowers and winemakers. The European Union (EU) was especially generous in supporting vignerons as domestic wine consumption fell from very high levels post-World War II, which led to massive 'wine lakes' that were disposed of by authorities selling at low prices to producers of brandy and various industrial products. Reforms of the EU's Common Agricultural Policy gradually moved away from such measures but nonetheless continued to support winegrowers using other means. The average extent of that support for the period 2007–12 is estimated to have raised the gross incomes of EU vignerons by 20% (Jensen and Anderson 2016 — Article 21).

Internationalization of winegrape varietal choices

Yet another aspect of internationalization of wine has to do with the vignerons' choice of winegrape varieties. Over the centuries, each winegrowing region of each European country gradually concentrated on varieties that best suited the region's terroir. Certainly, some varieties grew in many places (although often the name of each such variety differed between regions), but numerous regions had unique varieties. As wine production moved to other parts of the world over the past half-millennium, so too did a few of the more-prominent varieties of winegrapes as and when any local native grape varieties proved to be less suitable for wine production.

Reliable data on the distribution of winegrape varieties across the world were impossible to assemble until recently, because of the use of different local names for many varieties. However, DNA research has suddenly changed that: Robinson, Harding and Vouillamoz (2012) have identified 1368 commercially grown prime winegrape varieties and have attached the names of synonyms to them. With the help of that resource, Anderson (2013) has compiled the bearing area of those varieties as of 1990, 2000 and 2010 in more than 600 of the world's wine-growing regions. Those data reveal that there has been a considerable convergence of varietal choice across countries during the previous three decades toward a small number of so-called international varieties, mostly originating from France, Italy and Spain (Anderson 2014 — Article 22). More-detailed analysis of data for the United States shows a drift in that country toward the varieties dominant in France (Alston, Anderson and Sambucci 2015 — Article 23), as is also the case for Australia (Anderson 2016 — Article 24). The data in Anderson (2013) are to be updated during 2019–20.

Convergence in national alcohol consumption patterns

Just as there has been convergence across countries in winegrape varieties as the current globalization wave has proceeded, so too has there been convergence in national alcohol consumption patterns. In particular, countries that were beer- or spirits-focused in the early 1960s are now much more wine-focused. Australia is an extreme example of a country whose consumers have gradually moved from a strong spirits focus to a beer focus a century ago and, only belatedly, to a wine focus (Anderson 2018). Meanwhile, wine-dominant countries have seen a marked reduction in their volumes of wine consumption, even if they are still more wine-focused than other countries (Holmes and Anderson 2017 — Article 25). Various influences are responsible for that convergence, some of which are evolving regulations affecting alcohol consumption; but also important are technological changes that, together with taste changes as incomes grow, are altering the industrial organization of alcohol-producing industries (Anderson, Meloni and Swinnen 2018 — Article 26).

References reprinted in this volume

1. Wittwer, G., N. Berger and K. Anderson (2003), "A Model of the World's Wine Markets", *Economic Modelling* 20(3): 487–506, May.
2. Anderson, K., D. Norman and G. Wittwer (2003), "Globalisation of the World's Wine Markets", *The World Economy* 26(5): 659–87, May.
3. Anderson, K. and G. Wittwer (2013), "Modeling Global Wine Markets to 2018: Exchange Rates, Taste Changes, and China's Import Growth", *Journal of Wine Economics* 8(2): 131–58.
4. Anderson, K., J. Francois, D. Nelson and G. Wittwer (2016), "Intra-Industry Trade in a Rapidly Globalizing Industry: The Case of Wine", *Review of International Economics* 24(4): 820–36, September.
5. Anderson, K. (2017), "How Might Climate Changes and Preference Changes Affect the Competitiveness of the World's Wine Regions?" *Wine Economics and Policy* 6(2): 23–27, June.

6. Anderson, K. and G. Wittwer (2017), "U.K. and Global Wine Markets by 2025, and Implications of Brexit", *Journal of Wine Economics* 12(3): 221–51.
7. Anderson, K. and G. Wittwer (2018), "Cumulative Effects of Brexit and Other UK and EU-27 Bilateral Free-Trade Agreements on the World's Wine Markets", *The World Economy* 41(11): 2883–94, November.
8. Wittwer, G. and K. Anderson (2001), "Accounting for Growth in the Australian Wine Industry, 1987 to 2003", *Australian Economic Review* 34(2): 179–89, June.
9. Zhao, X., K. Anderson and G. Wittwer (2003), "Who Gains from Australian Generic Wine Promotion and R&D?", *The Australian Journal of Agricultural and Resource Economics* 47(2): 181–209, June.
10. Schamel, G. and K. Anderson (2003), "Wine Quality and Varietal, Regional and Winery Reputations: Hedonic Prices for Australia and New Zealand", *The Economic Record* 79(246): 357–69, September.
11. Wood, D. and K. Anderson (2006), "What Determines the Future Value of an Icon Wine? New Evidence from Australia", *Journal of Wine Economics* 1(2): 141–61, Fall.
12. Anderson, K. (2018), "Australian Wine Industry Competitiveness: Why so Slow to Emerge?" *Australian Journal of Agricultural and Resource Economics* 62(4): 507–26, October.
13. Anderson, K. (2013), "Is Georgia the Next 'New' Wine-Exporting Country?" *Journal of Wine Economics* 8(1): 1–28, Spring.
14. Anderson, K. and G. Wittwer (2015), "Asia's Evolving Role in Global Wine Markets", *China Economic Review* 35: 1–14, September.
15. Anderson, K. and K. Harada (2018), "How Much Wine Is *Really* Produced and Consumed in China, Hong Kong, and Japan?", *Journal of Wine Economics* 13(2): 199–220.
16. Anderson, K. (2001), "On the Impact of the Canada-United States Free Trade Agreement on Canadian Wine Imports", *Australian and New Zealand Wine Industry Journal* 16(1): 115–17, January/February.
17. Wittwer, G. and K. Anderson (2002), "Impact of the GST and Wine Tax Reform on Australia's Wine Industry: A CGE Analysis", *Australian Economic Papers* 41(1): 69–81, March.
18. Anderson, K. (2010), "Excise and Import Taxes on Wine Versus Beer and Spirits: An International Comparison", *Economic Papers* 29(2): 215–28, June.
19. Anderson, K. (with the assistance of N.R. Aryal) (2014), "Excise Taxes on Wines, Beers and Spirits: An Updated International Comparison", *Wine and Viticulture Journal* 29(6): 66–71, November/December.
20. Anderson, K., E. Valenzuela and G. Wittwer (2011), "Wine Export Shocks and Wine Tax Reform in Australia: Regional Consequences Using an Economy-Wide Approach", *Economic Papers* 30(3): 386–99, September.
21. Anderson, K. and H.G. Jensen (2016), "How Much Government Assistance Do European Wine Producers Receive?", *Journal of Wine Economics* 11(2): 289–305, August.

22. Anderson, K. (2014), "Changing Varietal Distinctiveness of the World's Wine Regions: Evidence from a New Global Database", *Journal of Wine Economics* 9(3): 249–72.
23. Alston, J., K. Anderson and O. Sambucci (2015), "Drifting Towards Bordeaux? The Evolving Varietal Emphasis of U.S. Wine Regions", *Journal of Wine Economics* 10(3): 349–78.
24. Anderson, K. (2016), "Evolving Varietal and Quality Distinctiveness of Australia's Wine Regions", *Journal of Wine Research* 27(3): 173–92, September.
25. Holmes, A.J. and K. Anderson (2017), "Convergence in National Alcohol Consumption Patterns: New Global Indicators", *Journal of Wine Economics* 12(2): 117–48.
26. Anderson, K., G. Meloni and J. Swinnen (2018), "Global Alcohol Markets: Evolving Consumption Patterns, Regulations and Industrial Organizations", *Annual Review of Resource Economics* 10: 105–32, October.

Other references cited

Alonso Ugaglia, A., J.-M. Cardebat and A. Corsi (eds.) (2019), *The Palgrave Handbook of Wine Industry Economics*, London and New York: Palgrave Macmillan.

Anderson, K. (ed.) (2004), *The World's Wine Markets: Globalization at Work*, Cheltenham: Edward Elgar.

Anderson, K. (2013), *Trade, Development and Agriculture: Essays in Economic Policy Analysis*, Singapore: World Scientific.

Anderson, K. (with the assistance of N.R. Aryal) (2013), *Which Winegrape Varieties Are Grown Where? A Global Empirical Picture*, Adelaide: University of Adelaide Press. Also freely available as an e-book at www.adelaide.edu.au/press/titles/winegrapes, and in Excel format at www.adelaide.edu.au/wine-econ/databases/winegrapes/

Anderson, K. (with the assistance of N.R. Aryal) (2015), *Growth and Cycles in Australia's Wine Industry: A Statistical Compendium, 1843 to 2013*, Adelaide: University of Adelaide Press. Also freely available as an e-book at www.adelaide.edu.au/press/titles/austwine, and in Excel format at www.adelaide.edu.au/wine-econ/databases/winehistory/

Anderson, K. (2018), "Evolving from a Rum State: A Comparative History of Australia's Alcohol Consumption", Revision of a paper presented at the annual conference of the AAEA, Washington DC, 5–7 August. Wine Economics Research Centre Working Paper 0418, November.

Anderson, K. (2019), "Asia's Emergence in Global Beverage Markets: The Rise of Wine". Wine Economics Research Centre Working Paper 0419, University of Adelaide, October.

Anderson, K., N. Berger and P. Spahni (1999), *Bilateral Trade Patterns in the World's Wine Markets, 1988 to 1997: A Statistical Compendium*, Adelaide: Centre for International Economic Studies.

Anderson, K., N. Berger and R. Stringer (1998), *Trends in the World's Wine Markets, 1961 to 1996: A Statistical Compendium*, Adelaide: Centre for International Economic Studies.

Anderson, K. and S. Nelgen (2011), *Global Wine Markets, 1961 to 2009: A Statistical Compendium*, Adelaide: University of Adelaide Press.

Anderson, K., S. Nelgen and V. Pinilla (2017), *Global Wine Markets, 1860 to 2015: A Statistical Compendium*, Adelaide: University of Adelaide Press. Also freely available as an ebook at www.adelaide.edu.au/press/titles/global-wine-markets, and in Excel format at www.adelaide.edu.au/wine-econ/databases/GWMhistory/

Anderson, K. and D. Norman (2003), *Global Wine Production, Consumption and Trade, 1961 to 2001: A Statistical Compendium*, Adelaide: Centre for International Economic Studies.

Anderson, K. and V. Pinilla (with the assistance of A.J. Holmes) (2017), *Annual Database of Global Wine Markets, 1835 to 2016*, freely available in Excel format at www.adelaide.edu.au/wine-econ/databases

Anderson, K. and V. Pinilla (eds.) (2018), *Wine Globalization: A New Comparative History*, Cambridge and New York: Cambridge University Press.

Anderson, K. and G. Wittwer (2001a), "US Dollar Appreciation and the Spread of Pierce's Disease: Effects on the World Wine Market", *Australian and New Zealand Wine Industry Journal* 16(2): 70–75, March/April.

Anderson, K. and G. Wittwer (2001b), "How Increased EU Import Barriers and Reduced Retail Margins Affect the World Wine Market", *Australian and New Zealand Wine Industry Journal* 16(3): 69–74, May/June.

Anderson, K. and G. Wittwer (2017), "The UK and Global Wine Markets by 2025, and Implications of Brexit", *Journal of Wine Economics* 12(3): 221–51, December.

Ashenfelter, O., D. Ashmore and R. Lalonde (1995), "Bordeaux Wine Vintage Quality and the Weather", *Chance* 8(4): 7–14.

Ashenfelter, O., O. Gergaud, K. Storchmann and W. Ziemba (eds.) (2018), *Handbook of the Economics of Wine, Volumes 1 and 2*, Singapore: World Scientific.

Berger, N. (2000), *Modelling Structural and Policy Changes in the World Wine Market into the 21st Century*, unpublished Master of Economics thesis, School of Economics, University of Adelaide, November.

Dixon, P., B. Parmenter, J. Sutton and D. Vincent (1982), *ORANI: A Multisectoral Model of the Australian Economy*, Amsterdam: North-Holland.

Holmes, A.J. and K. Anderson (2017), *Annual Database of National Beverage Consumption Volumes and Expenditures, 1950 to 2015*, Wine Economics Research Centre, University of Adelaide, at www.adelaide.edu.au/wine-econ/databases/

Johnson, H. (1989), *The Story of Wine*, London: Mitchell Beasley.

Osmond, R. and K. Anderson (1998), *Trends and Cycles in the Australian Wine Industry, 1850 to 2000*, Adelaide: Centre for International Economic Studies. Updated and hugely expanded to become Anderson (2015).

Robinson, J., J. Harding and J. Vouillamoz (2012), *Wine Grapes: A Complete Guide to 1,368 Vine Varieties, Including Their Origins and Flavours*, London: Allen Lane.

Unwin, T. (1991), *Wine and the Vine: An Historical Geography of Viticulture and the Wine Trade*, London and New York: Routledge.

Wittwer, G. (2000), *The Australian Wine Industry during a Period of Boom and Tax Changes*, unpublished PhD thesis, School of Economics, University of Adelaide, July.

A. Globalization of Wine

Chapter 1

A Model of the World's Wine Markets*

Glyn Wittwer[†], Nick Berger[‡] and Kym Anderson[†]

Abstract

This paper describes the theoretical and empirical structure of the World Multisectoral Wine Model, which uses some of the features of general equilibrium models. The model is disaggregated into the expanding premium and shrinking non-premium segments of the wine market. To illustrate its usefulness, we model the impact on the global market of the projected rapid premium supply expansion in New World wine production to 2005. The results show supply-induced falls in producer prices of New World producers are dampened or even reversed in the projection period by a growing consumer preference globally for premium wine. © 2002 Elsevier Science B.V. All rights reserved.

---

*First published in *Economic Modelling* 20(3): 487–506, May 2003. Corresponding author: K. Anderson. Phone: +61 8 8313 4712; E-mail: kym.anderson@adelaide.edu.au. Thanks are due to Australia's Grape and Wine Research and Development Corporation, its Rural Industries Research and Development Corporation, and the Australian Research Council for financial support.
[†]Centre for International Economic Studies, University of Adelaide, Adelaide, Australia
[‡]Productivity Commission, Melbourne, Australia

1. Introduction

The world wine market is the subject of increasing interest to Californian, Australian and other New World wine producers as their national outputs grow and they become more export oriented. Some fear that, with world wine consumption declining slightly while output is rising, the boom in the New World will be followed by a collapse in export prices. However, despite per capita consumption volumes declining in a number of significant wine-consuming nations in the past decade or so, consumers are substituting quality for quantity by moving up-market to premium wines. As well, wine consumption is increasing in non-traditional markets, again with the main focus on premium wine. In the 1990s the global demand for premium wine outstripped supply growth, causing unit values of bottled wine exports to increase.

New World producers account for most of the global growth in premium wine exports in the 1990s. Australia has been the leader in terms of export volumes among these producers, but Argentina, Chile, New Zealand, South Africa and the United States also are experiencing rapid export growth (Anderson, 2001). Wine-grape plantings in these nations in the latter 1990s will be reflected in substantial growth in the premium wine supply of New World producers in the first few years of the new millennium. This worries Old World traditional producers and exporters in Europe, where vineyard and winery upgrading has been on-going.

To project the impact of these recent changes in demand and supply (and of other prospective structural or policy changes) on the world wine market requires a multi-region global model that distinguishes between premium and non-premium grapes and wine and that identifies wines by region of origin. The present paper presents the theory and empirical base of such a model, the World Multisectoral Wine Model (WMWM). It also illustrates its usefulness by estimating the impact of the current rapid supply expansion in New World wine production on the global market by 2005.[1]

2. The structure of the WMWM model

The model consists of linearised expressions so as to be able to use GEMPACK software (Harrison and Pearson, 1994). This provides the

---

[1] Several other applications are provided in Anderson and Wittwer (2001).

relative simplicity of linearised algebra combined with software using multi-step solution procedures in order to obtain the solution accuracy of non-linear forms (Hertel et al., 1992).

2.1. Production

On the supply-side of the model, the multi-input product specification follows the separability assumptions of typical computable general equilibrium (CGE) models. For example, consider the production function for a single-product industry:

$$F(\text{inputs, output}) = 0 \qquad (1)$$

We write this as:

$$G(\text{inputs}) = \text{Output} \qquad (2)$$

The inputs in turn are derived from nested demands for intermediate inputs and primary factors. In the model, there are two grape industries plus three wine industries whose prices and outputs are endogenous. Intermediate inputs to these industries include grapes that are therefore both inputs and outputs in this model.

Figure 1 shows the structure of production in the World Multisectoral Wine Model for each region. Starting at the bottom left-hand corner of the diagram, producers choose a bundle of inputs from all sources (i.e. domestic and all import sources) so as to minimise the cost of each input, where the production function includes CES substitution possibilities. In percentage change terms, the demand for intermediate inputs i from source s by endogenous industry j in region $n(x_{is}^{jn})$ is related to the nested input demand x_i^{jn} in Eq. (3):

$$x_{is}^{jn} - a_{is}^{jn} = x_i^{jn} - \sigma_i^n \left(p_{is}^{jn} + a_{is}^{jn} - p_i^{jn} \right) \qquad (3)$$

In Eq. (3), p_{is}^{jn} is the source-specific input price and $\left(p_i^{jn}\right)$ the effective input price. The elasticity of substitution for intermediate inputs is σ_i^n. The source-specific preference shifter is a_{is}^{jn}. Next, we calculate the effective or nested price of the source-composite input, where S_{is}^{jn} refers to the sales share:

$$p_i^{jn} = \sum_s S_{is}^{jn} \left(p_{is}^{jn} + a_{is}^{jn} \right) \qquad (4)$$

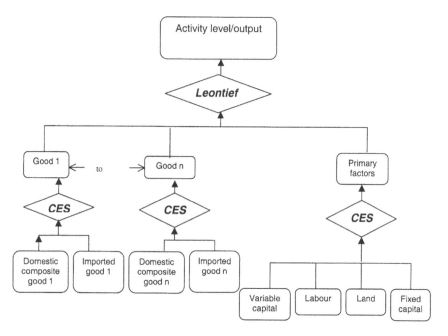

Figure 1. Structure of production.

The percentage change in the price of each intermediate input by regional source is set equal to the percentage change in the basic price $\left(p_{is}^o\right)$ of each input, assuming that there are no input taxes or margins:

$$p_{is}^{jn} = p_{is}^o \qquad (5)$$

The percentage change in effective inputs demanded is related to output $\left(x^{0jn}\right)$ in Eq. (6) via a Leontief function:

$$x_i^{jn} - (a_i^{jn} + a^{jn}) = x^{0jn} \qquad (6)$$

The variables a_i^{jn} and a^{jn} refer to percentage changes in effective intermediate and all-inputs unit requirements.

The next set of equations deals with primary factor demands. Within WMWM, there are four substitutable primary factors f. They are human capital, fixed capital, variable capital, and a fourth factor which for wine is labour and for grapes is 'harvest'. The latter factor is a composite of mechanical and manual labour inputs into grape harvesting, determined in a separate substitutable equation (not shown in Fig. 1). The percentage change in primary factors demanded (x_f^{jn}) is given by:

$$x_f^{jn} - a_f^{jn} = x_I^{jn} - \sigma_I^{jn}\left(p_f^{jn} + a_f^{jn} - p_I^{jn}\right) \qquad (7)$$

Percentage changes in the productivity of individual factors are given by a_{is}^{jn}, and the primary factor CES parameter by σ_I^{jn}. The composite quantities demanded are calculated in Eq. (8), where the subscript P refers to the primary factor composite:

$$x_P^{jn} - \left(a_P^{jn} + a^{jn}\right) = x^{0,jn} \qquad (8)$$

Eq. (9) computes the price term for effective factor demands:

$$p_P^{jn} = \sum_f S_f^{jn}\left(p_f^{jn} + a_f^{jn}\right) \qquad (9)$$

One of the primary factors, variable capital, is treated as perfectly mobile between grape and wine industries, so as to equalise the factor price:

$$p_K^{jn} = p_K^{n} \qquad (10)$$

The market clearing expression for variable capital is:

$$x_K^{n} = \sum_j S_K^{jn} x_K^{jn} \qquad (11)$$

Allocation of mechanical and manual inputs into grape harvesting in industry g (a subset of j) is determined by CES substitution in Eq. (12), while Eq. (13) computes the effective price:

$$x_h^{gn} - a_h^{gn} = x_H^{gn} - \sigma_H^{gn}\left(p_h^{gn} + a_h^{gn} - p_h^{gn}\right) \qquad (12)$$

$$p_H^{gn} = \sum_h S_h^{gn}\left(p_h^{gn} + a_h^{gn}\right) \qquad (13)$$

In the current version of the model, we assume that most factors used in grape and wine production are fixed. This is reasonable for the short to medium term, given the large fixed costs and partly irreversible nature of vineyard and winery investments. Labour is a mobile factor within each region but human capital is fixed, and all factors are assumed to be immobile internationally.[2] This degree of mobility ensures that in response to external shocks, most comparative static adjustments are through price (including changes in factor rewards) rather than output changes.

Equation (14) ensures zero pure profits in computing the producer price (p_1^{jn}), calculated using the cost shares for intermediate (S_i^{jn}) and primary inputs (S_P^{jn}):

$$p_1^{jn} - a_1^{jn} = \sum_i \left[S_i^{jn}(p_i^{jn} + a_i^{jn}) \right] + S_P^{jn}(p_P^{jn} + a_P^{jn}) \qquad (14)$$

2.2. Consumer prices

The relationship between producer and consumer prices $\left(p_{cs}^{wn} \right)$ is:

$$V_s^{wn} p_{cs}^{wn} = \left[B_s^{wn} + \sum_g T_s^{wng} \right] \left(p_{0s}^{w} + \sum_g t_s^{wng} \right) + \sum_u (M_s^{wnu} + p^{nu}) \qquad (15)$$

in which the upper-case terms refer to levels. The total consumption value of a transaction (V_s^{ws}), for sales from source s to region n, is equal to the basic value B_s^{wn} (i.e. at producer prices), plus all tariffs and consumer taxes on wine $\left(\Sigma_g T_s^{wng} \right.$, where g is the type of tax) plus margins $\left(\Sigma_u M_s^{wnu} \right.$, where u is the type of margin).

The variable t_s^{wng} denotes percentage changes in the power of a tax and p^{nu} is the percentage change in the margin price. Margins are used in the ORANI school of CGE models (Horridge et al., 1998) to distinguish between prices by type of sale. Here they are important because retail mark-ups are a large proportion of the total value of a wine, particularly in the case of on-premise consumption. Another type of margin within the u set is transport costs. In the present version of the model, margins are not added to the cost of intermediate inputs.

---

[2] In specific scenarios, we could alter the assumptions concerning international factor mobility, for example, by allowing wine industry human capital to be partly mobile between regions.

2.3. Consumer demands

Consumer demands are based on the Klein and Rubin (1948/1949) utility function:

$$U^n = \frac{1}{Q^n} \prod_j \left(X_c^{jn} - \psi_c^{jn}\right)^{\beta_{jn}} \qquad (16)$$

In levels terms, U^n represents utility, Q^n the number of households, X_c^{jn} the total consumption of good j, ψ_c^{jn} the subsistence component of this consumption and β_{jn} the marginal budget share of good j $\left(0 \leq \beta_{jn} \leq 1 \text{ and } \Sigma_j \beta_{jn} = 1\right)$. Also note that

$$\psi_c^{jn} = Q^n A_j^{Sn} \qquad (17)$$

where A_j^{Sn} is the individual household subsistence demand.

The maximisation of utility subject to the budget constraint $Y_n = \Sigma_j P_c^{jn} X_c^{jn}$ gives rise to the linear expenditure function of the following form:

$$P_c^{jn} X_c^{jn} = P_c^{jn} \psi_c^{jn} + \beta_{jn}\left(Y_n - \sum_j P_c^{jn} \psi_c^{jn}\right) \qquad (18)$$

Assume $V_n = \left(Y_n - \Sigma_j P_c^{jn} \psi_c^{jn}\right)$, which is the aggregate supernumerary expenditure. Eq. (18) then becomes

$$P_c^{jn} X_c^{jn} = P_c^{jn} \psi_c^{jn} + \beta_{jn} V_n \qquad (19)$$

By totally differentiating Eqs. (17) and (19) and dividing by $P_c^{jn} X_c^{jn}$, the percentage change in X_c^{jn} can be expressed as a function of the percentage changes in V_n, P_j, Q_n and A_j^{Sn}:

$$x_c^{jn} = \phi^{jn}\left(v_n - p_c^{jn}\right) + \left(1 - \phi^{jn}\right)\left(q_n + a_j^{Sn}\right) \qquad (20)$$

where $\phi^{jn} = \frac{V_n \beta_{jn}}{P_c^{jn} X_c^{jn}} = 1 - \frac{\psi_c^{jn}}{X_c^{jn}}$ is the supernumerary proportion of total expenditure on X_c^{jn}. The Frisch parameter γ_n is the (negative) ratio of total to luxury expenditure, given by $-\frac{Y_n}{V_n}$. Since $\beta_{jn} = \frac{\varepsilon_{jn} P_c^{jn} X_c^{jn}}{Y_n}$, where ε_{jn} is the expenditure elasticity of good j, it follows that $\phi^{jn} = -\frac{\varepsilon_{jn}}{\gamma_n}$.

Endogenous grape and wine types w are a subset of j. In applications of this model, non-grape and non-wine commodities comprise a single composite with an exogenously determined price. The supernumerary (a_j^{Ln}) and subsistence shifts (a_j^{Sn}) in preferences are related to the exogenous consumer preference shifter (a_c^{jn}):

$$a_j^{Sn} = a_j^{Sn} - \sum_j S_c^{jn} a_c^{jn} \qquad (21)$$

and

$$a_j^{Ln} = a_j^{Sn} - \sum_j \beta_{jn} a_j^{Sn} \qquad (22)$$

where the expenditure shares of aggregate consumption are given by S_c^{jn}.

We differentiate wine through disaggregation into wine types w, plus the Armington (1969) assumption of imperfect substitution by source d (1 = domestic, 2 = import composite) used to determine the domestic-import demands (x_d^{wn}):

$$x_d^{wn} - a_d^{wn} = x^{wn} - \sigma^{wn}(p_d^{wn} + a_d^{wn} - p^{wn}) \qquad (23)$$

In Eq. (23), σ^{wn} is the Armington elasticity and a_{cd}^{wn} the domestic-import preference shifter. Demands for imports from specific sources are determined in Eq. (24):

$$x_s^{wn} - a_s^{wn} = x_m^{wn} - \sigma_s^{wn}\left(p_s^{wn} + a_s^{wn} - p_m^{wn}\right) \qquad (24)$$

The parameter σ_s^{wn} is the elasticity of substitution between import sources. Subscript m refers to the import composite, and subscript s to the source of purchase. Hence, the demand for purchases by source entails a two-stage nesting process, between domestic purchases and a composite of imported purchases, and between different imports.

Next, we calculate the effective price of the source-composite wine commodity $\left(p_c^{wn}\right)$, where S_d^{wn} refers to the share of the sales of d in total sales to region n:

$$p^{wn} = \sum_d S_d^{wn}(p_d^{wn} + a_d^{wn}) \qquad (25)$$

The import composite price equation is:

$$p_m^{wn} = S_m^{wn}\left(p_m^{wn} + a_m^{wn}\right) \qquad (26)$$

2.4. Margins, market clearing equations and national income

The percentage change in the quantity of margin services (x_s^{wnu}) demanded is set equal to that of the wine type:

$$x_s^{wnu} = x_s^{wn} \qquad (27)$$

The market-clearing equation sets the supplies by source equal to the sum of demands (intermediate plus household) by region:

$$x^{0ws} = \sum_n \left(S_s^{wn} x_s^{wn}\right) + \sum_n \sum_i \left(S_{ws}^{in} x_{ws}^{in}\right) \qquad (28)$$

In Eq. (28), S_s^{wn} and S_{ws}^{in} are the shares of each sale in total sales of w, calculated at producer prices. In the present version of the model, only multipurpose grapes have sales as both intermediate inputs and household commodities.

Before calculating changes in income, we need to calculate the change in indirect taxes:

$$T^n t^n = \sum_w \sum_s \left[\left(B_{cs}^{wn} + \sum_g T_{cs}^{wng}\right)\sum_g t_{cs}^{wng} + \sum_g T_{cs}^{wng}\left(p_{0s}^w + x_{cs}^{wn}\right)\right] \qquad (29)$$

where t^n is the percentage change in tax and tariff revenue, and T^n the level of tax plus tariff revenue.

In comparative static runs (i.e. in which we assume that national endowments are unchanged), the change in income ($Y^n y^n$) is calculated as the percentage change in income earned by non-mobile factors multiplied by the non-mobile factor income level (F_h^{jn}, where subscript h is the non-mobile subset of all factors) in the grape and wine sectors, plus the percentage change in wine tax and tariff revenue.

$$Y^n y^n = \sum_j \sum_h F_h^{jn}\left(p_h^{jn} + x_h^{jn}\right) + T^n t^n \qquad (30)$$

The percentage change in income calculated in Eq. (30) appears in the consumption function, to determine nominal aggregate consumption (w_c^n), where (f_c^n) denotes shifts in savings:

$$w_c^n = \frac{Y^n}{C^n} y^n - f_c^n \qquad (31)$$

If changes in household expenditure equal changes in income (i.e., f_c^n is exogenous so the marginal propensity to save is set to zero), we can use Eq. (32), in which real aggregate consumption is solved (where p^n is CPI), to calculate changes in welfare:

$$x_c^n = w^n - p^n \qquad (32)$$

3. Product and regional disaggregation in the WMWM model

The database of WMWM in its present form includes six intermediate input commodities (chemicals, water, premium grapes, multipurpose grapes, non-premium wine, and other) and five endogenous outputs (premium winegrapes, multi-purpose grapes, premium wine, non-premium wine and non-beverage wine).

The model currently divides the world into 10 regions:[3] Western European wine Exporters (WEE), United Kingdom (UK), Germany (GER), Rest of Western Europe (OWE), Central & Eastern Europe (CEE), United States & Canada (USC), Australia (AUS), New Zealand (NZ), Other Southern Hemisphere wine Exporters (OSE), and the Rest of the World (ROW). The choice of aggregation requires further comment. Western European Exporters (France, Italy, Portugal and Spain) are the largest wine producers in the world and, together with other Western European nations, also the largest consumers, accounting for roughly half the global wine market. The United Kingdom is treated separately because of its importance as a destination for New World wine, and Germany because it is the world's largest wine-importing country. Four of the

---

[3] Anderson and Norman (2001) have compiled statistics for 47 regions for wine, from which a more disaggregated version of the model is being developed.

regions, Australia, New Zealand, United States and Canada, and Other Southern Hemisphere Exporters (Argentina, Brazil, Chile, Uruguay and South Africa) experienced rapid export growth in the 1990s and now account for more than one-quarter of world production and exports. North America is exceptional among New World regions, in that most sales growth is likely to be in its domestic rather than export markets. The Rest of the World accounted for over 20% of global grape production in the late 1990s but made only 4% of the world's wine (FAO, 2000). This group includes a number of nations with sizeable Moslem populations who consume little alcohol.

3.1. Production, consumption and trade data

The starting points for constructing a global database are the historical statistics compiled by Berger *et al.* (1998, 1999) that are based on FAO, OIV and (for trade data) UN sources. These relate to wine as a single commodity for years up to 1997. Given the importance we attach to distinguishing between the expanding premium and shrinking non-premium segments of the world wine market, a crucial part of database preparation was to estimate this split. We also updated the data to 1999. The resulting database is still subject to revision as new information comes to light. It has 23% of the value and 60% of the volume of world wine production in the non-premium category in 1999, similar to Rabobank estimates (Geene *et al.*,1999).

Disaggregated data for the Australian region were drawn from two official agencies (ABS, 1999, 2000; AWEC, 2000) and from a recent thesis by Wittwer (2000). ABS data for Australia distinguish between premium and non-premium wines by container, with premium wines referring to those distributed in bottles of 1.5 l or less. We have amended this slightly so that two-litre casks also are categorised as premium wine. Among the other Southern Hemisphere exporters, there are sufficient New Zealand industry data to estimate disaggregated production and sales, with non-premium production now being a small proportion of the total (WINZ, 2000). South African data indicate that a larger proportion of production is of non-premium quality than in other New World regions (SAWIS, 2000). Estimates of the split between premium and non-premium production for the remaining Southern Hemisphere exporters are based on

Jenster *et al.* (1993), but updated to reflect an increasing proportion of premium in total production in the New World.

The industry in a number of European nations is classified by quality, but such classifications vary from country to country. The publication by Onivins (1998) provides some indicators of the quality split of consumption and production in France. In Geene *et al.* (1999), Figure 2.10 provides a split between premium and other table wine for EU-12 consumption based on European Commission data. The premium proportion has been adjusted downwards in our database because, according to Geene *et al.*, this category may include some wine inappropriately classified as premium.

Aggregate per capita wine consumption is much lower in North America than in Western Europe, but the premium proportion of the total is higher. Data in WIC (2000) indicate that until 1999, the volume of North American exports exceeded that of Australia. But the unit value and total value were substantially lower. US producers, particularly premium suppliers, have been able to rely mostly on an ever-growing domestic market for increased sales, in contrast to Southern Hemisphere producers. The 1999 data used for Central and Eastern Europe, as for the Rest of the World, are based on the authors' best guesses of trends in the latter 1990s using available OIV and FAO statistics.

3.2. Price data

Some indicative winegrape price data are readily available for Australia (PISA, 1996; PGIBSA, 2000), South Africa (SAWIS, 2000), the United States (WIC, 2000) and New Zealand (WINZ, 2000). We assume that winegrapes account for approximately 25% of the costs of wine production (based on discussions with Winemakers' Federation of Australia). Otherwise, prices are based to a considerable extent on UN unit value trade data, as in Berger (2000). Onivins (1998) and Geene *et al.* (1999) also provide some guidance in estimating producer prices for winegrapes and wine.

3.3. Tax data

Berger and Anderson (1999) have compiled wine consumer and import tax rates in all the key wine countries. An important feature of that tax database, which is reflected in WMWM, is that ad valorem and volumetric tax rates are separately included, since changes in the latter (and hence a switch from one form to the other) affect the premium and non-premium markets to different extents.

3.4. Transport and related margins

We assume that transport costs for domestic wine sales are equal to 15% of the producer price for premium wine and (reflecting its lower unit value) 20% for non-premium wine. The corresponding transport costs assumed for imported wine are 25% for premium and 30% for non-premium wine. Based on discussions with the Winemakers' Federation of Australia, retail margins at liquor stores are assumed to be 33% of the tax-inclusive wholesale price for premium wine and 25% for non-premium wine. But since approximately one-fifth of wine consumption is on licensed premises with mark-ups typically exceeding 100%, the overall retail margins are assumed to be 46% for premium and 40% for non-premium wine.

4. Elasticities in the WMWM model

We impose Armington (1969) elasticities of substitution in consumption between domestic and imported wine of 8.0, higher than for beverages within the GTAP database for the global economy because of greater possibilities for substitution the more disaggregated a product category (Hertel, 1996). For substitution between different sources of wine imports, we chose an elasticity of 16.0.

The expenditure elasticities in the initial database are 1.5 for premium wine and 0.6 for non-premium, based on estimates for Australia (CIE, 1995). The Frisch parameter is initially –1.82 in Australia, the European nations and USC, and a slightly larger (absolute) value elsewhere, reflecting the latter's lower per capita incomes.

On the supply side, in which industry-specific factors are exogenous, the elasticity of substitution between primary factors is set at 0.5. Were we to allow for endogeneity of primary factors other than labour, supply within the model would be more price-responsive.

As better parameter estimates for the wine market become available, we can readily fit them into the model or (on the supply side) alter the theory of the model. For the time being, the GEMPACK software allows us to undertake systematic sensitivity analysis to track the influence of parameter choice (and policy and growth uncertainty) on modelled outcomes (Arndt and Pearson, 1996).

5. Projecting the WMWM model from 1999 to 2005

By way of illustrating its usefulness, the following application projects the model from 1999 to 2005 to estimate the impact of known winegrape plantings of the late 1990s on grape and wine producers and consumers in different regions of the world. Our assumptions concerning the projection are summarised in Table 1. In addition to using the macroeconomic assumptions of Hertel *et al.* (2001) and Anderson and Strutt (1999), we also assume that there is a taste swing from non-premium towards premium wine consumption among consumers, based on Wittwer and Anderson (2001). Also within the projection is the assumption of an effective market promotion by Australia, as called for in the Australian industry's wine marketing strategy released in November 2000 (WFA and AWBC, 2000), which is assumed to cause specific taste swings towards Australian wine in the UK, Germany, USC and OWE by 2005.

The main feature of the projected scenario is that despite a rapid increase in premium wine output in the New World regions (i.e. Australia, United States, Canada, New Zealand, and Other Southern Hemisphere Exporters), downward pressure on producer prices is either minor or reversed by positive income and taste effects in consumer demand. Table 2 shows the producer price changes. In Europe (for example, OWE) producer prices for premium winegrapes rise while those for wine fall. This assumes that in Europe there is little growth in premium winegrape production and a fall in non-premium production, without a matching reduction in wine processing capacity. Table 3 gives a decomposition of the projected changes in consumer demand, computed from Eq. (20) above. For example, in the UK, a major importer of wine, income growth alone accounts for 22.1% of consumption growth of relatively income-elastic premium wine. Downward price pressures, arising from output growth of

Table 1. Key assumptions in projecting from 1999 to 2005 (percentage change over the 6 years)

	AUS	WEE	OWE	UK[a]	GER	CEE	USC	OSE	NZ	ROW	World
Aggregate consumption	19.4	14.6	14.6	14.6	14.6	17.3	18.0	19.4	18.7	18.7	17.1
Population	6.0	0.6	0.6	0.6	0.6	1.6	6.8	8.7	5.0	4.9	4.7
Taste swing to premium	8.0	8.0	8.0	8.0	8.0	8.0	8.0	8.0	8.0	8.0	8.0
Fixed capital, premium grapes	130.0	10.0	10.0	—	10.0	10.0	50.0	80.0	100.0	15.0	23.6
Human capital, premium grapes	100.0	5.0	5.0	—	5.0	5.0	40.0	70.0	80.0	10.0	20.0
Fixed & human cap., multigrapes	10.0	−5.0	−5.0	—	−5.0	−5.0	−5.0	−5.0	−5.0	−5.0	−4.9
Fixed capital, premium wine	80.0	5.0	5.0	—	5.0	5.0	40.0	60.0	70.0	10.0	23.8
Human capital, premium wine	80.0	5.0	5.0	—	5.0	5.0	40.0	60.0	70.0	10.0	16.2
Fixed capital, non-premium wine	−25.0	−25.0	−25.0	—	−25.0	−25.0	−25.0	−25.0	−25.0	−25.0	−25.0
Human cap., non-premium wine	−30.0	−30.0	−30.0	—	−30.0	−30.0	−30.0	−30.0	−30.0	−30.0	−30.0
Variable capital, grape and wine	90.0	10.0	10.0	—	10.0	10.0	30.0	60.0	70.0	15.0	22.0
Total factor productivity, wines[b]	15.0	12.6	12.6	—	12.6	1.8	10.0	12.6	12.6	1.8	11.0

[a] The UK's proportion of global consumption is significant, while its proportion of global production is negligible.
[b] In addition, for premium grapes we have assumed that TFP declines by 1.4% in Australia between 1999 and 2005 due to quality improvements that require reduced yields per hectare. Elsewhere, we assume no change in grape TFP.

Sources: Anderson and Strutt (1999); Hertel *et al*. (2004); ABS (2000); and authors' own assumptions.

Table 2. Grape and wine producer price changes (% change from 1999 to 2005 in 1999 constant US dollars)

	AUS	WEE[a]	GER[a]	OWE[a]	CEE[a]	USC	OSE	NZ	ROW	World
Premium grapes	0.9	37.3	12.0	17.5	12.0	−4.0	−3.6	−2.7	−8.7	18.5
OSE growth[b]	(1.2)	(2.5)	(2.1)	(2.2)	(0.6)	(1.1)	(32.7)	(1.2)	(1.7)	(3.3)
Taste change[c]	(1.9)	(4.9)	(3.6)	(3.5)	(3.2)	(2.7)	(2.5)	(1.8)	(2.5)	(3.6)
Multipurpose grapes	1.8	8.8	3.4	8.7	4.7	19.0	33.8	−5.8	20.2	17.0
OSE growth[b]	(0.7)	(0.7)	(2.4)	(0.7)	(0.4)	(0.7)	(4.1)	(1.7)	(0.4)	(0.2)
Taste change[c]	(0.1)	(0.1)	(0.7)	(0.2)	(0.2)	(0.1)	(0.3)	(0.6)	(0.1)	(0.1)
Premium wine	1.5	0.7	−11.0	−4.8	9.2	−11.9	−10.2	−9.6	0.1	−3.8
OSE growth[b]	(1.2)	(1.0)	(0.9)	(1.1)	(0.4)	(0.8)	(2.7)	(1.1)	(1.1)	(1.1)
Taste change[c]	(1.9)	(2.0)	(1.6)	(1.7)	(2.0)	(2.0)	(1.6)	(1.7)	(1.6)	(1.8)
Non-premium wine	10.1	12.4	11.2	11.6	17.5	14.0	7.5	11.0	16.2	12.6
OSE growth[b]	(1.3)	(1.4)	(1.6)	(1.3)	(1.1)	(1.4)	(4.6)	(1.5)	(1.2)	(1.7)
Taste change[c]	(1.1)	(0.9)	(0.9)	(0.8)	(0.7)	(1.1)	(0.9)	(1.2)	(0.7)	(0.9)

[a] Alternative demand assumptions, based on Europe's shrinking share of global wine consumption, would alter the producer price outcomes in these columns.
[b] All OSE growth shocks are varied by ±80%, with standard deviations arising from this variation in parentheses.
[c] $a_c^m = 8 \pm 6$ for j = premium wine and all n.

Source: Authors' WMWM model results.

Table 3. Decomposition of growth in the volume of premium wine consumption (% change from 1999 to 2005)

Effect of Change in:	AUS	WEE	UK	GER	OWE	CEE	USC	OSE	NZ	ROW
Income	20.3	21.7	22.1	21.3	21.9	23.8	17.1	16.6	21.3	21.2
OSE growth[a]	(0.1)	(0.1)	(0.1)	(0.1)	(0.1)	(0.1)	(0.1)	(0.1)	(0.1)	(0.1)
Taste change[b]	(0.4)	(0.3)	(0.4)	(0.4)	(0.4)	(0.3)	(0.2)	(0.3)	(0.4)	(0.4)
Price	-0.8	-0.2	4.6	-4.5	0.9	-4.0	2.6	6.0	3.7	2.1
OSE growth[a]	(0.7)	(0.6)	(0.8)	(0.6)	(0.8)	(0.2)	(0.6)	(1.6)	(0.7)	(0.8)
Taste change[b]	(1.1)	(1.2)	(1.1)	(1.0)	(1.1)	(0.9)	(1.2)	(1.0)	(1.0)	(1.0)
Taste	8.9	8.7	8.8	8.5	8.7	8.8	9.0	9.2	9.1	9.1
OSE growth[a]	(0.0)	(0.0)	(0.0)	(0.0)	(0.0)	(0.0)	(0.0)	(0.0)	(0.0)	(0.0)
Taste change[b]	(4.1)	(3.9)	(4.1)	(3.9)	(4.0)	(4.0)	(4.1)	(4.2)	(4.2)	(4.2)
Population	6.9	0.7	0.7	0.7	0.7	1.8	7.7	10.0	5.8	5.7
OSE growth[a]	(0.0)	(0.0)	(0.0)	(0.0)	(0.0)	(0.0)	(0.0)	(0.0)	(0.0)	(0.0)
Taste change[b]	(0.1)	(0.0)	(0.0)	(0.0)	(0.0)	(0.0)	(0.1)	(0.2)	(0.1)	(0.1)
Total	35.3	30.9	36.2	25.9	32.2	30.4	36.4	41.8	39.8	38.1
OSE growth[a]	(0.8)	(0.7)	(0.9)	(0.6)	(0.9)	(0.2)	(0.7)	(1.9)	(0.8)	(1.0)
Taste change[b]	(4.6)	(3.5)	(4.5)	(4.0)	(4.2)	(3.5)	(3.6)	(4.7)	(4.8)	(4.7)

[a] All OSE growth shocks are varied by ± 80%.
[b] $a_c^m = 8 \pm 6$ for j = premium wine and all n.

Source: Authors' WMWM model results.

Table 4. Decomposition of growth in the volume of premium wine output (% change from 1999 to 2005)

Effect of Change in:	AUS	WEE	GER	OWE	CEE	USC	OSE	NZ	ROW
Local Market	16.1	17.3	25.0	24.0	27.4	40.7	22.8	21.0	30.3
OSE growth[a]	(0.4)	(0.4)	(0.5)	(0.3)	(0.1)	(0.7)	(1.2)	(0.4)	(0.5)
Taste change[b]	(2.1)	(1.9)	(2.8)	(3.1)	(2.9)	(3.1)	(2.6)	(2.4)	(3.3)
Import Substitution	−1.0	−1.0	−33.1	−13.5	−2.4	1.7	0.2	8.6	−16.3
OSE growth[a]	(0.0)	(0.1)	(0.1)	(0.5)	(0.2)	(0.5)	(0.1)	(0.0)	(1.2)
Taste change[b]	(0.1)	(0.1)	(1.3)	(2.0)	(0.7)	(1.3)	(0.0)	(0.1)	(2.6)
Export	109.9	1.9	21.9	7.5	−2.5	9.6	71.8	68.0	−0.6
OSE growth[a]	(0.6)	(0.5)	(0.8)	(0.3)	(0.2)	(0.4)	(17.4)	(0.6)	(0.1)
Taste change[b]	(2.2)	(1.6)	(1.5)	(1.0)	(0.5)	(1.3)	(3.0)	(2.5)	(0.5)
Total	125.1	18.1	13.7	18.0	22.5	52.0	94.8	97.6	13.4
OSE growth[a]	(0.2)	(0.3)	(0.3)	(0.5)	(0.3)	(0.3)	(18.7)	(0.2)	(0.9)
Taste change[b]	(0.3)	(0.6)	(0.6)	(0.8)	(2.0)	(0.8)	(1.3)	(0.3)	(1.3)

[a] All OSE growth shocks are varied by ± 80%.
[b] $a_c^{jn} = 8 \pm 6$ for j = premium wine and all n.
Source: Authors' WMWM model results.

the UK's main premium suppliers, account for a 4.6% increase. The assumed taste swing to premium consumption leads to an 8.8% increase. But population growth accounts for only 0.7% of total consumption growth of 36.2%.

Table 4 contains a decomposition of premium wine output growth. The method of decomposition is based on a modified version of market clearing Eq. (28) of the model. The X terms refer to sales from source s and the M terms to purchases by region r from other regions.

$$X^s x^s = \left(X^{ss} + \sum_s M^{sr} \right) x^{s*} + \sum_r X^{rs} x^{rs} - \sum_s M^{sr} m^{sr} \qquad (33)$$

In percentage change terms, total output of region s is x^s, local sales x^{s*}, exports x^{sr} and imports m^{sr}. The decomposed components of Eq. (33)

will not add exactly to $X^s x^s$ when large change solutions are computed.[4] To overcome this, we define an ordinary change variable q^s so that

$$X_0^s q^s = X^s x^s \tag{34}$$

where X_0^s is the initial quantity of total sales. In ordinary change terms,

$$q^s = q^l + q^x + q^m \tag{35}$$

where q^l is the local market contribution, q^x the export contribution and q^m the import replacement contribution. We define the local market contribution as the percentage change in local sales from local and imported sources, weighted by the value of locally sourced sales:

$$q^l = \frac{X^{ss} x^{s*}}{X_0^s} \tag{36}$$

The export contribution is $\frac{\Sigma_r X^{rs} x^{rs}}{X_0^s}$ and the import contribution is calculated from Eq. (35).

The decomposition shown in Table 4 reveals key differences between New World and European producers. In the New World, output growth of premium wine is large, and will be heavily reliant on export sales. In the European regions (WEE, Germany and OWE), local market growth accounts for most if not all output growth. Germany's relatively large import substitution and export growth are based on the assumption of a taste swing away from white wine in Germany towards red wine: this will induce an increase in both exports and imports in Germany, as that country produces predominately white wine. The United States and Canada, despite rapid output expansion, have sufficient local demand growth (through the various positive consumption effects shown in Table 3) to absorb a large proportion of their output growth.

The Systematic Sensitivity Analysis (SSA) facility of the GEMPACK software used to run WMWM allows us to explore how uncertainty

---

[4] The GEMPACK software used by WMWM may use multi-step solution procedures in large change cases (Harrison and Pearson, 1994). Such multi-step computation percentage changes are compounded, whereas ordinary changes are added.

relating to growth or other assumptions affects the modelled outcome. Although we have relatively accurate information on winegrape plantings for Australia, United States and Canada and New Zealand, the growth assumptions for the other regions are somewhat speculative. For example, we assume that in Europe, premium wine-grape production increases slightly while non-premium production falls sharply between 1999 and 2005, whereas it may be possible that adjustments to grape production in Europe could occur through quality upgrades with a much smaller change in net production.

We use SSA to consider uncertainty in two sets of assumptions: first, in wine output growth of Other Southern Hemisphere wine Exporters (OSE), and second, in the magnitude of the global taste swing towards premium wine consumption between 1999 and 2005. In each case, we vary the shocks by plus or minus 80% of the magnitude of the changes shown in Table 1. This applies to Table 1's growth in premium wine and winegrape factors for OSE in the 8th column, and the taste swing shown in the 3rd row. The estimated standard deviations associated with each set of uncertain shocks are shown in parentheses in Tables 2–4. In each set, the shocks are varied uniformly from their mean values, that is, without a bias towards the mean.

In the case of uncertainty in OSE growth, the standard deviation of the producer price change for OSE premium winegrapes (a non-traded input) is 32.7%, while for OSE premium wine (a traded commodity) it is only 2.7% (Table 2). With winemaking capacity virtually fixed, primary supply uncertainty transmits to uncertainty in the primary product price. In other regions, uncertain supply in OSE causes smaller standard deviations, for example, 1.2% for the price of both premium winegrapes and wine in Australia. The standard deviation of OSE's price effect is 1.6%, accounting for most of the uncertainty in overall consumption, which is 1.9% (Table 3). Elsewhere, the standard deviations of consumption growth are between 0.2 and 0.8% (Table 3). In the decomposition of output, as shown in Table 4, the only notable standard deviations are those for OSE's export contribution (17.4%) and total output (18.7%).[5]

---

[5]Although OSE remains a small contributor to global trade, a similar pattern emerges among the standard deviations using SSA to depict growth uncertainty in WEE. The standard deviation of the winegrape producer price for WEE again is large, as is that for the

Turning to uncertainty in the taste swing towards premium wine, the standard deviations of the winegrape producer prices are relatively large in all regions, being 1.9% in Australia, for example, and 4.9% in WEE, where we project a large increase in winegrape prices. This time the standard deviations for premium wine producer prices are only marginally smaller than for winegrapes (Table 2). The standard deviations with respect to consumption show that the direct uncertainty surrounding tastes accounts for most of the uncertainty in the consumption outcome (e.g. in Australia, the standard deviation of the taste change effect is 4.1%, and that of total consumption 4.6%, Table 3). But uncertain demand shifts imply uncertain prices. Hence, moderate standard deviations also appear for the price effect in each region (1.1% for Australia, Table 3). Overall, however, the uncertainty attributable to taste shifts is small relative to projected total consumption growth, which exceeds 30% in most regions (Table 3).

Finally, we examine output growth. While taste uncertainty provides uncertainty in both the local market and export effects, the impact on the totals is relatively small, as indicated by the respective standard deviations in Table 4. In Australia, for example, the standard deviations of the local market and export effects are 2.1 and 2.2%, respectively, yet that for total growth is only 0.3%. This indicates some interchange between local and export sales at the national level in the face of uncertainty surrounding the extent of the global demand shift.

6. Conclusion

WMWM models a small industry in the global economy and therefore essentially is a partial equilibrium model in practice, although it draws on some of the restrictions imposed on general equilibrium models, especially in modelling household demands. The supply side of the model in its present form is mostly exogenous, reflecting the medium-term constraints on adjustment in the winegrape and wine industry. As there are lags of four years or more between winegrape plantings and production, it is possible to project several years ahead on the basis of known plantings.

---

export contribution to WEE output, while other standard deviations with respect to WEE growth uncertainty are relatively small.

SSA helps the modeller explore uncertainty associated with unavailable plantings data in particular regions, or other assumptions involved in projecting from one time period to another. SSA is also a tool for analysing the implications of parameter or policy uncertainty (Wittwer, 2000).

In its present form, WMWM is well suited to analysing a rapid growth phase, as is occurring in the premium segment of production in the New World. The theory of supply within the model may need modifications to analyse the market as growth subsides. Useful modifications to the model may include developing a dynamic framework and depicting the partly irreversible nature of vineyard and winery investments. The structure of the model could be adapted readily to analyse other commodities. The world olive market, for example, is a similarly small industry suitable for modelling in this framework.

References

ABS (Australian Bureau of Statistics), 1999. Sales of Australian Wine and Brandy by Winemakers, Catalogue no. 8504.0. ABS, Canberra.

ABS (Australian Bureau of Statistics), 2000. Australian Wine and Grape Industry, Catalogue no. 1329.0. ABS, Canberra.

Anderson, K., 2001. Where in the World is the Wine Industry Going? Opening Plenary Paper at the AARES Annual Conference, Adelaide, 22–24 January (http://www.adelaide.edu.au/ CIES/0101.pdf).

Anderson, K., Norman, D., 2001. Global Wine Production, Consumption and Trade, 1961 to 1999. Centre for International Economic Studies, University of Adelaide.

Anderson, K., Strutt, A., 1999. Impact of East Asia's growth interruption and policy responses: the case of Indonesia. Asian Econ. J. 13 (2), 205–218.

Anderson, K., Wittwer, G., 2001. Projecting the World Wine Market to 2005: Impacts of Structural and Policy Changes, Paper for the Enometrics VIII Conference of the VDQS (Vineyard Data Quantification Society), Napa Valley, CA 21–22 May.

Armington, P.A., 1969. A theory of demand for products distinguished by place of production. IMF Staff Papers 16, 159–178.

Arndt, C., Pearson, K., 1996. How to Carry Out Systematic Sensitivity Analysis via Gaussian Quadrature and GEMPACK, GTAP Technical Paper No. 3, Preliminary version. Purdue University, West Lafayette.

AWEC (Australian Wine Export Council), 2000. Wine Export Approval Report (www.awbc.com.au/awec/export — statistics.html).

Berger, N., 2000. Modelling Structural and Policy Changes in the World Wine Market into the 21st Century, unpublished Masters dissertation. University of Adelaide.

Berger, N., Anderson, K., 1999. Consumer and import taxes in the world wine market: Australia in international perspective, Aust. Agribus. Rev. 7(3).

Berger, N., Anderson, K., Stringer, R., 1998. Trends in the World Wine Market, 1961 to 1996: A Statistical Compendium. Centre for International Economic Studies, Adelaide.

Berger, N., Spahni, P., Anderson, K., 1999. Bilateral Trade Patterns in the World Wine Market, 1988 to 1997: A Statistical Compendium. Centre for International Economic Studies, Adelaide.

CIE (Centre for International Economics), 1995. Generation of Demand Parameters for an Economy wide Model of the Grape and Wine Industry, Prepared for the Commonwealth Government Inquiry into the Wine Grape and Wine Industry, Canberra.

FAO (Food and Agricultural Organisation of the United Nations), 2000. Online database (www.apps.fao.org).

Geene, A., Heijbroek, A., Lagerwerf, A., Wazir, R., 1999. The World Wine Business. Rabobank International, Utrecht.

Harrison, J., Pearson, K., 1994. Computing solutions for large scale general equilibrium models using GEMPACK. Comput. Econ. 9 (2), 83–127.

Hertel, T. (Ed.), 1996. Global Trade Analysis: Modeling and Applications. Cambridge University Press, New York.

Hertel, T., Horridge, M., Pearson, K., 1992. Mending the family tree: a reconciliation of the linearization and levels schools of AGE modelling. Econ. Modelling 9, 385–407.

Hertel, T., Anderson, K., Francois, J., Martin, W., 2004. Agriculture and non-agricultural liberalisation in the millennium round. In: Ingco, M.D., Winters, L.A. (Eds.), Agriculture and the New Trade Agenda. Cambridge University Press, Cambridge and New York.

Horridge, J., Parmenter, B., Pearson, K., 1998. ORANI-G: A General Equilibrium Model of the Australian Economy, Centre of Policy Studies and Impact Project, prepared for an ORANI-G course at Monash University, 29 June-3 July (www.monash.edu.au/policy/ftp/oranig/oranidoc.pdf).

Jenster, P., Jenster, L., Watchurst, N., 1993. The Business of Wine: An Analysis of the Global Wine Industry. SMC Publishing, Lausanne.

Klein, L., Rubin, H., 1948. A constant-utility index of the cost of living. Rev. Econ. Stud. 15, 84–87.

Onivins (Office national inteprofessionnel des vins), 1998. Statisiques sur la filiere viti-vinicole. Onivins, Paris.

PGIBSA (Phylloxera and Grape Industry Board of South Australia), 2000. South Australian Winegrape Utilisation and Pricing Survey — 2000. PGIBSA, Adelaide.

PISA (Primary Industries South Australia), 1996. South Australian Winegrape Utilisation and Pricing Survey — 1996. South Australian Grape Advisory Committee and Phylloxera and Grape Industry Board of South Australia.

SAWIS (SA Wine Industry Information & Systems), 2000. South African Wine Industry Statistics NR 24. SAWIS, Suider Paarl.

WFA (Winemaker's Federation of Australia) and AWBC (Australian Wine and Brandy Corporation), 2000. The Marketing Decade: Setting the Australian Wine Marketing Agenda 2000 to 2010. WFA, Adelaide.

WINZ (Wine Institute of New Zealand), 2000. Online statistics (www.nzwine.com/statistics).

WIC (Wine Institute of California), 2000. Online statistics (www.wineinstitute.org/communications/statistics).

Wittwer, G., 2000. The Australian Wine Industry During a Period of Boom and Tax Changes, Unpublished Ph.D. dissertation. University of Adelaide.

Wittwer, G., Anderson, K., 2001. Accounting for growth in the wine Australian wine industry, 1986 to 2003. Aust. Econ. Rev. 34, 179–189.

Chapter 2

Globalisation of the World's Wine Markets*

Kym Anderson, David Norman and Glyn Wittwer

1. Introduction

Why does the wine industry attract so much attention? After all, it accounts for just 0.4 per cent of global household consumption, and vines cover only 0.5 per cent of the world's cropland (of which barely one-third produce winegrapes). Moreover, globally it is not a growth industry in that world wine production and consumption have been declining slightly over the past two decades. But to millions of investors and hundreds of millions of consumers, this industry provides a far more fascinating product than

---

*First published in *The World Economy* 26(5): 659–87, May 2003.

KYM ANDERSON is Executive Director of the Centre for International Economic Studies at the University of Adelaide in Australia. DAVID NORMAN is a Masters student at CIES in Adelaide. GLYN WITTWER was a Research Fellow at CIES in Adelaide when this research began before he moved to the Centre of Policy Studies at Monash University in Melbourne.

This paper is a revision of an Invited Paper for the Australian Conference of Economists, Adelaide, 1–3 October, 2002. The research on which the paper draws was funded by the Grape and Wine Research and Development Corporation, the Rural Industries Research and Development Corporation, and the Australian Research Council. Thanks are due to Nick Berger for his pioneering work in developing a prototype of the database and model used in this paper (see Berger, 2000) and to an anonymous referee for helpful comments.

its shares of global expenditure or GDP might suggest. Moreover, it provides an insightful case study of globalisation at work that involves primary, secondary and tertiary sectors of the economy, because the global average cost of a bottle of wine is shared roughly as follows: 10 per cent to the grapegrower, 30 per cent to the winery, 37 per cent to transporters, wholesalers and retailers, and 23 per cent to tax collectors (Wittwer, Berger and Anderson, 2003).

This paper begins with a brief history of wine industry globalisation over the past four millennia and then a review of recent developments. While globalisation is not new to the world's wine markets, its influence over the past decade or so has increased significantly. One indicator of that is the growth in the share of global production that is exported, which in volume terms rose from 15 to 25 per cent over the 1990s and in value terms is now around 40 per cent. While that influence has been very positive for stakeholders in much of the New World (North and South America, South Africa and Australasia), it has presented and will continue to present some serious challenges to Old World producers in both Western and Eastern Europe. Moreover, following a dramatic expansion in their vineyard plantings in the latter 1990s, New World regions too are beginning to face challenges as the grapes from those recent plantings add to the stocks of wine available for sale.

Looking forward, the paper then draws on a new model of the world's wine markets that distinguishes non-premium, commercial premium and super-plus premium wines in each of 47 countries or country groups spanning the world. It projects developments to 2005, based on trends in income, population and preferences on the demand side and vine acreage and productivity trends on the supply side of each market. The effect of a slowdown in the global economy in the medium term is also considered. Implications of recent and prospective developments on the key wine-exporting regions are exposed by the model's results. Finally, we explore the possibility that in the case of wine, the forces of globalisation and consequent market responses could well be such as to please both the pro- and anti-globalisation groups, while at the same time allowing both small and large firms in the industry to prosper.

2. Brief history of wine industry globalisation

An important aspect of globalisation is the movement of crucial inputs and know-how from established to new areas. The first systematic cultivation of grapevines for wine probably took place between and to the south of the Black and Caspian Seas at least 6,000 years ago. Production knowledge and cuttings of the best subspecies, *Vitis vinifera*, gradually spread west to Egypt, Greece and perhaps southern Spain by 2,500 BC. The Etruscans began vine cultivation in central Italy using native varieties before the 8th century BC, when the Greek colonists began to take cuttings to southern Italy and Sicily. Viticulture was introduced to southern France by the Romans around 600 BC, and was spread north in the 2nd and 1st centuries BC. It took only until the 4th century AD for winegrape cultivation to be well established in what we refer to now as the Old World of Europe, and in North Africa (Robinson, 1994, pp. 697–8). Meanwhile, the drinking of wine in the Middle East went into decline, following Mohammed's decree against alcohol in the 7th century AD (Johnson, 1989, pp. 98–101).

The first explorers of the New World took vine cuttings and know-how with them first to South America and Mexico in the 1500s and to South Africa from 1655. Attempts to export the same technology and varieties to the eastern part of North America from as early as 1619 were unsuccessful, and it took until the Spanish-Mexican Jesuits moved north from Baja California in the early 19th century before cultivation began to flourish in what is now the US State of California. The first grape cultivation in Australia began with cuttings imported by the earliest British settlers in 1788, while for New Zealand it was three decades later (Robinson, 1994, p. 666). In Australia most of the production up to the 1840s was for own-consumption or local markets (Osmond and Anderson, 1998). And even in the subsequent 150 years, Australia, and other New World wine producers, had very little impact on global wine markets, with more than three-quarters of the volume of world wine production, consumption and trade still involving Europe at the end of the 20th century (Table 1).

Table 1. Shares of major regions in world wine production and consumption volume and in value of exports and imports, including and excluding Intra-European union trade, 1988 and 1999 (per cent)

	Production Volume	Consumption Volume	Incl. Intra-EU15		Excl. Intra-EU15	
			Exports	Imports	Exports	Imports
W. European Exporters[a]						
1988	52.4	43.0	82.5	7.4	70.4	0.6
1999	56.7	36.2	74.2	9.2	55.5	0.8
Other Western Europe						
1988	7.1	16.6	8.5	62.8	7.2	25.0
1999	7.5	19.9	6.6	59.9	5.0	32.0
Europe's Transition Economies[b]						
1988	16.5	15.2	5.3	3.7	13.3	9.1
1999	10.2	16.1	2.7	2.5	5.5	5.1
North America						
1988	6.7	9.4	1.1	18.5	2.7	46.0
1999	7.5	9.8	3.6	17.7	7.4	36.1
Latin America						
1988	11.0	10.6	0.4	1.1	1.1	2.8
1999	9.0	8.6	5.0	2.6	10.4	5.2
South Africa						
1988	3.1	1.3	0.1	0.0	0.4	0.1
1999	2.8	1.7	1.4	0.1	2.8	0.2
Australia and N. Zealand						
1988	2.0	1.6	1.4	0.9	3.6	2.2
1999	3.2	1.8	5.8	0.9	11.8	1.9
China and Japan						
1988	0.5	0.8	0.0	3.2	0.1	8.1
1999	2.3	3.6	0.0	5.6	0.1	11.5
WORLD TOTAL (%)						
1988–90	100.0	100.0	100.0	100.0	100.0	100.0
1999	100.0	100.0	100.0	100.0	100.0	100.0
WORLD TOTAL (billion litres or US$)						
1988	27.6	24.7	6.7	6.7	2.7	2.7
1999	28.0	24.0	14.5	14.5	7.1	7.1
Growth rate (% p.a.)	**−0.5**	**−0.1**	**7.2**	**7.2**	**9.7**	**9.7**

Notes:
[a]France, Italy, Portugal and Spain.
[b]Central and Eastern Europe and the former Soviet Union.
Source: Anderson and Norman (2001).

3. Recent developments

While Europe accounted in value terms for all but 4 per cent of global wine exports (and three-quarters of wine imports) in the late 1980s, the world's wine markets since then have been going through major structural changes. In particular, the United States and several Southern Hemisphere countries (Australia, Argentina, Chile, New Zealand, South Africa and Uruguay) are beginning to challenge that European dominance in international markets. Between 1988 and 1999, this New World group's combined share of global wine exports grew from 3 to 16 per cent in value terms. When intra-European Union (EU) trade is excluded, Europe's decline in dominance is even more dramatic: from 82 per cent to 67 per cent, while the New World's share grows from 8 to 31 per cent (Figure 1).

Of the world's top ten wine exporting countries, which account for 90 per cent of the value of international wine trade, half are in Western Europe and the other half are New World suppliers. Europe's economies in transition from socialism account for much of the rest. Of those top ten, Australia is the world's fourth largest exporter of wine, after France (alone accounting in 2000 for more than 40 per cent), Italy (18 per cent) and Spain (9 per cent) — see Figure 2. The share of

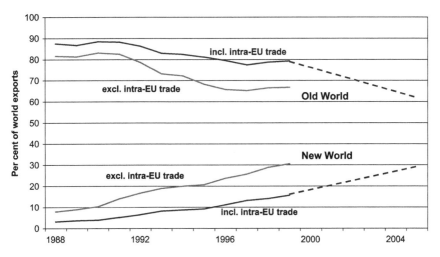

Figure 1. Shares of Old World and New World in the value of global wine exports
Source: Data are from the compilation by Anderson and Norman (2001).

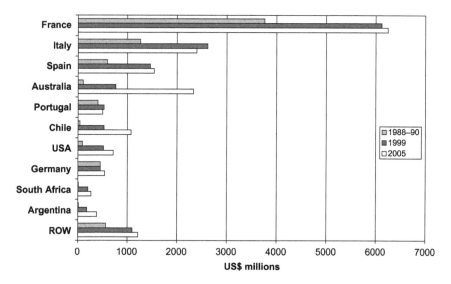

Figure 2. Wine export values, top ten countries
Source: Data are from the compilation by Anderson and Norman (2001).

France has dropped ten percentage points since the late 1980s, which with smaller drops for Italy and Germany have ensured that the shares of Australia and other New World suppliers have risen substantially in key import markets (Figure 3, where Old World is defined as France, Italy, Portugal, Spain, Greece, Bulgaria, Hungary and Romania). In 2000, half the value of all imports continued to be bought by the three biggest importers: the UK (with 18 per cent), the US (with 16 per cent) and Germany (with 14 per cent).

If the European Union is treated as a single trader and so intra-EU trade is excluded from the EU and world trade data, Australia moves to number two in the world and its share of global exports rises from 3 per cent to 11 per cent. It is this fact, in spite of Australia's small share of global production, that has made Australia suddenly a much more significant player in the global wine market. Meanwhile, the share of the other main New World exporters (Argentina, Chile, New Zealand, South Africa and the US) rose even faster, from 4 per cent to 21 per cent (Figure 1). That is, while Australia has done very well as an expanding wine exporter, it is not alone: the world wine market as a whole is becoming more internationalised and far more competitive, and most key New

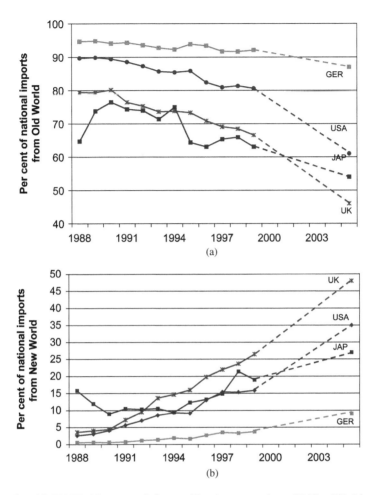

Figure 3. (a) Old World exporters' shares of key import markets. (b) New World exporters' shares of key import markets

Source: Data are from the compilation by Anderson and Norman (2001).

World suppliers are expanding their export sales (albeit from a lower base) nearly as fast or even faster than Australia, as is clear from Figure 4.

The rapid growth in wine exports over the past decade is ironic, in that it coincided with a slight decline in world wine production and consumption. Over the 1988–99 period global wine production fell at 0.5 per cent per year, and yet global wine trade rose by 5.3 per cent per year in volume terms and 7.2 per cent in nominal US dollar value terms (Table 2). As a

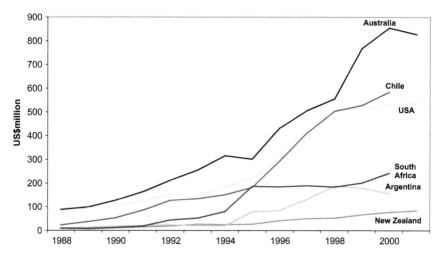

Figure 4. Value of wine exports by new world producers
Source: Data are updated from the compilation by Anderson and Norman (2001).

Table 2. Growth in wine production, consumption and export volume and value, major regions, 1988 to 1999 (per cent per year, from log-linear regression equations)

	Export Volume	Export Value	Production Volume	Consumption Volume
Western European Exporters[a]	4.4	5.8	−0.7	−1.6
Other Western Europe	1.4	5.5	−1.1	1.5
Europe's Transition Economies[b]	4.4	6.5	−3.1	0.6
North America	16.8	18.2	2.7	0.4
Latin America	22.7	30.9	−1.4	−2.2
South Africa	32.0	33.8	0.4	2 2
Australia	15.6	19.3	5.3	1.2
New Zealand	15.8	20.3	2.0	2.5
China	12.9	12.7	15.1	16.3
WORLD TOTAL	**5.3**	**7.2**	**−0.5**	**−0.1**

Notes:
[a]France, Italy, Portugal and Spain.
[b]Central and Eastern Europe and the former Soviet Union.
Source: Anderson and Norman (2001).

result, the trade orientation of the industry has increased substantially: hugely for the New World, but significantly also for Europe. Traditionally the countries producing wine were also the countries consuming it, with only about one-tenth of global sales being across national borders. The proportion traded rose a little over the 1980s but has since risen much more, so that now about one-quarter of the volume of sales is international.[1] That is, despite per capita wine consumption falling by 1.5 per cent per year over the 1990s globally, wine is becoming much more of an internationally traded product as consumption shrinks in the traditional producing countries (from a high base) and consumption expands in non-producing countries in Europe and East Asia (from a low base — see Figure 5).

Within the New World, the contributors to their high rates of export growth are various. Australia's exports grew rapidly because its production growth was much faster than its consumption growth. By contrast, in North America much slower production growth accompanied even slower growth in the aggregate volume of consumption. Meanwhile, in the southern cone of Latin America production actually declined, but less so than domestic consumption, allowing exports to boom (Table 3). Volumes of consumption per capita have become a little more equal across regions as a result but, as Table 3 shows, there is still a wide variance.

The differing production changes in turn are and will continue for some time to be due to diverging trends in the area under vines: slow declines in Europe at the same time as dramatic increases in parts of the New World. Those differing trends in vine area are important inputs into our projection of wine production to 2005 (see next section).

What is happening to the quality of the wine being traded? While France's strong position has changed little, New Zealand and to a lesser extent Australia have improved their positions considerably to rival the

---

[1] Anderson and Norman (2001). When expressed in *value* terms that share is considerably higher (almost 40 per cent, according to our model discussed in the next section), because most non-premium wine is not traded internationally.

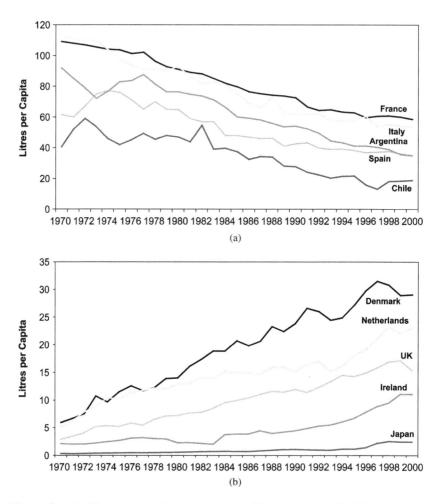

Figure 5. (a) Wine consumption per capita, traditional markets. (b) Wine per capita consumption, emerging markets

Source: Updated from Anderson and Norman (2001).

quality dominance of France's exports. New Zealand's average export price is well ahead of France's now, and Australia is just 50 cents per litre behind France. Meanwhile, the price of exports from other Southern Hemisphere suppliers and the US in 1999 was barely half the Australasian average. The quality of wine imported varies a great deal across countries

Table 3. Volume of wine production and consumption per capita, trade orientation, and price of exports, by region, 1988–90 and 1999

	Volume of Prod'n per Capita (litres pa)	Volume of Cons'n per Capita (litres pa)	Exports as % of Prod'n	Imports as % of Cons'n	Prod'n as % of Cons'n	Index of Comp. Adv.[d]	Export Unit Value (US$/l)
Western European Exporter[a]							
1988–90	98	63	21	7	156	6.34	1.88
1999	96	52	31	8	164	5.95	2.29
Other Western Europe							
1988–90	10	19	20	64	53	0.25	1.48
1999	7	21	25	72	35	0.23	2.11
Europe's Transition Economies[b]							
1988–90	9	8	5	3	108	0.36	0.77
1999	8	8	20	18	106	1.26	1.01
North America							
1988–90	7	8	3	19	89	0.08	1.75
1999	8	8	6	27	112	0.21	2.52
Latin America							
1988–90	0	0	9	38	96	0.02	0.73
1999	0	0	5	46	73	0.02	1.46
South Africa							
1988–90	15	14	2	1	110	0.38	1.13
1999	12	9	14	4	137	2.49	1.77
Australia							
1988–90	27	19	10	3	149	1.16	2.17
1999	45	20	30	6	228	5.16	2.98
New Zealand							
1988–90	15	14	7	16	102	0.39	2.61
1999	16	16	28	50	100	2.00	3.99
China							
1988–90	0.1	0.1	1	0	101	0.02	1.80
1999	0.4	0.4	1	7	94	0.02	1.27

(*Continued*)

Table 3. (Continued)

	Volume of Prod'n per Capita (litres pa)	Volume of Cons'n per Capita (litres pa)	Exports as % of Prod'n	Imports as % of Cons'n	Prod'n as % of Cons'n	Index of Comp. Adv.[d]	Export Unit Value (US$/l)
WORLD TOTAL							
1988–90	**5.4**	**4.6**	**15**	**18**	**117[c]**	**1.00**	**1.67**
1999	**4.7**	**4.0**	**25**	**29**	**117[c]**	**1.00**	**2.10**
Growth rate (% p.a.)	–1.0	–1.6	5.9	5.4	na	na	1.80
Memo item: EU-15							
1988–90	47	38	20	22	130	2.08	1.84
1999	48	34	30	37	139	2.18	2.19

Notes:
[a]France, Italy, Portugal and Spain.
[b]Central and Eastern Europe and the former Soviet Union.
[c]Production exceeds consumption globally because consumption is net of distillation and other industrial uses.
[d]The index of comparative advantage is defined as the share of wine in a region's merchandise exports divided by the share of wine in global merchandise exports.
Source: Anderson and Norman (2001).

too, although much less so now than in the late 1980s. The United States stands out a long way ahead of Japan and Switzerland, who in turn are a long way ahead of the United Kingdom and smaller EU countries. By contrast Germany, the world's biggest importer in volume terms, imports relatively low quality wine (Anderson, Norman and Wittwer, 2001, Figures 8(a) and (b)).

The Australian average unit export price (in nominal US dollars) rose at 3.8 per cent per year from 1988 to 1999 compared with the global average of 1.9 per cent, but that was exceeded by Chile (11.1 per cent), New Zealand (4.6 per cent), Argentina (4.1 per cent) and Uruguay (4.0 per cent), and not far behind was Italy (3.3 per cent). Clearly, all New World exporters are striving to raise the quality of their exports, albeit from different bases. Meanwhile, the average unit export price for Europe's big four exporters rose less than 1.5 per cent over those dozen years (Anderson and Norman, 2001).

4. Prospects to 2005 and beyond

What might be the net effect on global wine markets of current trends in grape and wine supply and demand? The trend towards premium and away from non-premium wine production and consumption, together with the data on new plantings (the most recent of which will take until 2005 to produce significant crops), provide enough information to attempt to project wine markets a few years into the present decade.

4.1. *A model of global wine markets*

To do such a projection requires a global model of grape and wine markets that differentiates not only according to country of origin but also as between premium and non-premium segments of each market and each bilateral trade flow. A prototype model for that purpose was reported on recently (Wittwer, Berger and Anderson, 2003). Since the compilation of the Statistical Compendium by Anderson and Norman (2001), that prototype has been improved considerably. Specifically, it now includes the same 47 countries/country groups shown in the Anderson/Norman compendium for 1999. It also divides premium wine into commercial and super premium classes, with the dividing lines between the three wine classes being somewhat arbitrarily set at US$1 and US$4 per litre at the wholesale pre-tax level in 1999 (equivalent to about AUD3 and AUD12 per 750 ml at the tax-inclusive retail level in Australia). The model's database has half the volume of global wine consumption in the non-premium category and one-sixth in super premium (following Geene *et al.*, 1999), while the value shares are one-fifth and two-fifths, the residual being commercial premium.

The projections model is based on perfectly competitive microeconomic theory. In each region, market demands and supplies reflect utility- and profit-maximising behaviour, with supplies equalling demands globally for each grape and wine product. Competitive prices are set equal to unit costs. While the model has several commodities it is partial equilibrium in the sense that the prices of intermediate inputs, other than grapes used in production of wine, are taken as given.

On the demand side, households consume 'other' products in addition to grapes and wine, where 'other' is a composite of all other goods and services. The theory of household demand employed is based on the Stone-Geary utility function. A consumption function allows the user to tie changes in household expenditure to changes in income. We impose Armington (1969) elasticities of substitution in consumption between domestic and imported wine of 8.0, slightly higher than for beverages within the GTAP database (Hertel, 1996) because of the greater possibilities for substitution the more disaggregated is a product category. For substitution between different sources of wine imports, we chose 16.0. The expenditure elasticities in the initial database are 1.7 for premium wine and 0.8 for super-premium wine, and 0.5 for non-premium, based on estimates for Australia (CIE, 1995). The Frisch parameter is initially −1.82 in Australia, the European Union and North America, and a slightly larger (absolute) value elsewhere, reflecting the latter's lower per capita incomes.

On the supply side, each region's wine is differentiated from the wine of each other region, so no region's domestically produced wine is a perfect substitute for wine imported from other regions. The model assumes that most factors used in grape and wine production are fixed. This is reasonable for the short to medium term, given the large fixed costs and partly irreversible nature of vineyard and winery investments. Labour is a mobile factor within each region but human capital is fixed, and all factors are assumed to be immobile internationally.[2] Each industry within the model uses intermediate goods that, together with a primary factor composite, are proportional to total output for a given production technology. The degree of mobility in the version of the model used here implies that in response to external shocks, comparative static adjustments are mostly through price (including changes in factor rewards) rather than output changes. The elasticity of substitution between primary factors is set at 0.5. Were we to allow for endogeneity of primary factors other than labour, supply within the model would be more price-responsive.

In its present form the model's database includes six intermediate input commodities (chemicals, water, premium grapes, multipurpose grapes, non-premium wine, and other), six endogenous outputs (premium

---

[2] In specific scenarios, we can of course alter the assumptions concerning factor mobility, for example, by allowing wine industry human capital to be partly mobile between regions.

winegrapes, multipurpose grapes, super premium wine, commercial premium wine, non-premium wine and non-beverage wine) and 47 regions.

4.2. *Projecting the database to 2005*

New World producers have planted unprecedented areas to premium winegrapes since the mid-1990s. These are modelled to translate into substantially increased premium winegrape supplies by the early years of the new millennium and, after allowing for lags associated with wine maturation, much larger volumes of sales by 2005. Assumptions about aggregate expenditure growth and population growth are based on World Bank projections as used by Hertel, Anderson, Francois and Martin (2002). Their total factor productivity growth assumption for the manufacturing sector is assumed to apply also to wine making. For the primary activity of winegrape production, we assume a small decrease in total factor productivity, because growers are seeking to decrease yields and chemical and water application in order to increase winegrape quality. Growers will be rewarded for upgrading their quality in the form of effective demand growth, since we also assume a continuation of the movement in consumer preferences away from non-premium and towards premium wines.[3] We also assume that there is a preference swing in Germany towards imported wines, due to growing domestic preferences for premium red wine (not produced in Germany) over premium white wine. Growth in primary factor use is based on available plantings data. We assume that the wine industry attracts an accommodating increase in other factor supplies to match the new plantings, and that there are no changes in consumer or import taxes on wine. Also as part of that base case, we assume that, between 2001 and 2005, consumers show an increasing preference for Australian wines over those from other regions in response to the major marketing strategy launched by the Australian

---

[3] In the latter 1990s, growers in New World countries such as Australia and the US received very high prices for winegrapes, with origin often mattering less than variety. Following the recent rash of plantings the premiums that were being paid in response to winegrape shortages are now being replaced by higher premiums for quality. With the increase in winegrape supply and falling demand for non-premium wine, growers are finding it more difficult to market low quality, high yielding grapes.

industry in November 2000 (WFA and AWBC, 2000). The extent of that shift is enough to reduce the projected decline in the producer price of Australian commercial premium grapes between 1999 and 2005 from 10 per cent to 2 per cent (while having little influence on producer prices in other countries). The resulting base case is examined in some detail below, before briefly looking at the implication of a slowdown in income growth in the medium term following the 11 September, 2001, disaster in New York and Washington DC.

Table 4 summarises the key growth assumptions in projecting the model from 1999 to 2005. The volume of world wine consumption is projected to grow at less than 1 per cent per year from 1999 to 2005, but the premium segments (44 per cent of global wine output in 1999) grow in aggregate at 3.7 per cent per year while output of non-premium wine declines slightly. The results for each country are too numerous to include, but trends to 2005 are shown in some of the figures above. Key points are as follows:

- The share of global wine production that is exported rises from 25 per cent in 1999 to 28 per cent by 2005 in volume terms, or from 37 to 39 per cent in value terms;
- The New World's share of global wine exports continues to grow, from 16 per cent in 1999 to 29 per cent in 2005, while the Old World's share falls further from 79 to 63 per cent (Figure 1);
- The value of wine exports from several of the New World countries continue to grow spectacularly, with Australia's nearly trebling between 2000 and 2005 and the Southern Cone's roughly doubling, but US exports grow somewhat slower as their domestic market absorbs much of their increase (Figure 2); and
- The New World surpasses the Old World's share of the United Kingdom market by 2005 (48 vs 46 per cent), having been less than half as large in 1999 (26 vs 67 per cent), and the gap closes in most other markets and especially the United States where the New World's share of the value of wine imports rises from 16 to 35 per cent as the Old World's falls commensurately from 81 to 61 per cent (Figure 3).

The projections numbers perhaps most sought after by producers are the prices they can expect to receive. For the world as a whole, the model's

Table 4. Assumed per cent changes in key markets in projecting global wine markets from 1999 to 2005

Factor Assumptions	FRA	ITA	POR	SPN	GER	UK	CEF	AUS	USA	ARG	CHILE	SAF
Premium grapes												
Human K	5.0	5.0	5.0	15.0	5.0	5.0	5.0	100.0	40.0	15.0	70.0	5.0
Fixed K	10.0	10.0	10.0	25.0	10.0	10.0	10.0	130.0	50.0	15.0	80.0	10.0
Non-premium grapes												
Human K	-5.0	-5.0	-5.0	-20.0	-5.0	-5.0	-5.0	10.0	-5.0	-15.0	-5.0	-5.0
Fixed K	-5.0	-5.0	-5.0	-20.0	-5.0	-5.0	-5.0	10.0	-5.0	-15.0	-5.0	-5.0
Super premium wine												
Human K	6.7	6.7	6.7	15.0	6.7	6.7	6.7	87.0	33.0	20.0	54.0	6.7
Fixed K	6.7	6.7	6.7	15.0	6.7	6.7	6.7	87.0	33.0	20.0	54.0	6.7
Commercial premium wine												
Human K	5.0	5.0	5.0	12.5	5.0	5.0	5.0	65.0	25.0	15.0	40.0	5.0
Fixed K	5.0	5.0	5.0	12.5	5.0	5.0	5.0	65.0	25.0	15.0	40.0	5.0
Non-premium wine												
Human K	-30.0	-30.0	-30.0	-30.0	-30.0	-30.0	-30.0	-30.0	-30.0	-30.0	-30.0	-30.0
Fixed K	-25.0	-25.0	-25.0	-25.0	-25.0	-25.0	-25.0	-25.0	-25.0	-25.0	-25.0	-25.0
Population	0.6	0.6	0.6	0.6	0.6	0.6	6.8	6.0	6.0	4.0	4.0	7.0
Aggregate expenditure	14.6	14.6	14.6	14.6	14.6	14.6	17.3	19.4	18.7	19.0	19.0	19.0
Preference changes (negative indicates reduced demand)												
Non-premium wine	-26.0	-26.0	-26.0	-26.0	-16.0	-16.0	-16.0	-16.0	-16.0	-16.0	-16.0	-16.0
Commercial premium wine	6.0	6.0	6.0	6.0	6.0	6.0	6.0	6.0	6.0	6.0	6.0	6.0
Super premium wine	10.0	10.0	10.0	10.0	10.0	10.0	10.0	10.0	10.0	10.0	10.0	10.0
Preference swing by source in all buying regions (negative indicates reduced demand)												
Non-premium wine	0.0	0.0	0.0	0.0	0.0	0.0	0.0	0.0	0.0	0.0	0.0	0.0
Commercial premium wine	-7.5	-7.5	-7.5	-7.5	0.0	0.0	-7.5	7.5	0.0	7.5	7.5	10.0
Super premium wine	-7.5	-7.5	-7.5	-7.5	0.0	0.0	-7.5	7.5	0.0	7.5	7.5	7.5

base case projects the 2005 price for non-premium wine to be the same as in 1999 in real terms. This comes about because the very slow growth in consumption is just matched by the change in projected supply as producers upgrade the quality of their vineyards and wineries. The global average producer prices of commercial premium and super premium wines are projected to decline slightly over the 1999–2005 period (by 7 and 3 per cent, respectively), because the supply growth outstrips the projected growth in the demand for premium wines (Table 5). Yet for all wine as an aggregate, the global average producer price rises 12 per cent. This reflects the fact that the average quality of the wine being produced around the world is rising, with global annual output expanding 13 per cent for commercial premium and 45 per cent for super premium wine while shrinking 10 per cent for non-premium wine. The wine producer price effects differ by country though: super premium prices fall

Table 5. Projected per cent change in grape and wine producer prices and outputs, 1999 to 2005, selected countries

	Commercial Premium Wine	Super Premium Wine	Premium Grapes
Price			
France	−5.7	−5.7	5.7
Spain	−12.0	−7.1	0.2
USA	−10.4	−1.3	−7.5
Chile	−5.4	−1.5	−3.8
Australia	−0.7	9.0	−0.9
WORLD TOTAL	**−6.7**	**−3.1**	
Output			
France	−0	22	12
Spain	22	33	26
USA	36	57	45
Chile	99	136	115
Australia	99	136	115
WORLD TOTAL	**13**	**45**	

Source: Authors' model results.

less than commercial premium, particularly in the countries where commercial volumes are rising rapidly (USA, Spain and Australia).

What have been the relative contributions of the different forces at work over the projection period? To answer that question, consider as an example the premium segment of the Australian industry. The base scenario projects that premium grape prices will hardly be any different in 2005 than in 1999 (a fall of just 0.9 per cent in real US dollar terms). It also projects little change in the producer price of commercial premium wines (−0.7 per cent), and a 9 per cent rise in super premium prices (much of which may have already happened during 1999–2001). How can that be, when we know there will be at least a doubling in premium grape and wine supplies as the large areas of newly planted vines come into full production in Australia over the next few years?

To answer that question the results are decomposed in Table 6 into six components. The first one is the expansion in supply in Australia and other New World wine exporting countries. On its own, it would depress premium grape prices by 31 per cent and premium wine prices by more than 40 per cent (row 1 of Table 6). The assumed upgrading of vineyards and wineries in the Old World further depresses international prices of premium relative to non-premium wines, which on its own would lower premium wine prices for producers in Australia by a further 10 per cent. However, there are four offsetting forces at work. One is the assumed overall global economic growth, which on its own would be enough to lift premium wine prices in Australia by about one-quarter over this period. The second is an assumed continuation of the gradual preference swing globally away from non-premium and towards premium wine, which adds another one-twelfth. The third is an assumed continuation of the gradual preference swing in the Northern Hemisphere towards fruit-driven New World styles, which adds another one-eighth. Had they been the only influences, the producer prices in Australia would have been projected to fall by about 3 per cent for super premium wine, 12 per cent for commercial premium wine, and 8 per cent for premium grapes. But that would have been to ignore the campaign launched in November 2000 to boost substantially the promotion of Australian wines abroad (WFA and AWBC, 2000). We assumed that will be capable of shifting out the demand for Australian premium wines enough to boost their average price by

Table 6. Decomposition of the projected changes in producer prices and outputs in Australia's premium wine industry, 1999 to 2005 (per cent change over the period)[a]

	Commercial Premium Wine	Super Premium Wine	Premium Grapes
Producer price change (per cent) due to:			
1. New World expansion in premium grape and wine supplies	−45.7	−41.6	−30.7
2. Old World resource re-allocation from non-premium to premium	−9.7	−11.8	−7.1
3. Global growth in population and per capita expenditure	24.6	27.7	17.3
4. Preference swing globally from non-premium to premium wine	7.2	9.1	5.4
5. Preference swing in N. Hemisphere towards New World fruit-driven wines	12.6	14.1	8.9
6. Enhanced Australian promotion drive (shifts Northern Hemisphere preferences toward Australian wine)	10.9	11.8	7.5
TOTAL	**−0.7**	**9.0**	**−0.9**
Production changes (per cent)	**99**	**136**	**115**

Note:
[a]Numbers do not add up exactly because of rounding.
Source: Authors' model results.

about 11 per cent, which in turn raises the price of premium grapes by 7.5 per cent (row 6 of Table 6).

Those results are based on World Bank projections of overall economic growth in the various countries of the world as of early 2001. Since then, there has been a substantial downgrading of those forecasts. We therefore explored the effects of halving the assumed rate of growth for the 1999–2005 period. A sample of results is shown in Table 7, for producer prices of premium grapes and wines in several countries. The first five rows of columns 1 and 2 show the depressing effect of lower incomes on premium wine prices, and slightly more so for super premium than for commercial premium wines (because of different income elasticities of demand). On average they would be dampened by about one-seventh,

Table 7. Decomposition of the additional effect on premium grape and wine producer prices of assuming slower global economic growth (which reduces household expenditure and causes wineries to expand processing capacity less) (per cent difference in 2005)

	Commercial Premium Wine	Super Premium Wine	Premium Grapes
Slower growth in household expenditure			
France	−13.7	−14.1	−18
Spain	−12.4	−14.4	−18
USA	−14.2	−16.2	−11
Chile	−13.6	−15.6	−8
Australia	−13.4	−14.9	−8
Slower growth in winery processing capacity			
France	4.4	4.4	5
Spain	4.7	4.6	2
USA	7.4	6.3	−8
Chile	8.6	8.2	−8
Australia	8.8	7.5	−20
TOTAL EFFECT			
France	−9.3	−9.7	−13
Spain	−7.7	−9.8	−16
USA	−6.8	−9.9	−19
Chile	−5.0	−7.4	−17
Australia	−4.7	−7.4	−28

Source: Authors' model results.

other things equal. But in fact other things would not be equal if there was such a downturn in the global economy. In particular, wineries could be expected to reduce their planned investments in processing capacity if their profits expectations were dampened. We assume Australia would reduce its sizeable planned investments by wineries over the period to 2005 by 15 per cent, and that other countries would reduce their more modest expansions by 25 per cent. The second set of rows in Table 7 shows that such a scaling back has a considerable offsetting effect on wine prices, especially in the New World countries where some major winery expansions would be delayed. However, such a postponement would depress New World grape prices, reinforcing the direct effect of an economic downturn. This is particularly so in Australia where premium grape supplies will be expanding fastest over the next four years. If the extent of slowdown in winery expansion is as great as modelled, the price of premium grapes in Australia in 2005 would be 28 per cent lower than they would otherwise have been, that is, 29 per cent instead of just 1 per cent lower than in 1999 (see Table 6). Wine prices, however, would be dampened much less because of that investment response by wineries. In Australia's case the commercial premium price would fall 5 instead of only 1 per cent between 1999 and 2005, and the super premium price would rise by only 2 per cent instead of rising by 9 per cent.

5. Conclusion

What the above projection exercise demonstrates is that the answer to the question as to where grape and wine producer prices might be in a few years' time is the same as the answer to all such economic questions, and that is: it depends. But a global model such as that used here is able is give an indication of the relative importance of different contributing factors under certain assumptions. As well, when circumstances change such as an unexpected economic downturn, the model can be rerun with just that change to see its likely effects.

In developing and using this model of the world's wine markets it does NOT follow that we think wine is just another primary commodity whose heterogeneity can be ignored. On the contrary, we have gone to considerable trouble to differentiate producers and consumers by country of origin and to sub-divide wine into three different qualities. The constraint on doing more than that is unavailability of reliable data, but that is not the main point we would stress. Rather, it is that the forces of supply and demand work as well for wine as for any other product, regardless of how much heterogeneity there is within the industry. Hence we can get a sense from the model of how prices might move *on average*, even if an individual producer, through his/her own actions, may be an outlier.

What, then, does globalisation mean for small regions and boutique producers? With increasing affluence comes an increasing demand for many things including product variety (the spice of life). Certainly homogeneous wines such as those in the basic Jacob's Creek family (which retail in Australia at just under AUD10 and which go abroad in whole shiploads at a time) are wonderfully easy to mass-market to newcomers to wine drinking through such outlets as supermarkets in the UK. However, over time, many of those consumers will look for superior and more-varied wines. They will begin to differentiate between grape varieties, between not just countries of origin but regions within them, and, with the help of wine critics such as Hugh Johnson in the UK, Robert Parker in the US and James Halliday in Australia, between brands and the various labels within a brand.[4] That preference for heterogeneity on the demand side, and the infinite scope for experimentation by vignerons on the supply side, ensures that there will always be small and medium producers alongside the few large corporations in the wine industry. Undoubtedly the forces of globalisation together with the boom in premium winegrape supplies will lead to more mergers, acquisitions and other alliances among wineries within and across national borders, but their success in the global marketplace is likely to continue to provide a slipstream in which astute smaller operators can also thrive.

References

Anderson, K. and D. Norman (2001), *Global Wine Production, Consumption and Trade, 1961 to 1999: A Statistical Compendium* (Adelaide, Centre for International Economic Studies, in print and CD-ROM versions).

Anderson, K., D. Norman and G. Wittwer (2001), 'Globalization and the World's Wine Markets: Overview', Paper presented at the Workshop on Understanding Developments in the World's Wine Markets (Adelaide, 11–12 October, http://www.adelaide.edu.au/CIES/0143.pdf).

Armington, P. A. (1969), 'A Theory of Demand for Products Distinguished by Place of Production', *IMF Staff Papers*, **16**, 159–78.

Berger, N. (2000), 'Modelling Structural and Policy Changes in the World Wine Market into the 21st Century', Unpublished Master's Dissertation (University of Adelaide, November).

---

[4] For empirical evidence of the growing extent of such discernment by consumers, see Schamel (2000) and Schamel and Anderson (2003). To date this preference for variety has not shown up in much growth in intra-industry trade except for North America (see Anderson and Norman, 2001, Table 49).

Berger, N. and K. Anderson (1999), 'Consumer and Import Taxes in the World Wine Market: Australia in International Perspective', *Australian Agribusiness Review*, **7**, 3 (June).
CIE (Centre for International Economics) (1995), 'Generation of Demand Parameters for an Economy-wide Model of the Grape and Wine Industry', Prepared for the Commonwealth Government Inquiry into the Wine Grape and Wine Industry (Canberra, February).
Geene, A., A. Heijbroek, A. Lagerwerf and R. Wazir (1999), *The World Wine Business* (Utrecht, Rabobank International).
Hertel, T. (ed.) (1996), *Global Trade Analysis: Modeling and Applications* (New York, Cambridge University Press).
Hertel, T., K. Anderson, J. Francois and W. Martin (2002), 'Agriculture and Non-Agricultural Liberalisation in the Millennium Round', in M. D. Ingco and L. A. Winters (eds.), *Agriculture and the New Trade Agenda from a Development Perspective* (Cambridge and New York, Cambridge University Press, forthcoming).
Johnson, H. (1989), *The Story of Wine* (London: Mitchell Beasley).
Osmond, R. and K. Anderson (1998), *Trends and Cycles in the Australian Wine Industry, 1850 to 2000* (Adelaide, Centre for International Economic Studies).
Robinson, J. (1994), *The Oxford Companion to Wine* (London, Oxford University Press).
Schamel, G. (2000), 'Individual and Collective Reputation Indicators of Wine Quality', Discussion Paper 00/09 (Centre for International Economic Studies, Adelaide University, March, www.adelaide.edu.au/CIES/wine.htm#other).
Schamel, G. and K. Anderson (2003), 'Wine Quality and Varietal, Regional and Winery Reputations: Hedonic Prices for Australia and New Zealand', *The Economic Record* **79**, 246, 357–69.
WFA (Winemakers' Federation of Australia) and AWBC (Australian Wine and Brandy Corporation) (2000), *The Marketing Decade: Setting the Australian Wine Marketing Agenda 2000–2010* (Adelaide, WFA).
Wittwer, G. and K. Anderson (2003), 'A Model of the World's Wine Markets', *Economic Modelling*, **20**, 3, 487–506.

Chapter 3

Modeling Global Wine Markets to 2018: Exchange Rates, Taste Changes, and China's Import Growth*

Kym Anderson[†] and Glyn Wittwer[‡]

Abstract

In this paper, we use a revised, expanded, and updated version of a global model first developed by Wittwer et al. (2003) to project the wine markets of its 44 countries plus seven residual country groups to 2018. Because real exchange rate (RER) changes have played a key role in the fortunes of wine market participants in some countries in recent years,

---

*First published in *Journal of Wine Economics* 8(2): 131–58, 2013. Revision of a plenary paper presented at the American Association of Wine Economists' Annual Conference, Stellenbosch, South Africa, June 26–29, 2013. Thanks are due to conference delegates for helpful comments and to Australia's Grape and Wine Research and Development Corporation for financial support under Project Number UA 12/08. Views expressed are solely those of the authors.

[†]Wine Economics Research Centre, School of Economics, University of Adelaide, Adelaide SA 5005 Australia; e-mail: kym.anderson@adelaide.edu.au (contact author).

[‡]Centre of Policy Studies, Monash University, Clayton Vic. 3168 Australia.

we use the model to analyze their impact, first retrospectively during 2007–11 and then prospectively during the period to 2018 under two alternative sets of RERs: no change, and a halfway return to 2009 rates. In both scenarios, we assume a return to the gradual trend toward premium wines and away from nonpremium wines. The other major development expected to affect the world's wine trade is growth in China's import demand. Alternative simulations provide a range of possibilities, but even the low-growth scenario suggests that China's place in global wine markets is likely to become increasingly prominent.

1. Introduction

Wine markets throughout the world have been hit by two major shocks in recent years. The first is the global financial crisis (GFC), which brought substantial changes in bilateral real exchange rates (RERs) and — due to the fall in income and wealth — a temporary decline in the quantity and quality of wine demanded in traditional markets. The second is the rapid economic growth in China (and other emerging Asian economies), which slowed only slightly when high-income economies went into recession after 2007. Because Asia's emerging economies are natural resource-poor, their rapid industrialization and economic growth have strengthened primary product prices and hence the RERs of natural resource-rich countries such as Australia. And because their income growth has led to a burgeoning middle class and enriched their elite, the demand for wine in Asia has surged. It has grown especially rapidly in China, leading to an increase in the U.S. dollar value of its wine imports of about 50 percent per year in both 2006–2009 and 2009–2012. That in turn has stimulated vineyard expansion and rapid growth in wine production in China, although not enough to match domestic demand growth. The wine industry in those Southern Hemisphere countries whose RERs strengthened has been hurt by that appreciation but helped by the growth in Asian wine import demand.

These recent shocks to the world economy matter to grape growers and winemakers in both the Old World and the New World far more than most past shocks. This is partly because of the move by most countries to flexible exchange rates since the 1980s and partly because in the past two decades the wine industry has become more globalized than ever. The share of global wine production exported has more than doubled between 1989 and 2009, rising from 15 percent (which was already above its peak in the first globalization wave a century earlier) to 32 percent, and it reached 41 percent in 2012. In the four biggest European wine-exporting countries, their export propensity rose over the two decades to 2009 from 20 to 35 percent, while for New World exporters it rose from just 4 percent to 37 percent (Anderson and Nelgen, 2011). In 2012, those shares reached 49 and 42 percent, respectively, according to OIV (2013). Moreover, these exporters are much more exposed now than in the past to import competition in their domestic market.

In the wake of these global shocks, the wine industry in numerous countries is struggling to anticipate where the world's wine markets are headed in the next few years. A formal model of economic behavior in those markets can assist in analyzing recent or prospective changes. The purpose of this paper is to use a revised, expanded, and updated version of the model of the world's wine markets developed by Wittwer *et al.* (2003) to project those markets to 2018. Because RERs have played a dominant role in the fortunes of some countries' wine markets in recent years, we first incorporate those changes to 2011 before considering two alternative paths over the 2011–2018 period for RERs: no change, and a halfway return to 2009 rates. In both scenarios, we assume a return to the pre-GFC gradual trend toward premium wines and away from nonpremium wines. Because growth in China's imports dominates the trade picture in both scenarios, another scenario is included in which we alter three variables that dampen China's import demand, to indicate the degree of sensitivity of results to our assumptions concerning those variables.

The paper begins in Section 2 by documenting an important consequence of the two changes in the world economy mentioned above (the global financial crisis and the rapid increase in Asia's share of global income and trade), namely, their impact on nominal and real exchange rates. Section 3 then outlines the revised model of the world's wine markets and the way in which changes in real exchange rates and other variables are applied as shocks. (Details of the model are included in the Appendix.) The model's simulation results of the effects of the dramatic exchange rate changes between 2007 and 2011 on producer prices are summarized in Section 4. Prospective changes to grape and wine markets by 2018 are then simulated for our two alternative paths for real exchange rates over the next five years (no change, and a halfway return to 2009 rates) and for a variation on projected conditions in the Chinese market, results of which are summarized in Section 5. Section 6 draws out implications of the findings for wine markets and their participants in the years ahead.

2. Exchange rate changes, 2007 to 2011

The shocks given to depict the changes between 2007 and 2011 in the international competitiveness of key countries in global wine markets are shown in the first three columns of Appendix Table 1(a). Column (1) shows nominal exchange rates relative to the U.S. dollar, ϕ_d, column (2) shows the price of the gross domestic product (GDP), P_d^g, and column (3) shows the price of consumer goods, P_d^c.[1] Column (4) shows the real exchange rate movement relative to the U.S. currency, ϕ_d^R. As outlined in the Appendix, this endogenous variable is calculated as: $\phi_d^R = P_d^g / [P_{"USA"}^g * \phi_d]$.

The fourth column of Appendix Table 1(a) provides observed changes in international competitiveness in 44 key wine-producing and wine-consuming countries between 2007 and 2011. It is clear that both rapidly growing East Asia (i.e., mainland China and, to a lesser extent, Japan and Southeast Asia) and that region's natural resource–rich trading partners (notably Australia among the significant wine-exporting countries) appreciated their real exchange rates heavily against the U.S. dollar (by 17–35 percent). Real exchange rates of other New World wine exporters (Argentina, Chile, New Zealand, South Africa) appreciated almost as much. By contrast, the British pound *depreciated* heavily against the U.S. dollar (by 18 percent), while in other West European countries — both wine-exporting and wine-importing — real exchange rates remained close to the U.S. dollar during that period in real terms.

The effect of these real exchange rate changes over that five-year period is analyzed first, leaving aside all other influences on the world's

---

[1] In the case of Argentina, the official CPI has been understating the inflation rate, so we have relied instead on Cavallo (2013).

wine markets during that time. To model that, we shock our global wine markets model with those RER changes. The results are presented in Section 4 below, preceded in Section 3 with an outline of the model and its database, where we also lay out the RER assumptions for the prospective analysis to 2018.

3. Revised model of the world's wine markets and its database

We have revised and updated a model of the world's wine markets that was first published by Wittwer *et al.* (2003). As explained in the Appendix, several significant enhancements have been made to that original model. Wine markets have been disaggregated into five types, namely, nonpremium (including bulk), commercial-premium, superpremium and iconic still wines, and sparkling wine.[2] There are two types of grapes, premium and nonpremium. Nonpremium wine uses nonpremium grapes exclusively, superpremium and iconic wines use premium grapes exclusively, and commercial-premium and sparkling wines use both types of grapes. The world is divided into 44 individual countries and seven composite regions.

The model's database is calibrated initially to 2009, based on the comprehensive volume and value data and trade and excise tax data provided in Anderson and Nelgen (2011). It is projected forward in two steps. The first step involves using actual aggregate national consumption and population growth between 2009 and 2011 (the most recent year for which data were available for all countries when the study began), together with the changes in real exchange rates reported in Appendix Table 1(b). The second step assumes aggregate national consumption and population grow from 2011 to 2018 at the rates shown in Appendix Table 2 and that real exchange rates over that period either (a) remain at

---
[2] Commercial-premium still wines are defined by Anderson and Nelgen (2011) as those between US$2.50 and $7.50 per liter pretax at a country's border or wholesale. Iconic still wines are a small subset above superpremium wines. They are assumed to have an average wholesale pretax price of $80 per liter and to account for just 0.45% of global wine production and consumption.

their 2011 levels or (b) return halfway to their 2009 rates (except for China, whose RER is assumed to continue to appreciate slightly, by 2 percent per year between 2011 and 2018). In each of those steps, a number of additional assumptions are made concerning preferences, technologies, and capital stocks.

Concerning preferences, there is assumed to be a considerable swing towards all wine types in China, as more Chinese achieve middle-class incomes. Because aggregate wine consumption is projected by the major commodity forecasters to rise by 70 percent over that seven-year period, we calibrate the increase in China's consumption to that in the most likely of our scenarios in which exchange rates revert halfway back from 2011 to 2009 rates. That implies a rise in per capita consumption from 1.0 to 1.6 liters per year. This may be too conservative. Per-capita wine consumption grew faster than that in several West European wine-importing countries in recent decades, and Vinexpo claims that China's 2012 consumption was already 1.4 liters per year. Because the middle class in China currently numbers around 250 million and is growing at 10 million per year (Barton *et al.*, 2013; Kharas, 2010) and because grape wine still accounts for only 4 percent of alcohol consumption by China's 1.1 million adults, large increases in the volume of wine demanded are not unreasonable to expect. However, if China's income growth were to grow more slowly than we assume and if that meant that China's RER did not continue to appreciate slightly, wine import growth would be slower. For the rest of the world, the long-term trend preference swing away from nonpremium wines is assumed to continue now that recession in the North Atlantic economies has bottomed out.

Both grape and wine industry total factor productivity is assumed to grow at 1 percent per year everywhere, while grape and wine industry capital is assumed to grow, net of depreciation, at 1.5 percent per year in China but zero elsewhere. This means that China's production rises by about one-sixth, one-quarter, and one-third for nonpremium, commercial-premium, and superpremium wines between 2011 and 2018 — which in aggregate is less than half that needed to keep up with the modeled growth in China's consumption. Of course, if China's wine production from domestic grapes were to grow faster than we assume in our base scenario, wine imports would increase less.

Given the uncertainty associated with several dimensions of developments in China's wine markets, we also compare the more likely of our two main scenarios to 2018 (in which RERs for all but China revert halfway back from 2011 to 2009 rates — call it Alternative 1) with a third scenario (call it Alternative 2) in which three dimensions are altered: China's aggregate expenditure growth during 2011–2018 is reduced by one-quarter (from 7.5 to 5.6 percent per year),[3] its RER does not change from 2011 instead of appreciating at 2 percent per year over that period, and its grape and wine industry capital is assumed to grow at 3 instead of 1.5 percent per year. Each of those three changes ensures a smaller increase in China's wine imports by 2018 in this Alternative 2 scenario. However, this should be considered very much a lower-bound projection because, even if China's GDP growth, industrialization, and infrastructure spending were to slow more than assumed in our Base and Alternative 1 scenarios, and there were less conspicuous extravagance and iconic gift-giving by business and government, Chinese households nonetheless are being encouraged to reduce their extraordinarily high savings rates and consume more of their income. In addition, grape wine is encouraged as an alternative to the dominant alcoholic beverages of (barley-based) beer and (rice-based) spirits because of its perceived health benefits and because it does not undermine food security by diminishing foodgrain supplies.

This global model has supply and demand equations and hence quantities and prices for each of the grape and wine products and for a single composite of all other products in each country. Grapes are not assumed to be traded internationally, but other products are both exported and imported. Each market is assumed to have cleared before any shock and to find a new market-clearing outcome following any exogenously introduced shock. An enhancement of importance to the present study is the

---

[3] According to one of China's most prominent economists and a former senior vice-president of the World Bank, "China can maintain an 8 percent annual GDP growth rate for many years to come .... China's per capita GDP in 2008 was 21 percent of per capita GDP in the United States. That is roughly the same gap that existed between the United States and Japan in 1951, Singapore in 1967, Taiwan in 1975, and South Korea in 1977. ... Japan's average annual growth rate soared to 9.2 percent over the subsequent 20 years, compared to 8.6 percent in Singapore, 8.3 percent in Taiwan, and 7.6 percent in South Korea" (Lin, 2013).

inclusion of exchange rate variables explicitly in the model. This enables us to distinguish between price impacts as observed in local currency units from those observed in U.S. dollars, as described in the previous section. All prices are expressed in real (2009) terms.

4. Impacts of exchange rate movements on competitiveness, 2007 to 2011

Major exchange rate changes occurred after 2007, so we first backcast the model from its 2009 base to 2007 and then shock it by just the changes in RERs that actually occurred between 2007 and 2011, as reported in Appendix Table 1(a). The first column of Table 1 summarizes those actual RER changes in key wine-exporting and wine-importing countries. If there were no other shocks to the world's wine markets over this 2007–11 period, what would those RER changes lead one to expect? Australia, for example, experienced the largest real appreciation among the wine exporters, so its wineries are among the ones to have been affected most adversely: receiving fewer Australian dollars for their exports and facing more foreign competition in their home market, so depressing their grape and wine prices. As for wine-importing countries, those whose real exchange rates appreciated most (notably China and Japan) would be expected to import more wine, all other things being equal. Meanwhile, for those experiencing a real depreciation, most notably the United Kingdom, wine imports would be expected to fall.

That is indeed what is shown in the other columns of Table 1, and the impacts of those shocks on bilateral wine trade volumes are summarized in Table 2. Specifically, the RER changes are responsible for declines in grape and wine production in the Southern Hemisphere, where RERs appreciated, and for slight production increases in the United States and Europe, where RERs changed relatively little.

Because Australia had the largest appreciation of all wine-exporting countries over that period, its winemakers, and hence grape growers, are estimated to have suffered among the largest reductions in domestic prices in real local currency terms from this shock: winegrape and commercial premium wine producer prices are reduced by one-eighth and superpremium wine prices by one-fifth. Large price reductions are estimated for

Table 1a. Estimated impact of 2007–2011 changes in real exchange rates on domestic prices (in real local currency) and quantities of wine — main exporters (changes in percent)

	Real Exchange Rate	Non-premium Grape Price	Premium Grape Price	Commercial Premium Wine[b] Producer Price	Super Premium Wine[b] Producer Price	Commercial Premium Wine[b] Prod. Volume	Super Premium Wine[b] Prod. Volume	Domestic Wine Consum. Volume (Model)	Domestic Wine Consum. Volume (Actual)
W. Europe 6[a]	0	6	5	5	5	2	2	0	(–10)
United States	0	3	4	2	4	1	2	–1	(2)
New Zealand	9	–1	–1	–1	–1	0	0	2	(0)
Chile	16	–8	–6	–8	–8	–2	–1	–2	(–5)
South Africa	23	–9	–8	–10	–12	–2	–2	1	(–1)
Argentina	24	–18	–17	–19	–18	–3	–3	5	(?)
Australia	33	–12	–13	–13	–19	–2	–3	4	(3)

[a]France, Italy, Spain, Portugal, Germany and Austria. [b]Commercial-premium wines are defined by Anderson and Nelgen (2011) as those between US$2.50 and $7.50 per liter pre-tax wholesale or at a country's border.

Source: Authors' model results.

Table 1b. Estimated impact of 2007–2011 changes in real exchange rates on domestic prices (in real local currency) and quantities of wine — main importers (changes in percent)

	Real Exchange Rate	Commercial-Premium Wine[a] Consumer Price	Super Premium Wine[a] Consumer Price	Domestic Wine Consum. Volume (Model)	Domestic Wine Consum. Volume (Actual)
United Kingdom	−18	8	8	−4	(−7)
Other W. Europe[b]	4	−2	−3	1	(na)
Japan	29	−9	−8	10	(−2)
China	35	1	2	0	(22)

[a]Commercial-premium wines are defined by Anderson and Nelgen (2011) as those between US$2.50 and $7.50 per liter pre-tax wholesale or at a country's border; [b]Other W. Europe (Belgium, Denmark, Finland, Ireland, the Netherlands, Sweden and Switzerland).
Source: Authors' model results.

Table 2. Impact of real exchange rate changes on export volume of wine-exporting countries 2007 to 2011 (in million liters)

	Exporter				
	Australia	Other Southern Hemisphere	United States	Western European Exporters	Other
Importer:					
United Kingdom	−33	−31	2	2	1
United States	−23	−38	0	6	0
Canada	−3	−10	4	6	0
New Zealand	0	0	0	0	0
Germany	−2	−13	1	7	−6
Other W. Europe[a]	−7	−24	2	32	9
China	5	8	2	7	2
Other Asia	−1	1	5	30	−1
Other countries	0	−3	3	75	1
Total world	−64	−110	19	167	6

[a]Other W. Europe (Belgium, Denmark, Finland, Ireland, the Netherlands, Sweden and Switzerland).
Source: Authors' model results.

Argentina, too (although its numbers are less reliable because the official underrecording of inflation required us to use a secondary source for consumer price index (CPI) changes, Cavallo, 2013). Associated with those local currency price reductions are declines in the volume of Australia's and Argentina's wine production as a result of RER changes. Those output changes over this five-year period are smaller than the price declines, though, reflecting the low elasticity of supply response to producer price downturns that are incorporated into the model.

As seen in Table 1, real prices in domestic currency terms decline in the other Southern Hemisphere countries as well, but by less than two-thirds as much as in Australia and Argentina. Furthermore, real grape and wine prices (again in domestic currency terms) *rise* in the United States and Western Europe, by between 2 and 5 percent, so output in those regions is estimated to have been boosted by recent RER movements. In short, those exchange rate shocks have been a major contributor to the decline in the international competitiveness of Southern Hemisphere wine producers since 2007.

The trade consequences of that set of exchange rate shocks also depend on how it affects wine consumption. Because of lower prices for both domestic and imported wines, Australian consumption is estimated to have been boosted by 4 percent because of these RER changes — which is close to the proportional change in *actual* consumption during that period (see last two columns of Table 1a). This suggests that the net effect on domestic consumption of all other influences over the period 2007–11 was close to zero.

In Europe's key wine-exporting countries and in the United States, by contrast, the rise in wine prices would have reduced domestic wine consumption in the absence of other influences. Other influences evidently were not absent, however. In the United States, wine consumption actually rose by 2 percent over that period, perhaps as the economy there began to recover in 2011 from the global financial crisis. In Western Europe's wine-exporting countries, by contrast, it fell by 10 percent, perhaps because in 2011 those economies were still recovering from the financial crisis.

Estimated changes in consumption in wine-importing countries are shown in Table 1b. The 18 percent real depreciation of the British pound against the U.S. dollar on its own caused the consumer price of wine in that market to rise to the point that estimated wine consumption fell 4 percent, which is less than the actual decrease over that period of 7 percent. Discrepancies arise when there is a nontrivial net effect of economic changes other than in RERs. For the UK, that would have been the income drop that resulted from the financial crisis during that period. In the case of China, its rapid income growth and increasing absorption of Western tastes meant that there was a substantial increase in wine demand there between 2007 and 2011, so observed wine consumption grew by 22 percent over that period despite almost no contribution (0.2 percent) from RER changes. As in the UK, other countries that went into recession had incomes fall between 2007 and 2011, which affected wine consumption. For example, Japan's actual wine consumption declined 2 percent even though RER changes on their own are estimated to have induced a 10 percent increase.

The negative impact on consumption of the real depreciation in the United Kingdom is bad news for all wine-exporting countries, but the impact is even worse for Australia (which was the second-most-important supplier in volume terms of wine to the UK market after Italy, and third in value terms after France and Italy). The first set of rows of Table 2 shows the impact on the UK's import volumes by country of origin. Australia and other Southern Hemisphere countries (most notably, South Africa) are the standout losers in this scenario, with annual demand for their wine falling by an estimated 64 ML — half of which is borne by Australia. By contrast, annual sales by the Old World and the United States to the UK are slightly higher (by 2ML each) as a consequence of RER movements between 2007 and 2011, as are Old World sales to North America and Western Europe — again at the expense of sales from the Southern Hemisphere.

That is, the modeled reduction in wine consumption in Europe and the United States is borne almost entirely by Australian and other Southern Hemisphere producers, whose wines become more expensive than domestically produced or Old World wines in the U.S. market. That set of RER shocks reduces the Southern Hemisphere's share of U.S. total wine consumption from 21 to 18 percent. The pattern of impact on bilateral wine trades with Canada, Germany, and other Western European wine-importing countries is not quite as severe, but in all those cases Australian and other Southern Hemisphere producers lose out to U.S. and Old World suppliers.

China remains the market in which wine exporters anticipate the highest rate of import growth in the future. China's renminbi appreciated in real terms more than most major currencies did between 2007 and 2011, the effect of which in isolation would be for China to increase its share of global wine consumption. Table 1b shows that real local currency prices of wine in China fell by one-sixth due to observed RER movements. This caused increased imports of wine from all sources, with increases from both the New World (15 ML including the United States) and Old World (7 ML) reported in Table 2. Those imports substituted for domestic wine, whose consumption is discouraged by the real appreciation. As for other Asian markets and the rest of the world, Southern Hemisphere producers again lose while the U.S. and Old World wine exporters gain.

In aggregate, RER movements over the 2007–2011 period are estimated to have reduced Australia's annual wine exports by 64 ML. This is one-third of the loss to all Southern Hemisphere exporters of 174 ML, and it contrasts with estimated export gains of 19 ML to the United States and 167 ML to Western Europe's key wine-exporting countries (last row of Table 2). This has reversed somewhat the massive gains of the Southern Hemisphere exporters at the expense of the Old World over the past two decades (Figure 1). It also strengthened the competitiveness of the US

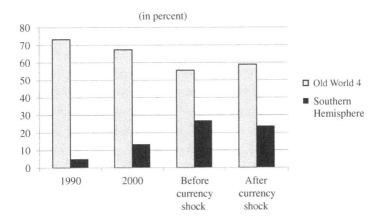

Figure 1. Shares in global wine export volume, 1990, 2000, and before and after real exchange rate changes during 2007–2011

Note: Old World 4 refers to France, Italy, Portugal, and Spain.

Source: Authors' model results.

wine industry relative to other New World wine producers in both the U.S. and European markets.

Clearly, Australia is the country whose wine trade has been most adversely affected by real currency changes since 2007. In addition to losing export sales, however, it has also seen a considerable increase in imports. One-third of the estimated extra imports due to currency changes are from New Zealand, because of the greater real appreciation of the Australian dollar compared with the New Zealand dollar. The bracketed numbers in Table 3 show that New Zealand's additional penetration of the Australian market is especially strong in the superpremium category (predominately Sauvignon Blanc and Pinot Noir), while France's is predominantly in sparkling wine and Italy's in commercial-premium wines.

How do the modeled outcomes compare with observed export changes in Australia? Historic data indicate that between 2006–2007 and 2010–2011, the volume of Australia's wine exports fell only slightly, from 768 ML to 727 ML; but, in domestic currency terms, exports dropped from almost AUD2.9 billion to just under AUD2.0 billion over that period (www.wineaustralia.com). Therefore, the modeled effect of RER changes slightly overstates the drop in the volume of wine exports, but the modeled drop in value — shown in Table 3 — is very close to the observed change.

These results suggest that RER changes go a long way toward explaining why market shares and producer prices have changed so much for some New World wine-exporting countries in recent years and in particular the improvement in competitiveness of the United States and European Union and the decline for Australian and other Southern Hemisphere exporters between 2007 and 2011. This only slightly reverses the trend of the previous 15 years, though (Figure 1). Nor does it necessarily mean that the era in which Australian and other Southern Hemisphere exporters have gradually increased their share of global wine exports is over. After all, RER changes can easily reverse — and indeed did in mid-2013. We turn now to consider the period to 2018, and in particular to examine how much a half-reversal of RER changes in 2009–2011 would affect wine exporters.

Table 3. Projected real producer price changes, in local currency, 2011 to 2018 (changes in percent)

	FRA	ITA	PRT	ESP	AUT	GER	AUS	NZL	USA	ARG	CHL	ZAF	CHN
(a) 2011 to 2018: Base scenario (assuming no RER changes from 2011)													
Non-premium wine	−24.9	−26.9	−26.0	−26.0	−26.3	−26.6	−15.3	−19.1	−23.4	−18.8	−17.7	−17.1	29.2
Commercial-premium	−2.0	−5.0	−4.3	−5.2	−8.3	−3.4	2.7	−1.3	−2.1	3.9	3.1	−0.2	93.2
Super-premium	37.9	37.4	41.8	35.5	30.0	35.1	49.7	42.9	40.7	46.4	45.8	54.0	164.4
Iconic still wine	41.2	41.8	42.3	41.9	39.9	40.9	44.8	45.2	46.4	85.3	61.6	84.3	119.5
Sparkling wine	4.2	4.8	5.0	5.1	3.3	3.0	8.3	7.7	7.7	34.9	9.9	7.8	8.9
Premium grapes	21.5	10.8	14.4	7.1	24.4	9.6	20.1	34.6	29.8	7.0	13.9	13.5	60.2
Non-premium grapes	−7.5	−18.6	−19.4	−15.9	−18.3	−12.8	−6.1	−10.6	−10.6	−3.8	−7.5	−11.9	28.8
(b) 2011 to 2018: Alternative 1 (assuming RERs return half-way from 2011 to 2009 rates)													
Non-premium wine	−25.5	−27.5	−26.4	27.0	−26.7	−27.4	−5.9	−14.2	−24.1	−17.2	−12.4	−12.1	20.8
Commercial-premium	−3.9	−7.2	−6.5	−7.3	−9.4	−5.8	19.0	6.4	−3.7	7.3	11.4	8.3	75.9
Super-premium	36.0	35.2	38.9	33.7	29.7	33.5	67.9	56.0	40.2	52.5	56.5	63.6	144.4
Iconic still wine	38.5	39.0	39.5	39.5	39.2	38.9	49.6	55.4	44.6	84.9	64.3	85.7	102.7
Sparkling wine	3.0	3.0	3.4	3.2	2.3	2.0	19.0	15.0	6.7	35.9	18.1	20.2	−0.2

(Continued)

Table 3. (Continued)

	FRA	ITA	PRT	ESP	AUT	GER	AUS	NZL	USA	ARG	CHL	ZAF	CHN
Premium grapes	19.7	8.4	11.9	4.9	23.8	7.9	34.6	45.9	29.0	10.5	23.5	24.9	52.4
Non-premium grapes	−9.2	−20.1	−20.7	−17.9	−19.5	−14.5	12.2	−1.2	−12.2	−0.9	1.3	−2.3	24.3
(c) 2011 to 2018: Alternative 2 (assuming also slower Chinese import growth)													
Non-premium wine	−26.9	−28.0	−26.8	−28.0	−27.1	−28.1	−11.7	−17.2	−26.0	−18.0	−16.3	−13.3	−16.0
Commercial-premium	−7.6	−9.7	−8.8	−9.8	−10.7	−8.8	12.2	2.7	−6.5	5.2	5.8	5.6	47.4
Super-premium	33.8	33.6	37.2	32.4	29.5	32.2	59.0	53.2	39.8	51.0	53.5	62.2	97.4
Iconic still wine	38.5	38.9	39.4	39.4	39.1	38.8	49.5	55.3	44.6	84.9	64.3	85.6	67.2
Sparkling wine	2.6	2.7	3.1	2.9	2.1	1.7	18.5	14.5	6.5	35.8	17.6	19.8	1.3
Premium grapes	17.7	6.1	9.7	2.5	23.1	6.3	29.8	42.8	27.8	8.4	17.7	21.7	36.8
Non-premium grapes	−11.7	−21.6	−22.1	−19.9	−20.7	−16.0	4.4	−6.0	−15.2	−2.5	−5.0	−4.9	6.1

Source: Authors' model results.

5. Projecting global wine markets to 2018

To project global wine markets forward, it is important first to update the model's 2009 baseline with known data. Sufficient data were available globally to calibrate the model to 2011 when the study began, so we project the model to that year first using actual aggregate national consumption and population growth together with actual changes in RERs between 2009 and 2011 and assumed changes in preferences, technologies, and capital stocks as described. After this new baseline is in place, the second step is to assume that aggregate national consumption and population grow from 2011 to 2018 at the rates shown in Appendix Table 2 and that preferences, technologies, and capital stocks continue to change as described above and that RERs over that period either remain at their 2011 levels (our Base Scenario) or return halfway to their 2009 rates (except for China) as reported in Appendix Table 1(b).[4] The latter RER changes began to happen in mid-2013, so this (our Alternative 1) scenario is more likely to be representative of the real world by 2018 than our Base Scenario. A third scenario (our Alternative 2) presents a lower-bound projection of what might happen to Chinese wine import demand if China's economy slowed by one-quarter, its RER ceased to appreciate, and simultaneously its domestic grape and wine production capital grew twice as fast.

The impacts of those three scenarios on real producer prices in the sector, in local currency units, are reported for the world's main wine-producing countries in Table 3. For the period to 2018, Australia's nonpremium grape and wine prices are projected to fall further if real exchange rates do not change from their 2011 levels, while superpremium and iconic still wine prices are projected to rise by more than 40 percent (Table 3a). If, however, RERs were to return halfway to what they were in 2009, real prices in Australia in local currency terms would rise above 2011 levels for all grape and premium wine types (Table 3b). The extent of those rises would be somewhat but not sub-

---

[4] In the first two scenarios presented here, China's RER is assumed to appreciate a further 2 percent per year over this projection period because of the country's assumed strong economic growth.

stantially less if China's import growth were to be slower as in the Alternative 2 scenario (Table 3c). Similar changes are shown for the other wine-exporting countries in the Base scenario, because that involves no RER or other country-specific changes: price changes for commercial-premium are minimal, and for superpremium wines the increases are in the 30–50 percent range.[5]

Given the assumptions that all countries enjoy productivity growth of 1 percent per year and that there is a taste swing against nonpremium wine, it is not surprising that all major suppliers are projected to expand their output of all wine types except nonpremium in the Base scenario. In the Alternative 1 scenario with the reversal in RER trends, however, those output increases would be greater in the Southern Hemisphere and less elsewhere (compare Tables 4a and 4b). If China's import growth were much slower, as in the Alternative 2 scenario, the increases would be up to one percentage point less except in China, where, by assumption in this scenario, its grape and wine capital and hence output would grow faster (Table 4c).

The income, population, and preference changes together mean that consumption volumes grow over the period to 2018 for all but nonpremium wine, but least so for commercial-premium. The percentage increases are similar in the three scenarios, but slightly less in the Alternative 1 scenario (altered currencies) and slightly more in the Alternative 2 scenario — except for China, where the differences are in the opposite direction (Table 5). This is consistent with the differences in local currency consumer price changes.

What is even more striking is the concentration of consumption growth and declines, as shown in Figure 2. In all scenarios, growth is concentrated in China, while there are substantial declines in aggregate consumption in the Old World, where the declining nonpremium wine segment is still substantial.

When this scenario is combined with the changes projected in production, it is possible to get a picture of what is projected to happen to wine trade. Table 6 provides projections for the main wine-trading regions. In

---

[5] Consumer prices move in the same direction as producer prices, but the changes are more muted because of the presence of trade and transport margins.

Table 4. Projected grape and wine output volume changes, 2011 to 2018 (in percent)

	FRA	ITA	PRT	ESP	AUT	DEU	AUS	NZL	USA	ARG	BRA	CHL	ZAF	CHN
(a) Base Scenario (assuming no RER changes from 2011)														
Non-premium wine	−9.0	−10.3	−11.7	−7.2	−11.7	−10.6	−8.1	−9.9	−5.0	−1.5	−7.4	−4.2	−14.0	17.9
Commercial-premium	6.4	5.9	6.0	5.7	2.6	6.5	8.1	5.5	5.9	7.2	7.9	7.3	5.1	25.9
Super-premium	15.1	15.1	15.6	15.4	14.6	15.0	15.3	18.9	15.5	15.6	17.1	15.3	18.4	29.1
Iconic still wine	15.7	15.9	16.1	16.1	15.9	15.4	15.4	19.1	15.8	12.6	14.2	15.0	18.1	34.2
Sparkling wine	8.6	9.2	9.3	9.3	8.5	8.6	11.4	10.3	9.6	12.0	10.1	11.9	9.8	0.3
Premium grapes	9.8	8.8	9.3	8.4	10.3	8.6	9.6	12.2	10.6	7.2	9.0	9.5	8.9	20.2
Non-premium grapes	6.0	2.3	1.5	3.4	2.0	4.7	6.1	3.8	4.9	5.2	3.7	5.2	0.3	17.8
(b) Alternative 1 (assuming RERs return half-way from 2011 to 2009 rates)														
Non-premium wine	−9.7	−11.0	−12.2	−8.3	−12.2	−11.6	1.4	−3.7	−5.6	−0.9	−2.2	−3.5	−6.2	17.2
Commercial-premium	5.6	5.0	5.1	4.9	2.0	5.6	13.4	9.6	5.2	8.3	11.6	9.1	10.1	24.6
Super-premium	14.9	14.9	15.3	15.2	14.6	14.8	18.0	20.4	15.4	16.7	18.1	15.4	19.2	28.4
Iconic still wine	15.3	15.6	15.8	15.9	15.8	15.2	16.3	20.1	15.6	12.8	14.2	15.1	18.1	32.9

(*Continued*)

Table 4. (Continued)

	FRA	ITA	PRT	ESP	AUT	DEU	AUS	NZL	USA	ARG	BRA	CHL	ZAF	CHN
Sparkling wine	8.2	8.7	8.8	8.8	8.1	8.3	15.1	12.6	9.3	12.2	12.6	13.5	15.2	−15.9
Premium grapes	9.6	8.5	9.0	8.1	10.3	8.4	11.4	13.0	10.5	7.7	10.1	9.7	10.5	19.7
Non-premium grapes	5.6	1.8	1.0	2.8	1.6	4.3	9.6	7.0	4.5	5.7	6.6	6.2	5.1	17.3
(c) Alternative 2 (assuming also slower Chinese import growth)														
Non-premium wine	−11.6	−11.6	−12.6	−9.4	−12.6	−12.6	−4.4	−7.3	−7.6	−1.3	−5.9	−3.9	−7.7	23.5
Commercial-premium	3.7	3.7	3.9	3.6	1.0	4.1	11.7	7.8	3.8	7.6	9.2	8.7	8.7	35.3
Super-premium	14.6	14.7	15.1	15.1	14.5	14.6	17.3	20.1	15.4	16.5	17.9	15.4	19.2	39.3
Iconic still wine	15.4	15.7	15.9	15.9	15.8	15.3	16.4	20.2	15.6	12.8	14.3	15.1	18.1	43.6
Sparkling wine	8.2	8.7	8.8	8.8	8.1	8.3	15.3	12.6	9.3	12.2	12.8	13.5	15.2	15.2
Premium grapes	9.5	8.2	8.7	7.8	10.2	8.2	11.0	12.8	10.4	7.4	9.4	9.7	10.1	30.9
Non-premium grapes	5.0	1.2	0.4	2.1	1.1	3.9	8.2	5.6	3.6	5.4	4.7	5.9	4.0	27.4

Source: Authors' model results.

Table 5. Changes in quantities of wine consumed, 2011 to 2018 (in percent)

	FRA	DEU	ITA	ESP	GBR	OW[a]	RUS	AUS	NZL	USA	ARG	BRA	CHL	ZAF	CHN	JPN
(a) Base scenario (assuming no RER changes from 2011)																
Non-premium	−12.7	−12.3	−12.4	−12.5	−12.7	−12.4	−9.1	−7.3	−7.6	−8.3	−1.3	−4.2	−5.1	−6.9	28.9	−13.9
Commercial-premium	−2.3	−1.8	−1.6	−1.6	−2.2	−2.0	4.7	4.0	2.7	2.5	12.7	9.4	7.4	7.5	87.3	−3.4
Super-premium	11.1	11.6	11.5	12.2	10.9	12.8	19.4	12.2	14.9	15.7	31.6	17.5	22.1	24.4	87.4	9.2
Iconic still wine	14.5	13.9	14.5	14.5	14.8	16.0	26.2	16.8	17.8	17.7	15.5	19.2	18.4	20.4	154.1	9.6
Sparkling wine	7.1	7.3	7.1	7.1	7.2	7.2	11.6	14.0	12.2	11.8	15.4	17.9	17.3	17.8	94.3	4.4
All wines	−2.9	−4.9	−7.8	−6.1	−4.1	−4.7	3.0	2.7	2.3	1.4	2.4	9.0	1.0	4.0	62.4	−1.1
(b) Alternative 1 (assuming RERs return half-way from 2011 to 2009 rates)																
Non-premium	−12.6	−12.1	−12.4	−12.4	−12.3	−12.2	−9.6	−8.7	−8.6	−8.1	−1.6	−4.5	−6.0	−7.5	31.1	−14.1
Commercial-premium	−1.9	−1.3	−1.2	−1.2	−1.6	−1.5	3.3	0.3	0.8	3.0	11.8	7.6	5.4	5.7	95.1	−3.5
Super-premium	11.7	12.2	12.2	12.8	12.1	13.3	16.5	6.0	10.6	15.9	29.0	16.4	18.1	21.4	99.6	8.6

(Continued)

Table 5. (Continued)

	FRA	DEU	ITA	ESP	GBR	OW[a]	RUS	AUS	NZL	USA	ARG	BRA	CHL	ZAF	CHN	JPN
Iconic still wine	16.0	15.2	16.1	15.8	16.9	16.7	21.3	12.8	12.5	19.2	15.3	17.4	16.8	19.7	177.0	8.6
Sparkling wine	7.3	7.6	7.4	7.4	7.5	7.5	10.4	10.7	10.2	12.1	15.0	15.4	14.9	14.6	104.3	4.0
All wines	−2.6	−4.4	−7.6	−5.8	−2.8	−4.0	−0.5	−0.1	0.9	2.6	2.0	6.2	−0.5	2.6	70.0	−1.8
(c) Alternative 2 (assuming also slower Chinese import growth)																
Non-premium	−12.4	−12.0	−12.3	−12.3	−12.0	−12.0	−9.5	−8.0	−8.0	−7.8	−1.4	−4.4	−5.3	−7.4	25.6	−13.8
Commercial-premium	−1.2	−0.7	−0.7	−0.6	−0.9	−0.9	3.6	1.6	1.7	3.7	12.3	8.1	6.7	6.3	72.7	−3.1
Super-premium	12.5	12.7	12.7	13.2	12.9	13.7	16.7	8.8	11.5	16.1	29.6	16.5	19.2	21.8	69.1	9.0
Iconic still wine	16.1	15.3	16.1	15.9	16.9	16.7	21.3	12.9	12.5	19.2	15.3	17.4	16.8	19.7	114.9	8.7
Sparkling wine	7.4	7.6	7.5	7.5	7.6	7.5	10.5	10.9	10.3	12.2	15.0	15.4	15.1	14.7	67.5	4.1
All wines	−2.2	−4.1	−7.4	−5.5	−2.2	−3.5	−0.1	1.2	2.3	3.6	2.3	6.7	0.3	3.0	46.2	−1.1

[a]Belgium, Denmark, Finland, Ireland, the Netherlands, Sweden, and Switzerland.
Source: Authors' model results.

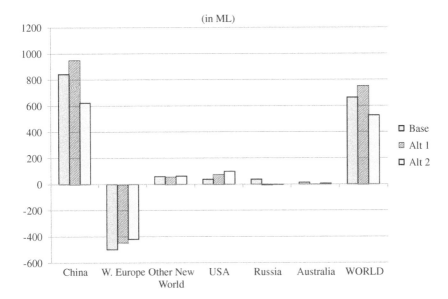

Figure 2. Changes in consumption of all wines, 2011 to 2018
Source: Authors' model results.

terms of volume, world trade expands 6 percent by 2018 in the Base Scenario, and 7 percent in the Alternative 1 scenario in which RERs change. Virtually all of that increase in those two scenarios is due to China's import growth. In the Alternative 2 scenario, in which China imports less, global trade also expands less (by only 4 percent). In terms of the real value of global trade, however, the upgrading of demand elsewhere means that China accounts for a smaller proportion of the growth in global import value, namely 36, 43, and 30 percent in the Base, Alternative 1, and Alternative 2 scenarios, respectively. In all three scenarios, the real value of global wine trade rises by about one-sixth (last row of Table 6).

It is not surprising that China is such a dominant force in these projections, given the dramatic growth in its wine consumption over the past dozen years (Figure 3), the expectation of continued high growth in its income over the next five years (albeit somewhat slower than in the past five years), and the assumption that China's winegrape production growth

Table 6. Projected changes in wine import and export volumes and real values, 2011 to 2018

	Volume (ML)			Real Value (US$ millions)		
	Base	Alt. 1	Alt. 2	Base	Alt. 1	Alt. 2
(a) Imports						
United Kingdom	−54	−36	−29	98	174	93
North America	−23	11	37	961	1,097	1,015
Other Europe	−122	−162	−140	1012	646	552
China	627	739	334	1,948	2,305	1,178
Other Asia	20	14	16	877	788	769
Other developing	152	133	141	498	311	318
WORLD	600	696	359	5,394	5,321	3,925
(b) Exports						
Australia	0	90	59	336	933	675
Other New World	78	219	75	469	954	597
Old World	538	412	263	4,370	3,489	2,653
WORLD	600 (6%)	698 (7%)	359 (4%)	5,394 (17%)	5,321 (17%)	3,925 (15%)

Source: Authors' model results.

cannot keep pace with domestic demand growth. As a result, China's share of consumption imported falls from its 2009 level of 85 percent to 57, 54, and 67 percent in 2018 the Base, Alternative 1, and Alternative 2 scenarios.

France is projected to become even more dominant in imports by China in the Base Scenario, in which exchange rates remain at 2011 levels. However, in the more likely Alternative 1 scenario with a reversal of recent exchange rate movements, the increase in China's imports from Australia is almost the same as that of France in value terms — and they lose equally if China's import growth slows further as in Alternative 2 (Figure 4a). In volume terms, it is Chile that enjoys the greatest increase in sales to China in the two Alternative scenarios (Figure 4b). The impacts of these changes on the shares of different exporters in sales to China are summarized in Figure 5. In the Base Scenario, France increases the dominance it had in 2009, in the Alternative 1 scenario Australia almost catches France, and in the Alternative 2 case Australia slightly overtakes

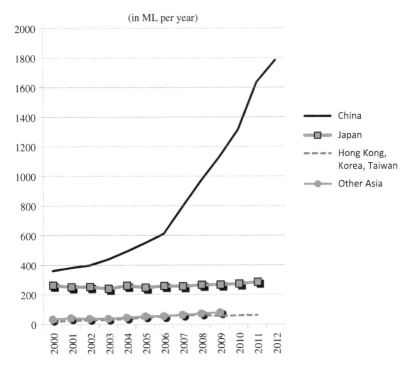

Figure 3. China's increasing dominance in Asian wine consumption, 2000 to 2012
Sources: Anderson and Nelgen (2011, table 16), updated for China from OIV (2013) and for other countries from Euromonitor International.

France. Meanwhile, all other exporters' shares remain less than half those of Australia and France (Figure 5).

Projected bilateral trade changes more generally are summarized in Table 7 for the most likely (Alternative 1) scenario. All major wine-producing regions benefit from China's burgeoning demands. In volume terms, that is slightly at the expense of growth in their exports to other regions, although not in value terms because of the modeled upgrading of quality in those other markets. For Australia and Other Southern Hemisphere exporters, growth in real export values in local currency terms will be even larger than in the U.S. dollar terms shown in Table 7 due to the modeled real depreciation of the currencies of this group. For example, Australia's export value growth of US$933 million converts to an Australian dollar increase of A$1.36 billion. Australia's projected vol-

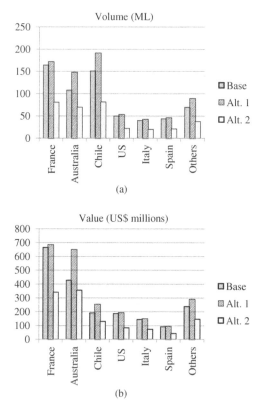

Figure 4. Changes in China's imports, by source, 2011–2018
Source: Authors' model results.

ume growth in this scenario is an extra 21 ML of wine per year exported to China during 2011 to 2018. That should be manageable, as it is the same rate of increase in Australia's sales to the United States during the first decade of this century.

6. Summary and implications for wine markets and their participants

The above results suggest that RER changes over the period 2007 to 2011 altered substantially the global wine export shares of the Old World and United States versus the Southern Hemisphere's New World exporters and especially Australia.

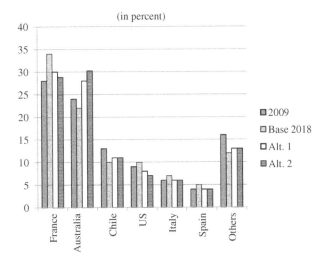

Figure 5. Shares of China's wine import value, by source, 2009 and 2018
Source: Authors' model results.

This development reversed somewhat the massive gains of the latter group at the expense of the Old World over the past two decades (Figure 1). The exchange rate changes also strengthened the competitiveness of the U.S. wine industry, relative to other New World wine producers, in both the U.S. and European markets. Given those results, it is not surprising that the comparison between scenarios involving no RER changes from 2011 versus a halfway return to 2009 RERs suggests that there would be a reversal in international competitiveness of the various exporting countries.[6]

The projections to 2018 reveal an even more striking prospect, however. It has to do with the continuing growth of China's net imports. China has already become by far the most important wine-consuming country in Asia (Figure 3) and, with a projected extra 620–940 ML to be added by 2018 to its consumption of 1,630 ML in 2011, that dominance is becom-

---

[6] Had we analyzed the effect of changes in real exchange rates over the dozen years to 2000, we would have predicted a dramatic growth in Australian wine exports because over that period Australia's currency depreciated in real terms by almost 30 percent. In fact, the volume and U.S. dollar value of Australia's wine exports grew 16 and 18 percent per year, respectively, over that period. An analysis of the effects of U.S. dollar appreciation at the turn of the century is provided by Anderson and Wittwer (2001).

Table 7. Changes in export volumes and values of wine-exporting countries in the Alternative 1 scenario, 2011 to 2018

	Exporter				
	Australia	Other Southern Hemisphere	United States	Western European Exporters	Other
(a) Volumes (ML)					
Importer:					
United Kingdom	−25	−10	−8	7	−1
United States	−14	−4	0	32	0
Canada	−4	−3	−4	8	0
New Zealand	−2	0	0	0	0
Germany	−3	−13	−4	−44	−12
Other West Europe[a]	−9	−17	−4	−6	−7
China	147	242	53	266	31
Other Asia	0	−1	0	14	−1
Other countries	−1	6	−7	114	−19
TOTAL WORLD	90	200	25	391	−8
(b) Values (US$ millions)					
Importer:					
United Kingdom	42	60	−27	107	−8
United States	115	167	0	542	17
Canada	33	46	−9	187	−2
New Zealand	9	0	0	4	−2
Germany	0	−4	−10	−65	−15
Other West Europe[a]	27	30	−13	643	−43
China	649	356	191	948	161
Other Asia	46	50	12	564	43
Other countries	11	93	−19	479	−95
TOTAL WORLD	933	798	125	3408	56

[a]Other West Europe = Belgium, Denmark, Finland, Ireland, the Netherlands, Sweden, and Switzerland.
Source: Authors' model results.

ing even greater. Because China's domestic production is projected to increase by "only" about 210–290 ML by 2018, its net imports are projected to rise by between 330 and 740 ML.

This modeling exercise suggests not only that RER changes go a long way toward explaining why market shares and producer prices have changed so much for New World wine-exporting countries in recent years — especially the decline in competitiveness for Australia and the improvement for the United States — but also that exchange rates are capable of playing a major role in the years ahead. But on top of that, the above projections point to the enormous speed with which China may become a dominant market for wine exporters. Although the recent and projected rates of increase in per-capita wine consumption in China are no higher than what occurred in several northwestern European countries in earlier decades, it is the sheer size of China's adult population of 1.1 billion — and the fact that grape wine still accounts for only 4 percent of Chinese alcohol consumption — that makes this import growth opportunity unprecedented. It would be somewhat smaller if China's own winegrape production increases faster, as in the Alternative 2 scenario, but certainly in as short a period as the next five years that is unlikely to be able to reduce the growth in China's wine imports very much, especially at the premium end of the spectrum.

Of course, these projections are not predictions. Where exchange rates move and how fast various countries' wine producers take advantage of the projected market growth opportunities in Asia will be key determinants of the actual changes in market shares over the coming years. Not all segments of the industry are projected to benefit, with nonpremium producers facing falling prices if demand for their product continues to dwindle as projected above. But exporting firms that are willing to invest sufficiently in building relationships with their Chinese importer/distributor — or in going into grape growing or winemaking in China — may well enjoy long-term benefits from such investments.

References

Anderson, K., and Nelgen, S. (2011). *Global Wine Markets, 1961 to 2009: A Statistical Compendium.* Adelaide: University of Adelaide Press. Freely accessible as an e-book at www.adelaide.edu.au/press/titles/global-wine/and as Excel files at www.adelaide.edu.au/wine-econ/databases/GWM/.

Anderson, K., and Wittwer, G. (2001). U.S. dollar appreciation and the spread of Pierce's disease: Effects on the world's wine markets. *Australian and New Zealand Wine Industry Journal,* 16(2), 70–75.

Anderson, K., and Strutt, A. (2012). Emerging economies, productivity growth, and trade with resource-rich economies by 2030. Revision of a paper for the 15th Annual Conference on Global Economic Analysis, Geneva, 27–29 June. Since published in the *Australian Journal of Agricultural and Resource Economics,* 58(4): 590–606, October 2014.

Barton, D., Chen, Y., and Jin, A. (2013). Mapping China's middle class. *McKinsey Quarterly,* June. www.mckinsey.com/insights/consumer_and_retail/mapping_chinas_middle_class/.

Cavallo, A. (2013). Online and official price indexes: Measuring Argentina's inflation. *Journal of Monetary Economics,* 60(2), 152–165. http://dx.doi.org/10.1016/j.jmoneco.2012.10.002.

Euromonitor International. (2013a). *Wine in the United Kingdom.* Accessed September 5, 2013, at http://www.euromonitor.com/wine-in-the-united-kingdom/report/.

Euromonitor International. (2013b). *Wine in Japan.* Accessed September 5, 2013, at http://www.euromonitor.com/wine-in-japan/report/.

Euromonitor International (2013c), *Wine in South Korea.* Accessed September 5, 2013, at http://www.euromonitor.com/wine-in-south-korea/report/.

Euromonitor International. (2013d). *Wine in Taiwan.* Accessed September 5, 2013, at http:// www.euromonitor.com/wine-in-taiwan/report/.

Kharas, H. (2010). The emerging middle class in developing countries. Working Paper 285, OECD Development Centre, Paris, January.

Harrison, J., and Pearson, K. (1996). Computing solutions for large General Equilibrium Models using GEMPACK. *Computational Economics,* 9(1), 93–127.

Lin, J.Y. (2013). Long live China's boom. Chazen Global Insights, Columbia Business School, New York, August 16, http://www8.gsb.columbia.edu/chazen/globalinsights/node/207/Long+Live+China%27s+Boom/.

OIV (Organisation Internationale de la Vigne et du Vin). (2013). *State of the Vitiviniculture World Market.* Paris, March (www.oiv.org).

Wittwer, G., Berger, N., and Anderson, K. (2003). A model of the world's wine markets. *Economic Modelling,* 20, 487–506.

World Bank. (2012). *World Development Indicators.* Washington, DC: World Bank. Accessed November 6, 2012, at www.worldbank.org.

Appendix: Revised model of the world's wine markets

A model of the world's wine markets was first published by Wittwer *et al.* (2003). That model has since been much revised and updated. Several significant enhancements have been made to that original model (which is still solved using GEMPACK software; see Harrison and Pearson,

1996). Wine types have been disaggregated from the original two to five types: non-premium (including bulk), commercial-premium, superpremium and iconic still wines, and sparkling wine. As in the original model, there are two types of grapes, premium and nonpremium. Nonpremium wine uses nonpremium grapes exclusively, superpremium and iconic wines use premium grapes exclusively, and commercial-premium and sparkling wines use both types of grapes. As for the model's regional dimension, the number of countries and country groups has expanded from 10 in the original model to 51: 44 individual countries and 7 composite regions. The model's database is calibrated to 2009, based on the data provided in Anderson and Nelgen (2011, especially Sections V, VI, and VII).

The model has supply and demand equations and hence quantities and prices for each of the grape and wine products and for a single composite of all other products. Grapes are not assumed to be traded internationally, but other products are both exported and imported. The model also includes excise and import taxes on each of the wine products and value-added taxes on all products. Each market is assumed to be in equilibrium before any shock and to find a new equilibrium following any exogenously introduced shock.

An enhancement of importance to the present study is the inclusion of exchange rate variables in the model. This enables us to distinguish between price impacts observed in the local currency from those observed in U.S. dollars.

Model equations

In the model, the grape and wine sectors minimize costs of intermediate inputs subject to weak constant elasticity of substitution (CES) between inputs. We assume that no intermediate inputs are imported from other countries. Intermediate demands are specified as follows:

$$X_{id}^c = f\left(X1_{id}, CES\left[P_{id}^c/P1_{id}\right]\right) \quad (1)$$

$$P1_{id} \cdot X1_{id} = \sum_c X_{id}^c \cdot P_{id}^c \quad (2)$$

where X_{id}^c is the quantity demanded of commodity c by grape or wine industry i in region d, P_{id}^c is the corresponding price, and $X1_{id}$ and $P1_{id}$ are the respective intermediate composite quantities and prices.

Two primary factors are employed in the sector: labor (the quantity of which is endogenous with perfectly elastic supply) and capital. Capital is usually treated as exogenous in quantity, with rates of return bearing all the adjustment in the various scenarios. This reflects the fact that both grapes (a perennial crop) and wine plant capacity adjust slowly to market signals:

$$L_{id} = f(F_{id}, CES[W1_{id} / PF_{id}]) \quad (3)$$

$$K_{id} = f(F_{id}, CES[R_{id} / PF_{id}]) \quad (4)$$

$$PF_{id} \cdot F_{id} = LL1_{id} \cdot W1_{id} + K_{id} \cdot R_{id} \quad (5)$$

Grape and wine producers are assumed to minimize costs subject to CES substitution between capital and labor. Equations (3) to (5) show primary factor demands for the labor composite $L1_{id}$ and capital K_{id} subject to a composite factor demand F_{id} by industry i in region d. The factor prices are $W1_{id}$ for composite labor, R_{id} for capital rentals, and PF_{id} for composite prices.

The composite factor demand F_{id} is proportional to total output Q_{id} subject to a primary-factor using technology A_{id}. Hence

$$F_{id} = Q_{id} \cdot A_{id} \quad (6)$$

The perfectly competitive zero pure profit condition is that total revenue, valued at the output price P_i^{0s} multiplied by Q_{id}, equals the total production cost:

$$P_i^{0s} \cdot Q_{id} = \sum_c P_{id}^c \cdot X1_{id}^c + \sum_0 W_{id}^0 \cdot L_{id}^0 + R_{id} \cdot K_{id} \quad (7)$$

Household demands follow a linear expenditure system in each region. We reduce the optimizing problem for household consumption of each commodity, subject to a budget constraint, to equations describing subsistence and discretionary demands. Aggregate subsistence expenditure $WSUB_d$ depends only on consumer prices $P3_{cd}$ for each commodity, and the number of households N, as per capita subsistence quantities $XSUB_{cd}$ subject to given preferences are constant.

$$WSUB_d = \sum_c P3_{cd} \cdot XSUB_{cd} \cdot N_d \qquad (8)$$

Discretionary expenditures for each commodity (the left-hand side of equation (9) are determined by the marginal budget share (β_{cd}) of aggregate discretionary expenditure. This aggregate is the bracketed term on the right-hand side of equation (9), where $W3TOT_d$ is aggregate nominal expenditure:

$$P3_{cd}(X3_{cd} - XSUB_{cd} \cdot N_d) = \beta_{cd}(W3TOT_d - WSUB_d) \qquad (9)$$

Because real aggregate consumption is usually exogenous in our partial equilibrium simulations, the linear expenditure system determines the consumption shares of individual final commodities (i.e., the five wine types plus a composite of all other consumption items), driven by changes in relative prices as faced by domestic consumers. The income elasticity of demand for each commodity is equal to the marginal budget share divided by the expenditure share. This varies from 0.5 for nonpremium wine to 2.5 for iconic still wine. The income elasticity of demand for other consumption is very close to 1.0, because wine accounts for an average of only 0.3 percent of aggregate expenditure globally and no more than 1.1 percent in any country (Anderson and Nelgen, 2011, table 166).

A new feature of our revised model of world wine markets is the inclusion of nominal exchange rates. These appear directly in the equation linking retail prices ($P3_{cd}^s$) to producer prices by country of origin (P_c^{0s}), where c denotes the wine type:

$$P3_{cd}^s = P_c^{0s} \frac{\phi_d}{\phi_s} T_{cd}^{tar} T_{cd}^{tax} + P_{cd}^m \qquad (10)$$

The exchange rates in the consuming (wine-importing) and producing (wine-exporting) regions are ϕ_d and ϕ_s respectively, expressed as local currency units per U.S. dollar. T_{cd}^{tar} is the power of the tariff in the consuming region and T_{cd}^{tax} the power of the domestic consumption (or excise) tax over and above any generic value-added or goods and services tax. P_{cd}^m is the price of margin m, assumed to be locally supplied, nontradable, and therefore unaffected by the exchange rate.

A given level of consumption for wine type c ($X3_{cd}$) is satisfied using the Armington assumption, in which wine from different countries of origin are imperfectly substitutable. First, domestic wine is imperfectly substitutable with a composite of imports:

$$X3_{cd}^{ss} = f(X3_{cd}, CES(P3_{cd}^{ss} / P3_{cd})) \quad ss = \text{domestic, imports} \quad (11)$$

Imports by origin $\left(X3_{cd}^{s}\right)$ are determined in a second CES equation:

$$X3_{cd}^{s} = f\left(X3_{cd}^{ss=imports}, CES\left(P3_{cd}^{s} / P3_{cd}^{ss=imports}\right)\right) \quad (12)$$

Shocks to international competitiveness

The focus of the present study is how changes in international competitiveness affect the world's wine markets. A crucial part of this exercise is explaining how prices determined outside the grape and wine markets influence these markets. Because the model is partial equilibrium, in order to depict the impacts of changes in international competitiveness, outside price changes need to be imposed as shocks on the model. The price of intermediate inputs shown in equations (1) and (2) is set equal to the price of GDP $\left(P_d^g\right)$ multiplied by a shifter F_d^c.

$$P_{id}^c = F_d^c P_d^g \quad (13)$$

If no specific price observations are available, the shifter F_d^c remains exogenous and unshocked, with the change in price being determined by a shock to the price of GDP. If observations are available for specific input price movements, the shifter F_d^w becomes endogenous, with P_{id}^c now exogenous and shocked.

$$W1_{id} = F_d^w P_d^g \quad (14)$$

Wage rates are treated similarly. In equation (14), if the wage shifter F_d^w is exogenous, changes in wage rates $W1_{id}$ are determined by changes in the price of GDP. If wage rate data are available, F_d^w becomes endogenous and wage rates are shocked directly.

$$P_{cd}^m = F_d^w P_d^g \quad (15)$$

The prices of trade and transport margins are also determined by the price of GDP if the shifter F_d^m in equation (15) is exogenous.

Changes in international competitiveness depend on changes in relative price levels and changes in nominal exchange rates. In equation (16), ϕ_s^R denotes real exchange rate movements relative to the U.S. dollar in wine-exporting regions (and for wine-importing countries simply replace the subscript s with d):

$$\phi_s^R = P_s^g / \left[P^{g\text{"USA"}} * \phi_s \right] \quad (16)$$

In equation (16), the nominal exchange rate for the United States is always unchanged, because nominal and real exchange rates are expressed in terms of U.S. currency.

We calculate real producer prices, $P_{i,loc}^{0s}$, as the producer price divided by the GDP deflator P_s^g:

$$P_{i,loc}^{0s} = P_i^{0s} / P_s^g \quad (17)$$

$P3_{cd}^s$ is converted to local currency prices in equation (10). To obtain real price changes in local currency terms, we deflate source-specific $P3_{cd}^s$ and source-composite $P3_{cd}$ wine consumption prices by $\text{CPI}(P_d^c)$:

$$P3_{cd,loc}^s = P3_{cd}^s / P_d^c \quad (18)$$

and

$$P3_{cd,loc} = P3_{cd} / P_d^c \quad (19)$$

Model calibration to market conditions

This revised model of the world's wine markets is calibrated to market conditions in 2009, as detailed in Anderson and Nelgen (2011, Section VI). This was only one vintage after the beginning of the global financial crisis and is assumed to provide a reasonable wine market benchmark against which to examine the impact of the major changes in real exchange rate changes since 2007.

Estimating the effects of exchange rate shocks, 2007 to 2011

The model enables us to ascribe shocks to depict changes in international competitiveness with information up to 2011 (the most recent year for which full data were available when this analysis began), from which it is then possible to project further ahead. Consumer price changes for the period 2007 to 2011 are available for each region from the World Bank (2012). Consumer prices are relevant because if in a scenario wine prices rise/fall relative to CPI in a given country, the quantity of wine consumed will decrease/increase for a given level of real aggregate household expenditure. Ideally, we would like to obtain nominal wage growth, producer price indexes, and margin prices for each country. If wage observations are available, F_d^w in equation (14) is made endogenous and wages are shocked directly. If more specific producer price indexes are available, we could make F_d^c in equation (13) endogenous and shock the indexes directly. And if we have margin price data, F_d^m becomes endogenous in equation (15) so as to shock margin prices directly. In the absence of more specific price data, each of the shifters in equations (13), (14), and (15) remains exogenous so the GDP price acts as a proxy.

Appendix Table 1. Cumulative changes in exchange rates and prices relative to the US dollar, 2007–11 (in percent)

	ϕ_d (1)	P_d^g (2)	P_d^c (3)	ϕ_d^R (4)		ϕ_d (1)	P_d^g (2)	P_d^c (3)	ϕ_d^R (4)
(a) 2007 to 2011									
FRA	−1.5	5.8	6.7	0.1	UKR	57.8	91.4	71.4	13.0
ITA	−1.5	6.5	8.6	0.7	TUR	28.5	35.4	35.7	−1.9
PRT	−1.5	4.3	6.9	−1.3	AUS	−18.9	16.2	13.0	33.4
ESP	−1.5	4.3	9.0	−1.3	NZL	−7.0	8.8	13.4	9.0
AUT	−1.5	6.9	9.1	1.1	CAN	−7.9	8.5	7.5	9.7
BEL	−3.9	7.3	10.5	4.0	USA	0.0	7.3	8.5	0.0
DEN	−1.4	10.3	10.1	4.1	ARG	32.8	77.2	100.0	24.3
FIN	−1.5	7.3	7.2	1.5	BRA	−14.1	34.4	24.1	45.8
DEU	−1.5	3.4	6.5	−2.2	CHL	−7.4	15.7	5.3	16.4
GRC	−1.5	11.3	14.1	5.3	MEX	13.7	26.0	23.3	3.3
IRL	−1.5	−7.7	1.0	−12.7	URU	−17.7	30.0	33.2	47.1

(*Continued*)

Appendix Table 1. (*Continued*)

	ϕ_d (1)	P_d^g (2)	P_d^c (3)	ϕ_d^R (4)		ϕ_d (1)	P_d^g (2)	P_d^c (3)	ϕ_d^R (4)
NLD	−1.5	4.2	7.5	−1.4	ZAF	3.1	35.8	30.8	22.8
SWE	−3.9	7.3	7.2	4.0	OAFR	5.3	52.7	61.9	35.2
CHE	−26.0	3.3	2.9	30.1	CHN	−15.1	23.2	14.5	35.1
GBR	24.9	10.4	14.2	−17.7	HKG	−0.2	4.8	13.0	−2.2
BUL	−1.6	22.0	23.3	15.5	IND	12.9	34.9	46.5	11.3
CRO	−0.4	13.0	12.2	5.7	JPN	−32.2	−5.8	−1.0	29.4
GEO	1.0	27.4	30.1	17.6	KOR	19.3	12.2	15.2	−12.4
HUN	9.5	16.3	20.5	−1.0	MAL	−11.0	14.3	11.3	19.6
MDA	−3.3	33.2	30.3	28.4	SGP	−16.5	0.7	15.9	12.5
ROM	25.0	31.9	27.8	−1.7	TWN	−15.1	23.2	14.5	35.1
RUS	14.9	55.6	47.6	26.2	THA	−11.7	14.5	12.1	20.7
(b) 2009 to 2011									
FRA	−0.1	2.4	3.7	−1.4	UKR	2.3	31.6	18.1	23.9
ITA	−0.1	1.7	4.3	−2.1	TUR	8.1	14.8	15.6	2.2
PRT	−0.1	1.7	5.1	−2.1	AUS	−24.4	6.4	6.3	35.5
ESP	−0.1	1.8	5.1	−2.0	NZL	−20.9	3.5	6.8	25.9
AUT	−0.1	3.9	5.1	0.0	CAN	−13.4	6.3	4.7	18.1
BEL	−0.1	3.7	5.8	−0.2	USA	0.0	3.9	4.8	0.0
DEN	0.2	4.7	5.1	0.6	ARG	10.8	35.3	45.0	17.5
FIN	−0.1	4.1	4.2	0.2	BRA	−16.3	15.8	12.0	33.1
DEU	−0.1	1.4	3.5	−2.4	CHL	−13.8	10.5	4.8	23.3
GRC	−0.1	3.4	8.2	−0.4	MEX	−8.1	9.8	8.2	14.9
IRL	−0.1	−1.5	1.6	−5.2	URU	−14.4	13.9	15.3	28.0
NLD	−0.1	2.5	3.7	−1.3	ZAF	−14.3	16.5	9.5	30.8
SWE	−15.2	1.9	4.2	15.6	OAFR[a]	7.0	22.4	22.5	10.1
CHE	−18.4	0.7	0.9	18.7	CHN	−5.4	15.0	8.9	17.0
GBR	−2.8	5.3	7.9	4.2	HKG	0.4	3.9	7.7	−0.4
BUL	0.0	7.9	6.8	3.8	IND	−3.6	17.1	21.9	16.9
CRO	1.1	3.1	3.3	−1.9	JPN	−14.7	−4.2	−1.0	8.1

(*Continued*)

Appendix Table 1. *(Continued)*

	ϕ_d (1)	P_d^g (2)	P_d^c (3)	ϕ_d^R (4)		ϕ_d (1)	P_d^g (2)	P_d^c (3)	ϕ_d^R (4)
GEO	1.0	18.5	16.2	13.0	KOR	−13.2	5.4	7.1	16.9
HUN	−0.6	6.7	9.0	3.3	MAL	−13.2	11.3	4.9	23.3
MDA	5.7	19.3	15.6	8.7	SGP	−13.5	9.1	8.2	21.4
ROM	0.0	10.9	12.2	6.8	TWN	−5.4	15.0	8.9	17.0
RUS	−7.4	29.3	15.9	34.4	THA	−11.1	8.1	7.3	16.9

Key: ϕ_d = nominal exchange rate change; P_d^g = change in GDP deflator; P_d^c = change in the consumer price index; ϕ_d^R = calculated change in real exchange rate. [a]Other Africa.
Source: Authors' compilation based on data downloaded from data.worldbank.org, and on estimated inflation rates for Argentina from Cavallo (2013).

Appendix Table 2. Cumulative consumption and population growth, 2011 to 2018 (in percent)

	Aggregate Consumption	Population
FRA	10.0	0.7
ITA	10.0	0.7
PRT	10.0	0.7
ESP	10.0	0.7
AUT	10.0	0.7
BEL	10.0	0.7
DNK	10.0	0.7
FIN	10.0	0.7
DEU	10.0	0.7
GRC	10.0	0.7
IRL	10.0	0.7
NLD	10.0	0.7
SWE	10.0	0.7
CHE	10.0	0.7
GBR	10.0	0.7
OWEN	10.0	0.7
BUL	23.1	1.9

(Continued)

Appendix Table 2. (*Continued*)

	Aggregate Consumption	Population
CRO	23.1	1.9
GEO	23.1	1.9
HUN	23.1	1.9
MDA	23.1	1.9
ROM	23.1	1.9
RUS	20.6	−1.7
UKR	23.1	1.9
OCEF	23.1	1.9
AUS	17.8	7.3
NZL	15.4	5.9
CAN	14.2	5.6
USA	15.5	5.2
ARG	30.0	4.9
BRA	27.3	3.8
CHL	23.4	5.0
MEX	22.0	4.6
URU	25.6	7.3
OLAC	25.6	7.3
ZAF	23.1	3.0
TUR	31.8	9.1
NAFR	31.8	9.1
OAFR	55.8	15.1
MEST	31.8	9.1
CHN	69.0	2.7
HKG	23.7	4.7
IND	63.1	7.0
JAP	7.1	−1.3
KOR	22.0	0.7
MYS	34.4	8.2
PHL	34.4	9.8

(*Continued*)

Appendix Table 2. (*Continued*)

	Aggregate Consumption	Population
SGP	18.6	5.6
TWN	34.6	2.3
THA	36.0	2.6
OAPA	32.2	11.2

Source: Projections from global economy-wide modeling by Anderson and Strutt (2012). OWEN = Other Western European, OLAC = Other Latin American and Caribbean, NAFR = North Africa, OAFR = Other Africa, MEST = Middle East, OAPA = Other Asia and the Pacific Islands.

Chapter 4

Intra-Industry Trade in a Rapidly Globalizing Industry: The Case of Wine*

Kym Anderson, Joseph Francois,
Douglas Nelson and Glyn Wittwer[†]

Abstract

This paper overviews the current structure and dynamics of international trade in wine with an emphasis on its intra-industry features. Using network analytic methods, we illustrate developments in the world's wine markets since the mid-1960s around a relatively stable core of countries. Those developments include both evolving demands for wine and, on the supply side, a rapidly emerging group of countries entering the core without displacing the original members. Not surprisingly, given that the analysis is based on bilateral trade in a single product, the developing patterns of intra-industry trade are quite consistent with the patterns revealed in the network analysis.

---

*First published in *Review of International Economics* 24(4): 820–36, September 2016.

[†] Nelson: Murphy Institute, Tulane University, New Orleans, LA 70118, USA. E-mail: dnelson@tulane.edu. Anderson: Wine Economics Research Centre, University of Adelaide, Adelaide SA 5005, Australia. Francois: World Trade Institute, University of Bern, 3012, Bern, Switzerland. Wittwer: Centre of Policy Studies, Victoria University, Melbourne, Victoria 8001, Australia. The authors dedicate this paper to David Greenaway: scholar of intra-industry trade, lover of wine.

1. Introduction

Wine is one of the oldest products to be traded over long distances (Johnson, 1989; Lukacs, 2012; Pellechia, 2006; Simpson, 2011; Unwin, 1991). Indeed, there is evidence of Bronze Age trade not only in wine but also in the paraphernalia needed to store, process and drink wine (Piggott, 1959). At the same time, wine is an archetypal differentiated product. In addition to red, white, rosé, various fortifieds and sparkling, there is differentiation by grape variety, terroir, technology, and, of course, by quality. While the data do not exist to tap these dimensions of differentiation over a significant time period, it would be surprising if there were not extensive trade between wine-producing countries. As with Staffan Linder's (1961) classic account of intra-industry trade, which provided inspiration for theoretical work rooted in monopolistic competition models (Helpman and Krugman, 1985) and systematic empirical work on intra-industry trade (Grubel and Lloyd, 1975; Greenaway and Milner, 1986), we expect wine varieties to reflect local preferences and production conditions. As consumers in other countries develop more sophisticated palates, we expect to see the development of a preference for variety in wine that, in turn, produces intra-industry trade. With newer wine-producing countries, we might expect to observe the development of this pattern directly in the data. Thus, in this paper, we use some basic network topological measures, along with standard intra-industry trade measures, to characterize the evolution of trade in wine — the "world wine web."

The viability of this study is underwritten to some extent by the dramatic growth in wine trade in the post-Second World War period on both the intensive and extensive margins. We are able to take advantage of data collection efforts that provide relatively long series of data on trade, production and consumption (e.g. Anderson and Nelgen, 2011). In this paper we characterize and explore a number of facts about the growth of the global wine industry, leaving theoretical development for later work. We begin with a narrative of recent developments in the world's wine markets. In subsequent sections we apply basic network measures to characterize the structure and dynamics of the product's international trade before providing a more detailed analysis of intra-industry trade in wine. Finally, we conclude with some projection analysis of future trends in global wine trade.

2. Recent trends in the world's wine markets

The past two decades have seen globalization of the world's wine markets proceed like never before, in both speed and breadth. There was a degree of trade expansion in the five decades prior to the First World War, but that was mostly in response to the outbreak of Phylloxera that destroyed the majority of vines in Europe and saw French wineries invest in huge plantings in North Africa (Meloni and Swinnen, 2014). Until the late 20th century, interactions between continents involved little more than the exporting of vine cuttings and of traditional production expertise. Indeed prior to 1990, most wine was consumed in the country of production (if one considers the French-owned vineyards in nearby French colonies of North Africa as part of France),[1] and those countries were mostly on or near the Mediterranean Sea.

The fall in transport and communication costs since the 1980s is largely responsible for the recent globalization of the industry. On the demand side, as incomes grew and access to television and the internet spread, so tastes broadened and an ever-greater variety of products has been sought by consumers, including for beverages.

On the supply side, the fall in travel and communication costs has made it more affordable for producers to consider exporting, for flying viticulturalists and winemakers to spread new technologies rapidly, and for some large wineries to also engage in cross-border mergers or acquisitions. Falling international trade costs plus deregulation of liquor retailing from the 1980s also allowed large supermarket chains to become the major buyers not only of branded bottled or bag-in-box wines but also of bulk wine for building their own house brands.

Retailing through such chain stores requires large quantities of homogenous wine year after year to justify national advertising campaigns. Producers in the New World were more adept at initially responding to that

---

[1] If Algeria, etc. are treated as separate countries, then France switched from being a net exporter of wine up to 1880 to being a net importer for the next 100 years, with a considerable degree of intra-industry trade during that period (Anderson and Pinilla, 2017), importing low-quality wine from North Africa and to a lesser extent southern European countries, and exporting mainly high-quality wines from Champagne, Bordeaux and Burgundy.

new demand, creating a huge new category of robust, fruity "commercial premium" wines that fall between expensive fine wines and cheap non-premium (or "table") wines.

The share of global wine production exported, which had always been below 15% and mostly Mediterranean or intra-European, grew dramatically from the late 1980s. By 2012 it exceeded 40%. The New World was the main contributor, with its share of global wine exports rising from 3% in the late 1980s to 25% (if sparkling wine is excluded) by 2004 (Anderson et al., 2003).

Recognizing their relatively poor performance, Europe's wine producers during the past decade have been adapting their practices to compete. The three leading European wine-exporting countries as a group now export almost half their production, up from just one-fifth a generation ago.

Simultaneously, New World producers are seeking to expand their exports of more expensive wines to complement their lower-end products. The next phase of wine's globalization therefore may involve a convergence whereby both groups produce terroir-driven super-premium wines alongside more affordable "commercial premium" branded wines. Meanwhile, cheap basic non-premium wines are continuing their demise in both Europe and the New World.

Technological developments are rapidly altering the means of exporting commercial premium wines. In the past decade or so the share of wine that is exported from the New World in bulk shipping containers has risen from less than 15% to more than 40% (and to 57% for Australia by 2014). Bottling in the country of destination is sometimes cheaper, and it lowers the cost and carbon footprint of shipping. By shipping in 24,000-litre bladders to fit 20-foot containers, this new shipping technology offers greater opportunities for buyers to blend wines from any region of the world as relative prices alter — and to meet changing retail demands in the destination country more rapidly.

Greater openness to trade means winemakers and hence grape growers are far more exposed now than pre-1990 to exchange rate volatility, and also to greater import competition in their domestic market as consumers are better able to choose from an ever-broader range of wines (Anderson and Wittwer, 2013). The share of imports in domestic

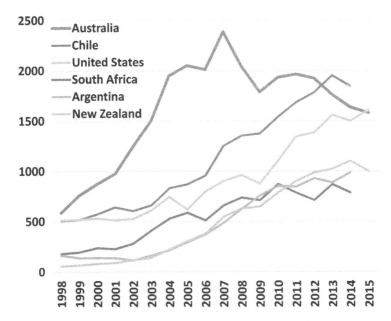

Figure 1. Value of wine exports, New World countries, 1995–2015 (US$million)
Source: Updated from Anderson (2015).

consumption in Australia, for example, rose from an average of 3% in 2000–2004 to 15% by 2013 in volume terms and around 20% in value terms (Anderson and Aryal, 2015). Wide fluctuations in exchange rates since the global financial crisis began in 2008 have substantially altered national rankings of New World wine-exporting countries (Figure 1).

Increased openness and international travel have also altered tastes and preferences not only on both sides of the North Atlantic but also in Asia. Nowhere has this been more obvious in the case of wine than in China. Chinese wine imports grew more than 50% per year during 2006–2012. With the number of middle class in China currently around 250 million and growing at around 10 million per year, and with grape wine accounting for less than 5% of alcohol consumption, further large increases in wine consumption are expected. How much of that Chinese demand will be supplied by domestic producers is difficult to guess. While import growth is likely to continue for the foreseeable future (Anderson and Wittwer, 2015), some exports also might begin to emerge from China in the future if there turns out to be a miss-match between the qualities of the wines produced and demanded domestically.

3. Structure of the world wine web

In this section, we apply tools of network analysis to data on global wine trade. We focus specifically on two interesting facts about the structure of the global wine economy: the overall growth in the breadth and depth of those markets, and the stability of the core of that economy.

Table 1 shows the evolution of total trade from 1964 to 2009. It is clear that the global wine economy expanded dramatically over this period. Even though the number of wine-trading countries increased by 50% (much of this being new countries, formed in a variety of ways, but some being new importing or exporting countries), the number of links between countries increased by 450% and the volume of trade increased more than 45-fold! This suggests that not only are more countries involved in importing and/or exporting wine, but these countries are trading with more partners and the links themselves involve more trade on average. Direct evidence of this is shown in Table 1.[2]

In network analysis, degree is simply the number of links between a given node (i.e. a national economy in our case) and other nodes. Because we consider both exports and imports as links, each node is potentially linked to every other node via exports and imports, thus we show both "out degree" (economies to which a given economy is linked by exports) and "in degree" (economies to which a given economy is linked by imports). The country that exported to the largest number of countries in 1964 (France) exported to 141 countries. In fact, France was the country with the maximum out degree in every year in our data, and by 2009 it was exporting to 190 countries.

Because we are also interested in the value of exports or imports of wine between a pair of countries, we represent the structure of trade by

---

[2] All of the statistics presented in Tables 1 and 2 were calculated in UCINET (Borgatti et al., 2013). This source is a handy overview of network empirics as well as basic applications using UCINET. The appendix to De Benedictis and Tajoli (2011) is a compact presentation of most of the definitions relevant to this paper.

Table 1. Network statistics on world wine web, all countries, 1964–2009

	1964	1969	1974	1979	1984	1989	1994	1999	2004	2009
No. of countries	152	157	196	193	191	195	216	213	225	230
No. of links	1,147	1,423	2,029	2,131	2,015	2,283	2,997	3,615	4,660	5,156
Total trade	587,858	704,647	1,829,924	4,118,851	3,873,040	6,888,756	8,853,214	14,299,819	21,076,262	26,721,601
Max out degree	141	148	169	173	168	165	183	181	195	190
Max weighted out	166,155	234,936	635,669	1,654,576	1,716,800	3,631,749	4,054,235	6,079,691	6,915,577	8,199,769
Median out degree	0	0	1	1	1	1	1	2	4	6
Median weighted out	0	0	1	1	1	5	10	19	28	88
Out centralization	0.7	1.8	2.9	2.9	2.1	2.5	2.3	2.3	2.2	2.1
Mean degree	8	9	10	11	11	12	14	17	21	22
Mean weighted deg.	3,867	4,488	9,336	21,341	20,278	35,327	40,987	67,135	93,672	116,181
Max in degree	34	36	56	51	58	65	60	75	80	86
Max weighted in	219,070	105,796	293,596	692,263	1,064,519	1,352,308	1,718,869	2,979,401	5,275,938	5,040,290
Median in degree	6	7	8	9	8	9	11	13	15	18
Median weighted in	116	211	282	596	454	951	1225	1,796	2,201	3,689
In centralization	0.9	0.8	1.3	1.2	1.3	0.9	1.0	1.1	1.6	1.4
Density	0.050	0.058	0.053	0.058	0.056	0.060	0.065	0.080	0.092	0.098

Source: Authors' calculations, based on UN COMTRADE data.

considering the links between a pair of nodes as weighted by the value of exports or imports. France was also the country with the highest total value of exports (weighted out degree) in every year except 1964 (when Algeria was the country with the highest weighted out degree, though 97% of its exports went to France).

The mean number of links rises strongly over this 45-year period, from 8 to 22, while the mean weighted degree increases by a factor of 49.[3] As we shall see, this growth is primarily a function of increasingly intensive trade among the core members of the world's wine economy, but it should be noted that the median country, which was not an exporter in 1964, was exporting to six countries in 2009.[4]

Table 1 shows similar growth in both the size and extent of importing in the world wine web. The largest importer in 1964 was sourcing wines from 34 supplier countries, and by 2009 this had more than doubled to 86 supplier countries. Similarly, the volume imported by the largest importer had increased by a factor of 23. Unlike the case of exports, where France dominated the entire period, the identity of the largest importer has changed over time. Over this period the UK, USA and Germany were the largest importers by value, with the UK often the largest by a substantial margin.[5] Over the first half of the period, the UK usually has the largest number of suppliers, while in the latter half of our sample period this is usually the USA. As with exports, we again find substantial growth in both the number of suppliers to and the imports of the median economy.

The previous two paragraphs suggest that the world wine web should have been growing progressively denser. The standard network-theoretic

---

[3] The mean degree and mean weighted degree are equal for in and out because, in either case, this is just total links divided by number of countries or total world trade in wine divided by number of countries.

[4] Note that the median country will vary from year to year. The point here is simply that the number of wine-exporting countries clearly increases, and increases substantially.

[5] An exception to this statement is that in the first two periods in our data (1964 and 1969), France is by far the largest importer. However in both of these years three quarters of its imports were from Algeria. As these imports shrank over time, France remained a sizable importer, but never one of the largest importers of wine.

definition/measure of density is simply the number of (unweighted) links observed in the data as a proportion of the number of possible links. With n countries, the number of possible links in a directed network (i.e. a network in which import links and export links are both possible) is just $[n(n-1)]$. Thus, density is the number in the second row of Table 1 divided by the number of possible links.[6] So, from 1964 to 2009, density doubles, even though the number of nodes (i.e. countries) increases by just 50%. That is, not only do countries have more trading partners on average, but also the world wine economy is more intensely interconnected. By way of comparison, the density of the entire world trade web, as reported by De Benedictis and Tajoli (2011), also doubles over this period; however, density of total trade for approximately comparable years ranges from 0.27 in 1970 to 0.40 in 2000.[7] One would expect the network for a single commodity to be far less dense than the network for all commodities; in this case the latter is around five times as dense as the wine trade network over the whole period.

While the world wine web extends quite broadly across the countries of the world, it is also the case that there is a small core of countries that accounts for most of this trade. One approach to identifying a core looks for a single country that dominates trade. Freeman's (1979) centralization measures seek to characterize the extent to which a network is dominated by a single node (importer or exporter). That is, centralization is a measure of compactness in the sense that a star network is maximally centralized (in a star network, every node except the center has degree one, while the center has degree $n - 1$). The centralization measures the extent to which the world wine web deviates from the star network. Thus, UCINET calculates the sum of the differences between the degree of the most central node and all other nodes, as a fraction of the maximum possible sum of differences in a network with n nodes. While the world wine web extends quite broadly across the countries of the world, it is also the case that there is a small core of countries that accounts for most of this trade.

---

[6] In 1964, with 152 countries, the denominator is 22,952, so density in 1964 is 1147/22,952 or 0.050, as reported in the final row of Table 1.
[7] De Benedictis and Tajoli (2011) report values at 10-year intervals, starting in 1960 and ending in 2000.

On the other hand, unsurprisingly given what we have just seen in Table 1, the level of concentration is quite low. However, we observe an interesting pattern of increasing concentration up to around 1979 and then a decline, which is especially pronounced for exports. This reflects the dominance early in our data period of traditional exporters (especially France), and then the rise of new exporters.

The low centralization reflects the existence of a number of sizable exporters and importers. Thus, we might be interested in the importance of a core set of countries. We can construct the core in a rough-and-ready way by considering the top dozen wine producers, exporters and importers in 2009.[8] Table 2 shows data illustrating the evolution of this core from 1964. The first thing to notice is that trade within this core rises from about half of world trade to nearly 90% before falling back to 80%.[9] As with the world wine web as a whole, the density of trade in the core nearly doubles over the period covered by our data. However, trade in the core is 10 times as dense as in the global wine economy as a whole. Centralization of this core is on the order of 10–20 times greater than that of the world economy as a whole, but still shows the same pattern of rising, then declining centralization.

---

[8] The top 12 producers in 2009 were: Italy, France, Spain, the USA, Argentina, Chile, China, Australia, South Africa, Germany and Portugal. The top 12 exporters were: France, Italy, Spain, Australia, Chile, Germany the USA, Portugal, South Africa, New Zealand, Argentina and the UK. The top 12 importers were: the UK, the USA, Germany, Canada, Belgium–Luxembourg, Netherlands, Japan, Switzerland, Sweden, Denmark, France and Russia. The union of these three lists gives a 21-country core as of 2009: France, Italy, Spain, the USA, Argentina, Australia, South Africa, Germany, Chile, China, Portugal, the UK, Canada, Belgium–Luxembourg, Netherlands, Japan, Switzerland, Sweden, Denmark, Russia and New Zealand. It should be noted that Russia does not enter our data until 1994, and that for consistency we work with Russia combined with other former Soviet republics.

[9] The 12 top exporters as of 2009 account for well over 90% of world trade in wine in every year in our sample, even though a number of these countries exported no wine, or very little wine, in the early years of our sample period. In fact, France, Italy, Spain and Portugal account for around 90% of world trade in wine in 1964 and 1969. Germany plays an increasing role, especially from 1979, and from 1999 Australia becomes a major world exporter of wine.

Table 2. Network statistics on core of world wine web (top 21 wine-trading countries), 1964–2009

	1964	1969	1974	1979	1984	1989	1994	1999	2004	2009
No. of countries	20	20	20	20	20	20	21	21	21	21
No. of links	204	230	273	282	285	317	370	368	391	391
Total trade	290,538	427,870	1,380,868	3,394,735	3,352,158	6,035,842	7,549,519	12,292,198	17,487,763	21,154,106
Global proportion	0.49	0.61	0.75	0.82	0.87	0.88	0.85	0.86	0.83	0.79
Mean degree	10.2	11.5	13.7	14.1	14.3	15.9	17.6	17.5	18.6	18.6
Mean weighted degree	14,527	21,394	69,043	169,737	167,608	301,792	359,501	585,343	832,751	1,007,338
Normalized degree	2.0	2.4	3.2	3.0	2.1	2.1	2.2	2.4	3.0	3.3
Density	0.5	0.6	0.7	0.7	0.8	0.8	0.9	0.9	0.9	0.9
Out centralization	19.2	22.3	24.6	24.9	18.5	23.0	21.6	21.5	20.0	20.9
In centralization	9.2	8.6	9.9	9.5	11.3	7.6	8.1	9.7	15.7	12.9

Source: Authors' calculations, based on UN COMTRADE data.

4. Intra-industry trade in wine

We now turn to analysis of the pattern of trade in wine based on the Grubel and Lloyd index of intra-industry trade. What we mean by intra-industry trade is the case where partners both import to and export from each other (also known as two-way trade) (Greenaway and Milner, 1986; Grubel and Lloyd, 1975). Two-way trade in wine can reflect, for example, consumer interest in final wine varieties that differ by country of origin, such as trade in different wine varieties for final consumption between France and Spain. However, a great deal of wine is traded in bulk and then mixed with domestic wine, or with wine imported from other countries, before packaging for final consumers (COGEA.S.r.l., 2014). In this sense, two-way trade in wine reflects demand at both the final and intermediate product levels.

On a bilateral basis, we define the intra-industry trade index (in this case for wine) $IIT_{i,j}$ between countries i and j as a function of imports by country j from i ($M_{i,j}$) and imports by country i from country j ($M_{j,i}$) as follows:

$$IIT_{i,j} = 1 - \left[\frac{|M_{i,j} - M_{j,i}|}{M_{i,j} + M_{j,i}}\right]. \qquad (1)$$

In equation (1), the main term in square brackets represents the share of bilateral trade that is classified as net trade, or as reflecting inter-industry trade. The remaining share is then the share of trade that is intra-industry or two-way, meaning it reflects trade that is balanced in both directions (where country i imports from country j and country j imports from country I to the same extent). Note there is symmetry with the definition in (1), where $IIT_{i,j} = IIT_{j,i}$.

Starting from equation (1) we can also define an intra-industry trade index for country j trade with the world as a whole (where we take all trading partners of j collectively). In formal terms, we define this aggregate index $IIT_{j,world}$ as follows:

$$IIT_{j,world} = 1 - \sum_i \left[\frac{|M_{i,j} - M_{j,i}|}{\sum_k M_{k,j} + M_{j,k}}\right]. \qquad (2)$$

We will work with both bilateral and aggregate IIT indexes as defined in equations (1) and (2). These are all calculated on the basis of trade data (bilateral imports) from the UN COMTRADE database.

Table 3 below presents the values of index $IIT_{j,world}$ for the 21 countries that account collectively for between 90% and 95% of global trade in

Table 3. IIT indexes,[a] top 21 wine-trading countries with the world, 1969–2009

	1969	1979	1989	1999	2009
Argentina (ARG)	0.354	0.428	0.056	0.288	0.029
Australia (AUS)	0.821	0.319	0.687	0.145	0.129
Belgium–Luxemburg (BLX)	0.180	0.069	0.132	0.127	0.137
Canada (CAN)	0.011	0.007	0.005	0.014	0.018
Switzerland (CHE)	0.033	0.081	0.030	0.084	0.054
Chile (CHL)	0.049	0.070	0.018	0.020	0.004
China (CHN)	0.978	0.597	0.256	0.192	0.023
Germany (DEU)	0.411	0.680	0.553	0.339	0.443
Denmark (DNK)	0.038	0.004	0.033	0.016	0.168
Spain (ESP)	0.024	0.011	0.094	0.164	0.171
France (FRA)	0.122	0.388	0.162	0.149	0.149
United Kingdom (GBR)	0.030	0.056	0.016	0.055	0.112
Hong Kong (HKG)	0.010	0.003	0.035	0.027	0.003
Italy (ITA)	0.328	0.156	0.250	0.160	0.142
Japan (JPN)	0.676	0.008	0.003	0.004	0.010
Netherlands (NLD)	0.419	0.078	0.061	0.121	0.117
Portugal (PRT)	0.005	0.088	0.337	0.465	0.298
Former Soviet Union (SVU)[b]	0.406	0.456	0.200	0.465	0.033
Sweden (SWE)	0.004	0.006	0.008	0.012	0.038
United States (USA)	0.017	0.030	0.161	0.376	0.367
South Africa (ZAF)	0.320	0.542	0.562	0.109	0.039

Notes: [a]The index of intra-industry trade is defined in equation (1) of the text. [b]For the former Soviet Union (SVU) we focus on trade between the Soviet Union, or countries that were part of the Soviet Union pre-1991, and the rest of the world.

Source: Authors' calculations, based on UN COMTRADE data.

wine over the period 1969–2009.[10] There are some significant changes over the 40 years in the table. For example, we see that for Argentina, Australia and South Africa there is a discernable drop in the IIT share of trade with the world. In the case of these countries and, as will become clearer when we turn to bilateral flows below, this reflects their rise over those four decades as net exporters to the rest of the world. In contrast, the IIT share of trade also fell dramatically for China, but in this case it is because of China's rise as a wine importer.

Globally, changes in net positions as exporters or importers are reflected in changes in the aggregate IIT indexes in Table 3. To better understand these changes, in Figure 2 we provide bilateral IIT indexes as defined in equation (1).[11] In comparing the pattern in 2009 with 1969, we see an increase in pair-wise relationships defined by a high share of IIT trade in total pair-wise trade, for example between Belgium–Luxemburg and Switzerland, South Africa and Argentina, and South Africa and France.

However, while we see more pairs engaged in IIT trade defined in trade share terms, much of this IIT takes place in the context of relatively low levels of total trade on a volume basis. For this reason, in Figure 3, we present the level of intra-industry trade for each of the dyads in the figures. In formal terms, we can define the level of intra-industry trade $LIIT_{i,j}$ as follows:

$$LIIT_{i,j} = \left(1 - \left[\frac{|M_{i,j} - M_{j,i}|}{M_{i,j} + M_{j,i}}\right]\right)\left(M_{i,j} + M_{j,i}\right). \tag{3}$$

In Figure 3, cells are scaled by the maximum value of $LIIT_{i,j}$ for the corresponding year relating to each Figure. On a level instead of a share basis, in 1969 the great bulk of two-way trade in wine was between France and Italy, with a smaller flow (approximately 25% of the France–Italy trade) between Germany and the Netherlands. What we see by 2009 is a spread of two-way trade. France and Italy still show the greatest level of

---

[10] Formally, we have taken the union of the set of the top 11 exporters and the top 15 importers for 2009. The combined share of these countries over time remains consistently between 90% and 95% on a value basis over the period 1969–2009. See note 8.

[11] The full set of figures for intervening decades are available as part of the on-line Appendix.

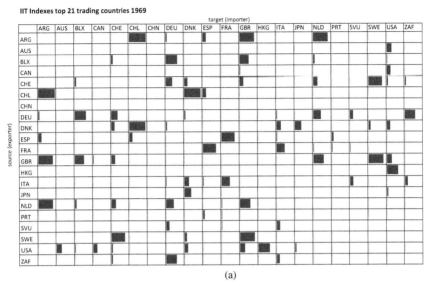

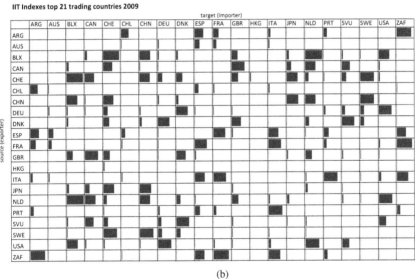

Figure 2. IIT Indexes, top wine-trading countries, 1969 and 2009

Notes: Cells are scaled by the maximum value for the IIT index. Countries are identified by the standard UN ISO 3 codes shown in Table 3.

Source: Authors' calculations based on UN COMTRADE data and equation (1) in text.

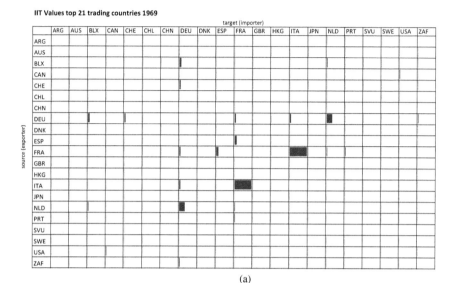

Figure 3. Level of IIT (Values), top 21 wine-trading countries, 1969 and 2009

Notes: Cells are scaled by the maximum value for inter-industry trade flows in the table. Countries are identified by the standard UN ISO 3 codes shown in Table 3.

Source: Authors' calculations based, on UN COMTRADE data.

intra-industry trade, reflecting bulk trade and well established blending patterns (COGEA, 2014). However, we also now have relatively high volumes of intra-industry trade between France and Spain, Germany and the USA, and Italy and the USA.

As a further step in decomposition, in Figure 4 we present net export positions by country pair. Again with reference to equation (1) we are now working with the value of the term $|M_{i,j} - M_{j,i}|$ entering into the right-hand side of equation (1). These figures provide a different perspective from the value of intra-industry trade in Figure 3. For example, while we have some growth in the value of two-way trade between France in the USA (Figure 3), there is also growth in net exports from France to the USA (Figure 4). In contrast, while we have had substantial growth in the level of intra-industry trade between France and Italy (Figure 3), there is little change in the pattern of net trade (Figure 4). This illustrates the growth of trade in wine primarily for final consumption in one case (the USA and France) vs trade for both final and intermediate consumption in the other case (France and Italy).

Another change evident from Figure 4 is the emergence of New World suppliers of wine, especially Australia (exporting to the USA and UK), but to a lesser extent South Africa (to Germany, UK and Sweden) and Chile (to the USA and UK). This pattern of change is especially evident when we examine the pattern of the British wine trade. Figure 5 presents the evolution of the UK's IIT trade and net import patterns from 1969 to 2009. In 1969, most trade was imports from France and Spain (left panel). We see high two-way trade indexes for Argentina, Belgium–Luxemburg, the Netherlands and Sweden (center panel). However, on a value basis, we see in the right panel of Figure 5 that this is primarily trade with the Netherlands (reflecting the role of both Britain and the Netherlands as re-export points). We have a substantial change in this pattern by 2009.

At the end of the period covered by Figure 5, Britain has a more diversified pattern of import suppliers, with Australia, Chile, Italy and South Africa all taking on more important positions, although still secondary *vis-à-vis* France; and while Italy has steadily picked up market share in the UK, Spain has dropped off over the same period (left panel). In addition, when we compare IIT indexes with IIT values, we see a shift away from the Netherlands: on an index basis, Canada now shows the greatest two-way trade intensity (center panel), although this is clearly at low actual values of intra-industry

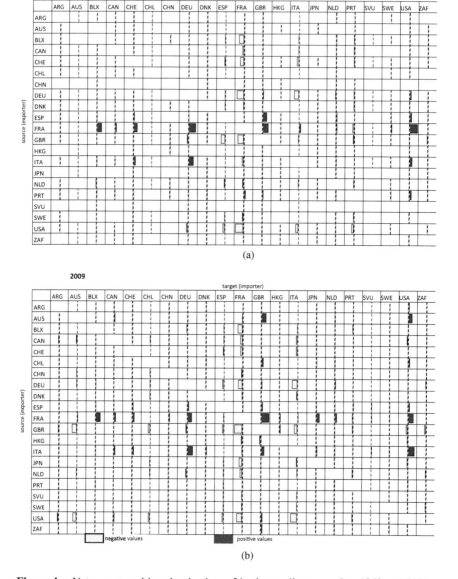

Figure 4. Net export positions by dyad, top 21 wine-trading countries, 1969 and 2009

Notes: Cells are scaled by the maximum value for net exports. Countries are identified by the standard UN ISO 3 codes shown in Table 3.

Source: Authors' calculations based, on UN COMTRADE data.

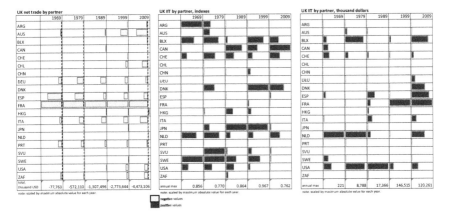

Figure 5. Evolution of UK trade composition in wine, 1969–2009

Notes: Cells are scaled by maximum value for each year. Countries are identified by the standard UN ISO 3 codes shown in Table 3.

Source: Authors' calculations based, on UN COMTRADE data.

trade (right panel). The most important partner on a value basis in terms of the UK's two-way trade is now France (right panel), even though on a relative or share basis this trade relationship remains one of net imports (left and center panels). We also see a growing pattern of two-way trade in wine with Denmark, both in share and value terms (center and right panels).

5. What next?

How might total and intra-industry trade in wine change in the coming years? Recent global wine modeling studies by Anderson and Wittwer (2013, 2015) show that the outcome is likely to depend very much on changes in real bilateral exchange rates and the propensity of China to import vs producing more of its own wine. Since those variables are notoriously difficult to predict, Anderson and Wittwer offer several scenarios. A summary of the bilateral trade consequences from their most likely scenario is provided in Table 4. It suggests the US$ value (in 2009 dollars) of global wine trade will rise by 19% between 2011 and 2018, but more than half of that rise is accounted for by imports of China and other Asian countries. The USA is the only other country shown in Table 4 whose imports rise by (slightly) more than the global average of 19%. US exports

Table 4. Projected changes in values of wine trade, 2011–2018 (US$million)

	FRA	BLX	DEU	GBR	OWEM[a]	RUS	OECA[a]	USA	CAN	CHN	JPN	OASIA[a]	AUS	NZL	RofWM[a]	World	% Change
FRA	0	202	35	121	363	32	24	337	119	683	176	382	3	3	151	2630	28
ITA	11	7	−52	0	95	23	12	161	51	148	19	26	2	1	24	528	9
PRT	41	16	−1	2	24	0	1	16	14	22	2	7	0	0	61	205	22
ESP	−17	−3	−47	−15	−23	0	2	28	4	94	3	7	0	0	13	46	2
DEU	0	0	0	−6	−4	1	3	13	1	63	1	5	0	0	3	80	7
USA	−2	−2	−10	−27	−11	−2	−1	0	−9	191	−4	16	0	0	−14	125	12
AUS	1	3	0	42	24	0	1	115	33	649	3	50	0	9	3	933	52
ARG	0	0	−1	−1	−6	−4	0	11	−3	33	−1	1	0	0	6	36	6
CHL	−1	−1	−5	−4	−7	−1	2	21	5	252	2	13	0	0	28	303	24
NZL	2	2	1	45	33	0	1	128	41	35	7	36	47	0	3	380	66
ZAF	0	2	2	20	13	1	1	7	5	35	1	3	1	1	18	109	18
RofWX[a]	−6	−4	−16	−3	−38	−28	−39	4	−4	100	21	11	11	−3	−60	−54	−3
World	27	221	−94	174	463	22	7	841	256	2305	231	557	63	11	236	5321	19
% change	4	15	−3	4	8	2	1	20	16	309	18	38	13	11	13	19	

Notes: [a]OWEM = other Western European wine importers (excl. France, Belgium/Luxembourg, Germany and Great Britain (UK)); OECA = other Eastern Europe and former Soviet Union (excl. Russia); OASIA = other Asia (excl. China and Japan); RofWM = other wine importers not shown here; and RofWX = other wine exporters not shown here. Other countries' acronyms are identified by the standard UN iso3 codes shown in Table 3.

Source: From modeling results summarized in Anderson and Wittwer (2013).

grow by only 12% though. By contrast, Australian and New Zealand wine exports are projected to grow by more than 50% over the same 8-year period (mostly destined for China), while their imports grow by only two-thirds the global average, thanks to their real exchange rates depreciating from their historically high 2011 rates in the scenario modeled.

6. Conclusions

This paper illustrates the benefits of network methods to the study of trade in a sector characterized by dynamic evolution of both production and consumption of a differentiated product. The takeaway message from this analysis is that the global wine industry is growing rapidly around a rather stable core of countries that are both sizable exporters and sizable importers. This trade reflects both trade in intermediate inputs (bulk wine for blending) and trade at the final product level. The growing demand for wine is increasingly being served by new wine exporters, without displacing the historical core of the wine producers. If new Chinese producers are able to move up market, they could become major participants in this core.

While our trade data do not permit us to distinguish quality at the dyadic level over the entire period, it is clear from the aggregate data on production and consumption that countries differ substantially in patterns of consumption, and production, by quality. By focusing on a single product, especially one characterized by extensive differentiation, future work should be able to provide more extensive analysis of the foundations of intra-industry trade and its evolution. In particular, the co-evolution of production and consumption has long been recognized as a phenomenon that is characteristic of sophisticated differentiated products.[12] Network methods provide an effective body of tools for characterizing and measuring precisely this sort of phenomenon. We have only scratched the surface of what is possible using these methods.

In addition, the close link between network methods and gravity modeling of trade provides a bridge between the sort of analysis presented in

---

[12] In addition to Linder's (1961) work, mentioned in the introduction, this has long been part of the product life cycle analysis of the evolution of trade relations (Vernon, 1966; Hufbauer, 1966).

this paper and the most common approach to empirical research on international trade in current trade research (Ward *et al.*, 2013; Fagiolo, 2010; Duenas and Fagiolo, 2013). By matching production, consumption and trade data over time (Anderson and Nelgen, 2011; Anderson and Pinilla, 2017), there is ample scope to examine in future work the causal relationships between these factors.

References

Anderson, K. and N. R. Aryal, *Growth and Cycles in Australia's Wine Industry: A Statistical Compendium, 1843 to 2013*, Adelaide, SA: University of Adelaide Press (2015).

Anderson, K. and S. Nelgen, *Global Wine Markets, 1961 to 2009: A Statistical Compendium*, Adelaide, SA: University of Adelaide Press (2011).

Anderson, K. and V. Pinilla, *Global Wine Markets, 1860 to 2016: A Statistical Compendium*, Adelaide, SA: University of Adelaide Press (2017).

Anderson, K. and G. Wittwer, "Modeling Global Wine Markets to 2018: Exchange Rates, Taste Changes, and China's Import Growth," *Journal of Wine Economics* 8 (2013):131–58.

——, "Asia's Evolving Role in Global Wine Markets," *China Economic Review* 35 (2015): 1–14.

Anderson, K., D. Norman, and G. Wittwer, "Globalisation of the World's Wine Markets," *World Economy* 26 (2003):659–87.

Borgatti, S. P., M. G. Everett, and J. C. Johnson, Analyzing Social Networks, Thousand Oaks, CA: Sage (2013).

COGEA.S.r.l., "Study on the Competitiveness of European Wines: Final Report," doi: 10.2762/56910, European Commission, Luxembourg Publications Office of the European Union, Luxembourg (2014).

De Benedictis, L. and L. Tajoli, "The World Trade Network," *The World Economy* 34 (2011): 1417–54.

Duenas, M. and G. Fagiolo, "Modeling the International Trade Network: A Gravity Approach," *Journal of Economic Interaction and Coordination* 8 (2013):155–78.

Fagiolo, G., "The International Trade Network: Gravity Equations and Topological Properties," *Journal of Economic Interaction and Coordination* 5 (2010):1–25.

Freeman, L. C., "Centrality in Social Networks' Conceptual Clarification," *Social Networks* 1 (1979):215–39.

Greenaway, D. and C. Milner, The Economics of Intra-industry Trade, Oxford: Basil Blackwell (1986).

Grubel, H. G. and P. J. Lloyd, Intra-industry Trade: The Theory and Measurement of International Trade in Differentiated Products, New York: Wiley (1975).

Helpman, E. and P. R. Krugman, *Market Structure and Foreign Trade: Increasing Returns, Imperfect Competition, and the International Economy*, Cambridge, MA: MIT Press (1985).

Hufbauer, G. C., Synthetic Materials and the Theory of International Trade, London: Duckworth (1966).

Johnson, H., Vintage: The Story of Wine, New York: Simon and Schuster (1989).

Linder, S. B., An Essay on Trade and Transformation, Stockholm: Almqvist & Wiksell (1961).

Lukacs, P., Inventing Wine: A New History of One of the World's Most Ancient Pleasures, New York: W. W. Norton (2012).

Meloni, G. and J. Swinnen, "The Rise and Fall of the World's Largest Wine Exporter — and Its Institutional Legacy," *Journal of Wine Economics* 9 (2014):3–33.

Pellechia, T., Wine: The 8,000-Year-Old Story of the Wine Trade, New York: Thunder's Mouth Press (2006).

Piggott, S., "A Late Bronze Age Wine Trade?", *Antiquity* 33 no. 130 (1959):122–23.

Simpson, J., *Creating Wine: The Emergence of a World Industry, 1840–1914*, Princeton, NJ: Princeton University Press (2011).

Unwin, T., Wine and the Vine: An Historical Geography of Viticulture and the Wine Trade, London: Routledge (1991).

Vernon, R., "International Investment and International Trade in the Product Cycle," *Quarterly Journal of Economics* 80 (1966):190–207.

Ward, M. D., J. S. Ahlquist, and A. Rozenas, "Gravity's Rainbow: A Dynamic Latent Space Model for the World Trade Network," *Network Science* 1 (2013):95–118.

Chapter 5

How Might Climate Changes and Preference Changes Affect the Competitiveness of the World's Wine Regions?*

Kym Anderson[†]

Abstract

Winegrape production is generally considered riskier in cool-climate regions than in warmer ones, yet more producers are looking to invest in such regions. A commonly stated reason is to hedge against global warming, but is there more to it than that? This note reflects on some other supply-side drivers as well as some drivers from the demand side of global wine markets. It first defines what characterizes a cool-climate region; and it ends by drawing implications for the economic future of such cool regions as compared with the world's warmer wine regions.

---

*First published in *Wine Economics and Policy* 6(2): 23–27, June 2017, following its presentation at the 9th International Cool Climate Wine Symposium, Brighton, England, 26–28 May 2016. Assistance from Peter Dry and Gregory Jones in defining cool climate regions is greatly appreciated, but they bear no responsibility for the selection chosen. This note is a variant of an article that first appeared in Australia's *Wine and Viticulture Journal* 31(5): 63–65, September/October 2016.

[†]Wine Economics Research Centre, School of Economics, University of Adelaide, Adelaide, SA 5005, Australia.

1. What defines a cool climate wine region?

There is no consensus on what defines a cool climate wine region. Certainly average temperature over the growing season is important (October-April in Southern Hemisphere, April-October in Northern), but so too are such aspects as months of growing season, rainfall distribution, wind exposure, frost prevalence and sunlight hours. Jones and Schultz (2016) believe an average growing season temperature (GST) should be between 13°C and 15°C: below 13°C means only non-vinifera (hybrid) varieties will prosper, and above 15°C tends to result in wines that are significantly less acidic.

2. Why riskier?

Growing winegrapes in cool climates is both riskier and more costly than in warmer regions for several reasons. If cool regions also have higher rainfall because they are near the coast, disease pressure is greater; or if they are far inland they face a higher risk of spring or fall frosts that could kill the weakest vines. Also, the shorter growing season raises the risk that grapes won't ripen sufficiently in the coldest vintages. Yields will tend to be lower on average too, raising production costs per ton, and they tend to be more variable from vintage to vintage, adding to marketing challenges (especially when compared with those warmer regions that allow irrigation). If the prevalence to hand prune and pick is greater in cooler regions, that too would make them costlier. One of the few offsetting factors is that longer summer daylight hours in higher latitudes can contribute more to photosynthesis.

3. How significant are cool climate wine regions?

The share of cool climate regions in the world's vineyard area depends of course on which regions are classified as cool. The set listed in Table 1 has

Table 1. Cool climate area by region and share of national winegrape area, 2010

Region	Bearing Area (hectares)	National Share (%)
Argentina		
Neuquen	1653	0.82
Rio Negro	1643	0.82
Total Argentina	**3295**	**1.64**
Australia		
Adelaide Hills	3861	2.54
Alpine Valleys	705	0.46
Australian Capital Territory	4	0.00
Beechworth	57	0.04
Bendigo	771	0.51
Canberra District (ACT)	105	0.07
Canberra District (NSW)	378	0.25
Coonawarra	5985	3.94
Grampians	506	0.33
Heathcote	1245	0.82
Henty	183	0.12
Macedon Ranges	224	0.15
Mornington Peninsula	752	0.50
Mount Benson	233	0.15
Mount Lofty Ranges — other	468	0.31
Port Phillip — other	68	0.04
Robe	644	0.42
Southern Highlands	202	0.13
Tasmania	1251	0.82
Tumbarumba	254	0.17
Wrattonbully	2818	1.86
Yarra Valley	2440	1.61
Total Australia	**23,153**	**15.25**
Austria		
Burgenland	13,842	30.40

(*Continued*)

Table 1. (*Continued*)

Region	Bearing Area (hectares)	National Share (%)
Niederosterreich	27,184	59.70
Steiermark	3867	8.49
Wien and other Bundeslander	640	1.40
Total Austria	**45,533**	**100.00**
Canada		
British Colombia	3995	39.56
Ontario	6102	60.44
Total Canada	**10,096**	**100.00**
Chile		
Del Bio Bio	3420	3.07
Valparaiso	8522	7.64
Total Chile	**11,942**	**10.71**
China		
Ningxia	11,152	37.74
Total China	**11,152**	**37.74**
Croatia		
Dalmatinska Zagora	602	2.90
Hrvatsko Primorje	210	1.01
Istra	3083	14.85
Moslavina	228	1.10
Plesivica	452	2.18
Podunavlje	3206	15.45
Pokuplje	41	0.20
Prigorje-Bilogora	791	3.81
Sjeverna Dalmacija	2333	11.24
Slavonija	3307	15.94
Srednja Juzna Dalm.	2972	14.32
Zagorje-Medimurje	1266	6.10
Other HR	2263	10.90
Total Croatia	**20,754**	**100.00**

(*Continued*)

Table 1. (*Continued*)

Region	Bearing Area (hectares)	National Share (%)
Czech Republic		
Cechy	785	4.83
Morava	15,457	95.17
Total Czech Republic	**16,242**	**100.00**
France		
Bas Rhin	6965	0.82
Cher	4027	0.48
Cote d'Or	9665	1.14
Haut Rhin	9190	1.09
Indre	424	0.05
Indre et Loire	10,443	1.23
Nievre	1611	0.19
Saone et Loire	13,486	1.59
Savoie	1323	0.16
Vendee	1318	0.16
Vienne	1091	0.13
Yonne	7131	0.84
Total France	**66,675**	**7.87**
Germany		
Ahr	550	0.54
Baden	15,830	15.51
Franken	6100	5.98
Hessische Bergstra E	420	0.41
Mittelrhein	450	0.44
Mosel-Saar-Ruwer	8970	8.79
Nahe	4160	4.08
Rheingau	3060	3.00
Rheinhessen	26,470	25.94
Rhein-Pfalz	23,460	22.99
Saale-Unstrut	700	0.69

(*Continued*)

Table 1. (*Continued*)

Region	Bearing Area (hectares)	National Share (%)
Sachsen	460	0.45
Wurttemberg	11,430	11.20
Total Germany	**102,060**	**100.00**
Hungary		
Badacsony	1618	2.32
Balatonboglar	3305	4.74
Balatonfelvidek	1025	1.47
Balatonfured-Csopak	2180	3.13
Bukk	1055	1.51
Csongrad	1513	2.17
Eger	5509	7.90
Etyek-Budai	1717	2.46
Hajos-Bajai	1982	2.84
Kunsag	22263	31.93
Matra	6294	9.03
Mor	730	1.05
Nagy-Somlo	598	0.86
Neszmely	1587	2.28
Pannonhalma	615	0.88
Pecs	777	1.11
Sopron	1919	2.75
Szekszard	2333	3.35
Tokaj	5994	8.60
Tolna	2526	3.62
Villany	2582	3.70
Zala	1592	2.28
Total Hungary	**69,715**	**100.00**
Japan		
Hokkaido	835	22.47
Nagano	754	20.30

(*Continued*)

Table 1. (Continued)

Region	Bearing Area (hectares)	National Share (%)
Yamagata	392	10.56
Yamanashi	632	17.01
Other Japan	1102	29.66
Total Japan	**3715**	**100.00**
Luxembourg	**1304**	**100.00**
New Zealand		
Auckland	543	1.70
Canterbury	320	1.00
Gisborne	2149	6.72
Hawkes Bay	4921	15.40
Marlborough	18,401	57.57
Nelson	813	2.54
Otago	1532	4.79
Waikato	147	0.46
Waipara	1442	4.51
Wairarapa	859	2.69
Other NZ	836	2.62
Total New Zealand	**31,964**	**100.00**
Slovakia		
Juznoslovenska	4141	32.77
Malokarpatska	3683	29.14
Nitrianska	2652	20.98
Stredoslovenska	1155	9.14
Tokajska	453	3.59
Vychodoslovenska	553	4.38
Total Slovakia	**12,637**	**100.00**
Slovenia		
Bela Krajina	365	2.23
Bizeljsko Sremic	907	5.54
Dolenjska	1476	9.02

(Continued)

Table 1. (*Continued*)

Region	Bearing Area (hectares)	National Share (%)
Prekmurje	564	3.45
Stajerska Slovenija	6374	38.97
Total Slovenia	**9686**	**59.22**
Switzerland		
Aargau	399	2.69
Basel-Landschaft	114	0.77
Bern	242	1.63
Fribourg	117	0.79
Geneva	1292	8.72
Graub• Nden	421	2.84
Jura	14	0.09
Lucerne	41	0.28
Neuchytel	591	3.99
Schaffhausen	478	3.22
Schwyz	38	0.26
St. Gallen	215	1.45
Thurgau	263	1.78
Ticino	1069	7.21
Valais	5070	34.21
Vaud	3819	25.77
Zurich	614	4.14
Other CH	25	0.17
Total Switzerland	**14,820**	**100.00**
United Kingdom	**1198**	**100.00**
United States		
Marin	62	0.03
Mendocino	6555	2.88
Monterey	15,600	6.84
San Luis Obispo	11,484	5.04
Santa Barbara	6512	2.86

(*Continued*)

Table 1. (*Continued*)

Region	Bearing Area (hectares)	National Share (%)
Santa Clara	609	0.27
Santa Cruz	160	0.07
Sonoma	22,265	9.77
Columbia Gorge	159	0.07
Columbia Valley	3023	1.33
Horse Heaven Hills	4283	1.88
Lake Chelan	100	0.04
Puget Sound	72	0.03
Rattlesnake Hills	647	0.28
Red Mountain	515	0.23
Snipes Mountain	285	0.12
Wahluke Slope	2689	1.18
Walla Walla Valley	528	0.23
Yakima Valley	5444	2.39
Chautauqua-Erie	7561	3.32
Finger Lakes	3801	1.67
Other New York	1508	0.66
Benton Co.	155	0.07
Columbia River	610	0.27
Douglas Co.	350	0.15
Jackson Co.	536	0.24
Josephine Co.	162	0.07
Lane Co.	341	0.15
Marion Co.	660	0.29
Other W. Valley	154	0.07
Polk Co.	928	0.41
Washington Co.	670	0.29
Yamhill Co.	2273	1.00
Illinois	373	0.16
Indiana	263	0.12

(*Continued*)

Table 1. (*Continued*)

Region	Bearing Area (hectares)	National Share (%)
Iowa	194	0.09
Michigan	1072	0.47
Minnesota	418	0.18
Ohio	436	0.19
Pennsylvania	1004	0.44
Virginia	1065	0.47
Total United States	**105,527**	**46.29**
World in 2010	**608,850**	**13.22**

Source: Author's compilation based on consultations with Peter Dry of the Australian Wine Research Institute, using regional data assembled in Anderson (2013).

been compiled with the help of Peter Dry of the Australian Wine Research Institute. It may include some regions that are slightly warmer than what Jones and Schultz (2016) consider cool, but even so it suggests they account for just 13 percent of the world's winegrape bearing area in 2010.

These regions may be more important economically than just those area data suggest, however. This would be the case if average winegrape prices in cool climate regions are sufficiently higher than those of warmer regions to offset the lower yields per hectare. Their wines may have an even larger share of the global wine market if the wine price to grape price ratio is above the world average.

Are these regions expanding? Certainly they are in Australia and New Zealand, and famously also (albeit from a very low base) in England (see Figure 1). But globally the area of the regions listed in Table 1 fell by one-sixth between 2000 and 2010, while the bearing area of warmer regions fell only one-tenth.

4. How different are cool climate winegrape varieties?

According to Jones (2006), there is a clear ranking of premium quality winegrape varieties in terms of their potential to ripen in different climates. That manifests itself in a quite different mix of varieties in cool as

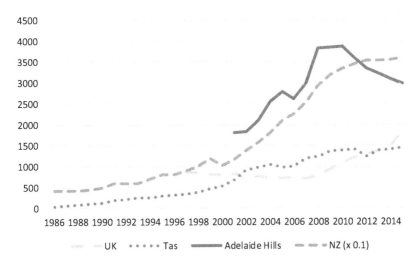

Figure 1. Vine bearing area in a selection of cool climate regions,[a] 1986 to 2015 (hectares)
[a]Note that New Zealand's area is ten times that shown on the above scale.
Source: Author's compilation from national sources.

distinct from warmer climates: among the top ten varieties globally in those two subsets of regions, there are only three that are common, namely Chardonnay, Cabernet Sauvignon and Merlot (Figure 2).

5. Supply-side determinants of the competitiveness of cool climate vignerons

Global warming is typically thought of as a major driver of new investment in cool climate wine regions, including from producers in warmer areas seeking to supplement supplies that can help them maintain their current styles of wines as well as add new ones (Ashenfelter and Storchmann, 2016). An opposite development took place between 1200 and 1600: the average temperature in Southern England fell about 1.3°C over those four centuries, and the gradual disappearance of England's vineyards after 1200 is often attributed to that cooling (Lamb, 1982, Grove, 1988) — although the British takeover of the Bordeaux region of France may have been the main reason for their demise.

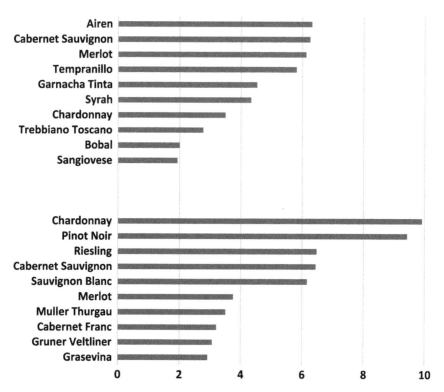

Figure 2. Shares of the top ten varieties in the bearing area of the world's cool and warmer regions, 2010 (percent; bars for cool regions are shown below the set for warmer regions)
Source: Derived from Anderson (2013) using the regional classification in Table 1.

Over time with global warming, the warmest of cool regions would no longer be capable of producing cool climate wine styles. However, that would be more or less offset by new plantings in areas at higher altitudes or latitudes that were previously too cold to grow winegrapes profitably. Evidence to support this expectation is provided by Ashenfelter and Storchmann (2010a, 2010b). They examine economic data from the Mosel region of Germany and find that a 1°C rise in GST increases gross earnings from Riesling by 30 percent.

Data compiled for Australia by Webb (2006), by contrast, suggest that in that country's hot winegrape regions, greater warming leads to lower prices and profits. This would add to a strengthening of the competitive edge of cool climate regions over hot ones.

Research and development can of course affect competitiveness. If cool climate regions have different R&D needs from warmer regions, it is a question of how R&D funding is allocated. Traditionally Australia has paid relatively little attention to cool climate viticultural research, in contrast to Germany and northern France (from whose research institutes more-northern European regions can borrow). Australia's cool climate regions may benefit from developing strategies to boost pertinent R&D investment collaboration with New Zealand.

Another supply-side influence on cool climate competitiveness is trade costs. Shipping small quantities of premium wine half-way around the world has been infeasible historically, which is a key reason why cool climate regions in the southern hemisphere had little presence in the main (i.e., northern hemisphere) markets for fine wine. Technological changes in ocean transportation of wine have helped to lower trade costs substantially over the past three decades however, and not only for commercial premium wines that are increasingly being shipped in bulk. That development is reducing the competitive disadvantage that southern hemisphere producers of fine wine, including from cool regions, have had to suffer until recently. Falling information and communication costs also have helped, by speeding the pace of technology transfer from the established centres of cool climate grape and wine research in Europe to the antipodes.

6. Demand-side determinants of the competitiveness of cool climate vignerons

Since it is relatively expensive to produce cool climate wines, they need to be able to command relatively high prices. A rise in the demand for them therefore depends on a rise in incomes of those wine consumers with a preference for that style of wine, or a preference shift toward that style. If both things happen simultaneously, prices of cool climate wines would rise even more than otherwise would have been the case. Regional marketing by cool climate producers may be able to reinforce such a preference switch, provided it is not more than offset by generic promotion by other regions.

Fine wines from cool regions have been produced since at least the 19th century, but only the elite could afford them. Unprecedented rises in per capita incomes since the 1980s, however, have boosted the demand for all luxury products, including wines. More specifically, higher incomes are raising the demand for higher-quality wines at the expense of low-quality wines, and for more styles and novel varieties. Also accompanying the higher incomes of such consumers is a greater tolerance — even a desire — for vintage variation in still wines of the sort that is more common in cool climates. So even though there has been a halving in global consumption of wine per capita since the 1950s, the demand for fine wines from cool regions can still grow. The challenge will be to be able to attract high-income customers in the wake of efforts by warmer regions to emulate the styles of cool-region wines, both still and sparkling.

7. Implications for southern hemisphere cool-climate regions

In addition to the above forces altering the competitiveness of cool climate wine regions in general, producers in cool regions of the Southern Hemisphere face the challenge of being relatively small both individually and collectively in each region. Smallness matters because it means the costs of focused R&D and of brand or regional promotion are subject to diseconomies of scale. It also means transport costs are relatively high. But as New Zealand has shown, these handicaps need not be insuperable. On the contrary, as producers in the relatively new cool regions gradually discover the varieties, clones and styles they can produce most profitably, so investments in their region could expand.

Appendix A. Supporting material

Supplementary data associated with this article can be found in the online version at http://dx.doi.org/10.1016/j.wep.2016.12.001.

References

Anderson, K., 2013. Which Winegrape Varieties are Grown Where? A Global Empirical Picture. University of Adelaide Press, Adelaide (Freely available as an ebook at <www.adelaide.edu.au/press/titles/winegrapes>).

Ashenfelter, O., Storchmann, K., 2010a. Using a hedonic model of solar radiation to assess the economic effect of climate change: the case of Mosel Valley Vineyards. Rev. Econ. Stat. 92 (2), 333–349.

Ashenfelter, O., Storchmann, K., 2010b. Measuring the economic effect of global warming on viticulture using auction, retail and wholesale prices. Rev. Ind. Organ. 37, 51 64.

Ashenfelter, O., Storchmann, K., 2016. Climate change and wine: a review of the economic implications. J. Wine Econ. 11 (1), 108–138.

Grove, J.M., 1988. The Little Ice Age. Methuen, London.

Jones, G., 2006. Climate change and wine: observations, impacts and future implications. Aust. New Zealand Wine Ind. J. 21 (4), 21–26 (20-July/August).

Jones, G. and Schultz H., 2016. Emerging Cool Climate Regions', Invited Paper presented at the 9th International Cool Climate Wine Symposium, Brighton, England, 26–28 May.

Lamb, H.H., 1982. Climate, History and the Modern World. Methuen, London.

Webb, L.B., 2006. The Impact of Projected Greenhouse Gas-induced Climate Change on the Australian Wine Industry (Unpublished PhD thesis). University of Melbourne, Parkville (October).

Chapter 6

U.K. and Global Wine Markets by 2025, and Implications of Brexit*

Kym Anderson[†] and Glyn Wittwer[‡]

1. Introduction

The United Kingdom's planned withdrawal from the European Union (Brexit) will affect markets for many products, including wine. Very little wine is produced in the United Kingdom (although the volume is now five times what it was in the 1980s), and wine has accounted on average for just 0.5% of U.K. merchandise imports since World War I. Over the past six decades, though, wine's share of U.K. alcohol consumption has steadily

---

*First published in *Journal of Wine Economics* 12(3): 221–51, 2017. The authors are grateful for helpful comments from referees and from L. Alan Winters, Jancis Robinson, Tamara Roberts, and other participants in a seminar at Chatham House in London on May 19, 2017. We also thank the U.K. Trade Policy Observatory of the University of Sussex and the Royal Institute for International Affairs for hosting the seminar.

[†]Kym Anderson, Wine Economics Research Centre, School of Economics, University of Adelaide, Adelaide, SA 5005, Australia; and Australian National University, Canberra, ACT 2600; e-mail: kym.anderson@adelaide.edu.au (corresponding author).

[‡]Glyn Wittwer, Professorial Fellow, Centre of Policy Studies, Victoria University, PO Box 14428, Melbourne, Vic. 8001, Australia; e-mail: Glyn.Wittwer@vu.edu.au.

risen, from 5% to more than one-third, so wine traders, distributors, and retailers as well as consumers are concerned about Brexit's potential impact. Among wine producers and consumers outside the United Kingdom, Brexit is also attracting considerable attention, because the United Kingdom has always accounted for a major share of the world's wine imports.

To examine how wine markets might be affected by the United Kingdom's exit from the European Union, it is necessary to look beyond just the immediate trade-reducing and trade-diverting effects of altering bilateral import tariffs that are the focus of the standard comparative static economic theory of (withdrawal from) customs unions. Because the process of exiting, establishing new trading arrangements, and adjusting to altered incentives is expected to spread over many years, and initially to slow the growth of U.K. incomes and to devalue the pound, one needs to begin with a projection of how wine markets would have looked without Brexit in several years and then show how that projected baseline might change under various Brexit scenarios and a replacement trade agreement between the United Kingdom and the EU27. We do that using a model of the world's wine markets projected to 2025.

This paper begins by briefly reviewing the United Kingdom's historic and present roles in global wine markets. It then outlines a model of the world's wine markets along with a description of the way in which the model projects and of how that projection can be altered to simulate the effects of Brexit and subsequent bilateral trade agreements on the United Kingdom and other countries. The model's resulting prospective changes to grape and wine markets by 2025 for a baseline case, followed by results for a range of alternative adjustments following Brexit, were included in this article. However, with the continuing developments over the following year this analysis was improved and appears as Chapter 7 in this volume. This chapter is thus a truncated version of the original article.

2. Historical backdrop: Wine in the United Kingdom and the United Kingdom in global wine markets

Wine has rarely accounted for more than 2% of U.K. merchandise imports, and since World War I, it has averaged just 0.5%. Also, prior to 1950, wine accounted for less than 4% of the volume of alcohol consumed

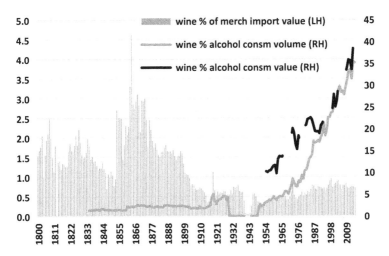

Figure 1. Wine's shares of U.K. merchandise import value and of volume and value of U.K. alcohol consumption,[a] 1800 to 2015 (%)

[a]Reliable wine consumption volume data are not available for the 1930s and 1940s, nor are value of alcohol consumption data pre-1955.

Sources: Compiled from data in Anderson and Pinilla (2017) and Holmes and Anderson (2017a, b).

in the United Kingdom (except briefly in the 1920s) and not much more as a share of alcohol expenditure. Over the past six decades, though, wine's share of U.K. alcohol consumption has steadily risen, and it now exceeds one-third in volume and value terms (Figure 1).

The United Kingdom is a key player in wine-trade circles, as it has always accounted for a major — and often the largest — share of the world's wine imports. Prior to 1960, the United Kingdom's share of the value of world imports of wine roughly matched its share for all merchandise: more than 20% in the 19th century, but steadily declining to around 10% by 1960. Since then, the two shares have diverged, with the all-goods share falling to around 4% while the wine share climbed back above 20% by the beginning of the twenty-first century. The United Kingdom's share of the volume of global wine imports has always been below its value share, but those two shares have converged since 1960 and are now both around 14% (Figure 2).

These two trends are summarized in Figure 3: The ratio of the United Kingdom's shares of world imports of wine to that of all goods rose from 1 to 4 between 1960 and 2000; and the ratio of the United Kingdom's

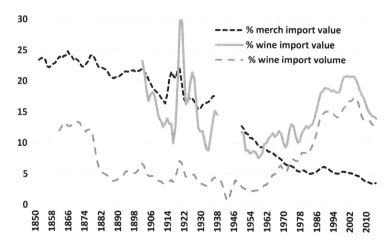

Figure 2. U.K. shares of value of world merchandise imports and of value and volume of world wine imports, 1850 to 2015 (%, 3-year averages to year shown)
Source: Compiled from data in Anderson and Pinilla (2017).

Figure 3. U.K. price relative to world price of wine imports, and U.K. wine-import intensity,[a] 1950 to 2015 (%)

[a] Import intensity is defined as the United Kingdom's share of the value of global wine imports divided by the United Kingdom's share of the world's total merchandise imports.
Source: Compiled from data in Anderson and Pinilla (2017).

average import price to the world average has come down from between 3 and 4 pre-1960 (when the United Kingdom was mostly importing relatively expensive wines from Bordeaux and Champagne) to about 1.2 by 1980 and is now close to 1.

Associated with the change in the average quality of U.K. wine imports are dramatic changes in the importance of different wine-exporting countries to U.K. imports and in U.K. shares in the wine exports of those countries.

Those recent shares are very different from what they were in 1995, when the New World was just beginning to expand its wine exports. But such changes are not unprecedented. Indeed, they changed considerably not only because of the changing global shares of the various wine-exporting countries but also because of changes in the United Kingdom's preferential trading arrangements, such as the 1703 Methuen Treaty with Portugal, the 1860 Cobden-Chevalier Treaty with France, and the 1932 Ottawa Agreement with Commonwealth countries (Tables 1 and 2).

In the middle rows of Table 1, the 2010–2014 shares of exporters in the international market are shown below their shares in the U.K. markets. For some countries, those two sets of shares are similar (France, Italy, Germany, Chile), while for others they are very different. The latter is most noticeable for the former colonies of Australia, New Zealand, and South Africa, whose shares in the United Kingdom are more than twice their shares in the rest of the world. Both shares for the EU27 exceed two-thirds. Many commentators expect the EU27 shares to drop and shares of, e.g., Australia and New Zealand to rise as a consequence of Brexit.

The United Kingdom's recent importance to producers in wine-exporting countries is clear from Figure 4. For seven key suppliers, the United Kingdom accounted in 2010–2014 for more than one-sixth of their wine-export earnings, and for three of them (Australia, the United States, and New Zealand), the United Kingdom was a market for more than one-third of their volume of wine exports.

Recent import duties and other taxes affecting the consumer prices of alcohol in the United Kingdom are summarized in Table 3, expressed per liter of beverage. Import and excise duties on wines vary according to their alcohol content. About one-third of U.K. wine imports arrive in bulk, perhaps half of which contain less than 13% alcohol, and one-tenth of imports are sparkling, so the volume-weighted average import duty is 13 pence per liter. This figure contrasts with the volume-weighted average excise tax on wine, which is 297 pence per liter. To that increase in the wholesale price is added perhaps a 25% retail margin for off-trade sales and well over a 100% margin for many restaurant sales before the 20% value-added tax

Table 1. Shares of U.K. wine imports from today's key wine-exporting countries, 1675 to 2014 and projected to 2025 without and with Brexit (%)

Volume	France	Spain	Portugal	Italy	Germany	South Africa	Australia	United States	Chile	New Zealand	Argentina	Other Countries	Total
1675–1696	25	42	23	1	9	0	0	0	0	0	0	0	100
1697–1862	5	26	49	1	3	2	0	0	0	0	0	14	100
1863–1919	26	26	22	0	0	0	2	0	0	0	0	25	100
1920–1940	12	18	32	0	0	5	14	0	0	0	0	20	100
1995:													
volume	32	10	3	18	14	3	7	3	2	1	0	7	100
value	43	9	4	13	10	2	8	3	2	1	0	5	100
2010–2014:													
volume	15	9	1	17	4	8	21	10	8	4	1	2	100
value	35	8	2	15	4	4	11	5	6	6	1	2	100
Exporters' share of world wine exports, 2010–2014:													
volume	*15*	*20*	*3*	*22*	*4*	*4*	*7*	*4*	*7*	*2*	*3*	*9*	*100*
value	*30*	*9*	*3*	*19*	*4*	*2*	*6*	*4*	*5*	*3*	*3*	*12*	*100*
2025 projected, no Brexit													100
volume	18.8	18.8	2.6	20.7	4.5	4.5	6.5	4.3	6.4	1.7	2.0	9.2	100
value	32.3	10.0	3.0	21.8	4.4	2.3	5.8	4.4	5.4	4.1	2.0	4.5	100
2025 projected, with Brexit													
volume	19.0	18.8	2.7	20.8	4.3	4.4	6.6	4.2	6.3	1.7	1.9	9.3	100
value	31.1	9.6	2.9	21.0	4.1	2.4	5.9	4.4	5.5	4.1	2.0	7.0	100

Sources: Compiled from data in Anderson and Pinilla (2017) to 1940, United Nations COMTRADE, https://comtrade.un.org/data/ for 1995–2014, and authors' model results for 2025.

Table 2. Taxes on British wine imports, by source, 1660–1862 (British pounds per kiloliter)

	France	Germany	Spain	Portugal	South Africa
1660–1665	7	9	8	8	
1666–1684	7	9	8	8	
1685–1691	14	20	19	18	
1692–1695	22	20	19	18	
1696	47	20	19	18	
1697–1702	51	25	23	22	
1703	52	27	24	23	
1704–1744	55	31	26	25	
1745–1762	63	35	30	29	
1763–1777	71	39	34	33	
1778	79	43	38	37	
1779	84	41	40	39	
1780–1781	92	49	44	43	
1782–1785	96	51	47	46	44
1786	65	51	37	37	37
1787–1794	47	51	32	32	37
1795	78	64	51	51	57
1796–1797	108	92	71	71	77
1798	111	96	73	73	79
1799–1801	107	92	71	71	77
1802	112	97	74	74	80
1803	131	109	87	87	87
1804	142	117	95	95	95
1805–1824	144	119	96	96	96
1825–1830	78	50	50	50	25
1831–1859	58	58	58	58	29
1860	32	32	32	32	32
1861	16	21	21	21	21
1862	11	26	26	26	26

Source: Summarized from Ludington (2013, Table A1).

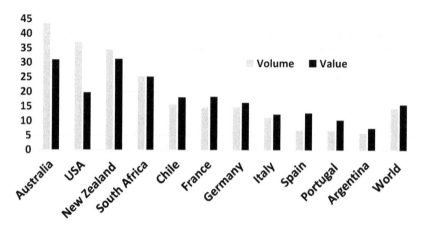

Figure 4. U.K. shares in wine exports of key wine-exporting countries, 2010–2014 (%)
Source: Compiled from data in Anderson and Pinilla (2017).

(VAT) is added. So the average import price in 2013–2015 of 222 pence per liter is escalated to 800 pence for off-trade sales and more than 1,300 pence for on-trade sales (which are about one-fifth of the total sales volume in the United Kingdom). The share of that latter retail price that is due to tariffs on wine imports is thus just 1%. The change in the United Kingdom's import trade regime from imposing such tariffs on wines currently imported free of duty from the European Union, Chile, and South Africa is therefore likely to be very minor. However, as becomes clear below, the effect of Brexit on wine sales involves far more than just the trade-reducing and trade-diverting effects of altering bilateral import tariffs.

3. Global wine markets model and database

Our model of the world's wine markets, first published by Wittwer, Berger, and Anderson (2003) and revised by Anderson and Wittwer (2013), disaggregates wine markets into four types: namely, nonpremium, commercial-premium, and superpremium still wines and sparkling wines.[1] There are two types of grapes: premium and nonpremium. Nonpremium wine uses nonpremium grapes exclusively, superpremium wines use premium grapes exclusively, and

---

[1] Commercial-premium still wines are defined by Anderson, Nelgen, and Pinilla (2017) to cost between US$2.50 and US$7.50 per liter pretax at a country's border or wholesale.

Table 3. Import duties, excise duties, and VAT affecting consumer prices of wine and other alcohol in the United Kingdom, April 1, 2017

VAT	20%
MFN import duties on wine:	£ per liter
-bottled still wine, <13% alc.	0.114
-bottled still wine, 13–15% alc.	0.134
-bottled still wine, 15–18% alc.	0.162
-bulk still wine, <13% alc.	0.086
-bulk still wine, 13–15% alc.	0.105
-bulk still wine, 15–18% alc.	0.134
-sparkling wine	0.278
Weighted average[a]	0.130
Excise duties on alcohol:	£ per liter
-still wine, <15% alc.	2.887
-still wine, 15-22% alc.	3.848
-sparkling wine, 5.5–8.5% alc.	2.795
-sparkling wine, 8.5–15% alc.	3.697
-spirits (assumed 40% alc.)	11.551
-beer (assumed 5% alc.)	0.954
VAT on alcohol	20%

[a]Assumes that one-third of U.K. wine imports arrives in bulk, that half has less than 13% alcohol, and that one-tenth of imports is sparkling.

Sources: HM Revenue, https://www.gov.uk/government/publications/alcohol-duty-rate-changes, for excise duties and VAT, accessed April 9, 2017; and Wine Australia (2015) for import duties, converted at the 2016 average exchange rate of £0.740634 per euro.

commercial-premium and sparkling wines use both types of grapes to varying extents across countries. The world is divided into 44 individual nations and 7 composite geographic regions that capture all other countries.

The model's database is calibrated to 2014, based on the comprehensive wine-market volume and value data and trade and excise-tax data provided in Anderson and Pinilla (2017) and in Anderson, Nelgen, and Pinilla (2017). It is projected assuming that aggregate national consumption, population, and real exchange rates change between 2014 and 2025 to the extent shown in Appendix Table 1.[2] The Brexit alternatives to that baseline also are projected to 2025.

Concerning preferences, we assume a continued considerable swing toward all wine types in China and a swing away from nonpremium wines in all other countries until 2025.

In our baseline scenario, grape- and wine-industry total-factor productivity are assumed to grow at 1% per year everywhere, while grape- and wine-industry capital is assumed to grow net of depreciation at 1.5% per year in China but zero elsewhere (consistent with the almost-zero growth in global wine production and consumption over the past two decades).

This global model has supply-and-demand equations and, hence, quantities, prices, and price elasticities for each of the grape and wine products and for a single composite of all other products in each country. Income elasticities of demand also exist for each final product. Grapes are assumed to not be traded internationally, but other products are exported and imported. Each market is assumed to have been in equilibrium before any shock and to find a new market-clearing outcome following any exogenously introduced shock.

4. Projecting global wine markets to 2025

Global wine production and exports are projected in the baseline from 2014 to 2025 consistent with past trends. The model's global volume of production (and consumption) rises little over that 11-year period (9%), made up of a 6% decline in nonpremium wine and a one-sixth rise in commercial-premium and superpremium wine. In real (2014 US$) value, though, global wine output and consumption increase by about 50% in total and 60% in the two premium categories. The international trade projections are similar, although a little larger, with the share of global wine production exported (equivalent to the share of global consumption imported) rising 2 percentage points between 2014 and 2025.

---

[2] The real exchange rate changes over the projection period are the changes expected in the nominal value of country i's currency relative to the U.S. dollar times the expected ratio of the GDP deflator for the United States versus that for country i.

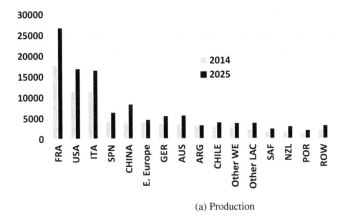

(a) Production

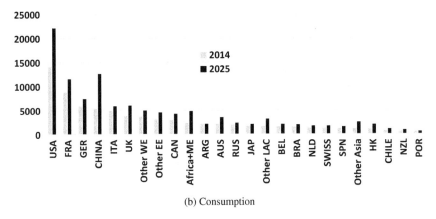

(b) Consumption

Figure 5. Value of wine production and consumption in key countries, 2014 and projected baseline for 2025 (2014 US$ million at winery/wholesale pretax prices)
Source: Authors' model results.

The baseline projection does not greatly alter the 2014 shares of various countries in global wine production, apart from China, because we assume vineyard expansion there is faster than elsewhere.[3] In value terms, this assumption means that China moves from fifth to fourth by 2025, behind France, the United States, and Italy. Spain remains barely ahead of Australia, and they and Germany take the next three places (Figure 5(a)). In total wine-production volume terms, China moves from sixth to fifth place, and Argentina drops from fifth to eighth (and from eighth to ninth in value terms).

---

[3] In fact, China's wine production fell steadily between 2012 and 2016, by a total of one-sixth, so China's wine imports may grow faster in practice than in this baseline projection.

When their products are subdivided into fine wines (superpremium still plus sparking), commercial-premium wines, and nonpremium wines, France and the United States retain the highest two places on the global ladder for fine-wine production, and Spain and Italy retain the top two places for nonpremium wine. As for commercial-premium wine production (defined to cost between US$2.50 and US$7.50 per liter pretax at a country's wholesale level or national border), Italy retains the top ranking over our projections period, but, at least in terms of value, China challenges France for second place.

The country rankings by projected value of total wine consumption change somewhat more than those for production by 2025, with China taking second place after the United States ahead of France and Germany, and then the United Kingdom slightly overtaking Italy to slip into fifth place (Figure 5(b)). The United States, France, and Germany retain the top three rankings for consuming fine wine, but Canada slightly overtakes Italy for fourth place, in terms of value at least. In the case of commercial-wine consumption, China strengthens its number-one position ahead of the United States, and the United Kingdom does likewise vis-à-vis Germany for third place.

As for the projected changes in consumption volumes, China is projected to dominate the increase in aggregate, although the United States is projected to lead the increase in consumption of fine wine. In Western Europe and in the Southern Hemisphere's New World countries, fine wines are projected to substitute for commercial wines (defined as the sum of commercial-premium and nonpremium wines), with almost no change in total wine consumption. Sub-Saharan Africa is the next region that is projected to take off, with its growth accounting for more than one-third of the rest of the world's increase in volume consumed.

Those differences in production versus consumption rankings are reflected in international trade. Figure 6 shows that France, Italy, and Spain remain the three dominant exporters of wine in aggregate value, but the rankings of the next few change, with Australia being slightly ahead of Chile, and the United States, Germany, and New Zealand being nearly tied for sixth place in value terms. France and Italy are even more dominant in fine-wine exports and remain so by 2025, while Italy outranks France in the commercial-premium export category, and Spain outranks Italy, Australia, and Chile in the nonpremium export class.

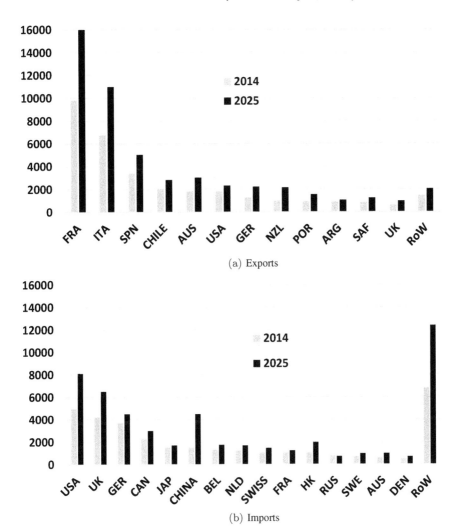

Figure 6. Value of wine exports and imports, key wine-trading countries, 2014 and projected baseline for 2025 (2014 US$ million)
Source: Authors' model results.

Among the importers, the United States and the United Kingdom are projected to continue to hold the first two places in 2025 in value terms, but China moves into third place slightly ahead of Germany, followed well behind by Canada, Hong Kong, Belgium-Luxembourg, the Netherlands, and Japan (Figure 6(b)). Other Africa (excluding South Africa) is projected to experience the largest increase in imports among all the other regions, followed by Other Asia, which becomes as big as Germany in value terms (Figure 7(a)). In terms of total volume of wine imports, Germany and the United Kingdom held the top two shares in 2014, but by 2025, the United Kingdom is projected to be well ahead of Germany (Figure 7 (b)). However, this projection ignores the effects of Brexit. Those are reported in the following chapter (Chapter 7) of this volume.

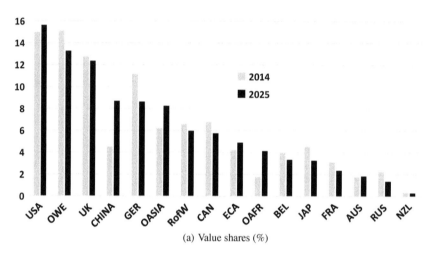

(a) Value shares (%)

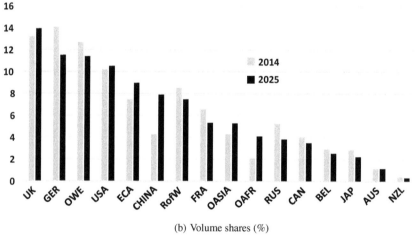

(b) Volume shares (%)

Figure 7. National shares of global wine import value and volume, 2014 and projected baseline for 2025 (%)
Source: Authors' model results.

Appendix Table 1. Cumulative consumption and population growth rates and changes in the Real Exchange Rate (RER) relative to the U.S. dollar, 2014 to 2025 without Brexit (%)

	Aggregate Consumption	Pop'n	RER		Aggregate Consumption	Pop'n	RER
France	18	4	−11	Australia	35	11	−17
Italy	11	2	−9	New Zealand	32	9	−26
Portugal	14	0	−9	Canada	27	8	−18
Spain	26	8	−9	United States	31	8	0
Austria	19	4	−7	Argentina	7	10	109
Belgium	20	7	−9	Brazil	16	8	−29
Denmark	22	2	−9	Chile	55	8	−2
Finland	21	3	−7	Mexico	42	12	−8
Germany	14	−2	−11	Uruguay	45	3	1
Greece	22	−1	−14	Other Latin America	60	10	−5
Ireland	42	12	−9	South Africa	36	12	−1
Netherlands	21	4	−9	Turkey	50	8	20
Sweden	24	9	−13	North Africa	53	11	0
Switzerland	18	8	−6	Other Africa	109	18	84
United Kingdom	32	6	1	Middle East	52	18	−12
Other West Europe	21	10	−1	China	79	3	5
Bulgaria	41	−7	7	Hong Kong	42	3	2
Croatia	20	−2	−1	India	134	13	17
Georgia	35	0	23	Japan	11	−3	−24
Hungary	25	−3	−11	Korea	38	1	−9
Moldova	49	−11	13	Malaysia	62	15	−16
Romania	45	−4	22	Philippines	75	18	7
Russia	18	−2	−8	Singapore	44	21	−22
Ukraine	22	−5	14	Taiwan	29	1	−13
Other East Europe	40	−5	48	Thailand	47	3	−9
				Other Asia	99	10	10

Source: Authors' compilation from projections by various international agencies and from global economy-wide modeling by Anderson and Strutt (2016).

References

Anderson, K., and Nelgen, S. (2011). *Global Wine Markets, 1961 to 2009: A Statistical Compendium.* Adelaide: University of Adelaide Press. Also available as an e-book at www.adelaide.edu.au/press/titles/global-wine.

Anderson, K., Nelgen, S., and Pinilla, V. (2017). *Global Wine Markets, 1860 to 2016: A Statistical Compendium.* Adelaide: University of Adelaide Press. Also to be available as an e-book at www.adelaide.edu.au/press/.

Anderson, K., and Pinilla, V. (with the assistance of A. J. Holmes). (2017). *Annual Database of Global Wine Markets, 1835 to 2016.* Wine Economics Research Centre, University of Adelaide, at www.adelaide.edu.au/wine-econ/databases/.

Anderson, K., and Strutt, A. (2016). Impacts of Asia's rise on African and Latin American trade: Projections to 2030. *World Economy,* 39(2), 172–194.

Anderson, K., and Wittwer, G. (2013). Modeling global wine markets to 2018: Exchange rates, taste changes, and China's import growth. *Journal of Wine Economics,* 8(2), 131–158.

Anderson, K., and Wittwer, G. (2015). Asia's evolving role in global wine markets. *China Economic Review,* 35, 1–14.

Armington, P. A. (1969). A theory of demand for products distinguished by place of production. *IMF Staff Papers,* 16, 159–178.

Holmes, A. J., and Anderson, K. (2017a). *Annual Database of National Beverage Consumption Volumes and Expenditures, 1950 to 2015.* Wine Economics Research Centre, University of Adelaide, posted at www.adelaide.edu.au/wine-econ/databases/.

Holmes, A. J., and Anderson, K. (2017b). Convergence in National Alcohol Consumption Patterns: New Global Indicators. *Journal of Wine Economics,,* 12(2), 117–148.

Ludington, C. C. (2013). *The Politics of Wine in Britain: A New Cultural History.* Basingstoke, U.K.: Palgrave Macmillan.

Wine Australia. (2015). *Export Market Guide: European Union.* Adelaide: Wine Australia.

Wittwer, G., Berger, N., and Anderson, K. (2003). A model of the world's wine markets. *Economic Modelling,* 20(3), 487–506.

Chapter 7

Cumulative Effects of Brexit and Other UK and EU-27 Bilateral Free-Trade Agreements on the World's Wine Markets*

Kym Anderson[†] and Glyn Wittwer[‡]

1. Introduction

Over the past six decades, wine's share of UK alcohol consumption has steadily risen from 5% to more than one-third, so UK wine traders, distributors and retailers as well as wine consumers are concerned about the UK's planned withdrawal from the European Union (Brexit). Brexit is also attracting the attention of wine producers and consumers outside the UK, because the UK accounts for a major share of the world's wine imports. This product thus makes an ideal case study of the various impacts of the Brexit vote and follow-on consequences on a commonly purchased product.

---

*First published in *The World Economy* 41(11): 2883–94, November 2018. The authors are grateful for financial assistance from the Faculty of the Professions, University of Adelaide.

[†]Economics, University of Adelaide, Adelaide, South Australia and Crawford School of Public Policy, Australian National University, Canberra, Australia.

[‡]Centre of Policy Studies, Victoria University, Melbourne, Victoria, Australia.

The immediate trade-reducing and trade-diverting effects of altering bilateral import tariffs are the focus of standard comparative static economic theory of (withdrawal from) a customs union. But the process of exiting, establishing new trading arrangements and adjusting to the altered incentives is inherently uncertain and expected to spread over many years, and initially to slow the growth of UK incomes and devalue the pound. Therefore, one needs to begin with a projection of how wine markets would have looked without Brexit in several years and then show how that projected baseline might change under various scenarios involving a replacement trade agreement between the UK and EU-27 and subsequent free-trade agreements (FTAs) with non-EU trading partners. We do that using a model of the world's wine markets projected to 2025.

The paper begins by summarising what trade theory would lead one to expect for a country leaving a customs union.[1] A model of the world's wine markets is then outlined, along with a description of the way in which the model projects forward and of how that projection can be altered to simulate the effects of Brexit and subsequent bilateral trade agreements on those markets. The model's results of prospective changes to grape and wine markets by 2025 for a baseline case are then summarised, followed by results for a range of additional adjustments following Brexit. They are then compared with the effects of a multilateral agreement to remove all wine import tariffs. Unrealistic though the latter is, it exposes the far bigger responses by wine producers and consumers that could emerge from a single multilateral undertaking than from several bilateral or regional FTAs. The final section draws out implications of the

---

[1] It was not yet certain as of mid-2018 whether the UK would seek to form a customs union with EU-27. But that would require the UK to retain the EU's tariff policy, continue to allow freedom of movement of labour and remain under the European Court of Justice — none of which Brexiteers want. We therefore ignore this possibility and, following Rollo, Borchert, Dawar, Holmes, and Winters (2016) and Smith (2017), assume that the UK will commit to the current EU tariff schedule at the WTO in the first instance and then seek a free trade agreement (FTA) with the EU-27. Other trading partners will want to wait and see what that FTA looks like before signing on to a bilateral FTA of their own with the UK. Meanwhile, the EU has been pursuing other bilateral trade agreements (see EC, 2015), but most of those too are unlikely to be completed before the settling of a new trade arrangement between the UK and EU-27.

findings for wine markets and their participants in the UK and abroad, both within and outside the EU.

2. Expected effects of leaving a customs union

When countries join a customs union and impose a common external tariff on imports from non-union countries, there can be net trade creation (depending on the height of the common external tariff relative to the previous national tariffs), but there will also be trade diversion (because of the new preference to producers within the union — see Viner, 1950). If the overall consequence of joining the union is trade-liberalising for a member, its real income is likely to rise. When a country leaves a union, the reverse happens, because the leaving country's tariffs will now apply to its imports from union countries as well as from the rest of the world (and its real income is likely to fall, assuming the leaver's tariff rates are not reduced). Hence, imports from the union will fall, because their preferential access to the leaving country will no longer apply. That is also the case for countries that enjoy a free trade agreement (FTA) with the union. Of significance to wine are the EU's FTAs with Chile and South Africa (although there are more than 30 other bilateral or regional FTAs with the EU that the UK may wish to replicate after its exit).

How large the trade-diverting impact of leaving the union will be on wine depends on the external tariff imposed on wine imports not only by the union but also by the leaving country. Some have suggested the UK should become the Hong Kong of Europe and go immediately to free trade on all products. Others have suggested that this would impose huge structural changes on the UK economy that its society would not tolerate, at least not without major compensation packages. But both groups agree that a new trade policy that sets most-favoured-nation tariff rates is needed before the UK can begin to negotiate new preferential trading arrangements with the EU-27, its FTA partners such as Chile and South Africa, or any other country. Rollo *et al*. (2016) suggest the most practical trade policy for the UK to adopt at the outset is the EU's tariff schedules previously agreed to at the World Trade Organization (WTO). In all but one of the Brexit scenarios examined below, we assume this will be the new UK trade policy commitment to WTO members, and that subsequent negotiations for preferential arrangements will take years, and any consequent agreements with the EU and others will be gradually implemented after that.

The impact of leaving a highly integrative customs union on wine markets comes not only from tariff changes, however. Also relevant are any effects the uncertainty associated with the decision to leave has on real UK incomes and the value of the pound. If the UK was to move to free trade on all products (the Hong Kong option), its per capita income could eventually rise, but only after considerable adjustment. Should instead the UK commit to the current EU tariff schedule at the WTO in the first instance, as we assume below, then its per capita income growth rate and the pound's exchange rates almost certainly will be lower for some time — at least until new trade agreement negotiations with the EU-27 and others are sufficiently advanced as to restore investor and consumer confidence in the UK economy. Support for that notion was provided initially by Campos (2016). A more-comprehensive assessment of macroeconomic effects by Dhingra et al. (2017), using a general equilibrium model, estimates welfare losses for the average UK household of 1.3% if the UK remains in the EU's Single Market (a softer Brexit than we consider below) and 2.7% if the UK leaves the Single Market (a "hard" Brexit). When the dynamic effects of Brexit on productivity are taken into account, those estimates more than treble to between 6.3% and 9.4% per capita, partly via falls in foreign investment (See also Born, Müller, Schularick, & Sedláček, 2017; Emerson, Busse, Di Salvo, Gros, & Pelkmans, 2017; Oberhofer & Pfaffermayr, 2017; Sampson, 2017).

The assumed adverse macroeconomic effects of Brexit will add to the initial impact of altered wine tariffs on aggregate wine consumption in the UK and hence on its bilateral trades in wine. They will make the loss of wine sales to the UK by EU (and Chilean and South African) suppliers greater than would otherwise be the case. And they reduce the likelihood that other countries' sales of wine in the UK will be higher than in the baseline. That is, even countries currently discriminated against by the EU-28's wine trade policy may be worse off because of Brexit if the adverse macroeconomic effects outweigh the positive trade-diverting effects on them.

3. Global wine markets model and database

We use a model of the world's wine markets summarised in Anderson and Wittwer (2013). It is a partial equilibrium model that follows the theory of computable general equilibrium (CGE) models (Dixon, Parmenter, Sutton, & Vincent, 1982). Unlike the CGE approach, the model depicts the input structures and sales patterns only of the grape and wine sectors, which comprise a small fraction of economic activity in wine-producing nations.

Consumers follow a linear expenditure function within the model, although aggregate consumption is assumed to be exogenous, given the small budget share of wine in total consumption. The model includes an expenditure function so as to project markets to 2025, since this requires projecting aggregate consumption growth with a distinction between fast-growing economies such as China and other emerging economies relative to slower-growing Western economies (see Table A1 in the Appendix), with a taste swing towards higher-quality wines and away from lower-quality wines and provision for higher-quality wines to have higher income elasticities than lower-quality wines. The linear expenditure system and provision for taste swings as formulated in the theory of the World Wine Model enable us to capture each of these attributes.

Wine from different national origins is assumed to be imperfectly substitutable, following the Armington (1969) assumption. The model is implemented using GEMPACK software (Harrison, Horridge, Jerie, & Pearson, 2014).

The World Wine Model disaggregates wine markets into four types, namely non-premium, commercial premium and super-premium still wines, and sparkling wine.[2] There are two types of grapes, namely premium and non-premium. Non-premium wine uses non-premium grapes exclusively, super-premium wines use premium grapes exclusively, and commercial premium and sparkling wines use both types of grapes to varying extents across countries. In the model's database, the world is divided into 44 individual nations and seven composite geographic

---

[2] Commercial premium still wines are defined by Anderson, Nelgen, and Pinilla (2017) to be those between US$2.50 and $7.50 per litre pretax at a country's border or wholesale.

regions that capture all other countries. That database is calibrated to 2014, based on the comprehensive wine market volume and value data and trade and excise tax data provided in Anderson *et al.* (2017). It is projected forward assuming aggregate national consumption, population and real exchange rates change between 2014 and 2025 to the extent shown in Table A1. The alternatives to that baseline also are projected to 2025. As for preferences, there is assumed to continue to be a considerable swing towards all wine types in China and a swing away from non-premium to premium wines in all other countries through to 2025. And in the baseline scenario, both grape and wine industry total factor productivity rates are assumed to grow at 1% per year everywhere, while grape and wine industry capital is assumed to grow net of depreciation at 1.5% per year in China but zero elsewhere.

Two alternative scenarios for the initial impact of Brexit are considered ("hard" and "soft"). In those scenarios, the rate of UK real GDP growth is only one-third or two-thirds as fast over the projection period (0.9% or 1.8% per year instead of 2.6%), and the UK pound will be 20% or 10% lower in real terms, than in the model's core baseline projection.[3] In both Brexit scenarios, it is assumed the UK applies the EU's external tariffs on wine at the end of the agreed transition period following the UK's formal triggering of Article 50.

We consider a "soft" Brexit to be the result of the UK negotiating, signing, implementing and responding to, by 2025, a free trade agreement (FTA) with the EU-27. We therefore modelled a subsequent scenario in which the pound and real incomes in the UK are as in our "soft" initial Brexit scenario but also involving an FTA between the UK and the rest of the EU that removes the tariffs on wine in UK trade with the EU-27.

Various additional bilateral FTAs are then assumed to be signed sequentially. Just prior to the Brexit decision, the EU announced it would

---

[3] The nominal US$ price of the pound in the fortnight following the Brexit vote on 23 June 2016 dropped 13% to US$1.30, and 16 months later the pound sat at a similar rate. Our choice of a low of 10% and a high of 20% aims to capture future possible rates while uncertainties remain. The average real wage in the UK fell in the first half of 2017 and projected real GDP growth during 2018–20 was revised down to 1.7% in the UK's latest Budget (HM Treasury, 2017).

be pursuing other bilateral trade agreements, with Australia and New Zealand as early possibilities (EC, 2015). The UK has signalled that it too will be looking to sign FTAs with non-EU trading partners as soon as it has settled a new trade arrangement with EU-27. Again Australia and New Zealand have been mentioned as early possibilities (they account for one-fifth of the value of UK wine imports), as have Chile and South Africa (whose share is one-sixth, with all other non-EU suppliers accounting for just one-eighth of UK wine imports). Each of these FTAs may have some trade-creating effects, but none is likely to have significant positive macroeconomic effects to offset the adverse macro-effects of the prolonged uncertainty introduced by Brexit. They will, however, have some trade-diverting effects that may offset each other, just as has happened with recent bilateral FTAs between wine-exporting countries and three Northeast Asian countries (see Anderson & Wittwer, 2015).

4. How might Brexit affect wine markets by 2025?

In the absence of Brexit, global wine production and exports are projected in the model's baseline from 2014 to 2025 to be consistent with past trends: the global volume of production (and consumption) rises little over that 11-year period (9%), made up of a 6% decline in non-premium wine and a one-sixth rise in commercial and super-premium wine. In real (2014 US$) value though, global wine output and consumption increase by about 50% as the average quality rises. The international trade projections are similar although a little larger, with the share of global wine production exported (= share of global consumption imported) rising two percentage points between 2014 and 2025. The baseline projection does not alter greatly the 2014 shares of various countries in global wine production. When subdivided into fine wine (super-premium still plus sparking), commercial premium wine and non-premium wine, France and the US retain the highest two places on the global ladder for fine wine production, and Spain and Italy retain the top two places for non-premium wine. As for commercial premium wine production (defined to be those between US$2.50 and $7.50 per litre pre-tax at a country's wholesale level or national border), Italy retains the top ranking over our projections period but, at least in terms of value, China challenges France for 2nd place.

France, Italy and Spain remain the three dominant exporters of wine in aggregate value. France and then Italy are even more dominant in fine wine exports, and remain so by 2025, while Italy outranks France in the commercial premium export category, and Spain outranks Italy, Australia and then Chile in the non-premium export class. Among the importers, the US and UK are projected to continue to hold the first two places in 2025 in value terms, but China moves into third place slightly ahead of Germany in the absence of Brexit.

4.1. Initial impact of Brexit

As mentioned earlier, we consider two alternative scenarios to capture the initial effects of Brexit ("hard" and "soft"). We assume that, following the UK's exit from the EU, the rate of UK economic growth would be only one-third or two-thirds as fast for the period to 2025, the British pound would be 20% or 10% lower in real terms than in our model's baseline projection, and the UK would apply the EU's external tariff on wine to imports from EU member countries (as part of establishing MFN rates via the WTO in order to then start new bilateral FTA negotiations). In the first of these initial scenarios, it is assumed the UK does not implement any new free trade agreements, particularly with the EU-27, Chile and South Africa. The second ("soft") scenario is assumed to be more pertinent if and when an FTA between the UK and EU-27 is agreed. Generally, the results are about half as big in the "soft" scenario, with the exception of the bilateral trade effects. To show the sensitivity of results to our assumptions, we point out the differences when the "soft" results are not close to half the results shown for the "hard" scenario.

As compared with the baseline scenario to 2025, in the "hard" Brexit scenario the consumer price of wine in 2025 is 16% higher in the UK in local currency terms (10% because of real depreciation of the pound, 8% because of the new tariffs on EU, Chilean and South African wines, and –2% because of slower UK income growth). The volume of UK wine consumption is 28% lower: 16% because of slower UK economic growth, 9% because of real depreciation of the pound and 3% because of the new tariffs. Super-premium still wine sales are the most affected, dropping by two-fifths, while sparkling and commercial wines would drop a bit less than one-quarter. Since the average price rises by more than the fall in the volume sold, the aggregate value of UK sales even in local currency terms would fall in this "hard" Brexit case. Under the "soft" Brexit scenario, the consumer price of wine in 2025 would be 11% higher in the UK and its volume of wine consumption would be 17% lower.

The volume of projected UK imports in 2025 is 427 million litres (ML) or nearly one-quarter lower in the "hard" scenario than in the baseline scenario, comprising 58 ML less sparkling, 31 ML less super-premium still wine and 339 ML less commercial wine. World imports would be lower by just 239 ML because imports by other countries would be 189 ML higher in response to the international prices of wines being lower in this scenario. In value terms, UK imports are $1.75 billion (or 27%) lower in 2025 because of "hard" Brexit: $1.13 billion because of lower incomes, $0.38 billion because of the fall in the pound and $0.14 billion because of the rise in wine import tariffs (Table 1). These aggregate trade impacts are a little more than half as large under the "soft" Brexit scenario.

Despite the levels of imports falling because of raised import tariffs, domestic consumption of all three quality categories of UK-produced

Table 1. Difference in 2025 projected volume and value of wine imports by the United Kingdom and the rest of the world as a consequence of the initial Brexit shock (million litres (ML) and 2014 US$ million, "hard" scenario)

	Volume (ML)					Value (US$ million)				
	NP + CP[a]	Super Pr[b]	Sparkling	Total	%	NP + CP[a]	Super Pr[b]	Sparkling	Total	%
ΔUK imports due to										
Lower incomes	−198	−20	−29	−247	58	−644	−253	−234	−1,131	65
Lower pound	−70	−10	−14	−93	22	−248	−127	−102	−476	27
Higher tariffs	−71	−1	−16	−87	20	−110	−8	−24	−143	8
Total	−339	−31	−58	−427	100	−1,001	−388	−360	−1,750	100
% diff. from base	23	32	33	25		24	32	32	27	
% of total cuts	79	7	14	100		57	22	21	100	
ΔRoW net imports	141	21	25	187		−126	129	−83	−79	
ΔWorld trade	−197	−10	−33	−240		−1,127	−259	−443	−1,829	

Notes: [a]Non-premium plus Commercial Premium still wines.
[b]Super-premium still wines.
Source: Authors' model results.

wine is lower with than without a "hard" Brexit, because of the shrunken demand for all wines resulting from the lowered UK incomes and their raised local price because of the devaluation of the pound. The pound's devaluation does make it easier for the UK to sell wines abroad though: their exports are 7 ML or nearly 5% higher in 2025 in the "hard" Brexit scenario, and UK production is 3% higher. Those UK exports (or re-exports of imported bulk wine after it is bottled in the UK) that go to EU-27 countries are reduced though because of the tariff now imposed at the new EU border.

Without Brexit, the UK's shares of global wine imports are projected to be slightly higher in volume terms in 2025 than in 2010–15, but two percentage points lower in value terms thanks to East Asia's expanding demand for imports of premium wines. With a "hard" Brexit, however, that value share would be a further two percentage points lower, and the volume share would be almost five points lower. Most of the trade effect of a "hard" Brexit is a large decline in net imports of wine by the UK with very little offsetting positive effect on trade in the rest of the world. The "soft" Brexit numbers are a bit more than half these for a "hard" Brexit.

The aggregate effect of a "hard" Brexit on the market shares of various wine-exporting countries in the UK is almost indiscernible. The projected 2025 shares are quite different from the actual 2014 shares for several countries. They are much smaller in 2025 for South Africa, Australia and New Zealand (and the US in volume terms) and are much larger in volume for Spain and in value for Italy. This is because wine-exporting countries benefit differentially from the varying rates of growth in net import demand for wine in non-UK countries in the no-Brexit baseline over this projection period. The most important projected changes are the increase in the real value of annual wine imports between 2014 and 2025 by China (200% or $3 billion), Other Asia (110% or $2.2 billion) and Africa (270% or $1.6 billion). More than half of Australia's increase in annual exports from 2014 to 2025 go to Asia, and more than half of South Africa's increase in exports go to other Africa.

Table 2 reveals that European, Chilean and South African wine exports are lowered by a "hard" Brexit, by 150 ML or US$1.2 billion in the case of the EU, with some of their exports diverted from the UK to EU-27 and other markets in competition with New World exporters.

Table 2. Difference in 2025 bilateral wine import volumes and values from key exporters by the UK and rest of the world (RoW) as a result of initial Brexit shock (ML and 2014 US$ million)[a]

	Volume (ML)				Value (2014 US$ million)			
	UK	RoW	World	(%)	UK	RoW	World	(%)
(a) "hard" Brexit scenario								
EU-27	−287	136	−150	(−1.7)	−1,187	−5	−1,192	(−3.1)
Chile	−59	35	−25	(−3.0)	−169	31	−138	(−4.8)
South Africa	−53	35	−18	(−3.2)	−105	20	−85	(−6.7)
USA	−7	−6	−13	(−2.4)	−75	−40	−115	(−5.0)
Australia	−4	−3	−7	(−0.9)	−25	−65	−90	(−3.0)
Argentina	−3	−9	−12	(−4.8)	−16	−39	−55	(−5.2)
New Zealand	−11	9	−2	(−0.9)	−162	71	−91	(−4.3)
Others	−2	−10	−12	(−0.2)	−11	−52	−63	(−4.4)
World	−427	187	−240	(−1.9)	−1,750	−79	−1,829	(−3.5)
(b) "soft" Brexit scenario								
EU-27	−178	82	−96	(−1.2)	−692	−43	−736	(−1.9)
Chile	−46	28	−18	(−2.4)	−128	36	−91	(−3.2)
South Africa	−43	29	−14	(−4.2)	−82	23	−59	(−4.7)
USA	1	−6	−5	(−1.1)	−23	−28	−51	(−2.2)
Australia	5	−10	−5	(−0.6)	19	−56	−38	(−1.3)
Argentina	0	−6	−6	(−2.6)	−3	−25	−29	(−2.7)
New Zealand	−5	4	−1	(−0.6)	−80	34	−46	(−2.2)
Others	0	−9	−9	(−0.1)	−1	−33	−34	(−2.4)
World	−266	112	−154	(−1.3)	−991	−92	−1,083	(−2.1)

Note: [a]Numbers in parentheses are the percentage difference between the Brexit and baseline scenarios for 2025 projected wine import volumes or values by source.
Source: Authors' model results.

While the US, Australia and Argentina sell only a little less into the UK, they sell less also to other countries. For Chile and South Africa, who lose their preferential access to UK (but not to EU-27) markets in this Brexit scenario, some of their exports are re-directed from the UK to EU-27 countries but again they export less overall. Global wine trade in 2025 would be less under this "hard" Brexit scenario by 240 ML (1.9%)

or $1.8 billion (3.5%). The percentage by which wine exporters' trade shrinks is greater for values than for volumes because of changes in relative prices of different-quality wines. Those differences are shown in the numbers in parentheses in Table 2.

A number of other points are worth making about Table 2. One is that Australia sells slightly more to the UK in the "soft" Brexit scenario, rather than slightly less as in the "hard" Brexit case. Evidently, the negative income and price (devaluation) effects do not more than offset the positive trade-diverting effect on Australian exports to the UK of removing preferences in the "soft" scenario. Second, New Zealand sells slightly more to non-UK countries under Brexit, despite greater competition from EU-27, Chile and South Africa. This anomaly is due to changes in the relative prices of different qualities of wine in global wine markets, bearing in mind that New Zealand has the world's highest average price for still wine exports. And third, the value (but not the volume) of exports of "other" countries to markets other than the UK is higher under Brexit. This too is due to changes in the relative prices of different qualities of wine in global wine markets.

4.2. *Subsequent impact of Brexit from a UK-EU-27 FTA*

The next most-likely step in the Brexit process is for the UK to negotiate a new trade arrangement with the EU-27. We therefore assume that a UK-EU-27 FTA with free bilateral wine trade is implemented and adjusted to by 2025, and that progress towards that end occurs soon enough that the adverse macroeconomic shocks from the initial impact of uncertainty over the Brexit process are confined to those assumed in our "soft" scenario outlined above.

This subsequent development in the Brexit process would reverse the sign of most of the initial effects of Brexit by 2025, but be only a partial offset to them because of our assumption of lost growth in the initial years of uncertainty. (The longer it takes before this FTA is finalised and implemented, the longer will the estimated initial adverse effects persist and so the larger will be the cumulative cost of Brexit to UK wine consumers and to grape and wine producers in wine-exporting countries.)

Table 3 summarises the subsequent trade effects for 2025. It suggests that only one-sixth of the loss in volume and one-twelfth of the loss in value of world trade in wine from the initial "soft" impact would be

Table 3. Difference in 2025 bilateral wine import volumes and values from key exporters by the UK and rest of the world (RoW) as a result of implementing a UK-EU-27 free-trade agreement (difference relative to initial "soft" Brexit shock, million litres [ML] and 2014 US$ million)[a]

	Volume (ML)				Value (2014 US$ million)			
	UK	RoW	World	("soft" w'out FTA)[a]	UK	RoW	World	("soft" w'out FTA)[a]
EU-27	67	−38	30	(−96)	169	−58	111	(−736)
Chile	−8	7	−1	(−18)	−27	22	−5	(−91)
South Africa	−5	5	0	(−14)	−14	11	−3	(−59)
USA	−4	2	−1	(−5)	−16	6	−10	(−51)
Australia	−7	6	0	(−5)	−26	19	−7	(−38)
Argentina	−2	1	0	(−6)	−6	4	−2	(−29)
New Zealand	−1	1	0	(−1)	−6	4	−2	(−46)
Others	−2	2	0	(−9)	−6	8	2	(−34)
World	40	−13	27	(−154)	69	16	84	(−1,083)

Note: [a]Numbers in parentheses are the world trade differences between the "soft" initial Brexit scenario before the FTA is implemented and the baseline scenario, copied from columns (3) and (7) of Table 2(b).
Source: Authors' model results.

restored. Most of that improved outcome is because of recovered imports from EU-27, commensurate with the latter's high share of UK imports (52% by value in 2013–14).

This subsequent (FTA) step in the Brexit process thus can be expected to restore by 2025 only a little of the initial adverse effects in the UK of the Brexit vote. The boost to world wine trade of just $84 million from this FTA is small because the EU's tariff on wine is so small (a weighted average of 13 pence per litre). As is evident from the final column of Table 1, the tariff itself is a very minor contributor to the adverse effect of Brexit, compared with the macro effects.

5. Effects of new bilateral FTAs with non-EU countries

The signing of new trade agreements affecting wine trade will not end with just the UK-EU-27 FTA. While President Trump has ruled out the planned Trans-Atlantic Trade and Investment Partnership (TTIP) between the EU and the US, the EU has signalled it wants other bilateral FTAs, including with Australia and New Zealand. So too does the UK, and it would also seek FTAs with other countries that currently have agreements with the EU, most notably Chile and South Africa in terms of wine trade importance. Meanwhile, in December 2017 an EU-Japan Economic Partnership agreement was finalised, which will see Japan's tariff on wine imports from the EU removed. In this section, we examine the cumulative impact of such a sequence of FTAs on the value of wine exports from key countries and globally.

Bilateral EU-27-Australia and EU-27-New Zealand FTA agreements add about half as much again to the global trade increase due to the UK-EU-27 FTA. Most of that extra benefit is enjoyed by the signing partners — more than offsetting their loss from the UK-EU-27 FTA — while a small additional loss of sales is imposed on other exporters (columns (1) and (2) of Table 4).

When new bilateral FTA agreements are then implemented between the UK and four Southern Hemisphere exporters, global exports expand a little further, benefiting not only Australia and New Zealand but also Chile

Table 4. Cumulative impacts of additional free-trade agreements (FTAs), and of multilateral free trade in wine, on the value of national and global wine exports in 2025 (difference relative to "soft" Brexit with UK-EU-27 FTA, in 2014 US$ million)

Exporter	Extra FTAs			Global free wine trade	% above 2025 base
	EU-27-ANZ FTA	EU-27-ANZ FTA + UK-NW[a] FTA	EU-27-ANZ FTA + UK-NW[a] FTA + EU-27-Jap FTA		
EU-27	122	105	188	2,137	6
Australia + NZ	30	45	44	368	8
Chile + S. Africa	−10	16	12	379	10
USA	−11	−18	−42	219	10
Rest of world	−1	3	3	451	13
World	131	150	222	3,553	7

Note: [a]"NW" includes Australia, NZ, Chile and South Africa.
Source: Authors' model results.

and South Africa but at the expense of exporters in the EU-27 and the US (column (3) of Table 4).

The new EU-Japan Economic Partnership agreement further boosts global wine exports, but in this case virtually all of that benefit is enjoyed by EU-27 exporters while other wine exports lose a little from this new preferential arrangement (column (4) of Table 4).

All of these prospective FTAs, even including the UK-EU-27 FTA, raise the value of world wine trade in 2025 by less than 0.5% compared with the original baseline projection for 2025. This is because the gross trade creation of each FTA is reduced by considerable trade diversion, whereby one exporter's gain is largely at the expense of other exporting countries.

To see how close those FTAs get the world to free international trade in wine, we also ran a scenario in which all import tariffs on wine are removed multilaterally. The results of that scenario are reported in the final two columns of Table 4. Clearly, the gains are far greater, and far more evenly spread among wine exporters, when all tariffs are removed simultaneously rather than just a few being removed preferentially. The value of world wine trade would be 7% greater in 2025 with all wine tariffs eliminated, which is sixteen times the cumulative increase from the above-listed sequence of FTAs.

6. Caveats and conclusions

The above simulations are just a few of many scenarios that could be modelled following the Brexit vote in June 2016. The sequence in which FTAs are signed and the speed with which they are implemented will matter (as was also the case with the sequential signing over the past decade of bilateral FTAs with Northeast Asian countries by Chile, Australia and New Zealand, see Anderson & Wittwer, 2015).

We have assumed above that no changes are made to alcohol excise duties in any country, including the UK following Brexit, when in fact they are scheduled to be progressively raised with inflation in the UK and some other countries. They may be raised in various countries for health reasons too, and possibly raised even more for wine relative to spirits and beer in the UK to offset the opposite effects of Brexit on those two domestic industries. Even without a change in relative consumer tax rates of beverages, consumption of local beers and spirits is likely to rise relative to wine consumption because of Brexit.

Brexit will be costly initially to UK consumers of wine (and of many other tradable products), because the domestic retail price in local currency tax-inclusive terms will be higher than otherwise and the volume of wine consumed domestically will be lower unless and until a UK-EU-27 FTA comes into force. Even if such an FTA does get signed, ratified by all 28 parliaments and implemented by 2025, the slower income growth in the interim will mean a smaller UK wine market in 2025. The volume reduction will be a blow to many participants in UK wine bottling, transporting, storing, wholesaling and retailing businesses, in addition to restaurants and pubs. Very little of that initial impact is because of higher import tariffs; most important is the assumed fall in UK real incomes relative to what they would have been if the UK vote in June 2016 had been to remain in the Single Market. A fall in real incomes will dampen growth in consumption of other beverages also.

Even with a UK-EU-27 FTA in place, EU-27 wine exporters are projected to export US$625 million less wine in 2025 thanks to Brexit, Chile and South Africa to export $158 million less wine, Australia and New Zealand export $93 million less, and Argentina and the United States $92 million less.

There will be great uncertainly for some time yet over the possible policy outcomes to flow from Brexit, and of their consequent sequential impacts on UK household disposable incomes, foreign exchange rates and bilateral wine tariffs. Meanwhile, the above projections under explicit assumptions provide some idea of how wine markets might be affected by the most likely first two stages of the Brexit process (agreeing on a new tariff schedule at the WTO, and agreeing to and implementing a UK-EU-27 FTA). In particular, they make clear that there could be non-trivial initial adverse impacts on the domestic wine market, effects that are likely to be much larger than just the direct impact of changes in bilateral tariffs. In any event, the net effect of Brexit on the welfare of the world's consumers and producers of wine as a whole will be negative not just initially but permanently unless new trade policy commitments by the UK with major wine-exporting countries are sufficiently more liberal than current arrangements.

As for the gains to wine producers and consumers that could emerge from a single multilateral undertaking to remove all import tariffs on wine, they would be even greater if that multilateral agreement involved liberalising all product markets and thus boosting global incomes. Unfortunately, however, the world's leaders seem disinterested in any such undertaking at present, as witnessed in the lack of any substantive communique resulting from the WTO's biennial Trade Ministerial Meeting in Buenos Aires in December 2017.

References

Anderson, K., Nelgen, S., & Pinilla, V. (2017). *Global wine markets, 1860 to 2016: A statistical compendium.* Adelaide, SA: University of Adelaide Press. Retrieved from www.adelaide.edu.au/press/titles/global-wine-markets

Anderson, K., & Strutt, A. (2016). Impacts of Asia's rise on African and Latin American trade: Projections to 2030. *The World Economy, 39*(2), 172–194. https://doi.org/10.1111/twec.12370

Anderson, K., & Wittwer, G. (2013). Modeling global wine markets to 2018: Exchange rates, taste changes, and China's import growth. *Journal of Wine Economics, 8*(2), 131–158. https://doi.org/10.1017/jwe.2013.31

Anderson, K., & Wittwer, G. (2015). Asia's evolving role in global wine markets. *China Economic Review, 35*, 1–14. https://doi.org/10.1016/jxhieco.2015.05.003

Armington, P. A. (1969). A theory of demand for products distinguished by place of production. *IMF Staff Papers, 16*, 159–178. https://doi.org/10.2307/3866403

Born, B., Müller, G. J., Schularick, M., & Sedláček, P. (2017). *The economic consequences of the Brexit vote.* DP12454. London, UK: Centre for Economic Policy Research. Retrieved from: https://cepr.org/active/publica tions/discussion_papers/dp.php?dpno=12454

Campos, N. F. (2016). Lousy experts: Looking back at the *ex ante* estimates of the costs of Brexit. In R. E. Baldwin (Ed.), *Brexit Beckons: Thinking ahead by leading economists* (Ch. 3, pp. 35–42). London, UK: CEPR.

Dhingra, S., Huang, H., Ottaviano, G., Pessoa, J. P., Sampson, T., & Van Reenen, J. (2017). The costs and benefits of leaving the EU: Trade effects. *Economic Policy, 32*(92), 651–705. https://doi.org/10.1093/epolic/eix015

Dixon, P., Parmenter, B., Sutton, J., & Vincent, D. (1982). *ORANI: A multisectoral model of the Australian economy.* Contributions to Economic Analysis 142, Amsterdam, the Netherlands: North-Holland.

EC (2015). *Trade for all: Towards a more responsible trade and investment policy.* Brussels, Belgium: European Commission.

Emerson, M., Busse, M., Di Salvo, M., Gros, D., & Pelkmans, J. (2017). *An assessment of the economic impact of Brexit on the EU27, IP/A/IMCO/2016-13, Study for the European Parliament, Brussels.* Retrieved from http:// www.europarl.europa.eu/studies

Harrison, J., Horridge, M., Jerie, M., & Pearson, K. (2014). *GEMPACK manual.* Melbourne, Vic.: GEMPACK Software.

HM Treasury (2017). *Spring budget 2017.* London, UK: HM Treasury.

Oberhofer, H., & Pfaffermayr, M. (2017). *Estimating the trade and welfare effects of Brexit: A panel data structural gravity model* (CESifo Working Paper No. 6828). Munich, Germany. Retrieved from CESifo website: http:// www.cesifo-group.de/DocDL/cesifo1_wp6828.pdf

Rollo, J., Borchert, I., Dawar, K., Holmes, P., & Winters, L. A. (2016). *The World Trade Organisation: A safety net for a post-Brexit UK trade policy?* Briefing Paper 1. UKTPO, University of Sussex. Retrieved from University of Sussex website: http://blogs.sussex.ac.uk/uktpo/files/2017/01/Briefing-paper-1-final-1.pdf

Sampson, T. (2017). Brexit: The economics of international disintegration. *Journal of Economic Perspectives*, *31*(4), 163–184. https://doi.org/10.1257/jep.31.4163

Smith, A. (2017). *Brexit: Hard truths and hard choices.* UKTPO blog. Retrieved from University of Sussex website: https://blogs.sussex.ac.uk/uktpo/2017/06/19/brexit-hard-truths-and-hard-choices/

Viner, J. (1950). *The customs union issue.* New York, NY: Carnegie Endowment for International Peace.

Appendix

Table A1. Assumed cumulative consumption and population growth rates and changes in the real exchange rate (RER)[a] relative to the US dollar, 2014 to 2025 without Brexit (%)

	Aggregate Consumption	Population	RER
France	18	4	−11
Italy	11	2	−9
Portugal	14	0	−9
Spain	26	8	−9
Austria	19	4	−7
Belgium	20	7	−9
Denmark	22	2	−9
Finland	21	3	−7
Germany	14	−2	−11

(*Continued*)

Table A1. (*Continued*)

	Aggregate Consumption	Population	RER
Greece	22	−1	−14
Ireland	42	12	−9
Netherlands	21	4	−9
Sweden	24	9	−13
Switzerland	18	8	−6
United Kingdom	32	6	1
Other W. Europe	21	10	−1
Bulgaria	41	−7	7
Croatia	20	−2	−1
Georgia	35	0	23
Hungary	25	−3	−11
Moldova	49	−11	13
Romania	45	−4	22
Russia	18	−2	−8
Ukraine	22	−5	14
Other E. Europe	40	−5	48
Australia	35	11	−17
New Zealand	32	9	−26
Canada	27	8	−18
United States	31	8	0
Argentina	7	10	109
Brazil	16	8	−29
Chile	55	8	−2
Mexico	42	12	−8
Uruguay	45	3	1
Other L. Am	60	10	−5
South Africa	36	12	−1
Turkey	50	8	20
North Africa	53	11	0

(*Continued*)

Table A1. (*Continued*)

	Aggregate Consumption	Population	RER
Other Africa	109	18	84
Middle East	52	18	−12
China	79	3	5
Hong Kong	42	3	2
India	134	13	17
Japan	11	−3	−24
Korea	38	1	−9
Malaysia	62	15	−16
Philippines	75	18	7
Singapore	44	21	−22
Taiwan	29	1	−13
Thailand	47	3	−9
Other Asia	99	10	10

Note: [a]RER changes over the projection period are the changes expected in the nominal value of country i's currency relative to the US dollar times the expected ratio of the GDP deflator for the US versus that for country i.

Source: Authors' compilation from projections by various international agencies and from global economy-wide modelling by Anderson and Strutt (2016).

B. Australia's Wine Internationalization

Chapter 8

Accounting for Growth in the Australian Wine Industry, 1987 to 2003[*]

Glyn Wittwer and Kym Anderson[†]

Abstract

A computable general equilibrium model of the Australian economy is used to account for the dramatic growth in Australia's wine industry between 1987 and 1999, and to project grape and wine volumes and prices to 2003. Export demand growth has made a major contribution to total output growth in premium wines, and accounts for most of the increase in the producer price of premium red wine. Domestic consumer preferences have shifted, mainly towards premium red wine, but there is also some evidence of growing demand for premium white wine since the mid 1990s. From the perspective of producers, productivity growth,

---

[*] First published in *Australian Economic Review* 34(2): 179–89, June 2001. The authors are grateful to John Creedy and an anonymous referee for helpful comments. Thanks are due to the Australian Research Council, the Grape and Wine Research and Development Corporation, the Rural Industries Research and Development Corporation, and the Winemakers' Federation of Australia for financially supporting the research program for which this study was undertaken.
[†]School of Economics and Centre for International Economic Studies, The University of Adelaide

while being less important than growth in domestic demand, appears to have more than offset the negative effects on suppliers of wine consumer tax increases. From the domestic consumers' perspective, however, tax hikes have raised retail prices much more than productivity gains have lowered them. The high and sustained levels of profitability resulting from export demand growth have led to a massive supply response in Australia. Even so, by 2003 Australian wine output will still be less than 5 per cent of global production.

1. Introduction

Between 1987 and 1999, the volume of Australian wine production increased by over 70 per cent. The composition of output also altered substantially, with premium output trebling (red more than white) while non-premium output changed little. The present study makes two contributions: first, it uses available data and an economy-wide model to assess the relative contributions of various demand and supply factors to the rapid growth and structural changes in the wine industry since 1987; and second, it uses those results to obtain a projection of industry trends to 2003.[1] Specifically, the article decomposes the effect on output and prices of wine of changes between 1987 and 1999 in (i) export demand for wine, (ii) domestic demand for wine, (iii) domestic wine taxes, (iv) grape and wine industry productivity, (v) changes in the rest of the economy and (vi) observed winegrape bearing area. This is done using a computable general equilibrium (CGE), 29-sector, two-region model of the economies of South Australia (where half the industry is located) and the rest of Australia. Known as FEDSA-WINE, it is a static model of Australia's economy in the ORANI family of models (Horridge, Parmenter and Pearson 1998; Madden 1995).

Drawing on insights from the historical growth accounting exercise, plus additional industry-specific information (most notably actual and intended winegrape plantings to 2000), we project the wine industry to

---

[1] Apart from being useful in its own right, we wanted to project forward the database so as to analyse the impacts of the GST and associated wine tax changes in July 2000 on the wine industry as of the early part of the present decade rather than the middle of the past decade (Wittwer and Anderson 2002).

2003. This provides insights into where the Australian wine industry is headed as the new plantings reach maturity.

Past CGE studies focusing on the Australian wine industry include Meagher, Parmenter, Rimmer and Clements (1985) and Centre for International Economics (1995a), both of which analyse the impacts of increasing consumption taxes on wine. We wish to examine more than just domestic demand issues, however, so we draw on the methodology of Dixon, Menon and Rimmer (2000).[2] This links the underlying theory of a CGE model with the available data. Since the focus here is on just the grape and wine industry, we are able to develop in one sense a simpler approach, utilising less data in a less elaborate CGE model with less disaggregation of non-wine sectors than the Dixon, Menon and Rimmer study, but in another sense more detail in that we allow for a degree of heterogeneity in the industry of focus. This is done by dividing both winegrapes and wine into three segments: premium red, premium white and nonpremium.

An overview of our methodology is given in the next section. Then Section 3 presents the results of decomposition of the historical changes. The projection of the wine industry to 2003 is detailed in Section 4. The article concludes in Section 5 with a summary of the findings.

2. Methodology

As explained in the Appendix, the FEDSA-WINE model solves a system of equations involving variables for prices and quantities for a particular year, to which the database is updated from the base year during the simulation. The equations follow the standard competitive economic theory of CGE models. Different combinations of variables (called closures) can be included in the exogenous set to solve the model. The method used

---

[2] Earlier demand studies of the Australian wine industry include Tsolakis, Reithmuller and Watts (1983), Clements and Johnson (1984), Clements and Selvanathan (1991), Oczkowski (1994), Centre for International Economics (1995b) and Clements, Yang and Zheng (1997). Earlier Australian CGE historical decomposition studies include Dixon, Malakellis and Rimmer (1997), Parmenter, Meagher and Higgs (1994) and Dixon et al. (2000).

Table 1. Selected variables in the historical and decomposition closures

Exogenous in historical simulation, endogenous in decomposition simulation (components of $X(HD')$)	Endogenous in historical simulation, exogenous in decomposition (corresponding components of $X(H'D)$)
Consumption, three wine types	Shifts in household preferences, wine
Producer prices, winegrapes	Markups on costs, winegrapes
Wine export volumes and f.o.b. prices	Shifts in foreign demand and domestic supply functions, wine
Employment, winegrapes and wine	Capital/labour bias in technical change, winegrapes and wine
Aggregate consumption	Shift in average propensity to consume
Exogenous in both historical and decomposition simulations (components of $X(HD)$)	Endogenous in both historical and decomposition simulations (components of $X(H'D')$)
Tax and tariff rates	Producer prices, except winegrapes
Population	Consumer prices, wine and other commodities
Winegrape bearing area	Capital stocks, all industries
Primary factor saving technical change	Demands for intermediate inputs (including margins services)
Rates of return on capital	

for accounting for past growth involves running the model twice, doing first an historical simulation and then a decomposition simulation. The two runs require different combinations of exogenous variables. Table 1 summarises the categorisation of key variables. Those that are exogenous in the historical simulation include observable variables for which data on historical changes are available. For each of the three wine types, we select as exogenous the following variables: household consumption, export volumes, and f.o.b. export prices. We also include producer prices for winegrapes and employment data for both winegrapes and wine. Observable macroeconomic variables (for example, aggregate consumption) are also part of this set, even though such variables are normally endogenous in CGE simulations. To estimate unobservable variables in the historical simulation, or ones for which data are unreliable (notably disaggregated wine prices), the observable variables are shocked by the observed change.

In the decomposition simulation, we revert to a more typical CGE closure. For example, household wine consumption is now endogenous. We isolate the effect of the taste shifter (estimated in the historical simulation) for the three wine types from the other shocks used to project the model between the end-point years (1987 and 1999). This provides an estimate of the contribution of domestic taste changes to the historical changes in the wine market. Similarly, the observable wine tax shocks in isolation provide an estimate of the historical impact of wine tax changes on the industry. Changes in aggregate household consumption and in population also contribute to changes in wine consumption through general economic effects.

3. Results

3.1 *The historical data*

Table 2 shows historical data for the Australian wine industry for 1987 and 1999. At the macroeconomic level, income growth allowed Australia's aggregate real consumption of goods and services to rise 43 per cent (in midpoint terms)[3] over the 12-year period. But consumption of wine rose by less than 10 per cent, despite the income and aggregate expenditure growth. However, within the wine category, there has been a dramatic switch in consumption in Australia from non-premium to premium (especially red) wine. There has also been a boom in wine exports. Australia's exports of premium wine grew more than 15-fold between 1987 and 1999, with the share of production exported rising from less than 5 to more than 30 per cent. To accommodate a rapid increase in premium (especially export) demand, plantings of premium winegrapes trebled over that period, with an accompanying increase (albeit with a three to five year delay) in Australian premium wine production.

---

[3] All changes are expressed in midpoint percentages, using the formula given in footnote (a) to Table 2. Midpoints are used as some key indicators, notably exports, have experienced rapid growth from low base levels in 1987.

Table 2. Growth in the Australian winegrape and wine industries, 1987 to 2003

	1987	Historical 1999	Midpoint Per Cent Change[a]	2003[b] (1)	Projected Midpoint Per Cent Change 1999–2003	2003[c] (2)
Population (total, millions)	16.3	19.0	15.3	19.2	1.0	19.2
Real aggregate consumption ($billion)[d]	220.7	340.1	42.6	383.3	22.5	377.0
Domestic consumption (megalitres)						
Premium red wine	22.4	62.5	94.5	92.2	38.4	88.8
Premium white wine	46.2	69.9	40.8	87.8	22.7	85.3
Non-premium wine	270.7	240.7	−11.7	240.0	−0.3	236.6
Wine, total	339.3	372.6	9.4	420.0	12.0	410.6
Production (megalitres)						
Premium red wine	64.9	270.5	122.6	587.6	73.9	590.0
Premium white wine	94.5	242.1	87.7	383.3	45.1	386.7
Non-premium wine	330.2	339.6	2.8	359.4	5.7	356.1
Wine, total	489.6	852.2	54.0	1330.2	43.8	1332.8
Wine exports (megalitres)						
Premium red wine	4.6	87.8	180.1	254.2	97.3	263.3
Premium white wine	5.4	82.6	175.5	149.1	57.4	153.2
Non-premium wine	14.0	45.7	106.2	75.9	49.6	76.1
Wine, total	24.0	215.5	159.9	479.2	75.9	492.6
Winegrape prices ($ per tonne)[d]						
Premium red grapes	653	1437	75.0	1213	−16.8	1219
Premium white grapes	874	813	−7.2	798	−1.9	802
Non-premium grapes	290	402	32.4	373	−7.5	376

Commonwealth and state consumer taxes (per cent)	19	41	—	48	48
Retail prices ($ per litre)					
Premium red wine	9.54	13.11	31.5	12.59	12.59
Premium white wine	10.00	11.46	13.6	11.36	11.29
Non-premium wine	3.17	3.71	15.6	3.65	3.59
Wine stocks (megalitres)					
Premium red wine	155	580	115.6	1253	1265
Premium white wine	205	350	52.3	601	608
Non-premium wine	170	160	-6.1	140	143
Area of bearing winegrapes ('000 hectares)					
Premium red grapes	9.4	41.3	125.8	63.1	63.1
Premium white grapes	10.9	28.4	89.1	32.5	32.5
Non-premium grapes	14.9	14.8	-0.7	16.4	16.4
Self-sufficiency ratio[e] (per cent)					
Premium red wine	111	234	—	358	412
Premium white wine	107	212	—	257	288
Non-premium wine	103	112	—	121	130

Notes: (a) Midpoint per cent change = $200(Z_f - Z_i)/(Z_f + Z_i)$ where Z_f and Z_i are the final and initial values of Z.
(b) This includes GST and Wine Equalisation Tax.
(c) This includes a real depreciation relative to the base case.
(d) All values are real, in 1995–96 dollars.
(e) Self-sufficiency ratio = $(Q - \Delta S)/C$, where Q is production, ΔS gross addition to stocks and C consumption.

Sources: Australian Bureau of Statistics (1999, 2000); Australian Wine and Brandy Corporation, unpublished data.

3.2 Export demand growth

Column 1 in Table 3 shows the effect of the estimated shift in the volume of export demand.

In the modelled decomposition of the observed period, export demand growth explains almost all the increase in producer prices for premium red wine (30.5 out of 31.2 per cent) and about one-fifth of total output growth (25.1 out of 122.6 per cent). This implies that the wine supply response was not sufficient by the end of the period, even after adding the increase

Table 3. Decomposition of wine industry changes, 1987 to 1999 (midpoint per cent change)

	Export Demand Growth (1)	Domestic Consumer Tastes (2)	Consumer Tax Changes (3)	Productivity (4)	Economic Growth (5)	Winegrape Area (6)	Total (7)
Premium red wine							
Output	25.1	30.1	−4.6	11.3	26.2	34.5	122.6
Producer price	30.5	2.6	−0.7	−5.6	15.5	−11.2	31.2
Consumer price	17.1	1.5	9.3	−3.1	13.3	−6.5	31.5
Domestic consumption	−15.4	61.6	−7.9	2.8	46.9	6.5	94.5
Export volume	114.2	−18.5	2.1	28.4	−38.3	92.2	180.1
Premium white wine							
Output	31.7	0.4	−4.0	10.9	31.6	17.2	87.8
Producer price	4.6	−0.2	−0.5	−5.6	6.2	−7.0	−2.4
Consumer price	2.6	−0.1	10.4	−3.2	7.9	−4.1	13.6
Domestic consumption	−1.5	3.4	−6.3	2.0	40.8	2.6	41.0
Export volume	104.4	−2.1	1.3	27.6	−1.4	45.7	175.5
Non-premium wine							
Output	3.2	−32.7	−3.3	1.8	34.9	0.2	4.0
Producer price	2.8	−0.6	−0.2	−4.6	6.0	−0.5	2.9
Consumer price	1.8	−0.4	10.8	−3.0	6.7	−0.3	15.6
Domestic consumption	−0.6	−38.4	−3.6	1.0	30.5	0.1	−11.1
Export volume	82.4	2.3	0.3	15.1	4.4	1.7	106.2

Source: Authors' FEDSA-WINE decomposition.

in winegrape area shown in the sixth column, to dampen upward price pressures.

By contrast, for premium white wine, the output increase attributable to export demand growth was relatively larger and the price increases smaller than for red wine. White winegrape prices were relatively high at the beginning of the period, indicating that demand for the premium white segment started at a high point (Table 2). Note that the static CGE framework and use only of end-point data do not explain the timing of the supply response, a point we discuss further in Section 4.

A high proportion of Australian non-premium wine is sold domestically, with the rest exported, mostly to New Zealand. Although non-premium export demand grew in the historical period, exports remained a small proportion of total output. Export demand growth contributed only 3 per cent to non-premium output growth, despite an increase in export volume of 82 per cent (Table 3).

3.3 Domestic consumer tastes

Column 2 of Table 3 provides an estimate of changes in consumption attributable to changing preferences rather than price, income or population growth effects. In the period from 1987 to 1996, we observed a taste swing against all alcoholic beverages except premium red wine. Between 1996 and 1999, there was also a preference change towards premium white wine consumption, with the net result that changing domestic consumer preferences explained almost none of the overall change in premium white wine production between 1987 and 1999. Increasing domestic preferences for premium red wine explain a significant part of the segment's output growth in the 12-year period (30 per cent out of total growth of 123 per cent). By reducing excess supply, this effect had a negative impact on export growth (−19 per cent). Emerging evidence of the health benefits of moderate red wine consumption may explain much of the increase in demand for red wine. The main reason for the swing against white is that demand for white was already strong in 1987 at a time when interest in premium wines was growing, whereas the histamine scare had for a time stopped consumers from turning to red wine. The negative consumption and output contributions in column 2 of Table 3 for non-premium wine reflect the growing preferences of consumers towards premium wine.

3.4 Increased consumer taxes and franchise fees

The Commonwealth Government introduced a 10 per cent wholesale sales tax on wine in August 1984, which had increased to 31 per cent by August 1993, before settling at 26 per cent in July 1995 after several adjustments. In addition, there were modest increases in State Government franchise fees on retail alcohol sales. The impact of increased taxes on domestic consumption had only a moderate effect on exports: 2 per cent for red, 1 per cent for white, and less than 1 per cent for non-premium exports (column 3 of Table 3). This is because output is reduced by the increase in consumption taxes: with imperfect substitution between domestic and export sales, producers bear a small part of the burden of the tax. The rest is borne by domestic consumers, evident in declines in consumption of 8, 6 and 4 per cent for premium red, premium white and non-premium wines. For each, the increase in consumer price due to the ad valorem tax increase was around 10 per cent.

3.5 Productivity changes

Within the database for 1996, the shares of labour, capital and agricultural land in Australia's GDP are 0.59, 0.40 and 0.01. Between 1987 and 1999, the increases in labour, capital and land inputs were 24, 58 and 0 per cent (Australian Bureau of Statistics 2000). Real GDP rose 50 per cent in this period, implying total factor productivity (TFP) growth of about 14 per cent for the economy overall. In the winegrape industry, changes in the bearing land area are known at a disaggregated level. For labour inputs, available data for both winegrapes and wine have been disaggregated by assuming that the premium segments are more labour-intensive than the non-premium segments. But changes in capital usage are unknown. These are estimated within the model, based on output growth, changes in the rate of return on capital (imposed to follow the direction of observed price changes) and imposed primary factor productivity growth. We use the economy-wide TFP calculation to ascribe productivity shocks, adjusting for differences between broad industry groups.[4]

The growing emphasis on quality in all stages of production in grape growing and winemaking implies that measures of productivity may understate the impact of new technologies on the industry. For example, a grape grower may raise the unit costs of production through practices that increase the quality and price of output, possibly without a productivity improvement — or even a decline — in quantitative terms. This emphasis on quality differs from an earlier understanding propounded by the Senate Standing Committee on Trade and Commerce (1977), which stresses that with technological improvements, winemakers could produce wine from inferior grapes. Now, much of the aim of the industry is to maximise profits through raising the quality of grapes. Nonetheless, mechanical harvesting and pruning are being used increasingly, not only in non-premium production but also in the 'commercial' or lower end of the premium spectrum, with a significant impact on quantifiable productivity. In particular, mechanisation and computerisation of irrigation have decreased the labour-intensity of winegrape production.

As for wineries, we can attribute much of the employment growth to an increasing proportion of premium in total wine production. Premium wine production per litre of output is substantially more labour-intensive than nonpremium production. Winemakers, for example, pay most attention to premium produce even in wineries where the volume of non-premium wine is substantially greater than the premium volume.

Column 4 of Table 3 indicates an order of magnitude (based on the economy-wide estimate) rather than a more precise estimate of the impact of productivity growth on wine producers and consumers. Productivity growth contributes proportionally more to export growth (28 per cent for red) than growth in domestic consumption (3 per cent for red). This reflects the effect of supply shifts along the relatively elastic export

---

[4] Consistent with the estimates of Dixon *et al.* (2000), greater shocks are imposed on mining and agriculture than other industries. The estimates of Knopke, Strappazzon and Mullen (1995) on agricultural productivity growth also imply higher growth than the economy-wide average for Australia. This is similar to the finding for many countries (Martin and Mitra 1999).

demand curves compared with less elastic domestic demand. Such growth also more than compensates for increases in consumer taxes on premium wine in the historical period, from the producers' perspective. However, the small consumer price declines arising from the productivity effect fall well short of compensating consumers for rising taxes in the period. The effect on premium wine output is proportionally larger than on non-premium wine. This is due to non-premium grapes being multi-purpose. That is, increased productivity increases grape availability for use as table and dried grapes as well as increased inputs into non-premium wine production. In addition, the non-premium wine segment is less export oriented, so there is less scope for expansion through excess supply shifts along the relatively elastic export demand curve.

3.6 *General economic growth and changes in other industries*

In the historical simulation, the task is to fit observed data at the macroeconomic and industry levels, beyond changes only in the wine industry. Observed macroeconomic data include GDP and primary factor endowments. The fifth column of Table 3 indicates the impact of changes in the economy not directly related to the wine industry. The column also includes the impact of productivity growth in non-wine industries and the observable change in the real exchange rate. To summarise, this indicates what would have happened to the wine industry without any wine industry-specific changes in the historical period.

General economic growth increases domestic consumption of each wine type through the expenditure effect. The expenditure effect is output increasing and export reducing. It is surprising therefore that this column makes a positive contribution to exports for non-premium wine. This appears to be due to rising apparent rates of return on capital in non-wine industries. In isolation, this lowers the ratio of the rate of return in the wine industry to that in other industries, thereby inducing a capital inflow to wine and increasing its excess supply.

3.7 *Observed changes in the bearing area of winegrapes*

The sixth column in Table 3 shows the impact of changes in the winegrape bearing area between 1987 and 1999. As we expect, the outward supply shifts implied by increased bearing area for premium winegrapes raise output and the excess supply, while lowering producer and consumer prices. The price effect induces an increase in domestic consumption. This change in plantings comprises only part of the supply response of the winegrape segments, as they can still respond to changing prices via primary factor substitutability.

There are two reasons why we have presented the effects of changes in the bearing area in a separate column. First, part of the motivation for decomposition was to assist in projecting future industry outputs (see Section 4 below). Plantings in a given year plus the year's bearing area allow us to obtain a relatively accurate projection of the bearing area several years into the future. Second, explaining the decision to invest in a vineyard may require more than the standard theory embedded in (even dynamic) CGE models.

A critical issue concerns the timing of vineyard investments in response to a change in market signals. The premium red segment started the period emerging from a time of great pessimism, in which the South Australian and Commonwealth Governments introduced a short-lived vine-pull scheme to encourage disinvestment in grape growing. Except for price falls in the recessive early 1990s, premium red winegrape producers rose throughout the past dozen years. We calculate that based on the new plantings of 1998 and 1999, the bearing area of premium red winegrapes will double between 1999 and 2003 (having almost doubled between 1996 and 1999). By contrast, growth in the bearing area of white winegrapes has been and will continue to 2003 to be only very gradual.

Viticulture's substantial fixed costs imply considerable supply irreversibility. Winegrape growing is extremely capital-intensive, with an investment required per hectare currently of at least $A30000 plus the costs of land and water rights. Also, there is a lag of at least three years before there is a positive cash flow. During several years of high and rising prices, as occurred in the late 1990s, growers may be able to recoup new investments quickly. After recovering those sunk costs, many growers would be able to maintain profitability in the event of a sharp fall in winegrape prices. Therefore, while a sustained boom in the wine industry has led to rapid plantings of vineyards, a subsequent fall in grape prices is unlikely to lead to a rapid reduction in production.[5]

---

[5] A formal framework for examining the investment decision of winegrape growers in the 1990s is the real options theory elaborated by Dixit and Pindyck (1994).

4. Projecting to 2003

We have projected FEDSA-WINE into the future and examine how different scenarios may impact on expected growth. This entails the use of macroeconomic projections plus the forecast increase in bearing area of the winegrape segments of the model (Table 4). We also impose primary factor productivity growth on both winegrapes and wines (and on the non-wine industries in the model). And we assume that export demand growth and domestic taste changes continue, based approximately on shocks estimated in the historical simulation (Table 4).

4.1 *The base case projection from 1999 to 2003*

The base projection, including the GST tax reforms (discussed in Wittwer and Anderson 2002) but excluding the recent currency devaluation (considered separately below), has domestic premium red wine consumption increasing from 63 Ml (megalitres) in 1999 to 92 Ml in 2003 (Table 2). In the same period, premium white wine consumption increases from 70 Ml to 88 Ml, and non-premium wine consumption decreases from 241 Ml to

Table 4. Changes to productivity, wine export demand and domestic wine preferences (midpoint per cent per annum)

	1987 to 1999	1999 to 2003
Primary factor productivity growth		
Winegrapes	1.0	1.6
Wine	1.2	0.9
Export demand growth		
Red premium wine	*16.0*	12.3
White premium wine	*13.7*	10.0
Non-premium wine	*11.9*	8.3
Domestic taste change		
Red premium wine	*5.4*	4.5
White premium wine	*0.1*	2.4
Non-premium wine	*–3.2*	–2.6

Source: Italicised numbers are estimated in the historical simulation.

240 Ml. The expenditure effect and increased preferences for premium wine add to the effect of falls in consumer prices. Population growth and falling prices almost offset the effect of the projected taste swing against non-premium consumption.

Production of premium red wine is projected to double between 1999 and 2003, with slower yet still substantial growth in white wine production. Due to this increase, the export supply of premium wine is projected to escalate in this period. Premium red wine exports increase from 88 Ml in 1999 to 254 Ml in 2003, premium white wine exports from 83 Ml to 149 Ml, and non-premium exports from 46 Ml to 76 Ml.

4.2 A real depreciation of the Australian dollar

In the wake of the East Asian financial crisis in the late 1990s, the Australian dollar appreciated against East Asian currencies but depreciated in real terms against other major currencies. In the first 10 months of 2000, the domestic currency devalued sharply against the US dollar. Sustained changes in the real exchange rate will alter outcomes, particularly for export-oriented industries including premium red and white wine. Relative to the 2003 base projection, which assumes no change in the exchange rate from 1999, a real devaluation that reduces aggregate consumption raises wine output and increases exports, with a decrease in domestic wine consumption (final column of Table 2). Multi-purpose grapes are diverted from winemaking to direct exports as table grapes, explaining the small output reduction for non-premium wine. Winegrape prices rise slightly along with the costs of production. During the present phase of rapid expansion in the wine industry, any real depreciation will favour wine export growth slightly. The converse effect would result from any recovery of the Australian dollar's real exchange rate to pre-Asian crisis levels.

5. Conclusion

In our analysis of the 1990s exceptional growth phase of the wine industry, we find using a static CGE model that expanding export growth explains a significant proportion of that output growth and, for the premium red segment, most of the observed price increase in the period from 1987 to 1999. With accelerated winegrape plantings in the late 1990s and expanding wine manufacturing capacity, the industry will rely increasingly on export sales over the next decade. A sustained depreciation of the Australian dollar will assist producers during the rapid expansion phase. Our modeling suggests only a modest fall in winegrape prices with expanding export supply by 2003. But for producer prices to remain firm, Australia's producers will need to continue successful export promotion as the wine export supply of other countries grows — an obvious area for further modelling development and analysis.

First version received May 1999;
final version accepted February 2001 (Eds).

Appendix 1: Details of the methodology used in the decomposition analysis

FEDSA-WINE solves a system of equations of the following form:

$$F(X) = 0 \qquad (1)$$

where F is an m-vector of differentiable equations, and X is an n-vector of variables for year t, $n > m$.

X includes variables for prices and quantities in year t, to which the database is updated from the base year during the simulation. The m equations follow the economic theory of CGE models, including supplies and demands reflecting utility- and profit-maximising behaviour, with supplies equalling demands, and perfectly competitive prices set equal to unit costs. Different closures or combinations of $n - m$ variables can be included in the exogenous set to solve the model. The method used for historical accounting involves running the model twice, doing first a historical simulation and then a decomposition simulation. To solve the model, we use version 7.0 of GEMPACK to decompose the shocks of large change simulations (Harrison, Horridge and Pearson 1999). The two runs require different combinations of exogenous variables. We can have four versions of X (as in Table 1):

$$X(HD), X(H'D), X(HD') \text{ and } X(H'D')$$

where H is exogenous and H' endogenous in the historical closure, and D is exogenous and D' endogenous in the decomposition closure.

$X(HD')$, for example, refers to variables exogenous in the historical simulation and endogenous in the decomposition simulation. This set includes observable variables for which data on historical changes are available. For each of the three wine types, we select as exogenous the following variables: household consumption, export volumes, and f.o.b. export prices. We also include producer prices for winegrapes and employment data for both winegrapes and wine. Observable macroeconomic variables (for example, aggregate consumption) are also part of the $X(HD')$ set. This set thus includes variables that are normally endogenous in CGE simulations. To estimate unobservable variables, the observable variables are made exogenous in the historical simulation and shocked by the observed change. The unobservable variables have an economic interpretation. By making aggregate consumption exogenous, for example, we obtain an estimate of the change in the average propensity to consume between the two end points (1987 and 1999) of the historical simulation.[6] Table 1 summarises the categorisation of key variables.

The Australian Bureau of Statistics publishes only a single price index for wine, and other surveys tend not to have representative expenditure weights for disaggregated wine types. Hence, wine prices are part of the $X(H'D')$ set. Variables with a large influence on disaggregated retail wine prices (p_i) include available winegrape prices (winegrapes account for about 25 per cent of wine production costs, Winemakers' Federation of Australia, personal communication) and tax shifters. Household demands for non-wine commodities are assumed in FEDSA-WINE to respond almost entirely to expenditure effects (induced by the imposed change in aggregate consumption) and price effects. Such data are available but they would add little to our understanding of changes in the wine industry.

$X(HD)$ includes observable changes in wine import tariff and consumer tax rates, c.i.f. import prices for wine, and population. CGE models generally are not used to explain these variables. This set also includes imposed primary factor productivity growth, as changes in capital stocks are not available to complete the picture of primary factor usage for winegrapes and wine.

---

[6] In simulating, we divided the time period into two, from 1996 back to 1987, and from 1996 to 1999. For brevity, we report the 12 years from 1987 to 1999 as one time period for most variables.

To illustrate the use of the historical and decomposition simulations of the period 1987 to 1999 in this study, we consider a general function (that is, not defining the functional form) for household demand within a CGE model:

$$x_i = (p_i, p_j, c, a_i, q) \qquad (2)$$

In percentage change terms, x_i and p_i denote the domestic consumption quantity and price of household good i, P_j is the price of other goods ($i \neq j$), c is aggregate household consumption, a_i denotes household preferences and q is population. For each of the three wine types in the database, x_i is observable and in the set $X(HD')$: it is exogenous in the historical run and endogenous in the decomposition run. Other observable variables include aggregate consumption, population growth and tax rates. The retail price p_i, as discussed above, is endogenous in all simulations. The unobservable residual a_i is in the set $X(H'D)$, and hence endogenous in the historical simulation: it provides an estimate of the taste change for each wine type.

In the decomposition simulation, x_i is endogenous. We isolate the effect of the taste shifter a_i (estimated in the historical simulation) for the three wine types from the other shocks used to project the model between the end points. This provides an estimate of the contribution of domestic taste changes to the historical changes in the wine market. Similarly, the observable wine tax shocks in isolation provide an estimate of the historical impact of wine tax changes on the industry. And c, through the expenditure effect, and q contribute to changes in wine consumption through general economic effects.

References

Australian Bureau of Statistics 1999, *Australian Wine and Grape Industry*, Cat. no. 1329.0, ABS, Canberra.

Australian Bureau of Statistics 2000, *Treasury Model of the Australian Economy*, Cat. no. 1364.0, ABS, Canberra.

Centre for International Economics 1995a, 'Additional simulations with the grape and wine industry model', report prepared for the South Australian Development Council, Canberra.

Centre for International Economics 1995b, 'Generation of demand parameters for an economy-wide model of the grape and wine industry', report prepared for the Commonwealth Government Inquiry into the Wine Grape and Wine Industry, Canberra.

Clements, K. and Johnson, L. 1984, 'The demand for beer, wine and spirits: A systemwide analysis', *Journal of Business*, vol. 56, pp. 273–304.

Clements, K. and Selvanathan, S. 1991, 'The economic determinants of alcohol consumption', *Australian Journal of Agricultural Economics*, vol. 35, pp. 209–31.

Clements, K., Yang, W. and Zheng, S. 1997, 'Is utility additive? The case of alcohol', *Applied Economics*, vol. 29, pp. 1163–7.

Dixit, A. and Pindyck, R. 1994, *Investment under Uncertainty*, Princeton University Press, Princeton, New Jersey.

Dixon, P., Malakellis, M. and Rimmer, M. 1997, *The Australian Automotive Industry from 1986–87 to 2009–10: Analysis Using the MONASH Model*, A report to the Industry Commission, Centre of Policy Studies and IMPACT project, Monash University.

Dixon, P., Menon, J. and Rimmer, M. 2000, 'Changes in technology and preferences: A general equilibrium explanation of rapid growth in trade', *Australian Economic Papers*, vol. 39, pp. 33–55.

Harrison, J., Horridge, M. and Pearson, K. 1999, 'Decomposing simulation results with respect to exogenous shocks', Preliminary Working Paper no. IP-73, Centre of Policy Studies and Impact Project, Monash University; available at http://www.monash.edu.au/policy/ELECPAPR/ip-73.htm.

Horridge, J., Parmenter, B. and Pearson, K. 1998, 'ORANI-G: A general equilibrium model of the Australian economy', paper prepared for ORANI-G course, Centre of Policy Studies and Impact Project, Monash University, 29 June–3 July; available at http://www.monash.edu.au/policy/ftp/oranig/oranidoc.pdf.

Knopke, P., Strappazzon, L. and Mullen, J. 1995, 'Productivity growth: Total factor productivity on Australian broadacre farms', *Australian Commodities*, vol. 2, pp. 486–97.

Madden, J. 1995, 'FEDERAL: A two-region multisectoral fiscal model of the Australian economy', in *Modelling and Control of National and Regional Economies 1995*, eds L. Vlacic, T. Nguyen and D. Cecez-Kecmanovic, Elsevier Science, Oxford.

Martin, W. and Mitra, D. 1999, 'Productivity growth and convergence in agriculture and manufacturing', Discussion Paper no. 99/18, Centre for International Economic Studies, University of Adelaide.

Meagher, G. A., Parmenter, B., Rimmer, R. and Clements, K. 1985, 'ORANI-WINE: Tax issues and the Australian wine industry', *Review of Marketing and Agricultural Economics*, vol. 53, pp. 47–62.

Oczkowski, E. 1994, 'A hedonic price function for Australian premium table wine', *Australian Journal of Agricultural Economics*, vol. 38, pp. 93–110.

Parmenter, B., Meagher, G. A. and Higgs, P. 1994, 'Technical change in Australia during the 1980s: Simulations with a computable general equilibrium model', *Economic and Financial Modelling*, vol. 1, pp. 61–80.

Senate Standing Committee on Trade and Commerce 1977, *Tax and the Wine and Grape Industries*, AGPS, Canberra.

Tsolakis, D., Reithmuller, R. and Watts, G. 1983, 'The demand for wine and beer', *Review of Marketing and Agricultural Economics*, vol. 51, pp. 131–51.

Wittwer, G. and Anderson, K. 2002, 'Impact of the GST and wine tax reform on Australia's wine industry: A CGE analysis', *Australian Economic Papers* vol. 41(1), pp. 69–81, March.

Chapter 9

Who Gains from Australian Generic Wine Promotion and R&D?*

Xueyan Zhao,[†] Kym Anderson and Glyn Wittwer

Abstract

The present paper estimates the distributions of aggregate returns from different types of research and promotion investments by the Australian grape and wine industry among grapegrowers, winemakers, domestic and foreign consumers, and the tax office. The results show that most of the gains from cost-reducing R&D in grape and wine production go to producers and that producers get a far larger share of the benefit from export promotion than from domestic promotion. Foreign consumers of Australian wine also enjoy a significant share of the benefits from Australian R&D. Sensitivity analysis shows that the key results hold for a wide range of parameter values.

---

* First published in *The Australian Journal of Agricultural and Resource Economics* 47(2): 181–209, June 2003. The authors are grateful for financial support from the Grape and Wine Research and Development Corporation, the Rural Industries Research and Development Corporation and the Australian Research Council. Thanks are due also to Julian Alston, the editors and two anonymous referees for valuable comments.

[†] XUEYAN ZHAO is with the Department of Econometrics and Business Statistics, whereas GLYN WITTWER was with the Centre of Policy Studies, both of Monash University before his Centre moved to Victoria University. KYM ANDERSON is with the School of Economics and Wine Economics Research Centre, University of Adelaide, Australia.

1. Introduction

During the latter half of the 20th century, the wine industry in many parts of the world has gradually become more professional in its approach to investing both in research and development (R&D) and in promotion. This has been particularly pronounced in the New World as the industry has corporatized and large firms have emerged,[1] and as export-orientated output has expanded.[2] Brand-level promotion can be, and is, undertaken by large and medium firms, but because most firms are small, even in the USA and Australia, many cannot afford mass media promotion campaigns. They therefore depend on generic promotion of their nation and region of origin. With respect to R&D, even large firms, let alone small ones, cannot, on their own, justify undertaking much large-scale research. In addition, the public good nature of both research and generic promotion is such that there is underinvestment unless these activities are funded collectively. Hence, grapegrowers and winemakers in countries such as Australia agree to pay a production-based annual levy to fund both these activities. The Australian Government supplements those funds, matching them in the case of R&D on a dollar-for-dollar basis up to 0.5% of the value of production.

Specifically, R&D via Australia's Grape and Wine Research and Development Corporation (GWRDC) is currently funded by a levy of $5 per tonne of grapes ($2 per tonne from grapegrowers on grapes received by wineries and $3 per tonne from wineries on the weight of grapes crushed for wine), which is matched by a similar grant from the Federal Government. There has been a significant increase in real dollar terms in the grape and wine R&D expenditure since the early 1980s as a result of industry expansion and past increases in the levy rate. The annual R&D expenditure for 2001–2002 reached $13 million in nominal terms

---

[1] The shares of national wine production held by the top five firms in 2000 are as follows: Australia 68%, New Zealand 80%, USA 73%, Argentina 50% and Chile 47%. In contrast, they are much lower in the Old World, where small cooperatives still dominate: 13% in France (excluding Champagne), 10% in Spain and 5% in Italy (Anderson et al. 2004).

[2] Between 1988 and 1999, wine production grew at 5.3% per year in Australia, 2.8% in the USA, 2.4% in Chile and Uruguay and 2.0% in New Zealand; the share of global wine production that is exported rose from 15 to 25% (Anderson and Norman 2001, Tables 11 and 32).

(GWRDC 2001). However, the producer proportion of that represents only approximately 0.3% of the value of production, well below the 0.5% limit to which matching government funding applies. Proposals are currently being considered by producers to raise the industry R&D levy and, possibly, to move to an *ad valorem* levy system. This would ensure the funding level moves with the product price as quality rises over time and/or as supply growth depresses some prices. The support for such a rise has been boosted by a recent benefit–cost study suggesting that the current portfolio of GWRDC research projects is expected to yield a 9:1 benefit/cost ratio and that a sample of past projects yielded ratios ranging from 7:1 to 76:1 (McLeod 2002).

Generic national promotion abroad is funded by a Federal Government grant plus a compulsory wine export levy based on the freight on board value of wine exported (0.2% of an exporter's first $10 million of sales, 0.1% for the next $40 million and 0.05% for sales beyond $50 million per year). The manager of those funds and provider of promotion is the Australian Wine and Brandy Corporation (AWBC; AWBC, 2001). Generic regional promotion is funded by voluntary membership of regional associations.

How should these funds be allocated and who benefits from the investment of the funds? Grape growers, winemakers and the government, on behalf of taxpayers and domestic consumers, are all interested in maximising the pay-offs from their investments. Issues of interest to various parties include the returns from research versus promotion, from R&D for grapes versus for wine, from cost-reducing R&D versus quality-enhancing R&D, and from domestic promotion versus export promotion. Both the aggregate returns from these broad types of investments and the distributions of total returns among groups, such as premium and non-premium grape growers, premium and non-premium winemakers, domestic retailers, taxpayers and domestic and overseas consumers, are of interest. For example, to what extent do premium producers benefit relative to producers of lower-quality wine? How do these outcomes change as the industry becomes more export orientated?

The distributional issue also relates to the question of who should pay for what types of investments: not only as between government and producers, but also as between grape growers and wineries. Just as the benefits from a new technology in one sector of an industry are distributed across all related producer and consumer groups, the costs of the R&D nominally paid by a producer group are also shared by various parties along the chain. For example, are the grape growers paying a larger share of the costs than their shares of R&D benefits? While the non-premium grape and wine producers pay a significant amount of the tonnage-based R&D levy, most of the funded R&D projects are targeted at premium grapes and wine. Are the non-premium producers paying more than their fair share? In addition, the impacts on the government treasury via both the Wine Equalisation Tax (WET) and the Goods and Services Tax (GST) from alternative investment choices are also relevant.

This Australian case study is particularly timely because of the planned increase in levy rate (proposed for 2003–2004) and a recently launched new marketing drive (WFA and AWBC 2001). As recent modelling results demonstrate (Anderson 2004; Anderson *et al.* 2004), the latter is going to be essential when the industry is in a vulnerable position due to the recent boom in plantings, which is translating into ever-greater supplies of premium wines on the international market.

The present paper aims to address these questions. The published literature on the economic evaluation of research and promotion expenditures is growing rapidly (Alston *et al.* 1995, 2002; Byerlee and Anderson 2002). One of the approaches has been the use of a partial equilibrium, comparative static framework to measure the effects on economic welfare within an industry (Freebairn *et al.* 1982; Wohlgenant 1993; Alston *et al.* 1999; Zhao *et al.* 2000b). This approach is adopted in the present paper because of its convenience in modelling disaggregated industry sectors and its moderate data requirements.[3] We use a multisectoral partial equilibrium model of the markets for two types of Australian grapes and wine (premium and non-premium) to study the distributions of returns from different types of research and promotion investments. The distinction between premium and non-premium is crucial, because one-third of the market is non-premium and, yet, virtually all the R&D and marketing

---

[3] An alternative approach is to use an economy wide, general equilibrium model (see, for example, Anderson and Nielsen 2002); however, this model is inappropriate for an industry as small as the wine industry with few close substitutes in production or consumption.

efforts are focused on just premium products in an attempt to raise quality as consumers continue to move upmarket.

Previous studies have shown that welfare distribution hinges crucially on input substitution possibilities in the post-farm sectors. Freebairn *et al.* (1982) conclude that if farm inputs and processing inputs are used in strictly fixed proportions in the processing sector, the distribution of returns among industry groups is the same, regardless of where along the chain funds are invested in R&D or promotion. However, Alston and Scobie (1983) show that when input substitution is possible, each sector receives a larger share of total benefits from investment in its own sector. In this case, farmers receive a larger share of returns from farm research than from post-farm research and promotion. Furthermore, Alston and Scobie (1983) show that farmers can even lose welfare from post-farm research if the input substitution elasticity is bigger in size than the demand elasticity for the retail product. Using a model involving two post-farm sectors, namely processing and marketing/distribution, Holloway (1989) showed further that the benefits to farmers also depend on the post-farm stage to which the research is directed. He derived analytical conditions in terms of market elasticities that are necessary and sufficient for the farmers to gain from various types of post-farm research. With this in mind, another objective of the present paper is to investigate the implication of the uncertainty in the values of many market elasticities for the returns to growers from alternative investments, including the possibility of growers losing welfare from wine research, in a vertically, as well as horizontally, disaggregated industry.

The model is presented first and the data and market parameters are described next. Results are then presented, followed by a section on sensitivity analysis of the results to changes in key elasticities. Discussion of the implications and related issues is provided in the final section of the present paper.

2. The model

The structure of the model of the Australian grape and wine industry is provided in Figure 1, where each rectangle represents a production function and each arrowed straight line represents the market for a product,

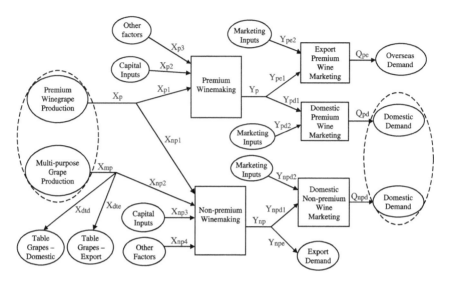

Figure 1. Structure of the model

with the arrowed end being the demand and the non-arrowed end being the supply of the product. Each oval represents a supply or demand schedule where an exogenous shift may occur.

Vertically, the industry is separated into the sectors of grape production, winemaking, wine marketing and final consumption. This enables us to study impacts of R&D and promotion investments on individual parts of the chain. Horizontally, the industry is disaggregated into premium and non-premium wine sectors. Grapes are divided into premium and multipurpose (non-premium). Grapes for uses other than winemaking account for only one-tenth of total usage. Sultana accounts for two-thirds of multipurpose grapes and approximately 5% of grape inputs into wine production. No reported variety is used exclusively for non-wine purposes so, for simplicity, we classify non-premium and multipurpose grapes as the same input (ABS 2001).

We assume that all sectors are profit maximisers and the technologies are characterised by constant returns to scale.[4] A set of demand and supply

---

[4] For an industry such as this, which has more than 1400 wineries and thousands more grape-growers of varying sizes, Diewert (1981) has shown that under very weak regularity

equations with general functional form is used to describe the relationships among various industry links in the chain (equations (1)–(37)). The impacts of alternative R&D and promotion investments are modelled as 15 exogenous variables that shift the relevant supply or demand curves, and the changes in prices and quantities resulting from new technologies or promotion are then solved to obtain the welfare implications for various industry groups. Variable notation is also shown in Figure 1.

2.1. Input supply to the premium and non-premium wine sectors

$$X_p = X_p(w_p, w_{mp}, T_{xp}, T_{Xmp}) \tag{1}$$

$$X_p = X_{p1} + X_{np1} \tag{2}$$

$$X_{p2} = X_{p2}(w_{p2}, T_{Xp2}) \tag{3}$$

$$X_{p3} = X_{p3}(w_{p3}, T_{Xp3}) \tag{4}$$

Equation (1) is the supply function for premium wine grapes, relating total quantity supplied X_p to own price w_p and the price of multipurpose grapes w_{mp}. In other words, it is assumed that the premium grape growers can shift some of the production to multipurpose grapes in response to changes in the relative prices of the two types of grapes. T_{Xp} and T_{Xmp} are the supply shifters representing the impacts of new technologies that reduce the costs of producing premium and non-premium grapes, respectively. The identity given in equation (2) shows that the premium grapes can be used for producing either premium wine (X_{p1}) or non-premium wine (X_{np1}). Equations (3) and (4) are supply functions for two other aggregated inputs to premium wine production. X_{p2} represents fixed capital, human capital and other inputs that are specific to premium wine making. Supplies of these inputs are relatively inelastic because they require specific skills that take time to supply. X_{p3} represents mobile factors, such as labour, chemical and other factor inputs, which are non-specific to

---

conditions it is reasonable to assume that the industry's aggregate production function can be approximated by constant returns to scale.

premium wine making. Supply of these inputs is much more elastic. T_{Xp2} and T_{Xp3} are supply shifters for X_{p2} and X_{p3}, respectively. T_{Xp2} can be used to represent technical changes in the premium wine making sector.

$$X_{mp} = X_{mp}(w_{mp}, w_p, T_{Xp}, T_{Xmp}) \tag{5}$$

$$X_{mp} = X_{np2} + X_{dtd} + X_{dte} \tag{6}$$

$$X_{np3} = X_{np3}(w_{np3}, T_{Xnp3}) \tag{7}$$

$$X_{np4} = X_{np4}(w_{np4}, T_{Xnp4}) \tag{8}$$

Equation (5) is the supply of multipurpose grapes relating the quantity supplied to own price and the price of premium grapes, with T_{Xp} and T_{Xmp} as the supply shifters. Prices for multipurpose grapes used for non-premium winemaking and for fruit are assumed to be the same w_{mp}. Equation (6) shows that multipurpose grapes can be used either for non-premium wine production or as dried and table grapes for domestic (X_{dtd}) or export (X_{dte}) markets. Equations (7) and (8) are supply functions for capital inputs (X_{np3}) and mobile inputs (X_{np4}), respectively, in non-premium wine production, with T_{Xnp3} and T_{Xnp4} as supply shifters.

2.2. Demand for table grapes

$$X_{dtd} = X_{dtd}(w_{mp}, N_{Xdtd}) \tag{9}$$

$$X_{dte} = X_{dte}(w_{mp}, N_{Xdte}) \tag{10}$$

Equations (9) and (10) are demand schedules for dried and table grapes for domestic (X_{dtd}) and export (X_{dte}) markets, respectively. N_{Xdtd} and N_{Xdte} are the respective demand shifters.

2.3. Output-constrained input demand of the premium wine sector

$$X_{p1} = Y_p^* c'_{Yp,1}(w_p, w_{p2}, w_{p3}) \tag{11}$$

$$X_{p2} = Y_p^* c'_{Yp,2}(w_p, w_{p2}, w_{p3}) \tag{12}$$

$$X_{p3} = Y_p^* c'_{Yp,3}(w_p, w_{p2}, w_{p3}) \quad (13)$$

The above three equations (11), (12) and (13) are the output-constrained input demand for X_{p1}, X_{p2} and X_{p3}, derived using Shephard's Lemma (Chambers 1991, p. 262). $c'_{Yp,i}(w_p, w_{p2}, w_p)$ ($i = 1, 2, 3$) are partial derivatives of the unit cost functions $c_{Yp}(w_p, w_{p2}, w_{p3})$ ($i = 1, 2, 3$).

2.4. Output-constrained input demand of the non-premium wine sector

$$X_{np1} = Y_{np}^* c'_{Ynp,1}(w_p, w_{mp}, w_{np3}, w_{np4}) \quad (14)$$

$$X_{np2} = Y_{np}^* c'_{Ynp,2}(w_p, w_{mp}, w_{np3}, w_{np4}) \quad (15)$$

$$X_{np3} = Y_{np}^* c'_{Ynp,3}(w_p, w_{mp}, w_{np3}, w_{np4}) \quad (16)$$

$$X_{np4} = Y_{np}^* c'_{Ynp,4}(w_p, w_{mp}, w_{np3}, w_{np4}) \quad (17)$$

Equations (14)–(17) are the output-constrained input demand for non-premium wine production, also derived using Shephard's Lemma. $c'_{Ynp,i}(w_p, w_{mp}, w_{np3}, w_{np4})$ ($i = 1,\ldots,4$) are partial derivatives of the unit cost functions $c_{Ynp}(w_p, w_{mp}, w_{np3}, w_{np4})$ ($i = 1, \ldots, 4$).

2.5. Market-clearing condition/supply of premium and non-premium wholesale wine

$$v_p = c_{Yp}(w_p, w_{p2}, w_{p3}) \quad (18)$$

$$v_{np} = c_{Ynp}(w_p, w_{mp}, w_{np3}, w_{np4}) \quad (19)$$

The aforementioned market-clearing conditions specify that unit prices for outputs equal the unit costs of production at the margin.

2.6. Destination of wine at the cellar door

$$Y_p = Y_{pd1} + Y_{pe1} \quad (20)$$

$$Y_{np} = Y_{npd1} + Y_{npe} \quad (21)$$

Equations (20) and (21) show that both premium and non-premium producer wines are destined for either domestic and export markets.

2.7. Supply of wine marketing inputs

$$Y_{pd2} = Y_{pd2}(v_{pd2}, T_{Ypd2}) \tag{22}$$

$$Y_{pe2} = Y_{pe2}(v_{pe2}, T_{Ype2}) \tag{23}$$

$$Y_{npd2} = Y_{npd2}(v_{npd2}, T_{Ynpd2}) \tag{24}$$

Equations (22)–(24) show that the supplies of marketing inputs (Y_{pd2}, Y_{pe2} and Y_{npd2}) relate to own prices (v_{pd2}, v_{pe2} and v_{npd2}) and other supply shifters (T_{Ypd2}, T_{Ype2} and T_{Ynpd2}), such as R&D, in marketing sectors. These include any technical changes that reduce marketing margins, such as new technologies with lower packaging costs, internet selling or labour market reforms in the retailing sector.

2.8. Output-constrained input demand of the wine marketing sectors

$$Y_{pd1} = Q^*_{pd} c'_{Qpd,1}(v_p, v_{pd2}) \tag{25}$$

$$Y_{pd2} = Q^*_{pd} c'_{Qpd,2}(v_p, v_{pd2}) \tag{26}$$

$$Y_{pe1} = Q^*_{pe} c'_{Qpe,1}(v_p, v_{pe2}) \tag{27}$$

$$Y_{pe2} = Q^*_{pe} c'_{Qpe,2}(v_p, v_{pe2}) \tag{28}$$

$$Y_{npd1} = Q^*_{npd} c'_{Qnpd,1}(v_{np}, v_{npd2}) \tag{29}$$

$$Y_{npd2} = Q^*_{npd} c'_{Qnpd,2}(v_{np}, v_{npd2}) \tag{30}$$

These are the output-constrained input demand for the three marketing sectors based on Shephard's Lemma.

2.9. Market-clearing condition for the marketing sectors

$$p_{pd} = c(v_p, v_{pd2}) \qquad (31)$$

$$p_{pe} = c(v_p, v_{pe2}) \qquad (32)$$

$$p_{npd} = c(v_{np}, v_{npd2}) \qquad (33)$$

These specify that the unit output price for each of the three marketing sectors is equal to the unit cost.

2.10. Final demand for wine

$$Y_{npe} = Y_{npe}(v_{np}, N_{Ynpe}) \qquad (34)$$

$$Q_{pd} = Q_{pd}(p_{pd}, p_{npd}, N_{Qpd}, N_{Qnpd}) \qquad (35)$$

$$Q_{pe} = Q_{pe}(p_{pe}, N_{Qpe}) \qquad (36)$$

$$Q_{npd} = Q_{npd}(p_{pd}, p_{npd}, N_{Qpd}, N_{Qnpd}) \qquad (37)$$

These are the demand functions for the four final wine products/markets. The N functions are demand shifters representing impacts of promotion or increases in product quality in individual markets. As can be seen from equations (35) and (37), the premium and non-premium wines are assumed to be substitutes in the domestic market.[5] Note that there is no marketing sector specified for exported non-premium wine, because this is a very insignificant segment of total production, accounting for less than 8% of the volume and 1% of the value of total sales. Similarly, given the relatively small volume of non-premium exports, the two wine types are not treated as substitutes in the export market.

The structural model described defines equilibrium in all markets. When a new technology or promotion disturbs the system, a displacement

---

[5] Cross-price effects from other substitutes, such as beer and spirits, are ignored because their cross-price elasticities are very small according to the literature review reported in Wittwer and Anderson (2002).

from the base equilibrium results. By totally differentiating the system of equations at the initial equilibrium, the displacement model that linearly relates changes of endogenous variables to changes in exogenous shifters can be derived with market elasticities as parameters. The displacement model is detailed in the Appendix. Definitions of all market parameters are given in Tables 1 and 2. Integrability conditions, such as symmetry and homogeneity conditions, have been imposed implicitly.

3. The data

The inputs required for solving the model in equations 1′–37′ in the Appendix are in three parts: (i) base equilibrium prices and quantities for all sectors and markets; (ii) market parameters that describe producer and consumer responsiveness to any price changes; and (iii) the values of exogenous variables that quantify the effects of R&D and promotion.

The database used for the base equilibrium for 2005 is adapted from the model of global wine markets outlined in Anderson *et al.* (2004) and Wittwer *et al.* (2003), which describe the sectoral disaggregation of the Australian wine industry as projected to 2005. We used a base of 2005 to capture the effect of recent expansion of the industry. Because it takes up to 7 years before newly planted vines are fully bearing in terms of quality and yield, the projection of production to 2005 is likely to be reasonably robust. The disaggregation between premium and non-premium wines is based on containers, with premium wines referring to those in bottles of 2.0 L or less.

The input cost structures for industry sectors are adapted and reconstructed from the database in Wittwer *et al.* (2003). Inputs other than grapes to the two winemaking sectors are grouped into two aggregated inputs: capital inputs and mobile factors. The inputs to wine marketing sectors are grouped into wholesale wine inputs and other marketing inputs. The cost structures for marketing sectors are based, in part, on the margin information in Wittwer *et al.* (2003), as are the splits among domestic and export destinations for both premium and non-premium wines. The base values and the resulting cost shares are summarised in Table 1.

Table 1. Base equilibrium values projected for 2005 (in AU$ million)

Grapes	
Premium grapes	
Total value	$TV_{Xp} = 1350$
Destinations	$\rho_{Xp1} = 0.96$, $\rho_{Xnp1} = 0.04$
Multi-purpose grapes	
Total value	$TV_{Xmp} = 450$
Destinations	$\rho_{Xdtd} = 0.26$, $\rho_{Xdte} = 0.42$, $\rho_{Xnp2} = 0.32$
Wine production	
Premium wine	
Total value	$TV_{Yp} = 4784$
Cost shares	$\kappa_{p1} = 0.27$, $\kappa_{p2} = 0.43$, $\kappa_{p3} = 0.30$
Non-premium wine	
Total value	$TV_{Ynp} = 652$
Cost shares	$\kappa_{np1} = 0.09$, $\kappa_{np2} = 0.24$, $\kappa_{np3} = 0.43$, $\kappa_{np4} = 0.24$
Marketing sectors and final wines	
Premium wine	
Domestic	
Before WET	$TV_{Ypd1} = 1436$
After GST	$TV_{Qpd}^* = 3452$
Cost shares for marketing	$\lambda_{pd1} = 0.59$, $\lambda_{pd2} = 0.41$
Export	
Producer value	$TV_{Ype1} = 3348$
f.o.b. value	$TV_{Qpe} = 3680$
Cost shares for marketing	$\lambda_{pe1} = 0.91$, $\lambda_{pe2} = 0.09$
Non-premium wine	
Domestic	
Before WET	$TV_{Ynpd1} = 560$
After GST	$TV_{Qnpd}^* = 1304$
Cost shares for marketing	$\lambda_{npd1} = 0.61$, $\lambda_{pd2} = 0.39$
Export	
Producer value	$TV_{Ynpe} = 46$

Source: Derived from the database used in Wittwer *et al.* 2003.
WET, Wine Equalisation Tax; GST, Goods and Services Tax; f.o.b., freight on board.

Table 2. Assumed market elasticities

Grape supply	
Low	$\varepsilon_{(Xp,wp)} = 0.4$, $\varepsilon_{(Xmp,wmp)} = 0.5$, $\varepsilon_{(Xmp,wp)} = -0.2$ ($\varepsilon_{(\Xi\pi,\omega\mu\pi)} = -0.07$)
Higher	$\varepsilon_{(Xp,wp)} = 0.8$, $\varepsilon_{(Xmp,wmp)} = 1.0$, $\varepsilon_{(Xmp,wp)} = -0.6$ ($\varepsilon_{(Xp,wmp)} = -0.22$)
Other winemaking input supply	
Low	
Premium	$\varepsilon_{(Xp2,wp2)} = 0.4$, $\varepsilon_{(Xp3,wp3)} = 5$
Non-premium	$\varepsilon_{(Xnp3,wnp3)} = 0.5$, $\varepsilon_{(Xp3,wp3)} = 5$
Higher	
Premium	$\varepsilon_{(Xp2,wp2)} = 0.8$, $\varepsilon_{(Xp3,wp3)} = 5$
Non-premium	$\varepsilon_{(Xnp3,wnp3)} = 1.0$, $\varepsilon_{(Xp3,wp3)} = 5$
Table grape demand	$\eta_{(Xdtd,wdtd)} = -0.6$, $\eta_{(Xdte,wdte)} = -5$
Input substitution for winemaking	
Premium	$\sigma_{(Xpi,Xpj)} = 0.1$ ($i, j = 1, 2$ and $3; i < j$)
Non-premium	$\sigma_{(Xnp1,Xnp2)} = 0.15$, rest $\sigma_{(Xnpi,Xnpj)} = 0.1$ ($i, j = 1, 2, 3$ and $4; i < j$)
Wine marketing input supply	
Premium	$\varepsilon_{(Ypd2,vpd2)} = 2$, $\varepsilon_{(Ype2,vpe2)} = 2$
Non-premium	$\varepsilon_{(Ynpd2,vnpd2)} = 2$
Input substitution for marketing	
Premium	$\sigma_{(Ypd1,Ypd2)} = 0.1$, $\sigma_{(Ype1,Ype2)} = 0.1$
Non-premium	$\sigma_{(Ynpd1,Ynpd2)} = 0.1$
Final wine demand	
Premium	$\eta_{(Qpd,ppd)} = -0.8$, $\eta_{(Qpe,ppe)} = -5.0$
Non-premium	$\eta_{(Qnpd,pnpd)} = -0.9$, $\eta_{(Ynpe,vnpe)} = -7.0$
Cross-price in domestic market	$\eta_{(Qnpd,ppd)} = 0.3$ ($\eta_{(Qpd,pnpd)} = 0.11$)

The market elasticity values used are given in Table 2. These are chosen according to limited empirical studies and subjective judgement.[6]

---

[6] See James and Alston (2002) for further discussion of the choice of elasticities for a quality disaggregated equilibrium displacement model of the Australian wine industry.

On the supply side, we choose a low and a high set, reflecting our uncertainty about these critical parameters. We have used 0.4 and 0.5 (premium and non-premium, respectively) for the low set of own-price supply elasticities and 0.8 and 1.0 for the high set of supply elasticities. Cross-price supply elasticities are assumed to range from a low of –0.2 to a high of –0.6 for multipurpose grapes with respect to premium grape price. The values for the other pair of the cross-price supply elasticities (–0.07 and –0.22) are determined using the symmetry condition. On the demand side, we have assumed much higher own-price elasticities for export markets (–5 for premium and –7 for non-premium) relative to the domestic market (–0.8 and –0.9). The analytical relationship provided in Dixon and Rimmer (2002, pp. 222–5) is used as a guide in choosing the export demand elasticities. We have also included a cross-price elasticity of final demand between premium and non-premium wine for the domestic market, and imposed the standard symmetry condition.

As explained in the model section, for the winemaking sectors, we have chosen inelastic supply elasticities for the fixed capital and human capital inputs (lows of 0.4–0.5 and highs of 0.8–1.0), due to the highly technical nature of the specialized fixed capital and human capital inputs, but a nearly perfectly elastic supply for other mobile inputs (a value of 5). For the supply elasticities for wine marketing inputs, we have used a less-than-perfectly elastic value of 2.

There are no empirical estimates for elasticities of input substitution between primary and other inputs in the winemaking and wine marketing sectors, yet the results of interest in this study hinge on these elasticity values. Wohlgenant (1993) has used 0.72 for USA beef and 0.35 for USA pork as a base case and half those values as an alternative case, based on an earlier empirical study (Wohlgenant 1989). Mullen *et al.* (1989) have used 0.1 for Australian wool. We have used a value of 0.1 for all sectors in the present study. Diewert (1981) pointed out that industry level production function generally exhibits more input substitutability than the plant level production function. For the input substitution between the two grape types in the non-premium winemaking sector, we have used an elasticity of 0.15. Both a substantial drop in the price ratio of warm-climate red winegrape prices to Sultana between 1997 and 2001 and prohibition in 2000 of the mislabelling of grape varieties on wine bottles and casks have reduced Sultana usage in wine. Nonetheless, Sultana remains important in non-premium production, making a small input-substitution parameter for grapes into non-premium production defensible (ABS 2001).[7]

There are 15 exogenous variables in the model that can be used to shift the various demand and supply schedules and, thus, to model the impacts of various R&D and promotion investments on various industry sectors. In the present study, we concentrate on estimating the impacts of five R&D and promotion scenarios:

1. Cost-reducing R&D in premium grape production (t_{Xp});
2. Cost-reducing R&D in premium winemaking (t_{Xp2});
3. Quality enhancing R&D for premium wine (n_{Qpd} and n_{Qpe});
4. Premium wine promotion in the domestic market (n_{Qpd}); and
5. Premium wine promotion in the export market (n_{Qpe}).

In each case, a 1% vertical parallel shift of the relevant supply or demand curve is assumed. In other words, we examine the impacts of a 1% cost reduction in the relevant sector in the case of cost-reducing R&D and a 1% increase in consumers' willingness to pay in the case of promotion or product quality improvement. The choice of a 1% shift is arbitrary. While the total welfare gain in dollar terms in each scenario will be proportional to the initial percentage shift, the distribution of the total benefit among industry groups is independent of the size of the initial shift (i.e. 1% here), as long as the shift is assumed parallel and relatively small in comparison with the equilibrium price level (Zhao *et al.* 2000b, p. 84).

4. Results for alternative R&D and promotion investments

With specified values for the base equilibrium, market elasticities and exogenous shifters, the equilibrium displacement model in equations 1'–37' in

---

[7] A back-of-the-envelope calculation from the observed relative prices and usage between 1997 and 2001 indicates a substitution elasticity of 0.3–0.4. Policy change about mislabelling for non-premium wine would have been the main factor driving the changes in usage. This makes the assumed value of 0.15 seem reasonable.

the Appendix is solved to obtain the percentage changes in all price and quantity variables for each policy scenario. Changes in economic surpluses for each of the industry groups involved and changes in wine tax revenues are then calculated. The results for the five scenarios are summarized in Table 3. For each case, total economic welfare gains in millions of Australian dollars and the proportional distribution among grapegrowers, wineries, retailers, domestic and overseas consumers, and government wine tax revenues are provided. These include the effects on the recently introduced WET and the GST.[8] In the interest of brevity, the price and quantity changes for each scenario are not presented, but they are available from the authors.

Some qualifications should be noted in examining the results. The total welfare benefits in dollar terms relate to 1% shifts in the relevant supply or demand curves. The relative costs that would be required to bring about the 1% shifts for alternative scenarios are not known and hence are not discussed in the present study. That is, we cannot say how costly reducing grape production costs by 1% through R&D is compared with increasing consumers' willingness-to-pay by 1% via promotion. Project-level cost–benefit analysis for R&D and empirical studies of wine advertising would be necessary in order to compare returns from alternative investments in dollar terms. In general, the total welfare gain for a 1% shift is related directly to the value of the market where the initial shift is involved. For example, looking at the total welfare gains in Table 3 for grape R&D (approximately $14 million) compared with export promotion (approximately $35 million), we note that we need a 3% cost reduction in premium grape production in order to gain the same total welfare gain in dollars as from a 1% increase in overseas consumers' willingness to pay.

However, the distribution of the total welfare gains among industry groups is independent of the size of the initial shift (Zhao et al. 2000b, p. 84). Hence, it is meaningful to compare the welfare distributions across alternative scenarios even without knowledge of the costs involved in the initial 1% shifts.[9]

---

[8] See Wittwer and Anderson (2002) for an analysis of those tax changes.

[9] Were the supply curve to shift in a non-parallel way, the welfare gain to producers would be different in aggregate terms and in its distribution among producers (see Lindner and Jarrett 1978).

Table 3. Total economic welfare changes (in 2001 $A million) and shares of total welfare changes (in percentage) to various groups from alternative investment scenarios: Low- and higher-elasticities cases

Non-Government Welfare Gains (% shares)	Scenario 1 Premium Grape Cost-Reducing R&D		Scenario 2 Premium Wine Cost-Reducing R&D		Scenario 3 Premium Wine Quality Enhancing R&D		Scenario 4 Premium Wine Domestic Promotion		Scenario 5 Premium Wine Export Promotion	
Supply elasticities	Low	High	Low	High	Low	High	Low	High	Low	High
Total welfare gain ($A million)	13.6	13.7	20.8	20.9	73.3	73.7	37.5	38.9	34.5	34.8
Distributions (%)										
ΔPS_{Xp}	42.9	33.2	23.7	22.6	22.6	19.5	2.2	2.3	45.0	38.4
ΔPS_{Xmp}	1.2	2.2	0.5	1.4	0.4	1.2	−0.2	0.0	1.1	2.4
$\Delta PS_{Xp} + \Delta PS_{Xmp}$ grape producers subtotal	44.1	35.5	24.2	24.0	23.0	20.7	2.0	2.3	46.1	40.8
ΔPS_{Xp2} (Premium wineries)	35.6	32.7	57.5	45.7	35.9	30.0	3.2	3.8	71.2	58.7
ΔPS_{Xnp3} (Non-premium wineries)	0.9	0.6	−0.7	−0.6	−0.8	−0.6	−1.6	−0.8	−0.5	−0.4
Wineries subtotal	36.5	33.3	56.8	45.1	35.1	29.3	1.7	3.1	70.7	58.3
$\Delta PS_{Xp3} + \Delta PS_{Xnp4}$ mobile factors gains	2.5	4.1	2.5	4.2	2.4	3.6	−0.1	0.3	4.9	7.2

Who Gains from Australian Generic Wine Promotion and R&D?

ΔPS_{Ypd2}	0.6	1.1	0.8	1.3	3.1	3.4	10.9	10.7	-5.3	-4.7
ΔPS_{Ynpd2}	0.1	0.1	-0.2	-0.3	-0.4	-0.5	-1.3	-1.1	0.5	0.4
ΔPS_{Ype2}	1.9	3.1	2.0	3.3	1.6	2.6	-1.1	-0.8	4.5	6.3
Marketing sector subtotal	2.6	4.3	2.6	4.3	4.4	5.6	8.5	8.7	-0.4	2.1
ΔCS_{Xdtd}	-0.3	-0.6	-0.1	-0.4	-0.1	-0.3	0.1	0.0	-0.3	-0.7
ΔCS_{Qpd}	5.9	9.7	6.1	10.1	18.2	21.1	77.6	74.4	-44.5	-38.4
ΔCS_{Qnpd}	1.3	1.7	-0.4	-0.6	0.1	-0.2	2.4	2.2	-2.8	-2.8
Domestic consumers subtotal	6.9	10.8	5.6	9.0	18.2	20.6	80.1	76.6	-47.6	-41.9
ΔCS_{Xdte}	-0.5	-0.9	-0.2	-0.6	-0.2	-0.5	0.1	0.0	-0.5	-1.0
ΔCS_{Qpe}	8.8	14.7	9.5	15.7	6.7	11.2	-5.2	-3.7	19.3	28.0
ΔCS_{Ynpe}	0.2	0.2	-0.1	-0.1	-0.1	-0.1	0.2	0.1	-0.3	-0.3
Overseas consumers subtotal	8.5	14.0	9.2	15.0	6.5	10.7	-4.9	-3.6	18.5	26.7
Tax revenue changes										
Wholesale sales tax	-1.0	-1.6	-0.8	-1.2	6.6	6.2	6.7	6.7	6.4	5.6
GST	-0.1	-0.3	-0.2	-0.3	3.8	3.7	6.0	5.9	1.3	1.2
Tax subtotal	-1.2	-1.9	-1.0	-1.5	10.4	9.9	12.7	12.6	7.7	6.8
Total percentage	100.0	100.0	100.0	100.0	100.0	100.0	100.0	100.0	100.0	100.0

Source: Authors' model results.
GST, Goods and Services Tax.

What do the results reveal? Consider the first column of Table 3. It shows how a 1% shift downwards in the premium grape supply curve because of productivity enhancing R&D would benefit mostly, but not only, premium producers. If supply response is small, 44% ($5.9 million) of the welfare gains would go to the grapegrowers and 37% to the makers of premium wine, whereas most of the rest is shared with domestic and overseas consumers (7 and 9%, respectively). Consumers benefit because they enjoy lower prices and higher quantities as a result of lower production costs. The total welfare gain is $13.7 million per year. To provide some perspective, this is roughly the budget of the GWRDC for 2002–2003. The *ad valorem* tax revenue from wine is reduced by approximately $0.2 million, because the increased quantity less than compensates for the reduced price, due, in part, to the relatively low price elasticity of demand assumed, so the wholesale and retail values for wine are both reduced as a result of the cost reduction. If the supply elasticities are higher, the net welfare gain per year is much the same, but a larger share (almost one-third) goes to consumers at the expense of grapegrowers, whose share falls from 44 to 36%, yet the share to winemakers is little different (from 36 to 33%).

If, instead, the cost-reducing R&D is directed towards premium winemaking rather than grape production, the majority of the short-run welfare gains (57%) goes to wineries and only 24% ($5.0 million) goes to grape-growers, with again, 15% going to consumers. The net benefit of that shock is $21 million per year, of which 9% goes to consumers abroad.[10] The total dollar benefit for a 1% reduction in winemaking inputs is greater than that for a 1% cost reduction in the grape R&D scenario ($14 million per annum), because of the large additional value added in the supply chain by the wineries. The share of the gain to wineries is smaller (45%) when higher supply elasticities are used. The consumers' share in that case is 24%, equalling the grapegrowers' share, which is similar in the low- and higher-elasticity cases.

---

[10] For simplicity, we assume throughout that, in the time-frame considered in the present study, there are no beneficial spillovers to producers abroad in terms of the new technologies lowering their costs of production or in terms of Australian generic promotion affecting (positively or negatively) the demand for non-Australian wine.

If, as a result of quality enhancing R&D anywhere along the chain of premium wine production, consumers are willing to pay more for a better Australian premium wine in both domestic and overseas markets, then grape producers (23%, $16.9 million), wineries (35%) and domestic consumers (18%) all gain significant shares in the low-elasticity case. This also holds in the higher-elasticity case, with some of the benefits shifting from grape and wine producers to overseas consumers, whose share rises from 7 to 11% of the total $73 million per year gain. Note that overseas consumers receive a lower proportion of total benefits from quality enhancing research than from the cost-reducing research shown in the first two scenarios. This is because scenario 3 involves simultaneous shifts in both domestic and export demand curves. The gross benefits to foreign consumers from better wine in overseas markets are offset by the increased demand in the domestic market, which forces the export price up and, thereby, makes overseas consumers worse off than they would be if there was no demand response in the home market.

This can be seen by turning to the effects of promotion on just one of those two markets for one of the two wine types. In the case of just domestic promotion of premium wine (a market that accounts for barely one-quarter of the total volume of Australian wine industry sales), only approximately one-quarter of the gains from such promotion would accrue to producers, retailers and tax revenues (see the fourth column of Table 3). Nearly 80% of the welfare gains go to domestic consumers, due to the taste change effect or improved product knowledge as a consequence of promotion.[11] Overseas consumers, in contrast, are worse off because of the higher price of Australian wine generated by that domestic promotion campaign. The opposite occurs with just overseas promotion, as in the final scenario.

---

[11] Controversies have long surrounded the question of how advertising changes consumers' preferences and, thus, their welfare. Although there are issues relating to the empirical implementations of alternative notions (Alston et al. 1999), there seems to be consensus that consumers gain welfare from advertising either because their knowledge about a product has changed (thus, product characteristics have changed that are objects in their decision functions) or their taste ordering has changed (thus, parameters in the decision functions have changed). See Dixit and Norman (1979).

The final scenario is of particular interest to those engaged in the industry's efforts to boost marketing abroad of Australian premium wine (WFA and AWBC 2001), because the distributional effects of such an initiative are very different from the effects of R&D and domestic promotion. Specifically, in the low-elasticity case, grapegrowers gain nearly half of the benefits (46%, $15.9 million) and premium winemakers gain more than half of the benefits, largely because of the high priced elasticity of export demand (–5.0, compared with –0.8 for domestic demand) relative to the elasticity of supply of specialised inputs in these sectors. In contrast, non-premium winemakers lose slightly from such promotion. Certainly overseas consumers benefit in the willingness-to-pay sense, enjoying 19% of the total measured welfare gain in the low-elasticity case.[12] These percentages add to more than 100 because domestic consumers lose substantially from the price-raising effect of the promotion abroad and its impact in reducing supplies on the domestic market. In the higher-elasticity case, the effects are similar but with more benefit/less loss to consumers and less benefit to both grape-growers and winemakers.

In comparing the benefit distributions from alternative investment scenarios, the grape and wine producers would prefer production research and export promotion. They would also prefer export to domestic promotion: the very different effects on producers from the two promotion scenarios are due to the differences in demand responsiveness in the two markets. Unlike domestic consumers, overseas consumers are highly price elastic in their demands and, consequently, enjoy only a small boost in welfare from a demand shift. As a result, the benefit flows back to producers. Between the two producer groups, grapegrowers would prefer grape production R&D and winemakers would prefer wine production R&D, due to the nonzero input substitution assumed. The benefits from quality enhancing research are more evenly shared among the two producer groups, the two consumer groups and the tax office than that from

---

[12] The 19% of $35 million benefit to consumers abroad from overseas promotion (scenario 5), less their 5% of $38 million loss from domestic promotion (scenario 4), approximates the net gain to overseas consumers of 6.5% of $73 million from the outward shift in the demand curve in both domestic and export markets following quality enhancing R&D (scenario 3).

cost-reducing production R&D and promotion. The government gains significant wine tax revenue from improved grape and wine quality and promotion, but loses slightly from new cost-reducing grape and wine production technologies.

There are interesting differences between the results of the present study and similar studies for other agricultural industries, such as beef or pork (e.g. Wohlgenant 1993; Zhao *et al.* 2000b). Post-farm processors and marketers collect insignificant shares of welfare gains from R&D and promotion if the supplies of processing and marketing inputs are assumed highly elastic. The processors in the present study, namely the wineries, are estimated to gain a significant share of benefits, partly because of the specialised skills required in winemaking and, thus, the inelastic supply elasticities assumed for winemaking inputs. This raises the more general question of how sensitive the results are to other elasticities.

5. Sensitivity analysis

As discussed in the Introduction, the value of the elasticity of substitution between farm and non-farm inputs and its relationship with the sizes of other market elasticities play important roles in estimating the distribution of benefits. The higher this elasticity is above zero, the greater the grapegrowers' interest in investing in farm research compared with post-farm research and promotion, *ceteris paribus*. Furthermore, the relative sizes of the input substitution elasticities in individual post-farm sectors are also likely to be important in determining the returns to farmers from research at different postfarm stages. With a multistage model involving a processing sector and a marketing/distribution sector, Holloway (1989) derived analytical conditions for farmers to gain from various types of post-farm research. In particular, he showed that when input substitution elasticities are the same for the two postfarm sectors ($\sigma_p = \sigma_d$), farmers will lose from processing or distribution research under the condition that those elasticities are bigger than the absolute value of the retail demand elasticity $|\eta|$. However, if $\sigma_p \neq \sigma_d$, the condition for farmers to lose from marketing/distribution research remains $\sigma_d > |\eta|$, but the condition for the processing research involves $(\sigma_d - \sigma_p)$ and its relationship with other parameters, such as retail demand η, the elasticity of supply of distribution inputs ε_d and cost shares in the distribution sector. For example, Holloway (1989) showed that farmers can gain significantly from distribution research but, at the same time, lose significantly from processing research if σ_p is large and σ_d is small, even when σ_p is smaller than $|\eta|$.

These previous findings have potential implications for the estimated returns to grape-growers from winemaking research (processing) and wine marketing research in the present study. Even though the horizontal disaggregation into differentiated products in our model makes Holloway's analytical conditions not directly applicable, his results for a single product model nonetheless suggest the potential importance of key parameters. Table 4 shows the sensitivity of our baseline results to such elasticity changes. We focus on the results for our first three scenarios in Table 3, which relate to a supply shift in grape production (farm research), a supply shift in winemaking inputs (processing research) and final demand shifts due to quality change (or promotion), all along the premium product chain.

Cases 1–3 in Table 4 assume equal input substitution elasticities for all post-farm sectors for both premium and non-premium products. The results show how the welfare distributions change as the value for the equal input substitution elasticities changes from zero (case 2) to 0.1 (baseline in case 1) and then to 0.5 (case 3). When fixed proportions are assumed in case 2, the distributions of benefits are very similar to the baseline case across all three scenarios and all parties are relatively indifferent as to where the investments occur. The shares are not exactly the same as they would be in the single product case, because only the premium curves are shifted in our multiproduct model and the benefits to producers relate to the sum of both premium and non-premium products. When we move to case 1 and then to case 3 as the input substitution elasticities increase, it is clear that grape growers will increasingly prefer grape cost-reducing research, wineries prefer wine cost-reducing research and consumers prefer improved final product quality. Note that because the value of 0.5 in case 3 is still smaller than the final demand elasticities (–0.8 for domestic premium and –5 for export premium), grape-growers still gain a positive share of returns from wine research.

In cases 4–8 in Table 4, we investigate the possibility of grape-growers losing welfare from wine research as we allow the input substitution

Table 4. Sensitivity of welfare shares (%) going to grape-growers, winemakers, domestic consumers and export consumers to different values of pertinent elasticities

Alternative Elasticities	Scenario 1 (Premium Grape Cost-Reducing Research)				Scenario 2 (Premium Wine Cost-Reducing Research)				Scenario 3 (Premium Wine Quality Enhancing Research)			
	Grape	Wine	DC	EC	Grape	Wine	DC	EC	Grape	Wine	DC	EC
Case 1 (Baseline) All $\sigma_p = 0.1, \sigma_d = 0.1$ $\eta = (-5, -7, -0.8, -0.9, 0.3, 0.11)$	35.5	33.3	10.8	14.0	24.0	45.1	9.0	15.0	20.7	29.3	20.6	10.7
Case 2 All $\sigma_p = 0, \sigma_d = 0$ $\eta = (-5, -7, -0.8, -0.9, 0.3, 0.11)$	27.7	39.4	11.1	14.6	28.3	40.0	9.0	15.1	20.9	29.6	20.6	10.3
Case 3 All $\sigma_p = 0.5, \sigma_d = 0.5$ $\eta = (-5, -7, -0.8, -0.9, 0.3, 0.11)$	54.5	19.1	9.5	12.5	13.8	57.8	9.3	14.3	19.2	27.9	20.3	11.8
Case 4 All $\sigma_p = 1.0, \sigma_d = 1.0$ $\eta = (-1, -1, -0.8, -0.8, 0.2, 0.08)$	57.2	−0.5	18.2	27.0	−0.4	52.6	19.4	30.3	9.9	14.6	29.2	28.9

(*Continued*)

Table 4. (Continued)

Alternative Elasticities	Scenario 1 (Premium Grape Cost-Reducing Research)			Scenario 2 (Premium Wine Cost-Reducing Research)				Scenario 3 (Premium Wine Quality Enhancing Research)			
	Grape	Wine	DC	EC	Grape	Wine	DC	EC	Grape	Wine	DC	EC
Case 5 All $\sigma_p = 1.3$, $\sigma_d = 1.3$ $\eta = (-2, -3, -0.8, -0.8, 0.2, 0.08)$	65.8	2.0	13.5	19.3	1.5	61.9	14.9	22.3	12.9	19.0	25.2	22.7
Case 6 All $\sigma_p = 1.3$, $\sigma_d = 0.1$ $\eta = (-2, -3, -0.8, -0.8, 0.2, 0.08)$	65.3	0.1	12.7	20.8	0.1	60.6	14.1	23.9	13.2	19.6	25.9	21.8
Case 7 All $\sigma_p = 1.3$, $\sigma_d = 0.05$ $\eta = (-2, -3, -0.8, -0.8, 0.2, 0.08)$	65.3	-0.1	12.6	20.9	-0.02	60.6	14.0	24.0	13.3	19.6	26.0	21.8
Case 8 All $\sigma_p = 1.3$, $\sigma_d = 0$ $\eta = (-2, -3, -0.8, -0.8, 0.2, 0.08)$	65.2	-0.2	12.6	21.0	-0.1	60.5	14.0	24.1	13.3	19.6	26.0	21.7

σ_p, any input substitution elasticities in the processing/winemaking sectors; σ_d, any input substitution elasticities in the marketing sectors; $\eta = (\eta_{(Qpe,ppe)}, \eta_{(Ynpe, vnpe)}, \eta_{(Qpd,ppd)}, \eta_{(Qnpd, pnpd)}, \eta_{(Qpd, pnpd)}, \eta_{(Qnpd, ppd)})$, final wine demand elasticities for, respectively, own-price export premium, own-price export non-premium, own-price domestic premium, own-price domestic non-premium, cross-price for domestic non-premium, cross-price for domestic premium; DC, domestic consumers; EC, export consumers.

elasticities to be different for the two post-farm sectors and the final demand elasticities to be smaller. As implied by the previous studies, the relationship between the input substitution elasticities for the winemaking (processing) sectors and marketing sectors, and their relative sizes in comparison with the final demand elasticities, are vital. Recall that we have used very elastic demand elasticities for export premium wine ($\eta_{(Qpe, ppe)} = -5$ for export compared with $\eta_{(Qpd, ppd)} = -0.8$ for domestic) in the baseline model and two-thirds of Australian premium wine is exported. As Australian wine builds its reputation in international markets and differentiates itself from wines of other countries, it may be that the elasticity of demand overseas for Australian premium wine becomes lower than the value we have chosen. In case 4, we use a set of much lower demand elasticities (with -1 for export premium and -0.8 for domestic premium) and an equal input substitution elasticity of 1.0 for all post-farm sectors. As expected, under such extreme assumptions, grape-growers would lose from wine cost-reducing research and wineries would lose from grape cost-reducing research.

Turning to cases 5–8, we assume a set of perhaps more realistic wine demand elasticities that are higher than those in case 4: -2 and -3 for export premium and non-premium, respectively, and -0.8 and -0.5 for domestic premium and non-premium, respectively. Grape-growers are still gaining positive returns from wine research when input substitution elasticities are assumed to be 1.3 for all post-farm sectors in case 5 and when the input substitution elasticity for wine marketing sectors are assumed to be 0.1 in case 6. However, when the input substitution elasticities in wine marketing sectors are further lowered to 0.05 (case 7) and then zero (case 8), grape-growers start to lose out from winemaking research.

So what can we conclude about the robustness of our results for the Australian wine industry from the sensitivity analysis in Table 4, bearing in mind that we have limited knowledge about the sizes of the input substitution elasticities and even the wine demand elasticities? If we believe that the possibility for input substitution is close to zero in both the winemaking and wine marketing sectors, then the interests of individual sectors in the industry in choosing where along the vertical chain to invest research or promotion funds will be closely aligned with total industry welfare gains. In contrast, if input substitution elasticities are larger than the baseline value of 0.1 and the final demand elasticities are smaller than the base values, each group will receive an even higher share than suggested in the base scenario from investment in its own sector: grape-growers will even more strongly prefer grape research, winemakers will prefer winemaking research and consumers will prefer quality improvement or promotion (see, for example, case 3). However, in the case of the Australian wine industry, we believe that the relationships between input substitution and final demand are unlikely to be such that grape-growers will lose from cost-reducing wine research or that winemakers will lose from cost-reducing grape research. The majority of Australian premium wine is exported and exported products from small countries tend to be demand elastic. Although it could be argued that the input substitution elasticities for winemaking and marketing sectors are likely to be larger than, say, 0.1, we believe it is unlikely that they are larger than the export demand elasticity for Australian wine. In addition, it is difficult to argue that the input substitution within the winemaking sector is significantly larger than that within the marketing sector (it would seem to be easier to argue the other way around), in which case the negative returns to growers in cases 7 and 8 are not relevant.

6. Implications and conclusions

Numerous qualifications need to be kept in mind in interpreting the base results. Obviously the numbers depend heavily on the elasticities assumed (see Table 2). The sensitivity analysis summarised in Table 4 shows how the baseline results will change for alternative values of key elasticities. It illustrates Holloway's (1989) conclusion, with a vertically and also horizontally disaggregated model, that the returns to the farm sector from alternative stages of post-farm research depend crucially on how the input substitution elasticities in post-farm sectors compare with the final demand elasticities and how the input substitution elasticities in different sectors compare with one another. Systematic accounting for uncertainty in market parameters, as undertaken in Zhao *et al.* (2000a), would provide further insights. In addition, this model captures only partial equilibrium effects within the Australian industry. The feedback from other related sectors in demand (such as beer and spirits), the spillover of new technologies to other industries (including the grape and wine industry abroad) and any social and environmental impacts (both positive and negative) are left unmeasured. However, the model does capture the change in wine tax revenue.

The present study has also ignored the impacts of any costs incurred in R&D and promotion. Both generic R&D and promotion are funded, in part, by producer levies, which, in effect, add to the production costs and shift the supply curves upwards. The net impacts to all groups concerned are determined by the distributions of both benefits and costs. It is assumed here that the magnitude of such shifts are small in comparison with the shifts resulting from R&D-induced productivity gains and the increases in willingness-to-pay due to quality enhancing R&D or generic promotion. This assumption is supported by the estimated high cost–benefit ratios in GWRDC research programmes (McLeod 2002). Similarly, costs in extending and adopting research outcomes are not considered. For example, in the case of implementing quality enhancing technologies, there may be extra costs in switching to different grape varieties or clones or buying new equipment for wineries.

The results suggest that the major direct winners from R&D within the grape and wine industry's markets will be producers, and more so as the industry becomes increasingly export focused over the next decade. This contrasts with findings for other industries: according to Baumol (2002), on average across all USA industries, producers receive only approximately one-quarter of the benefits from R&D. In addition, even though growers and winemakers contribute approximately 50% of the R&D funds in the form of statutory levies, they eventually offload some of the burden to consumers through the incidence of the levy, with the proportions as estimated in the first two columns of Table 3 (which includes overseas consumers, incidently). So the producers' real contribution is significantly less than 50% (Zhao 2002). From an Australian national point of view, producer levy funding of R&D has the advantage of making overseas consumers share the incidence of costs, as well as the benefits, of research.

Finally, with the industry reconsidering the R&D levy in light of the apparently high rewards from research to date (McLeod 2002) and the fact that the current levy is well below the 0.5% threshold that attracts maximum government matching funds, now is the time to question the method of levying in addition to raising its level. To date, it has been a weight-based measure, so research intensity has declined as a percentage of the gross value of production over the past decade as the price of wine has risen with quality improvements and with increased demand in export markets. One way to prevent this continuing is to switch to a value-based *ad valorem* levy rate.[13] In addition, because much of the R&D and promotion is focused on premium products, whereas non-premium producers pay a significant amount of the costs through the gravimetric levy, such a change would seem to be a more equitable way to levy producers.

References

Alston, J.M. and Scobie, G.M. 1983, 'Distribution of research gains in multistage production systems: comment', *American Journal of Agricultural Economics*, vol. 65, pp. 353–356.

Alston, J.M., Chalfant, J.A. and Piggott, N.E. 1999, *Advertising and Consumer Welfare*, CIES Discussion Paper 99/09, University of Adelaide.

Alston, J.M., Freebairn, J.W. and James, J.S. 2002, '(Some of) the economics of levy-funded research', presented at the Agricultural Research Conference in Honour of John Dillon, University of New England, Armidale, 20 September.

Alston, J.M., Norton, G.W and Pardey, P.G. 1995, *Science Under Scarcity: Principles and Practice for Agricultural Research Evaluation and Priority Setting*, Cornell University Press, Ithaca.

Anderson, K. 2004, 'The Internationalization of Australia's Wine Industry', in K. Anderson (ed.), *The World's Wine Markets*, Ch. 13, Edward Elgar, London.

Anderson, K. and Nielsen, C. 2002, 'Economic effects of agricultural biotechnology research in the presence of price-distorting policies', presented at the Agricultural Research Conference in Honour of John Dillon, University of New England, Armidale, 20 September. Since published in *Journal of Economic Integration*, vol. 19(2): 374–94, June 2004.

Anderson, K. and Norman, D. 2001, *Global Wine Production, Consumption and Trade, 1961–99: A Statistical Compendium*. Centre for International Economic Studies, Adelaide University, Adelaide.

Anderson, K., Norman D. and Wittwer G. 2004, 'Globalization in the world's wine markets', in K. Anderson (ed.), *The World's Wine Markets*, Ch. 1, Edward Elgar, London.

---

[13] See James and Alston (2002) for a discussion of the impacts of *ad valorem* versus per unit taxes for quality differentiated products.

Australian Bureau of Statistics (ABS) 2001, *Australian Grape and Wine Industry*, Australian Bureau of Statistics, Cat. no. 1329.0, Canberra.
Australian Wine and Brandy Corporation (AWBC) 2001, *Annual Report 2000–01*, Australian Wine and Brandy Corporation, Adelaide.
Baumol, W.J. 2002, *The Free-Market Innovation Machine*, Princeton University Press, Princeton.
Byerlee, D. and Anderson, J.R. 2002, 'Contemporary challenges in impact assessment of agricultural research programs', presented at the Agricultural Research Conference in Honour of John Dillon, University of New England, Armidale, 20 September.
Chambers, R.G. 1991, *Applied Production Analysis: A Dual Approach*, Cambridge University Press, Cambridge.
Diewert, W.E. 1981, 'The comparative statics of industry long-run equilibrium', *Canadian Journal of Economics*, vol. 14, pp. 78–92.
Dixit, A. and Norman, V.D. 1979, 'Advertising and welfare: Reply', *Bell Journal of Economics*, vol. 10, pp. 728–729.
Dixon, P.D. and Rimmer, M.T. 2002, *Dynamic, General Equilibrium Modelling for Forecasting and Policy: A Practical Guide and Documentation of MONASH*, North-Holland, Amsterdam.
Freebairn, J.W., Davis J.S. and Edwards G.W. 1982, 'Distribution of research gains in multistage production systems', *American Journal of Agricultural Economics*, vol. 64, pp. 39–46.
Grape and Wine Research and Development Corporation 2001, *Annual Operational Plan 2000/2001*, Grape and Wine Research and Development Corporation, Adelaide.
Holloway, G.J. 1989, 'Distribution of research gains in multistage production systems: Further results', *American Journal of Agricultural Economics*, vol. 71, pp. 338–343.
James, J. and Alston, J. 2002, 'Taxes and quality: A market-level analysis', *Australian Journal of Agricultural and Resource Economics*, vol. 46, pp. 417–445.
Lindner, R.J. and Jarrett, F.G. 1978, 'Supply shifts and the size of research benefits', *American Journal of Agricultural Economics*, vol. 60, pp. 48–58.
McLeod, R. 2002, *Ex Ante and Ex Post Cost Benefit Analysis of the GWRDC's Project Portfolio*, Grape and Wine Research and Development Corporation, Adelaide.
Mullen, J.D., Alston, J.M. and Wohlgenant, M.K. 1989, 'The impact of farm and processing research on the Australian wool industry', *Australian Journal of Agricultural Economics*, vol. 33, pp. 32–47.
Winemakers' Federation of Australia and Australian Wine and Brandy Corporation 2001, *The Marketing Decade: Setting the Australian Wine Marketing Agenda 2000–10*, Winemakers' Federation of Australia and Australian Wine and Brandy Corporation, Adelaide.
Wittwer, G. and Anderson, K. 2002, 'Impact of the GST and wine tax reform on Australia's wine industry: A CGE analysis', *Australian Economic Papers*, vol. 41, pp. 69–81.
Wittwer, G., Berger, N. and Anderson, K. 2003, 'A model of the world's wine markets', *Economic Modelling*, vol. 20, pp. 487–506.

Wohlgenant, M.K. 1989, 'Demand for farm output in a complete system of demand functions', *American Journal of Agricultural Economics*, vol. 71, pp. 241–252.

Wohlgenant, M.K. 1993, 'Distribution of gains from research and promotion in multistage production systems: The case of the US beef and pork industries', *American Journal of Agricultural Economics*, vol. 75, pp. 642–651.

Zhao, X. 2002, 'Who bears the burden and who receives the gain? The case of GWRDC R&D investments in the Australian grape and wine industry', *Proceedings of the NEC-63 Conference*, Washington DC, 21–22 October.

Zhao, X., Griffiths, W., Griffith, G. and Mullen, J. 2000a, 'Probability distributions for economic surplus changes: The case of technical change in the Australian wool industry', *Australian Journal of Agricultural and Resource Economics*, vol. 44, pp. 83–106.

Zhao, X., Mullen J., Griffith G., Griffiths W and Piggott R. 2000b, 'An equilibrium displacement model of the Australian beef industry', *Economics Research Report*, no. 4, NSW Agriculture, Orange.

Appendix
The model in equilibrium-displacement form

In the following, $E(.) = \Delta(.)/(.)$ represents a small relative change of a variable $(.)$.

Input supply to premium wine and non-premium wine sectors

$$EX_p = \varepsilon_{(Xp,wp)}(Ew_p - t_{Xp}) + \varepsilon_{(Xp,wmp)}(Ew_{mp} - t_{Xmp}) \quad (1')$$

$$EX_p = \rho_{Xp1}EX_{p1} + \rho_{Xnp1}EX_{np1} \quad (2')$$

where $\rho_{Xp1} = X_{p1}/(X_{p1} + X_{np1})$ and $\rho_{Xnp1} = X_{p1}/(X_{p1} + X_{np1})$ are quantity shares.

$$EX_{p2} = \varepsilon_{(Xp2,wp2)}(Ew_{p2} - t_{Xp2}) \quad (3')$$

$$EX_{p3} = \varepsilon_{(Xp3,wp3)}(Ew_{p3} - t_{Xp3}) \quad (4')$$

$$EX_{mp} = \varepsilon_{(Xmp,wmp)}(Ew_{mp} - t_{Xmp}) + \varepsilon_{(Xmp,wp)}(Ew_p - t_{Xp}) \quad (5')$$

$$EX_{mp} = \rho_{np2}EX_{np2} + \rho_{Xdtd}EX_{dtd} + \rho_{Xdte}EX_{dte} \quad (6')$$

where $\rho_{Xnp2} = X_{np2}/(X_{np2} + X_{dt})$ and $\rho_{Xdt} = X_{dt}/(X_{np2} + X_{dt})$ are quantity shares.

$$EX_{np3} = \varepsilon_{(Xnp3, wnp3)} \left(Ew_{np3} - t_{Xnp3} \right) \tag{7'}$$

$$EX_{np4} = \varepsilon_{(Xnp4, wnp4)} \left(Ew_{np4} - t_{Xnp4} \right) \tag{8'}$$

Demand for drying and table grapes

$$EX_{dtd} = \eta_{(Xdtd, wmp)} \left(Ew_{mp} - n_{Xdtd} \right) \tag{9'}$$

$$EX_{dte} = \eta_{(Xdte, wdte)} \left(Ew_{mp} - n_{Xdte} \right) \tag{10'}$$

Output-constrained input demand of the premium wine sector

$$EX_{p1} = -\left(\kappa_{p2}\sigma_{(Xp1,Xp2)} + \kappa_{p3}\sigma_{(Xp1,Xp3)} \right) Ew_{p} + \kappa_{p2}\sigma_{(Xp1,Xp2)} Ew_{p2}$$
$$+ \kappa_{p3}\sigma_{(Xp1,Xp3)} Ew_{p3} + EY_{p} \tag{11'}$$

$$EX_{p2} = \kappa_{p1}\sigma_{(Xp1,Xp2)} Ew_{p} - \left(\kappa_{p1}\sigma_{(Xp1,Xp2)} + \kappa_{p3}\sigma_{(Xp2,Xp3)} \right) Ew_{p2}$$
$$+ \kappa_{p3}\sigma_{(Xp2,Xp3)} Ew_{p3} + EY_{p} \tag{12'}$$

$$EX_{p3} = \kappa_{p1}\sigma_{(Xp1,Xp3)} Ew_{p} + \kappa_{p2}\sigma_{(Xp2,Xp3)} Ew_{p2}$$
$$- \left(\kappa_{p1}\sigma_{(Xp1,Xp3)} + \kappa_{p2}\sigma_{(Xp2,Xp3)} \right) Ew_{p3} + EY_{p} \tag{13'}$$

Output-constrained input demand of the non-premium wine sector

$$EX_{np1} = -\left(\kappa_{np2}\sigma_{(Xnp1,Xnp2)} + \kappa_{np3}\sigma_{(Xnp1,Xnp3)} + \kappa_{np4}\sigma_{(Xnp1,Xnp4)} \right) Ew_{p}$$
$$+ \kappa_{np2}\sigma_{(Xnp1,Xnp2)} W_{mp} + \kappa_{np3}\sigma_{(Xnp1,Xnp2)} Ew_{np3}$$
$$+ \kappa_{np4}\sigma_{(Xnp1,Xnp4)} Ew_{np4} + EY_{np} \tag{14'}$$

$$EX_{np2} = -\left(\kappa_{np1}\sigma_{(Xnp1,Xnp2)} + \kappa_{np3}\sigma_{(Xnp2,Xnp3)} + \kappa_{np4}\sigma_{(Xnp2,Xnp4)} \right) Ew_{mp}$$
$$+ \kappa_{np1}\sigma_{(Xnp1,Xnp2)} W_{P} + \kappa_{np3}\sigma_{(Xnp2,Xnp3)} Ew_{np3}$$
$$+ \kappa_{np4}\sigma_{(Xnp2,Xnp4)} Ew_{np4} + EY_{np} \tag{15'}$$

$$EX_{np3} = -\left(\kappa_{np1}\sigma_{(Xnp1,Xnp3)} + \kappa_{np2}\sigma_{(Xnp2,Xnp3)} + \kappa_{np4}\sigma_{(Xnp3,Xnp4)}\right)Ew_{np3}$$
$$+ \kappa_{np1}\sigma_{(Xnp1,Xnp3)}W_P + \kappa_{np2}\sigma_{(Xnp2,Xnp3)}Ew_{mp}$$
$$+ \kappa_{np4}\sigma_{(Xnp3,Xnp4)}Ew_{np4} + EY_{np} \quad (16')$$

$$EX_{np4} = -\left(\kappa_{np1}\sigma_{(Xnp1,Xnp4)} + \kappa_{np2}\sigma_{(Xnp2,Xnp4)} + \kappa_{np3}\sigma_{(Xnp3,Xnp4)}\right)Ew_{np4}$$
$$+ \kappa_{np1}\sigma_{(Xnp1Xnp4)}W_P + \kappa_{np2}\sigma_{(Xnp2,Xnp4)}Ew_{mp}$$
$$+ \kappa_{np3}\sigma_{(Xnp3,Xnp4)}Ew_{np3} + EY_{np} \quad (17')$$

Market-clearing condition/supply of premium and non-premium wholesale wine

$$Ev_p = \kappa_{p1}Ew_p + \kappa_{p2}Ew_{p2} + \kappa_{p3}Ew_{p3} \quad (18')$$

$$Ev_{np} = \kappa_{np1}Ew_p + \kappa_{np2}Ew_{mp} + \kappa_{np3}Ew_{np3} + \kappa_{np4}Ew_{np4} \quad (19')$$

Destination of wine at the cellar door

$$EY_p = \theta_{pd}EY_{pd1} + \theta_{pe}EY_{pe1} \quad (20')$$

$$EY_{np} = \theta_{npd}EY_{npd1} + \theta_{npe}EY_{npe} \quad (21')$$

Supply of wine marketing inputs

$$EY_{pd2} = \varepsilon_{(Ypd2,vpd2)}\left(Ev_{pd2} - t_{Ypd2}\right) \quad (22')$$

$$EY_{pe2} = \varepsilon_{(Ype2,vpe2)}\left(Ev_{pe2} - t_{Ype2}\right) \quad (23')$$

$$EY_{npd2} = \varepsilon_{(Ynpd2,vnpd2)}\left(Ev_{npd2} - t_{Ynpd2}\right) \quad (24')$$

Output-constrained input demand of the wine marketing sectors

$$EY_{pd1} = -\lambda_{pd2}\sigma_{(Ypd1,Ypd2)}Ev_p + \lambda_{pd2}\sigma_{(Ypd1,Ypd2)}Ev_{pd2} + EQ_{pd} \quad (25')$$

$$EY_{pd2} = \lambda_{pd1}\sigma_{(Ypd1,Ypd2)}Ev_P - \lambda_{pd1}\sigma_{(Ypd1,Ypd2)}Ev_{pd2} + EQ_{pd} \quad (26')$$

$$EY_{pe1} = -\lambda_{pe2}\sigma_{(Ype1,Ype2)}Ev_p + \lambda_{pe2}\sigma_{(Ype1,Ype2)}Ev_{pe2} + EQ_{pe} \quad (27')$$

$$EY_{pe2} = \lambda_{pe1}\sigma_{(Ype1,Ype2)}Ev_p - \lambda_{pe1}\sigma_{(Ype1,Ype2)}Ev_{pe2} + EQ_{pe} \quad (28')$$

$$EY_{npd1} = -\lambda_{npd2}\sigma_{(Ynpd1,Ynpd2)}Ev_{np} + \lambda_{npd2}\sigma_{(Ynpd1,Ynpd2)}Ev_{npd2} + EQ_{npd} \quad (29')$$

$$EY_{npd2} = \lambda_{npd1}\sigma_{(Ynpd1,Ynpd2)}Ev_{np} - \lambda_{npd1}\sigma_{(Ynpd1,Ynpd2)}Ev_{npd2} + EQ_{npd} \quad (30')$$

Market-clearing condition for the marketing sectors

$$Ep_{pd} = \lambda_{pd1}Ev_p + \lambda_{pd2}Ev_{pd2} \quad (31')$$

$$Ep_{pe} = \lambda_{pe1}Ev_p + \lambda_{pe2}Ev_{pe2} \quad (32')$$

$$Ep_{npd} = \lambda_{npd1}Ev_{np} + \lambda_{npd2}Ev_{npd2} \quad (33')$$

Final demand for wine

$$EY_{npe} = \eta_{(Ynpe,vnpe)}(Ev_{np} - n_{Ynpe}) \quad (34')$$

$$EQ_{pd} = \eta_{(Qpd,ppd)}(Ep_{pd} - n_{Qpd}) + \eta_{(Qpd,pnpd)}(Ep_{npd} - n_{Qnpd}) \quad (35')$$

$$EQ_{pe} = \eta_{(Qpe,ppe)}(Ep_{pe} - n_{Qpe}) \quad (36')$$

$$EQ_{npd} = \eta_{(Qnpd,ppd)}(Ep_{pd} - n_{Qpd}) + \eta_{(Qnpd,pnpd)}(Ep_{npd} - n_{Qnpd}) \quad (37')$$

Chapter 10

Wine Quality and Varietal, Regional and Winery Reputations: Hedonic Prices for Australia and New Zealand*

Günter Schamel[†] and Kym Anderson[‡]

We estimate hedonic price functions for premium wine from Australia and New Zealand, differentiating implicit prices for sensory quality ratings, wine varieties and regional as well as winery brand reputations over the vintages 1992–2000. The results show regional reputations have become increasingly differentiated through time (although less so for

---

*First published in *The Economic Record* 79(246): 357–69, September 2003. Thanks are due to the editor, referees and numerous colleagues for comments on earlier drafts presented at the AARES Conference in Adelaide in January 2001, the Enometrics VIII Conference in the Napa Valley in May 2001, and the CIES Workshop on Understanding Developments in the World's Wine Markets in Adelaide in October 2001; to Australia's Grape and Wine Research and Development Corporation, Rural Industries Research and Development Corporation, and the Australian Research Council as well as the German Academic Exchange Service (DAAD) for financial support; and to James Halliday and Peter Simic for kindly providing their very extensive tastings databases.

†Humboldt-University, Berlin, Germany

‡University of Adelaide, Adelaide, Australia

New Zealand). In particular, cool-climate regions are becoming increasingly preferred over other regions in Australia. In each country, price premia associated with both James Halliday's and Winestate magazine's sensory quality ratings, and with Halliday's winery ratings and classic wine designations, are highly significant.

1. Introduction

For more than a decade the wine industry has been booming in Australia and New Zealand. Both the area planted to vineyards and the volume of premium wine produced have grown at 7+ per cent per year on average since 1990, while the two countries' exports of wine have been growing at 15+ per cent per year (from a low base). Simultaneously, wine exports from California, South Africa and Chile have been soaring, such that the share of global wine production that is exported has risen from 15 to 30 per cent in just a dozen years. Yet per capita wine consumption has grown little in Australia and New Zealand and has been falling steadily in the traditional wine-consuming countries of Europe and the southern cone of Latin America, more than offsetting demand growth in the UK, the US, and (from a tiny base) East Asia (Anderson & Norman 2003). In each of these markets, however, there has been a dramatic substitution of quality for quantity: premium (bottled) wine sales are growing steadily while non-premium (cask) sales are declining (Anderson 2003; Anderson et al. 2003).

With global demand static and export supplies expanding rapidly, the average price of internationally traded wine is bound to come under pressure to decline in the coming years. In this more-competitive and more-globalised environment, the extent to which the price declines (or rises) for a particular group of producers will depend very much on the quality upgrading of its product absolutely, and relative to that of other producer groups, as perceived by consumers at home and abroad. This raises the question of what determines consumers' perceptions of quality when they buy newly released wine.

Many consumers, especially when they are new and inexperienced, are looking for guidance before purchasing wines. Often they are unsure about the quality of a wine they intend to purchase and turn to the published ratings of wine experts for guidance. This begs the question as to how expert ratings, in addition to grape variety and regional reputations, affect the price of wine. What are consumers willing to pay for such things as the reputation of the producing region as distinct from corporate brand reputation, or grape variety reputation, or the published ratings of wine writers/judges/critics; and how has that willingness to pay evolved over time?

This paper addresses this question as it relates to Australian and New Zealand wines, using a hedonic pricing model. Our analysis extends previous studies in a number of ways. First, we simultaneously examine two very large data samples of quality ratings (Halliday 2001 and Winestate 2001), each drawn from the same base population of wines and consumers, which enables us to make direct comparisons between them. Second, we are able to expose changes in reputations over the past decade when wine markets changed dramatically. Finally, we include indicators for sensory quality, producer reputation, variety, and regional origin for not only Australia but also New Zealand, which allows us to directly compare both countries on various grounds (e.g. regional and variety differentials).

The paper is structured as follows. In section 2 we briefly review the literature on hedonic pricing models and their application to wine. Section 3 presents the model and the two different data sets used in the analysis. Section 4 details our empirical results for the markets in Australia and New Zealand separately over nine vintages. The final section summarises what has been learnt and suggests areas for further research.

2. Previous studies

A number of studies apply hedonic price analysis to estimate implicit prices for wine quality attributes.[1] They are based on the hypothesis that any product represents a bundle of characteristics that define quality. Their theoretical foundation is provided in the seminal paper by Rosen (1974), which posits that goods are valued for their utility-generating attributes.

---

[1] This is to be distinguished from consumer perceptions over time of the changing quality of ultra-premium wines as they mature in bottle following the initial sale by the winery, as captured by time series of prices in the secondary auction markets. According to Ashenfelter (2000), Ashenfelter et al. (1995), Byron and Ashenfelter (1995) and Wood and Anderson (2002), key determinants of the vintage-to-vintage variation in the quality of maturing wines are a few straightforward weather variables in the growing season — information that consumers appear to have ignored in the past.

Rosen suggests there are competitive implicit markets that define implicit prices for embodied product attributes, and that consumers evaluate product attributes when making a purchasing decision. The observed market price is the sum of implicit prices paid for each quality attribute.

Since the quality of a particular bottle of wine cannot be known until it is de-corked and consumed, consumers' willingness to pay depends on reputations associated with that wine. In addition to quality ratings, consumers' perceptions of a wine's quality depends on producer reputation, the collective reputation of the wine region of production, and the grape variety (or varieties) used. Shapiro (1983) presents a theoretical framework to examine the effects of individual producer reputation on prices. He develops an equilibrium price–quality schedule for high-quality products, assuming competitive markets and imperfect consumer information, to demonstrate that reputation allows high-quality producers to sell their items at a premium that may be interpreted as a return from producer investments in building reputation. On the demand side of the market, too, it is costly for consumers to improve their information about product quality. In such an environment of imperfect information, learning about the reputation of a product or of some of its attributes can be an effective way for consumers to become better informed. A favourable producer or winery rating assigned by a wine expert, for example, may serve as a way to reduce consumers' decision-making costs.

Tirole (1996) presents a model of collective reputation as an aggregate of individual reputations where current producer incentives are affected by their own actions as well as collective actions of the past. He shows that new producers may suffer from past mistakes of older producers for a long time after the latter disappear, and derives conditions under which the collective reputation in such cases can be regained. A favourable collective reputation of a particular wine region relative to other regions may provide another effective means of reducing consumers' decision-making costs.

Roberts and Reagans (2001) examine market experience, consumer attention, and price–quality relationships for New World wines in the United States market. They argue that the attention paid to wine quality signals increases with the market experience of its producer and, because of spillover effects, with the experience of associated producers.

Schamel (2000) estimates a hedonic pricing model based on United States data for sensory quality ratings, individual wine quality and regional reputation indicators for two premium wine varieties: a white

(Chardonnay) and a red (Cabernet Sauvignon). That paper examines seven regions (Napa and Sonoma Valley, Sonoma County, Oregon, Washington State, Australia, Chile, South Africa) and includes observations from a pool of eight vintages between 1988 and 1995. However, it does not estimate coefficients for individual vintages. The estimated price elasticity of sensory quality is larger for white than red wine, but both regional reputation and individual quality indicators seem to be more important to red wine consumers in the United States. The results also suggest that the marketing of regional origin as a reputation attribute may have a higher payoff for regions primarily growing red wine.

Because wine consumers are uncertain about quality, we assume that, in addition to their own quality perceptions about grape varieties and growing regions, they use expert quality ratings for the wine and/or the winery in their buying decisions. Thus, consumer willingness to pay for a particular wine depends on a critic's quality rating of the wine and /or the producer, as well as their own reputation assessment for grape varieties and growing regions expressed through premia or discounts relative to a base region and variety. The present paper analyses such quality and reputation indicators for premium wines from Australia and New Zealand. For each country, we examine Halliday's (1999 and 2001) data sets for nine vintages. Moreover, we analyse a second data set with more than 12 500 tasting scores for premium wines for the same two countries and up to eight vintages (Winestate 2001). This enables us to compare hedonic pricing model results for two different data sets drawn from the same base population of wines and consumers and for the same vintages.

3. The data and hedonic price model

3.1. *The data*

In Table 1, we provide an overview of the data set from the well-known Australian wine critic James Halliday,[2] which we use to estimate the first

---

[2] Halliday data are made publicly available in annual books (see Halliday, 2001 and earlier editions). We were kindly provided with an integrated database for the whole period, however, which minimises any inconsistencies from one yearbook to the next. There was of course some inflation over the 1990s (though much less than in earlier decades), but that is not a major problem in this study as we assess each vintage separately rather than pool the series.

Table 1. Description of James Halliday's (JH) data set

Variable
Dependent Variable: Log(Price), Range A$5–300, NZ$7–90
Vintage Rating: 100-Point Scale, Range 70–97
Winery Rating: 5-Star Rating, Range 2.5–5 (NR = 2)
Classic Wine: 1 = Classic Rating; 2 = Not
Variety Dummies: Red
Cabernet Sauvignon
Cabernet Blends
Shiraz† (AUS)
Shiraz Blends (AUS)
Pinot Noir
Merlot (NZ)
Other Red
Variety Dummies: White
Chardonnay‡
Riesling
Gewurztraminer (NZ)
Sauvignon Blanc
Semillon (AUS)
Sweet White
Other White
Regional Dummies: South Australia
Adelaide Hills
Barossa Valley†
Clare Valley
Coonawarra
Eden Valley
McLaren Vale
Other SA
Regional Dummies: ACT and NSW
Canberra
Hunter Valley
Mudgee
Riverina
Other NSW
Regional Dummies: Victoria
Bendigo
Goulburn Valley
Grampians
Macedon Ranges
Mornington Peninsula
Pyrenees

(*Continued*)

Table 1. (*Continued*)

Variable
Yarra Valley
Other Vic.
Regional Dummies: Western Australia
Great Southern
Perth
Margaret River
Other WA
Regional Dummies: Tasmania and Queensland
Northern Tasmania
Southern Tasmania
Queensland
Regional Dummies: New Zealand
Auckland
Canterbury
Hawke's Bay
Marlborough‡
Wairarapa
Other NZ

† (Aus) and ‡ (NZ) indicate the reference dummies, which we dropped from the regressions.

set of hedonic price equations for each vintage from 1992 (1993 in the case of New Zealand) to 2000. The set includes 6866 observations from Australia and 1531 from New Zealand. For the Australian sample, the average quality rating is 87.2 points (range 70–97) and the average price is A$23.81 (range A$5–300). For New Zealand, the average quality rating is 88.6 points (range 73–97) and the average price is NZ$23.25 (range NZ$7–90). Halliday's value of sensory wine quality is defined by the variable *vintage rating* (100-point scale). He also provides a *winery rating* (2.5–5 stars) of the producer as a supplier of premium wine, and a *classic wine* classification in recognition of an outstanding wine. To evaluate differences in the willingness to pay for different grape varieties, we distinguish six different red and six white wine varieties or variety groupings, respectively. In order to assess the value of regional denominations in Halliday's sample, we distinguish wines from 27 different regions in Australia as well as six different regions in New Zealand. Separate equations are estimated for Australia and New Zealand. The endogenous variable (the tax-inclusive recommended retail price) is expressed in local dollars per 750 mL bottle.

Table 2 provides an analogous overview of our second data source from Australia's popular wine magazine *Winestate*.[3] It provides wine ratings for 12 625 combined observations for Australia and New Zealand. In contrast to the 100-point scale for sensory wine quality adopted by Halliday, *Winestate* uses a 5-star rating scheme, assigning between 3 and 5 stars but also using half-stars. (Some wines have no rating at all, which presumably implies less than 3 stars, so we assigned 2.5 stars for all non-rated wines.) For simplicity, we have given two points for every star, to avoid using decimals. From the *Winestate* tastings, a consistent set is available for each vintage from 1992 to 1999 (1994–99 in the case of New Zealand), amounting to 11 251 observations from Australia and 1374 from New Zealand. For the Australian sample, the average quality rating is 3.25 stars and the average price is A$19.56 (range A$5–385). For New Zealand, the average quality rating is 3.44 stars and the average price is NZ$20.59 (range NZ$9–90). In order to assess regional denominations, the *Winestate* sample allows us to distinguish 28 different regions for Australia and six different regions for New Zealand.

3.2. The model

Following conventional hedonic models, we propose that a bundle of quality attributes defines any premium wine. Consumer willingness to pay is a function of that bundle of wine quality attributes. In addition to wine experts' sensory quality ratings of a particular wine, of each vintage and of the winery producing it (such ratings books are commonly available for perusal in wine shops), willingness to pay for a wine also reflects consumers' perception of the varietal reputation and the reputation of the

---

[3] As pointed out by Oczkowski (1994; footnote 4), *Winestate* uses a panel of judges that changes over time and so it provides a less consistent set of assessments than that provided by Halliday. It also includes a value-for-money consideration in its ratings. Even so, we thought it was worth doing the comparative analysis to see to what extent the *Winestate* data support the findings based on Halliday's data.

Table 2. Description of the Winestate (WS) data set

Variable
Dependent Variable: Log(Price), Range A$5–385, NZ$9–90
Star Rating: 3, $3\frac{1}{2}$, 4, $4\frac{1}{2}$, 5 Stars (NR = $2\frac{1}{2}$)
Point Rating: Conversion of star rating to a 10-Point Scale, Range 5–10
Variety Dummies: Red
Cabernet Sauvignon
Cabernet Blends
Shiraz†
Shiraz Blends (AUS)
Pinot Noir
Merlot
Other Red
Variety Dummies: White
Chardonnay‡
Riesling
Sauvignon Blanc
Semillon
Sweet White (AUS)
Other White
Regional Dummies: South Australia
Adelaide Hills
Barossa Valley†
Clare Valley
Coonawarra
Eden Valley
McLaren Vale
Other Limestone Coast
Riverland
Langhorne Creek
Other SA
Regional Dummies: ACT and NSW
Canberra
Hunter Valley
Mudgee
Riverina
Other NSW
Regional Dummies: Victoria
Goulburn Valley
Mornington Peninsula
Rutherglen

(*Continued*)

Table 2. (*Continued*)

Variable
King Valley
Yarra Valley
Central & West Vic.
Other Vic.
Regional Dummies: Western Australia
Great Southern
Perth
Margaret River
Other WA
Regional Dummies: Tasmania and Queensland
Tasmania
Queensland
Regional Dummies: New Zealand
Auckland
Canterbury
Hawke's Bay
Marlborough‡
Nelson
Other NZ

† (Aus) and ‡ (NZ) indicate the reference dummies, which we dropped from the regressions.

producing region. An individual quality indicator such as a classic wine rating assigned by wine critics may also affect buying decisions.

Hedonic price analysis relates the price of a good to its utility-generating characteristics, and generates implicit prices for these characteristics. Thus, any quantitative or qualitative variable that affects consumer utility may be included in a hedonic price function. We formulate a model assuming that consumers, uncertain about the true sensory quality of a particular wine, adjust their willingness to pay using expert ratings of wine quality (vintage ratings) and of the wine producer as well as their own perception of varietal and regional reputations.[4]

The theoretical model described above limits the type of explanatory variables, but it does not restrict the functional form to be esti-

---

[4] Previous studies have included other variables such as cellaring potential, year of marketing and producer size (see, e.g. Oczkowski 1994). We did not have such variables available for our full time series, so cannot expect as high an adjusted R^2 value.

mated. In the empirical literature on hedonic wine pricing, a variety of different functional forms have been explored and reported. For example, Landon and Smith (1997) examine five different functions choosing the reciprocal square root form, Oczkowski (1994) reports a log-linear form, and Nerlove (1995) compares log-linear, log-log and Box-Cox transformations. The log-linear form has been applied in a number of published studies, including Oczkowski (1994, 2001), Nerlove (1995), and Combris *et al.* (1997). In our case, following Oczkowski, the results of applying a RESET-test to the linear, log-linear, and log-log functional forms lead us to prefer the log- linear specification, with log(Price) as the dependent variable (see Table 3). An examination of the correlation matrices for the coefficient estimates suggests that no serious degree of multicollinearity is present in the data. Moreover, we take note of the point stressed by Oczkowski (2001) that serious correlation between a single measure quality regressor and the error term would point to measurement errors and lead to inconsistent OLS (ordinary least squares) estimates. To test for that, we conducted a standard Hausman test using the average of the quality ratings

Table 3. RESET F-test statistics

Form	Sample	2000	1999	1998	1997	1996	1995	1994	1993	1992
Log-Linear	JH AUS	6.14*	6.65*	29.8	22.9	62.4	52.4	26.3	18.2	6.68*
	JH NZ	0.58**	7.70	6.23*	12.93	6.64*	8.91	1.89**	0.36**	—
	WS AUS	—	0.16**	0.30**	4.73*	19.6	0.04**	6.17*	4.99*	0.09**
	WS NZ	—	1.76**	1.60**	1.42**	2.37**	0.22**	0.04**	—	—
Log-Log	JH AUS	7.41	11.0	29.8	22.4	53.2	54.0	29.7	19.6	7.50
	JH NZ	0.55**	13.1	6.33*	14.3	6.73*	11.2	2.18**	0.38**	—
	WS AUS	—	0.08**	0.38**	5.02*	20.4	0.002**	5.46*	5.22*	0.18**
	WS NZ	—	0.35**	2.40**	0.74**	1.55**	2.05**	0.18**	0.09**	—
Linear	JH AUS	26.0	59.1	152.3	82.5	154.9	131.3	97.3	58.6	39.4
	JH NZ	0.09**	23.2	34.1	70.6	52.2	72.7	12.6	1.50**	—
	WS AUS	—	9.47	18.5	19.3	45.5	17.7	185.9	26.7	39.9
	WS NZ	—	2.05**	7.24	11.7	0.05**	1.05**	0.14**	—	—

**, * indicate significance at least at the 10 per cent and 1 per cent levels, respectively. JH, James Halliday; WS, *Winestate* magazine.

Table 4. Hausman χ^2-test statistics

Form	Sample	2000	1999	1998	1997	1996	1995	1994	1993	1992
Log-Linear	JH AUS	7.74	3.58**	15.4	5.81*	2.13***	2.42***	4.41*	0.28***	2.18***
	JH NZ	5.20*	1.35***	3.65**	6.61*	2.69***	0.54***	0.047***	2.60***	—
	WS AUS	—	0.52***	10.12	7.90	6.07*	29.4	16.7	8.72	0.51***
	WS NZ	—	3.18**	0.90**	0.002***	5.80*	0.08***	2.47***	—	—

***, **, * indicate significance at least at the 10 per cent, 5 per cent, 1 per cent level, respectively. JH, James Halliday; WS, *Winestate* magazine.

for each producer label as an instrumental variables.[5] As is clear from Table 4, where more than 30 subsets of data are shown, only in five cases were the results significant at the 1 per cent level and another five at the 5 per cent level. We therefore conclude that in this study we do not have a serious problem of dependence between the quality ratings and the error term.

4. What do the results show?

4.1. *Australia*

Tables 5 and 6 present the estimation results for Australia from the Halliday and *Winestate* samples, respectively. Shiraz and Barossa Valley are chosen as the comparator variety and region (necessary to avoid the dummy variable trap). Thus, all coefficients are relative to what a Shiraz produced in the Barossa Valley would sell for. The columns show the estimation results for each of the eight or nine subsamples of individual vintages. For the Halliday sample, the coefficients for 'vintage rating' and 'winery rating' measure the percentage price premia for a one-point increase in the 100-point scale, respectively. The dummy variable coefficients for variety and regional origin can be interpreted as a percentage price impact relative to a Barossa Valley Shiraz. The coefficient for 'classic wine' reports the percentage price premium for a wine that obtained this special recognition.

---

[5] There are 765 (923) different producers in the Halliday (*Winestate*) sample for Australia. For New Zealand, there are 203 (205) different producers in the Halliday (Winestate) data set.

Table 5. Regression results for Australia (Halliday data set)

Parameter	2000	1999	1998	1997	1996	1995	1994	1993	1992
CONSTANT	0.931*	−0.353	−0.734*	0.093	0.491**	0.503**	0.639**	0.340	−0.337
Vintage Rating	0.023*	0.036*	0.041*	0.032*	0.028*	0.029*	0.025*	0.029*	0.038*
Winery Rating	0.021	0.046*	0.051*	0.055**	0.093*	0.069*	0.093*	0.075**	0.082***
Classic Wine	0.066	0.055	0.159*	0.271*	0.235*	0.259*	0.281*	0.361=	0.275*
Cabernet Sauvignon	−0.243	0.034	−0.045	0.003	−0.059	−0.118**	−0.036	−0.104***	−0.020
Cabernet Blends	−0.444*	0.012	−0.070***	−0.038	−0.065	0.000	0.025	0.013	0.022
Pinot Noir	−0.223**	0.060	0.040	−0.013	−0.086	−0.092	−0.029	0.145	0.245
Shiraz Blends	−0.099	−0.111***	−0.133**	−0.038	−0.110	−0.236*	−0.278*	−0.322*	−0.302**
Other Red	−0.347*	0.073***	−0.009	0.008	−0.110**	−0.110***	−0.136***	−0.119	0.018
Chardonnay	−0.288*	−0.070**	−0.160*	−0.174*	−0.250*	−0.219*	−0.176*	−0.103***	−0.051
Riesling	−0.420*	−0.339*	−0.531*	−0.471*	−0.597*	−0.581*	−0.537*	−0.379*	−0.505*
Sauvignon Blanc	−0.336*	−0.178*	−0.318*	−0.290*	−0.421*	−0.391*	−0.334*	−0.631***	−0.406
Semillon	−0.324*	−0.187*	−0.316*	−0.356*	−0.446*	−0.421*	−0.419*	−0.368*	−0.302
Sweet White	−0.322**	−0.152**	−0.102	−0.337*	−0.375*	−0.200	−0.205	−0.359*	−0.457**
Other White	−0.316*	−0.183*	−0.382*	−0.353*	−0.423*	−0.513*	−0.447*	−0.466*	−0.186
Great Southern	0.267*	0.094	0.163*	0.192*	0.016	−0.087	−0.004	−0.015	−0.191
Perth	0.086	−0.070	−0.001	0.022	−0.293*	−0.088	−0.243**	−0.151	−0.115

(*Continued*)

Table 5. (*Continued*)

Parameter	2000	1999	1998	1997	1996	1995	1994	1993	1992
Margaret River	0.276*	0.212	0.278*	0.234*	0.163*	0.055	0.181**	0.173***	0.040
Other WA	0.233**	0.139**	0.297*	0.244**	0.123	0.059	0.040	0.008	−0.030
Adelaide Hills	0.301*	0.183*	0.183*	0.342*	0.136***	0.163***	0.164***	−0.006	−0.023
Clare Valley	0.234*	0.008	0.109**	0.073	−0.099***	−0.154**	−0.105	−0.097	−0.260**
Coonawarra	0.177***	0.032	0.112**	0.066	−0.095***	−0.067	−0.029	−0.065	−0.155
Eden Valley	0.152***	0.080	0.248*	0.288*	0.202**	0.185**	0.205**	0.006	0.287
McLaren Vale	0.056	0.063	0.171*	0.023	−0.099***	−0.150**	0.040	−0.007	−0.193***
Other SA	−0.194**	−0.126**	−0.126**	−0.084	−0.281*	−0.259*	−0.132	−0.119	−0.439**
Canberra	0.253*	0.205**	0.123	0.060	−0.087	−0.098	−0.120	0.055	−0.392**
Hunter Valley	0.163*	0.082***	0.086***	0.055	−0.119**	−0.166**	−0.165**	−0.231**	−0.407**
Mudgee	0.045	0.029	0.131	−0.085	−0.115	−0.346**	−0.323*	−0.483*	−0.523
Riverina	−0.280**	−0.211*	−0.180***	−0.332*	−0.434**	−0.573**	−0.304***	−0.404*	−0.171
Other NSW	0.252*	0.066	−0.008	0.022	−0.239*	−0.245**	−0.170***	−0.200***	−0.382
Bendigo	0.376*	0.073	0.148***	0.117	−0.141	−0.004	0.036	0.023	−0.265
Goulburn Valley	0.009	−0.064	0.074	−0.031	−0.199**	−0.093	0.083	−0.098	−0.074
Grampians	0.218**	0.206***	0.275*	0.188***	−0.020	0.170	0.029	−0.015	0.110
Macedon Ranges	0.322*	0.264*	0.388*	0.211**	0.214***	0.095	0.139	0.055	−0.190
Mornington Peninsula	0.310*	0.233*	0.221*	0.236*	0.158***	0.107	0.126	0.018	−0.541

Pyrenees	0.280**	0.262*	0.146	0.264*	0.056	0.141	0.151	0.168	0.071
Yarra Valley	0.212*	0.173*	0.200*	0.197*	0.056	0.051	0.075	-0.014	-0.075
Other Victoria	0.266*	0.087***	0.044	-0.006	-0.077	-0.033	-0.068	-0.065	-0.151
Northern Tasmania	0.259*	0.083	0.141***	0.120	0.085	-0.005	-0.105	0.142	-0.328
Southern Tasmania	0.386*	0.158*	0.149**	0.122	0.064	0.018	0.067	-0.232	-0.162
Queensland	0.105	0.147	-0.054	-0.073	0.089	-0.130	-0.249	-0.232	-0.015
No. of Observations	429	999	1281	1033	929	767	725	448	255
Adjusted. R^2 (per cent)	29.4	39.4	38.5	44.8	44.4	43.6	42.7	43.7	37.5
Average Retail Price (A$)	18.01	21.57	24.39	24.03	24.45	24.50	24.75	25.24	28.90
Average Vintage Rating (points)	87.0	86.8	87.8	87.5	86.9	86.6	87.1	86.5	87.9
Average Winery Rating (stars)	3.83	3.89	3.96	4.03	4.08	4.08	4.07	4.08	4.15
1-point price effect (A$)	0.41*	0.79*	1.01*	0.77*	0.68*	0.71*	0.62*	0.74*	1.10*
$\frac{1}{2}$-star price effect (A$)	0.19	0.50*	0.62*	0.66*	1.13*	0.84*	1.15*	0.94**	1.19***

***, **, * indicate significance at least at the 10 per cent, 5 per cent, 1 per cent level, respectively.

Table 6. Regression results for Australia (Winestate data set)

Parameter	1999	1998	1997	1996	1995	1994	1993	1992
CONSTANT	2.550*	2.641*	2.767*	2.699*	2.634*	2.419*	2.432*	2.183*
Vintage Rating	0.041*	0.045*	0.044*	0.060*	0.073*	0.092*	0.107*	0.156*
Cabernet Sauvignon	−0.003	−0.019	−0.062**	−0.054***	−0.125*	−0.042	−0.012	−0.238*
Cabernet Blends	−0.149*	−0.094*	−0.141*	−0.161*	−0.199*	−0.112**	−0.103	−0.315**
Shiraz Blends	−0.307*	−0.254*	−0.063	−0.258*	−0.140***	−0.012	−0.322*	−0.240
Pinot Noir	0.105**	0.087**	−0.022	−0.111**	−0.138*	−0.077	−0.011*	−0.357**
Merlot	−0.068	0.067**	−0.016	0.021	−0.097	0.083	0.219	0.039
Other Red	−0.115**	−0.076**	−0.254*	−0.187*	−0.282*	−0.155*	−0.239*	−0.215***
Chardonnay	−0.143*	−0.167*	−0.247*	−0.258*	−0.249*	−0.124*	−0.136*	−0.530*
Riesling	−0.250*	−0.371*	−0.440*	−0.491*	−0.525*	−0.417*	−0.347*	−0.567*
Sauvignon Blanc	−0.121*	−0.253*	−0.396*	−0.418*	−0.401*	−0.250**	−0.088	−0.504*
Semillon	−0.192*	−0.253*	−0.416*	−0.442*	−0.393*	−0.226*	−0.276*	−0.419*
Sweet White	−0.001	−0.116	−0.223**	−0.507*	−0.800*	−0.548*	—	—
Other White	−0.220*	−0.379*	−0.450*	−0.471*	−0.495*	−0.394*	−0.335*	−0.690*
Adelaide Hills	0.248*	0.231*	0.173*	0.121*	0.083***	0.064	−0.110	0.122
Clare Valley	0.103**	0.047	0.010	−0.043	−0.052	−0.082	−0.300*	−0.125
Coonawarra	0.089	0.186*	0.112*	0.105*	0.015	0.078***	−0.053	0.068
Eden Valley	0.147**	0.081	0.316*	0.377*	0.598*	0.905*	−0.414	0.088

McLaren Vale	0.038	0.156*	0.058***	0.007	0.008	−0.152*	−0.318*	−0.159
Other Limestone Coast	0.127*	0.146*	0.067	0.025	0.345**	0.070	−0.667***	—
Riverland	−0.254*	−0.312*	−0.288*	−0.454*	−0.626*	−0.609*	−0.644*	−0.429***
Langhorne Creek	0.059	0.039	0.090	−0.118	0.073	−0.193	−0.129	−0.253
Other SA	0.121	−0.048	−0.057	−0.164*	−0.208*	−0.280*	−0.237*	−0.128
Canberra	0.313***	0.130	0.154	0.030	−0.115	−0.141	−0.306***	−0.294
Hunter Valley	0.179*	0.123*	0.058***	0.057	0.019	0.036	−0.085	0.007
Mudgee	0.009	0.033	0.092***	−0.201*	−0.264*	−0.427*	−0.754*	−0.252
Riverina	−0.407*	−0.321*	−0.328*	−0.222*	−0.351*	−0.239**	−0.230	−0.018
Other NSW	−0.011	−0.003	−0.011	−0.099***	−0.073	−0.015	−0.225	—
Goulburn Valley	0.063	−0.113	−0.021	−0.143**	−0.066	−0.133***	−0.081	−0.303***
Mornington Peninsula	0.300*	0.325*	0.231*	0.211***	0.249*	0.053	−0.259***	0.181
Rutherglen	0.051	−0.019	−0.105***	−0.154**	−0.103	−0.132***	−0.296***	−0.277**
King Valley	0.157	0.063	−0.069	0.003	0.085	0.129	0.424***	0.226
Yarra Valley	0.068	0.253*	0.212*	0.128*	0.161*	0.167**	0.004	0.082
Central & West Vic.	0.187*	0.197*	0.161*	0.090***	0.068	0.060	0.000	0.129
Other Victoria	0.094	0.019	−0.069	−0.024	−0.192**	−0.204**	−0.302*	−0.073
Great Southern	0.219*	0.159*	0.133**	0.112**	−0.031	−0.084	−0.020	0.058
Margaret River	0.287*	0.270*	0.363*	0.347*	0.182*	0.084	0.131***	0.069
Perth	−0.013	0.020	0.017	−0.022	−0.072	−0.170***	—	−0.103

(Continued)

Table 6. (Continued)

Parameter	1999	1998	1997	1996	1995	1994	1993	1992
Other WA	0.186*	0.128**	0.035	−0.042	0.071	0.048	−0.280*	−0.357
Tasmania	0.292*	0.269*	0.208*	0.190**	0.199*	0.118	−0.162	0.411
Queensland	0.080	0.013	−0.102	0.047	−0.219	−0.008	−0.280	−0.329
No. of Observations	1345	2154	1993	2001	1551	1186	489	367
Adj. R^2 (per cent)	34.2	30.9	29.7	29.7	30.5	26.3	30.4	40.8
Average Retail Price (A$)	15.87	19.29	20.22	20.31	20.03	20.75	21.33	19.98
Average Vintage Rating (stars)	2.96	3.20	3.29	3.34	3.32	3.35	3.35	3.11
$\frac{1}{2}$-star price effect (A$)	0.65*	0.86*	0.88*	1.21*	1.46*	1.92*	2.28*	3.12*

***, **, * indicates significance at least at the 10 per cent, 5 per cent, 1 per cent level, respectively.

For the *Winestate* sample, the coefficients for 'rating' measure the percentage price premia for a one-point increase (on a 10 point scale), which may in turn be interpreted as the percentage price premium for a $\frac{1}{2}$ star rating increase.

Consider first the estimates using the Halliday data (Table 5). The parameters for vintage rating are all significant and fairly constant over time. The price premium is 3.1 per cent on average and varies between 2.3 per cent and 4.1 per cent for a one-point increase in the vintage rating for the 1992–2000 vintages. That amounts to between a 40 and 110 cents increase on an average-priced bottle of wine for each vintage over that period (see second to last row in Table 5). The coefficients for producer reputation ('winery rating') are significant at the 5 per cent level for all vintages except 1992 and 2000 (1992 is significant at 10 per cent). The price premium for an average-priced bottle of wine worth ($23.80) ranges between 50 and 115 cents for another $\frac{1}{2}$ star in Halliday's winery rating, and has been declining over the 1990s. Halliday's 'classic wine' rating is significant for all vintages in Australia except the three most recent vintages (which were incomplete samples because many premium reds from those vintages were still to be released), and adds a price premium between 16 and 36 per cent, other things equal. The downward trend in this coefficient reflects a premium paid for older vintages.

Turning to the wine variety dummies, the changes over time in the parameter values for varieties reflect relative changes in consumer tastes and preferences for the various varieties. For example, Semillon and Sauvignon Blanc parameters become less negative (that is, the price discount for them relative to Barossa Valley Shiraz decreases), implying that these varieties have become less unpopular over the latter 1990s. For the 2000 vintage, they attract about a one-third discount relative to Barossa Shiraz, other things equal. For Chardonnay, the discount is less whereas for Riesling it averaged almost 50 per cent. In general the reds attracted similar prices relative to Shiraz, and with few exceptions showed no significant difference for most individual vintages. Shiraz blends and other reds were sold at discounts of as much as 20 per cent or more below the Barossa Shiraz price for the early vintages, but this difference has since become insignificant. White wines all sell at a discount relative to

Barossa Shiraz and their parameters have become slightly more significant through time.

When examining the regional dummies, note that they clearly become more significant over time. For the 1992 vintage, only four regions are significantly different from the Barossa at the 5 per cent level, while for the 1998 vintage, 10 of the 26 regions are significantly different at the 1 per cent level and another four at the 5 per cent level.[6] This pattern indicates of an intensifying regional quality differentiation in Australia, with coefficients for some regions trending down while others are trending up. For example, the coefficients for wines from Tasmania first become significant in 1998 and then increase further as they became more popular with consumers relative to Barossa Valley wines. Strong upward trends are also evident for the newly developing ultra-premium cool-climate regions of the Adelaide Hills, Mornington Peninsula and Yarra Valley, with average premia up to 31 per cent. By way of contrast, the wines of the warm-climate irrigated region such as Other South Australia and Riverina become heavily discounted by the mid-1990s.

Turning to the estimates for the *Winestate* data (Table 6), the parameters for vintage rating are all significant but less constant over time compared to the Halliday coefficients. The price premium varies between 4 and 16 per cent for a $\frac{1}{2}$-star improvement in the sensory quality rating for the 1993–99 vintages. That is, a $\frac{1}{2}$-star increase in *Winestate*'s rating would yield an increase in the price per bottle between 65 and 312 cents on an average-priced bottle of rated wine for the 1992–99 vintages (see last row in Table 6). Unfortunately, the rating schemes are too different to allow a direct comparison of the price premia in the two data sets, since *Winestate* only publishes ratings of three or more stars and the two data providers vary in the extent to which they focus on commercial, super- and ultra-premium wines (as reflected in their different average prices).

For the variety dummies, the *Winestate* data confirm that the Semillon and Sauvignon Blanc parameters become less unpopular relative to Barossa Valley Shiraz over the latter 1990s. On average, the *Winestate* data also

---

[6] Because the data sets for the 1999 and 2000 vintages exclude many super- and ultra-premium reds that were still awaiting release, less store can be put on the results for those last 2 years.

confirm that they attract about a one-third discount relative to Barossa Shiraz, other things equal, with both coefficients following the declining discount trends observed with the Halliday data. For Chardonnay the discounts are slightly higher in the *Winestate* sample whereas for Riesling they are slightly lower. Among the reds, Merlot attracted similar prices to Shiraz (less than 5 per cent significance), but other red varieties including blends of Cabernet and Shiraz showed significant discounts below the Barossa Shiraz price, other things equal. Compared to the results from Halliday's data set, more of these parameters became significant as the decade proceeded.

When examining the regional dummies, notice again that they become increasingly significant over time, although the trend is more scattered and less clear than in the Halliday sample. In the sample the only region significantly different from the Barossa Valley for the '92 vintage at the 5 per cent level was Rutherglen, while for the 1998 and 1999 vintages about half the regions are significantly different at the 1 per cent level. Again, this pattern is an indication of an intensifying regional quality differentiation in Australia, with coefficients trending up or downward. Moreover, the *Winestate* data confirm the strong upward trends for the newly developing ultra-premium cool-climate regions (e.g. Adelaide Hills, Mornington Peninsula and Tasmania).

4.2. New Zealand

The results for New Zealand, shown in Tables 7 and 8, differentiate 10 varieties and five regions in each data set. (Absence of an entry means insufficient or no observations.) The Chardonnay variety and the region of Marlborough are chosen as the New Zealand bases. A number of interesting results, especially when compared with Australia's, are worth highlighting. For example, the parameters for Halliday's 'vintage rating' are all significant and fairly constant over time, with somewhat lower price premia for New Zealand as compared with Australia. The coefficients vary between 1.1 and 2.7 per cent, which translate into price premia between 21 and 64 cents calculated at the average NZ price for each vintage. The parameters for 'winery rating' also are mostly smaller and less significant for New Zealand than for Australia, while the 'classic wine' parameter is equally significant with the premia ranging between 14 and 34 per cent.

Table 7. Regression results for New Zealand (Halliday data set)

Parameter	2000	1999	1998	1997	1996	1995	1994	1993
CONSTANT	1.914*	1.073*	0.796**	1.031*	0.802**	1.294*	1.248*	0.944
Vintage Rating	0.011**	0.022*	0.023*	0.022*	0.024*	0.018*	0.019*	0.027**
Winery Rating	0.030	0.036**	0.061*	0.049**	0.039	0.042	0.048**	−0.057
Classic Wine	0.279	0.189***	0.343*	0.320*	0.185**	0.315*	0.171**	0.140
Cabernet Sauvignon	—	−0.099	0.131***	0.027	0.240***	0.157	0.170**	0.242
Cabernet Blends	—	0.239*	0.175*	0.311*	0.191**	0.476*	−0.034	—
Merlot	0.096	0.073	0.064	0.158	0.089	0.508*	0.110	−0.168
Pinot Noir	0.278*	0.254*	0.184*	0.112***	0.159***	0.069	0.049	0.133
Other Red	—	0.142	0.296*	—	0.363*	—	−0.155	—
Riesling	−0.118**	−0.321*	−0.385*	−0.304*	−0.365**	−0.359*	−0.505*	−0.462*
Gewurztraminer	—	−0.002	−0.229***	−0.138	−0.187	−0.063	−0.369*	−0.412
Sauvignon Blanc	−0.143*	−0.248*	−0.279*	−0.346*	−0.261*	−0.257*	−0.334*	−0.303***
Sweet White	0.301*	0.043	0.193	0.013	0.000	0.052	−0.021	−0.071
Other White	0.022	−0.100***	−0.184**	−0.187**	−0.193***	−0.253*	−0.363*	−0.271

Auckland	0.053	−0.081	−0.005	−0.042	−0.006	−0.056	−0.017	0.038
Canterbury	−0.005	0.014	0.114**	−0.023	0.096	−0.105	0.148**	0.086
Hawke's Bay	0.020	0.061	0.088**	−0.001	0.008	−0.096	−0.045	−0.144
Wairarapa	0.098	0.165*	0.083	0.100***	0.132***	0.080	0.088***	0.177
Other NZ	−0.053	0.079***	0.103**	0.011	0.101***	0.100	−0.009	0.045
No. of Observations	176	328	289	196	216	117	143	53
Adj. R^2 (per cent)	35.6	56.3	57.8	58.1	47.4	71.7	64.5	36.2
Average Retail Price (NZ$)	19.50	24.68	25.27	21.40	23.39	23.67	22.08	23.45
Average Vintage Rating (points)	89.5	89.0	89.3	88.7	87.3	86.7	89.0	88.2
Average Winery Rating (stars)	4.09	4.08	4.06	3.99	4.104	4.081	4.105	4.151
1-point price effect (NZ$)	0.21**	0.53*	0.59*	0.46*	0.57*	0.43*	0.43*	0.64**
½-star price effect (NZ$)	0.29	0.45**	0.77*	0.53**	0.46	0.50	0.53**	−0.67

***, **, * indicates significance at least at the 10 per cent, 5 per cent, 1 per cent level, respectively.

Table 8. Regression results for New Zealand (Winestate data set)

Parameter	1999	1998	1997	1996	1995	1994
CONSTANT	2.530*	2.963*	2.782*	2.608*	2.760*	2.804*
Vintage Rating	0.048*	0.014	0.042*	0.065*	0.041**	0.046***
Cabernet Sauvignon	—	0.032	0.031	0.170***	0.000	0.038
Cabernet Blends	—	−0.107	0.269*	0.289*	0.174**	−0.023
Merlot	—	0.032	0.150**	0.047	0.184**	—
Pinot Noir	—	0.352*	0.291*	0.218*	0.090	0.134
Shiraz	—	—	—	0.156	—	—
Other Red	0.115	−0.179*	0.014	0.145	0.178***	0.042
Riesling	−0.037	−0.212*	−0.256*	−0.220*	−0.282*	−0.343*
Sauvignon Blanc	−0.095***	−0.223*	−0.258*	−0.255*	−0.304*	−0.027
Semillon	—	−0.073	−0.096	−0.135	−0.335**	—
Other White	0.195*	−0.227*	−0.266*	−0.309*	−0.369*	−0.415***
Auckland	−0.061	−0.063	−0.099*	−0.067***	−0.089	−0.052
Canterbury	—	—	−0.157**	−0.041	−0.002	−0.138
Hawke's Bay	−0.111	0.005	0.147*	0.042	0.001	0.137
Nelson	−0.088	−0.118	−0.105***	−0.023	−0.098	—
Other NZ	0.124	−0.054	0.076	0.109**	0.116	0.040
No. of Observations	126	248	344	362	194	90
Adj. R^2 (per cent)	22.4	29.5	45.1	38.1	43.0	14.7
Average Retail Price (NZ$)	17.70	19.62	20.30	21.23	21.14	24.43
Average Vintage Rating (stars)	3.54	3.33	3.38	3.49	3.45	3.66
$\frac{1}{2}$-star price effect (NZ$)	0.85*	0.27	0.84*	1.37*	0.87**	1.12***

***, **, * indicates significance at least at the 10 per cent, 5 per cent, 1 per cent level, respectively.

Varietal differences are less pronounced in New Zealand too. Note that Riesling is discounted by about one-third and Sauvignon Blanc between one-seventh and one-third relative to the base variety (Chardonnay), whereas the reds enjoy considerable premia, other things equal.

Most strikingly, however, are the differences in the degree of regional differentiation between the two countries. For New Zealand, only one out of a total of 40 regional dummy coefficients over eight vintages is significantly different from the base region (Marlborough) at the 1 per cent level (plus just four others at the 5 per cent level), and the degree of difference is not large. Nor are any trends in the size or significance of coefficients obvious over time, unlike for Australia.

Very similar findings emerge for New Zealand from the *Winestate* data (Table 8) as those from the Halliday data (Table 7): vintage ratings are nearly all significant with no obvious trend over time, variety and regional differences are not pronounced, and nor are they becoming more significant over time.

Finally on the results, note that in all subsamples the variation in prices explained by the model (adjusted R^2) is higher for New Zealand, despite the much smaller sample sizes. Moreover, note that the estimation results are fairly consistent across the two different data sets for each country, although the Halliday data set has the higher explanatory power. In addition, the size of the price premia that consumers are willing to pay for higher-rated wines is consistently less in New Zealand than in Australia (especially bearing in mind that the NZ$ was worth only 70–85 per cent of the value of the A$ in the 1990s).

5. Implications and areas for further research

At least three clear lessons can be drawn from these results. One is that vintage ratings by independent writers/critics/judges (in this case those of *Winestate* magazine judges and for James Halliday, as well as his winery ratings and classic wine categorisation) appear to have a significant positive impact on the prices that consumers are willing to pay for premium wines, after taking into account their own reputation assessment for grape varieties and growing regions. This is equally true for Australia and New Zealand. It is consistent with the earlier study for Australia for 1991–92 by Oczkowski (1994) and with Schamel's (2000) findings for the United States (based in that case on ratings published in the U.S. magazine *The Wine Spectator*), and suggests consumers value this information in their quest for greater knowledge about available wines.

Second, the premia consumers are willing to pay for higher-rated wines (both Halliday's and *Winestate*'s) appear to have trended downwards slightly over the 1990s. This is true also for Halliday's winery ratings. This is consistent with wine consumers in these two countries becoming more confident in their own ability to discern the quality of different wines, and hence less reliant on critics' ratings.

The third lesson is not unrelated to the second. It is that there is a clear trend towards greater regional and varietal differentiation, at least within Australia. This too suggests a greater proportion of consumers are becoming more discerning, which presumably is being reflected in vineyard land prices in the various regions. Note, however, the weaker regional and varietal differentiation and the absence of any obvious price premia trend in New Zealand. The weaker varietal differentiation may reflect the relatively few varieties grown in New Zealand and (a point emphasised by Roberts and Reagans, 2001) the newness of many of its premium wine-producing regions. The lower price premia New Zealanders seem willing to pay for higher-rated wines and wineries compared with Australians may simply reflect the lower per capita incomes in New Zealand and their weaker preference for wine (their per capita consumption being only 80 per cent that of Australians, and being more heavily focused on non-premium wines).

The difference between the two markets in the degree of regional differentiation also may reflect the fact that Australia has more major premium regions that have been producing continuously for a long time than does New Zealand. The greater extent to which regional differentiation is increasing in Australia is partly a consequence of the rapid growth in the 1990s of new ultra-premium cool-climate regions, which are challenging the supremacy of the long-established regions. But another contributing factor is that, unlike New Zealand, Australia has introduced legislation (in 1993) to allow legal registration of regional names (technically, 'geographical indications').[7] That legislation is providing stronger rights over the intellectual property value of regional names, thereby raising the

---

[7] This was to enable Australia to fulfill its agreement with the European Union on trade in wine, following the Uruguay Round of multilateral trade negotiations. For details see www.awbc.com.au/arms/a_regions.html. An analysis of its possible effects can be found in Kok (1999).

rates of return on investments in regional promotion. Even though they cannot say anything about the profitability of such investments, the above results are not inconsistent with the view that price premia can be generated through such promotion. The European tradition of emphasising region in addition to nation of origin would appear to be gradually taking hold in Australia. It remains to be seen whether regional reputation indicators become more or less important over time. On the one hand, regions are investing more in generic promotion of their regions; but on the other, globalisation is causing individual wineries to agglomerate and put more emphasis on building their corporate brand reputation.

As for the signs and sizes of the premia/discounts attached to variety, they are consistent with common knowledge. But the fact that there are distinct premia for particular varieties, over and above a premium or discount for region of origin, distinguishes the Antipodes from Western Europe where varietal distinctions have until very recently been downplayed.

There is much scope for further empirical work of this sort. Two examples of other questions that might be addressed are mentioned by way of conclusion. First, to what extent are subnational regions beginning to enjoy a price premium in markets abroad, or is it still only national recognition ('Brand Australia') and corporate brands that matter in those export markets at this stage? An answer to this question would help to fine-tune the promotional efforts of wine companies and regional wine associations. If national generic promotion can be shown to pay abroad, the bodies responsible for national promotion[8] would find it easier to attract (i) funds for that generic promotion and (ii) support for regulation of wine exports to ensure the national reputation for quality exports is not tarnished.[9] This is especially crucial in light of Tirole's (1996) theoretical result, and the bitter experiences following wine scandals in Austria and

---

[8] The Australian Wine and Brandy Corporation and the Wine Institute of New Zealand, respectively.

[9] Care is needed in any such empirical work to separate the influences of quality upgrading national research and development on the supply side and promotional efforts on the demand side (see Zhao et al. 2003), as well as to distinguish corporate, regional and national generic promotion.

Italy in the 1980s, showing that producers can suffer for a very long time from previous mistakes.

Second, how well could hedonic pricing models be applied to better understand the demand for wine grapes by wineries? Various technical features of grapes contribute to the quality of the wines made from them, but in ways that are not very transparent to grape growers. As quantitative measures improve for measuring in the vineyard and/or weighbridge those attributes winemakers are looking for, so will the scope for addressing this issue with hedonic price modelling. This would build on the work begun by Golan and Shalit (1993) with respect to Israeli grapes, and a recent paper by Oczkowski (2002). If indeed weather variables during the grape growing season are crucial, as the empirical results of Ashenfelter (2000) and Wood and Anderson (2002) suggest, those too would need to be included in addition to such variables as grape sugar level, colour and acidity.

References

Anderson, K., (ed.) (2004) *The World's Wine Markets: Globalization at Work*, Edward Elgar, London.

Anderson, K. and Norman, D. (2003) *Global Wine Production, Consumption and Trade, 1961–2001: A Statistical Compendium*, Centre for International Economic Studies, Adelaide.

Anderson, K., Norman, D. and Wittwer, G. (2003) Globalization and the World's Wine Markets', *The World Economy* **26**, 659–87.

Ashenfelter, O. (2000) 'Liquid Assets: The International Guide to Fine Wines', *Optimus: The Magazine for the Private Investor* **2**.

Ashenfelter, O., Ashmore, D. and Lalonde, R. (1995) 'Bordeaux Wine Vintage Quality and the Weather', *Chance* **8**, 7–14.

Byron, R.P. and Ashenfelter, O. (1995) 'Predicting the Quality of the Unborn Grange', *Economic Record* **71**, 40–53.

Combris, P., Lecocq, S. and Visser, M. (1997) 'Estimation of a Hedonic Price Equation for Bordeaux Wine: Does Quality Matter?' *Economic Journal* **107**, 390–402.

Golan, A. and Shalit, H. (1993) 'Wine Quality Differentials in Hedonic Grape Pricing', *Journal of Agricultural Economics* **44**, 311–21.

Halliday, J. (1999) *Australia and New Zealand Classic Wines*, Harper Collins, Sydney.

Halliday, J. (2001) *Australia and New Zealand Wine Companion 2002*, Harper Collins, Sydney.

Kok, S. (1999) 'The Economics of Geographical Indications: A Case Study of the EU-Australia Wine Agreement', (Unpublished Honours Thesis), School of Economics, University of Adelaide.

Landon, S. and Smith, C. E. (1997) 'The Use of Quality and Reputation Indicators by Consumers: The Case of Bordeaux Wine', *Journal of Consumer Policy* **20**, 289–323.

Nerlove, M. (1995) 'Hedonic Price Functions and the Measurement of Preferences: The Case of Swedish Wine Consumers', *European Economic Review* **39**, 1697–716.

Oczkowski, E. (1994) 'A Hedonic Price Function for Australian Premium Table Wine', *Australian Journal of Agricultural Economics* **38**, 93–110.

Oczkowski, E. (2001) 'Hedonic Wine Price Functions and Measurement Error', *Economic Record* **77**, 374–82.

Oczkowski, E. (2002) 'Modelling Winegrape Prices in Disequilibrium', Paper presented at the 31st Annual Australian Conference of Economists, Adelaide, 1–3 October.

Roberts, P. W. and Reagans, R. (2001) 'Market Experience, Consumer Attention and Price-Quality Relationships for New World Wines in the US Market, 1987–99', GSIA Working Paper. Graduate School of Industrial Administration, Carnegie, Mellon University, Pittsburgh.

Rosen, S. (1974) 'Hedonic Prices and Implicit Markets: Product Differentiation in Pure Competition', *Journal of Political Economy* **82**, 34–55.

Schamel, G. (2000) 'Individual and Collective Reputation Indicators of Wine Quality', CIES Discussion Paper 0009. Centre for International Economic Studies. University of Adelaide.

Shapiro, C. (1983) 'Premiums for High Quality Products as Returns to Reputations', *Quarterly Journal of Economics* **98**, 659–79.

Tirole, J. (1996) 'A Theory of Collective Reputations with Applications to the Persistence of Corruption and to Firm Quality', *Review of Economic Studies* **63**, 1–22.

Winestate (2001) Tasting Data File 2001, Personal Communication with *Winestate* Magazine, Adelaide.

Wood, D. and Anderson, K. (2002) 'What Determines the Future Value of an Icon Wine? Evidence from Australia', CIES Discussion Paper 0233, Centre for International Economic Studies. University of Adelaide. Since published in *Journal of Wine Economics* **1**, 141–61.

Zhao, X., Wittwer, G. and Anderson, K. (2003) 'Who Gains from Australian Generic Wine Promotion and R & D?' *Australian Journal of Agricultural and Resource Economics* **4**, 181–202.

Chapter 11

What Determines the Future Value of an Icon Wine? New Evidence from Australia*

Danielle Wood[†] and Kym Anderson[‡]

Abstract

To what extent can the future price of icon wines be anticipated from information available at the time of their initial sale by wineries? Using a seemingly unrelated regression model we show that weather variables and changes in production techniques, along with the age of the wine, have significant power in explaining the secondary market price variation across different vintages of each of three icon Australian red wines. The results have implications for winemakers in determining the prices

---

*First published in *Journal of Wine Economics* 1(2): 141–61, Fall 2006. Revision of a paper presented at the Oenometrics X Conference, Budapest, 22–24 May 2003. Thanks are due to Orley Ashenfelter of Princeton University for inspiring this research, to Langton's Fine Wine Auctions for access to their database, to referees for helpful comments, and to the Australian Research Council for financial support. This research began while the authors were at the University of Adelaide. The views are the authors' own and in no way reflect the opinions of Australia's Productivity Commission or the World Bank.

[†]Productivity Commission, Melbourne, Australia. Email: dwood@pc.gov.au.

[‡]World Bank, University of Adelaide and CEPR, Washington DC. Email: kanderson@worldbank.org.

they pay for grapes and charge for their wines, and for consumers/wine investors as a guide to the prospective quality of immature icon wines.

1. Introduction

The Australian secondary wine auction market is characterised by large variations in price between different vintages of the same wine, relative to the wineries' initial release prices of these wines. Thus, there exists the potential for buyers to improve their investment returns by choosing to purchase those vintages that are under-priced at the time of release, relative to their future secondary market value. Similarly, wine producers could improve profits either by charging higher prices for the better vintages (reflective of the price those wines will receive later in the secondary market), or by holding back some of the better vintages to sell later as the wine's quality becomes more obvious.

An important question for both producers and buyers is: to what extent can the future prices of such icon wines be anticipated from information available at the time of first release? Tasting the young wine, even by professionals, is unreliable because the high tannin content makes them astringent to the palate in their early years.

Weather conditions during the grape-growing season, long recognised by vignerons as a determinant of the quality of a vintage, may provide an objective and easily quantifiable guide (Gladstones, 1992). Econometricians have tested this hypothesis for Bordeaux wines and found it is strongly supported (Ashenfelter, Ashmore and Lalonde, 1995). A more-limited test on just one Australian wine (Grange) using only three years of auction data gave promising results as well (Byron and Ashenfelter, 1995). The purpose of the present paper is to make use of the much larger database now available to test this hypothesis for a broader range of icon wines using additional years of auction data.

Specifically, a seemingly unrelated regression model is used to explain the variation in the secondary (auction) market price between different vintages of particular wines, using several weather variables plus dummy variables for capturing changes in winemaking and grape growing techniques over time (based on interviews with the chief winemakers of the relevant wineries). The model is estimated using auction price data for three South Australian icon red wines: two by Penfolds (Grange and St Henri), and one by Henschke's (Hill of Grace).[1] This attempt to explain the variation in price between different vintages of the same wine label is in contrast to numerous studies that seek to explain the variation in price between the same vintages of different labels (see Oczkowski (2001), Schamel and Anderson (2003) and the references therein).

The paper is structured as follows. We first review previous studies that attempt to quantify the relationship between weather conditions during the growing season and wine prices. We then discuss our choice of variables for explaining the relationship between quality and weather, production techniques and wine age. The next section presents the empirical results, while the final section draws out conclusions, offers some implications for winemakers and consumers/investors, and suggests areas for future research.

2. Previous literature

Ashenfelter, Ashmore, and Lalonde (1995) were the first to attempt an empirical explanation of the variation in price between different vintages of a Bordeaux index. They consider the variation in price between different vintages of a representative sample of thirteen Bordeaux wines (used to create a vintage price index). The paper uses weather conditions during the growing season that produced the wine to explain variation in the vintage price index. Ashenfelter *et al.* also include age as an explanatory variable to capture the effect of increasing scarcity and the opportunity cost of holding wine. They find that age alone can explain 21 per cent of the variation in the price index between vintages. However, the inclusion of three weather variables in the model increases the model's explanatory power (as measured by R^2) to 83 per cent.

The 'Bordeaux Equation' was modified for a single wine by Byron and Ashenfelter (1995) in a study of Penfold's icon wine, Grange, and by Fogarty (2000) in a study of an icon West Australian wine, Moss Wood. These studies found a number of weather variables and age to be significant explanators of variation in price of these wines (with R^2 of 0.82 and

---

[1] Some information on these classic wines is provided in Appendix 1 of Wood and Anderson (2003). For more details see Halliday (1998) and Read and Caillard (2000).

0.88, respectively). In addition, the models were demonstrated to have strong out-of-sample predictive power. The findings of these studies support the Ashenfelter *et al.* hypothesis that the secondary market price of a given vintage depends on the weather conditions that produce the vintage.

Jones and Storchmann (2001) more clearly articulate the relationship between weather and wine quality. They adopt a two-step approach to modelling the price variation of Bordeaux wines, both between different wines and across vintages. Firstly, they estimate a model to explain variation in sugar and acid content at harvest by climatic variables. Secondly, they use these two endogenously determined variables as explanatory variables in the price regression, thus highlighting the channel through which weather influences quality and hence price.

3. The model

What factors explain the variation in quality (and hence price) between different vintages of the three icon wines in this study? The potential quality of a wine is a product of the quality of the inputs (particularly grapes) and the winemaking techniques used to transform these inputs into the final product. The quality of grapes in turn is determined by the interaction of soil, topography, climate and grape growing techniques. Given that we are attempting to explain variation in price of different vintages of the same wine label, it is reasonable to treat soil quality, aspect, slope and altitude as constant between vintages. Thus, this study focuses on variations in weather and changes in grape growing and winemaking techniques as explanators of potential quality differentials. However, the actual quality of the wine at any point in time depends on whether it has yet reached or has passed its peak, and thus we also discuss the importance of age in explaining quality variation across vintages at any point in time.

3.1. Weather

The influence of weather conditions during the growing period on grape quality has been well established. In recognition of the importance of climate, winemakers develop grape growing techniques to maximise the beneficial aspects of climate while reducing weather-based fluctuations in quality. Smart (2001) argues that while all climate parameters can be important in influencing grape quality, temperature is undoubtedly the most important. Gladstones (1992) suggests an average daily temperature during the growing season (mid-September to March in southern Australia) of 20–22°C is optimal for the formation of colour, flavour and aroma compounds in red table wines. Thus, we assume that grapes grown under these optimal conditions will be of the best quality, and vintages produced from these grapes will receive the highest prices.

Ashenfelter, Ashmore, and Lalonde (1995) report a positive linear relationship between average temperature during the growing season and price for Bordeaux red wines. However, when considering the warmer Barossa region of South Australia where the average growing season temperature regularly exceeds the suggested optimum, Byron and Ashenfelter (1995) find a quadratic function to be the most appropriate way to model the effect of temperature on wine prices. The quadratic function they estimate is concave with a turning point of 19.05 degrees, just slightly below the temperature range Gladstones puts forward as optimal.

Temperature also has the potential to affect quality and yields through its variation. Gladstones points out that the biochemical processes of grape development are favoured by a low diurnal temperature range (i.e. the difference between the daily maximum and the nightly minimum temperatures). His argument is supported by Byron and Ashenfelter, who find a significant negative relationship between the price of Grange and the average temperature differential during its growing season.

The number of hours of sunshine is another variable important to grape quality, both directly and for its interaction with temperature. Gladstones (1992) suggests that sunshine hours during the growing season, particularly in early spring, have a positive influence on quality. However, previous statistical analyses (Ashenfelter *et al.*, 1995; Byron and Ashenfelter, 1995; Fogarty, 2000) fail to identify any statistically significant relationship between hours of sunshine and icon wine prices. This failure is likely to be linked to the correlation between sunshine hours and temperature, which makes isolating their effects difficult.

After temperature, Smart (2001) ranks rainfall as the next most important climatic determinant of grape quality. As Gladstones (1992) points out, it is the seasonal distribution of rainfall that is important. Rainfall during winter and early spring aids grape development, particularly since the three wines considered come from vineyards that rely wholly or mostly on precipitation. On the other hand, rainfall in the period prior to harvest can waterlog the soil and thus prove detrimental to both grape yield and quality. These effects find statistical support in the study by Ashenfelter *et al.* (1995), who report evidence of a negative relationship between rainfall prior to harvest and Bordeaux wine prices, and a positive relationship between rainfall during the winter preceding the vintage and price. While the study of Grange prices by Byron and Ashenfelter (1995) also finds statistical evidence of the detrimental effect of rainfall prior to harvest, they do not find any statistically significant relationship between winter rainfall and price.

Gladstones (1992) also suggests there is a positive relationship between wine quality and relative humidity in February, the last month of the growing season. This relationship is particularly important in the relatively warm wine regions in Australia where afternoon humidity is necessary to encourage ripening when February temperatures are high.

The final climatic variable listed by both Gladstones (1992) and Smart (2001) as important to grape quality is windiness. Wind can have both a positive and negative influence on quality. On the positive side, wind can help prevent frosts and provides air circulation to the vines (which lowers humidity). However, strong winds have the potential to harm grape quality (Hamilton, 1988). In South Australia, for example, hot dry summer winds can cause imperfect ripening.

3.2. Vineyard management techniques

In addition to these weather influences, changes in vineyard management techniques can explain quality differences between the grapes used to produce different vintages. Gladstones (1992) details a range of practices important to both grape yield and quality. The spacing of vines determines the exposure of vines to sunlight, water and soil nutrients and therefore affects both yield and quality. Also affecting sunlight exposure is the orientation of rows. The height of vines is also important, because it determines the amount of heat the vine is exposed to via radiation from the soil. Further improvement of the efficiency of light use can come from the adoption of a suitable trellising system and canopy management. Irrigation, fertilisation, artificial drainage and windbreaks are other vineyard management techniques that may be important influences on grape yield and quality.

3.3. Winemaking techniques

High-quality grapes are an essential but not sufficient condition for producing high-quality wines. It is only when quality grapes are combined with superior winemaking techniques that excellent wines are produced. All facets of winemaking — grape selection, pressing and crushing, fermentation and clarification — can impact on the final quality of the wine.

For the two Penfold wines considered in this study, grapes are selected from various sites to partly offset site specific quality variations from year to year. However, for Henschke's Hill of Grace — a single-vineyard wine — the absence of the option to blend to offset quality variation means that the choice of grapes is of utmost importance.

The technology used in juice extraction (grape crushing and pressing) is a determinant of the levels of tannins in the wine and therefore its taste and cellaring potential. The type of oak in which a wine is fermented and the length of maturation influences the distinctive quality of the wine as well as the cost of production and thus its market price. Also important is whether the barrels are new or used. Similarly techniques used in the clarification process — racking, filtering and fining — can impact on both the quality of the wine and the cost of production.

3.4. Age of the wine

A characteristic of icon wine of the sort considered in this study is their ability to develop and improve with age. These wines are characterised by a high content of tannins in their youth, making them unpleasant for early drinking. Then as the tannin content recedes, the quality gradually improves until the maximum quality is reached. This state can persist for a number of years or even decades before the quality begins to decline.

Age is also related to price because the scarcity of a given vintage is non-decreasing with time. As a wine ages, more of the given vintage stock is consumed so that scarcity, and hence price, increases. For this reason, icon wines past their optimal drinking age can still command increasing prices over time.

Although previous studies model the relationship between quality and age linearly (Ashenfelter *et al.*, 1995; Byron and Ashenfelter, 1995; Fogarty, 2000), it seems reasonable, given the nature of the maturation process, to model age as a cubic function: prices rising when the wine is young, plateauing out around optimal drinking time, before increasing again in value as the wine becomes an 'antique' wine.[2]

4. The data

4.1. *Price data*

Wine auctions are the principal secondary market for icon wines in Australia, aided by the fact that the liquor licensing laws in many states prohibit private sales of wine. Auction prices provide a comparatively high degree of price transparency, and therefore provide the best indication of the equilibrium value of a particular vintage of wine at any point in time. Langton's represent over 70 per cent of the wine auction market in Australia,[3] and they have kindly provided the price data for this study.

The data provided are the high and low sale price and the date for every occasion on which each of the three icon wines were traded over the period 1988–2000. From this, the unweighted average of the sale price for each vintage in each auction year is calculated for each of the three wines. The prices are unweighted because data on the volume of wine traded at each date are, unfortunately, not available. However, in so far as differences in volumes traded are not large and are randomly distributed for a given vintage, this should not unduly affect the analysis.

Because the wine auction market in Australia only really developed in the last decade, many of the vintages were not traded every year, particularly in the first few years. Thus, only the auction years which provide a sufficient number of observations are considered for each wine. They are 1992–2000 for Grange, 1994–2000 for St Henri, and 1995–2000 for Hill of Grace.

In addition, some of the earlier vintages of each wine are excluded from the analysis because they were too infrequently traded. The vintages that are included are: 1960–1986 for Grange, 1965–1991 for St Henri, and

---

[2] We thank an anonymous referee for this suggestion.
[3] Details are given in Langton (2001 and earlier editions).

1971–1991 for Hill of Grace (except no 1974 vintage exists for Hill of Grace).

For the later auction years for each wine, price data for a number of additional vintages are available. For example, in 2000, vintages of Grange up to 1995 were traded, yet only prices for vintages up to 1986 are included in our data set to ensure a balanced sample. This provides scope to test the out-of-sample forecast power of the model.

The unweighted average nominal price in each auction year is converted into real price using the Consumer Price Index with base year 2000.

4.2. Weather data

The weather data are sourced from the Australian Bureau of Meteorology's Climate Station at Nuriootpa in the heart of the Barossa Valley in South Australia. A major issue is determining the weather conditions during the growing season for Penfolds grapes, because they are sourced from various regions but in different proportions in each vintage. Because the exact percentages of grapes used from each region to produce a given vintage are not publicly available, it is not possible to create a weighted average weather index for each vintage. Mike Farmilo, the Chief Winemaker at Penfolds, suggested the Nurioopta Climate Station would be the most representative site for Grange, and indeed Byron and Ashenfelter (1995) found that the data from this station provided the best fit. Hence this study will also use Nurioopta as a representative Climate Station for Grange. St Henri, like Grange, also uses grapes primarily sourced from the Barossa region and so Nurioopta will be used as the representative station for this wine also. For Hill of Grace, a single site wine, Nurioopta is the closest Climate Station with sufficient data available.

4.3. Technological change data

Data on the major changes in viticultural management and winemaking techniques were collected by interviewing the Chief Winemakers at Southcorp (the producer of Penfolds) and Henschke. In the interviews John Duval from Penfolds and Stephen Henschke discussed what they considered to be the major changes in their grape growing and winemaking techniques over the sample period. These changes in technique are introduced in the model through a dummy variable at the time of the change, held to one after the change.

In recognition of the importance of grape quality to all its blended wines, Penfolds introduced the star quality system in 1983. This system helps overcome the possible principal agent problem with their grape growers, by offering them substantial bonuses in line with the number of stars (a measure of quality) that their grapes achieve. Penfolds management adopted this system to maintain the integrity of their top wines, by introducing a minimum star requirement for the grapes used to produce each wine. However, while it is likely the plan has improved quality (and reduced quality risks) since its introduction, the fact that it was phased in over a number of years makes it less likely to show up as significant than if it was introduced overnight.

Another innovation introduced across the two Penfolds wines was a change in grape-pressing techniques in 1990, again aimed at improving the quality of the wine produced.

Langton's 1998 *Fine Wine Investment Guide* suggests that early vintages of Hill of Grace (1971–1977) are not considered as distinguished as vintages produced from 1978 when Stephen and Pru Henschke took over the family winery. Thus, we include a dummy variable with a break at 1978 to see whether the data suggest this is indeed the case.

In addition, Stephen Henschke detailed two changes introduced during his period of managing the winery that may have improved the quality and hence the demand for the wines. In 1983, the wine was matured in new French Oak barrels for the first time. And in a further attempt to improve grape quality, a new trellising system was introduced in 1990.

It should be noted however, that many of the changes in viticultural management and winemaking techniques described would have led to higher production costs. For example, the new French oak adopted for the maturation of Hill of Grace is substantially more expensive than the new American oak that was used prior to 1983. Given that this is a highly differentiated product, these higher production costs could be reflected to some extent at least in a higher release price for the wine, and all else being equal, higher secondary market prices. Thus, any evidence of higher secondary market prices for vintages employing these improved techniques may reflect a 'pass through' of higher production costs along with a premium buyers are willing to pay for the superior quality of the wine.

5. Estimation methodology

Following the approach of Byron and Ashenfelter (1995), the relationship between price and the age, weather and technique variables are estimated separately for each auction year using an unconstrained seemingly unrelated regression (SUR) model. Because the regressors in each equation are identical, this is equivalent to equation by equation OLS (Greene, 2002).

A log linear functional form is adopted, reflective of the fact that the magnitude of the effect of age, weather and technique would be expected to rise with the price of the wine (Byron and Ashenfelter, 1995).

Wald coefficient tests are used to test whether the coefficients on the explanatory variables are identical across equations. Given that we would expect that the effect of age and quality on price should not differ substantially across auction years, this is an important step in establishing the credibility of the explanatory variables and the functional form (Byron and Ashenfelter, 1995). The constants in each equation, however, would not necessarily be the same across auction years. Rather these capture 'shifts' in prices across all vintages, due to macroeconomic conditions or changes in demand for a given brand of wine, for example.

The explanatory variables considered for each wine are:

Age_{it}: Age of vintage 't' in auction year 'i';
$RainH_i$: Total rainfall in January, February and March, (the period just prior to harvest) in the year that produced vintage 't';
$Temp_i$: Average daily growing season temperature, calculated by taking the average daily temperature (maximum + minimum)/2 and averaging these over the months October to March;
$TempD_i$: Average daily growing season temperature variation, calculated by taking (average monthly max — average monthly min) and averaging over the months October to March;
$Wind_i$: Average daily wind speed in November and December;
$Press_i$: A dummy variable for Penfolds wines with break at 1990, the year in which Penfolds changed their pressing technique;

SP$_i$: A dummy variable for Hill of Grace with a break at 1978, the year Stephen and Prue Henschke took over the family winery; and

Trellis$_i$: A dummy variable for Hill of Grace with break at 1990, the year a new trellising system was introduced.

To test a proposition outlined in section 3 — that maximum temperature may be a better predictor of grape quality than average temperature — we also estimate the models using average daily maximum temperature over the growing season in place of average daily temperature.

6. Results

The estimates from the unconstrained SUR models are presented in Tables 1, 2 and 3 for Grange, St Henri and Hill of Grace, respectively. The preferred models are derived using a general-to-specific modelling approach, using selection criteria such as log likelihood, to provide a guide to the best fitting model across all auction years.

Diagnostic tests (for heteroscedasticity, serial correlation and normality) are performed on the residuals from the OLS equations for each wine across each auction year. These results are also presented in the relevant tables. There is evidence of heteroscedasticity for some auction years for Grange. This is corrected for using White's heteroscedasticity correction (White, 1980), and the corrected standard errors are presented below the estimates.

Wald coefficient tests are performed to test whether the coefficients on the explanatory variables are identical across auction years. For the majority of coefficients these restrictions cannot be rejected, suggesting that preferences for particular characteristics of the wine (as imparted by the weather conditions during the grape-growing season) have not changed over the auction years considered. This implies that a constrained SUR model can be estimated. The estimates from the constrained SUR model are presented in Tables 4, 5 and 6. These results are discussed in more detail below.

6.1. *Age*

The estimated effect of age on price is not directly comparable across Grange, St Henri and Hill of Grace because of the different functional

Table 1. Unconstrained SUR (OLS) Estimates for Grange[a] (by auction year)

	1992	1993	1994	1995	1996	1997[b]	1998	1999[b]	2000[b]
Constant	1.73	2.16	−0.47	0.39	−0.16	−0.78	−2.03	−1.51	−0.75
	(1.48)	(1.50)	(1.43)	(1.69)	(1.55)	(1.48)	(2.06)	(1.96)	(1.79)
						(1.66)		(1.97)	(1.89)
Age	0.032**	0.034**	0.020**	0.017**	0.015**	0.011	0.020*	0.023**	0.026**
	(0.007)	(0.007)	(0.006)	(0.008)	(0.007)	(0.007)	(0.010)	(0.009)	(0.008)
						(0.009)		(0.011)	(0.010)
Temp	0.18**	0.24**	0.27**	0.24**	0.26**	0.30**	0.38**	0.38**	0.36**
	(0.067)	(0.07)	(0.06)	(0.07)	(0.07)	(0.07)	(0.09)	(0.09)	(0.08)
						(0.04)		(0.07)	(0.06)
TempD	−0.21**	−0.35**	−0.22**	−0.25**	−0.21**	−0.23**	−0.31**	−0.36**	−0.37**
	(0.09)	(0.09)	(0.08)	(0.11)	(0.10)	(0.09)	(0.18)	(0.12)	(0.11)
						(0.10)		(0.15)	(0.14)
RainH	−0.003**	0.004**	−0.004**	−0.005**	−0.005**	−0.005**	−0.006**	−0.006**	−0.006**
	(0.001)	(0.001)	(0.001)	(0.001)	(0.001)	(0.001)	(0.001)	(0.002)	(0.001)
						(0.001)		(0.002)	(0.002)

(Continued)

Table 1. (Continued)

	1992	1993	1994	1995	1996	1997[b]	1998	1999[b]	2000[b]
Wind	0.29**	0.36**	0.44**	0.46**	0.46**	0.52**	0.62**	0.63**	0.60**
	(0.11)	(0.11)	(0.11)	(0.13)	(0.12)	(0.11)	(0.16)	(0.15)	(0.14)
						(0.09)		(0.12)	(0.10)
Wind^2	−0.009**	−0.01**	−0.01**	−0.01**	−0.01**	−0.02**	−0.02**	−0.02**	−0.02**
	(0.003)	(0.003)	(0.003)	(0.004)	(0.003)	(0.003)	(0.005)	(0.004)	(0.004)
						(0.003)		(0.004)	(0.003)
R^2	0.79	0.81	0.78	0.71	0.74	0.76	0.72	0.76	0.79
DW stat	2.36	2.56	2.49	2.34	2.43	2.24	2.03	2.13	1.99
White's test F statistic	1.49	0.71	1.29	1.78	1.93	3.39**	1.75	2.21*	2.11*
Jarque-Bera test statistic	1.15	1.46	1.78	1.43	2.27	1.83	1.06	1.31	2.29

[a] $n = 27$. Standard errors are reported in parentheses below the estimates.
[b] There is evidence of heteroscedasticity for the 1997, 1999 and 2000 regressions. The second set of terms in parentheses under each coefficient are the White heteroscedasticity consistent standard errors (White 1980).
* Statistically significant at the 0.10 level.
** Statistically significant at the 0.05 level.

Table 2. Unconstrained SUR (OLS) Estimates for St Henri[a] (by auction year)

	1995	1996	1997	1998	1999	2000
Constant	1.08	3.66**	2.63**	1.71	2.99	3.52**
	(1.26)	(1.13)	(1.05)	(1.08)	(1.11)	(1.42)
Age	0.201**	0.217**	0.076	0.026	0.019	0.087
	(0.078)	(0.080)	(0.082)	(0.092)	(0.104)	(0.142)
Age^2	−0.013**	−0.013**	−0.006	−0.004	−0.003	−0.0007
	(0.005)	(0.005)	(0.005)	(0.005)	(0.005)	(0.007)
Age^3	0.0003**	0.0002**	0.0001	0.0001	0.000008	0.0001
	(0.0001)	(0.0001)	(0.00009)	(0.00009)	(0.00009)	(0.0001)
Temp	0.11**	0.006	0.017	0.11**	0.07	0.13**
	(0.63)	(0.05)	(0.05)	(0.05)	(0.05)	(0.06)
TempD	−0.14	−0.18**	−0.07	−0.12	−0.11	−0.26**
	(0.08)	(0.08)	(0.07)	(0.07)	(0.07)	(0.09)
RainH	−0.003*	−0.004**	−0.003**	−0.003**	−0.002**	−0.005**
	(0.001)	(0.0009)	(0.0009)	(0.0009)	(0.0009)	(0.0011)
Wind	0.21**	0.21**	0.21**	0.27**	0.19**	0.20**
	(0.09)	(0.08)	(0.07)	(0.07)	(0.07)	(0.09)
$Wind^2$	−0.007**	−0.006**	−0.006**	−0.008**	−0.006**	−0.006**
	(0.003)	(0.002)	(0.002)	(0.002)	(0.002)	(0.003)
R^2	0.50	0.58	0.61	0.70	0.62	0.64
DW stat	2.78	2.18	2.40	2.67	2.76	2.15
White's test F statistic	0.40	0.96	0.59	0.71	0.49	0.59
Jarque-Bera test statistic	0.74	0.22	1.58	0.19	0.18	0.61

[a] $n = 26$. Standard errors are reported in parentheses below the estimates.
*Statistically significant at the 0.10 level.
**Statistically significant at the 0.05 level.

forms adopted. For both St Henri and Hill of Grace, age is estimated to effect the secondary market price in a cubic fashion. The coefficients are significant for both wines, and remarkably similar between the two wines. The coefficients suggest that prices rise with age initially, reach a plateau, and then begin to rise again.

This result is consistent with the hypothesis that while quality determines the price of these wines in the initial years after their

Table 3. Unconstrained SUR (OLS) Estimates for Hill of Grace[a] (by auction year)

	1995	1996	1997	1998	1999	2000
Constant	−31.06	−71.56**	−40.74	−72.85**	−40.41	−53.91*
	(23.07)	(22.37)	(25.67)	(26.28)	(27.46)	(23.68)
Age	−0.185	0.800**	0.557*	0.368	0.443	0.718*
	(0.213)	(0.236)	(0.306)	(0.352)	(0.409)	(0.389)
Age^2	0.011	−0.054**	−0.038*	−0.022	−0.026	−0.039*
	(0.015)	(0.015)	(0.019)	(0.020)	(0.023)	(0.020)
Age^3	0.0002	0.001**	0.0008**	0.0004	0.0005	0.0006*
	(0.00003)	(0.0003)	(0.0004)	(0.0004)	(0.0004)	(0.0003)
Temp	3.43	7.59**	4.14	8.09**	4.49	5.79**
	(2.41)	(2.32)	(2.66)	(2.71)	(2.81)	(2.40)
TempD	−0.091	−0.203**	−0.109	−0.217**	−0.121	−0.155**
	(0.065)	(0.062)	(0.071)	(0.072)	(0.075)	(0.064)
Wind	0.708**	0.493**	0.748**	0.125	0.303	0.236
	(0.254)	(0.254)	(0.280)	(0.285)	(0.295)	(0.253)
$Wind^2$	−0.030**	−0.025**	−0.035**	−0.007	−0.014	−0.011
	(0.011)	(0.011)	(0.012)	(0.012)	(0.013)	(0.011)
Trellis	0.41*	0.55**	0.41	0.44	0.45	0.57**
	(0.25)	(0.24)	(0.27)	(0.28)	(0.29)	(0.24)
SP	0.21	0.13	0.12	0.27	0.16	0.05
	(0.15)	(0.14)	(0.16)	(0.17)	(0.17)	(0.15)
R^2	0.61	0.59	0.69	0.67	0.65	0.75
DW stat	2.03	2.23	2.65	2.28	2.32	2.07
White's test F statistic	1.72	1.29	0.91	1.60	1.14	1.67
Jarque-Bera test statistic	0.41	0.24	0.47	1.31	0.10	0.17

[a] $n = 20$. Standard errors are reported in parentheses below the estimates.
*Statistically significant at the 0.10 level.
**Statistically significant at the 0.05 level.

release, eventually relative scarcity becomes the price driver. The optimal drinking age should occur around the turning of the cubic function (where prices plateau). For both St Henri and Hill of Grace the estimated turning point (at age 22.6 for St Henri and 19.7 for Hill of Grace), is within the optimal drinking range for most of the vintages considered in the sample (Read and Caillard, 1994). After these wines

Table 4. Constrained SUR Estimates for Grange[a] (by auction year)

	1992	1993	1994	1995	1996	1997	1998	1999	2000
Constant	−0.04	0.07	0.20	0.26	0.45	0.58	0.62	0.57	0.62
	(1.10)	(1.10)	(1.10)	(1.10)	(1.10)	(1.10)	(1.10)	(1.10)	(1.10)
Age					0.022**				
					(0.005)				
Temp					0.26**				
					(0.05)				
TempD					−0.24**				
					(0.07)				
RainH					−0.004**				
					(0.0009)				
Wind					0.43**				
					(0.08)				
Wind^2					−0.013**				
					(0.002)				
R^2	0.71	0.72	0.77	0.70	0.70	0.70	0.67	0.71	0.74
R^2(pooled)[b]					0.82				

[a] $n = 27$. Standard errors are reported in parentheses below the estimates.
[b] Pooled R^2 gives the R^2 of the pooled OLS model with cross-section specific constants and cross-sectional SUR weights.
*Statistically significant at the 0.10 level.
**Statistically significant at the 0.05 level.

have passed their optimal drinking time their 'icon status' means they still have collector value well beyond their potential for drinking. That is, the vintages of St Henri still in circulation but possibly past their prime for drinking are mainly in the market as antiques, rather than as part of the market for fine drinking wine, with consumers implicitly valuing highly their scarcity.

For Grange, on the other hand, age is estimated to effect the secondary market price in a linear fashion. The age coefficient of 0.022 is significant and suggests that an extra year of aging corresponds to an average 2.2 per cent increase in the real price, *ceteris paribus*. This is slightly lower than previous studies (Ashenfelter *et al.*, 1995; Byron and Ashenfelter, 1995; Fogarty, 2000) which report estimated coefficients (based on nominal prices) of 0.035, 0.041 and 0.03, respectively.

Table 5. Constrained SUR Estimates for St Henri[a] (by auction year)

	1995	1996	1997	1998	1999	2000
Constant	1.73* (0.91)	1.90** (0.91)	2.06** (0.91)	2.13** (0.91)	2.18** (0.91)	2.11** (0.91)
Age			0.16** (0.03)			
Age^2			−0.010** (0.002)			
Age^3			0.0002** (0.00003)			
Temp			0.048 (0.040)			
TempD			−0.096* (0.062)			
RainH			−0.0029** (0.0008)			
Wind			0.21** (0.06)			
Wind^2			−0.006** (0.002)			
R^2	0.42	0.50	0.56	0.60	0.56	0.53
R^2(pooled)[b]			0.70			

[a]$n = 26$. Standard errors are reported in parentheses below the estimates.
[b]Pooled R^2 gives the R^2 of the pooled OLS model with cross-section specific constants and cross-sectional SUR weights.
*Statistically significant at the 0.10 level.
**Statistically significant at the 0.05 level.

Why should prices for St Henri and Hill of Grace rise at a diminishing rate over the first twenty years and eventually plateau before beginning to rise again, while prices for Grange continue to grow linearly with age? The longer-term cellaring potential for Grange may provide some explanation for this. According to Read and Caillard (1994), all but four of the vintages of Grange in our sample were still at their peak or were yet to reach their peak in the auction years considered. This is in contrast to St Henri and Hill of Grace for which many of the older vintages were well past their optimal drinking age. It may also be that Grange's longevity is

Table 6. Constrained SUR Estimates for Hill of Grace[a] (by auction year)

	1995	1996	1997	1998	1999	2000
Constant	−40.16** (13.35)	−39.89** (13.35)	−39.67** (13.35)	−39.55** (13.35)	−39.54** (13.35)	−39.56** (13.35)
Age			0.167** (0.066)			
Age^2			−0.010** (0.004)			
Age^3			0.0002** (0.00008)			
Temp			4.57** (1.43)			
Temp^2			−0.123** (0.038)			
Wind			0.284** (0.131)			
Wind^2			−0.012** (0.006)			
Trellis			0.169** (0.097)			
SP			0.038** (0.081)			
R^2	0.46	0.24	0.51	0.53	0.56	0.70
R^2 (pooled)[b]			0.76			

[a] $n = 20$. Standard errors are reported in parentheses below the estimates.
[b] Pooled R^2 gives the R^2 of the pooled OLS model with cross-section specific constants and cross-sectional SUR weights.
*Statistically significant at the 0.10 level.
**Statistically significant at the 0.05 level.

such that, well before the quality begins its eventual deterioration, the wine has already achieved 'antique' status — that is, it is sufficiently old and rare to be viewed as a collector's item. Because of the large number of years it takes for the wine to reach its peak, and then the large number of years for which it can maintain it (Read and Caillard, 1994), it is conceivable that a given vintage could be quite rare even when only in the middle of its 'recommended drinking age' period. In that case, the plateau in price as quality falls would not occur because the price will continue to be driven upward by the relative scarcity, resulting in a linear relationship between age and price.

6.2. Temperature

Temperature is found to have a significant effect on the secondary market price variation of the vintages for all three icon wines considered. No significant difference was found between the explanatory power of the models using average daily maximum temperature compared with using average daily temperature, so we report the results based on average daily temperature for ease of comparison with previous studies.

For Grange, and St Henri, the relationship between average daily growing season temperature and price is found to be best modelled linearly, with coefficients of 0.26 for Grange and 0.048 for St Henri. This suggests that a one degree increase in the average maximum growing temperature leads to a 26 per cent increase in the price of Grange and a 5 per cent increase in the price of St Henri. These estimates should be viewed in the context of the stability in average temperatures in the region. For example, over the period 1960 to 1986 the standard deviation in average daily temperature was only 0.69°C.

For Hill of Grace, the relationship between secondary market price and average maximum growing season temperature is found to be best approximated by a quadratic. That is, higher average maximum temperatures lead to higher secondary market prices up to the 18.6°C optimal level, but for temperatures higher than 18.6 degrees, the opposite is true. This is slightly below the 20–21 degree range that Gladstones suggests is optimal.

The diurnal temperature range is also found to be significant in explaining the variation in price between vintages for all of the wines considered. Consistent with the viticulture literature, the estimated relationship in each case is negative, suggesting that a large temperature range has a negative affect on the quality of the grapes in a particular vintage year.

6.3. Rainfall

The estimated effect of total rainfall in the period prior to harvest was remarkably consistent across the two Penfolds wines. In line with viticultural expectations, higher rainfall during this period has a negative effect on grape quality and thereby on secondary market prices. We estimate a one-millilitre increase in the total rainfall prior to harvest leads to an average 0.4 per cent decrease in the secondary market price of Grange and a 0.3 per cent decrease for St Henri. These estimates are also remarkably similar to those estimated in other studies (0.4 per cent for Ashenfelter *et al.* and 0.3 per cent for Byron and Ashenfelter). However, rainfall in the period prior to harvest was not shown to have a significant effect on the price for Hill of Grace.

Winter rainfall in the Ashenfelter *et al.* study was found to be significantly positively related to the secondary market price of Bordeaux wines. We find it to be positive but insignificant for all three Australian icon wines.

6.4. *Other weather variables*

Humidity, sunlight, and windiness were all discussed in section 3 as potentially important to wine quality. Humidity and sunshine hours were tested as explanators of secondary market prices in Byron and Ashenfelter (1995). They, like us, found those variables not to be statistically significant. However, we find windiness to be significant in explaining the price variation of all three wines we considered. In each case we found the variable to be best modelled as a quadratic, consistent with viticultural theory. The optimal wind speeds were estimated to be 11.8 kms per hour for Hill of Grace and slightly higher at 16.5 and 17.5 for Grange and St Henri, respectively. The model suggests that wind impacts negatively on the secondary market price once these optimal speeds are reached.

6.5. *Technological change*

Improvements in production techniques introduced by viticulturists and oenologists are shown to have a positive effect on the secondary market prices of their wines where they are significant. For Hill of Grace, consumers are increasingly willing to pay for vintages produced since the time that Stephen and Prue Henschke took over their family winery in

1978. Further, the improvement in grape quality as a result of a new trellising system in 1990 is also reflected in the secondary market prices of vintages produced from that year onwards. However, as noted earlier, if this change in technique increased production costs, the higher price may to some extent reflect the passing through of these higher costs.

6.6. *Goodness of fit*

The signs of all the coefficients in our model are in line with viticultural expectations. In addition, there are other indications that our model is explaining well the price variation between different vintages of the same wine. Firstly, the R^2 for both the constrained and unconstrained SUR models for each wine are quite high. This indicates that the weather and changes in production techniques, along with the age of the wine, explain from 24 to 77 per cent of the variation in prices for any given auction year.

Using pooled Ordinary Least Squares[4] to estimate the models provides a single R^2 for each model. These are 0.82 for Grange, 0.70 for St Henri and 0.76 for Hill of Grace. The models in each case demonstrate significantly superior explanatory power compared to models estimated with age as the only explanatory variable. The R^2 for the models with weather and technological change variables excluded are 0.62, 0.58 and 0.67 for Grange, St Henri and Hill of Grace, respectively. This suggests weather variation in Australia is less important in explaining prices than is the case for fine Bordeaux wines. Ashenfelter, Ashmore and Lalonde show that introducing weather variables into their model improves the R^2 from 0.21 based on age alone to 0.83. The greater importance of weather for Bordeaux is likely to be related to the much stronger variation in climatic conditions in that part of the world. For example, the temperature variation in Australia (0.69°C standard deviation in the average daily maximum over the period 1960 to 1986) is considerably less than that observed in Bordeaux. Also, because Ashenfelter, Ashmore, and Lalonde did not experiment with alternative functional forms for the age variable, it is possible that the low explanatory

---

[4] Using cross-section specific constants and cross-sectional SUR weights, such that the estimates are identical to the constrained SUR estimates reported.

power of their model based on age alone reflects the fact that age does not influence price in a linear fashion for the wines they considered.

Our model is found to be particularly robust to alternative specifications in each case. For each wine the regression was re-estimated by systematically dropping one of the vintage observations at a time. The coefficients in each of the models exhibited minimal variation, and there was shown to be no statistically significant change in the models' explanatory power (as measured by R^2) any of the times that each model was re-estimated. The coefficient values attributable to each of the explanatory variables were also shown to be remarkably robust to the inclusion of insignificant explanatory variables in each model.

Also, the actual price was almost always within the 95 per cent confidence bands around the estimated price for the in-sample estimates (see Figures 1, 2 and 3). Although in some cases the confidence intervals are quite large, the fact that the model tracks the peaks and troughs of the auction price data closely provides further evidence that it is capturing weather- and age-driven quality variations.

The out-of-sample forecast power of the models is also demonstrated in these figures. For Hill of Grace and St Henri, the out-of-sample vintages fall within the 95 per cent confidence interval estimates; for Grange, however, the actual prices in a few cases break out on the upper

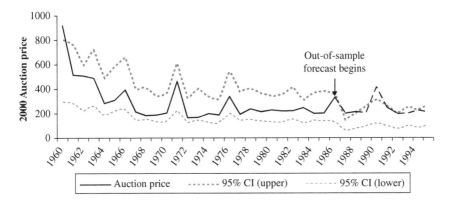

Figure 1. Actual and fitted auction prices: Grange[a]

[a]The fitted price is the mid-point between the 95 per cent confidence interval bands. The out-of-sample forecast is from the 1987 to the 1995 vintages.

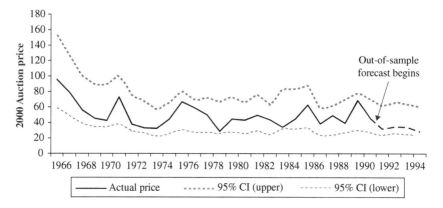

Figure 2. Actual and fitted auction prices: St Henri[a]

[a]The fitted price is the mid-point between the 95 per cent confidence interval bands. The out-of-sample forecast is from the 1992 to the 1995 vintages.

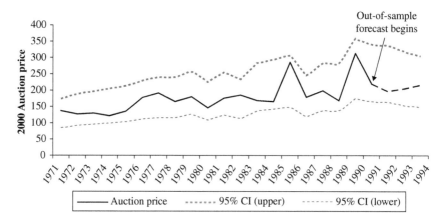

Figure 3. Actual and fitted auction prices: Hill of Grace[a]

[a]The fitted price is the mid-point between the 95 per cent confidence interval bands. The out-of-sample forecast is from the 1992 to the 1994 vintages.

side of this interval. This suggests that our model is under-predicting the prices of more-recent Grange vintages. While we were unable to obtain precise release price data for our study, anecdotal evidence suggests that release prices have increased strongly over the past decade for Grange (and more recently have also increased for Hill of Grace and St Henri). In that case, secondary market prices would be expected to rise if investors delay selling their product in the hope of achieving their expected return on their investment (based on historical returns when release prices were lower).[5]

7. Summary and conclusions

This study adds to the existing empirical literature on wine pricing by considering the determinants of secondary market price variation between different vintages of the same wine. Assuming that the price of a given vintage on the auction market is determined by the quality of the wine, the price variation between vintages can be attributed to differences in quality, which affects the consumers' willingness to pay (and the sellers' willingness to sell). In particular, extending the framework of Ashenfelter, Ashmore, and Lalonde (1995), we are able to explain econometrically these quality differences on the basis of weather conditions during the growing season and improvements in grape growing and winemaking techniques, in addition to age of the wine.

The theoretical plausibility of our models is supported by the fact that our estimates of the implicit prices imparted through superior weather conditions and winemaking techniques are in line with viticultural expectations. Our model is further validated by its robustness to alternative specifications, and by its high values for R^2.

Given that theoretical plausibility and statistical robustness of our models, we conclude that there is support for our hypothesis that the variation in consumers' willingness to pay for different vintages of aged icon wines is related to quality differentials across the vintages brought about by variations in age, weather and production techniques.

The findings of this study have implications for viticulturists, wine makers, wine consumers and investors. For viticulturists, the study provides an indication of the most appropriate climatic regions for growing

---

[5] It would be interesting to see whether more-recent vintages of St Henri and Hill of Grace are similarly selling for prices above those that would be estimated using historical data. If this were to be the case, then the release price or recommended retail price of the wines is an omitted variable in the estimated models. This does not invalidate our model as a predictor of vintage quality, however.

ultra-premium wine grapes. In the past, this decision has been based mainly on the understanding of the relationship between terroir (physical and hydrological aspects of soil, macro- and meso-climates, topography, etc.) and quality. However, by quantifying the relationship between weather and price, our study may allow a more detailed cost-benefit analysis of grape-growing prospects in different areas, given their climatic history.[6] For winemakers buying grapes from independent growers, the price paid could be set in part on the basis of the weather variables using the equations presented in this study, pending the development of more-reliable quantitative indicators of grape quality such as grape colour, baume, and pH using NIRS technology.[7]

For the wine consumer, our study provides an objective guide to the quality of immature icon wines. While the consumer has a number of avenues for establishing the quality of the wine once mature, such as expert tasters' opinions (see, for example, Schamel and Anderson, 2003), less information is available the further away are the peak drinking years of the wine. Since weather variables evidently provide a reliable indicator of future quality, our model provides a useful guide to the wine investor/consumer.

Although not explored in this study, due to difficulties in obtaining release price data, wine investors and/or producers may be able to benefit from a study of the efficiency of the primary (release) markets for icon wines. If the release price of a wine does not fully reflect all the weather features of its vintage, then wine investors could exploit the publicly available weather information and make economic profits by choosing to invest only in those vintages that are under-priced at the time of their release. Alternatively, winemakers could use that same information not only in setting their grape purchase price but also the wine release prices and/or quantities. For example, if the winemaker knows the weather conditions were exceptionally good for her/his grapes relative to others' grapes in the same region in a particular year, s/he would benefit from withholding some of that vintage for later sale once consumers realize how exceptional is that vintage.

---

[6] See Ashenfelter (1997) on how this hedonic approach can be applied to vineyard site selection.
[7] See Golan and Shalit (1993). For details of the progress being made in Near Infra Red Spectroscopy (NIRS) in Australia, see GWRDC (2001).

It would be interesting, although time-consuming, to go back through critics' ratings books to see the extent to which their ratings, when these wines were first released, provide better or worse guidance to consumers than the weather variables identified in the equations estimated in this study. Another interesting avenue for future research would be back-casting, to show the extent to which our model can track past auction price movements. Does the actual price approach the price predicted by our model (from below in good vintages and from above in poor vintages) as the wine ages? Is the pace of that convergence increasing over time as investors/consumers/producers learn more about weather and other determinants of quality (and in particular as viticulturalists find more-precise ways to compensate for adverse weather conditions)?

References

Ashenfelter, O. (1997). A hedonic approach to vineyard site selection. *Presentation to Fifth Annual Meeting of the Vineyard Data Quantification Society.*

Ashenfelter, O., Ashmore, D., and Lalonde, R. (1995). Bordeaux wine vintage quality and the weather. *Chance,* 8(4), 7–14.

Byron, R.P. and Ashenfelter, O. (1995). Predicting the quality of an unborn Grange. *Economic Record,* 71, 400–414.

Fogarty, J. (2000). Prices, age and weather. Unpublished Honours thesis, School of Economics, University of Western Australia, Perth.

Gladstones, J. (1992). Viticulture and the environment. Adelaide: Winetitles.

Golan, A. and Shalit, H. (1993). Wine quality differentials in hedonic grape pricing. *Journal of Agricultural Economics,* 44, 311–321.

Grape and Wine Research and Development Corporation (GWRDC) (2001). R&D highlights. Adelaide: GWRDC.

Greene, W.H. (2002). *Econometric Analysis,* Prentice Hall, 5th edition.

Halliday, J. (1998). Classic Wines of Australia. Sydney: Harper Collins, 2nd edition.

Hamilton, R.P. (1988). Wind effects on grape vines. In: *Proceedings of the Second International Symposium for Cool Climate Viticulture and Oeneology,* Auckland. pp. 65–68.

Jones, G.V. and Storchmann, K.H. (2001). Wine market prices and investment under uncertainty: An econometric model for Bordeaux Crus Classés. *Agricultural Economics,* 26(2), 115–133.

Langton, S. (2001). Fine wine buying and investment guide. Sydney: Media 21 Publishing Pty Ltd, 4th edition.

Oczkowski, E. (2001). Hedonic wine price functions and measurement error. *Economic Record,* 77(239), 374–382.

Read, A. and Caillard, A. (2000). The rewards of patience: A drinking and cellaring guide to Penfolds wines. 4th edition. Sydney: Penfolds Wines.

Schamel, G. and Anderson K. (2003). Wine quality and varietal, regional and winery reputations: Hedonic prices for Australia and New Zealand. *Economic Record*, 79(246), 357–369

Smart, R. (2001). Where to plant and what to plant. *ANZ Wine Industry Journal*, 16(4), 48–50.

White, H. (1980). A heteroskedastic-consistent covariance matrix estimator and a direct test for heteroskedasticity. *Econometrica*, 21, 149–170.

Chapter 12

Australian Wine Industry Competitiveness: Why so Slow to Emerge?*

Kym Anderson[†]

Abstract

Despite favourable growing conditions, Australia's production or exports of wine did not become significant until the 1890s. Both grew in the 1920s, but only because of government support. Once that support was removed in the late 1940s, production plateaued and exports diminished: only two per cent of wine production was exported during 1975–1985. Yet over the next two decades, Australia's wine production quadrupled and the share exported rose to two-thirds — before falling somewhat in the next 10 years. This paper explains why it took so long for Australia's production and competitive advantage in wine to emerge, why it took off spectacularly after the mid-1980s and why it fell in the

---

*First published in *Australian Journal of Agricultural and Resource Economics* 62(4): 507–26, October 2018. The author is grateful for helpful comments from four reviewers.
[†]Kym Anderson (e-mail: kym.anderson@adelaide.edu.au) is George Gollin Professor Emeritus at the School of Economics, University of Adelaide, and Honorary Professor at the Arndt-Corden Department of Economics, Australian National University, Canberra 2600, Australian Capital Territory, Australia.

10 years to 2016. It concludes that despite the recent downturn in the industry's fortunes, the country's international competitiveness is now firmly established and commensurate with its ideal wine-growing climate, notwithstanding the likelihood of further boom-slump cycles in the decades ahead.

1. Introduction

Why was Australia a net importer of wine until the 1890s? Why did exports then grow somewhat but then cease after World War II? And why, in just two decades from the mid-1980s, did Australia's wine production quadruple and the share of production exported rise from < 2 per cent to more than 60 per cent?[1] Answers to these questions are of great interest not only to current producers but also to potential industry investors (particularly from abroad). In addressing them, this paper explains why it took so long for Australia's production of and international competitiveness in wine to emerge, why the industry grew so spectacularly after the 1980s, and why it slipped back somewhat in the most recent decade before beginning to return to profitability after 2016. Such an explanation requires a perspective that is intersectoral (since other industries were expanding also in this settler economy) as well as international (since other settler countries in the New World also had the potential to become wine exporters).

The paper begins by outlining the determinants and some empirical indicators of wine industry competitiveness and trade specialisation. It then reviews briefly the long-run growth path for the industry as the domestic alcohol consumption pattern evolved and in the light of global wine market developments. A fuller explanation of why the country's production and trade in wine emerged as it did is then provided, by looking at each of several boom-plateau cycles the industry has gone through in the past 160 years. The final section summarises the findings.

---

[1] Between 1985 and 2010 the volume of Australian exports grew more than one hundred fold for wine while rising <80 per cent all other rural products (ABS 2010, table 25).

2. Determinants and indicators of an industry's intersectoral and international competitiveness

Standard Heckscher-Ohlin trade theory suggests a price-taking small open economy's export specialisation is determined by supply factors (relative factor endowments, and the relative factor intensities of production) assuming technologies and tastes are the same across countries and markets are undistorted by governments. Leamer (1987) developed that model for many goods and three factors of production: natural resource capital; produced capital; and labour. If the stock of natural resources is unchanged, rapid growth by one or more countries relative to others in their availability of produced capital per unit of available labour time would cause those economies to strengthen their comparative advantage in nonprimary products. By contrast, a discovery of minerals or energy raw materials or a rise in their real international price would strengthen that country's comparative advantage in mining and weaken its comparative advantage in agricultural and other tradable products. It would also boost national income and hence the demand for nontradables, which would cause mobile resources to move into the production of nontradable goods and services (Corden 1984; Freebairn 2015). As domestic transport infrastructure is developed, more of the country's products would move from the nontradable to the tradable category, and a fall in ocean transport costs also widens the range of products traded globally (Venables 2004). This is especially helpful for those countries most distant from key markets, but the benefit is not shared equally across the product range.

An important part of natural resource capital pertinent to wine is terroir, which refers to various aspects of such attributes as climate, topography, soils, and geology that determine the quality of the vine's growing environment. Experience has determined the best sites and most-suitable grape varieties in long-established wine regions. In new regions and where climate is changing rapidly, science is being used to speed the selection process (Gergaud and Ginsburgh 2008). The conventional wisdom is that winegrapes grow best between the 30° and 50° temperate latitude bands where rain is concentrated in the winter and summer harvest times are dry. Southern Australia is one of relatively few regions of the world with those climatic conditions.

Technologies are certainly transferable across countries, and for wine that transferability process has accelerated over the past two decades via both fly-in/fly-out vignerons and foreign direct investments. But new technologies in agriculture tend to be developed to save the scarcest factor of production, as reflected in relative factor prices. Thus, new labour-saving technologies can help high-wage countries remain competitive in winegrape growing.

For countries whose trade costs are too high for their wines to be internationally tradable, production is determined by the domestic demand for wine — which historically has differed greatly across countries, even controlling for income differences (Holmes and Anderson 2017b). Domestic demand is also relevant to smaller firms unable to cover the fixed cost of entering export markets, and even to a complete industry if it is too small to be able to afford generic promotion abroad. For these reasons, the size of the domestic market can be a contributor to an industry's productivity and hence competitiveness (Linder 1961; Krugman 1980), and can help explain a home-country bias in wine demand (Friberg *et al.* 2011).

In addition to these standard determinants of industry competitiveness, production and trade specialisation are also affected by market-distorting policies at home and abroad. Excise taxes on alcoholic beverage sales are common, and many countries also impose import taxes on beverages, especially those they do not produce. Hence, those taxes vary greatly across countries (Anderson 2010). Tariff preferences and export subsidies also affect wine trade patterns. Protection from imports for a country's other manufacturers weakens the international competitiveness of that country's wineries, while tariffs on wine imports themselves reduce competition from abroad but that tends to slow the speed with which quality of the domestic product is raised to the global frontier.

The most common empirical indicator of a national industry's comparative advantage in international trade is Balassa's (1965) 'revealed' comparative advantage (RCA) index: the share of wine in a nation's merchandise export earnings divided by that share for the world as a whole. The more that ratio is above (below) unity, the stronger is the country's comparative advantage (disadvantage) in wine as revealed by actual trade data — bearing in mind that actual trade data may be affected by governmental interventions in markets.

National volume indicators such as the share of wine production exported relative to those of other countries or the world, and wine production divided by wine consumption (the self-sufficiency indicator) are also helpful indicators of competitiveness. The share of consumption imported is also worth referring to, but it needs to be kept in mind that intra-industry trade (that is, simultaneous exporting and importing of a product) is to be expected the more heterogeneous is that product in terms of quality, variety or style — attributes that are demanded increasingly as incomes rise.

3. Australia's wine production and trade experience: Long-run trends

With the above influences on trade specialisation in mind, a brief overview of long-run developments in Australia's wine markets is provided in this section. It begins with domestic demand and imports before looking at domestic production and exports, and then places these developments in global perspective. The following section focuses on explaining how these developments affected the country's wine industry development during each of several boom-plateau cycles around an upward long-run trend.

3.1. Domestic demand for and imports of wine

Domestic alcohol consumption during the first 50 years of European settlement in New South Wales relied predominantly on imported spirits along with modest volumes of imported wines and beers, supplemented gradually by domestic (including illicit) spirits and beer production. Alcohol consumption rose hugely in the 1850s with the influx of male migrants and the boost in per capita incomes, due to the gold mining boom in Victoria. As the dominance of adult males in the population gradually fell during the next few decades, so too did the volume of per capita alcohol consumption. It was down to 5 L of alcohol per capita in the 1890s, to 4 L by the late 1920s, and below 3 L during the Great Depression of the early 1930s. Thereafter it rose steadily to a peak of 10 L in the mid-1970s, mostly of beer, before falling back to around 8 L by the early 1990s (Anderson 2015, Chart 34).

Spirits dominated in the first 100 years of European settlement partly because the settlers' peers back in Britain and Ireland drank spirits, and partly because it was the cheapest beverage per unit of alcohol to ship to the antipodes and was least likely to deteriorate on the trip. Meanwhile, beer was costly to produce domestically because Australia was a net importer of grain prior to the 1870s.

Even though wine continued to be the preferred beverage of only a small fraction of the population, its share of total alcohol consumption reached an average of seven per cent by the late 1860s and 12 per cent between 1890 and 1913. While this was low by the standards of southern Europe, it contrasts with Britain and New Zealand, where wine's share was barely 2 per cent in that latter period, and with the United States, where it was 3 per cent (Anderson and Pinilla 2017). It rose further during the two world wars when grain was kept for food rather than making beer, but otherwise showed a flat trend until the 1960s. By then, beer again comprised three-quarters of all alcohol consumption in Australia, with just one-eighth of the volume coming from wine (Anderson 2015, Chart 35).

Since the early 1960s, Australia's wine consumption per capita has increased faster than per capita income, at the expense of beer — the opposite of the global trend: the share of wine in Australia's total alcohol consumption was only half that of the world as a whole in 1960 but, by the mid-1970s, annual wine consumption per capita was twice its early 1960s average of 7 L in Australia, and it reached three times that earlier level by the turn of the century (Holmes and Anderson 2017a, b). Its per capita consumption level is now above the much-diminished levels of Argentina, Chile and Spain, and more than half of France and Italy. In 2015, it was three times the world average. Beer consumption has converged down to the world average, and spirits consumption has remained below half the global average (Anderson and Pinilla 2017).

Imports were the main source of wines consumed in Australia prior to 1860, but their share was below 20 per cent for the next four decades and then below five per cent for most of the 20th century. They expanded a little during the country's first big export-demand-driven mining boom that began in the mid-1970s, and expanded substantially in the subsequent mining investment boom from around 2005 (Figure 1).

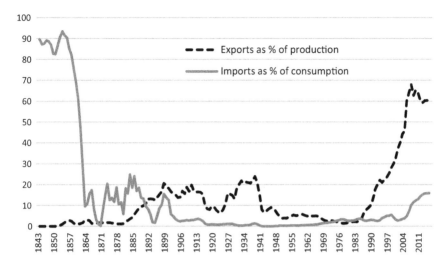

Figure 1. Exports as a per cent of wine production and imports as a per cent of wine consumption volume, Australia, 1843 to 2017 (3-year moving average around year shown). *Source*: Anderson and Pinilla (2017).

3.2. Domestic production and exports of wine

During their first 50 years, European settlers in New South Wales certainly experimented with imported vines and made wine to help satisfy their own demand (McIntyre 2012), but annual production (including for distillation into brandy) had yet to reach 100 kL by 1840. Even as new migrants began settling in Victoria, South Australia and Western Australia from the late 1830s, grape production expanded slowly. It would have grown faster had the demand for wool for Britain's booming textile mills not been so strong throughout the 19th century. Wool's high price and relatively low transport cost per dollar of product meant it dominated exports of Australia in every decade until the 1960s, apart from short periods when gold dominated during and following the gold rushes of the 1850s in Victoria and the 1890s in Western Australia (Anderson 2017).

Nonetheless, Australia's vine area, wine production and wine exports trace out rising trends over most of the past two centuries (Figure 2). Their respective annual compound growth rates over the 173 years from 1843 to 2016 are 2.8, 4.3 and 5.0 per cent. Exports expanded from the 1880s, and

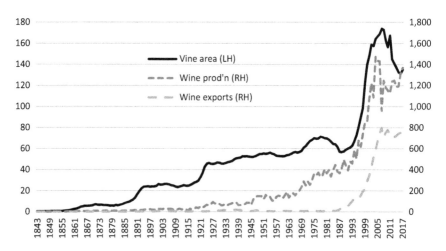

Figure 2. Vine bearing area, wine production and wine exports, Australia, 1843 to 2017 ('000 ha and ML).
Source: Anderson and Pinilla (2017).

accounted for 10–20 per cent of wine production for the first four decades of the Federation, but then shrank to around five per cent for the subsequent four decades. It took until the late 1980s before the industry took off with an export-led boom (Figure 1).

Two other indicators of the long-run trend in the wine industry's competitiveness vis-à-vis other industries in Australia are worth mentioning, since they are also useful in indicating cycles around long-run trends. One is the vine intensity of cropping: the area under vine has grown at about the same pace as the country's total crop area on average since the mid-19th century. The other is growth in production of wine relative to all products nationally (captured as the volume of wine production per $ of real GDP): Australia's wine output has grown only marginally faster than the economy's total output over the past two centuries (Anderson and Pinilla 2017).

3.3. Australia's wine production and trade in global perspective

Table 1 reveals that the volume of wine production per $ of real GDP in Australia was miniscule pre-World War II compared with the main

Table 1. Volume of wine production per $m of real GDP (KL)

	1860–1909	1910–1959	1960–1989	1990–1999	2000–2009	2010–2016
Australia	1.2	1.8	1.7	1.7	2.5	1.9
New Zealand	0.0	0.1	0.7	0.9	1.6	2.7
Argentina	5.7	13.9	11.9	5.5	4.4	3.3
Chile	9.5	15.5	9.5	2.6	3.6	4.2
South Africa	4.8	7.1	5.7	5.6	4.5	3.9
France	50.9	31.4	10.6	5.1	3.8	3.2
Italy	54.4	32.4	12.4	6.1	4.3	4.1
Spain	71.5	34.5	12.7	5.8	5.5	4.9
Portugal	61.1	58.7	19.7	6.2	4.4	4.4
Greece	26.5	24.9	7.2	3.4	2.6	2.1
Bulgaria	18.7	16.5	9.5	5.9	3.1	2.0
Hungary	16.7	12.6	7.9	6.7	4.9	2.9
Romania	16.0	28.5	10.6	8.4	6.1	4.2

Source: Anderson *et al.* (2017, table 135).

European producers, and small even relative to Argentina, Chile and South Africa. Since the 1950s that indicator has fallen greatly for those key producers, however, and is now only about twice Australia's. Similar convergences between Australia and these other countries have occurred in the share of vines in total crop area and in wine production per capita (Anderson *et al.*, 2017, tables 123 and 134).

As for trade, only twice before the 21st century did the export share of wine production in Australia exceed the world average, namely, in the lead-up to World War I and in the 1930s. Apart from the 1930s and World War II, the share of wine in Australia's total merchandise exports was always below that for the world as a whole until the 1990s. That is, Australia had a comparative disadvantage in wine pre-1990, according to the RCA index. Figure 3 shows that this index for Australia was never above unity prior to the late 1980s, and it was always well below 0.5 until 1925.

Even so, leaving aside the Western Cape of South Africa (whose vignerons have been producing for export markets since the mid-17th century),

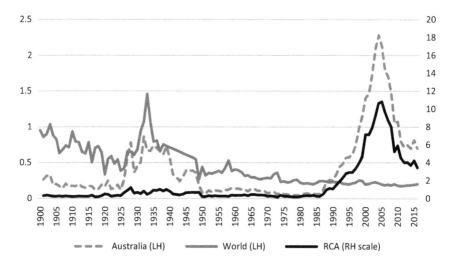

Figure 3. Wine exports as a per cent of total merchandise export value, Australia and the world (3-year moving average around year shown), and Australia's RCA index,[a] 1900 to 2016.

Note: [a]RCA refers to Balassa's (1965) index of 'revealed' comparative advantage in wine, defined as the share of wine in a nation's merchandise export earnings divided by that share for the world as a whole.

Source: Anderson and Pinilla (2017).

Australia led the way among New World countries[2] in reaching self-sufficiency during the first globalisation wave (Figure 4). Leading up to World War I and during the interwar period, among the New World countries, Australia also had the highest index of revealed comparative advantage in wine — although it was still less than unity and far lower than Europe's main wine exporters (Table 2). Like those other New World countries, it became self-sufficient with the help of import tariff protection. Then from the 1890s, Australia was a net exporter of wine. Its export propensity slumped somewhat during 1915–1925, rose over the subsequent two decades, but then dropped suddenly soon after World War II and stayed low for four decades before rising dramatically from the late 1980s (Figure 1). The most recent rise lasted nearly two decades. During that

---

[2] The New World refers to temperate climate countries settled by Europeans since the 1500s in the Americas, Australasia and South Africa.

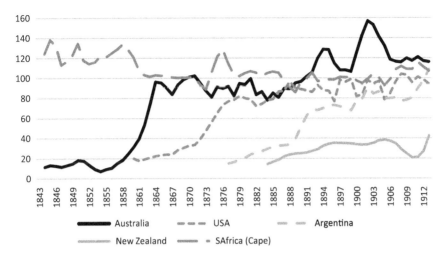

Figure 4. Wine self-sufficiency,[a] Australia and other New World wine exporters,[b] 1843 to 1914 (per cent, 3-year moving average around year shown).

Note: [a]Domestic production as a per cent of domestic consumption in volume terms. In value terms these lines would be lower, because the average price of New World imports were several times that of their exports.

[b]Chile was <1 per cent away from being 100 per cent self-sufficient in wine during 1860–1914.

Source: Anderson and Pinilla (2017).

time, Australia again led the New World in terms of its value of wine exports, but Chile and then New Zealand took the lead in terms of the comparative advantage index for wine as Australia's wine industry went into another slump from 2007 (Table 2).

4. The boom-slump cycles around Australia's wine growth path

As with most industries based on perennial crops, the wine industry is cyclical in all wine-producing countries. Even though Australia's area under vine has grown at about the same pace as the country's total crop area on average since the mid-19th century, and its wine output has grown only marginally faster than total GDP, around those long-run trends have been several distinct production cycles (Figure 5). This section examines the key developments contributing to the evolution of the Australian wine

Table 2. Index of 'revealed' comparative advantage in wine,[†] key exporting countries,[‡] 1900–2015

	France	Italy	Portugal	Spain	Greece	Bulgaria	Hungary	Australia	New Zealand	United States	Argentina	Chile	South Africa
1900–09	5.8	3.3	41.9	6.9	20.4	1.7	NA	0.3	0.0	0.1	0.0	0.1	0.0
1910–19	4.2	5.7	52.5	10.6	11.0	0.9	NA	0.2	0.0	0.1	0.1	0.2	0.1
1920–29	3.8	3.9	58.1	18.6	11.5	1.2	7.2	0.5	0.0	0.0	0.1	0.4	0.3
1930–39	3.5	3.2	22.6	3.6	4.3	0.3	3.2	0.8	0.0	0.0	0.0	0.8	0.9
1950–59	4.3	3.6	23.8	1.8	5.9	4.6	2.8	0.3	0.0	0.0	0.0	0.9	0.5
1960–69	5.3	3.0	23.7	12.4	4.1	11.8	4.9	0.4	0.0	0.0	0.0	0.4	0.5
1970–79	5.9	4.2	25.1	9.8	4.1	8.6	7.5	0.2	0.0	0.0	0.4	1.1	0.3
1980–89	8.1	4.3	17.3	6.4	2.4	6.2	6.2	0.5	0.2	0.1	0.5	1.4	0.2
1990–99	7.8	3.9	10.7	5.1	3.0	10.2	3.1	2.7	1.2	0.2	1.5	7.8	1.8
2000–09	7.8	5.3	8.5	4.9	2.0	4.2	0.7	8.4	7.2	0.4	3.7	12.6	4.9
2010–15	9.5	6.9	8.4	5.6	1.3	1.2	0.5	4.4	14.4	0.5	6.3	13.0	4.4
1900–2015	**6.0**	**4.3**	**26.6**	**7.8**	**6.4**	**4.6**	**4.0**	**1.7**	**2.1**	**0.1**	**1.1**	**3.5**	**1.3**

Note: [†]Balassa's (1965) 'revealed' comparative advantage (RCA) index is defined as the share of wine in a nation's merchandise export earnings divided by that share for the world as a whole.
[‡]Two other countries with high RCAs are Georgia and Moldova, whose annual RCAs during 1992–2015 averaged 27 and 63, respectively. During 1900–1969, Algeria's RCA averaged 67.
NA, not applicable.

Source: Compiled from Anderson and Pinilla (2017).

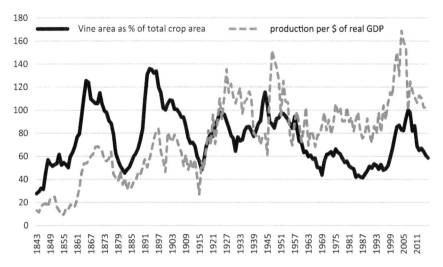

Figure 5. Vine area as per cent of total crop area and wine production per $ of real GDP, Australia, 1843 to 2016 (2007 = 100).
Source: Anderson and Pinilla (2017).

industry's intersectoral and international competitiveness within each of those cycles.[3]

4.1. *Australia's first wine cycle: 1855 to 1882*

The gold rush of the 1850s caused Australia's white population to almost treble and real GDP per capita to rise by 50 per cent that decade. Despite the expanded supply of labour, wages rose dramatically in the early 1850s. Many local men went to the Victorian goldfields too. That squeezed grape and wine production and profitability initially, with wine output in 1855 being only

---

[3] In the absence of producer price and hence production value data, the turning points of each cycle are chosen simply by inspecting annual vine bearing area and wine production data, both absolutely and relative to other sectors of the economy (as depicted in Figures 2 and 5, respectively). Each cycle starts with a boom in vine area, which is followed by a longer plateau (or at best a much slower rise) in planting that is associated with a fall in the share of vines in total crop area and in the production of wine relative to all products (captured by the volume of wine production per dollar of real GDP). Unless otherwise specified, the source of data referred to in this Section is Anderson (2015).

70 per cent of that in 1851. However, the increases in the continent's population and income were perceived correctly to lead to an expansion in domestic demand for wine. In response, the area of grapevines began to increase rapidly and by 1871 had expanded ten-fold, and wine production had increased 16-fold in those two decades.

The consequent growth in wine supplies was so fast that it outstripped the growth in domestic demand in each of Australia's colonies, so export outlets were sought. Intercolonial trade within the continent was one option. However, land and river transport costs were high, and each colony also sought to protect its local producers by imposing high import tariffs.[4] Fortunately, ocean shipping costs began to fall in this period, and Britain in 1860 abolished the import tariff preference for South African wine and in 1862 lowered its tariff on still wines by eighty percent. The cuts in UK table wine tariffs, together with the creation of off-licence retailing (thanks to Chancellor Gladstone's legislative changes in 1861), helped Australia's exports to Britain to quadruple over the 1860s and double again by the mid-1870s. This, however, was from a very low level first established in the mid-1850s: throughout the 1860s and 1870s Australia's modest wine exports amounted to < 3 per cent of its production (Figure 1).

Early exports from Australia were inhibited not only because the wine it produced was generally of extremely low quality (mostly dry red, shipped bulk in hogsheads only weeks after the grapes had been crushed), but also because up until then very little had been invested in securing quality packaging, marketing and distribution arrangements in Britain (Bell 1994). Producers suffered very low returns from the late 1860s as the rapid supply expansion outstripped demand growth. So poor were returns that the area of grapevines fell 10 per cent during the 1870s. Nonetheless, following the International Exhibition in Vienna in 1873, the official British report praised Australia's wines, and similar accolades (along with some critical reports) flowed from the International Exhibition of 1882 in Bordeaux.

---

[4] In 1860 the duties on wine coming into South Australia, Victoria and New South Wales were already quite high, but by the early 1890s they had been raised to near-prohibitive levels, equal to more than 100 per cent of the average export price of Australian wines.

4.2. The second cycle: 1882 to 1915

Successes in International Exhibitions, together with the prospect of forming an Australian Federation by the turn of the century which would see the removal of the high intercolonial trade restrictions, encouraged growers to expand the area under winegrapes in the 1880s. True, there were phylloxera[5] outbreaks in Geelong in the late 1870s and gradually in other parts of Victoria. But the Victorian Government responded with compensation for forced removal of diseased plants, and in 1890 offered subsidies of two pounds per acre ($10 per hectare) to replant with resistant stocks over the subsequent three years. As a result, Victoria's vine area more than doubled between 1889 and 1894. That planting, plus expanding vineyards in South Australia in anticipation of Federation, meant Australia's overall vineyard area and production of wine grew substantially during the 1880s/ early 1890s. Unfortunately that occurred just as the 1890s' Depression hit and domestic alcohol sales were plummeting.[6] So while wine production per capita doubled in the decade to 1895, wine consumption per capita fell by one-third during 1891–94.

Australia's vineyard expansions were soon followed by expansions of winery capacity and improvements in winemaking technology. This was associated with a concentration of winery ownership, which contributed to the industry's success in disposing of surpluses through exporting as the new century approached (Simpson 2011). By the turn of the century, production was three times its 1880 level, and one-sixth of the country's wine production was being exported (Figures 1 and 2). Australia's exports early in this cycle were helped partly by the reduced competition from France and other suppliers to Britain following the arrival and devastating spread of phylloxera in Europe in the 1870s and 1880s, with the vineyard area in France alone shrinking by two-fifths between 1870 and 1913. In the first decade of Federation, Australia had a stronger index of wine comparative

---

[5] Phylloxera is an insect pest originally native to eastern North America that infected France from the 1860s and spread to most of Europe's vineyards and to some in the New World (Campbell 2004).

[6] Between 1889 and 1894, real GDP per capita fell by 18 per cent, alcohol consumption per capita fell by 22 per cent, and wine consumption per capita fell by 26 per cent. It took until 1907 for real GDP per capita, and until 1905 for both wine and alcohol consumption, to return to their 1889 levels (Anderson 2015).

advantage than other New World countries, but it was still only a tiny fraction of that for Europe's wine-exporting countries (Table 2).

The build-up in Australia's exports during that first export boom was sustained through to World War I. The lowering of ocean transport freight rates and travel times contributed to the export take-off, probably due to the development of the steamship. Ocean transport costs from Australia were still nontrivial though, especially compared with those faced by expanding competitor wineries of southern Europe and North Africa.

Also influencing wine's competitiveness in the early years of Federation were new industry policies. Dried vine fruits were one of the first to be protected, receiving tariff protection that doubled the local price when first introduced in 1904. That year also saw the formation of the Australia Dried Fruits Association, which controlled over 90 per cent of domestic production and was able to raise the domestic price of grapes by diverting supplies to distilleries and/or to the dried fruit export market with the help of a government export subsidy. Higher grape prices raised the cost of producing wine, but that was offset by a tax on wine imports (which has prevailed to the present, although the most-favoured-nation rate is only 5 per cent currently).

Meanwhile, French producers invested heavily in vineyards in North Africa, especially Algeria. As soon as Algeria's vines were mature, their wine's access to the French market was assisted by the raising of near-prohibitive barriers to imports from the rest of the world (Meloni and Swinnen 2014). This trade policy development depressed prices for wines in Europe and contributed to the plateauing of Australia's vine area, wine production and wine exports during 1900–1915.

4.3. *The third cycle: 1915 to 1967*

Towards the end of and following World War I, there was another rapid expansion in Australia's vine area and wine output, both absolutely (Figure 2) and relative to other crops and to real GDP (Figure 5), followed by a long period of slow growth plus some disruptions during World War II and then a downturn in the 1950s. This was encouraged by the subsidised settlement on farms of ex-servicemen, particularly in the newly developed Murrumbidgee Irrigation Area of New South Wales and along the Murray

River. Annual output of wine more than doubled in the decade to 1925, leading to a grape glut. Having been fuelled by assistance with land development and irrigation infrastructure, the Australian Government felt obliged to further assist producers in the newly developed areas by offering from 1924 an export bounty on fortified wines. The bounty provided the equivalent of 8.8 cents per litre at a time when the average unit value of Australia's wine exports was <10 cents per litre.

Since an export subsidy is the equivalent of a production subsidy and a domestic consumption tax, this bounty dampened domestic fortified wine sales and table wine production, at the same time as boosting production and exports of fortified wines — and more so for lower-valued grapes and fortified wines, since the export bounty was a specific rather than an *ad valorem* duty. Australia's table wine production diminished substantially over the interwar period, reaching one-fifth of its 1923 level by the late 1930s.

Then in its June 1925 budget, the British Government introduced a tariff preference for wines from the British Empire. As a result, Australian exporters faced British per gallon tariffs of just two shillings on table wines and four shillings on fortified wines, compared with double those rates for wines imported by Britain from Europe. In the first two decades of the 20th century, France, Portugal and Spain supplied more than 80 per cent of UK wine imports when Australia's share was <10 per cent, but the latter rose to 24 per cent in the 1930s when Australia exported more to Britain than did France (Anderson and Pinilla 2017). This is reflected in Australia's RCA index, which in the interwar period averaged more than twice that just prior to World War I (Table 2). The total area of vines in Australia grew very little between the mid-1920s and the mid-1960s though, and it was five decades before the annual level of wine exports achieved in the late 1930s (artificially boosted to build stocks in Britain for the foreshadowed war) was again reached.

During World War II, domestic wine consumption rose. This was partly because beer and spirits sales were rationed, to boost foodgrain availability. Interstate trade in alcoholic beverages was banned during the war also, to conserve fuel. And the United Kingdom placed severe restrictions on wine imports from January 1941, providing only a small quota for Australia. That plus difficulties in obtaining space on ships meant

Australia's annual wine exports to Britain during 1940–1945 were only one-fifth those in the 1930s.

Following World War II, consumers in the United Kingdom moved away from wine once their wartime rationing of grain used in beer production was lifted. Partly this was because of long-established consumer preferences, but two policy changes gave a helping hand. One was that Britain raised its tariff on fortified wines five-fold in 1947 and kept it very high until the end of the 1950s (when it was lowered but was still double the interwar rate). The other was that, in Australia, the wine export bounty was no longer provided after 1947–48.

As for supply, despite new irrigation schemes at Loxton in South Australia and Robinvale in Victoria, the area of vines and wine production grew only slowly from the mid-1940s to the mid-1960s (Figure 3). During that time, the Korean War-induced wool price boom and then subsidies to other farm products such as wheat, milk and tobacco appealed more to farmers. As well, tighter restrictions on imports of manufactured goods boosted the import-competing industrial sector, while the removal of a ban on iron ore exports in the early 1960s triggered a mining boom. Both trade policy changes indirectly dampened producers' incentives in other industries producing tradables, including wine. As a consequence, wine production grew only three per cent per year between 1946 and 1966, and wine exports remained flat. Australia's index of comparative advantage in wine, which had risen to 0.8 by the 1930s, more than halved by the end of this cycle (Table 2).

The industry continued to be assisted throughout this cycle. Instruments included an import tariff on wine and brandy, a sales tax of 15 per cent on imported but not domestically produced wine, excise taxes on beer and spirits but not on wine, and a lower excise tax on brandy than on other spirits. The import tax on wine was nontrivial, which helps explain both the low share of imported wine in domestic consumption (Figure 1) and the relatively low overall level of wine consumption throughout this cycle.

The extent to which those support measures raised the domestic prices of grapes and wine is indicated by estimated nominal rates of assistance (NRAs). The NRA for drying grapes averaged 35 per cent in the interwar period and 10 per cent in the two decades thereafter. Meanwhile, the NRA for wine and brandy from import tariffs averaged 24 per cent over the 1950s and 1960s, which was above the average for other

Table 3. Nominal rates of assistance[†] to grape growing, wine making, all agriculture, and all manufacturing, Australia, 1904 to 2016

	Drying Grapes	Wine Grapes	All Agriculture	Wine and Brandy	All Manufacturing
1904–1909	91	NA	8	NA	31
1910–1919	62	NA	7	NA	29
1920–1929	35	NA	4	NA	30
1930–1939	34	NA	7	NA	51
1940–1949	6	NA	3	NA	42
1950–1959	7	NA	4	19	24
1960–1969	13	NA	9	30	22
1970–1979	20	38	8	39	18
1980–1989	20	18	5	20	13
1990–1999	13	10	4	9	6
2000–2016	<3	<4	1	<3	2

Note: [†]The nominal rates of assistance for wine and brandy manufacturing is underestimated for 1950–1968 as it is just customs revenue as % of import value.
NA, not applicable.
Source: Updated from Anderson (2015, table A9).

manufactures and nearly four times the average NRA for the agricultural sector (Table 3). This protection helped to stave off imports, but did not improve export competitiveness.

4.4. The fourth cycle: Domestic demand changes, 1967 to 1986

Britain hiked its tariff on fortified wines again in the late 1960s, and then joined the European Economic Community (EEC) in 1973 which provided duty-free access for wines from other EEC members. Meanwhile, a mining boom at home was reducing the competitiveness of Australia's nonmineral exporters, and simultaneously boosting incomes domestically. So for both demand and supply reasons, wine exports remained flat from the mid-1960s to mid-1980s and exports to the UK fell by nine-tenths. This drove the index of wine comparative advantage back to pre-World War I levels (Table 2). Grape and wine prices also remained low, particularly for reds.

Yet domestic demand began to grow, for several reasons. One was brand advertising plus generic promotion domestically by Australia's Wine Bureau. Another was the influx of wine-preferring immigrants from Southern Europe, who also influenced the per capita consumption of non-alcoholic beverages: tea-drinking shrunk by three-quarters while coffee-drinking expanded six-fold in Australia in the second half of the 20th century. Yet another factor was the fall in the real cost of air travel and discounts for under 25-year-olds. That encouraged young people to travel to Europe, where they were exposed to cultures in which wine is integral. As well, Australia's Trade Practices Act of 1974 made retail price fixing illegal and stimulated the emergence and gradual spread of liquor chain stores and wine discounting throughout the country.[7] Meanwhile, exports remained of minor and declining importance.

4.5. Australia's fifth cycle: Export take-off from 1986

The fifth boom began in 1986 not with a vine planting expansion but rather with a steady increase in exports to take advantage of the historically low value of the Australian dollar, while domestic consumers moved away from quantity and towards higher-quality wines as their disposable incomes grew. The export boom was so large as to raise wine's share of Australia's total merchandise value above one per cent for the first time in 1999, and to 2.3 per cent in 2004 just as mineral exports were taking off. Australia's wine export volume and value continued to grow until 2007, as did its share of global wine exports and its index of wine comparative advantage (Figures 1–6 and Table 2).

Associated with these changes were hikes in the prices of Australian wines, which stimulated vine plantings. The average price received for winegrapes in 1999 was four times that in 1986, even though the export price had risen 'only' 140 per cent (Figure 7). An important contributor to this production and export growth was owner-

---

[7] Similar income growth and deregulation of wine retailing in the UK and New Zealand led to the share of wine in their alcohol consumption growing even faster than Australia's, albeit from a lower base of 5 per cent in 1965 compared with Australia's 10 per cent. By 2010 those shares were 31 per cent for the UK and 35 per cent for both Australia and New Zealand (Anderson and Pinilla 2017).

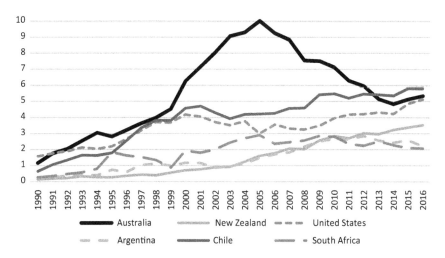

Figure 6. National shares of value of global wine exports, Australia and other New World countries, 1990 to 2016 (per cent).
Source: Anderson and Pinilla (2017).

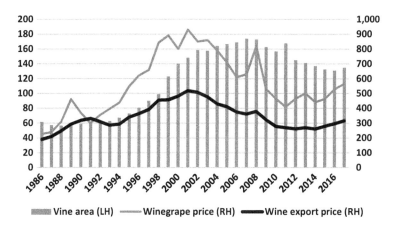

Figure 7. Vine bearing area, average winegrape price, and wine export price, Australia, 1986 to 2017 ('000 ha, A$ per tonne, and A$ per hectolitre).
Source: Updated from Anderson (2015).

ship concentration. This provided the opportunity to reap economies of scale not only in winemaking but also distribution and brand promotion, by producing large volumes of consistent, popular wines for specific supermarkets abroad.

The timing for this export surge was catalysed by a substantial depreciation of the Australian dollar in the mid-1980s, which was due to a sharp fall in prices of Australia's coal, grain and other primary export products. Together with low domestic prices for premium red grapes at the time, that depreciation — which persisted until the early 2000s — increased substantially the incentive to invest in developing overseas markets for Australian wine. Other factors that expanded demand abroad for Australian wine were food safety scares associated with Chernobyl in April 1986 and scandals involving additives in Austrian and Italian wines. Meanwhile, competition from other New World countries was minimal: from South Africa because of antiapartheid sentiment, from South America because of that region's macroeconomic and political instability, and from the United States because of the high value of its dollar relative to European currencies.

While this fifth boom was largely market-driven, it was also influenced by changes in government interventions. A steady reduction in Australia's manufacturing protection and in assistance to some of its other agricultural industries paralleled and thus offset the price-reducing effect of reductions in nominal rates of assistance to grape and wine producers (Table 3). Also, the imposition from 1984 of a wholesale sales tax on wine dampened domestic sales and thereby encouraged exporting.

In 1994–95 the wine industry developed and published a *Strategy 2025* document, laying out its targets for 30 years hence (AWF 1995). At the time those targets were considered rather optimistic, since they involved a threefold increase in the real value of wine production, 55 per cent of it for the export market. Getting halfway to those targets required having 80,000 hectares of winegrapes bearing enough for a crush of 1,100 kt to produce 750 million litres of wine at a wholesale pretax value of $3 billion ($4/L) in 1995–96 Australian dollars. By the turn of the century — that is, in just five vintages — the industry had reached the halfway point for achieving its targets 30 years out.

Meanwhile, several New World countries had begun to emulate the Australian export-led experience, leading to a growth spurt in their wine exports just a few years behind Australia's. Also, declining domestic consumption led several Old World suppliers plus Argentina and Chile to expand their exports. Thus Australian exporters began to face increasing competition just as the historically low value of the Australian dollar began its decade-long appreciation after 2001 in the wake of Australia's latest mining investment boom. The latter contributed greatly to the decline from that time in the local-currency price of Australia's wine exports (Anderson and Wittwer 2013), while other New World exports continued to grow (Figure 6). The volume of Australia's exports continued to expand each year until 2007 though, such was the need to dispose of rapidly growing stocks. The extent of the fall in the average wine export price from 2001 is as spectacular as its rise in the previous decade (Figure 7), as is the spike over those two decades in the index of wine comparative advantage (Figure 3). Meanwhile, the US$ average price of wine exports globally had risen to the Australian average price by 2007, and over the next seven years, the Australian price dropped to just 70 per cent of the world average (Anderson and Pinilla 2017).

The appreciating value of the Australian dollar also encouraged wine imports, which grew dramatically from the turn of the century (Figure 1). The surge in imports from New Zealand was particularly sharp from 2005, when the Australian Government agreed that New Zealand wineries could receive the same rebate as Australian producers of the 29 per cent wholesale tax on their wines sold in Australia (up to the ceiling of A$500,000 of sales per winery per year).

Has this fifth wine cycle ended? The two indicators in Figure 5 had not turned up as of 2016, and the 20 per cent depreciation of the real exchange rate between the March quarters of 2013 and 2016 reversed itself in the following seven quarters (a five per cent appreciation). However, the export volume and value indicators in Figures 1 and 2 have levelled off, and the average AUD prices of both winegrapes and wine exports have been rising since 2014 (Figure 7). An important contributor to that recent improvement has been the rapid growth in wine demand in Asia, especially China (Anderson and Wittwer 2015). If 2016 turns out to be the end of the latest wine cycle, then the fifth cycle will have had a similar length to the average of the previous four (a little over 30 years). However, and very importantly, the latest boom was nearly twice as long, and the following plateau or slump was less than half as long, as the average of earlier cycles.

5. Conclusion

The competitiveness of Australia's wine industry, while firmly established during the current globalisation wave, did not happen earlier for several reasons. One was high ocean transport costs for exporting wine relative to gold and wool which dominated Australia's exports for more than a century.

A second had to do with the small size of Australia's economy and of its domestic wine market, which together meant the industry was unable to reap the economies of scale needed to export sustainably to distant markets in the 19th century. That, more than French protectionism against all wine imports other than Algerian, explains why Australian wineries — like other New World producers — were unable to benefit from the production losses in Europe due to the phylloxera outbreak in the half century prior to World War I.

Third, the interwar period exports were artificially stimulated by an export bounty plus a UK tariff preference, which favoured exports of low-quality fortified wines at the expense of higher-quality table wines. Those exports promptly collapsed when those supports were removed in 1947–48.

Fourth, the wool boom of the early 1950s and the mining boom of the latter 1960s and 1970s reduced the international competitiveness of other tradables industries including wine, as did import quota and tariff protection to Australia's least-competitive manufacturing industries through to the 1980s. Mining's impact on the real exchange rate again dampened the wine industry's export performance increasingly through the first dozen years of the present century.

And fifth, the tariff import protection and relatively low excise taxation of wine and brandy shielded the wine industry somewhat from international competition, which would have slowed the speed with which the quality of the domestic industry's exports converged on the global quality frontier.

What of the future? The dramatic rise in the industry during its latest boom showed it is now capable of competing intersectorally and internationally as well as that of other key wine-exporting countries, notwithstanding the likelihood of more boom-plateau cycles of firm profitability in the decades ahead.

References

ABS (2018). *Balance of Payments and International Investment Position,* Cat. No. 5302.0. Australian Bureau of Statistics, Canberra.

Anderson, K. (2010). Excise and Import Taxes on Wine versus Beer and Spirits: An International Comparison, *Economic Papers* 29, 215–228.

Anderson, K. (with the assistance of N.R. Aryal) (2015). *Growth and Cycles in Australia's Wine Industry: A Statistical Compendium, 1843 to 2013.* University of Adelaide Press, Adelaide. Available from URL: http://www.adelaide.edu.au/press/titles/austwine [accessed 24 August 2018].

Anderson, K. (2017). Sectoral trends and shocks in Australia's economic growth, *Australian Economic History Review* 57, 2–21.

Anderson, K. and Pinilla, V. (with the assistance of A.J. Holmes) (2017). *Annual database of global wine markets, 1835 to 2016,* Available from URL: http://www.adelaide.edu.au/wine-econ/databases [accessed 24 August 2018].

Anderson, K. and Wittwer, G. (2013). Modeling Global Wine Markets to 2018: Exchange Rates, Taste Changes, and China's Import Growth, *Journal of Wine Economics* 8, 131–58.

Anderson, K. and Wittwer, G. (2015). Asia's evolving role in global wine markets, *China Economic Review* 35, 1–14.

Anderson, K., Nelgen, S. and Pinilla, V. (2017). *Global Wine Markets, 1860 to 2016: A Statistical Compendium.* University of Adelaide Press, Adelaide. Available from URL:http://www.adelaide.edu.au/press/titles/global-wine-markets [accessed 24 August 2018].

AWF (1995). *Strategy 2025: The Australian Wine Industry.* Winemakers' Federation of Australia for the Australian Wine Foundation, Adelaide.

Balassa, B. (1965). Trade liberalization and revealed comparative advantage, *Manchester School of Economic and Social Studies* 33, 99–124.

Bell, G. (1994). The London market for Australian wine, 1851–1901: A South Australian perspective, *Journal of Wine Research* 5, 19–40.

Campbell, C. (2004). *Phylloxera: How Wine Was Saved for the World.* HarperCollins Publishers, London.

Corden, W.M. (1984). Booming sector and Dutch disease economics: Survey and consolidation, *Oxford Economic Papers* 36, 359–380.

Freebairn, J. (2015). Mining booms and the exchange rate, *Australian Journal of Agricultural and Resource Economics* 59, 533–548.

Friberg, R., Paterson, R. and Richardson, A. (2011). Why is there a home bias? A case study of wine, *Journal of Wine Economics* 6, 37–66.

Gergaud, O. and Ginsburgh, V. (2008). Natural endowments, production technologies and the quality of wines in Bordeaux: Does terroir matter? *Economic Journal* 118, F142–F157.

Holmes, A.J. and Anderson, K. (2017a). *Annual Database of National Beverage Consumption Volumes and Expenditures, 1950 to 2015.* Wine Economics Research Centre, Adelaide, Available from URL:http://www.adelaide.edu.au/wine-econ/databases/alcohol-consumption [accessed 24 August 2018].

Holmes, A.J. and Anderson, K. (2017b). Convergence in national alcohol consumption patterns: New global indicators, *Journal of Wine Economics* 12, 117–148.

Krugman, P. (1980). Scale economies, product differentiation, and the pattern of trade, *American Economic Review* 70, 950–959.

Leamer, E.E. (1987). Paths of development in the three-factor, n-good general equilibrium model, *Journal of Political Economy* 95, 961–999.

Linder, S. (1961). *An Essay on Trade and Transformation*. Almqvist and Wiksell, Uppsala.

McIntyre, J. (2012). *First Vintage: Wine in Colonial New South Wales*. University of New South Wales Press, Sydney.

Meloni, G. and Swinnen, J. (2014). The rise and fall of the world's largest wine exporter — and its institutional legacy, *Journal of Wine Economics* 9, 3–33.

Simpson, J. (2011). *Creating Wine: The Emergence of a World Industry, 1840–1914*. Princeton University Press, Princeton, NJ.

Venables, A.J. (2004). Small, remote and poor, *World Trade Review* 3, 453–457.

C. Market Developments in Caucasia and Asia

Chapter 13

Is Georgia the Next "New" Wine-Exporting Country?*

Kym Anderson[†]

Abstract

The former Soviet republic of Georgia is reputedly the cradle of wine and has enjoyed at least 8,000 vintages. It has also been a major supplier of wine to Russia for at least 200 years, but to few other countries. In 2006, however, Russia imposed a ban on beverage imports from Georgia. Since then this relatively poor country, in which nearly half the population is rural and most farmers have a vineyard, has been seeking to develop new export markets for its wine. This paper assesses the potential for growth in Georgia's wine production and exports. It then outlines ways to address the challenges involved in trying to realize that

---

*First published in *Journal of Wine Economics* 8(1): 1–28, Spring 2013. Revision of a paper presented at a World Bank wine industry seminar, Tbilisi, Georgia, March 9, 2012, and at the Wine Pre-Conference Workshop, ICABR-EAAE Conference, Feudi di San Gregorio, Italy, June 24, 2012. The author is grateful for discussions with many people in Georgia and at the workshop, for very helpful referee comments, and for financial support from the World Bank and (for wine globalization research) Australia's Grape and Wine Research and Development Corporation. The views expressed are the author's alone.

[†]Wine Economics Research Centre, School of Economics, University of Adelaide, Adelaide SA 5005, Australia, e-mail: kym.anderson@adelaide.edu.au

potential, drawing on the experience of other countries that have rapidly expanded their wine exports in the past two decades. Implications for policy are drawn, particularly for ensuring that poverty is reduced as exports expand and the economy grows.

1. Introduction

Georgia, a country wedged between the Black and Caspian seas at the same latitude as the south of France, is reputedly the cradle of wine (McGovern 2003, 2009). It has experienced 8,000 vintages, is blessed with more than 500 indigenous *Vitis vinifera* wine grape varieties, and has an enviable reputation for hospitality involving lavish and lengthy feasts *(supra)*. In 2005 wine accounted to almost one-tenth of the value of all goods exported from Georgia, making wine exports around six times as economically important as in France, Italy, and Spain. Moreover, virtually every Georgian farm household grows grapes and produces wine. These households represent nearly half the country's households and employment and most of the poverty in this relatively poor country, in which one-third of the population survives on less than $2 a day.

For the past two centuries, including the Soviet era, Georgia has been a major supplier of wine to Russia and other members of the former Soviet Union's Commonwealth of Independent States (CIS). However, because very little Georgian wine has been exported elsewhere, it was a major blow when Russia, for political reasons, introduced a ban on wine imports from Georgia in 2006. As of March 2013, that embargo was still in place. That shock (compounded by a short war with Russia in August 2008) has required Georgian wine exporters to develop markets elsewhere, a task made considerably more difficult by the global financial crisis that began in 2008. Nonetheless, the country's agriculture minister announced in November 2011 that he wanted to see a near-trebling of wine exports by 2015.

This paper explores the prospects for growth in wine exports from Georgia. Section 2 offers a brief description of key indicators of Georgia's economy relative to those of its neighbors, highlighting the extraordinary importance of wine in the economy. That provides the background needed to assess the potential for growth in Georgia's wine production and exports, which is the focus of Section 3. Realizing that potential, however, will require the government and industry to work together on a wide range of fronts to attract the various crucial investments required. Those necessary conditions are enumerated in Section 4, based on the experience of other countries that have expanded their wine exports in the past two decades. Section 5 summarizes the paper's findings and lists several implications for policy, not least for ensuring that poverty is reduced as exports expand and the economy grows.

2. Key indicators of Georgia's economy and of wine's importance

The economy of Georgia is very open and by far the easiest in the region in which to do business. Its exports plus imports of goods and services amounted to 87 percent of its Gross Domestic Product (GDP) in 2010, when, according to the World Bank (2013), it ranked 9th of 185 countries in terms of the ease of doing business and had the most-improved ranking in the world in the period 2005–2012.

Yet, apart from Moldova, Georgia has the lowest gross national income per capita of the countries in the region bordering the Black and Caspian seas and has one of the region's most skewed distributions of income (greatest gap between rich and poor) and the largest proportion of households in poverty (World Bank, 2011).

Agricultural wages are around one-third those of nonfarm workers, and the incidence of poverty is nearly twice as high in rural as in urban areas. This is not surprising, given that the farm sector is dominated by small private farms with an average size of 1.2 hectares (ha) (93 percent are smaller than 2 ha). Even so, semisubsistence agriculture, which accounts for three-quarters of rural employment, is the main source of income for the majority of rural households, together with public transfers (World Bank, 2009). Most farmers have a vineyard and produce wine for self-consumption with family and friends, and some small and medium farm enterprises also sell grapes to commercial wineries, often under contract. Between 92 and 95 percent of the country's grapes are grown on family farms, and grapes account for around two-fifths of all fruit produced in Georgia. All but 8 percent of grapes are used for wine, the rest being consumed as table grapes (NSO, 2011a, 2011b).

The value of Georgia's wine output, including for subsistence consumption, amounted in 2009 to 0.7 percent of GDP, which is similar to that in Argentina and South Africa, only a little below France and Portugal's 0.9 percent and Chile's 1.2 percent, but well below Moldova's 4.6 percent (Anderson and Nelgen, 2011, tables 86 and 159).

Most nonfarm households in Georgia also consume wine as their alcoholic beverage of choice. Although it is commonly purchased from bulk containers rather than in labeled bottles, an expanding number of private wineries are developing brands and selling labeled bottles in the domestic market (while exported wine is shipped mainly in bottles). During 2006–10, exports comprised almost one-fifth of total wine production and nearly two-thirds of labeled bottles. Domestic wine consumption per adult, including from self-production, was estimated at around 17 liters in 2009. Wine is thus a nontrivial part of domestic household spending on food, beverages, and tobacco, which in 2010 accounted for 46 and 39 percent of Georgian rural and urban household expenditure, respectively.

Wine contributes to all three key sectors of the economy: primary production (grape growing), manufacturing (grape processing into wine and also brandy and *chacha*/grappa), and services (transporting of grapes and wine, marketing of wine, and the various activities associated with wine tourism). Commercial wine tourism is not something on which Georgians spend much time and money (since it has long been mainstreamed into the culture), but many international visitors to Georgia indulge in food and wine tourism activities to some extent. This component of the wine-producing industry is beginning to take off as a services export revenue earner.

Between 1995 and 2005, three-quarters of the country's wine export earnings came from Russia, and if combined with Ukraine that share rose to 90 percent. More than two-thirds of the earnings from exports of distilled spirits (brandy and *chacha*) also came from Russia.

The politically motivated decision by Russia in late March 2006 to ban imports of alcoholic beverages and bottled water from Georgia was therefore a major shock to the country's overall economy, particularly to its rural areas and especially to its wine industry.[1] The share of beverages in the total value of merchandise exports had grown from 11 percent to 15 percent in the first half of the previous decade, but during 2009–11 it was only half that share. Bottled water exports also halved. Wine's share of all goods and services exports fell from 5.4 percent to 1.3 percent between 2005 and 2010, and wine's share of just alcohol exports fell from 73 percent in 2005 to 33 percent in 2007, before recovering slightly to 40 percent in 2010: much of what would have been exported as wine was distilled, and exports of distilled alcohol doubled between 2005 and 2008 (NSO, 2012).

A striking feature of the Russian embargo is that Georgia's wine exports, while declining initially in quantity, have risen markedly in quality since 2006. Wine's average export price was only US$1 per liter in the late 1990s and $2 during 2000–2005, but by 2008 it averaged $3.50 and, despite the global financial crisis, was as high as $3.20 in 2011 (Figure 1).

Since the Russian embargo, the other CIS member countries have dominated as destinations for Georgian wine exports. By 2010 half the exports were still going to Ukraine and another one-quarter to other CIS members. Poland and the three Baltic countries that are former Soviet republics (Estonia, Latvia, and Lithuania) account for another one-eighth, while the United States and China each have a 2 percent share, and most of the rest goes to other members of the European Union (EU) (GWA, 2011). The current trade situation thus leaves a great deal of scope for diversifying Georgia's wine export destinations, since the entirety of Central and Eastern Europe plus the CIS (excluding Russia) accounted in 2005–9 for less than 7 percent of the volume of global wine imports, compared with more than 90 percent of wine exports from Georgia.

---

[1] This was preceded by two previous shocks: the anti-alcoholism campaign launched by Mikhail Gorbachev in 1985 led nearly three-quarters of Georgia's vineyards to be uprooted; and the economic collapse of the early independence years post-1991 damaged the industry further via widespread counterfeiting of Georgian wine in Russia. At the mid-1980s' peak, Georgia had around 120,000 ha of grapevines. That is comparable with the area in the early 2000s in Australia, Bulgaria, Chile, Greece, Moldova, and South Africa, and greater than in (East plus West) Germany. In recent years the bearing area has been around 50,000 ha.

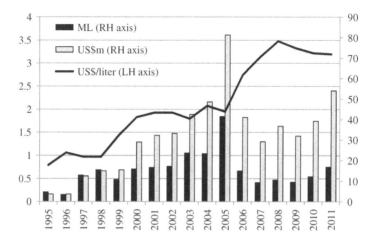

Figure 1. Wine export volume, value and average price, Georgia, 1995–2011
Sources: GWA (2011), NSO (2012).

3. Potential for growth in Georgia's wine production and export diversification

In exploring the growth potential for Georgian wine exports, it is helpful to review the basic determinants of comparative advantage in wine and then examine the available data for Georgia compared with other wine-exporting countries.

3.1. *Determinants of comparative advantage in wine*

There are numerous determinants of a country's comparative advantage in wine production, but of particular importance for wine are the three Ts of terroir, tradition, and technology.

Terroir refers to various pertinent aspects of climate, topography, soils, geology, and so on that determine the quality of the vine's growing conditions. Vineyard site selection therefore is crucial. Experience has determined the best sites and most-suitable grape varieties in long-established regions, whereas in new regions science must be used to speed the process of approaching the potential of any region to produce quality wine grapes (Gladstones, 1992). While Georgia has many suitable regions for growing various wine grape varieties and styles for its traditional markets, they have yet to be proven for other export markets.

Traditions determine not only how a product is produced but also the extent of local consumer demand. This is important for wine because typically local demand is the easiest and least costly for producers to satisfy, as there are relatively high fixed costs of entry into new export markets (Friberg *et al.*, 2011) — especially with unfamiliar styles and varieties. In Georgia, where the tradition of drinking (mostly unlabeled) wine with meals is already pervasive, domestic demand absorbs most of the grapes produced. What has been available for processing into labeled commercial wine for export has been sold almost exclusively in the larger Soviet (and post-Soviet) "home" market, which demanded a unique style of cheap semisweet red wine. Those two "home market" biases have not provided Georgia's wineries with experience in producing for bottled wine markets elsewhere that are very different from their traditional markets.

As for technology, there is always potential for improving on traditional production, processing, entrepreneurship, and marketing, whether by trial and error of practitioners over the generations or via formal investment in private and public research and development (R&D). The New World wine-producing countries have been more dependent on newly developed technologies than have producers in Western Europe, although both sets of countries have made major R&D investments — and expanded complementary tertiary education in viticulture, oenology, and wine marketing — over the past half-century (Giuliana *et al.*, 2011).

How important modern technology is relative to terroir in determining comparative advantage is a moot point. One recent statistical study suggests that terroir is not as dominant as is commonly assumed — even in regions as established as Bordeaux (Gergaud and Ginsburg, 2008). Another study, of vineyard sale values in Oregon, finds that while appellation reputation has some economic value, each location's physical attributes are not closely related to wine prices (Cross *et al.*, 2011). A recent book by Lewin (2010) begins its section on wine regions with the New World rather than the Old World, to emphasize that wines almost everywhere are manipulated by winemakers as they endeavor to make use of available knowledge to produce the products most desired by their customers. What they produce is increasingly being affected by how they can maximize profits through satisfying consumer demand.

New technology in agriculture has long tended to be biased in favor of saving the scarcest factor of production, as reflected in relative factor prices. Hayami and Ruttan (1985) emphasize that the focus of R&D investments thus has been driven in part by changes in factor prices, in particular by the rise in real wages. That has resulted in the development or adoption of labor-saving technology, such as mechanical harvesters and pruners for vineyards and super-fast bottling/labeling equipment for wineries in land-abundant, labor-scarce countries such as Australia. The adoption of labor-saving technology has helped countries with rapidly rising real wages retain their comparative advantage in what traditionally had been labor-intensive industries. This in turn means that poorer countries need to find sources of comparative advantage other than just low wages.

In Georgia, where real farm wages have remained relatively low, labor-intensive technology such as *qvevri*-based production (an ancient organic method involving large clay storage vessels), in addition to hand pruning and harvesting, has persisted. This is not inconsistent with Hayami/Ruttan theory, but it does mean that Georgia's traditional wine technology is very different from — and not necessarily more internationally competitive than — that of higher-wage wine-exporting countries.

Relative factor endowments also affect the comparative advantage of a country in terms of the quality of its exported products. New trade theory suggests that richer, capital-abundant countries will export higher-priced, higher-quality goods (Fajgelbaum *et al.*, 2011; Nayak, 2011). Relatively poor Georgia is therefore exceptional in exporting wine at an average price equal to or slightly above that for the world as a whole during 2005–2009.

A further set of influence on comparative advantage that can be important at certain times relates to currency exchange rate movements. A macroeconomic shock — such as Argentina's devaluation by two-thirds in late 2001 or a doubling in the Australian-U.S. dollar exchange rate over the past decade due largely to Australia's mining boom — have had major (and opposite) impacts on the international competiveness of wineries in those two Southern Hemisphere countries.

For Georgia, terroir and tradition have been the key domestic influences on its comparative advantage in wine production. Even so, there was some importation of exotic technologies and varieties from Western Europe in the nineteenth century and there was again following independence in 1991.

The international competitiveness of its wineries also has been heavily influenced by its long-established trade relations with Russia. Somewhat in contrast to the bilateral trade experience in the nineteenth century, during the Soviet era the choice of both technology and grape varieties in Georgia was focused on Russian demands for maximum quantities of semisweet, low-quality, mostly red wines (Kharbedia, 2010). With the dissolution of the Soviet Union in 1991 and even more so Russia's ban on imports of Georgian wine since 2006, the country now has a large degree of freedom to influence its future comparative advantage in wine.

To meet the agriculture minister's goal of trebling wine exports by 2015, total wine grape production would have to increase by one-quarter and wine grape and commercial bottled wine output would have to nearly triple. To examine what will be needed to meet that export goal in a sustainable way, it is helpful to review where Georgia is currently relative to other wine-exporting countries, especially those that have enjoyed rapid export growth in the past decade or two.

3.2. Georgia's wine comparative advantage

Trade data for the past decade reveal that Georgia's strong comparative advantage in wine is second only to that of Moldova. The indicator shown in Table 1 is wine's share of national merchandise exports relative to its share of global exports. However, the high value for Georgia has slipped a lot since the Russian import embargo, while those of several other countries (most notably, New Zealand and Argentina) have risen a great deal during the first decade of this century. That is also reflected in the share of Georgia's wine production volume (including noncommercial supplies) that is exported: it grew rapidly in the first half of the past decade to nearly 50 percent, but then fell sharply with the Russian ban and by 2010 had not yet returned to its 1995–99 average of 14 percent (Figure 2).

The country's wine comparative advantage is driven in large part by having ample terroir for wine grapes and by becoming familiar with that terroir by using it over millennia. Unlike elsewhere in the former Soviet Union, Georgia's vineyards were not decimated after the Union breakup: between 1992 and 1998 its wine production fell just 16 percent, compared

Table 1. Index of revealed comparative advantage in wine, Georgia and 12 other top countries, 2000–2009

	2000–2005	2006–2009
Moldova	96.1	45.9
Georgia	40.4	15.2
New Zealand	4.5	10.3
Chile	13.1	9.9
Macedonia	9.6	9.3
France	7.0	8.0
Portugal	8.2	7.8
Australia	8.5	7.0
Italy	4.4	5.0
South Africa	4.5	4.8
Argentina	2.7	4.6
Spain	4.4	4.4
Bulgaria	4.5	2.7

Note: Share of wine in value of national merchandise exports divided by share of wine in global merchandise export.

Source: Anderson and Nelgen (2011, table 75).

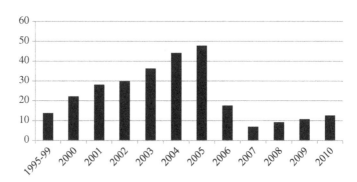

Figure 2. Export share of volume of wine production (including noncommercial), Georgia, 1995–2009, in percent

Source: A revision of data in Anderson and Nelgen (2011, tables 15 and 40), to account for noncommercial production.

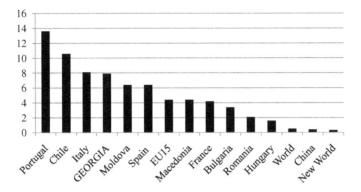

Figure 3. Share of crop land under vines, selected regions, 2009, in percent
Source: Anderson and Nelgen (2011, table 6).

with almost 60 percent in Russia and Moldova (Noev and Swinnen, 2004). One quick way of guessing the potential for expanding further is to look at the share of agricultural cropland under vines. As of 2009, Georgia ranked fourth in the world at 8 percent, after Portugal, Chile, and Italy and ahead of Moldova and Spain at 6 percent and Macedonia and France at 4 percent — and far ahead of the New World exporters at just 0.3 percent (Figure 3). Thus Georgia's potential for vineyard expansion may be not very great. True, Georgia's vineyard area was 2.5 times greater at its peak just before the Soviet anti-alcohol push in the mid-1980s to remove vines, but the quality of many of those vineyards was low.

Leaving aside the Russian market, Georgia is a relative latecomer to the tidal wave of wine export growth that has accompanied the past two decades of globalization. One symptom of that is the rise in the share of wine exported by both Western Europe and the New World. The share of EU wine that is exported has risen from one-sixth to more than one-third since the late 1980s. Far more dramatic, however, is the rise in that share for the New World, from just 2 percent to almost 40 percent (Anderson, 2004). Hence one-third of the world's wine is now consumed outside its country of production, while Georgia's share is less than one-eighth and much lower than for most of its East European wine-producing neighbors (Figure 4).

Being a latecomer to Western markets can have some benefits, in addition to well-known challenges. Recent history shows that it has been

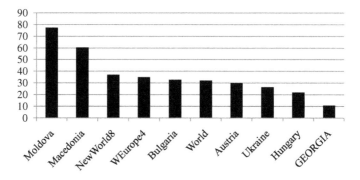

Figure 4. Share of wine production volume exported, selected regions, 2009
Source: Modified from data in Anderson and Nelgen (2011, table 51).

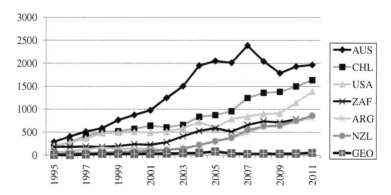

Figure 5. Georgian and New World wine exports, 1995–2011 in US$ millions
Source: Updated from Anderson and Nelgen (2011, table 63).

possible for several New World countries simultaneously to enjoy rapid growth in wine exports (Figure 5), in most cases from very low bases (Figure 6). In Argentina's case, the value of wine exports (in current U.S. dollars) grew at more than 20 percent per year in the decade since 2001, and New Zealand's at 25 percent, following Australia's 19 percent per year growth during the 1990s (Anderson and Nelgen, 2011, tables 63 and 127). Those experiences suggest that it would be technically possible for Georgia to expand its exports rapidly, if enough other supportive conditions are in place (see Section 4).

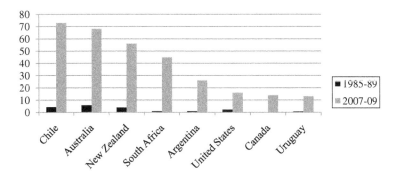

Figure 6. Share of wine production volume exported, New World countries, 1985–89 and 2007–9, in percent
Source: Anderson and Nelgen (2011, table 79).

The recent New World history also reveals that output expansion is not the only way to achieve export growth. The export growth in Argentina, Chile, and South Africa, for example, was possible without greatly expanding production initially. This is because it was accompanied by stagnant or falling domestic demand for wine. In New Zealand, production switched from low-quality wine for domestic consumers to high-quality wine mostly for export, while local demand was met largely by a doubling of wine imports over the first decade of this century. As for Australia, its export surge in the 1990s was preceded by a period of gradual decline in production, which meant that there was idle capacity ready and waiting to be used when the Australian dollar fell in value in the mid-1980s — as was also the case for Argentina after its devaluation in late 2001.

Georgia may well be in a somewhat comparable position now to that which Australia was in the mid-1980s and Argentina was in 2001, in the sense that both vineyards and winery capacity have been underutilized in Georgia since 2006.

Nor has Georgia's wine industry come under as much domestic competitive pressure from an export boom in other parts of its economy as occurred in Central and East European economies. Georgia is more like Hungary and Bulgaria in having a small share of its wine production exported, rather than like Moldova and Macedonia, where export sales dominate domestic sales (Figure 7), except that it currently has a much

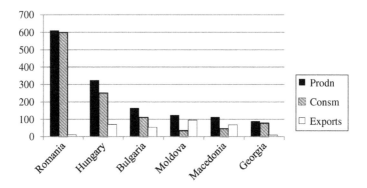

Figure 7. Volume of wine production, consumption (including noncommercial) and exports, Georgia and other transition economies, 2009, in million liters
Source: Modified from data in Anderson and Nelgen (2011) to include noncommercial consumption.

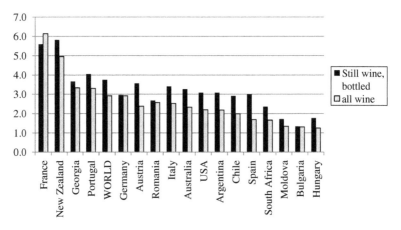

Figure 8. Average price of wine exports, selected countries, 2009, in US$/liter
Source: Anderson and Nelgen (2011, tables 76 and 79).

higher average price for its exports. The unit value of Georgia's wine exports in 2009, at US$3.33 per liter, was above the global average of $2.92 and within 4 cents of the West European average. While that is not as high as those of France or New Zealand, it is among the highest in the world and well above those of other New World exporters and transition economies (Figure 8). It is also far above Georgia's earlier averages of $1.05 and $1.92 per liter in 1995–99 and 2000–2005, respectively (Figure 1). Georgia's bottled still wine export price is only slightly higher (since Georgia normally has exported very little in bulk), but if inflated by the global average of 8.3 percent to allow for freight (the gap between fob and cif prices), it amounted to an average import price at destination of $3.96 in 2009. That is very close to that year's global average unit value of bottled still wine imports of $4.05 per liter. However, that world average is dominated by the large low-priced UK and German markets: most other significant importing countries have an average import price for bottled still wine well above $4 per liter.

4. What is needed to realize Georgia's full potential as a wine exporter?

Georgia has many natural advantages that could be further exploited in marketing its wine abroad. For example:

- a history of 8,000 vintages, longer than any other country;
- more than 500 unique *Vitis vinifera* wine grape varietals;
- a wide diversity of terroirs in which wine grapes can thrive;
- a unique and ancient organic production method *(qvevri),* possibly to be nominated for UNESCO cultural heritage protection;
- low-cost labor and viticultural land by Western standards;
- low chemical and water applications even in its modern styles of production;
- a unique and authentic food/wine/hospitality culture;
- a reputation (especially in Russia and among ex-Soviet diaspora) for approachable semisweet red wine and for high-quality brandy and *chacha* (grappa); and
- beautiful mountain-backed landscapes and stunning historical architecture at the eastern edge of Europe to add to the attractions for food-and-wine tourists.

While those advantages on their own are not enough to guarantee sales in new markets,[2] they can certainly be used to capture the initial attention of foreign wine writers, importers, and consumers via a generic

---

[2] Italy, for example, has had more than 2,000 vintages, has more than 400 wine grape varieties growing in a wide range of terroirs in very attractive settings, and is well known globally and appreciated for its food and wine culture.

"Wine of Georgia" marketing campaign. The advantage of still having the ancient *qvevri* production style, for example, is a genuine point of difference (as highlighted in DVDs by Kokochasvili [2011] and Lambert and Finlay [2011]) even if the shares of *qvevri* wine in Georgia's labeled wine production and exports remain small.

A prerequisite for launching a major generic or brand marketing campaign is having products ready in sufficient volume to be able to be well-positioned in clearly defined market segments. In their Export Market Development Action Plan, the Georgian Wine Association (GWA, 2011) has identified at least three broad quality segments in foreign markets for dry light still wine:

- nonpremium wine, typically sold in bulk;
- popular premium wine that new consumers often find attractive, mostly retailed in bottles (or bag-in-box, but increasingly in recent years New World wineries have exported in bulk before they or a supermarket bottle it in its destination country); and
- superpremium or fine wine, always exported in bottles.

According to Anderson and Nelgen (2011, tables 158, 169 and 170), these three segments in 2009 accounted for 37 percent, 50 percent, and 7 percent of the volume of global wine imports, respectively (with sparkling wine making up the remaining 6 percent), and for 11 percent, 58 percent, and 16 percent of the value of global wine imports, respectively (plus sparkling wine for the remaining 15 percent). The average export unit values per liter thus escalate across that range, from around US $0.90 for nonpremium in 2009 to $3.25 for commercial premium, $6.50 for superpremium, and $8.10 for sparkling wine (or $4.45 if French Champagne is excluded). The challenge for Georgian winemakers is to be cost competitive in supplying one or more of those market segments and at something less than those average prices, so as to entice newcomers to try their wine.

4.1. *Which market segments, which destinations to target, which varieties to focus on?*

Since Georgia already has a strong reputation in Russia, other CIS countries, and among ex-Soviet diaspora for its semisweet red wine and for its brandy and *chacha*, it will be able to build on that in non-CIS countries, beginning in cities or areas where the diaspora have settled. It will also be able to quickly return to the Russian market when it re-opens, should wineries so choose — although that market is slowly changing as it gains exposure to wines from non-CIS countries (Scholes, 2011). What is, or could be, Georgia's comparative advantages in the above three dry still wine segments outside Russia and therefore which countries should its wineries target?

The Georgian Wine Association (GWA) has identified six markets that it believes are worth targeting initially. Apart from the smallest of them (Poland), they are listed in Table 2. They comprise the world's three largest wine importers (the UK, the United States, and Germany) plus Ukraine and China. Around half the import volume of Germany and China is nonpremium (as is also the case for Russia), compared with just one-quarter for the other three. However, the average price of Georgian exports is a little above the average of the commercial premium category, and Table 2(b) suggests that fine-wine segment (superpremium) comprises a very small share of each of those markets — less than 5 percent — apart from the United States, where in 2009 it was 8 percent by volume and 18 percent by value.

There are marked differences between Western markets. The GWA's Development Action Plan (GWA, 2011) recognizes this and suggests the price points, varieties, and styles of Georgian wines that might be best targeted in each market. It suggests aiming for the low end of superpremium sales in all six countries, plus the diaspora market in the United States and Germany. It also recognizes the large size of the nonpremium market for bulk wine sales in China and Germany, presumably as a way of disposing of (unplanned?) low-quality wine. But it also suggests sales of commercial premium wines in China, Poland, and Ukraine, perhaps as a way of dealing with planned superpremium wine that did not quite reach that standard following difficult vintages.

Deloitte Consulting (2011), like many others, point out that the nonpremium market is chronically oversupplied globally and that the commercial premium segment has become extremely competitive, with very low margins thanks to the supermarket revolution on the buyer side and, on the seller side of the market, the economies of scale that are possible in commodity wine production in the relatively lightly populated New

Table 2. Volume, value, and unit value of wine imports and shares by quality, selected countries, 2009

	Volume (ML)	Value (US$ thousands)	Unit Value (US/liter)
(a) Volume, value, and unit value of wine imports			
China	173	457	2.65
Germany	1411	2770	1.96
Ukraine	17	47	2.77
United Kingdom	1277	4258	3.33
United States	927	4190	4.52

	Nonpremium	Commercial Premium	Superpremium	Sparkling	All Wines
(b) Share of volume and value of imports by quality (percent)					
China					
volume	46	50	3	1	100
value	14	75	8	3	100
Germany					
volume	52	41	2	5	100
value	18	59	6	17	100
Ukraine					
volume	27	67	1	5	100
value	7	79	3	11	100
United Kingdom					
volume	24	67	4	5	100
value	8	69	7	16	100
United States					
volumes	25	62	8	5	100
values	5	65	18	12	100
WORLD					
volumes	37	50	7	6	100
values	11	58	16	15	100

Note: The boundaries between the three still wine categories are US$2.50 and $7.50 per liter pre-tax at the border. The global average import unit values per liter thus escalate across that range, from around US$0.90 for nonpremium to $3.60 for commercial premium and $7.25 for superpremium (and $8.20 for sparkling wine, or $4.50 if French Champagne is excluded).

Source: Anderson and Nelgen (2011, section 6).

World. Differentiated products, by contrast, not only enjoy higher margins but are more recession-proof (see Gopinath *et al.*, 2011).

As for varieties, Georgia has been blessed with more than 500 indigenous varieties, of which more than half are currently still in production and others are in nurseries. In addition, Georgia imported Western wine grape varieties and production and processing technologies as long ago as the 1820s (Kharbedia, 2010, p. 33), and more have been planted in the past decade or so. Many indigenous varieties have names that consumers outside the CIS would struggle to remember and have flavor profiles that may be either too different or not different enough from those of international varieties to be easily marketable. Even the key indigenous varieties considered most likely to succeed abroad, such as red Saperavi and white Rkatsiteli, are produced in styles that those consumers might find not immediately approachable. Some wineries are therefore modifying the styles they produce, while others are blending those varieties with international ones. If the international name is placed first on the label of a 50:50 blend, a non-Georgian consumer might be less hesitant to try it once and more likely to enjoy it enough to remember the name when returning to the wine shop for more of the same (or of the adjacent bottle with only the indigenous variety).

Most New World countries have found that they initially became famous for just one or two varieties — as Austria has, since its recent resurgence as a wine exporter.[3]

The head of Austria's generic wine marketing agency warns that it is wiser to market the country rather than its signature varietal, lest the consumer tire of the latter (Carter, 2011). Argentina is aware of that risk, but its export success with Malbec has been so phenomenal that for the moment it continues to ride the wave.[4]

---

[3] This shows up in varietal intensity indexes, defined as the share of plantings to a variety in a country relative to its share globally. In 2000 Australia's Shiraz index was 9 (and Australia accounted for 4% of global planting of Shiraz), Argentina's Malbec index was 14 (6% of global planting), New Zealand's Savignon blanc was 19 (4% of global planting), and Austria's Grüner Veltliner was 81 (9% of global planting — see Anderson, 2010).

[4] In 2010, Argentina exported more than 4 million cases of Malbec to the United States, 20 times the amount it sent in 2002 and nearly double its 2008 volume. Malbec, which now represents 60 percent of Argentina's exports to the United States, was a rustic red with

How might Georgia first expand its grape and wine output for such export markets and then expand the demand for the final products in time for when they are ready for shipping? The key challenges are considered in turn below, drawing where appropriate on the experiences of other wine-exporting countries, before also considering the contribution that in-bound wine tourism could make.

4.2. *What is needed to expand export supplies?*

While Georgia's wineries and vineyards appear to have underutilized capacity at present, that may be more apparent than real. Old Soviet winemaking equipment was designed for large-scale production of low-quality semisweet red wine for the local market, and much of it is unsuitable for producing wines of sufficient quality to compete in other markets. Even *qvevri* production methods may need to be modified to ensure that they meet the demanding health standards of wine-importing countries.

Most small vineyards would require substantial upgrading before they could produce the grapes needed by a modern export-focused winery. For example, denser spacing of vines might be needed to raise grape quality; different varieties or even different clones may be needed before a contract is offered by a winery to a grower; and even then the winery may require a change in vineyard management practices to ensure that the grapes suit the style of wine for which they are to be used. The fact that so many Georgian farmers are struggling to sell their surplus grapes and yet new wineries are planting their own vineyards is an indication that the current grape output of smallholders is not meeting the needs of export-focused wineries.

---

little appeal outside the country before the surge in foreign investment following its devaluation by three-quarters at the end of 2001. However, the style has been transformed over the past decade to broaden hugely its appeal as a food wine even when drunk young. Wines of Argentina, the country's generic marketing agency, is now advancing its message by communicating directly to the consumer with events such as Malbec World Day. Having the cover story of the December 2011 issue of the U.S. magazine *Wine Spectator* (see Wesley, 2011) further boosted their sales in 2012.

Even more importantly, skilled viticulturalists, winemakers, and especially wine marketers capable of working together with grape growers are in short supply. Yet that collaboration is essential if small growers are to deliver wine grapes than can become a salable product on time and at the right price point in prospective markets abroad. In addition, the irrigation infrastructure also needs major improvements if it is to support production in dry years.

The fact that more investment is needed if Georgia's exportable surplus of wine is to expand substantially is similar to the situation faced by all the New World countries that chose to rapidly expand their wine exports in the past decade or two. In Australia's case, the industry attracted the required investment funds by developing a shared 30-year vision for the industry's future called Strategy 2025 (AWF, 1995). At the time many observers considered the targets in that document rather optimistic, since they involved a threefold increase in the real value of wine production, 55 percent of it for the export market. Yet so convincing was that document, and so intense and rapid was the subsequent investment, that the industry was more than halfway to meeting most of its 30-year targets in just six vintages (leading to excessive production in the subsequent decade; see Anderson, 2011).

Investment funds are required for altering or upgrading existing vineyards or planting new ones. They are needed even more immediately than for the building or upgrading wineries, bearing in mind that it takes a few years before grapes from new vineyards are available for producing the desired wine. Funds are also needed to finance the nontrivial costs of planning and then executing a marketing program for those wines. Those funds are required before, as well as when, the wines become ready to export to new markets.

In addition to finance for those investment needs of private firms, funds are required at an industry level for investment in collective goods and services, such as targeted viticultural, winemaking, and wine marketing education plus extension and leadership skills development, grape and wine research and development (R&D), generic promotion of the "Wines of Georgia" (see the next subsection), and more statistical data collection and up-to-date dissemination. Data are especially needed on the pace and nature of expansion in vineyard and winery capacity, as an aid to investors

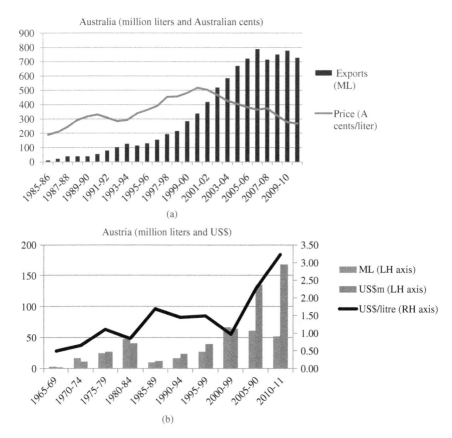

Figure 9. Wine export volume and average price, Australia and Austria, 1965–2011
Sources: Derived from data at the WINEFACTS part of www.wineaustralia.com and Anderson and Nelgen (2011, tables 117 and 127).

and so as to avoid the excessive exuberance in expanding that Australia experienced in the ten years following the release of its 30-year plan, which contributed to the subsequent decline in its average export price (see Figure 9a).

It would be a mistake to assume that Georgia can postpone an expansion of grape and wine R&D investment despite the facts that Georgia's traditional production methods are well known, having been passed down through generations, and that the published results of many research institutes abroad concerning alternative production methods can be readily accessed via the Internet, domestic R&D is still needed. The reason is that, apart from the *qvevri* method, there is almost no such thing as natural wine. On the contrary, there is great latitude for altering styles to suit various markets (Lewin, 2010). Since Georgia will target market niches requiring styles different from those of other suppliers, it needs its own R&D capability. In addition, there is clear evidence that a strong R&D base is needed not just for innovation but also to adapt technologies adoptable from abroad (Griffiths *et al.*, 2004). It is therefore laudable that a new Georgia Wine Institute is being established in Tsinandali, Kakheti (as announced in November 2011 by President Mikheil Saakashvili).

Some researchers are available locally, but additional ones will need to be recruited from the global pool or created by providing scholarships for promising students to undertake post-graduate studies in one of the world's major wine universities. Such training there has two important additional benefits: it will build links for future international collaboration in R&D, and it will provide a pool of lecturers for teaching undergraduate grape and wine science courses at Georgian universities.

To fund such R&D expansion and scholarships, a levy on producers might be required. Most wine firms in Georgia are too small to justify their own R&D facility. If foreign assistance grants are insufficient, and if the government believes that this activity would have too few spillover benefits beyond the wine industry to justify full public funding, then one possibility is to collect a small levy on all exported wine. That process could then also be used to help fund the generic promotion proposed in the next subsection. It could also be used to cover the cost of inspecting a sample of each wine destined for export, to ensure that only wine of sufficient quality is allowed to carry the words "Made in Georgia" on its label.

Small wine grape growers are unlikely to contribute to exports without having to agree to management disciplines. Currently there are hundreds of thousands of small wine grape growers and only a few dozen export-capable wineries. While those smallholders mostly produce grapes for home processing for their own consumption and for informal sale to friends, they could expand their sales to wineries if there were demand. To do so, however, they would need to forgo their reluctance to allow the commercial winery to determine the varieties grown, production techniques used, harvest time, sugar content, and so on. Moreover, they may be required to enter into a formal contract that would further limit their independence and flexibility, and even then there may be considerable uncertainty as to the final price that they would receive for their grapes.[5] To date, wineries exporting to new markets have signed up relatively few growers and have, instead, planted their own vineyards so as to be able to have full control of the wine grape production part of the supply chain. This issue is important for the alleviation of rural poverty, but it will also affect the optimal path of institutional innovation.

Experience in the rest of the world provides some guidance as to how the firm structure of the industry might evolve in Georgia. In all the New World wine-exporting countries, the firm structure is very skewed: the largest winery in each of those countries is responsible for between one-fifth and one-third of all domestic sales and the four largest for about three-fifths of domestic sales and an even larger share of export sales. By contrast, in Western Europe, apart from Portugal, the top four firms are responsible for only between 4 percent and 20 percent of domestic sales (Table 3). The Old World continues to be dominated by a large number of cooperatives, many of which do not penalize low-quality grape growers enough to prevent the delivery of fruit that can be used only for nonpremium wine or for industrial alcohol — hence the EU's history of wine lakes since the advent of its Common Agricultural Policy in the early 1960s. In particular, many cooperatives do not appear to be able to successfully export superpremium wines. Nor are they able to compete well in the international market, especially against the very large exporting firms of the New World, in supplying large quantities of consistent commercial premium wines for the major chain stores and supermarkets. Cooperatives are therefore not likely to be the answer for engaging more small growers in a wine export drive — not to mention

---

[5] In California both high-quality and low-quality wine grapes tend to be subject to contracts, with the former more likely to include provisions regarding the production process while the latter more likely to focus just on product attributes such as sugar content (Goodhue, 2011; Goodhue et al., 2003). Contracts are being used increasingly in Europe's transition economies to assist vertical coordination across various agri-food supply chains. See Dries et al. (2009) and Gorton et al. (2006) for examples from the dairy industry.

Table 3. Shares of four largest firms in domestic wine sales, Old World, New World, and transition economies, 2009, in percent

	Largest Firm	Second- to Fourth- Largest Firms	All Other Firms
Old World			
Austria	5	7	88
France	11	5	84
Germany	1	3	96
Italy	6	4	90
Portugal	62	23	15
Spain	11	10	79
New World			
Argentina	27	32	41
Australia	23	39	38
Chile	31	51	18
New Zealand	24	24	52
South Africa	34	4	62
United States	21	35	44
Transition Economies			
Bulgaria	13	26	61
Hungary	8	7	85
Romania	11	21	68
Russia	6	11	83
Ukraine	16	28	56

Source: Anderson and Nelgen (2011, table 33), based on Euromonitor International data.

that many Georgian farmers remain wary of returning to any form of collective.

The recent experience of New World wine countries suggests that the firms that survive and thrive as exporters are the larger and more-productive ones. This is consistent with empirical evidence from the international economics literature on manufacturers in general. That literature also reveals that the most-productive exporters of differentiated (branded) goods tend to be those who segment their markets and upgrade the quality of the products that they sell to high-income countries (Bastos and Silva, 2010; Flach, 2011). These findings suggest that small local firms such as Pheasant's Tears may be the exception rather than the norm among successful wine exporters, although in Southern Hemisphere countries there are some smaller wineries, which have been under family ownership for several generations, that have emerged as successful exporters.[6]

Given also how crucial it is to understand market niches and the distribution system in each destination country, a rapid expansion of wine exports from Georgia to the West is likely to require attracting foreign investors already very familiar with selling to those markets. This is especially the case because such experienced firms also are more likely to be at the technological frontier in viticulture, oenology, and wine marketing and to be able to access the substantial upfront finance that is required to plant new vineyards, construct or renovate a winery, and invest abroad in brand development.

One should be wary of expanding too rapidly. As already mentioned in connection with Figure 9(a), Australia's vineyard area and consequent wine production grew so quickly beginning in the mid-1990s that marketers simply could not find enough outlets for it all after the wine from new vines became available for sale, especially after the financial crisis emerged in the United States and the EU in 2007–08. The subsequent discounting and sales in bulk rather than in branded bottles is reflected in the rapid decline over the past decade in the unit value of Australian exports shown in Figure 9a. This led to a commensurate drop in grape prices (by more than one-third for Shiraz between 2008 and 2011 vintages). The same happened to New Zealand beginning in 2007: the unit value of its wine exports fell from US$6.65 in 2007 to $4.93 in 2010 (Anderson and Nelgen, 2011, table 79), with bulk wine's share of exports rising from 5 percent to 30 percent (NZW, 2011). One way to reduce the risk of oversupply is to collect and promptly disseminate accurate and comprehensive data on nursery sales, new plantings, vineyard renovations, and winery crushing and bottling capacity.

---

[6] See, for example, www.australiasfirstfamiliesofwine.com.au.

4.3. How to expand export demand?[7]

A case can be made for generic promotion to accompany and support private-sector promotion. Certainly, firms are capable of developing their own brands according to their competitive advantages and areas of difference but, especially in markets unfamiliar with the country's wines, they first need to draw attention to what the country has to offer in general. Empirical evidence supports this view for products overall,[8] and it is even more true for credence goods such as wine.

The experiences of other small economies provide guidance as to what generic promotion works well. Chile (www.winesofchile.com) and New Zealand (www. nzwine.com) are good examples. So, too, is Austria (www.austrianwine.com), a country in which, as in Georgia, the majority of wine grape growers have less than 1 ha of vines. All three countries have sought to associate their wines with their country and to emphasize the clean, green image of their beautiful vineyards against a background of snow-capped mountains — something that Georgia can surely emulate.

Austria provides a lesson on the importance of protecting the generic reputation of a country's wine quality. In 1985, a small proportion of Austrian wine was found to have been adulterated with a harmless but illegal additive to add body and sweetness. Austrian wine exports plummeted by four-fifths within a year and took more than a decade to recover. That recovery process has been characterized by raising the quality as well as image of Austria's exports (Carter, 2011). As a consequence, during the decade to 2011 the unit value of those exports nearly trebled (Figure 9b). This underscores the importance of Georgia's having in place sound procedures for testing the quality before approving the exportation of wines labeled "Made in Georgia."

---

[7] Demand for Georgian wines in the CIS countries is already well established, so attention in this section is focused on promoting Georgian wines in non-traditional markets in western Europe, North America, and East Asia.

[8] According to a recent cross-country study by Lederman *et al.* (2009), covering all exports not just wine, a 10 percent increase in the budget for generic export promotion on average leads to an increase in exports of between 0.6 percent and 1.0 percent. They also find diminishing returns to such expenditures, so the returns are even higher for those countries just beginning to grow their budget for such activities.

New Zealand has done well in promoting images of its countryside even though most of its customers in the Northern Hemisphere have not visited that distant place. That is good news for Georgia because, even though it is on the edge of Europe, to those living near the North Atlantic it is still considered remote (infrequent flights, unfamiliar airlines, troubled borders). If images can substitute for reality, they can buy time for Georgia to build its wine tourism (see the next subsection).

In the first decade of its export boom, Australia's generic promotion was considered highly successful. It promoted the idea of "sunshine in a bottle," of bold, upfront, fruity styles that appealed to newcomers to wine who were the target of supermarket promotions. But consumers — or at least wine columnists and other opinion leaders — gradually tired of the uniformity of styles. The reputation of Australian wine has gradually slipped in recent years as a consequence. This is ironic because it occurred just as many Australian winemakers were moving to more elegant, restrained styles to accompany fine foods (Hooke, 2011). As in Austria, the lesson is that while building a strong generic reputation is a slow process, the dismantling of that reputation can be swift. Australia is now investing heavily in rebuilding its reputation but with a focus on finer wines as well (www. apluswines.com).

Georgia can emphasize numerous points of difference to attract attention to its wines. Those differences, listed at the beginning of this section, include its wines' history, diversity, uniqueness, and authenticity. Its *qvevri* technology is especially appealing to wine enthusiasts. It could also appeal to a much wider clientele if it could be demonstrated that *qvevri* wine is healthier than wine as conventionally produced elsewhere. There is already some preliminary scientific evidence to support that claim (Diaz, 2011; Shalashvili *et al.*, 2010). If such studies were to be replicated and supplemented by other scientists, particularly in the countries that are to be targeted as export markets, they could be drawn on by wine writers in their reviews of Georgian wines. Meanwhile, some producers in Italy and Germany have been experimenting with the *qvevri* technology (*Newsweek,* October 31, 2011, pp. 50–51). This development should inspire encouragement among Georgian producers: imitation is the best compliment and, as with the article in *Newsweek,* it can generate additional — and free — publicity for Georgia.

Georgia's generic promotion should initially be country-wide rather than stressing specific regions. However, just as the Marlborough region now has 75 percent of New Zealand's wine grape area, so Kakheti has a similar proportion in Georgia. Hence that region will tend to become the best known, especially if it also continues to be the region where wine tourism is developing fastest. It is thus helpful that in 2011 the EU agreed to legally protect Georgia's geographical appellations. Other countries importing Georgian wine will now be encouraged to follow suit. This is particularly important in countries where there is a risk of counterfeit wine, as it provides not only recognition but also legal protection.

A single industry body could undertake generic promotion as well as administer generic R&D funds. Experience in New World countries suggests that a small country can achieve economies of size combining the roles of promotion, R&D, and regulatory oversight in one industry-owned organization, as in New Zealand (NZW, 2011, p. 21) and in Australia from July 2014 (WFA, 2012). That allows the returns from those three activities to be compared and the budget divided so as to maximize its overall return to the industry (and to the government, if it also is a financial stakeholder).

The budget for generic promotion and R&D should be in the millions of dollars. Australia and New Zealand each spend close to US1 cent per liter of wine produced on generic promotion (and associated regulatory functions), while Bordeaux spends more than 3 cents. Australia spends about 2 cents per liter on R&D, compared with about 1 cent in New Zealand. So if Georgia were to emulate Australia's spending pattern, with its annual production near 100 million liters per year that would suggest an annual budget of $1 million a year on generic promotion and $2 million a year on R&D and related extension activities initially (and to grow in parallel with the industry's output). Even if one were to exclude noncommercial production for the home market from the base of the calculus, about half those budgets would be required by 2015 if the president's aim of trebling the volume of exports between 2011 and 2015 is realized.

4.4. *What role for wine tourism?*

The potential for building wine tourism in Georgia is enormous, as eloquently explained by Taber (2009). A start has been made, with some wineries offering cellar-door tastings, but many other components need to be added, including more hotels ranging up to four- if not five-star (with Internet access, brewed coffee, and dependable hot water), similar-quality restaurants with waiters who can speak English and know how to serve wine with food (with some at least offering a *supra* experience), more paved roads connecting key sites, better road signage with a wine route symbols, information bays/kiosks, wine route maps and booklets in English and other key languages (with sample itineraries and contact details and opening times of each winery's cellar door and major restaurant), acceptance of major credit cards, and comprehensive multilingual websites to facilitate pretour planning. Two excellent DVDs have been produced to explain Georgia's uniqueness (Kokochasvili, 2011; Lambert and Finlay, 2011). If they are circulated widely, through being given to opinion-shaping visitors to take home and share with friends and colleagues, a better understanding of what Georgia has to offer can spread much faster than just via word of mouth.

To minimize travel time between venues, a clustering of cellar doors would help greatly, especially if the cluster included or was close to accommodations and dining as well as near historic sites such as the Tsinandali Estate or Alaverdi Monastery.[9] Given the heavy concentration of wine production in Kakheti, it would make sense to concentrate public infrastructure expansion in that area initially.

Investment financing is needed to build the infrastructure and facilities expected by today's international tourists from high-income countries, and then the construction phase can employ many low-skilled workers. This will thereby provide a major expansion in part-time off-farm earnings for farm households.

Once built, wineries, cellar-door outlets, restaurants, and hotels also require, on an ongoing basis, large numbers of employees who possess the full spectrum of skills. Post-secondary school training opportunities need to be created to teach those skills, such as in hospitality, vineyard management, winery tasks, and cellar-door operations. Then wine tourism could

---

[9] For more detailed suggestions from a visiting group of opinoin-shapers, see Deloitte Consulting (2011).

supplement employment- and income-creating opportunities from the expansion of grape and wine production in Georgia.

5. Implications for policy and poverty alleviation

The preceding discussion makes clear that the potential for growth in wine exports and in-bound wine tourism in Georgia is very real but also that many challenges remain. To realize that potential, investment is needed not only from the private sector but also from the government, beginning with Invest in Georgia, the national investment agency. That agency has a role in attracting investor interest to the industry and associated tourism opportunities. In conjunction with the GWA's Development Action Plan (GWA, 2011), Invest in Georgia can build awareness among prospective investors both domestically and abroad. The ex-Soviet diaspora is an obvious target group, but so are the large wine corporations that are already well established in the target markets.

The Georgian National Tourism Agency clearly also has a major role to play in developing in-bound tourism. The food-and-wine focus provides a major hook, though, so the industry needs to work with the tourism agency for them to reap mutual benefits. This linkage between the promotion of Georgian wine and Georgia as a tourist destination makes a strong economic case for government co-funding of wine promotion in selected markets abroad.

The government also has a key role in supporting investment in grape and wine R&D, in the tertiary education of viticulturalists, oenologists, and wine marketers, and in the post-secondary-school training of workers in the industry and the wine tourism sector. A strong economic case can be made for government co-funding of agricultural research in general, without which there inevitably will be underinvestment because the private sector is unable to capture all of society's gains from such investments (Alston and Fulton, 2012). The case for government funding is even stronger for grape and wine research in Georgia, given the contribution that it could make to expand dramatically the revenue from the low-performing grapevines of many low-income farm households (and even to encourage the replanting of vineyards that were pulled up beginning in the mid-1980s).

For the industry to produce in dry seasons, it needs reliable access to irrigation. Currently the irrigation infrastructure in Georgia is very run down. Creating the right institutions and putting the right policies in place for that to happen is a major challenge (see, e.g., Young, 2010), but it will have a high social payoff, as it would help not only the wine industry but also horticultural producers. Since that industry is very labor-intensive, it would add to the expansion of jobs in rural areas. If rural employment, too, became more export-focused, such jobs would include packing, processing, and transport activities. As countries such as Chile and Peru have found in the past two decades, this increase in rural employment can help boost rural development and alleviate poverty.

Finally, the government's current policy of providing a floor price for substandard grapes from growers unable to sell to commercial wineries and processing them in state-owned wineries (for eventual sale in bulk or for converting to industrial alcohol) needs to be reformed. Apart from the financial waste of such a policy (since costs are likely to exceed sales revenue of such state-owned wineries), it provides a disincentive for below-average growers to raise the quality of their product to a level acceptable to commercial wineries. If the resulting accumulation of low-quality wine is then exported in bulk to neighboring countries, there is the risk that it will be bottled and misrepresented for sale as Wine of Georgia (as has apparently already happened in Ukraine) and thus diminish the reputation of bottled wine exported directly from Georgia. Instead of offering price supports, the government would do better to provide financial supports to poor farm families via cash e-transfers with conditions such as to upgrade their wine grape production or to restructure away from grape growing and toward more profitable activities.

References

Alston, J.M. and Fulton, M. (2012). Sources of Institutional Failure and Underinvestment in Levy-Funded Agricultural Research. Paper presented at the 56th AARES Annual Conference, Fremantle, Western Australia, February 8–10.

Anderson, K. (ed.) (2004). *The World's Wine Markets: Globalization at Work.* Cheltenham, UK: Edward Elgar.

Anderson, K. (2010). Varietal intensities and similarities of the world's wine regions. *Journal of Wine Economics,* 5(2), 270–309.

Anderson, K. (2011). Contributions of the innovation system to Australia's wine industry growth. In Giuliana, E., Morrison, A. and Rabellotti, R. (eds.), *Innovation and Technological Catch-Up: The Changing Geography of Wine Production*. Cheltenham, UK: Edward Elgar. Chapter 4.

Anderson, K. and Nelgen, S. (2011). *Global Wine Markets, 1961 to 2009: A Statistical Compendium*. Adelaide: University of Adelaide Press, accessibleasane-bookatwww.adelaide.edu.au/press/titles/global-wine and as Excelspreadsheets at www.adelaide.edu.au/wine-econ/databases/GWM/.

AWF. (1995). *Strategy 2025: The Australian Wine Industry*. Adelaide: Winemakers' Federation of Australia for the Australian Wine Foundation.

Bastos, P. and Silva, J. (2010). The quality of a firm's exports: Where you export to matters. *Journal of International Economics*, 82(2), 99–111.

Carter, F. (2011). Austrian maverick: An interview with Willi Klinger. *Meininger's Wine Business International*, 6(5), 30–33.

Cross, R., Plantinga, A.J. and Stavins, R.N. (2011). The value of terroir: Hedonic estimation of vineyard sale prices. *Journal of Wine Economics*, 6(1), 1–14.

Deloitte Consulting (2011). *Wine Opinion-Shapers' Visit to Georgia: Compilation of Trip Reports*. Tbilisi: USAID Georgia, November.

Diaz, C. (2011). Studies of traditional winemaking methods based on spontaneous fermentation. Paper presented at the first Qvevri Wine Symposium, Georgia, September 15–18.

Dries, L., Germenji, E., Noev, N. and Swinnen, J.F.M. (2009). Farmers, vertical coordination, and the restructuring of dairy supply chains in Central and Eastern Europe. *World Development*, 37(11), 1742–1758.

Fajgelbaum, P., Grossman, G.M. and Helpman, E. (2011). Income distribution, product quality and international trade. *Journal of Political Economy*, 119(4), 721–765.

Flach, L. (2011). Quality upgrading and price heterogeneity: Evidence from Brazilian manufacturing exporters. Paper presented at the tenth Annual Postgraduate Conference, University of Nottingham, April 14–15. www.nottingham.ac.uk/gep/news-events/conferences/2011/postgrad-conf-14-04-11.aspx.

Friberg, R., Paterson, R.W. and Richardson, A.D. (2011). Why is there a home bias: A case study of wine. *Journal of Wine Economics*, 6(1), 37–66.

Gergaud, O. and Ginsburg, V. (2008). Natural endowments, production technologies and the quality of wines in Bordeaux: Does terroir Matter? *Economic Journal*, 118(529), F142-157. Reprinted in 2010 in *Journal of Wine Economics*, 5(1), 3–21.

Giuliana, E., Morrison, A. and Rabellotti, R. (eds.) (2011). *Innovation and Technological Catch-Up: The Changing Geography of Wine Production*. Cheltenham, UK: Edward Elgar.

Gladstones, J. (1992). *Viticulture and Environment*. Adelaide: Winetitles.

Goodhue, R.E. (2011). Food quality: The design of incentive contracts. *Annual Review of Resource Economics*, 3, 119–140.

Goodhue, R.E., Heien, D.M., Lee, H. and Sumner, D.A. (2003). Contracts and quality in the California wine grape industry. *Review of Industrial Organization*, 23(3–4), 267–282.

Gopinath, G., Itskhoki, O. and Neiman, B. (2011). Trade prices and the global trade collapse of 2008–2009. NBER Working Paper 17594, Cambridge, MA, November.

Gorton, M., Dumitrashko, M. and White, J. (2006). Overcoming supply chain failure in the agri-food sector: A case study from Moldova. *Food Policy*, 31, 90–103.

Griffiths, R., Redding, S. and van Reenen, J. (2004). Mapping the two faces of R&D: Productivity growth in a panel of OECD industries. *Review of Economics and Statistics*, 86(4), 883–895.

GWA (Georgian Wine Association) (2011). *Sector Export Market Development Action Plan (SEMDAP): Wine Sector.* Tbilisi: Georgian Wine Association.

Hayami, Y. and Ruttan, V.W. (1985). *Agricultural Development: An International Perspective*. Baltimore: Johns Hopkins University Press.

Hooke, H. (2011). Australia is the most under-appreciated wine country. *Decanter*, September 27.

Kharbedia, M. (2010). *Georgia: Cradle of Wine*. Tbilisi: Wine Club.

Kokochasvili, M. (2011). *The Cradle of Wine* [DVD]. Tbilisi: Young Directors Union New Studio.

Lambert, D. and Finlay, J. (2011). *That Crazy French Woman ... in Georgia* [DVD]. London: That Crazy French Woman Productions.

Lederman, D., Olarreaga, M. and Payton, L. (2009). Export promotion agencies revisited. Policy Research Working Paper 5125, World Bank, Washington DC, November.

Lewin, B. (2010). *Wine Myths and Reality*. San Francisco: Wine Appreciation Guild.

McGovern, P. (2003). *Ancient Wine: The Search for the Origins of Viticulture*. Princeton, NJ: Princeton University Press.

McGovern, P. (2009). *Uncorking the past: The Quest for Wine, Beer, and Other Alcoholic Beverages*. Berkeley: University of California Press.

Nayak, A. (2011). Does variety fit the quality bill? Factor-endowments driven differences in trade, export margins, prices and production techniques. Purdue University, West Lafayette, IN, May. www.auburn.edu/~azn0018/.

Noev, N. and Swinnen, J.F.M. (2004). Eastern Europe and the former Soviet Union. In Anderson, K. (ed.), *The World's Wine Markets: Globalization at Work*. Cheltenham, UK: Edward Elgar. Chapter 9.

NSO (National Statistical Office of Georgia) (2011a). *Agriculture of Georgia 2010*. Tbilisi: National Statistical Office of Georgia. www.geostat.ge.

NSO (National Statistical Office of Georgia) (2011b). *Households' Income and Expenditure 2010*. Tbilisi: National Statistical Office of Georgia. www.geostat.ge.

NSO (National Statistical Office of Georgia) (2012). *External Trade of Georgia*. Tbilisi: National Statistical Office of Georgia. www.geostat.ge.

NZW (New Zealand Winegrowers) (2011). *New Zealand Winegrowers Strategic Review*. Auckland: New Zealand Winegrowers, November.

Scholes, E. (2011). Russia's emerging wine culture. *Meininger's Wine Business International*, 6(4), 33–35.

Shalashvili, A., Ugrekhelidze, D., Targamadze, I., Zambakhidze, N. and Tsereteli, L. (2010). Comparison of wines of Georgian (Kakhethian) and European types according to quantitative content of phenolic compounds and antiradical efficiency. Paper presented at the 33rd OIV World Congress, Tbilisi, June 20–27.

Taber, G.M. (2009). *In Search of Bacchus: Wanderings in the Wonderful World of Wine Tourism*. New York: Scribner.

Wesley, N. (2011). Malbec's moment: How a forgotten red grape has revived Argentina and taken America by storm. *Wine Spectator*, December 15.

WFA (2012). Industry bodies seek merger of statutory authorities. Winemakers' Federation of Australia, Adelaide, 21 February. www.wfa.org.au/merger.aspx.

World Bank (2009). *Georgia: Agriculture and Rural Enterprise Development*. Washington, DC: World Bank.

World Bank (2011). *World Development Indicators*. Washington, DC: World Bank. http://data.worldbank.org/data-catalog/world-development-indicators/.

World Bank (2013). *Doing Business 2013*. Washington, DC: World Bank. www.doingbusiness.org/rankings/.

Young, M. (2010). *Environmental Effectiveness and Economic Efficiency of Water Use in Agriculture*. Paris: OECD.

Chapter 14

Asia's Evolving Role in Global Wine Markets*

Kym Anderson[†,‡,¶] and Glyn Wittwer[§]

Abstract

Over the past decade Hong Kong and China have become far more important to the world's wine markets, while Southeast Asia's imports of fine wine continue to grow steadily. This paper reviews recent developments in the light of comparative advantage theory before drawing on a model of global wine markets to project developments in Asia and elsewhere over the next five years under various economic growth, real exchange rate, and policy assumptions. It concludes that China is set to continue to be by far the most dominant player in Asia, and to change global markets for wines dramatically, just as it has been doing and will continue to do for so many other products.

---

*First published in *China Economic Review* 35: 1–14, September 2015. Thanks are due to the journal's referees for helpful comments and to the Australian Grape and Wine Authority for research funds under GWRDC Project UA 0804. Views expressed are the authors' alone.

[†] University of Adelaide, Australia
[‡] Australian National University, Australia
[§] Victoria University, Australia
[¶] Corresponding author.
E-mail addresses: kym.anderson@adelaide.edu.au (K. Anderson), Glyn.Wittwer@vu.edu.au (G. Wittwer).

1. Introduction

Rice wine is common in Asia, but wine made from grapes has had a very minor role traditionally. Prior to this century grape wine was consumed only by Asia's elite, and produced only in tiny quantities and mostly in just Japan and — from the late 1980s — China.[1] However, income growth and a preference swing towards this traditional European product have changed the consumption situation dramatically. China is also expanding its area of vineyards and is now the world's 5th largest producer of grape wine (hereafter called just wine), up from 15th as recently as 2001.[2] To date that supply expansion has not been able to keep up with China's growth in demand though, so wine imports have surged. Nor are those imports only of low quality. The average current US$ price of Asia's wine imports grew at 7% per year between 2000 and 2009, compared with only 5.5% in the rest of the world. By 2009 Asia's average import price was nearly 80% higher than the world average (and more than four times higher in the case of Hong Kong and Singapore). Even the unit values of China's imports of both still bottled and sparkling wines were above the global average by 2009 (Anderson & Nelgen, 2011). Meanwhile, shortly after removing its tariff on wine imports in February 2008, Hong Kong became the world's most important market for ultra-premium and iconic wines.

What is the future of Asia in the world's wine markets? Will China's wine production eventually exceed its needs domestically? Who else will satisfy Asia's growing thirst? What roles will excise and import taxes and preferential trade agreements play? How much will China's austerity drive, introduced in 2013, dampen conspicuous consumption of luxuries such as expensive wines?

---

[1] Winegrape production in China may have begun more than two millennia ago, but it would have been only for the ruling elite's pleasure (Huang, 2000 (pp. 240–246); McGovern, 2003, 2009). For developments in East Asian wine markets to the turn of this century, see Findlay, Farrell, Chen, and Wang (2004).

[2] China is also the world's largest producer of table grapes. Its total vineyard area surpassed that of France in 2014, at 799,000 ha compared with France's 792,000, and so now is 2nd only to Spain's 1.02 million ha (OIV, 2015).

This paper seeks to address these types of questions. It first draws on comparative advantage theory, then looks at the recent history in more detail before presenting some projections for the next five years under various assumptions about economic growth, real exchange rates, bilateral trade agreements, and China's austerity measures. It concludes that China — by far the most dominant player in Asia — is set to continue to change global markets for wines dramatically, just as it has been doing and will continue to do for so many other products.

2. Determinants of comparative advantage in wine

According to the workhorse theory of comparative advantage developed in the 20th century, we should expect agricultural trade to occur between relatively lightly populated economies that are well-endowed with agricultural land and those that are densely populated with little agricultural land per worker (Krueger, 1977). Leamer (1987) develops this model further and relates it to paths of economic development. If the stock of natural resources is unchanged, rapid growth by one or more countries relative to others in their availability of produced capital (physical plus human skills and technological knowledge) per unit of available labor time would tend to cause those economies to strengthen their comparative advantage in non-primary products. By contrast, a discovery of minerals or energy raw materials would strengthen that country's comparative advantage in mining and weaken its comparative advantage in agricultural and other tradable products, ceteris paribus. It would also boost national income and hence the demand for nontradables, which would cause mobile resources to move into the production of nontradable goods and services, further reducing farm and industrial production (Corden, 1984; Freebairn, 2015; Garnaut, 2014). As port etc. infrastructure is developed and costs of trading internationally fall for the country, more products would move from the nontradable to the tradable category (Venables, 2004).

At early stages of development of a country with a relatively small stock of natural resources per worker, wages would be low and the country is likely to have an initial comparative cost advantage in unskilled labor-intensive, standard-technology manufactures. Then as the stock of industrial capital grows, there would be a gradual move towards exporting manufactures that are relatively intensive in their use of physical capital, skills and knowledge. Natural resource-abundant economies, however, may invest more in capital specific to primary production and so would not develop a comparative advantage in manufacturing until a later stage of development, at which time their industrial exports would be relatively capital intensive.

The above theory of changing comparative has been used successfully to explain Asia's resource-poor first- and second-generation industrializing economies becoming more dependent on imports of primary products from their resource-rich trading partners (see, e.g., Anderson & Smith, 1981). It also explains well the 20th century flying geese pattern of comparative advantage and then disadvantage in unskilled labor-intensive manufactures as some rapidly growing economies expand their endowments of industrial capital per worker relative to the rest of the world — the classic example being clothing and textiles (Ozawa, 2009).

But how helpful is that theory for explaining comparative advantage in wine? Grape-based wine is dependent on winegrapes as an input, and they are too perishable to be transported internationally without at least the first stages of processing. The lowest-quality winegrapes and wine can be produced in less-than-ideal regions and sold as an undifferentiated commodity without a great deal of knowhow, but only at prices barely above the cost of production for most grapegrowers. To produce a higher-quality product that can be differentiated from other wines by consumers, and thus attract a higher price, requires far more technological knowledge and skills in grape growing, wine making and wine marketing in addition to access to high-quality vineyard land or at least grapes therefrom. To be economically sustainable the producer also needs ready access to financial capital to cover the very considerable up-front establishment costs and to finance the years when receipts fall short of outgoings, including the first seven years before cash income begins to exceed cash outlays. Secure property rights over the vineyard land are essential as well, since the lifetime of vines is at least 30 years and can be much longer.

Of particular importance as determinants of a country's competiveness in producing wine rather than other farm products are the three Ts of terroir, traditions, and technologies.

Terroir refers to various pertinent aspects of climate, topography, soils, geology, etc. that determine the quality of the vine's growing conditions. Vineyard site selection therefore is crucial. Experience has determined the best sites and most-suitable grape varieties in long-established regions, whereas in new regions science has to be used to speed the process of approaching the potential of any region to produce quality winegrapes. The conventional wisdom is that winegrapes grow best between the 30° and 50° temperate latitude bands north and south of the equator, and where rain is concentrated in the winter and summer harvest times are dry. Lower latitudes typically result in lower-quality winegrapes, although simultaneously moving to higher altitudes can help because temperatures decline about 5 °C per 1000 m of elevation (Ashenfelter & Storchmann, 2014; Gladstones, 1992).

Traditions determine not only how a product is produced but also the extent of local consumer demand. This is important for wine because typically local demand is the easiest and least costly for producers to satisfy, as there are relatively high fixed costs of entry into new export markets (Friberg, Paterson, & Richardson, 2011). Stigler and Becker (1977) argue that economists should begin by assuming tastes are stable over time and similar among people, and then focus on explaining differences in consumption patterns using standard determinants such as relative prices and real incomes. That view is supported for food even in the poorest settings. For example, recent studies in both India and China demonstrate that introducing subsidies to rice and wheat consumption does almost nothing to boost nutrition, as consumers tend to eat the same amount of nutrients but do so by switching from less-preferred coarse grains to now-subsidized rice and wheat (Jensen & Miller, 2011; Kaushal & Muchomba, 2013). Social norms and religion can also influence interest in consumption of alcoholic beverages, and those can alter with economic integration/globalization (Aizenman & Brooks, 2008).

Also, when preferences are non-homothetic, trade patterns can be affected by growth in domestic demand (Markusen, 2013). The income elasticity of demand for wine is typically below one and falling in traditional wine societies, but wine tends to have an income elasticity of demand greater than one in emerging economies in which wine is exotic (Fogarty, 2010). In such emerging economies its comparative advantage in wine would decline as per capita income rises unless its wine productivity grew sufficiently faster than domestic incomes, other things equal.

As for technologies, there is always potential to improve the efficiency of traditional production, processing, entrepreneurship and marketing, be that by trial and error of practitioners over the generations or via formal investment in private and public research and development (R&D). The New World wine-producing countries have been more dependent on newly developed technologies and less on terroir than have producers in Western Europe, although both sets of countries have made major R&D investments — and expanded complementary tertiary education in viticulture, oenology and wine marketing — over the past half-century (Giuliana, Morrison, & Rabellotti, 2011). Those technologies potentially are transferrable to other countries and can even become globalized, as has happened with grain technologies (Olmstead & Rhode, 2007). That process has been greatly accelerated over the past two decades through two mechanisms. One is the emergence of fly-in, fly-out viticulturalists and winemakers from both Old World and New World wine-producing countries (Williams, 1995). The decline in airfares has made it far more affordable for young professionals to work in both hemispheres each year, doubling their vintage experiences and learning and spreading new technologies quickly. The other mechanism is via foreign direct investment joint ventures: by combining two firms' technical and market knowledge, the latest technologies can be diffused to new regions more rapidly.

How important modern technologies are relative to terroir in determining wine comparative advantage is a moot point. One recent statistical study suggests terroir is not as dominant as is commonly assumed — even in regions as established as Bordeaux (Gerguad & Ginsburg, 2008). Another study, of vineyard sale values in Oregon, finds that while appellation reputation has some economic value, each location's physical attributes are not closely related to wine prices (Cross, Plantinga, & Stavins, 2011). A recent book by Lewin (2010) begins its section on wine regions with the New World rather than the Old World, to emphasize the point that wines almost everywhere are manipulated by winemakers as they endeavor to make use of available knowledge to produce the products most desired by their customers. What they choose to produce is increasingly being affected by how they can maximize profits through satisfying consumer demand, rather than by what they prefer to make with their available resources.

New technologies in agriculture have long tended to be biased in favor of saving the scarcest factor of production, as reflected in relative factor prices. Hayami and Ruttan (1985) emphasize that the focus of R&D investments has been driven in part by changes in factor prices, and in particular by the rise in real wages. That has resulted in the development and/or adoption of labor-saving technologies such as mechanical harvesters and pruners for vineyards and super-fast (even robotic) bottling/labeling equipment for wineries in viticultural land-abundant, labor-scarce countries. The adoption of labor-saving technologies has helped countries with rapidly rising real wages retain their comparative advantage in what traditionally had been (at least at the primary stage) a labor-intensive industry. This in turn means poorer countries need to find sources of comparative advantage other than just low wages.

Relative factor endowments affect the comparative advantage of a country in terms also of the *quality* of its exported products. New trade theory suggests richer, capital-abundant countries will export higher-quality and hence higher-priced goods (Fajgelbaum, Grossman, & Helpman, 2011; Nayak, 2011).

A further set of influences on comparative advantage that can be important at certain times relates to currency exchange rate movements. A macroeconomic shock such as Argentina's devaluation against the US dollar by two-thirds in late 2001, or a doubling in the Australian-US dollar exchange rate over the subsequent decade due largely to Australia's mining boom, have had major (and opposite) impacts on the international competiveness of wineries in those two Southern Hemisphere countries (Anderson & Wittwer, 2013).

3. Asia's wine production, consumption and trade to date

The previous section provides plenty of reasons for not expecting much winegrape production in most Asian countries: there is almost no tradition of wine consumption domestically; most people's incomes until very recently have been too low for wine to be a priority; there are very few regions with suitable terroir, especially where it is not hot and/or humid; and in numerous Islamic Asian countries their religion frowns on alcohol. It is thus not surprising that the only Asian countries with a significant area of grapevines (of which only a fraction is used in wine making) are parts of Japan, Korea and China. About 1% of South Korea's small crop area has been devoted to vines over the past two decades, and just 0.4% of Japan's since the 1970s, with little change in either country over those periods. By contrast, the share of crop area under vines in China has been growing rapidly, doubling since the turn of the century. Even so, that share in China is still not quite as high as in Japan, which suggests there is scope for substantially more expansion without encroaching very much on land used for food production (bearing in mind also that quality winegrapes grow better on poor slopes than on fertile flat land).[3] China has been open to foreign direct investment in vineyards and wineries, and has welcomed flying vignerons as consultants. It even seems to have found ways to provide adequate property rights for investors, notwithstanding the fact that farm land cannot be privately owned in China. Its vineyards are heavily focusing on red varieties (considered by Chinese people to be best for their health), especially ones originating in France.[4]

While it is true that India, Thailand and even Myanmar have some vineyards and have begun producing wine from them, the volumes are as yet insignificant.

China's volume of wine production has been growing more than twice as fast as its area under vines. This has been possible not just because the share of domestically grown grapes destined for wine has risen but also because China imports a lot of wine in bulk and blends it with wine made from Chinese grapes. This is legally feasible because national labeling

---

[3] Australia also had only 0.4% of its crop area under vines in 2008. By contrast, shares that year are as high as 4% in France, 6% in Spain and New Zealand, 8% in Italy and 14% in Portugal (Anderson & Nelgen, 2011, Table 6). It should be noted that the quality of grape and wine data for China are probably lower than for the other countries mentioned in this paper, but they are the best the authors have been able to assemble.

[4] In 2010, 96% of China's winegrape area was planted to red varieties (mostly Cabernet Sauvignon), and the country of origin of 97% of the varieties is France (Anderson, 2013, pp. 243 and 635).

laws are such that a bottle marked 'Product of China' is required to have only 10% local content.

Turning to consumption, there are only five Asian countries plus Hong Kong and Taiwan where per capita grape wine consumption has yet to exceed 0.2 litres per year. In each of those countries the level in 2012 is well above that of 2000, but the most dramatic increase has been in China (Figure 1(a)). Since that is also the most populous country, its growth has overwhelmingly dominated Asia's overall increase in wine consumption, which has nearly quadrupled since 2000 (Figure 1(b)). China accounted for barely half of Asia's wine consumption in 2000, but now it accounts for all but one-fifth. Similarly populous India, by contrast, has a wine industry

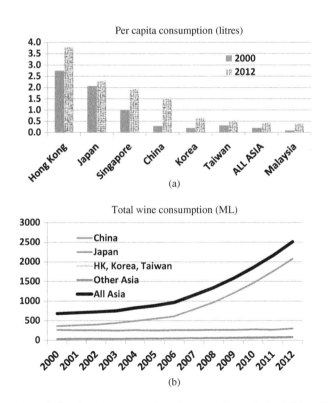

Figure 1. Per capita[a] and total consumption of grape wine in Asia, 2000 to 2012
[a]All other Asian countries consume less than 0.2 litres per capita per year.
Source: Updated from Anderson and Nelgen (2011) using Euromonitor International

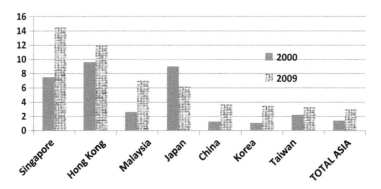

Figure 2. Wine's share of total alcohol consumption in Asia,[a] 2000 and 2009 (%)
[a]For all other Asian countries wine's share of alcohol consumption is less than 3%.
Source: Anderson and Nelgen (2011)

that is less than one-fiftieth the size of China's, notwithstanding its double-digit growth during the past decade.

During the first decade of this century wine doubled its share of Asia's recorded consumption of alcohol, but that brought it to just 3%, or only one-fifth of wine's global share of recorded alcohol consumption. The same handful of Asian countries are the only ones in which wine's share is above the Asian average (Figure 2).

So despite the recent rapid growth in wine consumption in Asia, the potential for further expansion remains enormous, given the current very low level of per capita consumption and share of wine in total alcohol purchases. The rapid aging and educating of the populations in Asia's emerging economies also lends itself to a continuing expansion of demand for wine there. Certainly the new Chinese Government's austerity drive has been discouraging consumption of expensive wines and other luxuries since 2013 but, as suggested below, that influence is much less on lower-quality wines, which are by far the most voluminous (as shown in Table 1).

No Asian country has yet produced grape wine for export in noticeable quantities. As for import dependence, it varied in 2009 from 15% in China (up from 8% in 2000–05) to 68% in Japan, 96% in Korea, and 100% for all other Asian countries (Anderson & Nelgen, 2011, Table 54). Thus China's share of Asian wine imports is much less than its share of consumption, especially when expressed in value terms because the unit value of China's imports in 2009 was only half the Asian average. Even so, China

Table 1. China's wine production, consumption and trade, by quality categories, 2009 (ML)

	Production	Imports	Consumption	Self-Sufficiency (%)
Non-premium	600	80	680	88
Commercial premium	344	86	430	80
Super premium	18	7	25	72
Total	962	173	1135	85

Source: Anderson and Nelgen (2011, Section VI)

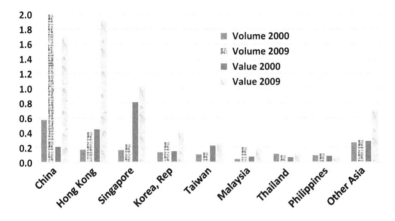

Figure 3. Shares in the volume and value of global wine imports, developing Asia, 2000 and 2009 (%)
[a]Japan's volume (value) shares are 5.8% (5.3%) in 2000 and 3.9% (2.1%) in 2009.
Source: Anderson and Nelgen (2011)

together with Hong Kong (which re-exports at least one-fifth of its wine imports to China) dominate Asia's aggregate wine imports (Figure 3).[5]

One needs to be careful not to diminish the role that some other Asian countries play as significant importers of high-quality wine though. As can be seen in Figure 3, the shares of those countries in the *value* of world imports far exceed their *volume* shares, reflecting the fact that the average price of their imports is well above that of most other countries. For small producers of super-premium wines, especially in nearby Australia, they are important and profitable markets.

---

[5] For Google motion charts on the growth of China's wine imports during 1997 to 2011, see Lewis (2013).

Table 2. Ad valorem consumer tax equivalent[a] of excise plus import taxes on alcoholic beverages, 2008 (%)

	Non-Premium Wine (A$2.50/l)	Commercial Premium Wine (A$7.50/l)	Super Premium Wine (A$20/l)	Beer (A$2/l)	Spirits (A$15/l)
China	32	25	25	18	21
Japan	32	11	4	0	12
Hong Kong	0	0	0	0	100
India	165	155	152	100	151
Korea	46	46	46	124	114
Philippines	22	12	9	10	35
Taiwan	23	14	12	2	23
Thailand	232	117	81	51	52
Vietnam	88	88	88	96	115

[a] At the prices shown in the column headings (expressed in Australian dollars), excluding VAT/GST. Vietnam rates refer to 2012.

Source: Anderson (2010), expanded to include China and Vietnam

Needless to say, Asian wine imports would be considerably larger if import tariffs and excise taxes on wine were less. In numerous Asian countries they exceed those for beer and spirits on a per-liter-of-alcohol basis (Table 2). The decision by Hong Kong to eliminate its tariff on wine imports in early 2008 is partly why its imports in Figure 3 are so much higher by the end than the beginning of the previous decade.

Even without any reforms of those taxes, consumption and imports of wine in Asia are destined to rise over the years to come. How much they might rise, and how much domestic wine production might expand to satisfy at least some of that demand increase, is not easy to predict. A recent study nonetheless has focused on projecting the world's wine markets over the next five years. The next section reports on its findings as they relate to Asia, and the following section uses the same global model to examine some recent policy changes.

4. Projecting the world's wine markets to 2018

Anderson and Wittwer (2013) have revised and updated a model of the world's wine markets that was first published by Wittwer, Berger, and

Anderson (2003). In it, wine markets are disaggregated into non-premium (including bulk), commercial-premium, and super-premium wines.[6] Two types of grapes are specified, premium and non-premium. Non-premium wine uses non-premium grapes exclusively, super-premium wines use premium grapes exclusively, and commercial-premium wines use both types of grapes. The world is divided into 44 individual nations and 7 composite regions.

The model's database is calibrated initially to 2009, based on the comprehensive volume and value data and trade and excise tax data provided in Anderson and Nelgen (2011, Sections V, VI and VII). It is projected forward in two steps. The first step involves using actual aggregate national consumption and population growth between 2009 and 2011 (the most-recent year for which data were available for all countries when the study began), together with changes in real exchange rates (RERs). The second step assumes aggregate national consumption and population grow from 2011 to 2018 at the rates shown in Appendix Table 1, and that RERs over that period either (a) remain at their 2011 levels or (b) return half-way to their 2009 rates (except for China, whose RER is assumed to continue to slightly appreciate, by 2% per year between 2011 and 2018). In each of those steps, a number of additional baseline assumptions are made regarding preferences, technologies, and capital stocks.

Concerning preferences, there is assumed to be a considerable swing towards consumption of all wine types in China, as more Chinese earn middle-class incomes. Since aggregate wine consumption is projected by the major commodity forecasters to rise by 70% rise over that 7-year period, the increase in China's consumption is calibrated to that in the more-likely scenario in which exchange rates revert half-way back from 2011 to 2009 rates. That implies a rise in per capita consumption from 1.0 to 1.6 l per year. This may be too conservative. Per capita wine consumption grew faster than that in several West European wine-importing countries in recent decades, and Vinexpo claims China's 2012 consumption was already 1.4 l. True, annual per capita wine consumption in Hong Kong is only 3 l, and Japan's is rarely above 2 l; but with the number of middle class in China currently around 250 million and growing at 10 million per

---

[6] Commercial–premium wines are defined by Anderson and Nelgen (2011) to be those between US$2.50 and $7.50 per liter pre-tax at a country's border or wholesale.

year (Barton, Chen, & Jin, 2013; Kharas, 2010), and with grape wine still accounting for less than 4% of alcohol consumption by China's 1.1 billion adults, it is not unreasonable to expect large increases in volumes of wine demanded. However, if China's income growth were to grow slower than the rate assumed in the base case, and if that meant China's RER did not continue to appreciate slightly, wine import growth would be slower. As for the rest of the world, the long trend preference swing away from non-premium wines is assumed to continue now that the great recession in the North Atlantic economies has bottomed out.

Both grape and wine industry total factor productivity is assumed to grow at 1% per year everywhere, while grape and wine industry capital is assumed to grow net of depreciation at 1.5% per year in China but zero elsewhere. This means that China's production rises by about one-sixth, one-quarter and one-third for non-premium, commercial-premium and super-premium wines between 2011 and 2018 — which in aggregate is less than half that needed to keep up with the modeled baseline growth in China's consumption. Of course if China's wine production from domestic grapes were to grow faster than the rate assumed in the base scenario, wine imports would increase less.

Given the uncertainty associated with several dimensions of developments in China's wine markets, the more likely of our two main scenarios to 2018 (in which RERs for all but China revert half-way back from 2011 to 2009 rates, called Alternative 1) is compared with a third scenario (called Alternative 2) in which three dimensions are altered: China's aggregate expenditure growth during 2011–18 is reduced by one-quarter (from 7.8 to 5.6% per year), its RER does not change from 2011 instead of appreciating at 2% per year over that period, and its grape and wine industry capital is assumed to grow at 3 instead of 1.5% per year. Each of those three changes ensures a smaller increase in China's wine imports by 2018 in this Alternative 2 scenario. However, this should be considered a lower-bound import projection because, even if China's growth in GDP, industrialization and infrastructure spending were to slow down more than assumed in the Base and Alternative 1 scenarios, Chinese households nonetheless are being encouraged to lower their extraordinarily high savings rates and consume more of their income. In addition, grape wine is encouraged as an alternative to the dominant alcoholic beverages of (grain-based) beer and spirits because of its perceived health benefits and because it does not undermine food security by diminishing foodgrain supplies.

This global model has supply and demand equations and hence quantities and prices for each of the grape and wine products and for a single composite of all other products in each country. Grapes are assumed to be not traded internationally, but other products are both exported and imported. Each market is assumed to have cleared before any shock, and to find a new market-clearing outcome following any exogenously introduced shock. All prices are expressed in real (2009) terms.

To project global wine markets forward, it is assumed that aggregate national consumption and population grow from 2011 to 2018 at the rates shown in Appendix Table 1 and that preferences, technologies, and capital stocks continue to change as described above, plus that RERs over that period either remain at their 2011 levels (the Base Scenario) or return halfway to their 2009 rates (except for China). The latter RER changes began to happen in mid-2013, so the Alternative 1 scenario is more likely to be representative of the real world by 2018 than the Base Scenario. The third scenario (Alternative 2) presents a lower-bound projection of what might happen to Chinese wine import demand if China's economy slows by one-quarter, its RER ceases to appreciate, and simultaneously its domestic grape and wine production capital grows twice as fast.

Table 3(a) suggests China's production of grapes and wine would grow at similar rates in the first two scenarios: by one-sixth for nonpremium wine and a bit over one-quarter for premium wines. In the third scenario those rises increase to one-quarter for nonpremium wine and to more than one-third for premium wines.

The income, population and preference changes together mean that Asian consumption volumes grow dramatically over the period to 2018 except in Japan where the increase is confined to super-premium wine (Table 4). For China the increase is around two-thirds in the first two scenarios and a little less than one-half in the third (slower growth) scenario, whereas for other emerging Asian countries they increase only one-seventh or one-sixth. Given the vast differences between Asian countries in their 2011 consumption levels though, China dominates the volume growth globally while Western Europe sees a decline in its consumption

Table 3. Projected grape and wine output volume changes for China, 2011 to 2018.[a] (%)

	BASE	ALT 1	ALT2
(a) Core scenarios to 2018			
Non-premium wine	18	17	24
Commercial-premium wine	26	25	35
Super-premium wine	29	29	39
Premium grapes	20	20	31
Non-premium grapes	18	17	27

	ALT 1	FTAs with NZ and Chile (% from ALT 1 Base)	FTA with Australia (% from NZ + Chile FTAs Scenario)	Austerity Scenario (% from 3 FTAs Scenario)
(b) Policy change scenarios: impacts relative to ALT 1 in 2018				
Non-premium wine	17.1	–0.1	–0.1	0.1
Commercial-premium wine	25.1	–0.1	–0.1	0.1
Super-premium wine	28.8	0.0	–0.1	–0.1
Premium grapes	19.9	0.0	–0.1	0.0
Non-premium grapes	17.4	0.0	–0.1	0.0

[a] 'Base' refers to the simulation assuming there are no changes in real exchange rates between 2011 and 2018; 'Alt. 1' assumes real exchange rates revert half way back from 2011 to 2009 rates by 2018 except for China's which appreciates 2%pa; and 'Alt. 2' assumes China's RER does not change from 2011, and its aggregate expenditure grows one-quarter less while its grape and wine capital grow twice as fast as in 'Alt. 1'. 'FTA' refers to removing the tariffs on China's wine imports from the country(ies) mentioned with whom it has signed a bilateral Free Trade Agreement. The 'Austerity' simulation assumes China's demand for super-premium wines expands by one-eleventh less than in the simulation involving the 3 FTAs.

Source: Authors' model results.

which dampens somewhat global consumption growth (Figure 4). The fall in Europe is mainly due to the hefty weight in its consumption of the declining non-premium wine sub-sector — continuing the trend in that region of the past three decades.

When combined with the changes projected in production, it is possible to get a picture of what is projected to happen to wine trade. Table 5 provides projections for the main wine-trading regions. In terms of volumes, world trade expands 6% by 2018 in the base scenario, and 7% in the Alternative 1 scenario in which RERs change. Virtually all of that increase

Table 4. Projected changes in quantities of wine consumed in Asia, 2011 to 2018 (%)

	China	Japan	Other Asia
(a) Base scenario (assuming no RER changes from 2011)			
Non premium wines	29	−14	0
Commercial-premium wines	87	−3	10
Super-premium wines	87	9	27
All wines	62	−1	17
(b) Alternative 1 (assuming RERs return half-way from 2011 to 2009 rates)			
Non-premium wines	31	−14	1
Commercial-premium wines	95	−4	9
Super-premium wines	100	9	27
All wines	70	−2	16
(c) Alternative 2 (assuming also slower Chinese import growth)			
Non-premium wines	26	−14	−1
Commercial-premium wines	73	−3	10
Super-premium wines	69	9	25
All wines	46	−1	14

Source: Anderson and Wittwer (2013).

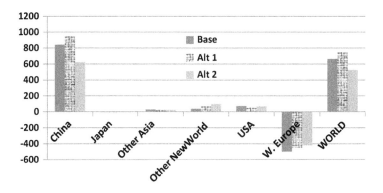

Figure 4. Projected changes in consumption of all wines, 2011-2018[a] (ML)

[a]'Base' refers to the simulation assuming there are no changes in real exchange rates between 2011 and 2018; 'Alt. 1' assumes real exchange rates revert half way back from 2011 to 2009 rates by 2018 except for China's which appreciates 2%pa; and 'Alt. 2' assumes China's RER does not change from 2011, and its aggregate expenditure grows one-quarter less while its grape and wine capital grow twice as fast as in 'Alt. 1'.

Source: Anderson and Wittwer (2013)

Table 5. Projected change in global wine import and export volumes and values, 2011 to 2018[a]

	Volume (ML)			Value (US$m)		
	Base	Alt. 1	Alt. 2	Base	Alt. 1	Alt. 2
(a) Imports						
China	627	739	334	1948	2309	1178
Japan	−10	−13	−10	262	235	230
Other Asia	30	24	26	615	520	539
United Kingdom	−54	−36	−29	98	179	93
North America	−23	11	37	961	1106	1015
Other Europe	−122	−176	−140	1012	740	552
Other	152	151	141	498	259	318
World	600	700	359	5394	5548	3925
(b) Exports						
Australia	0	90	59	336	933	675
Other New World	78	222	75	469	965	597
Old World	521	387	224	4370	3537	2653
World	600 (6%)	700 (7%)	359 (4%)	5394 (17%)	5548 (17%)	3925 (15%)

[a] 'Base' refers to the simulation assuming there are no changes in real exchange rates between 2011 and 2018; 'Alt. 1' assumes real exchange rates revert half way back from 2011 to 2009 rates by 2018 except for China's which appreciates 2% pa; and 'Alt. 2' assumes China's RER does not change from 2011, and its aggregate expenditure grows one-quarter less while its grape and wine capital grow twice as fast as in 'Alt. 1'.

Source: Anderson and Wittwer (2013)

in those two scenarios is due to China's import growth. In the Alternative 2 scenario, in which China imports less, global trade also expands less (by only 4%). In terms of the real value of global trade, however, the upgrading of demand elsewhere means that China accounts for smaller fractions of the growth in the global import value, namely 36%, 43%, and 30% in the Base, Alternative 1 and Alternative 2 scenarios, respectively. In all three scenarios China dominates Asian import growth, and the value of global wine trade rises by about one-sixth (last row of Table 5).

It is not surprising that China is such a dominant force in these projections, given the dramatic growth in its wine consumption over the past dozen years (Figure 1), the expectation of continued high growth in its income over the next five years (albeit somewhat slower than in the past five years), and the assumption that China's winegrape production growth cannot keep pace with domestic demand growth. As a result, China's share of consumption supplied domestically falls from its 2009 level of 85% to 57%, 54% and 67% in 2018 the Base, Alternative 1 and Alternative 2 scenarios for 2018, respectively.

France is projected to become even more dominant in imports by China in the Base scenario where exchange rates are assumed to remain at 2011 levels. However, in the more-likely Alternative 1 scenario with a part-reversal of recent exchange rate movements, the increase in China's imports from Australia is almost the same as that of France in value terms — and they lose equally if China's import growth slows further as in Alternative 2. In volume terms it is Chile that enjoys the greatest increase in sales to China in the two Alternative scenarios. The impacts of these changes on the shares of different exporters in sales to China's are summarized in Figure 5. In the Base case France increases the dominance it had in 2009, in the Alternative 1 scenario Australia almost catches France, and in the Alternative 2 case Australia slightly overtakes France. Meanwhile, all other exporters' shares remain less than half those of Australia and France.

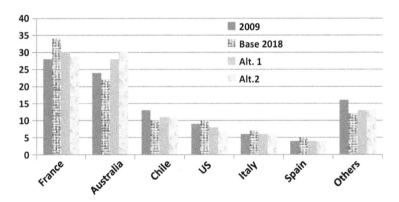

Figure 5. Shares of China's wine import value, by source, 2009 and projected 2018[a] (%)

[a]'Base 2018' refers to the simulation assuming there are no changes in real exchange rates between 2011 and 2018; 'Alt. 1' assumes real exchange rates revert half way back from 2011 to 2009 rates by 2018 except for China's which appreciates 2% pa; and 'Alt. 2' assumes China's RER does not change from 2011, and its aggregate expenditure grows one-quarter less while its grape and wine capital grow twice as fast as in 'Alt. 1'.

Source: Anderson and Wittwer (2013)

Projected bilateral trade changes more generally are summarized in Table 6 for the most-likely Alternative 1 scenario. All major wine-producing regions benefit from China's burgeoning demands. In volume terms that is slightly at the expense of growth in their exports to other regions, although not in value terms because of the modeled upgrading of quality in those other markets. For Australia and Other Southern Hemisphere exporters, projected growth in real export values in local currency terms is even larger than in the US$ terms shown in Table 6 due to the modeled real depreciation of the currencies of this group. For example, Australia's export value growth of US$933 million converts to an Australian dollar increase of AUD1360 million. Australia's projected volume growth in this scenario is an extra 21 ML of wine per year being exported to China during 2011 to 2018. That should be manageable, as it is the same rate of increase in Australia's sales to the United States during the first decade of this century.

5. Impacts on projections of recent policy developments: China's FTAs and austerity

The above results have not taken into account two recent developments that are affecting wine markets in China and in its import-supplying countries: the signing of several bilateral free-trade agreements (FTAs), and the anti-corruption/austerity drive that began in 2013 and has impacted heavily on official banqueting and expensive gift-giving.

Three pertinent FTAs involve the gradual lowering of tariffs on China's wine imports from wine-exporting countries. The general tariffs in 2008 were 14% on sparkling and still bottled wine and 20% on bulk wine. They have since been phased down to zero by 2012 for New Zealand and by 2016 for Chile. They will also be zero for Australia by 2016 for bottled wine and by 2018 for bulk wine.

To model the impact of those FTAs, we do so in two steps, starting with the Alternative 1 scenario from the previous section. In the first step we send to zero by 2018 the China tariffs on wine from Chile and New Zealand, they being the earlier FTAs (signed in 2006 and 2008, respectively). In the second step we then also phase out tariffs on China's wine

Table 6. Changes in export volumes and values of wine-exporting countries in the Alternative 1 scenario, 2011 to 2018[b]

Exporter: Importer:	Australia	Other Southern Hemisphere	United States	Western European Exporters	Other
(a) Volumes (ML)					
United Kingdom	−25	−10	−8	7	−1
United States	−14	−4	0	32	0
Canada	−4	−3	−4	8	0
New Zealand	−2	0	0	0	0
Germany	−3	−13	−4	−44	−12
Other W. Europe[a]	−9	−17	−4	−6	−7
China	147	242	53	266	31
Japan	−1	−3	−3	−5	−1
Other Asia	1	3	3	21	−1
Other countries	0	5	−8	112	−17
World	90	200	25	391	−8
(b) Values (US$m)					
United Kingdom	42	60	−27	107	−8
United States	115	167	0	542	17
Canada	33	46	−9	187	−2
New Zealand	9	0	0	4	−2
Germany	0	−4	−10	−65	−15
Other W. Europe[a]	27	30	−13	643	−43
China	649	356	191	948	161
Japan	4	9	−4	201	21
Other Asia	50	53	16	427	11
Other countries	4	81	−19	414	−84
World	933	798	125	3408	56

[a]Other W. Europe = Belgium, Denmark, Finland, Ireland, the Netherlands, Sweden and Switzerland.
[b]The 'Alternative 1' scenario assumes real exchange rates revert half way back from 2011 to 2009 rates by 2018 except for China's which appreciates 2% pa.
Source: Anderson and Wittwer (2013)

Table 7. Policy-induced wine consumption volume changes for China, 2018[a] (%)

	ALT 1 (% change from 2011)	FTAs with NZ and Chile (% from ALT 1 Base)	+FTA with Australia (% from NZ + Chile FTAs Scenario)	Austerity Scenario (% from 3 FTAs Scenario)
Non-premium wine	31	0.2	0.2	0.0
Commercial-premium wine	95	0.3	0.5	0.0
Super-premium wine	100	0.3	0.9	−9.2
All wines	70	0.3	0.4	−0.2

[a] 'Alt. 1' assumes real exchange rates revert half way back from 2011 to 2009 rates by 2018 except for China's which appreciates 2% pa. 'FTA' refers to removing the tariffs on China's wine imports from the country(ies) mentioned with whom it has signed a bilateral Free Trade Agreement. The 'Austerity' simulation assumes China's demand for super-premium wines expands by one-eleventh less than in the simulation involving the 3 FTAs.

Source: Authors' model results

imports from Australia, it being the most-recent country to sign a bilateral FTA with China (in 2014).

Tables 3(b) and 7 reveal that these FTAs will have almost no discernable impacts on grape and wine production or on wine consumption in China, especially compared with the changes between 2001 and 2018 expected from the Alternative 1 projections shown in the first column of those tables.

The FTAs' impacts on international trade in wine are somewhat more significant, but still not large. Table 8(b) suggests that Chile and New Zealand have been gaining market share in China (especially in volume terms for Chile), partly at Australia's expense; but with the signing of the Australia-China FTA those trade gains for Chile and New Zealand are to be somewhat reduced while Australia's export gain will more than offset the reduction it otherwise would have suffered from those two earlier-signed FTAs. From China's viewpoint it benefits more in volume than value of wine imports from the earlier two FTA's, in contrast to adding the FTA with Australia which boosts value much more than volume of its wine imports.

The impact of the three FTAs on bilateral trade patterns is summarized in Table 9. China's imports from its new FTA partners in the

Table 8. Policy-induced changes in global wine import and export volumes and values, 2018

	Volume (ML)			Value (US$m)		
	ALT 1 (ML change from 2011)	FTAs with NZ and Chile (ML from ALT 1[a] Base)	+ FTA with Australia (ML from NZ + Chile FTAs Scenario)	ALT 1 ($m change from 2011)	FTAs with NZ and Chile ($m from ALT 1[a] Base)	+ FTA with Australia ($m from NZ + Chile FTAs Scenario)
(a) Imports						
China	739	52	4	2309	34	86
Japan	-13	0	0	235	0	0
Other Asia	24	0	0	520	0	1
United Kingdom	-36	-1	-2	179	3	7
North America	11	-5	-9	1106	0	0
Other Europe	-176	-1	-1	740	4	1
Other	151	0	0	259	0	0
World	700	43	-6	5548	43	104
(b) Exports						
Australia	90	-1	10	933	-11	135
Other New World	222	44	-11	965	60	-18
Old World	387	0	-5	3537	-5	-12
World	700	43	-6	5548	43	104

[a] 'Alt. 1' assumes real exchange rates revert half way back from 2011 to 2009 rates by 2018 except for China's which appreciates 2% pa. 'FTA' refers to removing the tariffs on China's wine imports from the country(ies) mentioned with whom it has signed a bilateral Free Trade Agreement.
Source: Authors' model results

Table 9. Marginal impact of three FTAs on export volumes and values of wine-exporting countries in the Alternative 1 scenario, 2011 to 2018[b]

Exporter: Importer:	Australia	Other Southern Hemisphere	United States	Western European Exporters
(a) Volumes (ML)				
United Kingdom	−10	−2	1	7
United States	−13	−5	0	3
Canada	−2	−1	1	2
New Zealand	−1	0	0	0
Germany	−1	−2	0	1
Other W. Europe[a]	−4	−3	0	5
China	42	54	−6	−30
Japan	0	−1	0	1
Other Asia	−1	0	0	1
Other countries	−1	−4	1	3
World	9	36	−3	−7
(b) Values (US$m)				
United Kingdom	−15	−1	2	22
United States	−23	−5	0	23
Canada	−5	−1	2	6
New Zealand	−1	0	0	1
Germany	−1	−1	0	3
Other W. Europe[a]	−7	−5	1	13
China	187	76	−23	−104
Japan	−2	−1	0	2
Other Asia	−7	−2	1	6
Other countries	−2	−2	1	11
World	125	58	−16	−17

[a] Other W. Europe = Belgium, Denmark, Finland, Ireland, the Netherlands, Sweden and Switzerland.
[b] The 'Alternative 1' scenario assumes real exchange rates revert half way back from 2011 to 2009 rates by 2018 except for China's which appreciates 2% pa.
Source: Authors' model results

Southern Hemisphere will grow at the expense of its imports from the United States and Europe, and those FTA partners' wine exports to countries other than China will shrink — although by less than the increase in their exports to China. That is, global trade creation outweighs trade diversion from these FTAs in the case of wine, according to these results, as also confirmed in the bottom rows of Table 8(a) and (b).

The other policy development of significance to wine is China's austerity drive. We simulate that with a leftward shift in China's domestic demand for super-premium wines sufficient to reduce the projected expansion during 2011–18 in those quality wines by 9.2% (see Table 7). That has very little impact on China's grape and wine production (last column of Table 3), and only a minor influence on the overall *volume* of wine imports by China. However, austerity drive's impact on the *value* of China's wine imports and of France and Australia's wine exports to China are non-trivial, because the drive is depressing the prices of super-premium wines. As a result, the estimated value of China's imports will be $80 million less in 2018, with Australia and France bearing most of that fall: their exports are lower by about 2%, or $19 million and $46 million, respectively (Table 10).

6. Summary and implications

China has already become by far the most important wine-consuming country in Asia, and the above projections point to the enormous speed with which China may become an even more dominant market for wine exporters, with a projected extra 620–940 ML to be added by 2018 to its consumption of 1630 ML in 2011. Since China's domestic production is projected to increase by 'only' about 210–290 ML by 2018, its net imports are projected to rise by between 330 and 740 ML — or 50 ML more once the full impact of the three FTAs with Southern Hemisphere countries are felt. Certainly the recent austerity drive is going to dampen the growth in super-premium and iconic wine sales in China, but because those quality wines are still only a small share of the total sales volume the drive's impact on China's aggregate wine consumption and imports is very minor.

While the recent and projected rates of increase in per capita wine consumption in China are no faster than what occurred in several

Table 10. Impact of China's austerity drive on global wine import and export volumes and values, 2018[a]

	Volume (ML)		Value (US$m)	
	ALT 1 (ML change from 2011)	Austerity Scenario (ML from ALT 1 Base)	ALT 1 ($m change from 2011)	Austerity Scenario ($m from ALT 1 Base)
(a) Imports				
China	739	−3	2309	−80
Other Asia	11	1	755	−6
UK + Other Europe	−212	0	919	−3
North America	11	1	1106	2
Other	151	0	259	0
World	700	−1	5548	−87
(b) Exports				
Australia	90	0	933	−19
Other New World	222	0	965	−10
France	185	−1	2657	−46
Other Old World	202	0	880	−12
World	700	−1	5548	−87

[a] 'Alt. 1' assumes real exchange rates revert half way back from 2011 to 2009 rates by 2018 except for China's which appreciates 2% pa. The 'Austerity' simulation assumes China's demand for super-premium wines expands by one-eleventh less than in the simulation involving the 3 FTAs.
Source: Authors' model results.

northwestern European countries in earlier decades, it is the sheer size of China's adult population of 1.1 billion — and the fact that grape wine still accounts for less than 4% of Chinese alcohol consumption — that makes this import growth opportunity unprecedented. It would be somewhat less if China's own winegrape production increases faster, as in the Alternative 2 scenario above, but certainly in as short a period as the next five years that is unlikely to be able to reduce the growth in China's wine imports very much, especially at the super-premium end of the spectrum and notwithstanding that country's recent austerity drive.

Of course these projections are not predictions. Where exchange rates move, and how fast various countries' wine producers take advantage of the projected market growth opportunities in Asia, will be key determinants of the actual changes in market shares over the coming years. Not all segments of the industry are projected to benefit, with non-premium producers in both the Old World and the New World facing falling prices if demand for their product continues to dwindle as projected above. But those exporting firms willing to invest sufficiently in building relationships with their Chinese importer/distributor — or in grapegrowing or winemaking as joint venturers within China — may well enjoy long-term benefits from such investments, just as others have been doing and will continue to do for so many other products besides wine.

Meanwhile, the super-premium wine market in several other East Asian economies will remain an important and growing area of profitable sales for exporters such as Australia. The three largest Islamic countries in Asia (Bangladesh, Indonesia and Pakistan), by contrast, are far more remote possibilities. India potentially could be more important sooner, but internal and external trade restrictions and high taxes have to date confined the rapid growth in sales (but from a very low base) to domestic firms in India.

Appendix

Appendix Table 1. Cumulative consumption and population growth, 2011 to 2018

	Percent	
	Aggregate Consumption	Population
France	10.0	0.7
Italy	10.0	0.7
Portugal	10.0	0.7
Spain	10.0	0.7
Austria	10.0	0.7
Belgium	10.0	0.7
Denmark	10.0	0.7
Finland	10.0	0.7
Germany	10.0	0.7
Greece	10.0	0.7

(*Continued*)

Appendix Table 1. (*Continued*)

	Percent	
	Aggregate Consumption	Population
Ireland	10.0	0.7
Netherlands	10.0	0.7
Sweden	10.0	0.7
Switzerland	10.0	0.7
United Kingdom	10.0	0.7
Other W. Europe	10.0	0.7
Bulgaria	23.1	1.9
Croatia	23.1	1.9
Georgia	23.1	1.9
Hungary	23.1	1.9
Moldova	23.1	1.9
Romania	23.1	1.9
Russia	20.6	−1.7
Ukraine	23.1	1.9
Other E. Europe	23.1	1.9
Australia	17.8	7.3
New Zealand	15.4	5.9
Canada	14.2	5.6
United States	15.5	5.2
Argentina	30.0	4.9
Brazil	27.3	3.8
Chile	23.4	5.0
Mexico	22.0	4.6
Uruguay	25.6	7.3
Other L. Am	25.6	7.3
South Africa	23.1	3.0
Turkey	31.8	9.1
North Africa	31.8	9.1
Other Africa	55.8	15.1

(*Continued*)

Appendix Table 1. (*Continued*)

	Percent	
	Aggregate Consumption	Population
Middle East	31.8	9.1
China	69.0	2.7
Hong Kong	23.7	4.7
India	63.1	7.0
Japan	7.1	–1.3
Korea	22.0	0.7
Malaysia	34.4	8.2
Philippines	34.4	9.8
Singapore	18.6	5.6
Taiwan	34.6	2.3
Thailand	36.0	2.6
Other Asia	32.2	11.2

Source: Projections from global economy-wide modeling by Anderson and Strutt (2012)

References

Aizenman, J., & Brooks, B. (2008). Globalization and taste convergence: The cases of wine and beer. *Review of International Economics, 16(2),* 217–233.

Anderson, K. (2010, June). Excise and import taxes on wine vs beer and spirits: An international comparison. *Economic Papers, 29*(2), 215–228.

Anderson, K. (2013). *Which winegrape varieties are grown where? A global empirical picture.* Adelaide: University of Adelaide Press (Freely accessible as an e-book at www.adelaide.edu.au/press/titles/winegrapes and as Excel files at www.adelaide.edu.au/wine-econ/databases/winegrapes).

Anderson, K., & Nelgen, S. (2011). *Global wine markets, 1961 to 2009: A statistical compendium.* Adelaide: University of Adelaide Press (Freely accessible as an e-book at www.adelaide.edu.au/press/titles/global-wine and as Excel files at www.adelaide.edu.au/wine-econ/databases/GWM).

Anderson, K., & Smith, B. (1981). Changing economic relations between Asian ADCs and resource-exporting developed countries. In W. Hong, & L. Krause (Eds.), *Trade and growth in the advanced developing countries.* Seoul: Korea Development Institute Press.

Anderson, K., & Strutt, A. (2012, August). The changing geography of world trade: Projections to 2030. *Journal of Asian Economics, 23*(4), 303–323.

Anderson, K., & Wittwer, G. (2013). Modeling global wine markets to 2018: Exchange rates, taste changes, and China's import growth. *Journal of Wine Economics, 8*(2), 131–158.

Ashenfelter, O., & Storchmann, K. (2014, March). Wine and climate change. *AAWE working paper no. 152* (www.wine-economics.org).

Barton, D., Chen, Y., & Jin, A. (2013, June). Mapping China's middle class. McKinsey Quarterly (www.mckinsey.com/insights/consumer_and_retail/mapping_chinas_middle_class).

Corden, W. M. (1984, November). Booming sector and Dutch disease economics: Survey and consolidation. *Oxford Economic Papers, 36*(3), 359–380.

Cross, R., Plantinga, A. J., & Stavins, R. N. (2011). The value of terroir: Hedonic estimation of vineyard sale prices. *Journal of Wine Economics, 6*(1), 1–14.

Fajgelbaum, P., Grossman, G. M., & Helpman, E. (2011, August). Income distribution, product quality and international trade. *Journal of Political Economy, 119*(4), 721–765.

Findlay, C. F., Farrell, R, Chen, C, & Wang, D. (2004). EastAsia. In K. Anderson (Ed.), *The world's wine markets: Globalization at work.* Cheltenham UK: Edward Elgar (Ch. 15).

Fogarty, J. J. (2010). The demand for beer, wine, and spirits: A survey of the literature. *Journal of Economic Surveys, 24*(3), 428–478.

Freebairn, J. (2015). Mining booms and the exchange rate. *Australian Journal of Agricultural and Resource Economics, 59*(4), 533–548.

Friberg, R., Paterson, R. W., & Richardson, A. D. (2011). Why is there a home bias: A case study of wine. *Journal of Wine Economics, 6*(1), 37–66.

Garnaut, R. (2014, July). Australia and resources in the Asian century. *Australian Journal of Agricultural and Resource Economics, 58*(3), 301–313.

Gerguad, O., & Ginsburg, V. (2008, June). Natural endowments, production technologies and the quality of wines in Bordeaux: Does terroir matter? *Economic Journal,* 118(529), F142-F157 (Reprinted in *Journal of Wine Economics 5*(1): 3–21, 2010).

Giuliana, E., Morrison, A., & Rabellotti, R. (Eds.). (2011). *Innovation and technological catch-up: The changing geography of wine production.* Cheltenham UK: Edward Elgar.

Gladstones, J. (1992). *Viticulture and environment.* Adelaide: Winetitles.

Hayami, Y., & Ruttan, V. W. (1985). *Agricultural development: An international perspective.* Baltimore MD: Johns Hopkins University Press.

Huang, H. T. (2000). Biology and biological technology, Part 5: Fermentations and food science. *Volume 6 in the series of books on science and civilization in China.* Cambridge and New York: Cambridge University Press.

Jensen, R. T., & Miller, N. H. (2011). Do consumer price subsidies really improve nutrition? *Review of Economics and Statistics, 93*(4), 1205–1223.

Kaushal, N., & Muchomba, F. (2013, September). How consumer price subsidies affect nutrition. *NBER working paper 19404.* Cambridge MA: National Bureau of Economic Research.

Kharas, H. (2010, January). The emerging middle class in developing countries. *Working paper 285*. Paris: OECD Development Centre.

Krueger, A. O. (1977). *Growth, distortions and patterns of trade among many countries.* Princeton, NJ: International Finance Section.

Leamer, E. E. (1987). Paths of development in the three-factor, n-good general equilibrium model. *Journal of Political Economy, 95*(5), 961–999.

Lewin, B. (2010). *Wine myths and reality.* San Francisco: Wine Appreciation Guild.

Lewis, G. (2013). Winners and losers in the global wine industry. Google motion charts at http://23inhouse.com/wine-data/charts.html

Markusen, J. R. (2013, July). Putting per-capita income back into trade theory. *Journal of International Economics, 90*(2), 255–265.

McGovern, P. (2003). *Ancient wine: The search for the origins of viticulture.* Princeton NJ: Princeton University Press.

McGovern, P. (2009). *Uncorking the past: The quest for wine, beer, and other alcoholic beverages.* Berkeley CA: University of California Press.

Nayak, A.(2011, May). Does Variety Fit the Quality Bill? Factor-Endowments Driven Differences in Trade, Export Margins, Prices and Production Techniques, mimeo, Purdue University, West Lafayette IN. www.auburn.edu\~azn0018

OIV (2015, May). *Le vignoble mondial.* Paris: Organisation Internationale de la Vigne et du Vin.

Olmstead, A. L., & Rhode, P. W. (2007). Biological globalization: The other grain invasion. In T. J. Hatton, K. H. O'Rourke, & J. G. Williamson (Eds.), *The new comparative economic history: Essays in honor of Jeffrey G. Williamson.* Cambridge MA: MIT Press (Ch. 5).

Ozawa, T. (2009). *The rise of Asia: The 'flying-geese' theory of tandem growth and regional agglomeration.* London: Edward Elgar.

Stigler, G.J., & Becker, G. S. (1977, March). De Gustibus Non Est Disputandum. *American Economic Review, 67*(2), 76–90.

Venables, A.J. (2004, November). Small, remote and poor. *World Trade Review, 3*(3), 453–457.

Williams, A. (1995). *Flying winemakers: The new world of wine.* Adelaide: Winetitles.

Wittwer, G., Berger, N., & Anderson, K. (2003, May). A model of the world's wine markets. *Economic Modelling, 20*(3), 487–506.

Chapter 15

How Much Wine Is *Really* Produced and Consumed in China, Hong Kong, and Japan?*

Kym Anderson[†] and Kimie Harada[‡]

Abstract

Statistics on the wine market in countries where it is not traditionally produced or consumed are estimates using simple methods. In northeast Asia those statistics are exaggerated for a combination of several reasons. One is a labelling issue: imported bulk wine is able to be added to domestically produced wine without the front label having to declare the bottle may contain foreign product. Similar freedom applies to wine made from imported grape juice concentrate. A second (particularly in

---

*First published in *Journal of Wine Economics* 13(2): 199–220, 2018. The authors gratefully acknowledge helpful comments from Professor Huiqin Ma of China Agricultural University in Beijing, anonymous referees, and participants in a seminar at Kyoto University and a session of the AARES Annual Conference (Adelaide, 7–9 February 2018).

[†]Wine Economics Research Centre, School of Economics, University of Adelaide, Adelaide SA 5005; and Crawford School of Public Policy, Australian National University, Canberra, ACT 2600; e-mail: kym.anderson@adelaide.edu.au (corresponding author).

[‡]Chuo University, Tokyo, Japan; and Visiting Fellow, Crawford School of Public Policy, Australian National University, Canberra, ACT 2600; e-mail: kimie.hara.harada@gmail.com.

China) is a double-counting issue: domestic wine produced in one region of the country may be blended with wine produced in and packaged for final sale from another region, with both regions claiming it as their contribution to national wine output. A third possibility is a smuggling issue: some wine re-exports and imports are unrecorded. These possibilities of the wine market being exaggerated are significant for firms seeking to export to and sell in such countries, especially in the fast-growing ones of northeast Asia. This article shows the extent to which estimates for the region could change for such indicators as per capita wine consumption, wine self-sufficiency, and the region's share of global wine consumption, when alternative assumptions are made in response to these issues.

1. Introduction

Statistics on the grape wine market in countries where such wine is not traditionally produced or consumed are often weak or non-existent. If domestic production is insignificant, consumption is usually assumed to be equal to imports less any reexports (plus net changes in stocks if such data are available). Where there is enough domestic production for wine output statistics to be collected, however, there is a risk those statistics are exaggerated, for two possible reasons. The first reason is if imported bulk wine or wine made from imported concentrated grape juice can be added to domestically produced wine without having to declare on the bottle's front label that the product in the bottle is of mixed or foreign origin (a labelling issue). The second reason, particularly in China, is a double-counting issue. Double counting occurs when domestic wine produced in one region of the country is blended with wine produced in and packaged for final sale from another region: If both regions report inter-regionally traded wine as a product of their respective regions, there will be a degree of double counting in the national wine output data. When domestic production is so exaggerated, and domestic consumption is assumed (typically by analysts outside the country who are handicapped by a language barrier) to be domestic production plus net imports, then consumption also is overstated for that country.

It is also possible that apparent consumption estimates will be inaccurate to the extent that wine re-exports or imports are unrecorded when transported from one customs territory to another. This smuggling issue is more likely to occur, the greater the difference between those territories' wine taxes.

A further confusion can arise if rice "wine" consumption data are added to the data for grape wine consumption, as Euromonitor International does in its wine industry reports. Rice "wine" is made in numerous Asian countries but each under a different name (e.g., sake in Japan, mijiu in China, cheongju in Korea). Typically, it is at least 15% alcohol, brewed differently than beer, and looks and is drunk like a clear spirit. If it is not to be put in a separate category, then for the purpose of analysing grape wine markets it could be included in the spirits category. In the rest of this article the term "wine" refers just to that made from fresh grapes or grape juice concentrate.[1]

The possibility of wine production and/or consumption "data" being overstated is significant for several reasons. Obviously statistical agencies have an interest in ensuring the accuracy of their published data. Firms seeking to evaluate prospects for selling wine or other beverages in such countries also require accurate data. Furthermore, those concerned with health and social issues associated with excessive alcohol consumption want accurate data on both the aggregate quantity and — because social costs associated with excess consumption typically differ across beverage types — the mix of alcohols consumed.

Now is a good time to focus on this issue because of a new wine regulation in Japan, drafted in 2015 and effective from October 2018,[2] and also because China has been reviewing and revising its wine-related regulations. This year marks the tenth anniversary of the decisions by China's special administrative regions (SARs) of Hong Kong and Macau to eliminate — in February and August 2008, respectively — their taxes on

---

[1] In the Harmonized System of the United Nations (2018), grape-based wines are classified in trade statistics as Harmonised System 2204 ("Wines of fresh grapes, including fortified wines, and grape must"). Grape juice concentrate is part of Harmonised System 2009, defined as "Fruit juices (including grape must) and vegetable juices, unfermented and not containing added spirit."

[2] Japan's new standards on labelling and geographical indications for wine, sake, and other alcohol beverages are detailed in National Tax Agency (2015) and Uytsel (2015).

wine and beer (Yoon and Lam, 2012). That has distinguished those customs territories from mainland China where wine attracts an import tariff of 14% (or 20% if in containers larger than two litres) plus a consumption tax of 10% and a value-added tax of 17%, cumulating to close to 50%. This is pertinent because the most important emerging grape wine markets in the present decade are in greater China (Anderson and Wittwer, 2015), and that policy reform has made it more lucrative for China's SARs to illicitly re-export wine to mainland China. The incentive for such illicit trade is beginning to diminish though, as more wine-exporting countries sign free trade agreements with China (most recently Australia and Georgia following Chile and New Zealand, all of whose wine will be imported duty free by the end of this decade; and prospectively the European Union).

This article reports grape wine production, consumption, and trade estimates currently available for (mainland) China, Hong Kong, Macau, and Japan, and then offers an alternative set of estimates to show how they change such indicators as per capita wine consumption, wine self-sufficiency, the share of wine in total alcohol consumption, and the region's share of global wine production and consumption. Those indicators are important because our alternative estimates suggest they are even lower than is commonly believed. This underscores the considerable potential for growth in wine exports to greater China and Japan, and has implications for wine sales in Hong Kong and Macau versus imports to those territories for re-export to mainland China.

The next section of the article summarizes the commonly used statistics for the wine markets of these countries. Section 3 reports possible amendments to those statistics, showing how they would change under certain assumptions, and what those changes imply for various summary indicators of wine market trends over the past two decades in this important region. The final section draws out implications of the findings, especially for exporters of wine to northeast Asia.

2. Common sources of wine data for Northeast Asia

International analysts lacking northeast Asian language skills typically rely on wine production data for the region from the United Nations' Food and Agriculture Organization (FAO) (www.fao.org/faostat/en) and, for estimates of the latest updates, the Paris-based International Organisation of Vine and Wine (OIV) (www.oiv.int). Trade data also are available from the FAO and, more comprehensively and with all bilateral flows, from the United Nations's Statistical Office (https://comtrade.un.org/data), again with estimated updates from the OIV. All those sets of annual data are reliant on national government statistics being submitted to these international agencies. Commercial data providers such as the Global Trade Atlas (www.ihsmarkit.com/maritime-global-trade-atlas.html) assemble the most-recent trade data on an ongoing monthly basis, but access is not free. An Italian group produces updates of wine import volume and value data every six months and allows free downloads at www.winebynumbers.it

Wine consumption data are far more difficult to come by internationally. The Organisation for Economic Co-operation and Development (OECD) provides total alcohol consumption data for its member countries (hence Japan and the Republic of Korea) from the early 1960s and for major emerging economies (including China, India, and Indonesia) from 2000 (www.oecd.org/health/health-statistics.htm). The World Health Organization (WHO) provides those same data for all United Nation member countries disaggregated into wine, beer, spirits, and other beverages (see http://apps.who.int/gho/data/node.main.A1026?lang=en?showonly=GISAH). Again, both international agencies rely on national government statistics being submitted to them. Commercial providers with more up-to-date data for subscribers, or for a fee, include Euromonitor International (www.euromonitor.com) and International Wine and Spirit Research (https://www.theiwsr.com).

A way to check on consumption volume data, to fill gaps in historical series, or to avoid paying a fee to commercial data providers, is to add domestic production to imports net of exports. So long as there are no net changes in wine stocks over the period considered (e.g., a calendar year), this would be as reliable as the production and trade data. Indeed, it may be what some countries do to obtain their official consumption statistics. It is also what Anderson and Pinilla (2017) did to fill gaps when unable to find official national consumption statistics, except they use not just current-year production but rather the average of that plus the two previous years' production. That calculation not only smooths the time series but also captures the reality that not all wine is consumed in the year of production. Especially in the case of reds it is common to let the wine mature first in barrels and then in bottles; even after sale from the winery it may be stored for some time by wholesalers, retailers, restaurants, and even households before consumption. For the relatively new China market, however, we assume that wine is consumed in the year of domestic production or import.

3. Alternative wine market statistics for Japan, China, Hong Kong and Macau

We begin with Japan, the most mature of these northeast Asian markets, before turning to the most important and fastest growing wine market in Asia, namely mainland China.[3] Imports and exports of Hong Kong and Macau are also considered. Even though the latter are far smaller markets, they are related to China's via their re-exports, and they provide an indication of how other Asian countries' wine consumption might grow as their per capita incomes approach the higher levels of those two customs territories.

3.1. Japan

No less than 43 of Japan's 49 prefectures produce grape wine, mostly by small wineries that grow their own grapes and do not blend their product with material from other regions or abroad (Takahashi et al., 2017). While domestic wine produced in one region is seldom blended with wine produced in another region of Japan (see Appendix Table 1), wine is also "produced" in a few prefectures with large ports (Kawasaki et al., 2011). Firms in the latter prefectures bottle imported bulk wine and/or wine they make by adding sugar and yeast to imported unfermented grape juice concentrate (Shimamura, 2008). The front label of these bottles of wine declare they are produced in Japan, and although the back label notes that they may contain imported material, that note may be in a smaller size font.[4]

---

[3] Even in Japan, there is little economic research on its wine industry. Oda (2001) suggests topics for further wine industry research in countries where people did not drink wine on a regular basis, but now enjoy rapid wine consumption growth.

[4] To date Japan has had no laws governing the labelling of wine made from grapes, only the industry's own regulations. New wine labelling guidelines have been proposed by the

Official wine production data for Japan were not always reported to the United Nations' FAO, so for some years FAO has inserted unofficial data (1969–1973) or its own estimates (1974–1976 and from 2010). However, data from the National Tax Agency (2016) provide estimates of official grape wine production (including that using imported material) from 1973 and official grape wine consumption from 1988. Leading up to the planned implementation of Japan's new wine labelling law effective October 2018, official data also have been published for 2013 to 2015 that separate wine produced solely from domestic grapes and that produced using imported product (see National Tax Office, 2017 and earlier editions). Also available from official sources are wine import data by container, from which it is possible to get the share of total imports that come in bulk form (more than two litre containers) from 1988 (Ministry of Finance, 2017).

The annual volumes of Japanese wine production, consumption, and trade according to these official data are reported in Table 1(a). If we define "apparent consumption" as the sum of net imports plus the three-year average of production in that year and the two preceding years, then Table 1(a) shows it to be quite close to the National Tax Agency's estimate of Japan's consumption. The "apparent consumption" data suggest Japan's annual per capita consumption of wine has grown from below 0.3 litres as of 1975 (0.4 in 1975–1979) to almost three litres by 2016. They also suggest Japan's wine self-sufficiency has fallen from 75% in 1975 (62% in 1975–1979) to 28% by 2016.

Since the data in Table 1(a) overstate consumption and self-sufficiency to the extent imported material are included in the domestic production estimate, two adjustments need to be made. One is to make the very reasonable assumption that all wine imported in bulk containers is blended with domestic wine and/or sold in bottles front-labelled "Product of Japan" and recorded as such by the statistician. That adjustment brings per

---

National Tax Agency (2015) and are scheduled to come into effect from October 2018. They define "Wine of Japan" as wine made only from grapes harvested in Japan, as distinct from most other domestic wine which is produced using imported bulk wine or concentrated grape juice.

Table 1a. Japan's official wine production, official consumption, imports, exports and apparent consumption, 1975 to 2016 (kilolitres, litres, and %)

	Prod'n (KL)	Imports (KL)	Exports (KL)	Prod'n + Net Imports (KL)	Official Consm. (KL)[b]	Official Consm. p.c. (L)[a]	SSR (%)[a]
1975–1979	27,800	20,446	203	45,044	na	0.40	62
1980–1984	47,000	39,543	87	82,323	82,200	0.69	57
1985–1989	57,400	58,065	112	112,552	109,200	0.92	51
1990	68,000	86,025	253	152,772	134,000	1.24	45
1991	62,000	75,223	229	141,994	127,000	1.14	44
1992	60,000	68,370	184	131,519	124,000	1.05	46
1993	58,000	65,048	244	124,804	108,000	1.00	46
1994	64,000	89,707	276	150,098	123,000	1.20	43
1995	75,000	107,669	302	173,034	144,000	1.38	43
1996	84,000	107,351	265	181,420	159,000	1.44	46
1997	119,000	145,185	582	237,269	225,000	1.88	50
1998	146,000	321,392	421	437,304	298,000	3.46	33
1999	120,000	188,635	533	316,435	278,000	2.50	38
2000	103,000	165,746	859	287,887	266,000	2.27	36
2001	101,000	169,144	842	276,302	253,000	2.18	37
2002	105,000	167,938	328	270,610	259,000	2.13	39
2003	89,000	161,182	448	259,068	237,000	2.03	34
2004	80,000	166,543	413	257,463	226,000	2.02	31
2005	99,000	158,034	372	246,996	238,000	1.94	40
2006	81,000	166,243	462	252,448	229,000	1.98	32
2007	81,000	166,664	347	253,317	230,000	1.99	32
2008	83,000	171,760	370	253,057	227,000	1.99	33
2009	83,000	180,740	367	262,707	240,000	2.07	32
2010	88,000	193,853	222	278,298	262,000	2.18	32
2011	95,000	208,345	252	296,760	290,000	2.32	32
2012	99,000	257,126	174	350,952	321,000	2.75	28
2013	88,293	263,244	237	357,104	332,000	2.80	25
2014	95,098	270,425	208	364,347	351,000	2.87	26
2015	100,921	280,071	284	374,557	370,000	2.96	27
2016	102,000	268,639	226	367,753	na	2.90	28

capita consumption down to 2.7 rather than 2.9 litres and self-sufficiency down to 23% rather than 28% for 2016 (Table 1(b)).[5]

Furthermore, it is necessary to separate domestic wine production made from imported grape juice concentrate from that derived by fermenting fresh local grapes. Precise estimates of wine production from local grapes are available for 2013, 2014, and 2015 (14.3, 15.1, and 16.9 ML, respectively — see National Tax Agency (2017) and earlier editions). Those volumes average just one-fifth of the volumes in Table 1(b) for those years. They do not alter the apparent consumption per capita estimate in Table 1(b), but they do bring down the 2013–2015 self-sufficiency estimate from 22% to just 4% if it is assumed that the four-fifths difference is all due to wine made from imported concentrate. Had that same ratio of four-fifths been relevant for adjusting the production numbers in Table 1(b) for all years prior to 2013, then, as shown in Table 1(c), self-sufficiency is just 10% in 1975-1979.[6] Low though these revised self-sufficiency estimates appear, they are consistent with a claim made two decades ago by JETRO (1998), that less than 10% of wine bottled in Japan is made from domestically produced grapes.

The extent of the impact of all these adjustments on estimates of Japan's wine consumption per capita and on its self-sufficiency in wine are shown graphically in Figure 1.

3.2. China (Mainland)

The annual volumes of wine production, consumption, and trade according to official data reported in Table 2(a), suggest China's per capita consumption has grown from the turn of the century from below 0.2 litres

---

[5] Most documents written in Japan, such as Takahashi et al. (2017), use official data and so their quoted per capita consumption and self-sufficiency numbers are the higher ones in Table 1. Takahashi et al. (2017) is the first introductory book in both English and Japanese languages on Japan's wineries.

[6] While data are available on unfermented (non-alcoholic) grape juice concentrate imports by Japan (Harmonised System code 200961 and 200969), the factor needed to convert those tonnes into litres of wine with 12% alcohol is impossible to know because it depends on the brix content of each shipment of concentrate. During 2010–2016, the value of Japan's imports of grape juice concentrate averaged 7.4% of the value of its wine imports.

Table 1b. Japan's wine production, apparent consumption and self-sufficiency, assuming all imported bulk wine is bottled in and sold as a product of Japan, 1975 to 2016 (kilolitres, litres, and %)

	Bulk % of Imports[c]	Prod'n (KL)	Prod'n + Net Imports (KL)	Apparent Consumption Per Cap. (L)[a]	SSR (%)[a]
1975–1979	35	18,070	36,364	0.32	50
1980–1984	35	30,550	67,320	0.57	45
1985–1989	33	38,434	93,818	0.77	41
1990	30	47,693	132,360	1.07	36
1991	32	42,298	122,245	0.98	35
1992	26	44,194	112,914	0.91	39
1993	25	43,385	108,096	0.86	40
1994	19	51,534	135,802	1.08	38
1995	24	57,032	158,017	1.26	36
1996	24	63,755	164,526	1.31	39
1997	24	89,955	214,850	1.71	42
1998	21	115,117	410,579	3.25	28
1999	27	87,731	285,703	2.26	31
2000	18	83,989	260,500	2.06	32
2001	15	85,951	254,192	2.00	34
2002	14	89,880	254,217	2.00	35
2003	15	76,095	244,710	1.92	31
2004	14	68,880	244,415	1.92	28
2005	15	84,447	234,136	1.84	36
2006	16	68,202	239,624	1.88	28
2007	16	68,364	239,988	1.88	28
2008	17	68,973	239,903	1.88	29
2009	18	68,475	248,977	1.96	28
2010	19	71,720	263,354	2.07	27
2011	18	78,090	280,855	2.20	28
2012	17	81,873	334,180	2.62	24
2013	19	71,694	340,226	2.67	21
2014	20	76,269	346,829	2.74	22
2015	21	80,131	355,818	2.81	23
2016	22	79,866	347,169	2.74	23

Table 1c. Japan's wine production, apparent consumption and self-sufficiency, assuming all imported bulk wine and some concentrate is made into wine,[d] 1975 to 2015 (kilolitres, litres, and %)

	Prod'n from Imported Grape Juice Concentrate (KL)[d]	Prod'n from Local Grapes (KL)[d]	Prod'n + Net Imports (KL)	Apparent Consumption Per Capita (L)[a]	SSR (%)[a,e]
1975–1979	14,456	3,614	36,364	0.32	10
1980–1984	24,440	6,110	67,320	0.57	9
1985–1989	30,748	7,687	93,818	0.77	8
1990	38,154	9,539	132,360	1.07	7
1991	33,839	8,460	122,245	0.98	7
1992	35,355	8,839	112,914	0.91	8
1993	34,708	8,677	108,096	0.86	8
1994	41,227	10,307	135,802	1.08	8
1995	45,625	11,406	158,017	1.26	7
1996	51,004	12,751	164,526	1.31	8
1997	71,964	17,991	214,850	1.71	8
1998	92,093	23,023	410,579	3.25	6
1999	70,185	17,546	285,703	2.26	6
2000	67,191	16,798	260,500	2.06	6
2001	68,761	17,190	254,192	2.00	7
2002	71,904	17,976	254,217	2.00	7
2003	60,876	15,219	244,710	1.92	6
2004	55,104	13,776	244,415	1.92	6
2005	67,558	16,889	234,136	1.84	7
2006	54,562	13,640	239,624	1.88	6
2007	54,691	13,673	239,988	1.88	6
2008	55,178	13,795	239,903	1.88	6
2009	54,780	13,695	248,977	1.96	6
2010	57,376	14,344	263,354	2.07	5
2011	62,472	15,618	280,855	2.20	6
2012	65,498	16,375	334,180	2.62	5

(*Continued*)

Table 1c. (*Continued*)

	Prod'n from Imported Grape Juice Concentrate (KL)[d]	Prod'n from Local Grapes (KL)[d]	Prod'n + Net Imports (KL)	Apparent Consumption Per Capita (L)[a]	SSR (%)[a,e]
2013	57,388	14,306	351,300	2.76	4
2014	61,196	15,073	365,315	2.88	4
2015	63,212	16,919	380,708	3.01	4

[a] The final two columns assume consumption equals net imports plus the average of production in that and the previous two years.
[b] The official consumption estimates are from the National Tax Agency (2016).
[c] The share of bulk in total wine imports in 1975–1987 is assumed to be 35%, the same as in 1988.
[d] Production from local grapes, once grape juice concentrate is taken into account, is assumed to be one-fifth of production shown in Table 1(b), the same as the average share in 2013–2015, the only years for which actual data are available from the National Tax Agency (2016).
[e] In Table 1(c) self-sufficiency is production from local grapes as a percent of apparent consumption (with the latter including wine made from imported grape juice concentrate).
Source: See text.

to 1.28 litres by 2016. They also suggest China's wine self-sufficiency has fallen from 100% in 1995–1996 to 64% by 2016.

Much of the wine that is imported by China in bulk containers is bottled as is or blended with domestic wine and sold in bottles labelled "Product of China." If all such imported bulk wine was recorded as Chinese production by the statistician, then per capita consumption would have reached just 1.17 rather than 1.28 litres by 2016, and self-sufficiency would be 61% rather than 64% (Table 2, panel (b)). These alternative numbers for this adjustment are lower-bound estimates because they have removed all of the imported bulk wine from the official "production" data, whereas in practice some of that wine may have carried a correct country of origin label and not been counted as domestic production.

Furthermore, if there is double counting of domestic wine production because it is internally traded between provinces in bulk before being bottled but counted as output in the source province as well as the desination province, per capita consumption and self-sufficiency would be even lower than official data suggest. For example, if domestic production is only two-thirds of that recorded as official production, in addition to

How Much Wine Is Really Produced and Consumed in China? 391

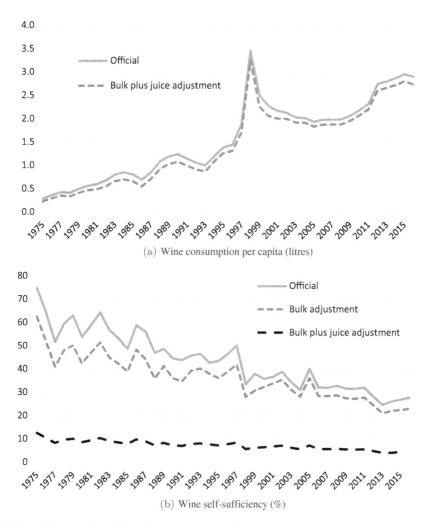

Figure 1. Japan's estimated wine consumption per capita and wine self-sufficiency under alternative assumptions,[a] 1975 to 2016 (litres and %)

[a] The middle line assumes all of Japan's bulk wine each year is sold as product of Japan; and the lowest line assumes in addition that a portion of the grape juice concentrate imported into Japan is converted into wine.

Source: See Table 1.

Table 2. China's wine production (official, and under alternative assumptions), trade and apparent consumption, 1995 to 2016 (kilolitres, litres, and %)

	(a) Official Data						(b) Assuming All Bulk Imports Are Blended with Chinese Wine				
	Prod'n (KL)	Imports (KL)	Exports (KL)	Consm.[a] (KL)	Consm.[a] p.c.(L)	SSR (%)	Bulk (%) of Imports	Prod'n (KL)	Consm. (KL)	Consm. p.c. (L)	SSR (%)
1995	220,000	712	2,622	218,090	0.18	101	37	219,737	217,827	0.18	101
1996	180,000	4,355	2,900	181,455	0.15	99	31	178,638	180,093	0.15	99
1997	190,000	33,578	2,779	220,799	0.18	86	58	170,422	201,221	0.16	85
1998	210,000	46,227	3,268	252,959	0.20	83	83	171,413	214,372	0.17	80
1999	230,000	43,658	4,531	269,127	0.21	85	91	190,232	229,359	0.18	83
2000	330,000	34,571	4,200	360,371	0.29	92	92	298,171	328,542	0.26	91
2001	355,000	29,220	2,967	381,253	0.30	93	91	328,467	354,720	0.28	93
2002	370,000	30,224	2,287	397,937	0.31	93	86	344,071	372,008	0.29	92
2003	399,000	41,404	2,004	438,400	0.34	91	88	362,431	401,831	0.31	90
2004	449,000	44,105	2,038	491,067	0.38	91	83	412,336	454,403	0.35	91
2005	498,000	53,971	2,712	549,259	0.42	91	80	454,935	506,194	0.39	90
2006	502,000	115,507	3,789	613,718	0.47	82	82	407,562	519,280	0.40	78
2007	653,000	148,240	9,285	791,955	0.60	82	71	548,290	687,245	0.52	80
2008	812,000	164,861	5,378	971,483	0.73	84	64	706,325	865,808	0.65	82
2009	968,840	172,881	1,483	1,140,238	0.86	85	46	888,644	1,060,042	0.80	84
2010	1,088,810	286,040	1,450	1,373,400	1.03	79	48	951,774	1,236,364	0.92	77
2011	1,156,860	365,535	1,916	1,520,479	1.13	76	33	1,036,603	1,400,222	1.04	74
2012	1,376,620	394,282	2,038	1,768,864	1.31	78	31	1,255,052	1,647,296	1.22	76
2013	1,178,360	377,541	1,900	1,554,001	1.14	76	24	1,089,076	1,464,717	1.08	74
2014	1,160,990	383,431	3,670	1,540,751	1.13	75	21	1,079,206	1,458,967	1.07	74
2015	1,148,000	552,088	8,221	1,691,867	1.23	68	26	1,002,768	1,546,635	1.12	65
2016	1,137,400	638,000	9,950	1,765,450	1.28	64	23	993,563	1,621,613	1.17	61

	(c) Assuming Production Is Two-Thirds of Official, and All Bulk Imports Also Blended					(d) Assuming Also Smuggling from HK[b]			
	Prod'n (KL)	Consm. (KL)	Consm. p.c. (L)	SSR (%)	Extra HK Exports to China (KL)	Consm. (KL)	Consm. p.c. (L)	SSR (%)	Unrecorded as % of China's Recorded Wine Imports
2000	187,656	218,027	0.17	86	487	219,052	0.18	86	1.4
2001	210,128	236,381	0.19	89	504	236,867	0.19	89	1.7
2002	220,512	248,449	0.19	89	518	248,953	0.20	89	1.7
2003	229,426	268,826	0.21	85	512	269,343	0.22	85	1.2
2004	262,662	304,729	0.24	86	849	305,241	0.24	86	1.9
2005	288,935	340,194	0.26	85	1,024	341,042	0.27	85	1.9
2006	240,228	351,946	0.27	68	1,788	352,969	0.28	68	1.5
2007	330,618	469,573	0.36	70	2,882	471,361	0.37	70	1.9
2008	435,658	595,141	0.45	73	3,466	598,023	0.46	73	2.1
2009	565,696	737,094	0.55	77	4,247	740,560	0.57	76	2.5
2010	627,190	911,780	0.68	69	6,168	916,026	0.70	68	2.2
2011	686,436	1,050,055	0.78	65	9,246	1,0562,23	0.81	65	2.5
2012	822,725	1,214,969	0.90	68	9,338	1,224,214	0.93	67	2.4
2013	710,820	1,086,461	0.80	65	9,556	1,095,799	0.83	65	2.5
2014	697,691	1,077,452	0.79	65	11,167	1,087,007	0.82	64	2.9
2015	619,582	1,163,449	0.85	53	13,671	1,174,616	0.88	53	2.5
2016	598,767	1,226,817	0.89	49	13,579	1,240,488	0.92	48	2.1

[a]Consm. is apparent consumption in KL, calculated as production plus imports minus exports; Consm. p.c. (litres per capita) is apparent consumption divided by total population; and SSR, the self-sufficiency ratio, is shown as production divided by apparent consumption (expressed as a percentage).

[b]The volume smuggled into China is assumed to be equal to an extra 50% of Hong Kong's total official re-exports.

Sources: Authors' calculations, starting with official production and trade numbers reported by the FAO, WHO, and OIV

imported bulk wine being counted as a product of China, then per capita consumption in 2016 would have reached only 0.89 litres rather then 1.28 litres and self-sufficiency would be 49% rather than 64% (Table 2, panel (c)). This is close to the suggestion made by one of China's leading wine reporters, having discussed the issue and its possible contributing factors with leading industry insiders (Boyce, 2017, 2018).

Finally, in addition to some recorded imports to Hong Kong and Macau being subsequently recorded as re-exported to China, it is believed that a portion also is transported to the mainland without being recorded, that is, it is smuggled so as to avoid one or more of China's three taxes on wine consumption. If the extent of such smuggling amounted to half as much again as Hong Kong has been re-exporting officially,[7] that would mean 2% higher consumption in China but the self-suffiency rate would be an extra percentage point lower (compare Table 2, panel (c) and Table 2, panel (d)).

The extent of the impact of these adjustments on estimates of China's wine consumption per capita and on its self-sufficiency in wine are shown in Figure 2 (where the adjustment including some smuggling is not shown as it is very close to the heavy black lines). The extent of their impact on estimated production in China of wine, if narrowly defined to be made from local grapes, are shown in Figure 3 (along with similarly adjusted production estimates for Japan).

3.3. *Hong Kong and Macau*

If Hong Kong's wine exports to China are in fact more than what are documented in official records, it makes a much bigger difference to Hong Kong's apparent wine consumption per capita than to China's. To use the previous example, if the extent of such smuggling amounted to

---

[7] The extent of such smuggling is unknowable, but informed commentators believe it has been non-trivial. See, for example, the comments by numerous key players in the Hong Kong market that were collated by Robinson (2018) on the tenth anniversary of the decision to abolish Hong Kong's wine import taxes. The reduction in Hong Kong's wine import tariff from 80% in February 2006 down to 40% starting in March 2007 and zero from March 2008, and of Macau's from 15% to zero after 27 August 2008, would have increased the incentive to smuggle imported wine from those territories to the mainland.

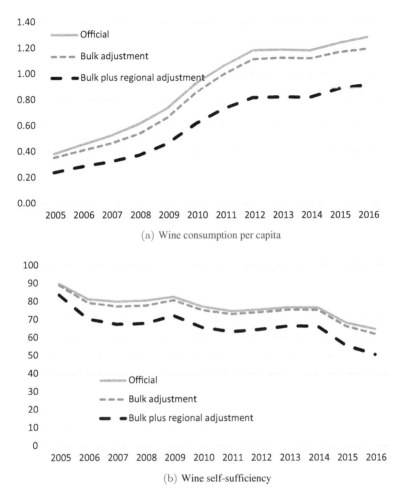

Figure 2. China's estimated wine consumption per capita and wine self-sufficiency under alternative assumptions,[a] 2005 to 2016 (litres and %)

[a]"Bulk adjustment" assumes all of China's bulk imports each year are blended with domestically produced wine before being bottled and sold as a Product of China; "Bulk plus regional adjustment" assumes domestically produced wine is only two-thirds of the official amount because of double counting due to wine of one region being blended in another region and counted by both regions, before imported bulk wine is blended into the mix prior to bottling.

Source: See Table 2.

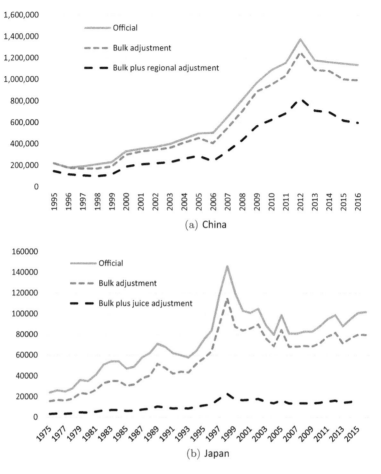

Figure 3. Estimated wine production in China and Japan's under alternative assumptions,[a] 1975 to 2016 (kilolitres)

[a]For explanation of assumptions, see note a of Figures 1 and 2.

Sources: See Tables 1 and 2.

half as much again as Hong Kong has been officially re-exporting, then Hong Kong's apparent consumption is only 3.0 litres instead of 4.9 litres per capita in 2015–2016 (see Table 3). That is much closer to the average annual 2.4 litres consumption level in Singapore in recent years.

Table 3. Wine imports, re-exports and consumption, Hong Kong (under alternative assumptions[a]) and Macau, 2000 to 2016 (kilolitres and litres)

	Hong Kong								Macau			
	Imports Recorded (KL)	Re-Exports Recorded (KL)	Net Imports Recorded (KL)	Consm.[b] Per Cap. (litres)	Re-Exports as % of Import Volume	Assumed Extra HK Exports to China (KL)	Amended Net Imports (KL)	Amended Consm.[b] Per Cap. (Litres)	Imports Recorded (KL)	Re-Exports Recorded (KL)	Net Imports Recorded (KL)	Consm.[b] Per Cap. (Litres)	Re-Exports as % of Import Volume
2000	10,135	973	9,162	1.38	10	487	8,676	1.30	905	53	852	1.97	6
2001	10,798	1,007	9,791	1.46	9	504	9,288	1.38	963	14	949	2.17	1
2002	10,925	1,035	9,890	1.46	9	518	9,373	1.39	1,193	33	1,160	2.61	3
2003	11,200	1,023	10,177	1.49	9	512	9,666	1.42	1,197	50	1,147	2.54	4
2004	13,440	1,697	11,743	1.71	13	849	10,895	1.59	1,463	26	1,437	3.13	2
2005	15,124	2,047	13,077	1.90	14	1,024	12,054	1.75	1,551	23	1,528	3.26	2
2006	18,336	3,576	14,760	2.13	20	1,788	12,972	1.87	1,919	21	1,898	3.95	1
2007	23,357	5,763	17,594	2.52	25	2,882	14,713	2.11	2,654	78	2,575	5.22	3
2008	30,327	6,932	23,395	3.33	23	3,466	19,929	2.84	3,518	225	3,293	6.49	6
2009	34,837	8,493	26,344	3.73	24	4,247	22,098	3.13	4,826	247	4,579	8.79	5
2010	39,984	12,336	27,648	3.94	31	6,168	21,480	3.06	6,128	589	5,539	10.37	10
2011	48,197	18,491	29,706	4.20	38	9,246	20,461	2.89	7,710	777	6,933	12.69	10
2012	50,525	18,675	31,850	4.45	37	9,338	22,513	3.15	6,839	na	na	na	na
2013	50,122	19,111	31,011	4.31	38	9,556	21,456	2.99	na	na	na	na	na
2014	52,514	22,334	30,180	4.18	43	11,167	19,013	2.63	5,355	740	4,615	7.59	14
2015	63,390	27,342	36,048	4.95	43	13,671	22,377	3.07	6,011	44	5,966	10.14	1
2016	62,935	27,157	35,778	4.87	43	13,579	22,200	3.02	5,932	554	5,378	8.97	9

[a] Unrecorded re-exports to the mainland are assumed to be 50% of Hong Kong's total recorded re-exports.
[b] Apparent consumption per capita, assumed to be net imports divided by population.

Source: Authors' calculations, starting with official trade numbers reported in Anderson and Pinilla (2017).

Macau has less than one-tenth of the population and hence a much smaller economy than Hong Kong, but it has had a similarly higher and rapidly rising per capita income and demand for wine imports, and a similar proximity to mainland China. It abolished its 15% wine import tax in August 2008, six months after Hong Kong. Its apparent per capita consumption of wine, when defined as recorded net imports, have been about twice that of Hong Kong's over the past two decades. However, its recorded re-exports have been a far smaller proportion of its reported imports than is the case for Hong Kong (Table 3). If there is no smuggling out of Macau, then it has by far the highest per capita wine consumption in Asia at more than twice that of Hong Kong's, three times that of Japan's, and four times that of Singapore's. That seems unlikely, however, notwithstanding the possibly considerable consumption by high-income gambling tourists in Macau (most of whom come from the mainland). A more likely explanation for these comparative data is that a large share of Macau's wine imports have been smuggled to mainland China. That would be consistent with the rapid growth in China's demand for fine wine imports during 2005–2012 and its subsequent slowdown following the austerity and anti-corruption measures Beijing introduced in December 2012 (Table 2, panel (a) and Table 4), as well as with the rapid rise in the average price of wine imports into greater China during 2005-2012 and their plateauing thereafter — in contrast to the rest of the world where average import prices fell from 2008 because of the global financial crisis (Figure 4).

4. Implications of revised statistics for wine exporters

These alternative estimates of wine market statistics for northeast Asia alter nontrivially the estimates of the share of wine in the region's alcohol consumption. Those shares are already presumed to be very low by world standards, but the earlier noted adjustments mean they may be even lower than previous estimates suggest. Nonetheless, since the turn of the century, even these alternative estimated shares have doubled for China, and gone up by about 50% for Hong Kong and Japan, at a time when wine's share of alcohol consumption in the rest of the world has shrunk by about

Table 4. Grape wine's share of total alcohol consumption, China, Hong Kong, Japan, and the World 2000 to 2015 (%)

	China Base	China Amended[a]	Hong Kong Base	Hong Kong Amended[b]	Japan Base	Japan Amended[c]	World Average
2000	1.4	0.8	10.9	10.4	4.4	4.0	16.1
2001	1.6	0.9	11.4	10.8	4.2	3.9	16.2
2002	1.7	1.0	11.2	10.7	4.2	3.9	16.6
2003	1.8	1.1	11.3	10.8	4.0	3.8	16.4
2004	1.9	1.1	12.5	11.7	4.0	3.8	16.5
2005	2.1	1.2	13.3	12.4	3.8	3.6	15.8
2006	2.2	1.3	14.4	12.9	3.9	3.7	15.2
2007	2.1	1.3	16.4	14.1	3.9	3.7	14.7
2008	2.2	1.3	20.3	17.8	4.0	3.8	14.0
2009	2.3	1.4	21.9	19.1	4.0	3.8	13.3
2010	2.4	1.6	22.3	18.2	4.2	4.0	12.8
2011	2.9	2.0	23.1	17.1	4.5	4.2	12.7
2012	3.1	2.1	23.8	18.1	5.2	5.0	12.8
2013	3.1	2.1	23.0	17.1	5.2	5.1	12.6
2014	3.0	2.1	22.4	15.4	5.4	5.4	12.7
2015	na	na	na	na	5.4	5.4	na

[a]Assuming that China's wine production is two-thirds of the official estimate, all bulk imports into China are blended with local wine, and the volume of wine smuggled into China is equal to an extra 50% of Hong Kong's total official wine re-exports.
[b]Assuming the volume of wine smuggled from Hong Kong to China is equal to an extra 50% of Hong Kong's total official wine re-exports.
[c]Assuming all imported bulk wine is bottled in and sold as a product of Japan.
Sources: Base estimates are from Anderson and Pinilla (2017); other estimates are based on the assumptions in Tables 1, 2, and 3.

one-quarter (Table 4). Little wonder that the world's wine exporters are paying close attention to sales in this region, which is one of the fastest growing globally (Anderson and Wittwer, 2015).

The more-than-doubling of apparent per capita consumption in Hong Kong and Macau based on official trade statistics, following the abolition of their wine import tariffs in 2008, imply very high price elasticities of demand for wine — especially in Macau where the tariff

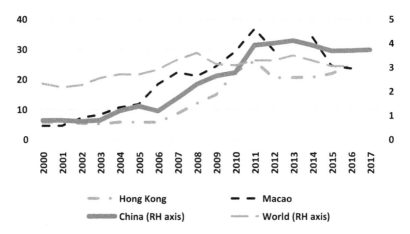

Figure 4. Average price of wine imports, China, Hong Kong, Macau and the World, 2000 to 2017 (current US$ per litre)
Source: United Nations (2018).

had been just 15% before being abolished. This lends support to the claims by insiders of non-trivial informal or smuggled trade in wine to the mainland.

These alternative estimates mean foreign suppliers may face considerably less competition in the Chinese and Japanese markets from local producers than official data imply. They also suggest the potential for increased per capita consumption in the region is even greater than previously thought, including in Hong Kong. True, these alternative estimates also suggest the rise in the share of the region in global wine consumption since the turn of the century has been overstated. That increase, from 2.9 to 8.4%, becomes one from 2.2 to 6.3% using these alternative estimates (Table 5). Even so, that amended increase in the combined share for these three economies is still huge compared with the proportional increase in their share of global income, which rose from 18 to 22% between 2000 and 2016 (World Bank, 2017). The scope for further growth in northeast Asia's wine consumption and imports would still seem very considerable though, when its 6–8% share of global wine consumption is compared with its 22% share of global income.

Table 5. Shares of China and Japan in global wine production and consumption, official and alternative estimates, 2000 to 2016 (%)

	China Base	China Amended	Japan Base	Japan Amended	China + Japan, Base	China + Japan, Amended
(a) Production						
2000	1.18	1.07	0.37	0.06	1.55	1.13
2001	1.32	1.22	0.38	0.06	1.70	1.28
2002	1.44	1.34	0.41	0.07	1.85	1.41
2003	1.50	1.36	0.33	0.06	1.83	1.42
2004	1.47	1.35	0.26	0.05	1.73	1.40
2005	1.77	1.62	0.35	0.06	2.12	1.68
2006	1.77	1.44	0.29	0.05	2.06	1.49
2007	2.47	2.08	0.31	0.05	2.78	2.13
2008	3.00	2.61	0.31	0.05	3.31	2.66
2009	3.56	3.26	0.30	0.05	3.86	3.31
2010	4.05	3.54	0.33	0.05	4.38	3.59
2011	4.25	3.81	0.35	0.06	4.60	3.87
2012	5.27	4.81	0.38	0.06	5.65	4.87
2013	4.11	3.80	0.31	0.05	4.42	3.85
2014	4.24	3.94	0.35	0.06	4.59	4.00
2015	4.16	3.63	0.37	0.06	4.53	3.69
2016	4.26	3.72	0.38	0.06	4.64	3.78
(b) Consumption						
2000	1.59	0.97	1.27	1.15	2.86	2.12
2001	1.66	1.03	1.20	1.11	2.86	2.14
2002	1.72	1.08	1.17	1.10	2.89	2.18
2003	1.87	1.15	1.11	1.05	2.98	2.20
2004	2.03	1.26	1.07	1.01	3.10	2.27
2005	2.36	1.46	1.06	1.00	3.42	2.46
2006	2.62	1.51	1.08	1.02	3.70	2.53

(*Continued*)

Table 5. (*Continued*)

	China Base	China Amended	Japan Base	Japan Amended	China + Japan, Base	China + Japan, Amended
(b) Consumption						
2007	3.32	1.98	1.06	1.01	4.38	2.99
2008	4.13	2.54	1.08	1.02	5.21	3.56
2009	4.88	3.17	1.12	1.07	6.00	4.24
2010	5.82	3.88	1.18	1.12	7.00	5.00
2011	6.20	4.31	1.21	1.14	7.41	5.45
2012	7.06	4.89	1.40	1.33	8.46	6.22
2013	6.32	4.46	1.45	1.43	7.77	5.89
2014	6.27	4.42	1.48	1.49	7.75	5.91
2015	6.77	4.70	1.50	1.52	8.27	6.22
2016	6.98	4.90	na	na	na	na

Sources: Estimates are based on the assumptions in Tables 1(c) and Table 2, panel (b) plus the global estimated production and consumption in Anderson and Pinilla (2017).

References

Anderson, K., and Pinilla, V (with the assistance of A.J. Holmes) (2017). *Annual Database of Global Wine Markets, 1835 to 2016*. Wine Economics Research Centre, University of Adelaide, posted at www.adelaide.edu.au/wine-econ/databases (accessed 29 November 2017).

Anderson, K., and Wittwer, G. (2015). Asia's evolving role in global wine markets. *China Economic Review*, 35, 1–14.

Boyce, J. (2017). China wine watch: Have imports already overtaken local production? Grape Wall of China, posted at http://www.grapewallofchina.com/ (accessed 20 May 2017).

Boyce, J. (2018). Do imported wines now have a majority of the market? Grape Wall of China, posted at http://www.grapewallofchina.com/2018/03/22/imports-top-local-wines-china-market/ (accessed 24 March 2018).

JETRO. (1998). *Japanese Market Report, Regulations and Practices: Wine*. Report No. 15, March, Tokyo: Japan External Trade Organization.

Kawasaki, N., Nagatani, T., Yamakawa, R., Nakamura, Y., Iba, H., Ueda, N., Ochiai, K., and Oda, S. (2011). An empirical analysis on the sustainable business of a regional small winery, from the viewpoint of product portfolio based on potential sources of grape. *Journal of ASEV Japan*, 22(1), 22–30.

Ministry of Finance. (2017). *Trade Statistics of Japan*. http://www.customs.go.jp/toukei/info/ index.htm (accessed 28 September 2017).

National Tax Agency (of Japan). (2015). Notice on establishing labelling standards for manufacturing process and quality of wine. Notice No.19, Tokyo: National Tax Agency, October. http://www.nta.go.jp/shiraberu/zeiho-kaishaku/kokuji/151030_3/index.htm and in English at http://www.nta.go.jp/foreign_language/sake/geographical/01.htm and http://sakefanworld.info/ja/sake_GI/pdf/GI_en.pdf (accessed 28 September 2017).

National Tax Agency (of Japan). (2016). 2016 Factsheet [Kajitsushi Seizogyo no Gaikyo]. http://www.nta.go.jp/shiraberu/senmonjoho/sake/shiori-gaikyo/seizogaikyo/kajitsu/pdf/h27wine-shosai.pdf (accessed 28 September 2017).

National Tax Agency (of Japan). (2017). 2017 Factsheet [Kajitsushi Seizogyo no Gaikyo]. http://www.nta.go.jp/shiraberu/senmonjoho/sake/shiori-gaikyo/seizogaikyo/kajitsu/pdf/28wine.pdf (accessed 9 March 2018).

Oda, S. (2001). Targets and topics for wine industry research. *Natural Resource Economics Review* [Seibutsu Shigen Keizai Kenkyu, Kyoto University], 21, 197–215.

Robinson, J. (2018). Hong Kong celebrates 10 duty-free years. *Jancis Robinson blog,* 27 February. Available at https://www.jancisrobinson.com/articles/hk-celebrates-10-duty-free-years (accessed 27 February 2018).

Shimamura, A. (2008). *Kanzen Kokusan Shugi.* Tokyo: Toyo Keizai.

Takahashi, T., Harada, K., Saito, H., and Kobayashi, K. (2017). *Wines of Japan.* Tokyo: Ikaros Publications.

United Nations. (2018). *COMTRADE database.* United Nations, Department of Economic and Social Affairs, Statistics Division, Trade Statistics, posted at https://comtrade.un.org/data/ (accessed 5 March 2018).

Uytsel, S.V (2015). Geographical indications in Japan. Rochester, NY: SSRN. Available at https://papers.ssrn.com/sol3/papers.cfm?abstract_id=2692450 (accessed 28 September 2017).

World Bank. (2017). *World Development Indicators.* Washington, DC: World Bank. http://data-bank.worldbank.org/data/reports.aspx?source=WDI-Archives (accessed 28 September 2017).

Yoon, S., and Lam, T.-H. (2012). The alcohol industry lobby and Hong Kong's zero wine and beer tax policy. *BMC Public Health,* 12(717), 1–12.

Appendix

Table A1. Winegrape production in Japan, by growing region and crushing region, March 2016 (tonnes)[a]

Place of Production \ Place of Wine Making	Sapporo, Hokkaido	Sendai, Fukushima Pref. (Yamagata Prefecture)	Kanto Area (Nagano Prefecture)	Tokyo Area (Yamanashi Prefecture)	Kanazawa, Ishikawa Prefecture	Nagoya, Aichi Prefecture	Osaka	Hiroshima Prefecture	Takamatsu, Kagawa Prefecture	Fukuoka Prefecture	Kumamoto Prefecture	Okinawa Prefecture	Grape Used for Wine Making
Sapporo, Hokkaido	**3,364**	232 (162)	-	61 (61)	153	-	5	-	8	-	35	-	3,858
Sendai, Fukushima (Yamagata prefecture)	-	**2,460 (1,555)**	3 (-)	24 (-)	-	-	-	-	-	-	-	-	2,487 (1,572)
Kanto area (Nagano prefecture)	169 (129)	159 (1)	**6,566 (6,137)**	589 (193)	17 (2)	1 (1)	15 (3)	48 (48)	-	-	-	-	7,566 (6,516)
Tokyo (Yamanashi prefecture)	8 (8)	348 (244)	448 (437)	**7,442 (7,432)**	-	12 (12)	4 (4)	2 (1)	-	-	-	-	8,263 (8,249)
Kanazawa, Ishikawa prefecture	20	4 (4)	1 (1)	29 (29)	**171**	-	9	-	-	-	-	-	234
Nagoya, Aichi prefecture	-	-	33 (33)	25 (25)	-	**55**	9	1	-	-	-	-	122
Osaka	-	194 (171)	54 (54)	148 (147)	3	-	**496**	-	10	-	-	-	905
Hiroshima prefecture	147	15 (-)	-	170 (170)	-	-	3	**638**	1	-	-	-	974
Takamatsu, Kagawa prefecture	-	-	-	-	-	-	-	-	**46**	-	-	-	46
Fukuoka prefecture	x	x	x	x	x	x	x	x	x	x	x	x	x
Kumamoto prefecture	-	48 (30)	-	82 (82)	-	-	14	4	7	0	**596**	-	750
Okinawa prefecture	x	x	x	x	x	x	x	x	x	x	x	x	x
Productuin volume of wine grapes	3,708	3459 (2428)	7105 (6704)	8597 (8586)	345	68	554	693	73	21	631	-	25,254

[a] "-" and "x" stand for "not applicable" and "protected information," respectively. Information is protected for regions with just a few wineries.

Source: National Tax Agency (2016).

D. Distortions to Wine Producer Incentives and Consumer Prices

Chapter 16

On the Impact of the Canada-United States Free Trade Agreement on U.S. Wine Exports*

Kym Anderson[†]

In their article on the impact of the Canada-United States Free Trade Agreement (CUSFTA) on United States wine exports, Heien and Sims (1999) note that the volume of US wine exports to Canada doubled and its value more than trebled between 1988 and 1994 as CUSFTA was progressively implemented. They attribute the remarkable growth in the quantity and quality of that bilateral wine trade somewhat to the preferential removal of the import tariff on U.S. wine but mostly to the removal of some key nontariff import barriers. The latter included discriminatory

---

*First published in *Australian and New Zealand Wine Industry Journal* 16(1): 115–17, January/February 2001. Kym Anderson is Professor of Economics and Executive Director of the Wine Economics Research Centre at the University of Adelaide. Financial assistance of the Australian Research Council is greatly acknowledged. For details of the Wine Economics Research Centre and its publications, visit its website at www.adelaide.edu.au/wine-econ

Centre for International Economic Studies, School of Economics, University of Adelaide, SA 5005 AUSTRALIA

listing practices (only a small subset of importable wines were listed by the monopolized liquor stores (control boards) in each Canadian province), discriminatory pricing policies (those boards marked up imported wine much more than domestic labels), discriminatory distribution practices (imported wine attracted a higher distribution service charge), and local content rules (domestic labels in British Columbia had to contain at least 80 per cent B.C. wine so as to be eligible for the discriminatory treatment favoring local wines).

Useful though their analysis is, Heien and Sims leave unanswered many questions about that bilateral trade growth. First, did the U.S. *share* of Canada's total wine imports grow? Second, did Canada's share of *U.S.* wine exports grow (since total U.S. wine exports grew rapidly in the 1990s)? Third, did U.S. wine sales in Canada grow faster than those of other 'New World' wine-exporting countries? In particular, did the U.S. penetration of Canada's wine market grow less rapidly relative to that of other foreign suppliers after 1995 when CUSFTA implementation had ended and implementation of the multilateral Uruguay Round Agreement on Agriculture began (given that NAFTA added no further liberalization of Canada-U.S. wine trade)? And fourth, to what extent was the quality upgrading of Canada's wine imports confined to U.S. wines? These questions are addressed in turn before drawing out some implications from this single-industry study of the role of bilateral/regional integration agreements as stepping stones to freer global trade.

If all that CUSFTA introduced was a drop in barriers to U.S. wine exports to Canada, the U.S. share of Canada's wine imports would have grown progressively during the 7-year period (1989 to 1995) over which CUSFTA was implemented — and beyond, if there were delayed responses to promotion of U.S. wines. Table 1 shows that the U.S. share grew in 1989 from 7.5 to 9.0 per cent, but it fell slightly in 1990 when Canadian imports from Southern Hemisphere wine exporters surged. True, the U.S share grew again during 1991–93, but thereafter it plateaued in the 15–17 per cent range.

What about Canada's share of U.S. wine exports? That share jumped from 22 to 26 per cent in 1989. But it rose only a little more after that first year, peaking at 28 per cent in 1993 before falling steadily to 17 per cent by 1997 (column 6 of Table 1) — well below the U.S. share of Canada's

Table 1. Value and sources of Canada's wine imports and their shares of U.S. and world wine exports

(current U.S. $ million and per cent by value)

	Value of Canada's Wine Imports (US $ million)	Percentage of Canada's Imports from:					Canada's Imports as a % of:	
		United States	Australia	Other 'New World'[a]	Western Europe	Rest of World	U.S. Exports	World Exports
1988	206	7.5	2.7	1.6	86.4	1.8	21.5	3.2
1989	276	9.0	3.0	2.0	84.0	2.0	26.0	4.1
1990	295	8.4	4.3	3.2	82.7	1.4	23.1	3.6
1991	281	11.7	4.3	4.5	77.9	1.6	26.4	3.4
1992	295	14.2	4.6	7.0	72.2	2.0	26.4	3.4
1993	283	15.6	5.1	7.6	70.0	1.7	28.2	3.7
1994	305	15.8	5.5	7.4	70.2	1.5	25.5	3.5
1995	324	15.1	4.7	8.5	70.1	1.6	20.6	3.2
1996	377	17.0	5.6	10.3	65.0	2.1	19.3	3.3
1997	409	16.7	6.0	12.5	63.1	1.7	16.8	3.3

[a] Argentina, Brazil, Chile, New Zealand, South Africa, and Uruguay.

Source: Calculated from United Nations trade value statistics as summarized by Berger, Spahni and Anderson (1999, Table 22).

imports of non-wine merchandise, which was 22 per cent in 1997. During that decade Canada's share of *world* wine trade rose significantly only in 1989 too, thereafter falling back to average in the 1990s barely above its 1988 share of 3.2 per cent (final column of Table 1). And even in that first year of CUSFTA, exports from the U.S. accounted for less than one-seventh of the growth in the total value of Canadian wine imports.

As it happens, this was a period of rapid expansion of wine exports from both the United States and several other 'New World' suppliers not just to Canada but generally (Anderson and Berger 1999). As a consequence, global exports of wine almost doubled during the decade to 1997, and the shares of 'New World' suppliers in international wine trade rose rapidly from a low base — at the expense of Western European suppliers. Column 2 of Table 2 shows that the U.S. share trebled. To what extent, then, can the growth in U.S. wine sales to Canada

Table 2. Value and sources of world wine exports (current U.S. $ billion and per cent by value)

	(Current U.S. $ billion and per cent by value)					
		Percentage of World Wine Exports from:				
	Value of World Wine Exports (US $ billion)	United States	Australia	Other 'New World'[a]	Western Europe	Rest of World[b]
1988	6.4	1.1	1.4	0.8	94.2	2.5
1989	6.7	1.4	1.5	1.1	93.1	2.9
1990	8.1	1.3	1.6	1.3	93.0	2.8
1991	8.1	1.5	2.0	1.8	91.7	3.0
1992	8.8	1.8	2.4	2.6	90.2	3.0
1993	7.6	2.0	3.3	3.2	87.4	4.1
1994	8.7	2.2	3.6	3.3	87.1	3.8
1995	10.0	2.4	3.3	4.1	86.2	4.0
1996	11.4	2.9	4.1	5.5	81.6	5.9
1997	12.3	3.3	4.8	6.7	79.1	6.1

[a] Argentina, Brazil, Chile, New Zealand, South Africa, and Uruguay.
[b] Mostly Central and Eastern Europe and the former Soviet Union.
Source: Calculated from United Nations trade statistics as summarized by Berger, Spahni and Anderson (1999, Table 22).

be accounted for simply by the growth in the contribution of U.S. exports to world trade in wine?

One way to net out the impact of the latter is to calculate the index of intensity of wine trade between the U.S and Canada. That index is the share of the exporting country's wine exports going to Canada divided by Canada's share of world wine imports or, equivalently, the exporting country's share of Canada's wine imports (from Table 1) divided by that exporting country's share of world wine exports (from Table 2). The numbers so calculated are summarized in Table 3. They show that in 1988 the intensity of U.S. wine exports to Canada was already extremely high: the U.S. share of Canadian imports was 6.7 times larger than the U.S. share of global wine exports. That intensity index *fell* slightly, rather than increased, in 1989 and 1990 as CUSFTA began to be implemented. It then rose slightly during the next two years,

Table 3. Index of intensity of wine exports to Canada, by source[a]

	United States	Australia	Other 'New World'[b]	Western Europe	Rest of World
1988	6.70	1.97	2.00	0.92	0.72
1989	6.34	2.05	1.82	0.90	0.48
1990	6.36	2.76	2.54	0.89	0.50
1991	7.56	2.14	2.50	0.85	0.53
1992	7.89	1.91	2.68	0.80	0.67
1993	7.68	1.53	2.38	0.80	0.70
1994	7.18	1.42	2.24	0.81	0.40
1995	6.29	1.42	2.07	0.81	0.40
1996	5.86	1.37	1.87	0.80	0.36
1997	5.06	1.25	1.87	0.80	0.28

[a] The intensity of trade index is the share of the value of each exporting country's/region's wine exports going to Canada divided by Canada's share of world wine trade (or equivalently, the exporting country's/region's share of Canada's wine imports divided by that country's/region's share of world wine trade when just export data are used).

[b] Argentina, Brazil, Chile, New Zealand, South Africa, and Uruguay.

Source: Calculated from United Nations trade value statistics as summarized by Berger, Spahni and Anderson (1999, Table 22).

but it fell steadily after 1992 and was below 5.1 by 1997. Meanwhile, the index of intensity of other 'New World' wine export trade to Canada rose considerably more, in proportionate terms, than that for the U.S. from the late 1980s to the early 1990s (from 2.0 to around 2.7), and the relatively low index of intensity of European wine sales to Canada deteriorated further.

Heien and Sims also point to the quality upgrading of U.S. wine exports to Canada as CUSFTA was being implemented. To what extent was that confined to imports from just the U.S.? The final row of Table 4 shows the average price of world wine exports to all markets in 1997 was 20 per cent above the 1988–90 average in current U.S. dollar terms, whereas that for wine exports just to Canada was 37 per cent higher. The price of U.S. exports to Canada, however, rose 126 per cent over those ten years, or three times more than the average for Canada's wine imports. The average price for Southern Hemisphere exports to Canada, by comparison, was only two-thirds greater in 1997 than in the late 1980s. Thus

Table 4. Unit value of wine exports to Canada (and to the world), by source[a] (current U.S. cents per litre)

	United States	Australia	Other 'New World'[b]	All Exporters
1988–90	106 (176)	211 (217)	89 (115)	185 (176)
1991–93	137 (179)	234 (215)	130 (152)	202 (189)
1994–96	188 (225)	294 (273)	120 (137)	224 (197)
1997	240 (252)	371 (331)	151 (177)	255 (212)
1997/ 1988–90	*2.26 (1.43)*	*1.76 (1.52)*	*1.70 (1.54)*	*1.37 (1.20)*

[a] Values in parentheses refer to exports to the world.
[b] Argentina, Brazil, Chile, New Zealand, South Africa, and Uruguay.
Source: Calculated from United Nations trade value and volume statistics as summarized by Berger, Spahni and Anderson (1999, Tables 21 and 22).

the quality upgrading of U.S.-Canada wine trade referred to by Heien and Sims was not only substantial in absolute terms but also relative to the quality upgrading of Canada's imports from other countries, including other 'New World' suppliers, and to the upgrading of global wine trade.

Apart from this quality feature, however, the above data suggest (a) that Canada has not opened up its wine market any more rapidly than other wine importers over the decade examined and (b) in so far as Canada has expanded its wine imports in absolute terms, the growth of U.S. sales in that market has not been outstanding relative to sales growth by Southern Hemisphere wine exporters, including during the CUSFTA implementation period.

Two implications follow from these data. First, when a bilateral free-trade agreement mainly involves the removal of non-tariff barriers including trade-inhibiting domestic practices, it is possible for third-country exporters to enjoy much of the benefit of that liberalization. In that sense a bilateral or regional free trade agreement can indeed be a stepping stone to freer global trade. But second, that benefit to exporters may not be large. In particular, if the removal of one series of trade-inhibiting measures is accompanied by the introduction of other anti-trade measures, as Heien and Sims document was the case in Canada, the growth in that country's imports can be dampened. Certainly the decline in Canada's self-sufficiency ratio from 22 to 18 per cent during the 1988–97 period (Berger, Spahni and Anderson 1999, Table 8) is in the right direction for a country with a strong and increasing comparative disadvantage in wine production, but that is simply a continuation of past trends.[1] It and the lack of growth in Canada's share of global wine imports during the 1990s together suggest (a) CUSFTA has had only a modest impact and (b) there may be considerable scope still for further wine market liberalization in Canada.

References

Anderson, K. and N. Berger (1999), 'Australia's Re-Emergence as a Wine Exporter: The First Decade in International Perspective', *Australian and New Zealand Wine Industry Journal* 14 (6): 26–38, November/December.

Berger, N., K. Anderson and R. Stringer (1998), *Trends in the World Wine Market, 1961 to 1996: A Statistical Compendium,* Adelaide: Centre for International Economic Studies.

Berger, N., P. Spahni and K. Anderson (1999), *Bilateral Trade Patterns in the World Wine Market, 1988 to 1997: A Statistical Compendium,* Adelaide: Centre for International Economic Studies.

Heien, D. and E.N. Sims (2000), 'The Impact of the Canada-United States Free Trade Agreement on U.S. Wine Exports', *American Journal of Agricultural Economics* 82(1): 173–182, February.

---

[1] Domestic wine production as a percentage of consumption in Canada was two-thirds in the early 1960s, one-half in the early 1970s, and one-third in the early 1980s, compared with about one-sixth in the late 1990s (Berger, Anderson and Stringer 1998, Table 12).

Chapter 17

Impact of the GST and Wine Tax Reform on Australia's Wine Industry: A CGE Analysis*

Glyn Wittwer and Kym Anderson[†]

Abstract

This study analyses the impacts of the Goods and Services Tax (GST) introduced on 1 July 2000, and the associated wine tax reform, on both the premium and non-premium segments of the grape and wine industry using a computable general equilibrium (CGE) model of the Australian economy. Through input cost reductions, the grape and wine industry is projected to gain from the GST tax package. Thus the industry can still gain even though wine consumption is taxed a little more heavily after than before the introduction of the GST. This is particularly so for the export-oriented premium wine segment. A switch from the current *ad valorem* to a revenue-neutral volumetric tax on wine under the GST is shown also to favour the premium segment of the industry, but at the expense of the non-premium segment.

---

*First published in *Australian Economic Papers* 41(1): 69–81, March 2002. Centre for International Economic Studies, University of Adelaide, SA 5005. The authors are grateful for the comments and suggestions of Peter Dixon and Brian Parmenter. They also acknowledge the financial and informational support of the Australian Research Council, the Grape and Wine Research and Development Corporation and the Rural Industries Research and Development Corporation.

[†]University of Adelaide

1. Introduction

For more than a century government policies in Australia and overseas have contributed much to the boom-bust cycles in the Australian wine industry (Osmond and Anderson 1998). While the 1990s boom was mainly the result of sustained export demand growth, a key question given the influence of government policy historically on the wine industry is how the broad-based goods-and-services tax (GST) package introduced on 1 July 2000, and possible future amendments to wine taxation in particular, are likely to affect the industry.

Would the switch to a GST help or hurt the wine industry? As it turned out, wine is one of the few commodities subject to a wholesale sales tax (WST) that the Coalition government targeted for continued taxing at the wholesale level. More than that, it has had an increase in taxation under the GST package. The increase came in two forms. One was the replacement of the previous 41 per cent WST with a 'wine equalisation tax' (WET) at the wholesale level of 29 per cent which, with a subsequent GST of 10 per cent at the retail level, is equivalent to a 4 to 6 percentage point rise at the wholesale level. The other source of revenue arises from wine that is consumed on licensed premises, through the GST on the on-premise service charge. Consequently, the 29 per cent WET on wine imposed by the Commonwealth in place of the previous WST raises the wine tax rate significantly.

This study uses a computable general equilibrium (CGE) model of the economies of South Australia (where half the national wine industry is located) and rest of Australia to model the impacts of the GST package on the Australian wine industry. This model, FEDSA-WINE (Wittwer 2000), is based on earlier Australian CGE models, ORANI-G (Dixon et al. 1982; Horridge et al. 1998), FEDERAL (Madden 1992) and MMRF (Naqvi and Peter 1996). It includes a detailed fiscal module at both the Commonwealth and state levels. Earlier CGE studies of the wine industry deal with wine taxation alone rather than a generalised movement from direct towards indirect taxation (Meagher et al. 1985; CIE 1995a). The justification for using a general equilibrium rather than partial equilibrium approach is the importance of indirect effects. These include changes in the costs of production of the wine industry brought about by the abolition of wholesale sales taxes, the expenditure effect of the GST package and the impact of the package on wine exports. Only the change in taxation can be calculated from partial analysis. The remaining effects require data, parameters and behavioural equations beyond those concerning only the wine industry.

2. The FEDSA-WINE simulation model

The main focus of this study is the impact of the introduction of the GST package on the wine industry plus the impact on South Australia relative to the rest of Australia. The household demand equations play an important part in analysing impacts. In FEDSA-WINE, these equations are based on the Klein-Rubin (1949) utility function with directly additive preferences

$$U = \frac{1}{Q} \prod_i (X_i - \psi_i)^{\beta_i} \quad (1)$$

Domestic consumption of each commodity is divided into supernumerary and subsistence components. In levels terms, U represents utility, Q the number of households, X_i the total consumption of good i, ψ_i the subsistence component of this consumption and β_i the marginal budget share of good i ($0 \leq \beta_i \leq 1$ and $\Sigma \beta_i = 1$).

The maximisation of utility subject to the budget constraint $Y = \Sigma_i P_i X_i$ gives rise to the linear expenditure function for good i of the following form

$$P_i X_i = P_i \psi_i + \beta_i \left(Y - \sum_i P_i \psi_i \right) \quad (2)$$

Assume $V = (Y - \Sigma_i P_i \psi_i)$, which is the aggregate supernumerary expenditure, then equation (2) becomes

$$P_i X_i = P_i \psi_i + \beta_i V \quad (3)$$

Next, we totally differentiate equation (3) and divide by $P_i X_i$

$$\frac{dP_i X_i + P_i dX_i}{P_i X_i} = \frac{\psi_i dP_i}{P_i X_i} + \frac{\beta_i dV}{P_i X_i} \frac{V}{V} \quad (4)$$

We rearrange (4) to express the percentage change in X_i as a function of the percentage changes in V and P_i

$$x_i = \phi_i (v - p_i) \qquad (5)$$

where $\phi_i = (V\beta_i/P_i X_i) = 1 - (\psi_i/X_i)$, i.e., the supernumerary proportion of total expenditure on X_i. The Frisch parameter γ is the (negative) ratio of total to luxury expenditure, given by $-(Y/V)$. Since $\beta_i = \varepsilon_i P_i X_i / Y$ where ε_i, is the expenditure elasticity of good i, $\phi_i = -\varepsilon_i / \gamma$. Hence, we can rewrite (5) as

$$x_i = -\frac{\varepsilon_i}{\gamma}(v - p_i) \qquad (6)$$

The RHS of (6) divides the change in household consumption into expenditure $\left(-\frac{\varepsilon_i}{\gamma}v\right)$ and price $\left(\frac{\varepsilon_i}{\gamma}p_i\right)$ effects.

FEDSA-WINE disaggregates wine into three categories. This distinguishes the premium red and premium white segments from the non-premium wine. The premium segments are growing rapidly while the non-premium segment is relatively static, in both consumption and production terms. Movements in consumer preferences are evident from changing wine budget shares. In 1987, the shares were 14 per cent for premium red wine, 30 per cent for premium white wine and 56 per cent for non-premium wine. The respective shares in 1999 were 35 per cent, 31 per cent and 34 per cent (Wittwer 2000). Similarly, export growth has favoured the premium segments. Exports of premium red wine grew from 5 megalitres (Ml) in 1987 to 88 Ml in 1999. Premium white exports grew from 5 Ml to 83 Ml and non-premium exports from 14 Ml to 46 Ml in the same period (AWEC 2000). Since the industry is changing rapidly, the FEDSA-WINE database has been updated to 2003 to reflect sales weights of the present decade rather than those of the 1990s (Wittwer 2000).

2.1. Parameters

Most available estimates of cross-price and own-price elasticities include wine as a single aggregated commodity. They also rely on data from periods prior to the marked taste changes of the past few years (Abdulla and

Duffus 1988; Clements and Selvanathan 1991). Such estimates of domestic demand elasticities drawing on pre-1990s data may be more applicable to non-premium than premium wine, given the change in budget shares since the 1980s. In FEDSA-WINE, the expenditure elasticities imposed are 2.0 for premium red wine, 1.2 for premium white wine and 0.6 for non-premium wine.[1]

Although Australia's share of the global trade is small, around four-fifths of exports are to four destinations, the UK, the USA, New Zealand and Canada. In the UK, Australia's exports account for 13 per cent of consumption at present, and in New Zealand, over 50 per cent (Berger *et al.*, 1999; AWEC 2000). The export demand elasticities in FEDSA-WINE are −6.5 for each wine type, derived from simulations with a global wine model using Armington (1969) elasticities of 4.0 and elasticities of substitution between different imports of 8.0 in each destination (Wittwer *et al.*, 2001).

2.2. *Closure*

The scenarios examined in this paper all concern the long run. National employment is fixed, with wages therefore varying with labour income. Regional shares of national employment are endogenous. We assume that capital is reallocated between industries to leave the rate of return unchanged from the base case in all industries. At the macroeconomic level, real government spending and real investment are exogenous. The latter implies that domestic savings are sufficient only to maintain domestically funded investment at base case levels. The balance of trade surplus is set equal to the increase in returns to capital, to pay foreign capital owners for additional capital that they finance. Real consumption is the only endogenous component of domestic absorption in these scenarios. The Commonwealth public sector borrowing requirement (PSBR) is exogenous

---

[1] The only study to include disaggregated wine types and to be based on relatively recent data, by CIE (1995a), estimates that premium red wine has an expenditure elasticity of 2.45, premium white wine 1.38, and non-premium wine 0.35. We have adopted these parameters with some modifications to reflect the different expenditure weights in our more-recent data.

and the income tax rate (both personal and corporate) endogenous.[2] The PSBRs of the two state governments in the database also are exogenous, by endogenising transfers from the Commonwealth to the states. The numeraire is the consumer price index.

In each scenario, indirect taxes on intermediate inputs into production are reduced by about one third. Most taxes on capital creation are removed, except for new taxes on housing construction. It turns out that the broad-based tax on household consumption excluding food increases consumption tax revenue by about 40 per cent in this scenario, despite the removal of most wholesale sales taxes (the exceptions being alcoholic beverages, tobacco and fuel).[3]

The first scenario reported depicts the comparative static long-run impacts of introducing the GST and the 29 per cent WET on the wine industry. In the second scenario, we depict the effect of policy uncertainty. This entails shocking wine consumption tax shifters by the mean of two politically possible extremes, one being no WET at all under the GST, the other a volumetric WET to raise the tax rate to the equivalent of the pre-GST beer rate. We use systematic sensitivity analysis (SSA) to vary the tax rate between these two extremes. Finally, the third and fourth scenarios examine the impacts of introducing a top-up tax on wine in a volumetric form, set equal to the pre-GST beer rate.

3. Results

A top-up tax of 22 per cent would be necessary, in addition to the GST, to raise the same revenue as the current 41 per cent WST on wine.[4] The

---

[2] The modelled income tax cuts are less than those introduced by the Coalition government with the GST package. Dixon and Rimmer (1999) note that the GST package included a fiscal stimulus, implying that future (i.e. long run) direct tax cuts will be smaller than otherwise.

[3] Some details of the GST package changed during this study due to compromises between the Coalition government and the Democrats. FEDSA-WINE, with only 29 sectors (of which six are wine related), is not sufficiently disaggregated to capture all details in other sectors.

[4] To convert a GST (g) plus top-up tax (t) on the retail sale to a WST (w) equivalent, $w = g(1 + m)(1 + t) + t$, where m is the retail price margin. For a 29% top-up tax, a 10% GST

Coalition government instead, after negotiating with the Democrats, settled on a 29 per cent top-up tax (the so-called 'wine equalization tax' or WET) but with exemption of $300,000 of direct (cellar door plus mail order) sales from the WET, plus partial exemptions for a winery's direct sales up to $580,000.[5] How significant is the exemption? About 6 per cent of domestic sales are direct at present. Given that larger wineries will usually have in excess of $580,000 of direct sales, the proportion of domestic sales that will be exempt from the top-up tax is likely to be only a fraction of the 6 per cent. The exemption therefore will have little effect on the average top-up tax paid by consumers. Hence we ignore the tax concessions on direct sales in the following analysis.

3.1. The first scenario: Introducing the GST package with a 29% WET

Dixon and Rimmer (1999) use a back-of-the-envelope (BOTE) model to explain some of the key impacts of the GST. We use some of their findings from the BOTE model to help explain our long run results. This model contains one good (grain) produced domestically by a constant-returns-to-scale production function of labour and capital inputs. It includes one imported good, vehicles. Grain and vehicles are investment and consumption goods formed as Cobb-Douglas functions. The costs of hiring labour and capital equate to the value of their marginal products. The model also includes different types of taxes.

The marginal product of capital (a negative function of K/L) is given by

$$M_k = \rho . T_q . T_g . T_i . \left(\frac{P_v}{P_g} \right)^{\alpha_{vi}} \qquad (7)$$

---

and 33% retail margin, the wholesale tax equivalent $w = 0.10(1 + 0.29)(1 + 0.33) + 0.29 = 0.46$. The GST applied to on-premise markups raises w further, with the actual level depending on the on-premise share in total wine consumption and the size of the on-premise margin, as shown in Wittwer (2000), p. 187.

[5] The latter concession is in addition to the 15 per cent WST rebate (to encourage wine tourism) on direct sales. Wineries with more than $580,000 of direct sales do not receive the WET exemption at all.

The marginal product of labour is

$$M_l = W_{rb}.T_c.T_g.\left(\frac{P_v}{P_g}\right)^{\alpha_{vc}} \tag{8}$$

where is the after-tax rate of return divided by the unit cost of capital. W_{rb} is the after-tax real wage rate. T_c, T_q, T_g and T_i are the powers of taxes on consumption, capital income, production (used as a proxy for taxes on intermediate inputs) and investment. P_v/P_g is the terms of trade. The shares of vehicles and grains in consumption and investment are α_{vc}, α_{gc}, α_{vi} and α_{gi}, such that $\alpha_{vc} + \alpha_{gc} = 1$ and $\alpha_{vi} + \alpha_{gi} = 1$.

In the GST package, taxes on income, production and investment decrease, so that in equation (7), $T_q.T_g.T_i$ decreases. In the long run, we assume that the after-tax rate of return is constant. Therefore, at constant terms of trade, a move from direct to indirect taxes results in a decrease in M_k, so that K/L increases. Since labour is fixed by assumption in the long run, an increase in capital raises K/L. This increases M_l, and implies that real after-tax wages also rise.

Within our modelling, national capital stocks increase relative to the base case by 3.0 per cent. And real after-tax wages rise by 1.0 per cent. The terms of trade decline by 0.5 per cent, small enough not to alter the direction of these outcomes.[6] The increased income arising from the increase in M_l leads to an increase in real consumption of 0.25 per cent, with a slightly larger gain in South Australia (0.36 per cent, Table 1). South Australia does slightly better than the rest of Australia in the scenario because two important industries in the state, cars and wine, gain from the package. In the case of cars, a sharp cut in the tax rate on sales occurs in the package, thereby expanding output.

This change in tax mix will lower the costs of production relative to CPI. At the industry level, the outcome of the GST depends largely on the movement in costs relative to other industries. If the cost decrease is of a

---

[6] Export prices fall due to export volume growth along the export demand curves of FEDSA-WINE, which have finite elasticities. Import demands, on the other hand, are assumed to be infinitely elastic, so that import prices do not change. Hence the terms of trade decline.

Table 1. Effects of the GST package with different wine tax options (mean % change from base case)

Scenario	1: Parameter Uncertainty[a]				2: Policy Uncertainty[b]			
Wine Output Fan Decomposition	Local Market	Export	Import Share	Total	Local Market	Export	Import Share	Total
Premium red	0.67 (0.04)	1.10 (0.33)	−0.01 (0.01)	1.76 (0.36)	4.30 (3.07)	0.56 (0.46)	−0.24 (0.19)	4.62 (2.40)
Premium white	0.35 (0.03)	0.89 (0.27)	0.04 (0.03)	1.29 (0.26)	2.79 (2.08)	0.55 (0.30)	−0.43 (0.39)	2.89 (1.37)
Non-premium	1.02 (0.02)	0.32 (0.12)	0.00 (0.00)	1.35 (0.13)	0.18 (2.70)	0.33 (0.03)	0.04 (0.12)	0.54 (2.56)
Prices[c]	Input Costs		Consumer		Input Costs		Consumer	
Premium red	−4.49		0.01		−4.27		−5.59	
Premium white	−4.45		0.28		−4.27		−5.74	
Non-premium	−4.79		−1.67		−4.76		2.36	
Services	−2.64		4.98		−2.61		5.01	
Other	−4.98		−5.32		−4.94		−5.36	
All sectors	**−3.33**		**0.00**		**−3.30**		**0.00**	
Wine tax revenue		16.5				0.4		
Wine Consumption	Price Effect	Expend. Effect	Total		Price Effect	Expenditure Effect	Total	
Premium red	−0.01	1.54	1.53		6.84	1.53	8.36	
Premium white	−0.19	0.92	0.73		4.24	0.92	5.16	
Non-premium	0.56	0.46	1.03		−0.46	0.45	−0.02	
Macroeconomic								
Real appreciation		2.46				2.43		
Capital stocks		3.01				2.98		
Real after-tax wage		1.03				1.03		
Supernumerary consumption		1.40				1.36		

(*Continued*)

Table 1. (*Continued*)

Wine Consumption	Price Effect	Expend. Effect	Total	Price Effect	Expenditure Effect	Total
Real consumption						
–Australia		0.25			0.25	
–South Australia		0.36			0.54	
–Rest of Australia		0.25			0.23	

Notes: [a]In scenario 1 with a 29% WET on wine, SSA is used to vary the export demand elasticities for each wine type: –6.5 ± 4. Estimated standard deviations for national output changes, based on these parameter ranges, are in parantheses.
[b]The shocks ascribed to the power of the consumption tax are: premium red –3 ± 14, premium white –3 ± 14 and non-premium 10.5 ± 27.5. Estimated standard deviations for national output changes, based on these ranges of shocks, are in parentheses.
[c]Price relative to CPI.
Source: Authors' FEDSA-WINE projections.

larger magnitude than the economy-wide average, this should induce a relatively larger movement of productive resources into the industry than the national average. The premium red and premium white wine industries export around half of their output by 2003, and so changes in their international competitiveness are also relevant.

The package introduces new taxes on service industries, many of which produce non-tradables (although tourism and education make relatively important contributions to exports). The GST package thus raises the price of non-tradables relative to tradables, resulting in a real exchange rate appreciation. Hence, we subtract the appreciation effect from an industry's cost reduction to calculate its gain in international competitiveness.

Premium red wine, the most export-oriented segment of the wine industry, has an input cost reduction of 4.5 per cent (relative to CPI), as does premium white, while that for non-premium wine is 4.8 per cent. The industry average cost reduction is 3.3 per cent: the average reduction in non-service industries is 5.0 per cent and in services 2.6 per cent. The difference between services and non-services is mainly due to the removal of wholesale taxes on intermediate inputs, with service industries being relatively less intensive in the use of taxed inputs than other industries. Therefore, the wine industry improves its competitiveness relative to other industries in the domestic market, but not relative to other non-service industries. In the scenario, the real exchange rate appreciates by 2.5 per cent (Table 1). Therefore, for an industry to improve its international competitiveness in the scenario, its unit cost reduction must exceed the real appreciation induced by the tax package, as the latter raises costs relative to foreign competitors.[7] Since the unit cost reduction for each wine segment exceeds the real appreciation, the tax reform package has a positive effect on international competitiveness.

Wine sold for domestic consumption introduces a complication. In addition to its relative cost reduction, there is also a change in its real consumer price. For non-premium wine, the tax increase with the GST package is more than offset by the unit cost reduction. For premium wines, however, the price increase is slightly larger than CPI (0.01 per cent for red and 0.28 per cent for white) due to the assumption that a higher proportion than that for non-premium wines is consumed on licensed premises. This makes premium wine consumption more exposed to the GST on the on-premise mark-up, and therefore subject overall to a higher effective tax increase.

Turning to equation (6), we can decompose the price and expenditure effects on household wine consumption. The pre-simulation values of $-\frac{\varepsilon_i}{\gamma}$ are 1.10, 0.66 and 0.33 for premium red, premium white and non-premium wines respectively. The national increase in supernumerary expenditure v is 1.40 per cent in the first scenario. Domestic consumption of the respective wine types increases by 1.53 per cent, 0.73 per cent and 1.03 per cent (Table 1). The change in premium red consumption calculated from (6) comprises a price effect of –0.01 (= 1.1 × –0.01) and an expenditure effect of 1.54 (= 1.1 × 1.40), for a total increase of 1.53 per cent. The two effects calculated for premium white wine are –0.19 (= 0.66 × –0.28) and 0.92 (= 0.66 × 1.40), totalling 0.73 per cent. And for non-premium wine, the price effect is 0.56 (= 0.33 × –1.67), the expenditure effect 0.46 (= 0.33 × 1.40) and the total 1.03 per cent. Decomposition shows us that expenditure effects dominate price effects.

One way of explaining industry outputs is through the market clearing assumption of the model: the percentage change in output is a weighted

---

[7] The average cost reduction we calculate (3.3%) is greater than the projected real appreciation (2.5%). But to calculate an economy-wide gain in international competitiveness, we should use more disaggregated data. In addition, sectoral export values rather than sector costs may be more appropriate weights for calculating the average cost reduction.

sum of percentage changes in sales volumes, decomposed by sales point. In quantity terms, let D denote domestic production, L_d local sales of domestic product and X exports. The market-clearing equation is

$$Dd = L_d l + Xx \tag{9}$$

The variables l and x are the percentage changes in local sales and exports that contribute to the percentage change in output d. Next, we obtain an expression for the change in local sales (l^*) in order to account for the effect of import replacement on domestic output

$$Ll^* = L_d l + Mm \tag{10}$$

where L is the total quantity of local sales from all sources, M the level of imports and m the percentage change in imports. The modified market-clearing equation becomes

$$Dd = Ll^* + Xx - Mm \tag{11}$$

In computing large change solutions, the decomposed components of equation (11) will not add exactly to Dd.[8] To overcome this, we define an ordinary change variable q so that

$$PD_q^0 = PDd, \tag{12}$$

where D^0 is the initial quantity of total sales, and P is the price level that is updated during the solution procedure. To decompose total output, let

$$q = q_l + q_x + q_m, \tag{13}$$

where q_l is the local market contribution, q_x the export contribution and q_m the import replacement contribution (each in ordinary change terms) to total output. The local market contribution to percentage change in domestic production is defined as the percentage change in local sales from local and imported sources, weighted by the value of locally sourced sales

$$q_l = \frac{L_d l^*}{D^0}. \tag{14}$$

---

[8] This is because multistep computation percentage changes are compounded, whereas ordinary changes are added.

The export contribution is $q_x = \frac{Xx}{D^0}$. Finally, the import contribution is calculated as a residual from equation (13). This decomposition method is known as 'Fan decomposition'.[9]

For each of the three wine types, at the national level, the local market contribution explains only part of the proportional increase in output in the first scenario. For premium red wine, this contribution is 0.67 per cent out of the total increase in output of 1.76 per cent. For premium white wine, the contribution is 0.35 out of 1.29 per cent (Table 1). Although the consumer price of both premium wines rises slightly, the expenditure effect, through the increase in real incomes, dominates the local market contribution. The increase in international competitiveness of the premium wine segments translate to increased exports, as domestic consumption increases absorb only part of the increased output. The local market contribution explains virtually all the output increase for non-premium wine, due to the relatively small export weighting in total non-premium sales. Tax revenue collected from on-premise and off-premise wine consumption rises by 16.5 per cent due to a rise in the effective tax rate, relative to the pre-GST WST rate, and a slight increase in domestic consumption.

Systematic sensitivity analysis (SSA) can indicate the extent to which parameter choice influences modelled outcomes (Arndt 1996; Arndt and Pearson 1996). In this study, where we do not use formally estimated export demand elasticities, SSA is especially important. Hence, the wine export demand elasticities were varied uniformly from their base values by plus or minus 4 (i.e., -6.5 ± 4). This SSA method implies that any point in the range is equally likely to be the true parameter value as any other, with no bias towards mid-range values. The standard deviations for the contributions to national wine output percentage changes, based on the parameter range, appear in Table 1. In the first scenario, uncertainty surrounding export demand elasticities for premium wines translates to uncertainty in output changes, with standard deviations of 0.36 per cent for red and 0.26 per cent for white wine. For non-premium wine, export

---

[9] The method is named after Mr Fan Mingtai of the Beijing Institute of Quantitative and Technical Economics.

demand parameter choice is less critical, as sales are mostly to the domestic market.[10]

3.2. The second scenario: Using SSA to depict policy uncertainty

Under the proposed GST with a top-up *ad valorem* WET, interest remains in alternative tax proposals, including a volumetric WET. Some lobbyists continue to advocate a volumetric tax on wine as a more direct means of addressing the alleged negative externalities associated with alcohol abuse. Some groups are also seeking higher taxes on wine, given that taxes on beer and spirits are higher than on wine in Australia (Wittwer 2000, Table F.1). Setting the tax on wine to the pre-GST levels applying to beer therefore is one political possibility.

Others argue that Australia's wine tax is already excessive by the standards of other wine-producing nations, which may provide a case for lower taxes (Berger and Anderson 1999). The sole purpose of most varieties of wine grapes is as an input into wine production. Hence, grape prices are highly sensitive to changes in market conditions for wine and, at least in the short run, taxation policies. This sensitivity might explain why there was no consumption tax on wine in Australia until 1984, apart from a two-year period in the early 1970s. Much of the impending massive increase in wine grape supply will coincide with the first few vintages under a GST. In response to industry concerns of falling prices, and the possibility that the tax hike on wine under the GST may shoulder a disproportionate share of the blame for this, the Commonwealth government may consider, in extreme political circumstances, reducing the top-up tax on wine.

---

[10] FEDSA-WINE's long-run closure assumes costless capital reallocation. An alternative assumption, to reflect a degree of risk aversion among investors, is that the rate of return on capital attracts premiums (discounts) as capital stocks increase (decrease). If we use this method to diminish the growth in capital stocks arising from the GST package to 1.0 per cent (approximately the long-run increase modelled by Dixon and Rimmer, 1999), aggregate household consumption does not change relative to the base case. This makes the percentage change in output more dependent on exports, and more sensitive to export demand parameter choice.

In the second scenario, systematic sensitivity analysis is used to address this policy uncertainty by varying the consumer tax on wine. The maximum shock applied to wine is equal to the pre-GST beer rate of taxation using a volumetric top-up tax. The minimum shock applied is equal to a GST with no top-up tax. The mean shocks entail a decrease in the tax on premium wine and a substantial increase in the tax on non-premium wine. These are equivalent to introducing a partly volumetric top-up tax.

For premium wines, the local market contribution (driven by positive price and expenditure effects) explains most of the total increase in output for premium wines. This is because a lower rate of taxation induces more imports and diverts sales from exports. The mean output gains are higher than in the first scenario, being 4.6 per cent for premium red wine and 2.9 per cent for premium white wine (Table 1). The standard deviations of the total output changes, although relatively large, are smaller than for the local market contributions alone, indicating substitution between domestic and overseas sales. The respective standard deviations for the local contributions and total outputs indicate that although the premium segments remain sensitive to the rate of consumer taxes on wine, the sensitivity is smaller than if the segments were less export oriented. Note that the output gains in scenario one for premium wines are below the range of gains implied by the means and standard deviations in the second scenario. This indicates that the 29 per cent WET on wine as part of the GST package is not a good outcome for the premium segment of the industry (using the pre-GST beer rate of taxation as a worst-case tax scenario).

The non-premium segment presents a different picture. The range of shocks imposed implies that there is only a small probability that the tax rate on non-premium wine will decrease. The outcome for the segment is dominated by the local market contribution. In the long run, the non-premium wine segment can withstand a moderate consumer tax increase without a loss of output, due to the relative cost reduction of the industry as a result of the GST. A revenue-neutral volumetric WET (which the mean shocks in scenario two approximate, with a wine tax revenue increase over the base case of only 0.4 per cent) as part of the GST package appears not to be output reducing for the non-premium segment, as non-premium output expands in scenario two. But raising the volumetric tax per unit of alcohol above the revenue-neutral rate would remove the gains in competitiveness arising from the GST package entirely for the non-premium wine segment.

National welfare, as measured by real consumption, barely changes between scenarios one and two. But the gain in real consumption is larger in South Australia in scenario two than scenario one. The proportion of premium wine in total wine production is larger in South Australia than the rest of the nation, so that a volumetric tax favours the region slightly.[11]

The introduction of a revenue-neutral volumetric WET would have a positive price effect on premium wine output and a negative price effect on non-premium wine. The outcome would be positive for the premium segments and ambiguous for the non-premium segment. A volumetric tax implies a large increase in taxes on non-premium wine, so the difference between the no top-up tax option and a volumetric WET option (at the pre-GST beer rate of taxation) is greater for non-premium than premium wines. Hence, the estimated standard deviation of output arising from policy uncertainty is greater for the non-premium segment, despite its relatively small income (and hence own-price) elasticity.

3.3. Modelling a volumetric top-up tax under alternative demand assumptions

The substitution effect arising from changes in consumer prices may have two parts: specific substitution, in which the marginal utility of income is held constant; and general substitution, in which goods compete for an extra dollar of income. The Klein-Rubin based linear expenditure system, as used in FEDSA-WINE, assumes preference independence. This implies there are no specific substitution possibilities.

The Klein-Rubin assumption may be appropriate in a model in which all commodities represent broad aggregations of different classes of goods. As disaggregation increases, some goods become more alike

---

[11] The change in tax instrument explains part of the additional gain in real consumption in South Australia. The remainder is attributable to the lower increase in wine tax revenue in scenario two than scenario one relative to the base case, as increased wine taxes penalise the state.

and consequently are more likely to display specific substitution at least within a group of goods. The three wine types in FEDSA-WINE are candidates for specific substitutability. Here, we model the introduction of the GST package with a volumetric tax, applied at the pre-GST beer rate of taxation. Two different household demand assumptions are used in modelling wine consumption. The third scenario uses the Klein-Rubin type as in the previous scenarios. The fourth scenario uses modified household demand equations, based on the methodology of Clements and Smith (1983), and used previously by Meagher et al. (1985) and CIE (1995b), to allow for specific substitutability between wine types.

Clements and Smith describe how to include a block of commodities for which own- and cross-price parameters have been estimated into a linear expenditure system. The utility function is divided into two, in this case, a set of wine commodities (S_w) containing the first w commodities, and a set of non-wine commodities (S_r)

$$U(X_1, ..., X_n) = U_1(X_1 ..., X_w) + U_2(X_{w+1}, ..., X_n) \quad (15)$$

Demand for a composite wine commodity is determined within a Stone-Geary utility function, as for the non-wine commodities in the model.

Let us first note the relationship between the unconditional Slutsky parameters (π_{ij}) and the uncompensated price elasticities (η_{ij}), where S_i is the expenditure share of good i

$$\eta_{ij} = \pi_{ij} / S_i - S_j \varepsilon_i \quad (16)$$

In the preference-independent Stone-Geary form, the unconditional Slutsky matrix is

$$\pi_{ij} = \frac{1}{\gamma}\left[\beta_i \left(\delta_i - \beta_j\right)\right] \quad (17)$$

with $\delta_{ij} = 1$ and $\delta_{ij} = 0$ for $i \neq j$. A composite wine commodity W forms part of the linear expenditure system. However, within the wine block, if we have additional own- and cross-price parameter estimates, the unconditional Slutsky matrix for wine commodities becomes

Table 2. Demand parameters in the modified demand system of FEDSA-WINE

	Conditional Slutsky Coefficients (× 100)			Uncompensated Unconditional Price Elasticities, 2003 Database		
	π_{i1}^w	π_{i2}^w	π_{i3}^w	η_{i1}	η_{i2}	η_{i3}
Premium red	−0.21	0.14	0.07	−1.16	0.04	0.11
Premium white	0.14	−0.24	0.10	0.05	−0.81	0.12
Non-premium	0.07	0.10	−0.17	0.18	0.16	−0.71

$$\pi_{ij} = \pi_{ij}^w + \frac{1}{\gamma}\left[\beta_w(1-\beta_w)\right]\beta_i'\beta_j' \tag{18}$$

In (18), π_{ij}^ω is the matrix of conditional Slutsky parameters, β_W is the marginal budget share of the wine composite, and $\beta_i' = (\beta_i / \beta_w)$ is the conditional marginal budget share of each wine type. Equation (17) calculates the Slutsky parameter when one or both of i and j are in the set S_r, and equation (18) applies only when both i and j are S_w. In the absence of estimated parameters specifically applicable to the wine disaggregation of the model, imposed Slutsky parameters are used in the modified system of demand for wine, as shown in Table 2.

A volumetric top-up tax on wine introduced at the equivalent of the pre-GST beer rate results in output increases for both premium wines. However, the local market effect switches sign, from being slightly negative with preference independence to being positive if the wine types are specifically substitutable. With the standard demand form, the output of the non-premium wine segment of decreases by 3.4 per cent, whereas with specific substitutability, the decline is 7.2 per cent (Table 3).

Non-premium grapes, unlike premium grapes, are multi-purpose, being sold as either inputs to non-premium wine, or as table or dried grapes. Since the wine boom started in the late 1980s, table and dried grape exports have declined as wine exports have grown (ABS 1999). A tax increase on non-premium wine increases the availability of non-premium grapes for export. In the case of the Klein-Rubin demand form, the export effect almost completely offsets the local market effect, so that there is little change in output. With the Clements-Smith modification, the

Table 3. Pre-GST beer rate on wine in GST package, % change from base case

Scenario:	3				4			
Household Demand Form	Clements-Smith Modification				Klein-Rubin			
Fan Decomposition	Local Market	Export	Import Share	Total	Local Market	Export	Import Share	Total
Non-premium grapes	−3.02	1.88	−0.01	−1.21	−1.30	1.05	0.00	−0.26
Wine								
Premium red	0.21	1.21	0.02	1.45	−0.57	1.32	0.06	0.80
Premium white	0.27	0.94	0.08	1.29	−0.55	1.06	0.20	0.70
Non-premium	−7.87	0.42	0.33	−7.18	−3.95	0.38	0.22	−3.37

Source: Authors' FEDSA-WINE projections.

export effect offsets less of the drop in local market sales, so that output declines by 1.2 per cent.

4. Conclusion

The premium segments of the wine industry could still gain from the GST package even though it was accompanied by a substantial increase in the wine consumption tax. This is because the package is likely to increase the international competitiveness of the export-oriented premium segments of the industry, partly offsetting the adverse impact on the domestic market of any wine tax hike. For non-premium wine, where the total outcome is more dependent on domestic sales, an increase in the top-up tax on non-premium wine beyond the 29 per cent WET imposed on 1 July 2000 (e.g., by introducing a volumetric tax) could eliminate the benefit of lower input costs arising from the GST package.

The two main reasons for having a top-up tax on wine are to collect revenue and to address any net negative externalities arising from wine consumption. In principle the GST should have eliminated the first reason by raising sufficient revenue from taxing all consumption of goods and services at an appropriate uniform rate. As to the second reason, if there are net negative externalities, the most direct approach would be to tax the source of the externality, namely alcohol, which suggests a volumetric tax should be used. But the perceived health benefits of moderate wine consumption are encouraging the industry to argue that the net externalities are positive, not negative, and so the WET should be removed. In the end it is likely that political sensitivities, rather than difficult-to-resolve debate over the size of the net externalities from wine consumption, will determine the taxes imposed on wine.

References

ABS 1999, *Australian Wine and Grape Industry*, Catalogue no. 1329.0.

Abdulla, A. and Duffus, G. 1988, 'The Demand for Wine in Australia', Contributed paper to the Australian Economics Society Annual Conference, Australian National University.

Armington, P. 1969, 'The Geographic Pattern of Trade and the Effects of Price Changes', *IMF Staff Papers*, vol. 17, pp. 176–199.

Arndt, C. 1996, 'An introduction to systematic sensitivity analysis via Gaussian quadrature', GTAP Technical Paper No. 2, Purdue University.

Arndt, C. and Pearson, K. 1996, 'How to carry out systematic sensitivity analysis via Gaussian quadrature and GEMPACK', GTAP Technical Paper No. 3, Purdue University.

AWEC 2000, *Wine Export Approval Report*, Australian Wine Export Council, March.

Berger, N. and Anderson, K. 1999, 'Consumer and Import Taxes in the World Wine Market: Australia in International Perspective', *Australian Agribusiness Review*, Vol. 7, June.

Berger, N., Spahni, P. and Anderson, K. 1999, *Bilateral Trade Patterns in the World Wine Market, 1988 to 1997, A Statistical Compendium*, Centre for International Economic Studies.

CIE 1995a, 'Additional simulations with the grape and wine industry model', Prepared for the South Australian Development Council, Centre for International Economics.

CIE 1995b, 'Generation of demand parameters for an economy-wide model of the grape and wine industry', Prepared for the Commonwealth Government Inquiry into the Wine Grape and Wine Industry, Centre for International Economics.

Clements, K. and Selvanathan, S. 1991, 'The economic determinants of alcohol consumption', *Australian Journal of Agricultural Economics*, vol. 35, pp. 209–231.

Clements, K. and Smith, D. 1983, 'Extending the consumption side of the ORANI model', Impact Project Preliminary Working Paper No. OP-38, University of Melbourne.

Dixon, P., Parmenter, B., Sutton, J. and Vincent, D. 1982, *ORANI: A Multisectoral Model of the Australian Economy*, North-Holland, Amsterdam.

Dixon, P. and Rimmer, M. 1999, 'Changes in Indirect Taxes in Australia: A Dynamic General Equilibrium Analysis', *Australian Economic Review*, vol. 32, pp. 327–348.

Horridge J., Parmenter, B. and Pearson, K. 1998, *ORANI-G: A General Equilibrium Model of the Australian Economy*, Centre of Policy Studies and Impact Project, Monash University.

Klein, L. and Rubin, H. 1949, 'A constant-utility index of the cost of living', *Review of Economic Studies*, vol. 15, pp. 84–87.

Madden, J. 1992, 'The Theoretical Structure of the Federal Model', CREA Paper No. TS-02, Centre for Regional Economic Analysis, University of Tasmania.

Meagher, G.A., Parmenter, B., Rimmer, R. and Clements, K. 1985, 'ORANI-WINE: Tax issues and the Australian wine industry', *Review of Marketing and Agricultural Economics*, vol. 53, pp. 47–62.

Naqvi, F. and Peter, M. 1996, 'A Multiregional, Multisectoral Model of the Australian Economy', *Australian Economic Papers*, Vol. 35, pp. 94–113.

Osmond, R. and Anderson, K. 1998, *Trends and Cycles in the Australian Wine Industry, 1850 to 2000*, Centre for International Economic Studies.

Wittwer, G. 2000, *The Australian Wine Industry During a Period of Boom and Tax Changes*, unpublished Ph.D. dissertation, University of Adelaide.

Wittwer, G., Berger, N. and Anderson, K. 2001, 'Modelling the world wine market to 2005: Impacts of structural and policy changes,' Contributed Paper for the AARES Annual Conference, Adelaide, 23–25 January.

Chapter 18

Excise and Import Taxes on Wine Versus Beer and Spirits: An International Comparison*

Kym Anderson[†]

Abstract

Nearly all countries tax the domestic consumption of alcoholic beverages. However, the rates of taxation, and the tax instruments used, vary enormously between countries. This study provides estimates, for a wide range of high-income and developing countries, of the consumer tax equivalents (CTEs) of wine, beer and spirits taxes as of 2008. It encompasses wholesale sales taxes, excise taxes and import tariffs expressed both in dollars per litre of alcohol and as a percentage of what the

---

*First published in *Economic Papers* 29(2): 215–28, June 2010. Revision of a paper presented at the AARES/AAWE Workshop on *The World's Wine Markets by 2030*, Adelaide Convention Centre, 8–9 February 2010. Thanks are due to Jayanthi Thennakoon for research assistance, and to GWRDC (Project Number UA08/04) and the University of Adelaide's Wine2030 Research Network for financial support. The views expressed are the author's alone and not necessarily those of any of the funders.

JEL classifications: H21, H22, H23, F13

Correspondence: Kym Anderson, School of Economics, University of Adelaide, North Terrace campus, Adelaide, SA 5005, Australia. Email: kym.anderson@adelaide.edu.au

[†] University of Adelaide

wholesale price would be without those taxes (as many taxes are volumetric and so their percentage CTE rates vary with the price of the product). The wine CTE tends to be lower in countries with a large wine industry, by which standard Australia is shown to have relatively high wine CTEs at least for premium wine. However, because Australia uses a percentage tax rather than the far more commonly used volumetric tax measure, it has a relatively low rate for non-premium wine.

1. Introduction

Ten years ago, the Australian Government introduced a goods-and-services tax (GST). In doing so, it replaced the wholesale sales tax on wine of 41 per cent with a top-up wholesale Wine "Equalisation" Tax (WET), which, together with the GST, brought in roughly the same tax revenue from domestic wine consumers as the tax it replaced.[1] Alternative proposals, pushed by some firms in the beer and spirits industries and by anti-alcohol interest groups, suggested that the WET should be much higher and volume based.[2] Australia's rate of wine consumer taxation was shown by Berger and Anderson (1999) to be high by OECD standards at that time, and especially by the standards of significant wine-producing/exporting countries. But Australia's type of wine tax is unusual in being *ad valorem* (a percentage of the wholesale price) rather than specific (in cents per litre of alcohol).

---

[1] Government revenue raising is a significant, but not the only, reason for the current tax. Its relevance should have diminished in the context of a major tax reform that introduced a general GST in 2000. An additional motivation for taxing wine and other alcoholic beverages is to offset perceived negative health, crime, road accident and other social externalities resulting from excessive alcohol consumption. In the case of wine, however, there is evidence of positive health benefits from moderate drinking, especially of red wine. Assessments of those externalities and other aspects affecting the optimal type and rate of taxation of different alcoholic beverages are provided in, for example, Pogue and Sgontz (1989), Kenkel (1996), Cnossen (2007, 2009), Clarke (2008), Carpenter and Dobkin (2010), and Freebairn (2010).

[2] For an empirical analysis of these and other wine tax options for Australia at that time, using an economy-wide model, see Wittwer and Anderson (2002). A contemporary empirical analysis of options under consideration currently, with a focus on their distributional consequences for Australia's various wine regions, is available in Anderson *et al.* (2010).

The Australian Government is again considering major tax reform, following a review of the overall Australian tax system, namely the Henry Review, which was completed at the end of 2009 (Henry, 2009). As part of that new review, the question of wine and other alcohol tax rates and instruments has come into focus — encouraged somewhat by the call by the World Health Organization (2009) for stronger measures to reduce the harmful use of alcohol, and the recent adoption of tougher measures in such countries as France and the United Kingdom.

Australia's wine industry has argued that the rate of taxation of wine should not be raised because they claim (a) it is still high by international standards and (b) wine is drunk mainly by adults in moderation with food rather than being the main beverage of choice for young binge drinkers such that it has fewer social costs than other forms of alcohol (WFA, 2010). This study examines that first claim by comparing recent tax measures for Australia with those of other countries, as a contribution to the debate. In doing so, tax rates for other alcoholic beverages are also compiled, as the optimal wine tax is not independent of the tax rates affecting the consumption of substitute products. The taxes normally considered are domestic excise taxes, but countries can — and some do — use import taxes at their border as an additional or alternative way of raising the consumer price. Hence, they are also considered here.[3]

This study begins by reviewing the basic economics of taxing wine assuming that there are two different types of domestic consumers. It then reviews the data available and the methodology for comparing rates of taxation across countries. Estimates are then presented on the domestic alcohol taxes in Australia and forty-five other high-income and developing countries that together account for more than 90 per cent of global wine consumption. The tax rates are expressed both as *ad valorem* equivalents and as volumetric rates (per litre of alcohol), and at a selection of price points. The latter is helpful for considering the impact these taxes are having on different types of consumers; but it is also helpful for analysts

---

[3] Export subsidies could also raise the consumer price, but they have been minor in the past and are mostly phased out now. The effect of government policies on grape and wine producer incentives are ignored here, as wine is a traded product and so those supply-side effects mainly influence the share of production exported rather than the price paid by domestic consumers.

seeking to use these estimates in economic models of wine markets in which the distinction is made between, say, non-premium, commercial premium and super-premium wines. The *ad valorem* consumer tax equivalents (CTEs) of import tariffs on those products are then presented, both on their own and then in combination with domestic taxes so as to get a set of overall consumer tax rates. The final section draws out implications for the ongoing tax reform debate in Australia.

2. The economics of taxing wine

The simplest way of modelling the effects of wine consumer taxation in an open economy such as Australia's, in which two-thirds of wine production is exported and (until very recently) only a tiny fraction of still wine consumption is imported, is to use a partial equilibrium diagram, assume that the country is a price taker, and examine the effects on such things as domestic prices, quantities consumed domestically and exported, and national economic welfare. In Figure 1a, it is assumed further that there are no externalities associated with producing, consuming or trading wine, so the marginal private and social benefits (MSB_f and MPB_f) coincide as do the marginal and social costs of production (MSC_f and MPC_f). If P_f is the free-trade price, then with no government intervention $O_f Q_f$ units are produced, $O_f C_f$ units are consumed domestically and $C_f Q_f$ is exported. An *ad valorem* tax on domestic consumers of 100t per cent (or an equivalent volumetric tax) would lower the domestic consumption (and raise exports) by $C_f' C_f$ units, raise the government revenue by area acmn, but reduce the consumer welfare by area admn. Hence, there would be a net reduction in national economic welfare of area acd.

Figure 1a may well apply to the fine wine market. Indeed, it may understate the national welfare cost of such taxation if, as suggested by extensive reviews of the health science literature (such as by Lippi *et al.*, 2010 and Karmel, 2010), moderate wine consumption can have net positive health externalities depending on the social setting. In what follows, it is assumed that Figure 1a applies to the fine wine market, and that its demand curve is unaffected by the consumer price of basic wine (zero elasticity of substitution between fine and basic wine).

Excise and Import Taxes on Wine Versus Beer and Spirits 441

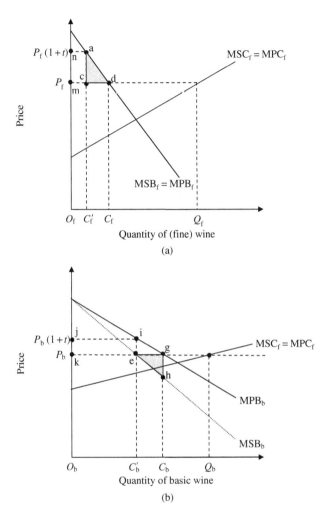

Figure 1. The market for wine in a small, open, wine-exporting economy: (a) (Fine) wine with no externalities; (b) Basic wine with a negative consumption externality (Source: Author's depiction)

The market for basic wine, in contrast, looks more like Figure 1b, in which (i) the domestic demand curve (MPB_b) is more elastic than in Figure 1a because beer and basic spirits are assumed to be substitutes for basic wine, especially for binge drinkers simply wanting alcohol (see table 4 of Srivastava and Zhao, 2010), and (ii) the marginal social benefit curve (MSB_b) is increasingly below MPB_b because of the negative externalities on society associated with excessive alcohol consumption.[4] If P_b is the free-trade price for basic wine, then with no government intervention O_bQ_b units are produced, O_bC_b units are consumed domestically and C_bQ_b units are exported. An *ad valorem* tax on domestic consumers of 100t per cent would lower the domestic consumption (and raise exports) of basic wine by $C_b'C_b$ units, raise the government revenue by area eijk and reduce the consumer welfare by area gijk, but it would reduce the externality on the rest of the society by area ighe. Hence, there would be a net improvement in national economic welfare of area ghe from this tax on basic wine.

If the tax on consumption of basic wine also applied to higher-priced fine wine at the same *ad valorem* rate, the dollar tax per unit would be higher on the latter than the former, and the national welfare gain from the taxing of basic wine would be reduced by the welfare loss in the fine wine market, e.g. area acd in Figure 1a.

If area acd in Figure 1a exceeds area ghe in Figure 1b, society could be worse off overall. The likelihood of an overall loss to society is higher, the bigger are the ratios of P_f to P_b and C_f to C_b. As those ratios have been rising over time in the course of income growth in Australia, so too has that likelihood of an overall loss from the current *ad valorem* WET. One way to reduce that loss prospect is to have a lower *ad valorem* rate for fine wine but, if that is too politically difficult to introduce (e.g. because only richer people drink fine wine — see figure 4 of Srivastava and Zhao, 2010), then a change from a common *ad valorem* WET to a common volumetric WET would be a more covert way of achieving a similar outcome.

The optimal rate of the volumetric WET would be difficult to determine even if the only reason for government intervention was to overcome the negative externalities associated with excessive alcohol consumption.

---

[4] It is common for analysts to represent the adverse social effects of excessive alcohol by raising the marginal cost curve. In the closed-economy framework of such analyses (e.g., Pogue and Sgontz, 1989; Kenkel, 1996), that will generate the same optimal tax rate as is generated by including them as a reduction in national marginal benefit. In the more-appropriate small open economy case of the Australian wine market, however, it is only domestic consumption that is generating the externality for the nation, hence the need to represent that externality on the demand side of the diagram (Corden, 1997).

One reason is that the marginal net gain in Figure 1b from raising the WET on basic wine consumption has to be equated with the marginal net loss in Figure 1a from raising the WET on fine wine consumption. Britten-Jones *et al.* (1987) show that both the slopes of the marginal benefit curves and the gap between the MSB_b and MPB_b curves affect that calculus. The gap between the MSB_b and MPB_b curves is not independent of other policy initiatives aimed at more-directly curbing adverse effects of excess alcohol consumption, such as information programs, enforcement of drink-driving laws, restrictions on advertising alcoholic beverages, liquor-licensing laws that regulate on-premise consumption and ban sales to young people, and the extent of subsidies to health care. Another complexity is that the slope of the MPB_b curve depends on the elasticities of substitution between basic wine and other alcoholic beverages. The position of that curve is further to the right, the higher the taxes on such beverages as beer and spirits (and the lower the elasticities of substitution between wine and alternative stimulants such as illicit drugs and petrol sniffing).

The supply and demand characteristics mentioned in the two preceding paragraphs, including the rates of tax on non-wine beverage consumption, vary across countries and over time. There is thus no reason in principle to expect the optimal wine tax rates to be the same across countries, or to change in the same way as economic growth and structural changes occur.

Countries also differ in the extent to which they are "small" in the sense of being price takers in the international market for basic and fine wines. Fine wines especially tend to be differentiated products, so a country's export demand curve for them would be somewhat downward sloping, rather than horizontal as in Figure 1. Altering that assumption would not affect the above qualitative conclusions regarding the optimal consumer tax, but it would affect the outcome quantitatively for producers because the tax would shift more sales to the export market and thereby depress the price received for them. That means a tax reform that replaced a uniform *ad valorem* tax on all domestic wine consumption with a uniform volumetric tax (whose *ad valorem* equivalent was therefore higher for basic wine but lower for fine wine) would raise relative returns to producers of fine wine and hence encourage grapegrowers and winemakers to upgrade the quality of their products.

With this analysis in mind, we turn now to examining the cross-country empirical evidence on alcohol tax rates.

3. Methodology and data sources

As specific (volumetric, dollars per litre of beverage or of alcohol) as well as *ad valorem* (percentage) tax rates are used in many countries, the CTE in percentage terms typically varies with the price of wine. This distinction is important because in recent years, the world wine market has been characterised by a trend towards premium wine consumption, and in some traditional wine-consuming countries the volume of non-premium wine consumption has fallen greatly. We therefore identify the tax type (specific or *ad valorem)* and express the CTE in terms of dollars per litre or bottle as well as an *ad valorem* equivalent for standard beer and spirits and for three different retail pre-tax wine prices: for non-premium wine (A$2.50/litre at the wholesale pre-tax level), for mid-range commercial premium wine (A$7.50/litre) and for super-premium wine (A$20/litre). The chosen price for non-premium wine, such as sold in casks (A$2.50/litre wholesale pre-tax), with a 29 per cent excise tax (WET), a 33 per cent mark-up to retail and the 10 per cent GST, implies a retail price in Australia of $18.90 for a four-litre cask. For commercial premium wine, A$7.50/litre wholesale implies, with a 29 per cent excise tax (WET), a 50 per cent mark-up to retail and 10 per cent GST, a retail price of $12 for a 750-millilitre bottle; and for super-premium wine (A$20/litre wholesale) and the same mark-ups as commercial premium implies a retail price of almost $32 for a 750-millilitre bottle. Two types of sparkling wine also are considered, at wholesale pre-tax prices of A$7.50 and A$25/litre. In making these calculations we assume that wine and beer degree alcohol contents are 12 and 4 per cent, respectively, and that the absolute alcohol content for spirits is 40 per cent.

The CTE is defined as the percentage by which the pre-tax wholesale price has been raised by beverage taxes (but not including the GST or VAT).[5] To estimate it, numerous assumptions have to be made. First, the

---

[5] Most countries also have a value-added or GST applying to beverages, but since those taxes apply at the retail level to most other goods as well we do not add them to the

CTE is assumed to apply also at the retail level, on the assumption that the wholesale-to-retail margin is *ad valorem*. If in fact those margins are somewhat independent of the product price, then our CTE estimate will overstate the impact on consumers at the retail level.

Second, we assume that imported and domestically produced wines are perfect substitutes. That is, we assume that the domestic prices of all wines, not just those imported, are raised by the amount of any import tariff. The tariff portion of the price is then also subject to any domestic consumer tax. Given the heterogeneous nature of wine, it is unlikely that the average price of all wine will increase by the full amount of any wine tariff, and more so the less substitutability there is between domestically produced and foreign wines (the degree of which in practice differs by the country of origin). This assumption inflates the estimated CTE above its true value in countries that are significant producers of wines that differ from those countries' imports. However, this is more or less offset by our inability to include estimates of the contribution to the true CTE of non-tariff barriers to wine imports.

Third, neither the average pre-tax retail prices of a bottle of commercial or super-premium wine or a litre of non-premium wine, nor the shares of each of these types in national wine consumption, are reliably known for more than a handful of countries. Hence an average CTE for each country is not calculated for wine as a group. Instead, we calculate the CTE at price levels that approximate the average prices in Australian dollars for the three chosen categories of wine sold in Australia in 2008. For each of beer and spirits we use, for simplicity of comparison, only one representative price for standard product (A$2 and A$15 per litre at the wholesale pre-tax level, respectively).

The primary source for domestic tax data are national government websites plus the European Commission (2008) and the OECD (2006, 2008). The import tariffs are taken from the WITS database (World Bank and UNCTAD, 2009). Depending on the importing country, a bottle of wine could face a specific (volume-based) tariff, an *ad valorem* (value-based)

---

beverage-specific taxes. However, for completeness, they are reported in the appendix of Anderson (2010), along with the foreign exchange rates used to convert specific tax rates expressed in national currencies to a common currency.

tariff and/or a tariff based on the volume of alcohol in the product. Specific tariffs based on volume are the most popular in Europe and the United States, whereas *ad valorem* tariffs based on product value are the norm in the Asia-Pacific region with the exception of Japan and Malaysia.

4. CTE calculations

Summaries of the estimates of the CTE by tax instrument for the various beverages, expressed both in dollars and in percentages, are shown in Tables 1–3, each of which is discussed in turn.[6]

Table 1 shows the CTE for still wine, beer and spirits (excluding VAT or GST) in 2008, expressed as a percentage of selected wholesale pre-tax prices. Relative to other wine-exporting New World countries, and certainly European wine-exporting countries, Australia does indeed have higher *ad valorem* equivalent excise taxes on wine at all three price points. However, Australia's wine tax rates are lower than their counterparts in wine-importing countries, shown in the second half of Table 1, except in the case of wines above the commercial premium range. Furthermore, Australia has higher excise taxes also for beer and spirits than the average for either of those two groups of other countries. Thus by that international standard wine is lightly taxed relative to beer and spirits in Australia. The only group of wine consumers in Australia who could claim to be relatively highly taxed are those who buy super-premium wines — unlike consumers in most other countries because they have volumetric rather than *ad valorem* wine taxes. This is ironic, as consumption of expensive fine wines is least likely to contribute to the social problem of binge drinking.[7] There is no obvious economic justification for this type of penalising of consumers of high-quality wine, given the presence of tiered income tax rates that can deal adequately with any income distributional issues society may have.

---

[6] Appendix tables 1–6 of Anderson (2010) detail the rates used as the basis for calculating the CTEs.

[7] The story is much the same as for sparkling wines, that is, only consumers of the super-premium product could be considered relatively highly taxed in Australia (see appendix table 6 of Anderson, 2010).

Table 1. Ad valorem consumer tax equivalent of excise taxes on still wine, beer and spirits, July 2008[†] (as a per cent of the wholesale pre-tax prices shown in column heads)

	Non-Premium Wine (A$2.50/L)	Commercial Premium Wine (A$7.50/L)	Super Premium Wine (A$20/L)	Beer (A$2/L)	Spirits (A$15/L)
New World net wine exporters					
Argentina	3	3	3	4	18
Australia	29	29	29	76	171
Canada	26	9	3	1	31
Chile	15	15	15	15	27
New Zealand	85	28	11	42	103
South Africa	10	3	1	0	24
United States	23	8	3	1	31
Unweighted average	27	11	9	10	39
European net wine exporters					
Austria	0	0	0	20	44
Bulgaria	0	0	0	8	25
France	2	1	0	0	64
Germany	0	0	0	8	57
Greece	0	0	0	11	48
Hungary	0	0	0	21	44
Italy	0	0	0	24	35
Portugal	0	0	0	3	43
Romania	0	0	0	7	30
Slovak Republic	0	0	0	15	41
Slovenia	0	0	0	0	31
Spain	0	0	0	1	37
Switzerland	0	0	0	na	55
Unweighted average	0	0	0	10	43
High-income country net wine importers					
Belgium	31	10	4	17	77
Czech Republic	0	0	0	9	49
Denmark	54	18	7	0	89

(*Continued*)

Table 1. (Continued)

	Non-Premium Wine (A$2.50/L)	Commercial Premium Wine (A$7.50/L)	Super Premium Wine (A$20/L)	Beer (A$2/L)	Spirits (A$15/L)
Estonia	44	15	5	0	57
Finland	154	51	19	1	143
Iceland	*252*	*84*	*32*	1	*26*
Ireland	180	60	23	1	173
Japan	32	*11*	*4*	0	*11*
Latvia	28	9	4	0	39
Lithuania	34	11	4	0	49
Luxembourg	0	0	0	8	46
Netherlands	45	15	6	0	66
Norway	*253*	*84*	*32*	0	*202*
Poland	27	9	3	18	60
Sweden	151	50	19	1	234
United Kingdom	162	54	20	1	119
Unweighted average	91	30	11	0	90
Developing country net wine importers					
Brazil	10	10	10	40	60
Hong Kong	0	0	0	0	100
India	15	5	2	0	1
Korea	*33*	*33*	*33*	*94*	*94*
Malaysia	204	68	26	6	26
Mexico	25	25	25	25	*50*
Philippines	15	5	2	1	25
Taiwan	13	4	2	2	23
Thailand	173	58	22	9	0
Turkey	*183*	*61*	*23*	63	*304*
Unweighted average	67	27	14	24	68

Notes: [†]Tax rates in italics refer to January 2007. Wine and beer degree alcohol contents are assumed to be 12 and 4 per cent, respectively; the absolute alcohol content for spirits is assumed to be 40 per cent.
Source: Author's compilation based on Anderson (2010, appendix tables 1 and 2).

Table 2. Excise taxes on alcoholic beverages per litre of alcohol for still wine, beer and spirits, July 2008[†] (A$ at the wholesale pre-tax prices shown in column heads)

	Non-Premium Wine (A$2.50/L)	Commercial Premium Wine (A$7.50/L)	Super Premium Wine (A$20/L)	Beer (A$2/L)	Spirits (A$15/L)
Memo: Unweighted average, all high-income OECD countries					
	11.3	12.0	13.7	5.3	28.4
New World net wine exporters					
Argentina	0.6	1.9	5.0	2.0	6.8
Australia	6.0	18.1	48.3	38.0	64.1
Canada	5.4	5.6	5.0	0.5	11.6
Chile	3.1	9.4	25.0	7.5	10.1
New Zealand	17.7	17.5	18.3	21.0	38.6
South Africa	2.1	1.9	1.7	0.0	9.0
United States	4.8	5.0	5.0	0.5	11.6
Unweighted average	5.7	8.5	15.5	9.9	21.7
European net wine exporters					
Austria	0.0	0.0	0.0	10.0	16.5
Bulgaria	0.0	0.0	0.0	4.0	9.4
France	0.4	0.6	0.0	0.0	24.0
Germany	0.0	0.0	0.0	4.0	21.4
Greece	0.0	0.0	0.0	5.5	18.0
Hungary	0.0	0.0	0.0	10.5	16.5
Italy	0.0	0.0	0.0	12.0	13.1
Portugal	0.0	0.0	0.0	1.5	16.1
Romania	0.0	0.0	0.0	3.5	11.3
Slovak Republic	0.0	0.0	0.0	7.5	15.4
Slovenia	0.0	0.0	0.0	0.0	11.6
Spain	0.0	0.0	0.0	0.5	13.9
Switzerland	0.0	0.0	0.0	na	20.6
Unweighted average	0.0	0.0	0.0	4.9	16.0
High-income country net wine importers					
Belgium	6.5	6.3	6.7	8.5	28.9
Czech Republic	0.0	0.0	0.0	4.5	18.4
Denmark	11.3	11.3	11.7	0.0	33.4

(*Continued*)

Table 2. (*Continued*)

	Non-Premium Wine (A$2.50/L)	Commercial Premium Wine (A$7.50/L)	Super Premium Wine (A$20/L)	Beer (A$2/L)	Spirits (A$15/L)
Estonia	9.2	9.4	8.3	0.0	21.4
Finland	32.1	31.9	31.7	0.5	53.6
Iceland	*52.5*	*52.5*	*53.3*	0.5	*9.8*
Ireland	37.5	37.5	38.3	0.5	64.9
Japan	*6.7*	*6.9*	*6.7*	0.0	*4.1*
Latvia	5.8	5.6	6.7	0.0	14.6
Lithuania	7.1	6.9	6.7	0.0	18.4
Luxembourg	0.0	0.0	0.0	4.0	17.3
Netherlands	9.4	9.4	10.0	0.0	24.8
Norway	*52.7*	*52.5*	*53.3*	0.0	*75.8*
Poland	5.6	5.6	5.0	9.0	22.5
Sweden	31.5	31.3	31.7	0.5	87.8
United Kingdom	33.8	33.8	33.3	0.5	44.6
Unweighted average	18.8	18.8	19.0	1.8	33.8
Developing country net wine importers					
Brazil	2.1	6.3	16.7	20.0	22.5
Hong Kong	0.0	0.0	0.0	0.0	37.5
India	*3.1*	*3.1*	*3.3*	0.0	*0.4*
Korea	6.9	20.6	55.0	47.0	35.3
Malaysia	*42.5*	*42.5*	*43.3*	3.0	*9.8*
Mexico	5.2	15.6	41.7	12.5	18.8
Philippines	3.1	3.1	3.3	0.5	9.4
Taiwan	2.7	2.5	3.3	1.0	8.6
Thailand	36.0	36.3	36.7	4.5	0.0
Turkey	*38.1*	*38.1*	*38.3*	31.5	*114.0*
Unweighted average	14.0	16.8	24.2	12.0	25.6

Notes: †Tax rates in italics refer to January 2007. Wine and beer degree alcohol contents are assumed to be 12 and 4 per cent, respectively; the absolute alcohol content for spirits is assumed to be 40 per cent.
Source: Author's compilation based on Anderson (2010, appendix tables 1–5).

Table 3. Ad valorem consumer tax equivalent of excise plus import taxes on alcoholic beverages, 2008[†] (per cent)

	Non-Premium Wine (A$2.50/L)	Commercial Premium Wine (A$7.50/L)	Super Premium Wine (A$20/L)	Beer (A$2/L)	Spirits (A$15/L)
New World net wine exporters					
Argentina	21	21	21	17	31
Australia	30	30	30	76	171
Canada	26	9	3	1	31
Chile	17	17	17	16	28
New Zealand	86	29	12	42	103
South Africa	35	28	26	0	24
United States	23	8	3	1	31
Unweighted average	34	20	16	22	60
European net wine exporters					
Austria	21	7	3	20	44
Bulgaria	21	7	3	8	25
France	23	8	3	0	64
Germany	21	7	3	8	57
Greece	21	7	3	11	48
Hungary	21	7	3	21	44
Italy	21	7	3	24	35
Portugal	21	7	3	3	43
Romania	21	7	3	7	30
Slovak Republic	21	7	3	15	41
Slovenia	21	7	3	0	31
Spain	21	7	3	1	37
Switzerland	22	7	3	0	55
Unweighted average	21	7	3	10	43
High-income country net wine importers					
Belgium	52	17	7	17	77
Czech Republic	21	7	3	9	49
Denmark	75	25	10	0	89
Estonia	65	22	8	0	57

(*Continued*)

Table 3. (*Continued*)

	Non-Premium Wine (A$2.50/L)	Commercial Premium Wine (A$7.50/L)	Super Premium Wine (A$20/L)	Beer (A$2/L)	Spirits (A$15/L)
Finland	175	58	22	1	143
Iceland	*252*	*91*	*35*	3	26
Ireland	202	60	26	1	173
Japan	*32*	*11*	*4*	0	*12*
Latvia	49	16	7	0	39
Lithuania	55	18	7	0	49
Luxembourg	21	7	3	8	46
Netherlands	66	22	9	0	66
Norway	*253*	*84*	*32*	0	*202*
Poland	48	16	6	18	60
Sweden	172	58	22	1	234
United Kingdom	183	61	23	1	119
Unweighted average	109	36	13	4	90
Developing country net wine importers					
Brazil	22	22	22	50	77
Hong Kong	0	0	0	0	100
India	*165*	*155*	*152*	100	*151*
Korea	46	46	46	124	114
Malaysia	*na*	*na*	*na*	na	*na*
Mexico	28	28	28	26	52
Philippines	22	12	9	10	35
Taiwan	23	14	12	2	23
Thailand	232	117	81	51	52
Turkey	*240*	*118*	*80*	63	*305*
Unweighted average	87	57	48	47	101

Notes: †The most recent year available for tariffs is used if 2008 is not available. It is assumed that the tariff for wine in containers of more than two litres applies to non-premium wine and that the rate for smaller containers applies to the other wine types. The tariffs on imports into the EU-27 apply only to non-EU imports and so affect only a small volume of total imports for most member countries.

Source: Author's compilation based on Anderson (2010).

In Table 2, the CTEs are expressed not as percentages of the wholesale price but rather as dollars per litre of alcohol. These present a mirror to the numbers just summarised, in that they confirm (a) that low-quality wines below about A$7.50 are lightly taxed in Australia relative to most other countries except those that are net exporters of wine, and (b) that the alcohol in beer and spirits is taxed more in Australia than in most other countries, so making low-quality wine an even cheaper source of alcohol relative to non-wine sources in Australia than elsewhere.

Those first two tables refer only to domestic taxes on alcohol. Many countries also impose import duties on beverages at their border, which are the equivalent of a production subsidy and a consumption tax on like goods. These duties are low but often specific tariffs for most high-income countries,[8] but they are nontrivial for numerous developing countries. When the import duties (shown in Anderson, 2010, appendix table 7) are converted to *ad valorem* equivalents and combined with the *ad valorem* excise taxes shown in Table 1, Australia's relative position does not change much *vis-a-vis* other high-income countries, but the CTEs of developing countries now look higher compared with Australia's (Table 3). Even so, when illustrated as in Figures 2 and 3, Australia is seen as an outlier in terms of its high taxes on high-priced wines, whereas it is seen as more towards the low-tax end of the spectrum for non-premium wines.

In short, on a volume of alcohol basis, Australia's super-premium wine consumers face a CTE more than three times the unweighted average for high-income OECD countries of 14 per cent, whereas its non-premium consumers face a CTE of only half the unweighted average for that country group of 11 per cent (row 1 of Table 2).[9] Meanwhile Australia's beer and spirits CTEs are about seven times and more than twice the unweighted

---

[8] The calculated CTEs for North America are "lower bound" estimates of the true CTEs as the price effects of state monopoly controls on the distribution of alcohol in Canada, and myriad state-controlled non-tariff barriers to wine trade into the United States, have not been quantified. It is alleged, for example, that the Liquor Control Board of Ontario (possibly, the world's biggest importer of wine) applies a two-thirds mark-up on imported wine.

[9] Unweighted averages are shown because each taxing entity (country) is an equally interesting observation regardless of its size. In any case, calculating consumption-weighted averages would be problematic because data on consumption by wine price point are not readily available.

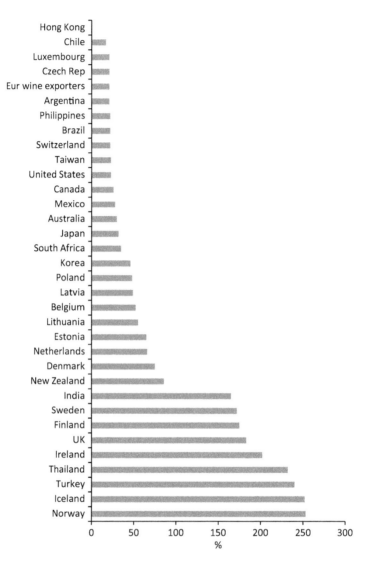

Figure 2. Ad valorem consumer tax equivalent of excise plus import taxes on non-premium wine, 2008 (per cent)
Source: Table 3.

Excise and Import Taxes on Wine Versus Beer and Spirits 455

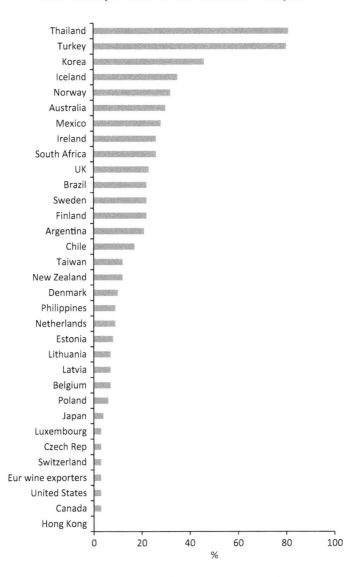

Figure 3. Ad valorem consumer tax equivalent of excise plus import taxes on super premium wine, 2008 (per cent)
Source: Table 3.

averages for high-income countries of 5 and 28 per cent, respectively. Hence relative to other beverage consumption, non-premium wine in Australia is taxed at well below the high-income country average and super-premium wine is taxed at far above that group's average — and to an even larger degree when the high-income country average is weighted according to the volume of wine consumption, as the largest consuming countries (France, Italy, Germany and Spain, accounting for around 40 per cent of global wine consumption) have the lowest taxes.

5. Implications for Australia's tax reform debate

The above international comparison provides a number of pointers of relevance to the Australian alcohol tax reform debate, including the following:

- Among the New World wine-exporters, Australia is the highest-taxing country for 750-millilitre bottles of wine above about A$7.50 wholesale pre-tax (and wine consumption is not taxed at all in most European wine-producing countries except slightly via a specific tariff at the European Union's external border).
- Even for non-premium wine retailing at <$20 for a four-litre cask, among the New World wine-exporters only New Zealand has (at 85 per cent) an *ad valorem* equivalent wine tax rate above Australia's.
- Among the wine-importing high-income countries, for 750-millilitre bottles of wine above A$7.50 wholesale pre-tax, the only countries with *ad valorem* equivalent wine tax rates above Australia's are the United Kingdom, Ireland and the Nordic countries.
- Even for the wine-importing developing countries for which data have been found, for 750-millilitre bottles of wine above $7.50 wholesale pre-tax only half have *ad valorem* equivalent wine tax rates above Australia's, namely, Korea, Malaysia, Thailand and Turkey (and India if import duties are included).
- Nonetheless, on a volume of alcohol basis, Australia's super-premium wine consumers face a CTE more than three times greater than the unweighted average high-income countries of 14 per cent, whereas its non-premium consumers face a CTE of only half that country group's average of 11 per cent.

- Since Australia's beer and spirits CTEs are about seven times and more than twice unweighted averages for high-income countries, relative to other beverage consumption Australia's non-premium wine is taxed at well below average and super-premium wine is taxed at well above the high-income country average.

Notwithstanding those comparisons, there has been strong lobbying by the health community for higher volumetric taxation of alcohol consumption in Australia, and by the beer and spirits industries for greater tax equality across types of alcoholic beverages. It is therefore not surprising that Australia's 2009 Henry review of taxation has focused on both the level of wine taxation and on whether the tax measure should remain *ad valorem*. Meanwhile, fine wine producers, especially those unable to afford the high start-up costs of exporting, have been supportive of a switch to volumetric taxation (so long as it does not involve an overall hike in wine taxes). If that switch does materialise, it will encourage more Australian vignerons to produce, and more Australians to consume, finer wines; and, in doing so, it is likely to bring Australia's wine tax system closer to a socially optimal regime.[10]

References

Anderson, K. (2010), 'Excise and Import Taxes on Wine vs Beer and Spirits: An International Comparison', Working Paper 0510, Wine Economics Research Centre, University of Adelaide, March. Available at: http:// www.adelaide.edu.au/wine-econ.

Anderson, K., Valenzuela, E. and Wittwer, G. (2010), 'Wine Export Demand Shocks and Wine Tax Reform in Australia: Regional Consequences Using an Economy-Wide Approach', Working Paper 0210, Wine Economics Research Centre, University of Adelaide, February. Available at: http://www.adelaide.edu.au/wine-econ. Since published in *Economic Papers*, 30(3), 386–99, September 2011.

Berger, N. and Anderson, K. (1999), 'Consumer and Import Taxes in the World Wine Market: Australia in International Perspective', *Australasian Agribusiness Review,* **7**, June. Available at: http://www.agrifood.info/ review/1999/Berger.html.

---

[10] It would have major implications for the regional distribution of winegrape production, however, especially in the short term. For an economywide modelling analysis of what impacts a change in the type and rate of tax on wine might have on wine and other beverage consumption in Australia, and on the wine industry's regional production and exports, see Anderson *et al.* (2010).

Britten-Jones, M., Nettle, R.S. and Anderson, K. (1987), 'On Optimal Second-Best Trade Intervention in the Presence of a Domestic Divergence', *Australian Economic Papers*, **26**, 332–6.
Carpenter, C. and Dobkin, C. (2010), 'Alcohol Regulation and Crime', NBER Working Paper 15828, Cambridge, MA.
Clarke, H. (2008), 'The Economist's Way of Thinking About Alcohol Policy', *Agenda*, **15**, 27–44.
Cnossen, S. (2007), 'Alcohol Taxation and Regulation in the European Union', *International Tax and Public Finance*, **14**, 699–732.
Cnossen, S. (2009), 'Excise Taxation in Australia', Paper presented at a conference on Australia's Future Tax System, University of Melbourne, 18–19 June. Available at: http://www.taxreview.treasury.gov.au.
Corden, W.M. (1997), *Trade Policy and Economic Welfare* (revised edition). Clarendon Press, Oxford.
European Commission (2008), *Excise Duty Tables: Part 1: Alcoholic Beverages*. European Commission, Brussels.
Freebairn, J.W. (2010), 'Special Taxation of Alcoholic Beverages to Correct Market Failures', *Economic Papers*, **29**(2), 200–14.
Henry, K. (2009), *Australia's Future Tax System: Report to the Treasurer* (The Henry Review). The Treasury, Canberra, December. Available at: http://www.taxreview.treasury.gov.au.
Karmel, C. (2010), 'Heart Disease, Cirrhosis of the Liver, and Changing Alcohol Consumption in Ten Countries, 1960–2007', Paper presented at pre-AARES Conference Workshop on The World's Wine Markets by 2030, Adelaide, 8–9 February. Available at: http://www.adelaide.edu.au/wine-econ/events/2030workshop/.
Kenkel, D.S. (1996), 'New Estimates of the Optimal Tax on Alcohol', *Economic Inquiry*, **34**, 296–319.
Lippi, G., Franchini, M. and Guidi, G.C. (2010), 'Red Wine and Cardiovascular Health: The 'French Paradox' Revisited', *International Journal of Wine Research*, **2**, 1–7.
OECD (2006), *Consumption Tax Trends*. OECD, Paris.
OECD (2008), *Consumption Tax Trends*. OECD, Paris.
Pogue, T. and Sgontz, L. (1989), 'Taxing to Control Social Costs: The Case of Alcohol', *American Economic Review*, **79**, 235–43.
Srivastava, P. and Zhao, X. (2010), 'What Do the Bingers Drink? Microeconometric Evidence on Negative Externalities and Drinker Characteristics of Alcohol Consumption by Beverage Types', *Economic Papers*, **29**(2), 229–50.
WFA (2010), *Pre-Budget Submission 2010–11*. Winemakers' Federation of Australia, Adelaide.
Wittwer, G. and Anderson, K. (2002), 'Impact of the GST and Wine Tax Reform on Australia's Wine Industry: A CGE Analysis', *Australian Economic Papers*, **41**, 69–81.

World Bank and UNCTAD (2009), *World Integrated Trade Solution (WITS) Database.* World Bank and Geneva: United Nations Conference on Trade and Development, Washington, DC. Available at: wits.worldbank.org, accessed December.

World Health Organization (2009), *Strategies to Reduce the Harmful Use of Alcohol: Draft Global Strategy.* Report by the Secretariat to the Executive Board's 126th Session, EB126/13, Geneva, 3 December.

Chapter 19

Excise Taxes on Wines, Beers and Spirits: An Updated International Comparison*

Kym Anderson (with the assistance of Nanda Aryal)[†]

Australia's rate of wine consumer taxation was shown by Berger and Anderson (1999) to be high by OECD standards in the late 1990s, and especially by the standards of significant wine producing/exporting countries. That was also true when those numbers were updated to 2008 by Anderson (2010). Australia's type of wine tax is unusual in being ad valorem (a percentage of the wholesale price) rather than specific (in cents per litre of alcohol), so the comparison depends on what price level is the focus of attention.

The Australian Government considered undertaking major tax reform following a review of the overall Australian tax system (Henry 2010). As part of that review, the question of wine and other alcohol tax rates and instruments came into focus — encouraged somewhat by the call by the World Health Organisation (2009) for stronger measures to reduce the harmful use of alcohol, and the recent adoption of tougher measures in such countries as France and the United Kingdom.

---

*First published in *Wine and Viticulture Journal* 29(6): 66–71, November/December 2014.

[†]Wine Economics Research Centre, School of Economics, University of Adelaide, Adelaide, South Australia 5005. Email: kym.anderson@adelaide.edu.au

It has been argued that the rate of taxation of wine should not be raised because (a) it is still high by international standards and (b) wine is drunk mainly by adults in moderation with food rather than being the main beverage of choice for young binge drinkers such that it has fewer social costs than other forms of alcohol (WFA 2010). This paper examines that first claim by comparing recent tax measures for Australia with those of other countries as a contribution to the debate. In doing so, tax rates for other alcoholic beverages are also compiled, since the optimal wine tax is not independent of the tax rates affecting consumption of substitute beverages.

The present paper reviews the data available and the methodology for comparing rates of taxation across countries. Estimates are then presented of the domestic alcohol taxes in Australia and the other high-income and key developing countries that together account for more than 90 per cent of global wine consumption. The tax rates are expressed both as ad valorem equivalents and as volumetric rates per standard drink of alcohol,[1] and at a selection of still wine price points. The latter is helpful for considering the impact these taxes are having on different types of consumers; but it is also helpful for analysts seeking to use these estimates in economic models of wine markets in which the distinction is made between, say, non-premium, commercial premium and super-premium wines (as in Wittwer and Anderson 2003 and Anderson and Wittwer 2013).

1. At a glance

- For commercial premium wines (retail AUD$12), Australia's 29% is the highest tax rate among the significant wine-exporting countries: the majority have zero taxes on such wines, France has 0.7%, South Africa 4%, the United States 6% and Canada 8%.
- At higher price points, only Korea and Norway among OECD countries have a higher tax rate than Australia's 29%.
- When expressed in Australian cents per standard drink of alcohol, Australia's wholesale tax for commercial premium wines (22 cents) is

---

[1] One standard drink in Australia is 12.5ml of pure alcohol (and so is equivalent to 250ml of beer at 5% alcohol or 12.5o Plato, or 100ml of wine at 12.5% alcohol, or 31.25ml of spirits at 40% alcohol). Thus, the specific tax rate becomes an A$ tax per standard drink by multiplying by 0.000125 the regular-strength beer, wine and spirits tax rates per hectolitre per degree of alcohol. See www.alcohol.gov.au

the same as New Zealand's in 2012, but at any higher price point Australia's tax exceeds New Zealand's.
- Wine is taxed less than spirits in all countries but Japan, and is taxed at a similar or lower rate than beer in all but a handful of countries.
- Australia is taxing wine relative to other alcoholic beverages more than most wine-exporting countries, the main exception being Chile where beer is very lightly taxed.

2. Methodology and data sources

In the many countries in which specific (volumetric, dollars per litre of beverage or of alcohol) tax rates are used without or with ad valorem (percentage) rates, the consumer tax equivalent (CTE) in percentage terms varies with the price of wine. This distinction is important because in recent years the world wine market has been characterised by a trend towards premium wine consumption, and in some traditional wine-consuming countries the volume of non-premium wine consumption has fallen greatly. We therefore identify the tax type (specific and/or ad valorem) and express the CTE in terms of dollars per standard alcoholic drink as well as an ad valorem equivalent.

Specifically, CTEs are calculated for regular beer (5% alcohol, A$2/litre wholesale pre-tax) and spirits (40% alcohol, A$15/litre wholesale pre-tax) and for wines at four different wholesale pre-tax prices assuming all have an alcohol content of 12.5%: non-premium still wine (A$2.50/litre at the wholesale pre-tax level), mid-range commercial premium still wine (A$7.50/litre), super-premium still wine (A$20/litre), and sparkling wine (A$25/litre).

For non-premium wine such as those products sold in casks (A$2.50/litre), given a 29% excise tax (WET), a 33% mark-up to retail, and the 10% GST, a retail price in Australia of $18.90 for a four-litre cask can be implied. For commercial premium wine, A$7.50/litre wholesale implies, with a 29% excise tax [WET], a 50% mark-up to retail and 10% GST, a retail price of $12 for a 750ml bottle; and for super-premium and sparkling wine (A$20 and $25 per litre, respectively), the same mark-ups as commercial premium implies a retail price of around $32 and $40, respectively, for a 750ml bottle.

The ad valorem consumer tax equivalent (CTE) is defined as the percentage by which the pre-tax wholesale price has been raised by beverage taxes (but not including the GST or VAT).[2] To estimate it, numerous assumptions have to be made.

First, the CTE is assumed to apply also at the retail level, on the assumption that the wholesale-to-retail margin is ad valorem. If, in fact, those margins are somewhat independent of the product price, then our CTE estimate will overstate the proportional impact of the tax on consumers at the retail level.

Secondly, neither the average pre-tax retail prices of a bottle of commercial or super-premium wine or a litre of non-premium wine, nor the shares of each of these types in national wine consumption, are reliably known for more than a handful of countries. Hence, an average CTE for each country is not calculated for wine as a group. Instead we calculate the CTE at price levels that approximate the average prices in Australian dollars for the three chosen categories of still wine sold in Australia in 2014. For beer, spirits and sparkling wine we use, for simplicity of comparison, only one representative price for each of those products (A$2, $15 and $25 per litre at the wholesale pre-tax level, respectively).

The primary source for domestic tax data are the OECD (2012) and the European Commission (2014), supplemented by national government websites for a few additional countries not included in those official publications.[3] These sources express the specific taxes in national currency per hectolitre per degree of alcohol if the tax instrument is not an ad valorem percentage.

3. Consumer tax equivalent (CTE) calculations

Tables 1 and 3 show the excise taxes in 2012 and 2014 for wines, beers and spirits expressed as a percentage of the selected wholesale pre-tax

---

[2] Most countries also have a value-added or goods-and-services tax applying to beverages, but since those taxes apply at the retail level to most other goods as well, we do not add them to the beverage-specific taxes. However, for completeness they are reported in Table 1. The foreign exchange rates used to convert specific tax rates expressed in national currencies to the Australian currency are reported in Tables 2 and 4, based on Reserve Bank of Australia rates on 3 January 2012 and 1 July 2014 (RBA 2014).

[3] For example, United States rates for 2014 are obtained from www.taxadmin.org/fta/ and those for Argentina in 2010 and 2014 from http://infoleg.mecon.gov.ar/infolegInternet/anexos/35000-39999/38621/texact.htm

prices shown at the top of each column. They do not include the VAT or GST (shown in the final column), which would be added at the retail level. For commercial premium wines (the sort that would retail at A$12 for a 750ml bottle in Australia inclusive of GST), those rates are depicted in Figure 1, where it is clear that in 2012 Australia's 29% was the highest tax rate among the significant wine-exporting countries: the majority have zero taxes on such wines, France has 0.7%, South Africa 4%, the United States 6% and Canada 8%. At higher price points, such as for the super premium wine category in the middle of Table 1, only Korea and Norway among OECD countries had a higher tax rate than Australia's 29%.

Tables 2 and 4 show the excise taxes in 2012 and 2014 for wines, beers and spirits expressed in Australian cents per standard drink of alcohol. They are converted from the national currencies at the exchange rates shown in the final column. In 2012 Australia's wholesale tax per standard drink is the same as New Zealand's for commercial premium wines (22 cents) but is higher at any higher price point above A$7.50/ litre. It compares with zero in Argentina, 3 cents in South Africa, 5 cents in the United States, and 6 cents in Canada — and just 1 cent in France and zero in the other Old World wine-exporting countries. That indicator for wines can be expressed as a percentage of those for other beverages, as in Figures 2 and 3. Wine is taxed less than spirits in all but Japan, and it is taxed at a similar or lower rate than beer in all but a handful of countries. Again, Australia is taxing wine relative to other alcoholic beverages more than most wine-exporting countries, the main exception being Chile where beer is very lightly taxed.

The unweighted averages of the OECD countries' 2012 rates are shown at the bottom of Tables 1 and 2. Australia's rate is twice the average for commercial premium wines and almost four times the averages for super premium and sparkling wines. Only for non-premium wine is it below those averages, and only slightly.

Acknowledgements

Thanks are due to the Winemakers' Federation of Australia for funding this update of earlier work undertaken in 2010 under GWRDC Research Project UA 0804. The update is part of the WFA's effort to increase public knowledge about the nature and extent of Australia's wine taxation.

Table 1. Ad valorem consumer tax equivalent of excise taxes on wines, beers, and spirits,[b] 1 January 2012 (as % of the wholesale pre-tax prices per litre shown in column heads)

		Non-Premium Wine $2.50	Commercial Premium Wine $7.50	Super Premium Wine $20	Sparkling Wine $25	Beer $2	Spirits $15	VAT/GST (%)
Argentina	AR	0.0	0.0	0.0	0.0	8.0	20.0	21
Australia	AU	29.0	29.0	29.0	29.0	107.1	184.4	10
Austria	AT	0.0	0.0	0.0	0.0	15.8	33.6	20
Belgium	BE	23.7	7.9	3.0	8.1	13.5	58.9	21
Canada	CA	23.7	7.9	3.0	2.4	74.7	29.9	-15
Chile	CL	15.0	15.0	15.0	15.0	15.0	27.0	19
Czech Rep.	CZ	0.0	0.0	0.0	4.6	3.9	37.2	20
Denmark	DK	71.9	24.0	9.0	9.6	26.9	67.7	25
Estonia	EE	36.8	12.3	4.6	3.74	17.1	47.7	20
Finland	FI	157.4	52.5	19.7	15.7	94.3	154.9	23
France	FR	2.0	0.7	0.3	0.5	8.7	55.8	20
Germany	DE	0.0	0.0	0.0	6.9	6.2	43.8	19
Greece	EL	0.0	0.0	0.0	0.0	20.5	82.4	23
Hungary	HU	0.0	0.0	0.0	2.4	14.6	30.8	27
Ireland	IE	132.1	44.0	16.5	26.4	49.5	104.7	23
Israel	IL	0.0	0.0	0.0	0.0	137.4	110.3	16
Italy	IT	0.0	0.0	0.0	0.0	18.5	26.9	21
Japan	JP	40.5	13.5	5.1	4.0	34.8	13.5	5

Excise Taxes on Wines, Beers and Spirits 467

Korea	KR	33.0	33.0	33.0	33.0	94.0	91.0	10
Luxembourg	LU	0.0	0.0	0.0	0.0	6.2	35.0	15
Mexico	MX	25.0	25.0	25.0	25.0	25.0	50.0	16
Netherlands	NL	35.8	11.9	4.5	12.2	17.3	50.6	19
New Zealand	NZ	86.1	28.7	10.8	8.6	51.8	251.5	15
Norway	NO	343.1	114.4	42.9	34.3	178.7	292.4	25
Poland	PL	17.8	5.9	2.2	1.8	13.7	37.3	23
Portugal	PT	0.0	0.0	0.0	0.0	58.09	37.3	23
Slovak Rep.	SK	0.0	0.0	0.0	4.0	11.3	36.6	20
Slovenia	SI	0.0	0.0	0.0	0.0	31.5	33.6	20
South Africa	ZA	12.0	4.0	1.5	3.6	17.8	35.7	10
Spain	ES	0.0	0.0	0.0	0.0	31.4	27.9	18
Sweden	SE	122.0	40.7	15.3	12.2	58.7	189.0	25
Switzerland	CH	0.0	0.0	0.0	0.0	43.7	80.0	8
Turkey[a]	TR	40.3	13.4	5.0	25.5	63.0	90.6	18
UK	UK	145.5	48.5	18.2	18.7	70.1	102.7	20
USA	US	18.3	6.1	2.3	4.5	53.4	25.2	0
OECD av.[c]		40.3	15.4	7.6	8.9	42.6	73.9	18

[a] Turkey still wine data are for 2010
[b] Wine and beer degree alcohol contents are assumed to be 12% and 4%, respectively; the absolute alcohol content for spirits is assumed to be 40%.
[c] Unweighted average

Table 2. Excise taxes on alcoholic beverages per standard drink of alcoholic for wines, beers and spirits, 1 January 2012 (Australian cents at the wholesale pre-tax prices per litre shown in column heads)

		Non-Premium Wine $2.50	Commercial Premium Wine $7.50	Super Premium Wine $20	Sparkling Wine $25	Beer $2	Spirits $15	Exchange Rate (local currency per AUD)
Argentina[b]	AR	0	0	0	0	8	10	4.47
Australia[b]	AU	7	22	58	73	54	86	1.00
Austria	AT	0	0	0	0	8	16	0.79
Belgium	BE	6	6	6	20	7	28	0.79
Canada	CA	6	6	6	6	37	14	1.04
Chile	CL	4	11	30	38	8	13	533.62
Czech Rep.	CZ	0	0	0	11	2	17	20.44
Denmark	DK	18	18	18	24	13	32	5.91
Estonia	EE	9	9	9	9	9	22	0.79
Finland	FI	39	39	39	39	47	68	0.79
France	FR	1	1	1	1	4	26	0.79
Germany	DE	0	0	0	17	3	21	0.79
Greece	EL	0	0	0	0	10	39	0.79
Hungary	HU	0	0	0	6	7	14	250.94
Ireland	IE	33	33	33	66	25	49	0.79
Israel	IL	0	0	0	0	69	17	3.97
Italy	IT	0	0	0	0	9	13	0.79

Japan	JP	10	10	10	10	17	6	79.09
Korea[b]	KR	8	25	66	83	47	43	1184.17
Luxembourg	LU	0	0	0	0	3	16	0.79
Mexico[b]	MX	6	19	50	63	13	23	14.19
Netherlands	NL	9	9	9	30	9	24	0.79
New Zealand	NZ	22	22	22	22	26	118	1.31
Norway	NO	86	86	86	86	89	137	6.13
Poland	PL	4	4	4	4	7	17	3.54
Portugal	PT	0	0	0	0	29	17	0.79
Slovak Rep.	SK	0	0	0	10	6	17	0.79
Slovenia	SI	0	0	0	0	16	16	0.79
South Africa	ZA	3	3	3	9	9	17	8.33
Spain	ES	0	0	0	0	16	13	0.79
Sweden	SE	31	31	31	31	29	89	7.07
Switzerland	CH	0	0	0	0	22	38	0.97
Turkey[a]	TR	10	10	10	64	32	42	1.94
UK	UK	36	36	36	47	35	48	0.66
USA	US	5	5	5	12	28	13	1.03
OECD av.[c]		10	12	15	22	22	34	

[a] Turkey still wine data are for 2010
[b] Argentina, Australia, Chile, Korea and Mexico have an ad valorem tax on non-premium, commercial premium and super premium wires
[c] One standard drink in Australia is 12.5ml of pure alcohol, and so is equivalent to 250ml of beer at 5% alcohol or 12.5o Plato, or 100ml of wine at 12.5% alcohol, or 31.25ml of spirits at 40% alcohol.
[d] Unweighted average

Table 3. Ad valorem consumer tax equivalent of excise taxes on wines, beers and spirits,[b] 1 July 2014 (as a % of the wholesale pre-tax prices per litre shown in column heads)

		Non-Premium Wine $2.50	Commercial Premium Wine $7.50	Super Premium Wine $20	Sparkling Wine $25	Beer $2	Spirits $15	VAT/GST (%)
Argentina	AR	0.0	0.0	0.0	0.0	8.0	20.0	21
Australia	AU	29.0	29.0	29.0	29.0	116.9	221.3	10
Austria	AT	0.0	2.2	0.0	5.8	18.1	46.3	20
Belgium	BE	33.0	11.0	4.1	11.3	16.7	81.8	21
Chile	CL	15.0	15.0	15.0	15.0	15.0	27.0	19
Czech Rep.	CZ	0.0	0.0	0.0	4.9	4.2	39.9	21
Denmark	DK	85.2	28.4	10.6	11.0	27.1	77.4	25
Estonia	EE	49.2	16.4	6.2	4.9	22.7	63.4	20
Finland	FI	196.3	65.4	24.5	19.6	116.0	175.8	24
France	FR	2.3	0.8	0.3	0.5	26.5	66.4	20
Germany	DE	0.0	0.0	0.0	7.9	7.1	50.3	19
Greece	EL	0.0	0.0	0.0	0.0	23.5	94.6	23
Hungary	HU	0.0	0.0	0.0	30.0	18.7	41.1	27

(*Continued*)

Ireland	IE	246.1	82.0	30.8	49.2	81.6	164.3	21
Italy	IT	0.0	0.0	0.0	0.0	24.4	36.4	22
Luxembourg	LU	0.0	0.0	0.0	0.0	7.2	40.2	15
Netherlands	NL	51.0	17.0	6.4	14.7	17.2	65.1	21
New Zealand	NZ	104.8	34.9	13.1	10.5	65.5	127.3	15
Poland	PL	21.9	7.3	2.7	2.2	16.9	52.7	23
Portugal	PT	0.0	0.0	0.0	0.0	68.3	48.3	23
Slovak Rep.	SK	0.0	0.0	0.0	4.6	13.0	41.7	20
Slovenia	SI	0.0	0.0	0.0	0.0	43.8	51.0	22
South Africa	ZA	11.4	3.8	1.4	3.6	17.1	36.5	14
Spain	ES	0.0	0.0	0.0	0.0	36.0	35.2	21
Sweden	SE	145.4	48.5	18.2	14.5	70.1	212.6	25
UK	UK	1974.8	65.9	24.7	25.3	86.5	136.2	20
USA[a]	US	19.9	6.6	2.5	4.9	58.2	27.5	0

[a] USA data are for 2012

[b] Wine and beer degree alcohol contents are assumed to be 12% and 4%, respectively; the absolute alcohol content for spirits is assumed to be 40%.

Table 4. Excise taxes on alcoholic beverages per standard drink of alcoholic for wines, beers and spirits, 1 July 2014 (Australian cents at the wholesale pre-tax prices per litre shown in column heads)

		Non-Premium Wine $2.50	Commercial Premium Wine $7.50	Super Premium Wine $20	Sparkling Wine $25	Beer $2	Spirits $15	Exchange Rate (local currency per AUD)
Argentina[b]	AR	0	0	0	0	8	10	7.72
Australia[b]	AU	7	22	58	73	58	99	1.00
Austria	AT	0	0	0	14	9	22	0.69
Belgium	BE	8	8	8	28	8	38	0.69
Chile[b]	CL	4	11	30	38	8	13	523.83
Czech Rep.	CZ	0	0	0	12	0	19	19.03
Denmark	DK	21	21	21	27	14	36	5.13
Estonia	EE	12	12	12	12	11	30	0.69
Finland	FI	49	49	49	49	58	82	0.69
France	FR	1	1	1	1	13	31	0.69
Germany	DE	0	0	0	20	4	24	0.69
Greece	EL	0	0	0	0	12	44	0.69
Hungary	HU	0	0	0	8	9	19	216.17
Ireland	IE	62	62	62	123	41	77	0.69
Italy	IT	0	0	0	0	12	17	0.69

Excise Taxes on Wines, Beers and Spirits

Luxembourg	LU	0	0	0	4	19	0.69
Netherlands	NL	13	13	37	9	31	0.69
New Zealand	NZ	26	26	26	33	60	1.08
Poland	PL	5	5	5	8	25	2.88
Portugal	PT	0	0	0	34	23	0.69
Slovak Rep.	SK	0	0	13	6	20	0.69
Slovenia	SI	0	0	0	22	24	0.69
South Africa	ZA	3	3	9	9	17	10.06
Spain	ES	0	0	0	18	17	0.69
Sweden	SE	36	36	36	35	100	6.35
UK	UK	49	49	63	43	64	0.55
USA[a]	US	5	5	12	29	13	0.95

[a] USA data are for 2012
[b] Argentina, Australia and Chile have an ad valorem tax on wines
[c] One standard drink in Australia is 12.5ml of pure alcohol, and so is equivalent to 250ml beer at 5% alcohol or 12.5o Plato, or 100ml of wine at 12.5% alcohol, or 31.25ml of spirits at 40% alcohol.

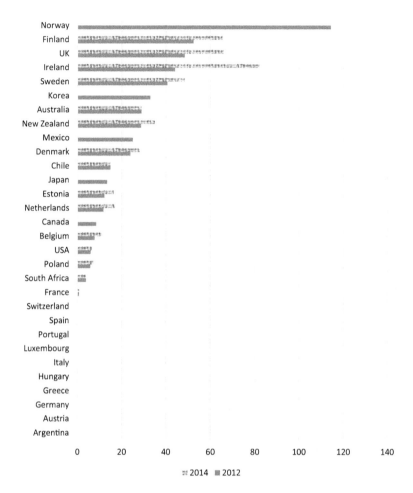

Figure 1. Ad valorem consumer tax equivalent of excise on commercial premium wines, 1 January 2012 and 1 July 2014 (percent)

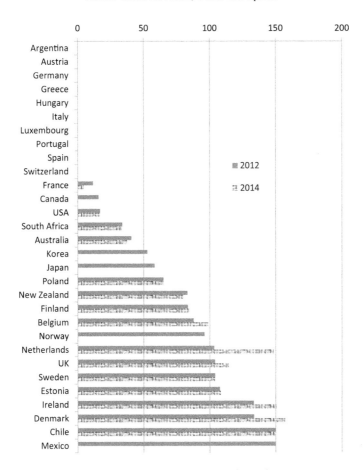

Figure 2. Specific consumer tax on commercial premium wines as a percentage of that on beers per standard drink, 1 January 2012 and 1 July 2014 (percent)

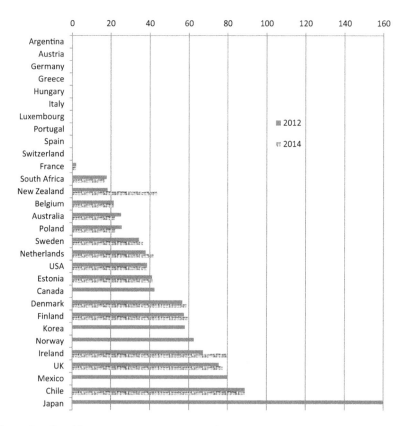

Figure 3. Specific consumer tax on commercial premium wines as a percentage of that on spirits per standard drink, 1 January 2012 and 1 July 2014 (percent)

References

Anderson, K. (2010) Excise and Import Taxes on Wine vs Beer and Spirits: An International Comparison, Economic Papers 29(2): 215–28, June.

Anderson, K. and G. Wittwer (2013) Modeling Global Wine Markets to 2018: Exchange Rates, Taste Changes, and China's Import Growth, Journal of Wine Economics 8(2): 131–58.

Berger, N. and K. Anderson (1999), "Consumer and Import Taxes in the World Wine Market: Australia in International Perspective", Australasian Agribusiness Review 7(3). June. http://www.agrifood.info/review/1999/Berger.html

European Commission (2014) Excise Duty Tables: Part 1: Alcoholic Beverages, Brussels: European Commission, accessed 19 August 2014. http://ec.europa.eu/taxation_customs/resources/documents/taxation/excise_duties/alcoholic_beverages/rates/excise_duties-part_i_alcohol_en.pdf

Henry, K. (2010) Australia's Future Tax System: Report to the Treasurer (The Henry Review), Canberra: The Treasury, www.taxreview.treasury.gov.au

OECD (2012) Consumption Tax Trends 2012: VAT/GST and Excise Rates, Trends and Administration Issues, Paris: OECD Publishing, accessed 19 August 2014. http://dx.doi.org/10.1787/ctt-2012-en

RBA (2014) Exchange rates, daily, Sydney: Reserve Bank of Australia, accessed 19 August 2014. http://www.rba.gov.au/statistics/historical-data.html

Wittwer, G. and K. Anderson (2002) Impact of the GST and Wine Tax Reform on Australia's Wine Industry: A CGE Analysis, Australian Economic Papers 41(1): 69–81, March.

Chapter 20

Wine Export Shocks and Wine Tax Reform in Australia: Regional Consequences Using an Economy-Wide Approach*

Kym Anderson,[†] Ernesto Valenzuela[‡] and Glyn Wittwer[§]

Abstract

We provide economy-wide modelling results of the national and regional implications of two current challenges facing the Australian wine industry: a decline in export demand, and a possible change in the

---

*First published in *Economic Papers* 30(3): 386–99, September 2011. Revision of a Contributed Paper presented at the AARES/AAWE Workshop on *The World's Wine Markets by 2030*, Adelaide Convention Centre, 8–9 February 2010. We are grateful for helpful referee comments. Thanks also are due to Jayanthi Thennakoon for research assistance and to the GWRDC (Project Number UA08/04) and the University of Adelaide's Wine2030 Network for financial support. The views expressed are the authors' alone and not necessarily those of any of the funders.

[†] School of Economics and Wine Economics Research Centre, University of Adelaide

[‡] School of Economics, University of Adelaide, Adelaide, SA; and

[§] Centre of Policy Studies, Monash University, Melbourne, VIC, Australia

Correspondence: Kym Anderson, School of Economics and Wine Economics Research Centre, University of Adelaide, Adelaide, SA 5005, Australia. Email: kym.anderson@adelaide.edu.au

tax on domestic wine sales following the Henry Review of Taxation. The demand shock causes regional GDP to fall in the cool and warm wine regions, but not in the hot wine regions unless the shock is large. A change from the current *ad valorem* tax to a similarly low volumetric tax on domestic wine sales causes regional GDP to rise in the cool and warm wine regions, partly offsetting its fall due to the export demand shock, but GDP in the hot wine regions would fall substantially. The switch to a volumetric tax as high as the standard beer rate would raise tax revenue and lower domestic wine consumption by more than one-third. However, it would induce a one-third decrease in production of non-premium wine as its consumer price would rise by at least three-quarters (while the average price of super premium wines would change very little). This would exacerbate the difference in effects of a tax reform on GDP in hot versus warm and cool wine regions.

1. Introduction

The Australian wine industry has been facing a number of challenges of late. Some of them are weather-related (bushfires, extreme heatwaves, drought and associated unavailability of adequate water, excessive rain or frost in some areas). Some are due to the rapid expansion in Australia's vineyard plantings in the past fifteen years, followed by similarly rapid expansions in other New World wine-exporting countries. But two other challenges are the focus of this paper. One is the current decline in export demand for premium wines, in part due to the recent global financial crisis and the consequent recession in many economies and also to the mining boom-induced appreciation of the Australian dollar. The other is the prospect of a change in the consumer tax on domestic wine sales, following the Henry Review of Taxation in Australia completed in 2010[1] together with pressure from those con-

---

[1] The Henry Review comes a decade after the introduction in Australia of a 10 per cent goods-and-services tax (GST), at which time the excise tax on wine was replaced by not only the GST at the retail level but also a Wine Equalization Tax (WET) at the wholesale level. The WET was so called because, by setting it at 29 per cent, it together with the GST generated about the same tax revenue for the government as the former excise tax on wine. For an analysis of the impact of that tax reform of a decade ago on the Australian wine

cerned with the health effects of alcohol consumption (see, e.g., Byrnes et al., 2010).

The reason we consider these two challenges together is because the export demand shock has occurred since the databases of existing models of the Australian economy were prepared. Its effects thus need to be simulated first, as a way of re-basing such models, before exploring the effects of any tax changes that may take place after 2010. Also, one set of proposed consumer tax changes — from the current *ad valorem* tax to a volumetric wine tax — would lead to a fall in domestic sales of non-premium wines but possibly an increase in sales of more-expensive wines, depending in part on the extent to which the tax reform also involved raising the wine tax rate in order to bring it closer to the rates applying to other beverages on a volume-of-alcohol basis.[2] Meanwhile, a decline in demand for exports of premium wine could have the opposite effects. Given that the hot winegrape-growing regions of Australia produce most of Australia's nonpremium wine while the cool regions specialise in producing super premium wine (with warm regions having more of a mix of both plus commercial premium wines), these challenges have profoundly differing implications for the various regional economies in Australia, hence the focus of the present study on the regional dimension.

One of the motivations for taxing alcohol is to address negative externalities associated with consumption (Freebairn, 2010). Studies assessing externalities by alcohol type, including that by Srivastava and Zhao (2010), find that the incidence of binge drinking in Australia is highest for RTDs and full-strength beer and lowest for bottled wine. Theory would suggest the rates of taxation of these beverages should be similarly ranked if there are no other policy motivations (Anderson, 2010b).

---

industry, see Wittwer and Anderson (2002). A fuller history of wine consumer taxation in Australia can be found in Anderson (2010a).

[2] If the 29 per cent *ad valorem* wholesale tax on wine were to be replaced by the excise tax applying to standard-strength beer (A$0.82 per litre of alcohol), then wines retailing above about A$18 per 750 ml bottle would potentially be cheaper, assuming a retail mark-up margin of one-third the wholesale price (Anderson, 2010b).

The paper is structured as follows. In the next section, we explain the regional economy-wide modelling approach used. We then present the results from four simulations: two alternative export demand shocks (one more negative than the other), followed by two alternative tax reforms that change the current *ad valorem* wine tax of 29 per cent to a volumetric tax (one that brings the new wine tax up to the rate applying to beer of less than 3 per cent alcohol, the other to the higher rate applying to standard-strength beer). The final section draws together the implications of the findings.

2. The modelling approach

The approach to be taken in this analysis is to use an economy-wide model of the Australian economy that is capable both of distinguishing between the three types of wine just mentioned (non-premium, commercial premium and super premium) and of showing the impacts at a disaggregated regional level. For that purpose, we use the ORANIG model (see http://www.monash.edu.au/policy/oranig.htm), which has been modified to generate what we call the ORANIG06-WINE model, which is based on 2006 data for the Australian economy. The national economy has been disaggregated into thirty-six regions, all but six of which are wine-intensive regions. While this model is regional only in a top-down manner, it is appropriate for analysing an external demand shock and a national policy issue such as a change in national alcohol taxes, because in both cases it is defensible to assume that wine prices would change across all regions by the same proportion for each of the three wine types.[3] The advantage of modifying ORANIG for analysing a change in the national tax on wine consumption is that it is relatively straightforward to make the desirable disaggregation of alcoholic beverages into numerous sectors with a top-down specification.[4]

---

[3] Even in the ORANIG model some industries are designated as "local". These include Utilities, Construction, Trade, Transport, BankFinIns, OwnerDwellng and PersOthSrv. In these sectors, regional output changes follow changes in regional income, which captures regional multiplier impacts, so output changes will differ across regions for these industries.

[4] By contrast, modifying a multi-region bottom-up model such as the TERM model of the Australian economy (www.monash.edu.au/policy/term.htm) would require more compli-

ORANIG has been modified to create ORANIG06-WINE as follows:

- The published 2001–02 national input-output database has a single wine, spirits and tobacco sector and a single beer sector. The former is split into three types of wine (non-premium, commercial premium and super premium), plus spirits and tobacco and the beer sector is split into non-premium and premium types. A new ready-to-drink sector, RTDs, is created partly from spirits and partly from the soft drinks sector.
- The database is updated to 2005–06 to reflect available national accounts and international trade data, using the ADJUST procedure devised by Mark Horridge (see http://www.monash.edu.au/policy/archivep.htm TPMH0058). Value-added data in the model's 2005–06 three wine sub-sectors and its grape sector in each wine region and climate zone are summarised in Table A1, the shares of gross value of wine production from the three sub-sectors are shown for each region in Table A2, and the model's structure of costs in wine production that year are summarised in Table A3.[5]
- The model also includes a top-down regional module that separates out all the significant wine regions of Australia (Table A1). The wine regions are also classified into three climatic zones: cool, warm and hot. In 2005–06, one-tenth of the value added in grape production

---

cated coding and large amounts of detailed regional data.

[5] The data available to split each region's wine output and value added into three quality categories are very limited. Better data are available on the distribution of winegrape prices (see AWBC, 2009), but they are only an approximate guide because grapes are often transported after harvest to another region for processing. Anderson *et al.* (2010) divide the 2008 crush into three quality categories by assuming grapes valued at less than A$550 per tonne were non-premium and those above A$1200 were super premium. Those dividers suggest nearly one-third of the crush volume and one-sixth of the crush value was non-premium that year, while one-sixth of the crush volume and a little over one-third of the crush value was super premium, hence around half was commercial premium winegrapes (Anderson *et al.*, 2010, tables 20–21). Based on similar regional winegrape price and quantity data for 2006 and information about inter-regional grape movements, we have allocated a distribution across the three wine types for each region. Those guesses imply that, as shown in Tables A1 and A2, a bit over one-third in value terms is commercial premium and one-half is super premium. Since these are close to the opposite of the winegrape value shares adopted by Anderson *et al.* (2010), the implicit dividing line used here between the commercial and super premium categories is at a slightly lower quality level.

came from cool regions, two-thirds from warm regions and not quite one-quarter from hot regions as defined (bottom of Table A1, based on the regional classifications shown in the final column).[6]
- Indirect taxes on both household consumption and intermediate inputs are split into three: GST, *ad valorem* top-up taxes and volumetric taxes. Given the significance of on-premise alcohol consumption, this allows us to account for on-premise taxes in the hotels and restaurants sector. The significance of this is that, as on-premise markups typically exceed 100 per cent, we do not overestimate the impacts of particular tax scenarios which would arise from treating all alcohol consumption as if purchases were at off-premise prices. The tax revenue raised from alcohol consumption taxes, according to the model's 2005–06 database, is summarised in Table A4.
- ORANIG06-WINE also contains a small fiscal module, so as to allow for direct taxation. This enables us to maintain the government's budget balance in policy scenarios. In the event that a wine tax policy change is not budget-neutral, there is an accommodating direct tax rate shift to maintain overall fiscal budget neutrality.

Models in the ORANI family (Dixon *et al.*, 1982) usually have a linear expenditure system (LES) of household demand. The advantage of LES in an economy-wide model is that it models expenditure and price effects with relatively few parameters (n parameters in a system of n commodities). The disadvantage is that there are no specific cross-price effects, with cross-price elasticities being determined by expenditure effects alone. This system is satisfactory for relatively broad groups of commodities, as are usually found in published input-output tables, but it is undesirable in the context of finely disaggregated commodities that are potentially substitutable, and particularly in a policy scenario in which there is the assumption of such substitution, as in the present case of a wine tax switch. LES is

---

[6]We use the same criteria as Anderson *et al.* (2010) in categorising regions into climate zones, as follows. Hot zone: mean January and February temperatures each above twenty-three degrees and Growing Degree Days above 2200; Cool zone: mean January and February temperatures each below twenty degrees and Growing Degree Days below 1550. The data for those variables by region have been carefully compiled by Webb (2006), pp. 239–240 and Section 2.1.

unsatisfactory because a revenue-neutral tax switch is likely to entail negligible expenditure effects and significant price effects; hence, a modification that allows for price substitution, even if at the expense of commodity-specific expenditure elasticities, is appropriate. We modified household demands accordingly, by grouping alcohol consumption into three nests, namely beer, wine and spirits/RTDs. Each of the three has an expenditure elasticity (or marginal budget share) within the LES. Household demand for beer is a constant elasticity of substitution (CES) nest of two beer types, while wine consumption is a CES nest of three types. Finally, spirits and RTDs form a CES nest that is part of the LES. We do not allow for cross-price effects between, for example, non-premium wine and beer types.[7] However, we include below a sensitivity analysis section in which we explore the effects on our results of altering the CES between the three wine types from the default value of 2.0 to either 0.5 or 4.0.

3. Applying the model: Estimating effects of export demand and tax reform shocks

Four sets of simulation results are reported in this section: two alternative export demand shocks (one more negative than the other), followed by two alternative tax reforms that change the current *ad valorem* wine tax of 29 per cent to a volumetric tax (one that brings the new wine tax up to the rate applying to light-strength beer, the other to the higher rate applying to standard-strength beer).

---

[7] The extent to which preference independence applies for different types of alcohol has been debated in the literature. We could have chosen ostensibly more elaborate demand forms, such as a translog system (Dixon *et al.*, 1992) or CRESH (Hanoch, 1971). Each of these forms allows for different pairwise elasticities of substitution, although the restrictions of each system may erode their intuitive appeal. That is, target cross-price elasticities between alcohol types regarded as close substitutes may be confounded by the adding-up conditions of the system. Our choice to not allow cross-price effects is vindicated by the recent estimates by Ramful and Zhao (2008), using a trivariate probit formulation, which allows for the three alcoholic beverages to be modelled jointly to account for correlation *via* unobserved personal characteristics. Their estimates of own- and cross-price elasticities suggest the cross-price elasticities between wine and beer and between wine and spirits for Australian consumers are very low.

The first export demand shock assumes there is a 20 per cent decline in super premium wine export demand coupled with a 10 per cent rise in commercial premium wine export demand (both measured in value terms), and no change in non-premium demand. As of early 2009, that seemed a reasonable characterisation of the type of shock the industry would face in 2009–10. By mid-2009, however, it was clear that the shock was going to be more severe, with demand for commercial premium wine falling even more than that for super premium and with total export sales falling by about $650 million from the 2006 level. Specifically, the second export demand shock assumes there is a 10 per cent decline in super premium wine export demand — less severe than initially feared — but with a 33 per cent decline in commercial premium wine export demand (and again no change in non-premium demand).

Once that second shock to the model's database is in place, follow-on changes from the current *ad valorem* domestic wine consumption tax of 29 per cent to a volumetric tax are explored. The first tax simulation raises the wine tax to the rate applying to beer with less than 3 per cent alcohol (A$28 per litre of alcohol), and the second tax simulation raises the wine tax to the rate applying to beer with more than 3 per cent alcohol (A$40.82 per litre of alcohol). To make it easy to compare results across the simulations, the effects of each of the two tax scenarios are presented as additional to the effects of the second export demand shock. Throughout, a long run setting is used in which capital stocks adjust so as to maintain pre-simulation rates of return, although the rental on land used in the grapes sector may vary relative to the base case in the long run.

3.1. *A change in demand for Australian wine exports*

With the recession in high-income countries from 2008, demand for Australian super premium wine exports has shrunk, as consumers eat out less and tighten their spending. Substitution to lower quality premium wines has been occurring, and initially it was thought that this would result in an increase in commercial premium demand. To simulate that shock, we assume in our first scenario that, relative to 2005–06, there is a 20 per cent reduction in export demand for Australia's super premium wine but a 10 per cent increase in export demand for commercial premium wine. The estimated macroeconomic effects of this shock, shown in column 1 of Table 1, reveal that this involves a slight decline in Australia's overall exports and imports, real GDP and real household income. In the second and more-severe export demand shock, involving just a 10 per cent reduction in export demand for Australia's super premium wine but a 33 per cent decline in export demand for commercial

Table 1. Simulation results: Effects on Australia's macroeconomy (per cent change)

	Changes to Wine Export Demand: 20% Decline in Super Premium and 10% Rise in Commercial Premium	Changes to Wine Export Demand: 10% Decline in Super Premium Wine and 33% Decline in Commercial Premium	Switch to Volumetric Wine Tax at the Beer Rate of A$28/LAL[†]	Switch to Volumetric Wine Tax at the Beer Rate of A$40.82/LAL[†]
Real household income	−0.006	−0.03	−0.04	−0.05
Real investment	0.001	0.00	−0.00	0.00
Real govt spending	0.000	0.00	0.00	0.00
Export volume	−0.047	−0.27	−0.02	−0.02
Import volume	−0.048	−0.28	−0.01	−0.01
Real GDP	−0.003	−0.01	−0.02	−0.03
Aggregate employment	0.000	0.00	0.00	0.00
Average real wage	0.001	0.01	−0.15	−0.24
Aggregate capital stock	−0.002	−0.01	−0.00	0.00
GDP Price Index	−0.005	−0.03	0.08	0.12
Consumer Price Index	−0.004	−0.02	0.14	0.22
Export Price Index	−0.004	−0.02	0.00	0.01
Real devaluation	0.005	0.03	−0.08	−0.12

Notes: LAL, litres of alcohol. [†]The tax simulations use as their base the resulting data after the export demand shock of a 10 per cent decline in super premium wine coupled with a 33 per cent decline in commercial premium. That is, they are the additional effects due to just the tax change.
Source: Authors' model simulation results.

premium wine, shown in column 2 of Table 1, those declines are somewhat greater but still small.

With the first demand shock, regional GDP falls in the cool and warm wine regions (by 0.1 and 0.2 per cent, respectively) but rises in the hot wine regions (by 0.2 per cent), as shown at the bottom of column 1 of Table 2. This is mostly because, as shown at the bottom of column 1 of Table 3, the volume of wine production falls in the cool and warm wine regions (by 5.7 and 2.5 per cent, respectively) but rises in the hot wine regions (by 1.9 per cent). With the more-severe export demand shock, by contrast, regional GDP falls in all three climate zones because wine production falls not only in the cool and warm regions but also in the hot wine regions, by 6.1, 8.5 and 9.0 per cent, respectively (bottom of column 2 of Tables 2 and 3, with impacts for specific wine regions shown in the bulk of those tables).

The aggregate national change in wine production with the first demand shock is a small increase of 1.6 per cent. This is made up of a fall in super premium wine output of 8.3 per cent and a rise of 5.5 per cent for commercial premium (and no significant change for non-premium wine), while the gross value of grapes in aggregate would fall nationally by just 0.5 per cent (column 1 of Table 4). By contrast, there is an aggregate national decline in the gross value of wine production with the second, more-severe export demand shock of 9.8 per cent, with super premium wine falling just 3.7 per cent but commercial premium wine production falling 17 per cent (and again no significant change for non-premium wine). In that second case, grape production falls nationally by almost 5 per cent (column 2 of Table 4).

3.2. *A switch from an* ad valorem *to a volumetric domestic wine consumption tax*

What if, on top of the more-severe export demand shock, there was a change from the current *ad valorem* tax on domestic wholesale wine sales of 29 per cent to a volumetric tax equal to that applied to beer in

Table 2. Simulation results: Effects on regional GDP, all sectors (per cent change)

	Changes to Wine Export Demand: 20% Decline in Super Premium and 10% Rise in Commercial Premium	Changes to Wine Export Demand: 10% Decline in Super Premium Wine and 33% Decline in Commercial Premium	Switch to Volumetric Wine Tax at the Beer Rate of A$28/LAL[†]	Switch to Volumetric Wine Tax at the Beer Rate of A$40.82/LAL[†]
RoNSW	0.01	0.03	−0.013	−0.01
NwcstlNSW	0.02	0.02	−0.007	−0.01
HunterBalNSW	0.02	−0.05	−0.016	−0.03
CentTbleNSW	0.05	−0.03	−0.073	−0.09
OrangeNSW	0.01	0.00	0.010	0.01
STbleIndNSW	0.00	−0.05	−0.017	−0.02
LMrmbNSW	0.20	−0.76	−2.601	−2.89
MrryDrlngNSW	0.26	−1.34	−1.086	−1.31
RoVIC	0.00	−0.01	−0.004	0.00
YarraRngVic	−0.11	0.03	0.212	0.23
MorningtnVic	−0.05	0.03	0.113	0.13
WCentrlHLVic	−0.07	−0.53	0.129	0.09
WOvnsMrryVic	−0.10	−0.78	−0.274	−0.36
EOvensMurVic	−0.02	−0.19	−0.064	−0.09
SWGoulbuVic	0.00	−0.05	−0.052	−0.06
WstMalleeVIC	0.04	−0.17	−0.131	−0.15
EMalleeVic	0.04	−0.37	−0.194	−0.24
DrlngDwnsQld	0.00	−0.02	−0.012	−0.02
RoQLD	0.01	0.05	−0.007	−0.01
RoSA	−0.04	−0.26	0.004	0.00

(*Continued*)

Table 2. (Continued)

	Changes to Wine Export Demand: 20% Decline in Super Premium and 10% Rise in Commercial Premium	Changes to Wine Export Demand: 10% Decline in Super Premium Wine and 33% Decline in Commercial Premium	Switch to Volumetric Wine Tax at the Beer Rate of A$28/LAL[†]	Switch to Volumetric Wine Tax at the Beer Rate of A$40.82/LAL[†]
SAdelaideSA	-0.10	-0.11	0.176	0.18
BarossaSA	-0.94	-2.27	1.511	1.47
MtLoftRanSA	-0.19	-0.19	0.316	0.33
FleurieuSA	0.00	-0.66	-0.004	-0.06
LwrNthSA	-0.29	-0.83	0.455	0.43
RiverLndSA	0.54	-2.14	-1.523	-1.89
UpperSESA	-0.09	-0.65	0.091	0.04
LowerSESA	-0.16	-0.19	0.162	0.15
NMetroWA	0.01	0.04	0.002	0.01
RoWA	0.01	0.06	-0.007	-0.01
VasseWA	-0.75	-0.82	1.223	1.27
KingWA	-0.18	-0.44	0.294	0.29
TAS	-0.02	0.04	0.052	0.06
NT/ACT	0.00	0.01	0.001	0.00
Total, Australia	-0.00	-0.01	-0.077	-0.12
Wine climatic zones				
Hot	0.2	-1.0	-1.4	-1.7
Warm	-0.2	-0.5	0.3	0.3
Cool	-0.1	-0.1	0.1	0.1

Notes: LAL, litres of alcohol. [†]The tax simulations use as their base the resulting data after the export demand shock of a 10 per cent decline in super premium wine coupled with a 33 per cent decline in commercial premium. That is, they are the additional effects due to just the tax change.

Source: Authors' model simulation results.

Table 3. Simulation results: Effects on regional volume of wine production (per cent change)

	Changes to Wine Export Demand: 20% Decline in Super Premium and 10% Rise in Commercial Premium	Changes to Wine Export Demand: 10% Decline in Super Premium Wine and 33% Decline in Commercial Premium	Switch to Volumetric Wine Tax at the Beer Rate of A$28/LAL[†]	Switch to Volumetric Wine Tax at the Beer Rate of A$40.82/LAL[†]
RoNSW	−1.3	−8.2	−4.2	−6.6
NwestlNSW	−0.1	−11.0	−1.2	−4.1
HunterBalNSW	−0.1	−11.0	−1.2	−4.1
CentTbleNSW	4.9	−15.3	−11.0	−15.7
OrangeNSW	−1.4	−10.4	2.8	0.3
STblelndNSW	−1.3	−8.2	−4.2	−6.6
LMrmbNSW	1.5	−4.7	−25.0	−28.0
MrryDrlngNSW	3.8	−11.9	−15.6	−19.8
RoVIC	−1.7	−9.3	0.8	−1.5
YarraRngVic	−7.4	−4.5	12.9	12.9
MorningtnVic	−7.6	−4.4	13.5	13.5
WCentrlHLVic	−1.6	−10.3	3.2	0.8
WOvnsMrryVic	−1.3	−8.2	−4.2	−6.6
EOvensMurVic	−1.3	−8.2	−4.2	−6.6
SWGoulbuVic	−1.3	−8.2	−4.2	−6.6

(Continued)

Table 3. (Continued)

	Changes to Wine Export Demand: 20% Decline in Super Premium and 10% Rise in Commercial Premium	Changes to Wine Export Demand: 10% Decline in Super Premium Wine and 33% Decline in Commercial Premium	Switch to Volumetric Wine Tax at the Beer Rate of A$28/LAL[†]	Switch to Volumetric Wine Tax at the Beer Rate of A$40.82/ LAL[†]
WstMalleeVIC	3.8	−11.9	−15.6	−19.8
EMalleeVic	3.8	−11.9	−15.6	−19.8
DrlngDwnsQld	−1.3	−8.2	−4.2	−6.6
RoQLD	−1.3	−8.2	−4.2	−6.6
RoSA	−1.5	−10.4	3.1	0.6
SAdelaideSA	−5.0	−6.8	8.8	7.8
BarossaSA	−3.8	−8.1	6.7	5.2
MtLoftRanSA	−6.4	−5.5	11.2	10.8
FleurieuSA	0.0	−11.7	0.5	−2.5
LwrNthSA	−3.4	−8.5	6.4	4.7
RiverLndSA	4.4	−13.8	−13.0	−17.5
UpperSESA	−1.6	−9.9	1.9	−0.5
LowerSESA	−5.5	−6.4	9.6	8.7

NMetroWA	-1.5	-10.4	3.1	0.6
RoWA	-1.3	-8.2	-4.2	-6.6
VasseWA	-6.3	-5.7	11.2	10.6
KingWA	-3.8	-8.1	7.1	5.6
TAS	-8.2	-3.8	14.6	14.8
NT/ACT	-1.2	-8.2	-4.2	-6.6
Total, Australia	-1.6	-8.4	0.2	-1.9
Wine climatic zones				
Hot	1.9	-9.0	-18.8	-18.9
Warm	-2.5	-8.5	0.5	0.4
Cool	-5.7	-6.1	8.9	8.9

Notes: LAL, litres of alcohol. †The tax simulations use as their base the resulting data after the export demand shock of a 10 per cent decline in super premium wine coupled with a 33 per cent decline in commercial premium. That is, they are the additional effects due to just the tax change.

Source: Authors' model simulation results.

Table 4. Simulation results: Effects on volume of Australia's grape and wine production (per cent change)

	Changes to Wine Export Demand: 20% Decline in Super Premium and 10% Rise in Commercial Premium	Changes to Wine Export Demand: 10% Decline in Super Premium Wine and 33% Decline in Commercial Premium	Switch to Volumetric Wine Tax at the Beer Rate of A\$28/ LAL[†]	Switch to Volumetric Wine Tax at the Beer Rate of A\$40.82/ LAL[†]
Grapes	−0.5	−4.6	0.2	−0.2
Wine				
Non–premium	0.0	0.1	−31.0	−33.2
Commercial premium	5.5	−17.3	−8.3	−13.4
Super premium	−8.3	−3.7	14.7	15.0
Total wine[‡]	1.6	−9.8	−11.9	−15.1

Notes: LAL, litres of alcohol. [†]The tax simulations use as their base the resulting data after the export demand shock of a 10 per cent decline in super premium wine coupled with a 33 per cent decline in commercial premium. That is, they are the additional effects due to just the tax change.
[‡]Using volumes of production as weights.
Source: Authors' model simulation results.

Australia?[8] We simulate that tax shock first at the low-alcohol beer rate of A\$28 per litre of alcohol and then at the standard beer rate of A\$40.82.

Either tax change would further reduce, albeit slightly, Australian aggregate exports and imports (Table 1). In the hot wine regions the extra tax would lower regional GDP, while in the warm and cool regions the tax change would cause regional GDP to rise slightly, nearly offsetting the negative effects there of even the larger of export demand shock (Table 2). This is because wine production rises in the cool and warm wine regions (by about 9 and 0.5 per cent, respectively) but falls in the hot wine regions (by 19 per cent)

---

[8]A key motivation for taxing alcohol, in addition to raising government revenue, is to address negative externalities associated with consumption. Studies assessing externalities by alcohol type, including by Srivastava and Zhao (2010), find that the incidence of binge drinking is highest for consumers of ready-to-drink spirits-based sweet beverages (RTDs) and full-strength beer, and are lowest for bottled wine and light beer. This is the rationale behind our chosen scenarios.

following either of the two tax reforms (see bottom three rows of columns 3 and 4 of Table 3). When combined with the export shock, this leads to declines of 8 and 10 per cent for the warm and hot wine regions, respectively, but a net increase in cool-climate wine production of 2.8 per cent.

The aggregate national change in wine production following the switch from *ad valorem* to volumetric taxation of wine consumers is a decline of 12 per cent if the lower volumetric tax applies and 15 per cent if the higher one applies. But the compositional changes are large: super premium wine output rises 15 per cent but commercial premium output falls between 8 and 13 per cent and the output of non-premium wine falls by almost one-third (columns 3 and 4 of Table 4). When combined with the second export shock, the larger tax change would result in changes of 11, –31 and –33 per cent for super premium, commercial premium and non-premium wine production, respectively. That amounts to a decline in aggregate national wine production of 25 per cent.

The large non-premium change in response to the switch to a high volumetric tax is not surprising, given that half of domestic wine sales are non-premium and their consumer price would rise by at least three-quarters. The impact of those tax changes on the volume of domestic consumption of non-premium wine are thus even larger: it falls by 60–65 per cent, or nearly three times as much as the decline in domestic sales of commercial premium wine (whose consumer price would rise by 22 or 33 per cent). By contrast, the average price of super premium wine would change very little (–3 or 2 per cent), but the quantity consumed would rise (by about one-quarter) because the tax change would make it relatively cheaper *vis-a-vis* lower quality wines. In aggregate, the retail price of wine to domestic consumers would be roughly 50 per cent higher and the aggregate volume of wine consumed domestically would be just over one-third lower (Table 5).

3.3. Sensitivity analysis of results

In addition to depending on the data that go into the model, these results also depend on numerous parameters. They are particularly sensitive to the assumed elasticity of substitution in consumption between the three wine types. The default elasticity is 2.0, causing total alcohol tax revenue

Table 5. Effects of wine tax changes on the volume and price of household consumption of wine in Australia (per cent change)

	Switch to Volumetric Wine Tax at the Beer Rate of A$28/LAL[†]		Switch to Volumetric Wine Tax at the Beer Rate of A$40.8/LAL[†]	
	Volume	Price	Volume	Price
Non–premium	−60	73	−65	92
Commercial premium	−21	22	−26	33
Super premium	25	−3	26	2
Total wine	−34[‡]	44	−38[‡]	58

Notes: LAL, litres of alcohol. [†]The tax simulations use as their base the resulting data after the export demand shock of a 10 per cent decline in super premium wine coupled with a 33 per cent decline in commercial premium. That is, they are the additional effects due to just the tax change. [‡]Unweighted sum of wine volumes.
Source: Authors' model simulation results.

to rise by about $535 million per year when the volumetric tax is set at the light beer rate, or by $910 million if it were to be set at the standard beer rate of $40.82 per litre of alcohol rather than at the current 29 per cent *ad valorem* rate. But if that elasticity is instead 0.5 (or 4.0), Table 6 suggests that the rise in alcohol tax revenue is about one-third more (or more than one-third less).

That elasticity assumption makes little difference to the change in aggregate domestic volume of wine production, but it makes big differences to the composition of both output and consumption: Table 7a shows that instead of falling 33 per cent, non-premium wine output would fall 14 per cent (45 per cent) if the elasticity was 0.5 (4.0), while instead of rising 15 per cent, super premium wine output would rise 1 per cent (28 per cent) if the elasticity was 0.5 (4.0). This is because the volume of domestic consumption of non-premium wine would fall 27 per cent (88 per cent) if the elasticity was 0.5 (4.0) instead of 65 per cent in the default case, while instead of rising 26 per cent, super premium wine consumption volume would rise 1 per cent (52 per cent) if the elasticity was 0.5 (4.0), as shown in Table 7b.

One final caveat. Throughout we have ignored the fact that in recent years the government has provided a rebate of the Wine Equalization Tax

Table 6. Sensitivity analysis of effects on alcohol tax revenue of a switch to a volumetric wine tax at the beer rate (A$million)

	Wine CES = 0.5	Wine CES = 2.0 [Default Value]	Wine CES = 4.0
(a) Volumetric wine tax at the light beer rate of A$28/LAL[†]			
Beer	−1	−1	−1
Spirits	−1	−1	−1
Wine	787	537	314
Total tax	785	535	312
(b) Volumetric wine tax at the standard beer rate of A$40.82/LAL[†]			
Beer	−1	−1	−1
Spirits	−2	−2	−1
Wine	1233	912	637
Total tax	1230	909	635

Notes: LAL, litres of alcohol; CES, constant elasticity of substitution. [†]Showing sensitivity to change in the elasticity of substitution in consumption between wine types from the default value of 2.0.
Source: Authors' model simulation results.

to those wineries with annual domestic sales below $1.72 million. That rebate amounted to around $110 million in 2006, the model's base year, and to about twice that in subsequent years because New Zealand wineries have also qualified for the rebate on their sales in the Australian market under the Closer Economic Relations agreement between the two countries. Had that rebate been incorporated in the baseline, the benefits estimated above from such a tax change for super premium producers and cool-climate regions would be less; and were it to be discontinued under a volumetric tax scheme, smaller premium wineries and their associated growers may be worse off rather than better off from the tax reform.

4. Conclusion

As is clear from the caveats in the previous section, the above results are very much dependent on both model parameters and the less-than-perfect data available on wine taxes net of rebates and prices and quantities of the three different types of wines and associated grapes produced in the

Table 7. Sensitivity analysis of effects on the volumes of sectoral outputs and domestic wine consumption from a switch to a volumetric wine tax at the beer rate of $40.82/LAL[†] (per cent)

	Wine CES = 0.5	Wine CES = 2.0 [Default Value]	Wine CES = 4.0
(a) Sectoral output volume			
RTDs	−0.15	−0.08	−0.03
Beer premium	−0.05	−0.05	−0.04
Beer non-premium	−0.05	−0.05	−0.05
Spirits	−0.20	−0.18	−0.18
Grapes	−1.2	−0.2	0.5
Wine non-premium	−13.7	−33.2	−45.1
Wine commercial premium	−4.8	−13.4	−20.5
Wine super premium	0.7	15.0	28.4
Total wine	−6.8	−15.1	−20.2
(b) Volume of domestic wine consumption			
Non-premium	−27	−65	−88
Commercial premium	−12	−26	−48
Super premium	1	26	52
Total wine[‡]	−7.2	−4.0	−1.5

Notes: LAL, litres of alcohol; CES, constant elasticity of substitution. [†]Showing sensitivity to change in the elasticity of substitution in consumption between wine types from the default value of 2.0. [‡]Value share-weighted sum of wine volumes

Source: Authors' model simulation results.

various wine regions of Australia. For example, the lower the degree of substitutability between different wine types, the less effective would be a switch from *ad valorem* to volumetric taxing of domestic wine consumption aimed at discouraging binge consumption of non-premium wine; and the higher the WET rebate for smaller growers, the less likely it is that they (and possibly consumers of their super premium wines) would gain from a switch to volumetric wine taxation. But better data and new parameter estimates are unlikely to alter the clear conclusion from the above analysis that both the decline in demand abroad for Australian wine and the prospect of a change in the method of taxing domestic wine consumption are adding non-trivially to the industry's current challenges of disposing of excess stocks of wine that have built up in recent years.[9]

References

Anderson, K. (2010a), 'Reforming Taxes on Wine and Other Alcoholic Beverage Consumption', *Economic Papers*, **29** (2), 197–9.

Anderson, K. (2010b), 'Excise and Import Taxes on Wine versus Beer and Spirits: An International Comparison', *Economic Papers*, **29** (2), 215–28.

Anderson, K., Nelgen, S., Wittwer, G. and Valenzuela, E. (2010), 'Economic Contributions and Characteristics of Grapes and Wine in Australia's Wine Regions', Working Paper 0110, Wine Economics Research Centre, University of Adelaide, February. Available at: http://www.adelaide.edu.au/wine-econ.

AWBC. (2009), 'Australian Winegrape Prices and Tonnes Crushed', Available at: https://www.awbc.com.au/winefacts/data/category.asp?catid=3.

Byrnes, J.M., Cobiac, L.J., Doran, C.M., Vos, T. and Shakeshaft, A.P. (2010), 'Cost-Effectiveness of Volumetric Alcohol Taxation in Australia', *Medical Journal of Australia*, **192**(6), 439–43.

Dixon, P.B., Parmenter, B.R., Sutton, J. and Vincent, D.P. (1982), *ORANI: A Multisector Model of the Australian Economy*. North-Holland, Amsterdam.

Dixon, P.B., Parmenter, B.R., Powell, A.A. and Wilcoxen, P.J. (1992), *Notes and Problems in Applied General Equilibrium Economics*. North-Holland, Amsterdam.

Freebairn, J.W. (2010), 'Special Taxation of Alcoholic Beverages to Correct Market Failures', *Economic Papers*, **29**(2), 200–14.

Hanoch, G. (1971), 'CRESH Production Functions', *Econometrica*, **39**, 695–712.

Ramful, P. and Zhao, X. (2008), 'Individual Heterogeneity in Alcohol Consumption: The Case of Beer, Wine and Spirits in Australia', *Economic Record*, **84**(265), 207–22.

Srivastava, P. and Zhao, X. (2010), 'What Do the Bingers Drink? Micro-econometric Evidence on Negative Externalities of Alcohol Consumption by Beverage Types,' *Economic Papers*, **29**(2), 229–50.

Webb, L.B. (2006), *The Impact of Projected Greenhouse Gas-induced Climate Change on the Australian Wine Industry*. Unpublished PhD thesis, University of Melbourne, Parkville, October.

Wittwer, G. and Anderson, K. (2002), 'Impact of the GST and Wine Tax Reform on Australia's Wine Industry: A CGE Analysis', *Australian Economic Papers*, **41**(1), 69–81.

---

[9] The further appreciation of the Australian dollar since this analysis was completed (of almost one-fifth against the US dollar in the twelve months to May 2011) has added to the decline in demand to Australia's wine exporters.

Appendix

Table A1. Value added by grapes and wine sub-sectors, by region, Australia, 2005–06 (A$million)

	Grapes	Non-Premium Wine	Commercial Premium Wine	Super Premium Wine	Climate Zone
RoNSW	17	24	58	75	Warm
NwcstlNSW	5	0	25	33	Warm
HunterBalNSW	5	0	11	14	Warm
CentTbleNSW	2	0	4	5	Warm
OrangeNSW	1	0	2	2	Warm
STblelndNSW	2	1	2	3	Warm
LMrmbNSW	16	36	42	5	Hot
MrryDrlngNSW	11	5	5	1	Hot
RoVIC	63	0	125	162	Warm
YarraRngVic	7	0	11	27	Cool
MomingtnVic	3	0	8	10	Cool
WCentrlHLVic	2	0	7	9	Cool
WOvnsMrryVic	6	7	16	21	Warm
EOvensMurVic	1	1	2	3	Cool
SWGoulbuVic	2	1	3	4	Warm
WstMalleeVIC	3	1	1	0	Hot
EMalleeVic	20	3	4	1	Hot
DrlngDwnsQld	2	2	4	6	Warm
RoQLD	7	10	24	32	Hot
RoSA	10	13	32	41	Warm
SAdelaideSA	23	0	76	98	Warm
BarossaSA	25	0	60	156	Warm
MtLoftRanSA	6	0	6	16	Cool
FleurieuSA	10	0	9	11	Warm
LwrNthSA	11	1	10	26	Warm
RiverLndSA	38	30	35	5	Hot
UpperSESA	9	0	14	18	Warm

(*Continued*)

Table A1. (*Continued*)

	Grapes	Non-Premium Wine	Commercial Premium Wine	Super Premium Wine	Climate Zone
LowerSESA	7	0	14	18	Cool
NMetroWA	1	2	6	7	Hot
RoWA	16	13	31	40	Warm
VasseWA	14	0	23	60	Warm
KingWA	6	0	9	24	Warm
TAS	7	0	14	18	Cool
NT/ACT	1	1	3	4	Warm
Total, Australia	357	124	686	965	
Wine climatic zones					
Hot	95	85	111	44	
Warm	229	65	519	805	
Cool	35	1	66	106	

Source: Database of the ORANIG06-WINE model. Column 1 is provisional, pending the availability of more-precise grape data from the Australian Bureau of Statistics.

Table A2. Shares of non-premium, commercial premium and super premium wine in the gross value of Australian wine production, by region, 2005–06 (per cent)

	Non-Premium (%)	Commercial Premium (%)	Super Premium (%)	Climate Zone
RoNSW	20	39	41	Warm
NwcstlNSW	6	56	38	Warm
HunterBalNSW	6	56	38	Warm
CentTbleNSW	11	89	0	Warm
OrangeNSW	1	50	49	Warm
STblelndNSW	20	39	41	Warm
LMrmbNSW	72	28	0	Hot
MrryDrlngNSW	31	69	0	Hot
RoVIC	8	43	49	Warm
YarraRngVic	1	6	93	Cool

(*Continued*)

Table A2. (*Continued*)

	Non-Premium (%)	Commercial Premium (%)	Super Premium (%)	Climate Zone
MorningtnVic	0	5	95	Cool
WCentrlHLVic	0	49	51	Cool
WOvnsMrryVic	20	39	41	Warm
EOvensMurVic	20	39	41	Cool
SWGoulbuVic	20	39	41	Warm
WstMalleeVIC	31	69	0	Hot
EMalleeVic	31	69	0	Hot
DrlngDwnsQld	20	39	41	Warm
RoQLD	20	39	41	Hot
RoSA	0	49	51	Warm
SAdelaideSA	1	23	76	Warm
BarossaSA	1	33	67	Warm
MtLoftRanSA	1	13	86	Cool
FleurieuSA	1	60	40	Warm
LwrNthSA	0	35	65	Warm
RiverLndSA	20	80	0	Hot
UpperSESA	4	47	50	Warm
LowerSESA	1	20	79	Cool
NMetroWA	0	65	35	Hot
RoWA	0	65	35	Warm
VasseWA	0	15	85	Warm
KingWA	0	32	68	Warm
TAS	0	1	99	Cool
NT/ACT	20	39	41	Warm
Total, Australia	12	37	51	
Wine climatic zones				
Hot	40	50	10	
Warm	7	38	55	
Cool	2	18	81	

Source: Anderson *et al.* (2010) and database of the ORANIG06-WINE model.

Table A3. Cost structure of wine production in Australia, 2005–06 (per cent)

	Labour	Capital	Grapes	Intermediate Inputs, Land and Other Costs	Total
Non-premium	6	19	6	69	100
Commercial premium	9	22	15	54	100
Super premium	12	26	13	49	100
Total wine	10	24	13	53	100

Source: Database of the ORANIG06-WINE model.

Table A4. Alcohol tax revenue, Australia, 2005–06 (A$million)

Beer	1966
Spirits and Ready To Drink	1775
Wine	893[†]
Total alcohol taxes	4634[†]

Note: [†]This does not exclude rebates to small wineries.
Source: Database of the ORANIG06-WINE model.

Chapter 21

How Much Government Assistance Do European Wine Producers Receive?*

Kym Anderson[†] and Hans G. Jensen[‡]

Abstract

The European Union's (EU) long-standing financial support for its wine industry has been nontrivial but very difficult to estimate. The Organization for Economic Cooperation and Development's (OECD) generic producer support estimate methodology has been able to capture some of the supports, but it excludes such measures as subsidized distillation of low-quality wine, grants to promote wine generically, protection via import tariffs, and grubbing-up premiums. Nor does the OECD disaggregate EU supports to individual member countries. This article provides a new set of more complete estimates of support to EU wine producers. It also reveals how unevenly those supports are spread across EU member countries. The

---

*First published in *Journal of Wine Economics* 11(2): 289–305, August 2016. The authors are grateful for very helpful comments from two referees and for funding support from the University of Adelaide and the University of Copenhagen. The views expressed are the authors' alone.

[†] School of Economics, University of Adelaide, Adelaide, South Australia 5005, Australia, and Australian National University; e-mail: kym.anderson@adelaide.edu.au

[‡] Institute of Food and Resource Economics, University of Copenhagen, 1958 Frederiksberg C, Denmark; e-mail: hans@ifro.ku.dk

new estimates suggest that during 2007–2012, annual assistance amounted to approximately 700 euros per hectare of vines or 0.15 euros per liter of wine produced in the EU as measured at the winery gate. That is equivalent to a nominal rate of direct plus indirect producer assistance of approximately 20%.

1. Introduction

For decades the European Union (EU) and its predecessors have had a Common Market Organization (CMO) for wine that has heavily regulated or influenced the quantity, quality, and price of wine grapes and wine produced in the EU (Gaeta and Corsinovi, 2014; Meloni and Swinnen, 2013; Spahni, 1988). Following a review in 2006 (European Commission, 2006), the policy went through a major reform in 2008, which included a 3-year grubbing-up program that paid growers to remove vines. Meanwhile, financial support for generic promotion of EU wines has been expanding considerably and is budgeted for further expansion during 2014–2018.

The Organization for Economic Cooperation and Development (OECD) has tracked support for farm industries in its member countries since 1986. In the case of the EU (but not other member countries) that has included support for the wine industry. However, using the OECD's generic methodology means that various support measures are not included in its producer support estimates (PSEs). It also means support is shown only for the EU as a whole, not for individual EU member countries. The omitted measures include subsidies for distillation of low-quality wine and any domestic price-raising effect of tariffs on imports of non-EU wines. The industry has also benefitted, along with other farm industries, from non-product-specific support to the rural sector of EU member countries. That support is treated as a generic rural benefit rather than supporting winegrowers or producers of any other particular agricultural product.

This article is not meant as a criticism of that generic OECD methodology. Rather, its purpose is to provide a set of more complete estimates of government support to EU wine producers because many other countries' wine producers are struggling and would like to compare the types and extent of EU support with that from their own government.

The focus is on the period 2007 to 2012, after which the OECD changed its generic methodology. We show how much the level and types of support have altered over that period and how unevenly they are spread across EU member countries. The article begins by describing the data sources. Results presented in tables and figures are then discussed, and the final section draws out implications and concludes.

2. Data

The OECD's PSE database has altered its methodology several times since it was first released more than two decades ago. The latest version, uploaded in July 2015 (OECD, 2015), not only has updated numbers to 2014 but also has altered past numbers back to 1986. The latest estimates are summarized in Table 1. They suggest EU wine producers benefited from transfers from consumers and taxpayers to the extent of about 800 million euros per year in the latter 1980s and the 1990s, but that this fell to less than 500 million euros per year in the past 10 years. Most of that was market price support prior to the policy reforms that began in the early 1990s, but these estimates suggest that has now

Table 1. OECD estimates of direct transfers[a] to wine producers and their nominal rate of direct producer protection,[b] European Union (EU-28), 1986–2014 (annual averages)

	1986–1992	1993–1999	2000–2006	2007–2013	2014
Transfers to producers (million euros per year)[a]	858	705	716	417	489
Of which, transfers due to market price support (million euros per year)	848	769	255	51	0
Nominal rate of direct protection (NRP, %)[b]	8.6	6.4	1.7	0.3	0.0

Notes: [a]The Organization for Economic Cooperation and Development's (OECD) single commodity transfers do not include such supports as subsidies to distill unwanted wine and to promote wine generically, grubbing-up premiums, price support from import tariffs, or any proportion of non-product-specific assistance to the agricultural sector and rural areas. [b]Based on OECD's estimate of nominal protection coefficient (NPC), where NRP = 100(NPC–1). The NRP expresses the estimated direct transfer as a percentage of the gross value of wine production (net of assistance).
Source: OECD (2015).

disappeared, with producer returns being raised by just 0.3% during 2007–2013 and zero in 2014 (see the nominal rate of protection [NRP] row in Table 1), down from approximately 7% in the latter 1980s and 1990s. This recent estimate, however, is not consistent with the fact that tariffs still apply on the EU's wine imports from all countries without a free-trade or association agreement with the EU-28. Those tariffs would have some positive impact on the domestic price of wine in EU countries, but the OECD chooses not to try to measure that because of the heterogeneous nature of wines.

It is possible to amend the OECD's estimates using the data contained in its database plus data available from Eurostat. In the Appendix (Table A1), we focus on aggregated EU-27 wine production from 2007 to 2012 and domestic support given directly to the industry's producers. That table is built up following the OECD's PSE structure prior to its latest methodology revision, which categorizes payments as either "single commodity transfers" or group commodity transfers. To that we have added a pro rata fraction of "all commodity transfers," based on wine's share of agriculture's gross value of production,[1] and "other transfers to producers" that are specific to grape and wine production. At the top of that table, the value of production (at the farm gate, inclusive of transfers) is taken directly from the PSE tables and originates from the Eurostat Dissemination Database, formerly New Cronos database, the official EU data portal. The single farm payment scheme data for wine are from the European Commission (2013) because the OECD no longer itemizes those payments by commodity.[2]

---

[1] For example, all commodity transfer payments given to the agricultural sectors of EU countries in 2012 amounted to €18.7 billion, of which €11.6 billion was national payments (according to information provided by the OECD) and the remainder was EU-funded payments. We allocated that residual to member countries in proportion to their national payments. The types of support that amounted to more than 5% of that 2012 total are as follows: investments in agricultural holdings (25%), fuel tax rebates/subsidies (22%), less-favored area payments (16%), environmentally friendly production (10%), disaster payments (6%), and extensive management of land (6%).

[2] Note also that the EU's Farm Accountancy Data Network provides subsidy information on a per hectare basis, albeit just for their sample farms, at http://ec.europa.eu/agriculture/rica/database/database_en.cfm.

The Appendix (Table A2) includes additional payments not specifically linked to the wine industry and specified by the OECD as "general services support estimates" (GSSEs), again for the EU-27 as a whole and for the period 2007 to 2012. These include some general payments from which the wine industry could benefit, so these are calculated as a pro rata fraction based on wine's share of agriculture's gross value of production within the EU-27 each year.

It might be argued that basing shares on gross production value in these two tables exaggerates the shares attributable to the wine industry because wine's share of total agricultural production exceeds considerably its share of total utilized agricultural land (4.2% compared with 1.8% in 2012, for example). For that reason we also calculated how much lower the total support would be had we used the land share instead of the production value share to calculate that nondirect assistance. It turns out to be about one-ninth lower (see Table 2 notes).

Tables A3 and A4 in the Appendix are structured the same as Tables A1 and A2, but they decompose the EU-27 data into the various receiving member countries, but just for 2012 in the interests of space. The GSSE payments in the OECD database that are not commodity specific are allocated in Table A4 to each member country using (1) official (but not publicly available) EU data taken from the Clearance Audit Trail System database that includes both EU-funded and national payments by member states and (2) wine CMO financial execution data on the national support program (European Commission, 2013).

In all tables, support payments are expressed in millions of euros. The vine bearing area and wine production volumes are shown as well, allowing the calculation of support per hectare of vines and per liter of wine produced. Those summary estimates are depicted in Figures 1 and 2 just for 2012, and the key forms of support since 2007 are summarized in Figure 3.

Table 2 aggregates the data at the bottom of Tables A1 and A2 for the years 2007 to 2012. These can now be compared with the OECD's estimates of transfers to producers, as summarized in Table 1. In Table 2 we report also what our estimates imply in terms of a nominal rate of assistance (NRA). The NRA is broader than the OECD's NRP in Table 1, the latter referring just to price-support measures, whereas the NRA also

Table 2. Direct plus other support to wine producers and their nominal rate of assistance,[a] European Union (EU-27), 2007–2012

	2007	2008	2009	2010	2011	2012[b,c]	2007–2012 Average
Total (direct + other) support (million euros)	2,225	2,488	2,495	2,189	2,364	2,285	2,341
Of which, direct support (million euros)	1,415	1,295	1,172	1,053	978	924	1,140
Nominal rate of total producer assistance[a] (NRA, %)	19.3	22.0	23.2	20.3	18.8	18.7	20.4
Total support per hectare of vines (€)	616	702	716	655	734	712	689
Total support per kiloliter of wine produced (€)	140	157	154	141	152	144	148

Notes: [a]NRA is total support as a percentage of gross value of wine production (net of assistance). The NRA is broader than the Organization for Economic Cooperation and Development's nominal rate of direct protection in Table 1, the latter referring just to price-support measures, whereas the NRA also includes the other transfers to producers that may not alter the price they receive for their output but are part of the total support shown in row 1 of this table (see Anderson et al., 2008).

[b] An assumption in Tables A2 and A4 (see Appendix) is that wine's share of some general services supports is proportional to the gross value of total agricultural production. If instead it is proportional to the share of vines in the total area of land used for agriculture, the numbers in the 2012 column other than for direct support would be one-tenth lower.

[c] The tariffs in EU wine imports had a weighted average in 2011 of 5.8% when expressed in ad valorem terms (estimated from the latest Global Trade Analysis Project Version 8 database; see http://www.gtap.org). Had they raised the domestic producer price in 2012 by a full 5.8% (an upper bound; or by just 1% as a possible lower bound), the market price support in 2012 would have been not zero but 788 million euros (or 136 million euros), thereby raising total producer support by the same amount. The 2012 NRA would then be not 18.7% but 26.4% (or 20.0%), the support per hectare of vines would rise from 712 to 946 (or 754) euros, and support per kiloliter of wine produced would rise from 144 to 191 (or 152) euros.

Source: Authors' calculations based on Tables A1 and A2 (see Appendix).

includes the other identified transfers to producers that may not alter the price they receive for their output (see Anderson et al., 2008).

3. Results

The comparison of Tables 1 and 2 suggests that the OECD estimates, at least since 2007, understate considerably the full extent of government support to the EU wine industry. In contrast to the OECD's estimate of an average transfer of less than 500 million euros per year during 2007–2012,

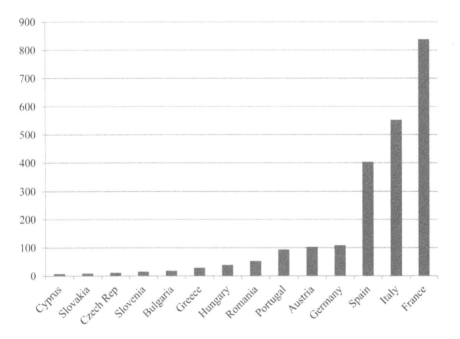

Figure 1. Total support to wine producers, individual European Union member countries in million euros, 2012
Source: Authors' calculations by summing final rows of Tables A3 and A4 (see Appendix).

our Table 2 suggests the number is more than 2,300 million euros per year — and it has not been declining (see also Figure 3a). This implies that gross returns are about one-fifth above what they would be without those supports (an average NRA for the 2007–2012 period of 20.4%). That annual assistance amounts to approximately 700 euros per hectare of vines, or 0.15 euros per liter of wine produced in the EU as measured at the winery gate (Table 2 and Figure 2).

Even these new estimates probably understate the transfers to producers. One reason the numbers in Table 2 are likely to be understated is because the effect of tariffs on imports of non-EU wine in raising producer prices is not included. An upper bound on the extent to which tariffs raised the domestic producer price in 2012 is 5.8%, which is the import-weighted average tariff that year when converted to ad valorem terms. A lower bound might be one-sixth of that (bearing in mind that the EU accounts for a large share of the global wine market and thus is hardly a

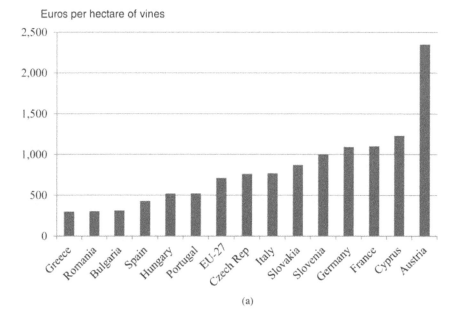

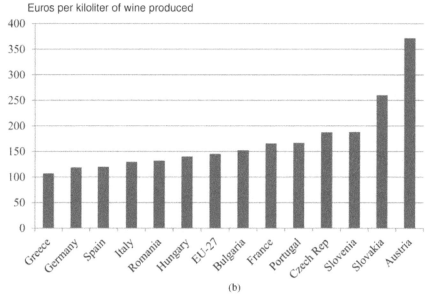

Figure 2. Total support to wine producers per hectare and per kiloliter of wine, individual European Union member countries, 2012

Source: Authors' calculations by summing final rows of Tables A3 and A4 (see Appendix).

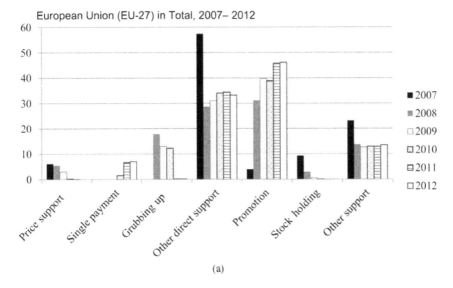

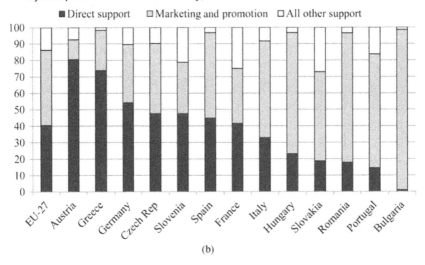

Figure 3. Shares of European Union wine producer supports by measure, 2007–2012 (%)
Source: Authors' calculations from Tables A1 to A4 (see Appendix).

price taker). As reported in Table 2 notes, the 2012 NRA would then be not 18.7% but 26.4% (or 20.0%), the estimated support per hectare of vines would rise from 712 to 946 (or 754) euros, and the support per kiloliter of wine produced would rise from 144 to 191 (or 152) euros.

However, the numbers in Table 2 assume wine's shares of general services supports are proportional to the gross value of total agricultural production. Had we assumed they are proportional to the share of vines in the total area of land used for agriculture, the numbers in the 2012 column of that table, apart from direct support, would be one-tenth lower. This may more or less than offset the effect of omitting tariff protection.

It might also be argued that payments for grubbing up vines should be omitted because they are unrelated to current production and are reducing the future EU (and hence global) supply of wine. However, because this article is trying to estimate not price distortions but financial support to the industry, their inclusion is appropriate.

In addition to an overview estimate of the size of payments given to the wine sector in the EU-27 as a whole, there is also an interest in the allocation of payments between EU member countries. In the Appendix (Tables A3 and A4), estimates of the individual payments by country are given for the year 2012 for all of the EU-27's wine-producing countries. These are summarized in Figures 1 and 2. Of course, France, Italy, and Spain get the lion's share of total payments, being by far the largest wine producers (Figure 1). However, per hectare support ranges from 300 euros in Greece to 2,350 euros in Austria (Figure 2a), and support per liter of wine produced ranges from 0.11 euros in Greece to 0.37 euros in Austria (Figure 2b).

By far the largest — and still growing — category of support is for marketing and generic promotion of EU wines. It accounts for about two-fifths of the estimated total in aggregate (Figure 3a). Direct price supports were most important in 2007, but since then they have been eclipsed by other direct supports and support for marketing and promotion. Although grubbing-up support was nontrivial during the 2008–2010 reform period, those payments are no longer being made. In 2012, direct supports were relatively more important to the Czech Republic, Germany, Slovenia, and Spain, whereas marketing and promotion supports were relatively more important to Bulgaria and Romania (Figure 3b).

4. Implications and conclusion

According to our new estimates, government support for European wine producers continued unabated between 2007 and 2012, albeit in changing forms. The support per hectare of vineyard in 2011 and 2012 exceeded 700 euros in the EU in aggregate and more than 1,000 euros in Austria, Cyprus, France, and Germany. That almost certainly exceeds the support provided by governments in any other major wine-producing country. It is equivalent to an average of 0.15 euros per liter of wine produced and more than 0.25 euros in Cyprus (at 1.02 euros, not shown in Figure 2b), Austria, and Slovakia.

Generic promotion accounted for a growing share of total EU support, amounting in 2012 to 0.009 euros per liter of wine produced. By contrast, Australia's expenditure per liter on generic promotion that year was half that amount (Anderson and Aryal, 2015). The EU provided a total of 522 million euros for wine promotion during 2008/2009 to 2012/2013 (Table A2), and, despite the uncovering of many misappropriations, that expenditure is to be more than doubled to 1,156 million euros for the period 2013/2014 to 2017/2018 (European Court of Auditors, 2014). Given that this promotion item (an average annual 231 million euros) is but one-tenth of the total support to the EU industry in 2012, it is little wonder that other wine-producing countries worry about their ability to compete in international markets against supported EU producers. True, vineyard planting restrictions may have reduced the extent to which the previously mentioned financial supports add to EU wine output and exports (Deconinck and Swinnen, 2015), but they are being relaxed. The empirical impact of past area restrictions and their recent relaxation is a topic worthy of further research.

References

Anderson, K. (with the assistance of Aryal, N.R.) (2015). *Growth and Cycles in Australia's Wine Industry: A Statistical Compendium, 1843 to 2013*. Adelaide, South Australia, Australia: University of Adelaide Press.

Anderson, K., Kurzweil, M., Martin, W., Sandri, D., and Valenzuela, E. (2008). Measuring distortions to agricultural incentives, revisited. *World Trade Review,* 7(4), 675–704.

Deconinck, K., and Swinnen, J. (2015). The economics of planting rights in wine production. *European Review of Agricultural Economics,* 42(3), 419–440.

European Commission. (2006). *Communication from the Commission to the Council and the European Parliament: Towards a Sustainable European Wine Sector.* COM (2006) 319 and SEC (2006) 770. Brussels, Belgium: Commission of the European Communities.

European Commission. (2013). *Wine CMO Financial Execution 2012.* Commission Regulation EC 555/2008. Brussels, Belgium: Commission of the European Communities. Accessed March 15, 2015, at http://ec.europa.eu/agriculture/wine/reforms/index_en.htm.

European Court of Auditors. (2014). *Is the EU Investment and Promotion Support to the Wine Sector Well Managed and Are Its Results on the Competitiveness of EU Wines Demonstrated?* Special Report No. 9. Luxembourg: Publications Office of the European Union.

Gaeta, D., and Corsinovi, P. (2014). *Economics, Governance, and Politics in the Wine Market: European Union Developments.* London: Palgrave Macmillan.

Meloni, G., and Swinnen, J. (2013). The political economy of European wine regulation. *Journal of Wine Economics,* 8(3), 244–284.

Organization for Economic Cooperation and Development (OECD). (2013). Producer and Consumer Support Estimates database. Accessed March 2015 at http://www.oecd.org/tad/agricultural-policies/producerandconsumersupportestimatesdatabase.htm#country.

Organization for Economic Cooperation and Development (OECD). (2015). Producer and Consumer Support Estimates database. Accessed July 20, 2015, at http://www.oecd.org/tad/agricultural-policies/producerandconsumersupportestimatesdatabase.htm#country.

Spahni, P. (1988). *The Common Wine Policy and Price Stabilization.* Aldershot, UK: Avebury.

Appendix

Table A1. Direct supports for wine producers, European Union (EU-27), 2007–2012 (million euros)

	2007	2008	2009	2010	2011	2012
Value of production (at farm gate, inclusive of price support)	13,769	13,785	13,266	12,954	14,937	14,523
Single commodity transfers (SCTs)						
Market price support	136.9	137.0	74.7	5.5	2.2	0.0
National output payments for wine	1.2	0.4	0.1	0.0	0.0	0.0
Agri-monetary (labor insurance 35%) wine	−0.3	0.0	0.0	0.0	0.0	0.0
Restructuring and conversion of vineyards	447.8	−3.7	−5.2	−10.4	0.0	0.0
Vineyard restructuring national expenditures	17.9	4.7	2.2	3.3	3.1	4.0
Payments for wine in most remote regions	1.7	2.5	2.5	2.5	2.5	2.5
Area payments for wine national expenditures	0.0	0.0	0.8	0.8	0.8	0.7
Payments for integrated production of wine: Rural Development Regulation (RDR) expenditures	5.5	9.6	10.9	11.9	11.0	11.4
Payments for integrated production of wine: national expenditures	8.5	10.7	10.6	10.3	10.6	10.2
Vineyard improvement/restructuring national expenditures	7.0	0.3	0.3	0.3	0.1	0.1
Total SCT	626.1	161.6	96.9	24.3	30.4	29.1
Group commodity transfers (GCTs)						
Total GCTS Investments in vineyards, national expenditures	6.2	6.9	25.9	14.3	5.5	9.9

(*Continued*)

Table A1. (Continued)

	2007	2008	2009	2010	2011	2012
All commodity transfers (ACTs)						
Wine's share of total ACT payments (based on gross value of production)	683.2	669.1	727.0	711.7	782.9	718.9
Other transfers to producers (OTPs)						
Single payment scheme	0.0	0.0	0.0	33.4	156.6	159.9
Permanent abandonment premiums in respect of areas under vine	97.7	12.9	0.0	0.1	0.0	0.0
Grubbing-up scheme (following wine reform of 2007/2008)	0.0	444.1	322.7	269.2	4.8	4.9
Other	1.9	0.2	0.0	0.2	−2.7	1.0
Total OTP	99.6	457.1	322.7	302.8	158.8	165.7
Total direct support (SCT + GCT + ACT + OTP)	1,415.2	1,294.8	1,172.4	1,053.0	977.5	923.6
Total EU-27 vineyard area (1,000 ha)	3,609	3,545	3,487	3,342	3,219	3,209
Total EU-27 wine production (billion liters)	15.91	15.81	16.22	15.48	15.57	15.90
Direct support per hectare of vines (€)	392	365	336	315	304	288
Direct support per thousand liters of wine produced (€)	89	82	72	68	63	58

Sources: Authors' calculations building on producer support estimates by Organization for Economic Cooperation and Development (2013) and single farm payments from European Commission (2013).

Table A2. Other supports for wine producers, European Union (EU-27), 2007–2012 (million euros)

	2007	2008	2009	2010	2011	2012
General services support estimate						
H. Research and development						
Wine's share of total payments (based on gross value of production)	85.4	85.9	91.3	77.9	34.7	125.2
I. Agricultural schools						
Wine's share of total payments (based on gross value of production)	55.5	49.7	52.5	59.0	63.8	93.8
J. Inspection services						
Wine's share of total payments (based on gross value of production)	26.8	29.0	31.1	27.8	22.5	13.9
K. Infrastructure						
Wine's share of total payments (based on gross value of production)	182.0	154.9	138.2	115.8	130.8	75.7
L. Marketing and promotion						
Aid for the use of must	164.2	21.5	1.7	0.6	0.0	0.0
National support programs for the wine sector (EC 479/2008 EU funded)						
Promotion	0.0	35.2	87.2	111.7	142.5	145.4
Restructuring and conversion	0.0	263.8	368.6	406.4	585.1	594.3
Ongoing plans N 1493/1999	0.0	62.4	31.9	19.5	6.3	4.8
Green harvesting	0.0	0.1	16.8	24.6	7.6	0.8
Harvest insurance	0.0	2.0	38.3	31.2	36.9	42.2
Investments	0.0	18.6	74.3	74.4	141.3	209.6
By-product distillation	0.0	85.5	95.9	85.5	92.0	49.1

(*Continued*)

Table A2. (*Continued*)

	2007	2008	2009	2010	2011	2012
Portable alcohol distillation	0.0	145.1	165.5	15.9	11.8	0.0
Crisis distillation	0.0	50.0	19.2	10.6	-0.6	0.0
Concentrated grape must	0.0	84.6	78.8	62.4	46.8	0.3
Marketing aid to producer groups in most-remote regions (processing of Madeira wine)	0.5	0.5	0.4	0.0	0.0	0.0
Marketing aid to producer groups in most-remote regions (marketing of Madeira wine)	0.4	1.4	1.2	0.0	0.0	0.0
Marketing aid to producer groups in most-remote regions (quality wine)	2.2	2.4	2.8	2.9	2.9	0
Wine's share of total payments (based on gross value of production)	84.1	24.7	10.2	5.7	10.0	6.0
M. Public stock holding						
Intervention for products of the wine-growing sector	73.8	34.2	0.2	0.3	0.0	0.0
Buying-in of alcohol from compulsory distillation	128.3	36.6	12.1	1.6	0.1	0.0
Wine's share of total payments (based on gross value of production)	4.6	3.3	3.2	0.6	0.5	0.1
N. Miscellaneous						
Wine's share of total payments (based on gross value of production)	1.9	2.1	1.5	1.8	1.7	0.2
Total other support	809.6	1,193.5	1,322.8	1,136.1	1,386.8	1,361.4
Total EU-27 vineyard area (1,000 ha)	3,609	3,545	3,487	3,342	3,219	3,209
Total EU-27 wine production (billion liters)	15.91	15.81	16.22	15.48	15.57	15.90
Other support per hectare of vines (€)	224	337	379	340	431	424
Other support per thousand liters of wine produced (€)	51	75	82	73	89	86

Sources: Authors' calculations building on producer support estimates by Organization for Economic Cooperation and Development (2013).

Table A3. Direct supports for wine producers, European Union (EU-27), by country, 2012 (million euros)

EU-27 Wine Year 2012	EU-27	Bulgaria	Czech Republic	Germany	Greece	Spain	France	Italy	Cyprus	Hungary	Austria	Portugal	Romania	Slovenia	Slovakia
Value of production	14,523	38	31	1,189	29	1,699	8,064	2,101	5	106	524	372	202	99	43
Single commodity transfers (SCTs)															
Market price support	0.0	0	0	0	0	0	0	0	0	0	0	0	0	0	0
National output payments for wine	0.0	0	0	0	0	0	0	0	0	0	0	0	0	0	0
Agri-monetary (labor insurance 35%)	0.0	0	0	0	0	0	0	0	0	0	0	0	0	0	0
Restructuring/conversion of vineyards	0.0	0	0	0	0	0	0	0	0	0	0	0	0	0	0
Vineyard restructuring national expenditures	4.0	0.0	0.0	0.0	0.0	0.0	0.0	0.0	0.0	0.0	0.0	0.0	3.9	0.0	0.0
Vineyard restructuring	0.0	0.0	0.0	0.0	0.0	0.0	0.0	0.0	0.0	0.0	0.0	0.0	0.0	0.0	0.0
Payments for wine in remote regions	2.5	0.0	0.0	0.0	2.5	0.0	0.0	0.0	0.0	0.0	0.0	0.0	0.0	0.0	0.0
Area payments for wine national expenditures	0.7	0.0	0.0	0.0	0.0	0.0	0.0	0.0	0.0	0.0	0.0	0.0	0.0	0.0	0.0
Payments for integrated production of wine: RDR expenditures	11.4	0.0	1.5	0.0	0.0	0.0	0.0	0.0	2.0	0.0	7.2	0.0	0.0	0.7	0.0
Payments for integrated production of wine: national expenditures	10.2	0.0	1.4	0.0	0.0	0.0	0.0	0.0	1.8	0.0	6.4	0.0	0.0	0.7	0.0

(*Continued*)

Table A3. (Continued)

EU-27 Wine Year 2012	EU-27	Bulgaria	Czech Republic	Germany	Greece	Spain	France	Italy	Cyprus	Hungary	Austria	Portugal	Romania	Slovenia	Slovakia
Vineyard improvement/ restructuring national expenditures	0.1	0.0	0.0	0.0	0.1	0.0	0.0	0.0	0.0	0.0	0.0	0.0	0.0	0.0	0.0
Total SCT	29.1	0.0	2.9	0.0	2.6	0.0	0.0	0.0	3.7	0.0	13.6	0.0	3.9	1.4	0.0
Group commodity transfers (GCTs)		0.0	0.0	0.0	0.0	0.0	0.0	0.0	0.0	0.0	0.0	0.0	0.0	0.0	0.0
GCT5 Investments in vineyards, national expenditures	9.9	0.0	2.0	0.0	0.0	2.1	0.0	0.0	0.0	5.8	0.0	0.0	0.0	0.0	0.0
Total GCT	9.9	0.0	2.0	0.0	0.0	2.1	0.0	0.0	0.0	5.8	0.0	0.0	0.0	0.0	0.0
All commodity transfers (ACTs)		0.0	0.0	0.0	0.0	0.0	0.0	0.0	0.0	0.0	0.0	0.0	0.0	0.0	0.0
Wines share of total ACT payments	718.9	0.2	0.9	59.0	3.0	32.7	348.2	180.4	0.3	3.2	60.6	13.4	5.5	6.2	1.8
Total ACT	718.9	0.2	0.9	59.0	3.0	32.7	348.2	180.4	0.3	3.2	60.6	13.4	5.5	6.2	1.8
Other transfers to producers (OTPs)		0.0	0.0	0.0	16.0	142.7	0.0	0.0	0.0	0.0	0.0	0.0	0.0	0.0	0.0
Single payment scheme	159.9	0.0	0.0	0.0	0.0	0.0	0.0	0.0	0.0	0.0	0.0	0.0	0.0	0.0	0.0

Permanent abandonment premiums	0.0	0.0	0.0	0.0	0.0	0.0	0.0	0.0	0.0	0.0	0.0	0.0	0.0
Grubbing-up scheme	0.0	0.0	0.0	0.0	0.0	3.0	0.1	1.7	0.0	0.0	0.0	0.0	0.0
Other	1.0	0.0	0.0	0.0	0.0	0.0	0.1	0.1	0.0	0.1	0.1	0.1	0.0
Total OTP	165.7	0.0	0.0	0.0	16.0	145.8	0.2	1.8	0.0	0.1	0.1	0.1	0.0
Total direct support (SCT + GCT + ACT + OTP)	923.6	5.8	59.1	21.7	180.6	348.4	182.1	9.1	74.3	13.5	9.5	7.6	1.8
Vineyard area (1,000 ha)	3,209	16	100	99	943	761	718	7	76	44	180	177	16	11
Total wine production (billion liters)	15.90	0.07	0.92	0.28	3.37	5.08	4.27	0.01	0.28	0.28	0.56	0.41	0.09	0.04
Direct support per hectare of vines (€)	288	367	594	218	192	458	254	600	120	1,704	75	54	466	172
Direct support per thousand liters of wine (€)	59	89	64	79	54	69	43	473	32	267	24	23	89	49

Sources: Authors' calculations building on producer support estimates by Organization for Economic Cooperation and Development (2013) and single farm payments from European Commission (2013).

Table A4. Other supports for wine producers, European Union 27 (EU-27), by country, 2012 (million euros)

EU-27 Wine Year 2012	EU-27	Bulgaria	Czech Republic	Germany	Greece	Spain	France	Italy	Cyprus	Hungary	Austria	Portugal	Romania	Slovenia	Slovakia
H. Research and development															
Wine's share of total payments	125.2	0.0	0.3	1.1	0.1	0.5	103.6	17.9	0.0	0.1	0.3	0.1	0.1	0.9	0.2
I. Agricultural schools															
Wine's share of total payments	93.8	0.0	0.1	0.4	0.0	0.9	83.6	1.8	0.0	0.3	4.5	1.3	0.4	0.2	0.1
J. Inspection services															
Wine's share of total payments	13.9	0.0	0.0	1.5	0.0	0.1	7.9	1.9	0.0	0.4	0.0	0.3	0.0	0.8	1.0
K. Infrastructure															
Wine's share of total payments	75.7	0.2	0.7	8.1	0.4	11.2	13.2	22.1	0.0	0.5	1.4	13.6	1.4	1.4	1.5
L. Marketing and promotion															
National support programs for the wine sector (EC 479/2008 EU funded)															
Promotion	145.4	0.0	0.0	1.2	3.3	38.3	17.1	73.6	0.0	0.0	1.2	9.2	0.7	0.8	0.1
Restructuring and conversion	594.3	17.7	3.2	16.9	3.9	163.7	108.5	154.4	3.7	22.6	2.2	50.9	41.2	4.2	1.3
Ongoing plans N 1493/1999	4.8	0.0	0.0	0.0	0.0	0.1	1.7	0.0	0.0	0.0	0.2	0.0	0.0	0.0	2.8
Green harvesting	0.8	0.0	0.0	0.0	0.0	0.0	0.0	0.8	0.0	0.0	0.0	0.0	0.0	0.0	0.0
Harvest insurance	42.2	0.6	0.0	1.5	0.0	0.0	0.0	35.1	0.2	0.0	0.0	4.3	0.2	0.0	0.3

How Much Government Assistance Do European Wine Producers Receive? 525

Investments	209.6	0.0	2.0	19.2	0.0	0.0	118.4	55.2	0.8	5.7	7.6	0.0	0.0	0.0	0.7
By-product distillation	49.1	0.0	0.0	0.0	0.0	7.8	34.7	5.2	0.0	0.8	0.0	0.7	0.0	0.0	0.0
Portable alcohol distillation	0.0	0.0	0.0	0.0	0.0	0.0	0.0	0.0	0.0	0.0	0.0	0.0	0.0	0.0	0.0
Crisis distillation	0.0	0.0	0.0	0.0	0.0	0.0	0.0	0.0	0.0	0.0	0.0	0.0	0.0	0.0	0.0
Concentrated grape must	0.3	0.0	0.0	0.0	0.0	0.0	0.0	0.3	0.0	0.0	0.0	0.0	0.0	0.0	0.0
Wine's share of total payments M. Public stock holding	6.0	0.0	0.0	0.1	0.0	0.6	1.8	2.5	0.0	0.0	0.7	0.2	0.0	0.0	0.0
Wine's share of total payments N. Miscellaneous	0.1	0.0	0.0	0.0	0.0	0.0	0.0	0.1	0.0	0.0	0.0	0.0	0.0	0.0	0.0
Wine's share of total payments	0.2	0.0	0.0	0.2	0.0	0.0	0.0	0.0	0.0	0.0	0.0	0.0	0.0	0.0	0.0
Total other support	1,361.4	18.6	6.4	50.2	7.7	223.1	490.4	370.7	4.6	30.4	29.1	80.5	44	8.4	7.8
Vineyard area (1,000 ha)	3,208	60	16	100	99	943	761	718	7	76	44	180	177	16	11
Total wine production (billion liters)	15.90	0.12	0.07	0.92	0.28	3.37	5.08	4.27	0.01	0.28	0.28	0.56	0.41	0.09	0.04
Other support per hectare of vine (€)	424	310	400	502	78	237	644	516	657	400	661	447	249	525	709
Other support per thousand liters of wine (€)	86	155	91	55	28	66	97	87	460	109	104	144	107	93	195

Sources: Authors' calculations building on producer support estimates by Organization for Economic Cooperation and Development (2013) and European Commission (2013).

E. Internationalization of Winegrape Varietal Choices

Chapter 22

Changing Varietal Distinctiveness of the World's Wine Regions: Evidence from a New Global Database*

Kym Anderson[†]

Abstract

Consumers are always looking for new types of wines. Producers compete for their attention by trying to product differentiate at the same time as they are responding to technological improvements, climate change, and evolving demand patterns. In doing so, wineries are increasingly highlighting their regional and varietal distinctiveness. This paper examines the extent to which the choice of winegrape varieties in wine

---

*First published in *Journal of Wine Economics* 9(3): 249–72, 2014. Revision of a paper presented at the Annual Conference of the American Association of Wine Economists, Stellenbosch, South Africa, June 26–29, 2013. The author is grateful for meticulous research assistance by Nanda Aryal in compiling the database and indicators, for helpful comments from two anonymous referees, and for financial assistance from Australia's Grape and Wine Research and Development Corporation (Project Number UA 12/08). Views expressed are the author's alone.

[†]Wine Economics Research Centre, School of Economics, University of Adelaide, Adelaide SA 5005, and Crawford School, Australian National University, Canberra, ACT 2600; e-mail: kym.anderson@adelaide.edu.au.

regions has already changed over the first decade of the twenty-first century in both the Old World and New World. In doing so, it reports a varietal intensity index of different regions and an index of similarity of varietal mix between regions. The study is based on a new database of vine-bearing areas circa 2000 and 2010 for nearly 1,300 DNA-distinct winegrape varieties, spanning over 600 regions in 44 countries that together account for 99 percent of the world's wine production.

1. Introduction

The dramatic globalization of the world's wine markets over the past two or three decades has generated countless new wine consumers. This has added to both the opportunities and the competitive challenges for producers seeking to differentiate their product to attract the attention of consumers. Consumers, in turn, are always looking for new types of wines and more so as wines within at least the lower-priced product ranges become more homogeneous, with the multinationalization of both wineries and wine retailers.

One strategy for producers has been to display grape varietal names on wine bottle labels. Its success, especially for lower-priced New World wines, has led to demands in the European Union (EU) for freeing up labeling laws so as to allow such labeling there also. Meanwhile, producers in the New World are increasingly realizing the marketing value of going beyond country of origin to regional labeling as another form of product differentiation — something that has long been practiced by Europe's traditional producers.

In addition to striving to differentiate their product, producers are also well aware of the impact that climate changes (higher temperatures, more extreme weather events) are having on their winegrapes. Adaptation strategies include switching to warmer-climate or more-resilient grape varieties and relocating to a higher latitude or altitude to retain the current mix of grape varieties. Especially in the New World, where regions are still trying to identify their varietal comparative advantages and where regulations do not restrict varietal choice, winegrowers are continually on the lookout for attractive alternative varieties that do well in climates similar to what they expect theirs to become in the decades ahead. Moreover, the biotechnology revolution is providing breeders with new opportunities, which is increasing the interest in exploring traits of little-known varieties.

Some people also are concerned that the diversity of winegrapes is narrowing to a few "international" varieties. Johnson and Robinson (2013, p. 8) note that vignerons are at last beginning to respond by reverting to neglected local varieties in the Old World and by exploring alternatives to the main "international" varieties in the New World. But how severe is the current concentration compared with earlier times, and how different is the concentration in the Old World compared with the New World?

These biodiversity concerns, together with marketing and climate adaptation needs, are generating a rapidly growing demand for information on which winegrape varieties are grown in the world's various wine regions. Since 1971, *The World Atlas of Wine* has provided a great deal of information about where winegrapes are grown (the seventh edition is Johnson and Robinson [2013]). That and other wine atlases have been complemented by a new book by Robinson, Harding, and Vouillamoz (2012), which provides a detailed guide to 1,368 of the world's commercially grown "prime" varieties and their various synonyms, based on the latest DNA research. However, neither of those seminal books, nor any other wine atlas or wine encyclopedia, provides comprehensive global data on the bearing areas of winegrapes by region and variety.[1]

This paper draws on a newly compiled global database (Anderson and Aryal, 2013) to estimate several indicators that capture changes over the first decade of the twenty-first century in the varietal mix of the world's wine regions. It builds on an earlier study of more limited data for 2000 by Anderson (2010) in several ways: it has data for 2010 as well as 2000; it includes more than 30 additional countries so that the sample now covers as much as 99 percent of global wine production; it is far more detailed in terms of having more than 600 regions and 2,000 varieties (of which

---

[1] The handbook by Fegan (2003) provides information for 2000 on key regions in the main wine-producing countries, and on the key varieties in those countries, but it does not provide a matrix of variety by region data. That is also true of two other sources of global wine varietal information, namely JKI (2013) and OIV (2012).

almost 1,300 are "primes" and the rest are their synonyms), compared with only 166 regions and 258 varieties previously; and it has removed spurious differences in varietal mixes resulting from the use of different varietal names for what have been shown recently to be DNA-identical varieties (thanks to the painstaking scientific work that led to the book by Robinson *et al.*, 2012).

The paper is structured as follows. Section 2 describes the database. Section 3 defines two key indexes that have been calculated to help summarize the data. Those data are then used to provide an empirical picture of the changing varietal distinctiveness of the world's wine regions. This is done in Section 4 by answering a sample of questions which, in the process, provide a sense of the breadth of the database. (Space limitations prevent us from highlighting the depth of the database in terms of its within-country regional detail.) The final section discusses possible extensions and other uses of the database.

2. The new database

Data on the bearing area of winegrapes are available by variety and region for most key wine-producing countries. In the case of the EU countries, area data are available from one source (Eurostat, 2013), while for other countries they are typically available online from a national wine industry body or the national statistical agency. The United States and Canada, where data are collected at the state/provincial level and only for those with significant wine production, are key exceptions.

The years chosen correspond to the most recent decadal agricultural census periods of the European Union, which were 1999 or 2000 and 2009 or 2010. For the non-EU countries, data have been sought for the earlier year in the Northern Hemisphere and the latter year in the Southern Hemisphere. Inevitably, not all other countries or regions had data for exactly those vintages, but in most cases the data refer to vintages that were only six months apart.

The raw data have been compiled by Anderson and Aryal (2013), and various indicators from that database have been assembled in comprehensive tables and figures by Anderson (2013). Appendix Table 1 lists the countries included and their relative importance in the global bearing area of winegrapes and in wine production, and it also shows the other countries reported to be producing wine (although collectively the latter group accounts for just 1 percent of global wine output).

Of the 44 countries included in Appendix Table 1, reliable area data for 2000 were unavailable for nine of them (China, Japan, Kazakhstan, Mexico, Myanmar, Peru, Thailand, Turkey, and Ukraine). The combined share of global wine production of those nine countries in 2000 was only 1.6% (compared with 5.1% in 2010), but their varietal contributions are included as a group (called "Missing 9 in 2000") by assuming each of them had (i) the same varietal distribution in 2000 as in 2010 and (ii) a national area that was the same fraction of its 2010 area then as was its national wine production volume. As well, the global bearing area of the world's 50 most important varieties in 1990 has been estimated using data in Fegan (2003).

The number of winegrape regions in each country for which bearing area data are available varies greatly across the sample of 44 countries (Appendix Table 2). And the number is not the same for each country in the two chosen years, which means that some regional detail is necessarily lost through aggregation when we seek to compare varietal mixes of each region in the two sample years. Nonetheless, even for that comparative exercise there are as many as 410 matching regions globally.

Thus the database on which this volume draws involves two years (2000 and 2010, plus some 1990 data), more than 600 regions (in 44 countries), and nearly 1,300 prime varieties. Such a large three-dimensional database potentially has 1.5 billion numbers in its cells (many of which are zeros). It can be sliced in three ways: across regions, years, or varieties. To assist in digesting such large spreadsheets, it is helpful to summarize the data by calculating a pair of indexes.

3. Two indexes

In addition to regional and varietal shares, two indexes that are used in the next section are defined in turn in this section: the varietal intensity index, and the varietal similarity index.

3.1. *Varietal intensity index*

A varietal intensity index is defined as a variety's share of a region's winegrape area divided by that variety's share of the global winegrape bearing area. The varietal intensity index is thus a complement to share information in that it indicates the importance of a variety in a region not relative to other varieties in that region but, rather, relative to that variety in the world.

Specifically, define f_{im} as the proportion of the bearing area of grape variety m in the total winegrape-bearing area in region or country i such that the proportions fall between 0 and 1 and sum to 1 (i.e., there is a total of M different grape varieties across the world, and $0 \leq f_{im} \leq 1$ and $\Sigma_m f_{im} = 1$). For the world as a whole, f_m is the bearing area of grape variety m as a proportion of the total global winegrape area, and $0 \leq f_m \leq 1$ and $\Sigma_m f_m = 1$. Then the varietal intensity index, V_{im} for variety m in region i, is:

$$V_{im} = f_{im}/f_m \qquad (1)$$

3.2. Regional similarity index

An index of varietal similarity has been defined by Anderson (2010) to measure the extent to which the varietal mix of one region or country matches that of another region or country or the world. It can also be used to compare the varietal mix of a region or country over time. In defining the index, Anderson (2010) borrows and adapts an approach introduced by Griliches (1979) and Jaffe (1986). That approach has been used subsequently by Jaffe (1989), and by others, including Alston, Norton, and Pardey (1998) and Alston et al. (2010, ch. 4), to measure interfirm or interindustry or interregional technology spillover potential.

The mix of grape varieties is a form of revealed preference or judgment by vignerons about what is best to grow in their region. That judgment is affected by not only terroir but also past and present economic considerations, including current expectations about future price trends, plus the sunk cost that would be involved in grafting new varieties onto existing rootstocks or grubbing out and replacing existing varieties.

The vector of grape varietal shares defined above, $f_i = (f_{i1},..., f_{iM})$, locates region i in M-dimensional space. Noting that proximity is defined by the direction in which the f-vectors are pointing, but not necessarily their length, Jaffe (1989) proposes a measure called the "angular separation of the vectors", which is equal to the cosine of the angle between them. If there were just two varieties, m and n, and region i had 80% of its total vine area planted to variety m whereas only 40% of region j was

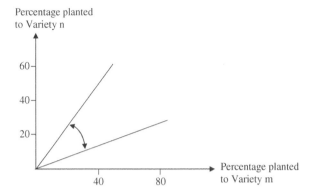

Figure 1. Angular separation between two regions, each growing two grape varieties

planted to variety m, then their index of regional similarity is the cosine of the arrowed angle between the two vectors (Figure 1). When there are M varieties, this measure is defined as:

$$\omega_{ij} = \frac{\sum_{m=1}^{M} f_{im} f_{jm}}{\left(\sum_{m=1}^{M} f_{im}^2\right)^{1/2} \left(\sum_{m=1}^{M} f_{jm}^2\right)^{1/2}}, \quad (2)$$

where again f_{im} is the area of plantings of grape variety m as a proportion of the total grape plantings in region i such that these proportions fall between 0 and 1 and sum to 1 (i.e., there is a total of M different grape varieties across the world, and $0 \leq f_{im} \leq 1$ and $\sum_m f_{im} = 1$). This makes it possible to indicate the degree of varietal mix "similarity" of any pair of regions. The index also can be generated for each region relative to the average of the world's N regions, which we call ω. In short, ω_{ij} measures the degree of overlap between f_i and f_j. The numerator of Equation (2) will be large when i's and j's varietal mixes are very similar. The denominator normalizes the measure to unity (that is, 1) when f_i and f_j are identical. Hence, ω_{ij} will be 0 for pairs of regions with no overlap in their grape varietal mix, and 1 for pairs of regions with an identical varietal mix. For cases in between those two extremes, $0 < \omega_{ij} < 1$. It is conceptually similar to a correlation coefficient. Like a correlation coefficient, it is completely symmetrical in that $\omega_{ij} = \omega_{ji}$ and $\omega_{ii} = 1$. Thus the results can be summarized in a symmetrical matrix with values of 1 on the diagonal, plus a vector that reports the index for each region relative to the global varietal mix.

4. The changing varietal distinctiveness of the world's wine regions

There are vast differences between countries in their winegrape-bearing areas. The three biggest, France, Italy, and Spain, accounted for 54% of the world's winegrape vineyard area in both 2000 and 2010. The next biggest is the United States, but its share is less than 5%. The same four countries dominate global wine production volume and value[2] (accounting for 60% in aggregate). However, the 2010 rankings among them in wine production differ considerably from that in winegrape area: France and Italy are ahead of Spain in wine production volume, and France and the United States are well ahead of Italy and Spain in terms of the value of wine production, followed by Germany and Australia. One reason for these differing rankings is that the huge La Mancha region of Spain has bush vines sparsely planted to the drought-resistant but low-quality Airen variety, much of whose grapes are often used to produce brandy rather than wine.

The global area of winegrapes has declined by almost 6% over the first decade of the twenty-first century. This is despite increases of around 30% in the United States and Georgia, 40% in the Czech Republic, and 220% in New Zealand. The biggest decreases were in Spain (13%), Portugal (20%), and several countries in southeastern Europe. That overall decline continues an earlier trend: the global area fell 8% in the final decade of the twentieth century.

A glimpse of how the varietal distinctiveness of the world's wine regions has changed over the decade to 2010 can be seen by interrogating the database to answer the following questions:

- Has varietal diversity of the world's vineyard increased or decreased over that decade? Did the change in the New World differ from that in the Old World?

---

[2] The pretax wholesale value of wine data are estimated for 2009 by Anderson and Nelgen (2011, table 175).

- How are those changes reflected in the global area rankings of varieties?
- Are red winegrapes becoming more prominent? In just some or many countries?
- How has the varietal intensity of each country changed since 2000?
- How similar is each country's varietal mix to that of other countries and to the world aggregate mix? How much has each country's varietal mix changed since 2000?

4.1. Changing varietal diversity of the world's vineyard

The extent of varietal concentration in the world's vineyard increased nontrivially between 2000 and 2010. This increase in concentration/ decrease in diversity can be seen in Figure 2a, where the 2010 cumulative curve is well above that for 2000. Indeed the six-percentage-point difference for most of the first 40 varieties continues right through to the 1290th variety. Moreover, that decline in diversity is almost equally as strong in the Old World as in the New World, even though the extent of diversity is greater in the Old World (Figure 2b).

Another way to explore the diversity issue is to examine what share of the global area is devoted to varieties by their country of origin. Between 2000 and 2010, the global winegrape share devoted to varieties of French origin rose from 26% to 36%. Particularly striking is the high and increasing dominance of French varieties in the New World's vineyards: that share averaged 67% in 2010, up from 53% in 2000. It compares with an increase from 20% to 27% for the Old World's vineyards. The next most important country of origin is Spain, accounting for 26% of the world's area in 2010, down from 28% in 2000, which is just a little above Spain's own share of the global bearing area of 22–24%. Third is Italy, whose country of origin share is almost the same as the country's share of global area, 13%.[3] No other country can lay claim to being the origin of more than 3% of the world's winegrape varieties in terms of bearing area.

---

[3] However, in terms of *number* of varieties, Italy's global winegrape share is more than three times that of Spain. Of the 1,289 prime varieties identified for 2010, the most popular country of origin is Italy with 328, followed by Portugal (196), France (120), and Spain (88). Then three other countries contribute between 55 and 70 varieties each (Hungary, the United States and Croatia). Most of the remaining varieties are from Southeastern Europe and the countries surrounding the Black Sea.

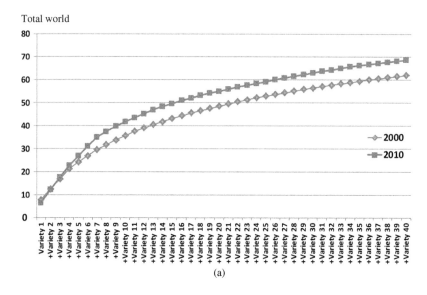

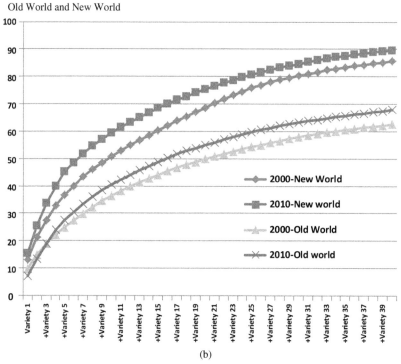

Figure 2. Cumulative varietal shares of global winegrape area, 2000 and 2010 (%)

Varietal concentration is also reflected in the share of the total area of winegrapes for a country or the world that is held by the top variety, or the cumulative shares of the top few varieties. Globally, the top 35 varieties accounted for 59% of the world's winegrape bearing area in 2000, but by 2010 that share was 66%. At the national level, in 2010 as many as 12 of the 44 countries had more than one-third of their total area under just their top variety. Perhaps even more striking is that only 6 of the 44 countries have less than one-third of their total winegrape area under their top three varieties. Those numbers of countries had changed from 7 and 7 in 2000, respectively, again indicating a rapid increase in varietal concentration.

4.2. Changes in global area rankings of varieties

The changes in varietal concentration in the world's vineyard are reflected in the marked changes in the global rankings of varieties over the period between 1990 and 2010. Cabernet Sauvignon and Merlot have more than doubled their shares to take them from 8th and 7th to 1st and 2nd places, and Tempranillo and Chardonnay have more than trebled their shares to take 4th and 5th places, while syrah has jumped from 35th to 6th. Sauvignon Blanc and Pinot Noir are the other two to move into the top ten. These have all been at the expense of Airen, which has fallen from 1st to 3rd, Garnacha from 2nd to 7th, Trebbiano Toscana from 5th to 9th, and Sultaniye (main synonym: Thompson seedless) from 3rd to more than 35th. As a consequence, the world's top 35 varieties as ranked in 1990 shows a quite different mix and rank ordering to the comparable chart for 2010 (Figure 3).

4.3. Changes in shares of red and white varieties

Among other things, these changes in varietal diversity have been accompanied by a rise in the overall share of red varieties in the global winegrape area: from 49% to 56% in the decade to 2010. That share varies hugely across countries, though, from 96% in China and even higher in North Africa to just 12% in Georgia and 8% in Luxembourg (Figure 4a). And the red/white mix has changed far more in some countries than in others, whether looked at in terms of red's share of the national total or in

Top varieties in 1990, compared with 2000 and 2010

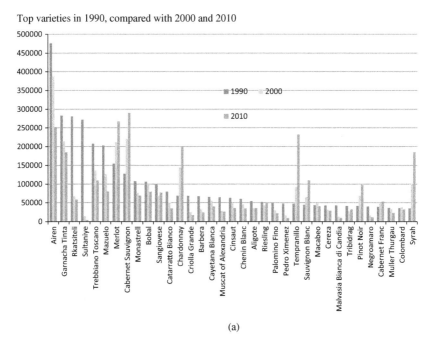

(a)

Top varieties in 2010, compared with 1990 and 2000

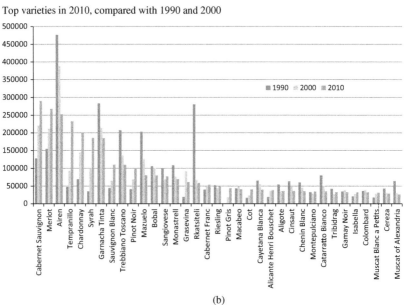

(b)

Figure 3. World's top 35 varieties in 1990, 2000 and 2010 (ha)

national hectares. Of the countries that have increased the share of red varieties in their national mix, the majority are in the Old World (Figure 4b). In hectares, the largest rises in winegrape area are in Spain, the United States, and Italy while the largest falls are in Romania, Bulgaria, and France. Within the red and white winegrape categories, the cumulative shares indicate that the varietal concentration increased almost equally for red and white winegrapes over the 2000 to 2010 period.

4.4. *Changes in varietal intensity indexes*

The varietal intensity index, defined above as a variety's share of a country's total winegrape area divided by that variety's share of the global winegrape area, complements national share information in that it indicates the importance of a variety in a country not relative to other varieties in that country but, rather, relative to that variety in the world. It also complements information on a country's share of the global area for a variety.

As an example, Cot (main synonym: Malbec) was the third-largest variety in terms of area in Argentina in 2000 but the largest variety in 2010 (15.4% of the national winegrape area), when it accounted for 76% of the world's Cot plantings. Since that variety represented only 0.88% of the global area of all varieties in that year, Argentina's Varietal Intensity Index (VII) for that variety was (0.154/0.088 =) 17.5 in 2010, which compares with 16.2 in 2000. For Argentina, Cot is not even in the top ten varieties ranked according to the VII, though, because there are numerous varieties that are unique to Argentina and that therefore have an even higher VII. In fact when a variety is grown only in that country, its VII is necessarily the inverse of the proportion of the global winegrape area accounted for by that country — and so is identical for each unique variety in that country and year (so 1/0.043 = 22.9 for Argentina in 2010).

Another example that helps to illustrate the difference between the national share of a variety and its VII is Syrah (main synonym: Shiraz). This is the most important variety in Australia, and its share of Australia's total winegrape area rose from 22% to 28% in the decade to 2010. However, over that period Syrah became more important in numerous other countries as well (Figure 5a). Its share of the global vineyard area

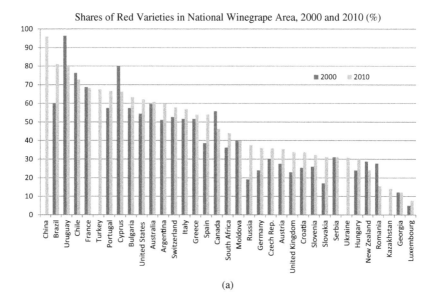

(a)

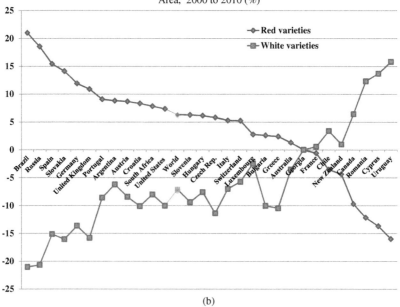

(b)

Figure 4. Changing importance of red varieties in national winegrape area, 2000 to 2010 (%)

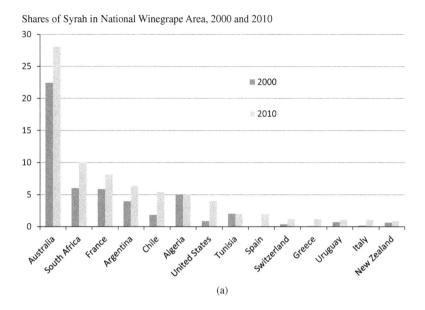

(a)

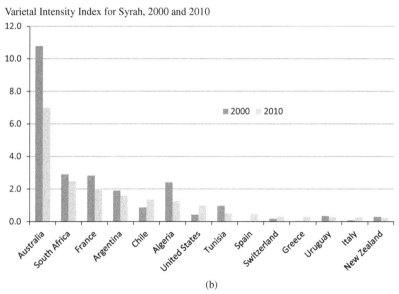

(b)

Figure 5. Changing importance of Syrah in selected countries, 2000 and 2010

thus rose from 2.1% in 2000 to 4.0% in 2010. As a result, Australia's share of Syrah's global area fell from 29% to 23% and so Syrah's VII for Australia fell from 11 to 7 over that decade (while the VII for countries such as the Chile and the United States rose — see Figure 5b).

A fall in the VII for Australia is not unique to Syrah. Indeed, of all 15 varieties for which there were more than 1,000 hectares in production in Australia in 2010, there are only four whose VII rose after 2000. Only a small fraction of that can be explained by an increase in size of Australia's share of the global area, since its share rose only marginally over that decade (from 2.7% to 3.3%). The much more important reason for the decline in VII for most of the key varieties in Australia is that the country's mix of varieties is becoming more similar to the global average (see next subsection).

4.5. *Changes in varietal similarity indexes*

An index of similarity of varietal mix between countries or over time, as defined in Section 3.2, provides an indication of how closely the shares of different varieties in the winegrape area in one location match the shares in another location or in the world (or in that same location in another time period). The closer (further away) that match, the closer the index is to 1 (0). That is, the index will be 0 for pairs of countries with no overlap in their winegrape varietal mix, and 1 for pairs of regions with an identical varietal mix. For the in-between cases, the index is conceptually similar to a correlation coefficient and, like a correlation coefficient, it is symmetrical.

Given the heterogeneity across regions and even countries in their varietal mix, several types of questions can be answered with the help of the varietal similarity index (VSI). The first is: how similar (or different) is each country's mix of varieties from the global average? For Australia, for example, its VSI was 0.45 in 2000, but it rose to 0.62 by 2010. That is, as suggested at the end of the previous section, Australia's varietal mix moved a long way toward the global average varietal mix in the first decade of the twenty-first century. Indeed, France and (marginally) the United States are the only two countries with a closer match to the world average in 2010, whereas nine other countries had a higher VSI than Australia in 2000 (Figure 6a). Bear in mind, though, that there is still a wide range of VSIs across the regions within Australia vis-à-vis the world, ranging from 0.25 to 0.61 in 2000 and from 0.30 to 0.70 in 2010.

A second use of the VSI is in examining, for any one region or country, how close its varietal mix in 2010 is to that in 2000. Figure 6b shows that while some countries have an across-time VSI close to 1, for others it is much lower, which reflects considerable changes in the varietal mix of their bearing areas over that decade. The RSIs between the two years range from highs of 0.99 (Switzerland) and 0.97 (France and Austria) to lows of 0.32 (United Kingdom) and 0.25 (Russia). The fact that the VSI with the world rose between 2000 and 2010 for each of the five biggest New World countries and for two of the three biggest Old World countries (Figure 6c) is a further reflection of the recent increase in varietal concentration in the world's vineyard over that decade.

A third use of the VSI is in examining the extent to which a country has a varietal mix similar to that of other countries. In both 2000 and 2010, the New World countries have varietal mixes closest to other New World countries, whereas the varietal mixes of Old World countries are closest to one of their neighbors (Table 1).

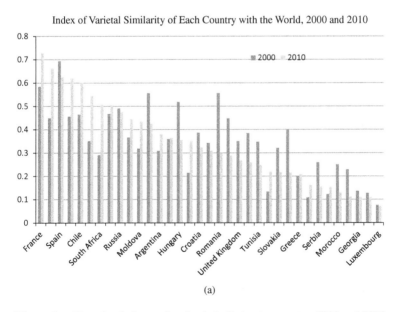

Figure 6. Changing indexes of varietal similarity, by country, 2000 and 2010

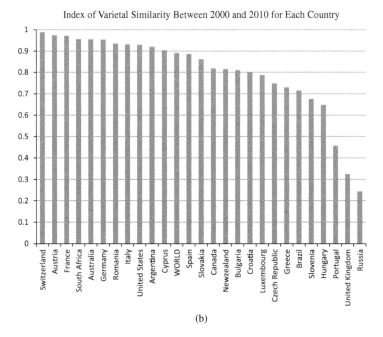

(b)

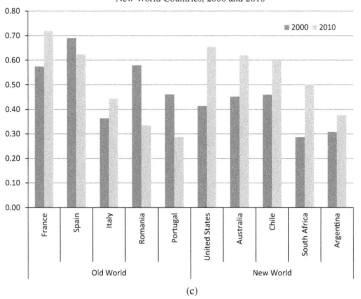

(c)

Figure 6. (*Continued*)

Changing Varietal Distinctiveness of the World's Wine Regions 547

Table 1. Each country's six most-similar winegrape countries in the world according to the varietal similarity index, 2000 and 2010

a. 2000

Algeria	0.70	TN	0.66	FR	0.19	AU	0.17	MA	0.17	US	0.16	CL
Argentina	0.31	AU	0.28	CL	0.20	CA	0.19	ZA	0.19	US	0.19	FR
Armenia	0.837	RU	0.74	RO	0.71	SI	0.68	HU	0.52	DE	0.50	GE
Australia	0.63	CL	0.55	US	0.47	FR	0.47	NZ	0.44	ZA	0.43	CA
Austria	0.71	SK	0.69	CZ	0.26	HU	0.21	RS	0.20	LU	0.19	HR
Brazil	0.33	CA	0.30	PT	0.29	RO	0.28	MD	0.28	SI	0.25	HU
Bulgaria	0.42	CL	0.37	MD	0.29	RU	0.29	GE	0.28	CA	0.28	AU
Canada	0.61	US	0.55	NZ	0.47	CL	0.43	AU	0.37	FR	0.34	SI
Chile	0.63	AU	0.50	US	0.47	CA	0.42	BG	0.41	NZ	0.40	FR
Croatia	0.76	SI	0.73	RS	0.70	HU	0.68	RO	0.65	SK	0.54	CZ
Cyprus	0.25	PT	0.20	MA	0.18	RO	0.16	SI	0.16	RU	0.14	HU
Czech Rep.	0.87	SK	0.70	HU	0.69	AT	0.64	DE	0.60	SI	0.55	RO
France	0.66	DZ	0.52	TN	0.47	AU	0.45	US	0.40	CL	0.37	CA
Georgia	0.60	RU	0.50	AM	0.38	MD	0.29	BG	0.10	RO	0.09	SI
Germany	0.64	CZ	0.63	HU	0.59	RO	0.59	LU	0.56	SI	0.52	AM
Greece	0.28	PT	0.27	RO	0.25	SI	0.24	HU	0.23	RU	0.18	MA
Hungary	0.88	SI	0.88	RO	0.70	HR	0.70	CZ	0.70	RU	0.68	AM
Italy	0.32	FR	0.23	US	0.19	CA	0.16	CL	0.15	NZ	0.14	AU

(Continued)

Table 1. (Continued)

Luxembourg	0.59	DE	0.40	CZ	0.27	SK	0.20	AT	0.17	NZ	0.15	CH
Moldova	0.46	NZ	0.38	CL	0.38	GE	0.37	BG	0.35	US	0.33	CA
Morocco	0.46	PT	0.33	TN	0.28	RO	0.27	RU	0.26	SI	0.22	HU
New Zealand	0.66	US	0.55	CA	0.47	AU	0.46	MD	0.41	CL	0.36	ZA
Portugal	0.719	RO	0.68	SI	0.62	RU	0.62	HU	0.46	MA	0.45	HR
Romania	0.94	SI	0.88	HU	0.78	RU	0.74	AM	0.72	PT	0.68	HR
Russia	0.84	AM	0.78	RO	0.74	SI	0.70	HU	0.62	PT	0.60	GE
Serbia	0.73	HR	0.67	SK	0.54	SI	0.48	HU	0.45	CZ	0.41	RO
Slovakia	0.87	CZ	0.71	AT	0.67	RS	0.65	HR	0.61	HU	0.56	SI
Slovenia	0.94	RO	0.88	HU	0.76	HR	0.74	RU	0.71	AM	0.68	PT
South Africa	0.56	US	0.44	AU	0.36	NZ	0.36	CL	0.31	FR	0.24	CA
Spain	0.20	RO	0.19	SI	0.18	HU	0.17	PT	0.16	RU	0.16	AM
Switzerland	0.23	NZ	0.22	CA	0.19	MD	0.18	FR	0.15	LU	0.13	US
Tunisia	0.70	DZ	0.52	FR	0.33	MA	0.26	PT	0.14	RO	0.14	RU
United Kingdom	0.60	RO	0.60	SI	0.56	HU	0.50	RU	0.49	AM	0.44	PT
United States	0.66	NZ	0.61	CA	0.56	ZA	0.55	AU	0.50	CL	0.45	FR
Uruguay	0.27	CL	0.24	CA	0.19	FR	0.19	BG	0.18	PT	0.18	AU
Old World	**0.77**	**ES**	**0.59**	**RO**	**0.59**	**SI**	**0.55**	**HU**	**0.52**	**RU**	**0.50**	**FR**
New World	**0.79**	**CL**	**0.79**	**AU**	**0.75**	**US**	**0.61**	**ZA**	**0.60**	**CA**	**0.55**	**FR**

Changing Varietal Distinctiveness of the World's Wine Regions 549

	World	0.69	ES	0.58	RO	0.58	SI	0.57	FR	0.54	HU	0.51	RU
b. 2010													
Algeria		0.70	TN	0.55	FR	0.31	MX	0.20	TR	0.18	MM	0.18	US
Argentina		0.37	AU	0.36	CL	0.31	US	0.30	CN	0.29	ZA	0.27	FR
Armenia		0.79	RO	0.59	KZ	0.50	GE	0.32	SI	0.30	UA	0.26	HR
Australia		0.72	US	0.70	TH	0.67	CL	0.64	MM	0.62	ZA	0.58	FR
Austria		0.79	SK	0.71	CZ	0.43	HU	0.26	SI	0.26	HR	0.20	RS
Brazil		0.37	MD	0.14	UA	0.12	UY	0.08	RO	0.08	US	0.07	BG
Bulgaria		0.59	JP	0.56	CL	0.55	CN	0.54	US	0.49	MX	0.48	FR
Canada		0.66	US	0.54	JP	0.51	AU	0.49	FR	0.45	CL	0.45	UK
Chile		0.90	CN	0.75	US	0.67	AU	0.65	RU	0.58	ZA	0.57	JP
China		0.90	CL	0.59	RU	0.59	US	0.55	BG	0.53	MX	0.48	AU
Croatia		0.78	RS	0.77	SI	0.50	HU	0.50	SK	0.39	RO	0.39	CZ
Cyprus		0.15	MX	0.12	TN	0.10	FR	0.10	AU	0.10	CL	0.09	DZ
Czech Rep.		0.85	SK	0.71	AT	0.57	DE	0.56	HU	0.44	SI	0.39	HR
France		0.58	AU	0.57	US	0.55	DZ	0.52	JP	0.49	CA	0.49	CL
Georgia		0.91	KZ	0.63	UA	0.50	AM	0.38	MD	0.19	BG	0.13	RU
Germany		0.57	CZ	0.41	LU	0.39	CA	0.35	UK	0.33	CH	0.30	SK
Greece		0.27	BG	0.26	MA	0.24	MX	0.22	RO	0.21	SI	0.18	AM

(Continued)

Table 1. (Continued)

Country												
Hungary	0.61	SK	0.58	SI	0.56	CZ	0.50	HR	0.43	AT	0.37	RS
Italy	0.35	FR	0.35	US	0.29	BG	0.28	JP	0.27	CA	0.25	AU
Japan	0.68	US	0.59	BG	0.57	CL	0.54	CA	0.52	FR	0.49	RU
Kazakhstan	0.91	GE	0.68	UA	0.59	AM	0.44	MD	0.21	BG	0.20	RO
Luxembourg	0.41	DE	0.33	CZ	0.2	SK	0.19	CA	0.12	HU	0.12	SI
Mexico	0.53	CN	0.51	CL	0.49	BG	0.43	FR	0.41	ZA	0.41	US
Moldova	0.86	UA	0.48	RU	0.44	US	0.44	KZ	0.43	CL	0.41	NZ
Morocco	0.33	TN	0.26	EL	0.21	BG	0.19	MX	0.17	DZ	0.14	SI
Myanmar	0.69	TH	0.64	AU	0.63	NZ	0.45	ZA	0.38	FR	0.32	TR
New Zealand	0.63	MM	0.41	MD	0.38	ZA	0.36	CL	0.36	CA	0.35	US
Peru	0.11	HU	0.07	SK	0.06	MX	0.05	CZ	0.05	SI	0.04	MM
Portugal	0.32	ES	0.14	MX	0.14	MM	0.13	TH	0.12	AU	0.10	AR
Romania	0.79	AM	0.46	SI	0.39	HR	0.35	RS	0.32	HU	0.30	BG
Russia	0.65	CL	0.59	US	0.59	CN	0.49	JP	0.48	MD	0.48	UA
Serbia	0.78	HR	0.60	SI	0.43	SK	0.37	HU	0.35	RO	0.27	CZ
Slovakia	0.85	CZ	0.79	AT	0.61	HU	0.50	HR	0.47	SI	0.43	RS
Slovenia	0.77	HR	0.60	RS	0.58	HU	0.47	SK	0.46	RO	0.44	CZ
South Africa	0.62	AU	0.60	US	0.58	CL	0.49	TH	0.47	FR	0.45	MM
Spain	0.32	PT	0.17	MX	0.16	FR	0.13	DZ	0.11	MM	0.10	AR

Switzerland	0.47	UK	0.30	CA	0.28	US	0.25	FR	0.24	NZ	0.23	MD
Thailand	0.70	AU	0.69	MM	0.49	ZA	0.36	TR	0.33	FR	0.24	AR
Tunisia	0.70	DZ	0.40	MX	0.36	FR	0.33	MA	0.17	EL	0.15	IT
Turkey	0.40	MX	0.39	AU	0.36	TH	0.32	MM	0.26	FR	0.23	ZA
Ukraine	0.86	MD	0.68	KZ	0.63	GE	0.48	RU	0.37	CL	0.36	BG
United Kingdom	0.53	US	0.47	CH	0.45	CA	0.34	AU	0.33	JP	0.31	NZ
United States	0.75	CL	0.72	AU	0.68	JP	0.66	CA	0.60	ZA	0.59	RU
Uruguay	0.41	FR	0.36	BG	0.32	CL	0.31	JP	0.30	US	0.30	CN
New World	**0.87**	**US**	**0.87**	**CL**	**0.84**	**AU**	**0.72**	**ZA**	**0.70**	**CN**	**0.64**	**FR**
Old World	**0.74**	**ES**	**0.64**	**FR**	**0.46**	**BG**	**0.46**	**US**	**0.43**	**MX**	**0.43**	**IT**
World	**0.72**	**FR**	**0.65**	**US**	**0.62**	**ES**	**0.62**	**AU**	**0.60**	**CL**	**0.55**	**BG**

Key: Algeria (DZ), Argentina (AR), Armenia (AM), Australia (AU), Austria (AT), Brazil (BR), Bulgaria (BG), Canada (CA), Chile (CL), China (CN), Croatia (HR), Cyprus (CY), Czech Rep. (CZ), France (FR), Georgia (GE), Germany (DE), Greece (EL), Hungary (HU), Italy (IT), Japan (JP), Kazakhstan (KZ), Luxembourg (LU), Mexico (MX), Moldova (MD), Morocco (MA), Myanmar (MM), New Zealand (NZ), Peru (PE), Portugal (PT), Romania (RO), Russia (RU), Serbia (RS), Slovakia (SK), Slovenia (SI), South Africa (ZA), Spain (ES), Switzerland (CH), Thailand (TH), Tunisia (TN), Turkey (TR), Ukraine (UA), United Kingdom (UK), United States (US), Uruguay (UY)

5. Possible extensions and other uses of the database

Space limitations prevent our drilling down to the regional level within countries, but Anderson (2013) also provides similar share, VII and VSI information for more than 600 regions within 29 of the 44 countries discussed here, full details of which are accessible at Anderson and Aryal (2013).

The regional VSI information in particular may be helpful for producers thinking of altering their varietal mix or relocating to a region with a higher latitude or altitude so as to maintain their firm's current varietal mix in view of global warming. If predictions of climate change were compiled for those 600 + regions, along with their consequent expected changes in the location and productivity of production of the various winegrape varieties across the world, a projected set of VSIs could be calculated to provide a sense of the prospective changes in any region's competition from any other regions that have had, or in the future will have, a similar pattern of varietal specialization.

Likewise, new technological developments — including as an adaptive response to climate change — will alter the VIIs and VSIs, depending on the extent of those new technologies' impact on the varietal mix of each region and any interregional and international spillovers of those new technologies. Indeed, the VSI could be useful in providing a basis for gauging the potential for interregional spillovers of new variety-specific technologies. If those possible changes in international competitiveness were aggregated to the national level, they could be fed in as shocks to the supply side of a model of the world's wine markets (such as that used by Anderson and Wittwer [2013]) to project their impact on grape and wine prices and on wine production, consumption, and trade.

While this paper provides a great deal of information about which winegrapes have been grown in various parts of the world during the first decade of the twenty-first century, it leaves open the question of *why* those varieties have been produced where they are. Is it driven mainly by what grows best in each location (the terroir explanation)? Gergaud and Ginsburgh (2008) argue that even in Bordeaux that has not been the main explanation. Is the increasing concentration on major French varieties because non-French producers — particularly in newly expanding wine-producing countries — find it easier to market them because of France's strong reputation in those varieties? Might part of the explanation also be that those varieties do well in a wide range of growing environments or have been found to be desirable for blending with traditional varieties of a region? These and other centripetal forces during the first decade of the twenty-first century apparently have dominated the possible centrifugal forces mentioned in the Introduction. It remains to be seen whether the latter will be strong enough to dominate the former over the next decade or so. If China is the country with the greatest expansion of winegrape area in the next few years, and if its new plantings remain focused on key French red varieties, the concentration of the world's varietal mix may continue to increase for some time yet.

References

Alston, J.M., Andersen, M.A., James, J.S., and Pardey, P.G. (2010). *Persistence Pays: U.S. Agricultural Productivity Growth and the Benefits from Public R&D Spending.* New York: Springer.

Alston, J.M., Norton, G.W., and Pardey, P. (1998). *Science Under Scarcity: Principles and Practice for Agricultural Research Evaluation and Priority Setting.* London: CAB International.

Anderson, K. (2010). Varietal intensities and similarities of the world's wine regions. *Journal of Wine Economics* 5(2), 270–309.

Anderson, K. (2013). *Which Winegrape Varieties Are Grown Where? A Global Empirical Picture.* Adelaide: University of Adelaide Press. Available at www.adelaide.edu.au/press/winegrapes/.

Anderson, K., and Aryal, N.R. (2013). *Database of Regional, National and Global Winegrape Bearing Areas by Variety, 2000 and 2010.* Available at www.adelaide.edu.au/wine-econ/databases/.

Anderson, K., and Nelgen, S. (2011). *Global Wine Markets, 1961 to 2009: A Statistical Compendium.* Adelaide: University of Adelaide Press. Available at www.adelaide.edu.au/press/titles/global-wine/.

Anderson, K., and Wittwer, G. (2013). Modeling global wine markets to 2018: Exchange rates, taste changes, and China's import growth. *Journal of Wine Economics*, 8(2), 131–158.

Eurostat. (2013). Basic vineyard survey. Available at http://epp.eurostat.ec.europa.eu/portal/page/portal/statistics/search_database/.

Fegan, P.W. (2003). *The Vineyard Handbook: Appellations, Maps and Statistics,* rev. ed. Springfield, IL: Phillips Brothers for the Chicago Wine School.

Gergaud, O., and Ginsburgh, V. (2008). Endowments, production technologies and the quality of wines in Bordeaux: Does terroir matter? *Economic Journal,* 118, F142–57. [Reprinted in *Journal of Wine Economics,* 5 (2010), 3–21.]

Griliches, Z. (1979). Issues in assessing the contribution of R&D to productivity growth. *Bell Journal of Economics,* 10, 92–116.

Jaffe, A.B. (1986). Technological opportunity and spillovers of R&D: Evidence from firms' patents profits and market value. *American Economic Review,* 76(5), 984–1001.

Jaffe, A.B. (1989). Real effects of academic research. *American Economic Review,* 79(5), 957–970.

JKI (Julius Kuhn-Institut). (2013). *Vitis International Variety Catalogue.* Institute for Grapevine Breeding, Federal Research Centre for Cultivated Plants, Geilweilerhof. Available at www.vivc.de.

Johnson, H., and Robinson, J. (2013). *World Atlas of Wine,* 7th ed. London: Mitchell Beasley.

OIV. (2012). *International List of Vine Varieties and Their Synonyms.* Paris: Organisation Internationale de la Vigne et du Vin (International Organisation of Vine and Wine). Available at www.oiv.org.

Robinson, J., Harding, J., and Vouillamoz, J. (2012). *Wine Grapes: A Complete Guide to 1,368 Vine Varieties, Including Their Origins and Flavours.* London: Allen Lane.

Appendix

Table A1. National shares of global winegrape area and wine production volume, 2000 and 2010

Sampled Wine-Producing Countries	Share (%) of Global Area		Share (%) of Global Wine Production		Non-Sampled Wine-Producing Countries	Share (%) of Global Wine Prod., 2010
	2000	2010	2000	2010		
Spain	23.97	22.13	13.11	12.16	Macedonia	0.31
France	17.54	18.23	21.19	21.19	Belarus	0.08
Italy	12.91	13.47	19.72	16.31	Uzbekistan	0.08
United States	3.56	4.91	8.02	8.76	Albania	0.06
Argentina	4.08	4.33	5.00	5.03	Montenegro	0.06
Romania	4.51	3.67	1.95	1.46	Turkmenistan	0.06
Portugal	4.16	3.52	2.72	2.24	Lebanon	0.05
Australia	2.65	3.27	2.91	4.03	Cuba	0.04
Chile	2.31	2.40	2.02	3.40	Madagascar	0.03
Germany	2.11	2.20	3.93	2.86	Egypt	0.03
South Africa	1.90	2.17	2.62	3.40	Azerbaijan	0.03
Moldova	1.82	1.93	0.33	0.45	Bolivia	0.03

(*Continued*)

Table A1. (Continued)

Sampled Wine-Producing Countries	Share (%) of Global Area		Share (%) of Global Wine Production		Non-Sampled Wine-Producing Countries	Share (%) of Global Wine Prod., 2010
	2000	2010	2000	2010		
Hungary	1.76	1.50	1.34	0.90	Lithuania	0.02
Serbia	1.40	1.49	0.59	0.78	Israel	0.02
Bulgaria	1.95	1.21	0.62	0.56	Bosnia & Herz.	0.01
Greece	1.03	1.17	1.41	1.13	Belgium	0.01
Ukraine		1.13		0.93	Zimbabwe	0.01
Brazil	1.07	1.06	1.09	1.20	Malta	0.01
Morocco	1.01	1.05	0.14	0.11	Paraguay	0.01
Georgia	0.76	1.03	0.25	0.33	Latvia	0.01
Austria	0.98	0.98	0.90	0.72	Kyrgyzstan	0.01
New Zealand	0.20	0.69	0.21	0.65	Ethiopia	0.01
Algeria	0.61	0.65	0.15	0.19		
China		0.64		5.68		
Russia	1.14	0.55	0.99	2.24		
Croatia	1.21	0.45	0.70	0.18		
Tunisia	0.34	0.36	0.15	0.08		
Slovenia	0.48	0.35	0.14	0.09		
Czech Rep.	0.23	0.35	0.19	0.17		
Switzerland	0.31	0.32	0.45	0.38		
Turkey		0.28		0.09		
Slovakia	0.32	0.27	0.16	0.10		
Armenia	0.23	0.24	0.02	0.02		
Canada	0.17	0.22	0.17	0.19		
Cyprus	0.37	0.19	0.20	0.04		
Uruguay	0.18	0.16	0.34	0.22		
Kazakhstan		0.15		0.06		
Mexico		0.12		0.15		
Japan		0.08		0.26		

(Continued)

Table A1. (Continued)

Sampled Wine-Producing Countries	Share (%) of Global Area		Share (%) of Global Wine Production		Non-Sampled Wine-Producing Countries	Share (%) of Global Wine Prod., 2010
	2000	2010	2000	2010		
Peru		0.08		0.22		
Luxembourg	0.03	0.03	0.05	0.04		
United Kingdom	0.02	0.03	0.00	0.00		
Thailand		0.00		0.00		
Myanmar		0.00		0.00		
"Missing 9 in 2000"	1.63	n.a.	5.14	n.a.		
Rest of the world	1.06	0.96	1.06	0.96		
Sample total	**98.94**	**99.04**	**98.94**	**99.04**	**Nonsample total**	**0.96**

Table A2. Number of regions and prime varieties, by country, 2000 and 2010

Country	Code	2000		2010	
		No. of Regions	No. of Varieties	No. of Regions	No. of Varieties
Algeria	DZ	1	8	1	8
Argentina	AR	3	31	28	111
Armenia	AM	1	6	1	6
Australia	AU	76	43	94	40
Austria	AT	4	33	4	35
Brazil	BR	1	19	1	101
Bulgaria	BG	1	21	6	16
Canada	CA	1	20	2	76
Chile	CL	8	38	9	54
China	CN			10	17
Croatia	HR	1	7	13	72
Cyprus	CY	1	2	1	15
Czech Rep.	CZ	1	10	2	32
France	FR	29	285	45	96

(*Continued*)

Table A2. (*Continued*)

Country	Code	2000		2010	
		No. of Regions	No. of Varieties	No. of Regions	No. of Varieties
Georgia	GE	1	21	1	21
Germany	DE	13	68	13	91
Greece	EL	13	60	13	56
Hungary	HU	1	32	22	137
Italy	IT	103	323	110	396
Japan	JP			5	15
Kazakhstan	KZ			6	15
Luxembourg	LU	1	11	1	10
Mexico	MX			5	17
Moldova	MD	1	39	1	39
Morocco	MA	1	8	1	8
Myanmar	MM			1	11
New Zealand	NZ	10	22	11	45
Peru	PE			4	30
Portugal	PT	9	80	9	266
Romania	RO	1	18	8	25
Russia	RU	1	11	2	55
Serbia	RS	1	4	1	4
Slovakia	SK	1	11	6	35
Slovenia	SI	1	6	10	21
South Africa	ZA	9	68	9	68
Spain	ES	36	159	36	150
Switzerland	CH	18	51	18	58
Thailand	TH			1	13
Tunisia	TN	1	9	1	9
Turkey	TR			7	35
Ukraine	UA			1	22
United Kingdom	UK	1	9	1	44

(*Continued*)

Table A2. (*Continued*)

Country	Code	2000		2010	
		No. of Regions	No. of Varieties	No. of Regions	No. of Varieties
United States	US	61	84	89	129
Uruguay	UY	1	8	1	41
"Missing 9 in 2000"	M9	1	101	n.a.	n.a.
Sample total		**414**	**1,018**	**611**	**1,289**

n.a.=not available.

Chapter 23

Drifting Towards Bordeaux? The Evolving Varietal Emphasis of U.S. Wine Regions*

Julian M. Alston[†], Kym Anderson[‡] and Olena Sambucci[§]

Abstract

In an ever-more-competitive global market, vignerons compete for the attention of consumers by trying to differentiate their product while also responding to technological advances, climate changes and evolving

---

*First published in *Journal of Wine Economics* 10(3): 349–78, 2015. The authors are grateful for meticulous research assistance by Nanda Aryal in compiling the database and indicators, for helpful comments from an anonymous reviewer, Jim Lapsley and participants at the AAWE Conference in Walla Walla WA in June 2014, and for financial assistance from the Australian Grape and Wine Authority (GWRDC Project Number UA 12/08) and the National Institute of Food and Agriculture, U.S. Department of Agriculture, under award number 2011-51181-30635 (the VitisGen project). Views expressed are the authors' alone

[†] Department of Agricultural and Resource Economics and Robert Mondavi Institute, Center for Wine Economics, UC Davis, Davis, CA 95616. e-mail: julian@primal.ucdavis.edu (corresponding author).

[‡] Wine Economics Research Centre, School of Economics, University of Adelaide, Adelaide SA 5005 Australia and Crawford School of Public Policy, Australian National University, Canberra, Australia. e-mail: kym.anderson@adelaide.edu.au

[§] Department of Agricultural and Resource Economics, UC Davis, Davis, CA 95616. e-mail: sambucci@primal.ucdavis.edu

demand patterns. In doing so, they highlight their regional and varietal distinctiveness. This paper examines the extent to which the winegrape varietal mix varies within and among states of the United States and relative to the rest of the world, and how that picture has been evolving. It reports varietal intensity indexes for different regions, indexes of similarity of varietal mix between regions and over time, and price-based quality indexes across regions and varieties within and among the three west-coast States. Broadly speaking, the mix of winegrape varieties in the United States is not very different from that in the rest of the world and, since 2000, it has become even less differentiated and closer to that of France and the world as a whole. But individual U.S. regions vary considerably in the mix of varieties in which they specialize and in the quality of grapes they produce of a given variety; and region-by-variety interactions have complex influences on the pattern of quality and production. We use measures of regional varietal comparative advantage and a Nerlovian partial adjustment model to account for some of the shifting varietal patterns in the U.S. vineyard and in winegrape production.

1. Introduction

Growers face many questions in deciding which variety of winegrapes to plant, including choices about which clone among perhaps dozens available for a chosen variety. It is widely understood that different varieties can be expected to do better or worse in particular locations, depending on soil types, topography, and local climate — sometimes referred to as terroir. The value of the grapes produced will depend on these factors, in interaction with the market demands for wines having particular flavor profiles and other relevant characteristics, including the varietal name itself in some cases.

Varietal choices are made more difficult because the variety-by-location interactions that determine the value of a particular variety vary significantly over space (sometimes over very short distances) and time (sometimes over very short intervals). While differences in their terroir and economic history of wine have led to enduring systematic differences in the varietal mix among producing regions, changes in patterns of demand, and in the structure of the (increasingly internationally interconnected) global markets for wine, have contributed to systematic shifts in the varietal mix among locations on a shorter time scale. Actual or expected changes in climate also may have contributed.

One source of shifting emphasis on particular varieties is changes in the demand for wine, reflecting changes in population and income, and shifting preferences both among wines and between wines and other beverages. The globalization of the world's wine markets has encouraged wine consumers to seek new types of wines, and has generated many new wine consumers, while some traditional wine consumers have drifted to other beverages. Seeking to attract and retain consumer attention, producers differentiate their products. Traditionally the Old World emphasized regional differences and restricted both the range of varieties grown in each region and the use of varietal labelling on bottles (see, e.g., Gaeta and Corsinovi, 2014). In contrast, in the United States and other New World countries differentiation has been mainly through varietal labeling, although gradually more emphasis is being given also to regional and even single vineyard labeling.

Another source of shifting varietal emphasis is changes on the supply side. The observed mix of grape varieties reflects judgement by vignerons about what is best to grow in their region. That judgement is affected not only by terroir but also by past and present economic considerations, including expectations about future price trends and the cost involved in grafting new varieties onto existing rootstocks or grubbing out and replacing existing varieties. Climate changes (higher temperatures, more extreme weather events) mean that the structure of the variety-by-location relationships is changing (see, e.g., Ashenfelter and Storchmann, 2016), and they are causing changes in comparative advantages even in places not affected directly, since it is a worldwide phenomenon and a global marketplace. Producers are well aware of the impacts climate changes are having on their winegrapes. Adaptation strategies include switching to warmer-climate or more-resilient grape varieties, and sourcing more from regions with a higher latitude or altitude or closer to the sea. Especially in regions and sites whose varietal comparative advantages are still unclear, winegrowers are continually searching for varieties that do well in climates similar to what they expect theirs to become in the future.

Are places becoming more similar, reflecting a shared incentive to shift towards currently more-generally favored varieties? Or are they becoming more differentiated, reflecting better-linked markets and more clearly defined comparative advantage? What role is played by the demand for a complete portfolio of varietal wines from a particular region, regardless of sub-regional comparative advantages in every other sense? To address such questions requires detailed information on what winegrape varieties are grown where, and how those patterns are changing.

Recently, Anderson and Aryal (2013) compiled a global database for 2000 and 2010 to serve these broad purposes.[1] This paper draws on that newly compiled global database plus additional new U.S. data to generate several indicators that capture recent changes in the varietal mix in the United States and its wine regions vis-à-vis the rest of the world. Regional and varietal shares of national and global bearing area and production of winegrapes are reasonably straightforward measures to compute and interpret when data are available — subject to the vagaries of varietal names as discussed and addressed satisfactorily by Anderson and Aryal (2013) by adopting the prime names chosen by Robinson *et al.* (2012) and listed in the online supplementary Appendix Table B-3. We report these measures for various aggregates. In addition, we use several other indexes as used by Anderson (2014): (a) a varietal intensity index (VII), (b) a varietal similarity index (VSI), and, using winegrape price as a proxy for quality, (c) a regional quality index (RQI) and (d) a varietal quality index (VQI). The online supplementary Appendix B provides detail on the data used to compute these indexes.

The paper is structured as follows. Section 2 provides an overview of the U.S. wine industry and its economic geography and relevant history. This provides a foundation for the subsequent discussion of the regional-

---

[1] The 2010 database includes more than 640 regions in 48 countries, thereby covering 99 percent of global wine production; and it includes more than 2,000 varieties, of which 1,548 are 'primes' and the rest are their synonyms (according to Robinson, *et al.*, 2012). To make the data more digestible, various summary charts and tables are published in a 700-page volume (Anderson, 2013). The database is periodically being revised and expanded, most recently in May 2014. The listing of countries in the original database in Anderson (2013), and their numbers of regions and varieties, are provided in the online supplementary Appendix Tables B-1 and B-2.

cum-varietal structure of production. A set of empirical pictures of the changing varietal distinctiveness of U.S. wine regions is presented in Section 3. Section 4 then analyzes regional and varietal quality differences within the United States, as reflected in winegrape prices. Section 5 presents a more formal statistical analysis of the role of measures of economic incentives in the evolving production patterns. The final section summarizes and synthesizes the findings and concludes the paper.

2. An overview of U.S. wine production regions

The U.S. wine industry is young by Old World standards, especially in its current incarnation that began to develop after 13 years of Prohibition, which ended in 1933. As in the rest of the New World, during recent decades the U.S. wine industry has grown rapidly: production has increased by about 75% since 1980. These and other changes took place in the context of some fundamentals that remained largely constant and determine the regional patterns of comparative advantage that favor wine production on the West Coast, especially in California (see, e.g., Lapsley, 1996; Sumner *et al.*, 2004; Olmstead and Rhode, 2010).

In 2010, the United States produced 3.7 million tons of grapes crushed for wine, with a farm value of $2.3 billion — representing about 10% of the world's wine volume. Of the U.S. total winegrape area of 228 thousand hectares in 2010, four states accounted for over 96%: California (CA), 79.7%; Washington (WA), 7.8%; New York (NY), 5.6%; Oregon (OR), 3.0%. Of these, only New York is not on the West Coast. In 1990, California alone accounted for 88.1% of the total and New York accounted for 8.9%. In the 20 years since, while the total U.S. winegrape area increased by about 50%, the winegrape area shrunk slightly in New York while growing rapidly in Oregon (four-fold) and Washington State (six-fold). California differs from the other major producing states, and itself contains several distinct wine production regions that differ in terms of their terrain, climate, soil types, mixture of varieties grown, and quality of grapes and wines produced. Data on production and prices of winegrapes in California are available in some cases by county (of which there are 58, not all of which grow wine grapes) and in others by crush district (of which there are 17). Some crush districts contain several counties or parts of counties.

In this paper we use data for California on the basis of crush districts, in some cases derived from data that were originally available on the basis of counties, which requires some assumptions if counties are divided across crush districts. But for most of the work we aggregate the crush districts into five regions, defined such that each county fits entirely into one of the five regions (see online supplementary Appendix Table A-1 and Appendix Figure A-1 for details).[2] Treating each of the other significant wine-producing states (i.e., WA, OR, and NY) as a region, we have eight primary U.S. wine-producing regions comprising these three plus the five in California. We have more-complete information on the industry in the West Coast states, and some of our detailed analysis is restricted to these three states. Table 1 includes some detail on the salient features of the eight main U.S. wine-producing regions we have identified.

Several distinct patterns are apparent as illustrated in Figure 1. First, California dominates the national total area, volume and value of wine production. Second, the regional shares differ significantly among measures of area, volume, and value of production. In particular, the Southern Central Valley has a much larger share of volume compared with area and especially value of production, while the North Coast region (mainly Napa and Sonoma) has a much smaller share of volume compared with area and value of production. These patterns reflect the relatively high yield per acre (and correspondingly low price per ton) of grapes from the Southern Central Valley and the conversely low yield and high price per ton in the North Coast.

Figure 2 illustrates graphically the links between the price per ton, yield per acre, and the implications for shares of value and volume of production of winegrapes across U.S. regions (and crush districts

---

[2] Varietal quality and specialization vary at a much finer spatial scale than these regional aggregates can reveal. Hence, our use of aggregated data entails some loss of information about patterns of absolute and comparative distinctiveness and specialization at the local level. For example, within the North Coast region we have both Napa and Sonoma counties, each of which contains several distinct sub-regions and appellations, reflecting significant differences in soil types and climate (e.g., ranging from cool Carneros at the southern end of the Napa Valley up to Calistoga in the northern end), known for different styles of wine and varietal mixes.

Table 1. Characteristics of U.S. winegrape growing regions, 2011 data

Region	Crush District	Total Acreage	Volume (tons)	Crush Price ($/ton)	Value ($ millions)
North Coast	3	58,894	166,619	2,083	347.1
(NC)	4	45,801	121,872	3,390	413.1
	Total	104,695	288,491	2,635	760.2
Central Coast	7	47,726	209,196	1,100	230.1
(CC)	8	47,949	158,171	1,217	192.5
	Total	95,675	367,367	1,150	422.6
Southern Central Valley	14	26,286	362,861	372	135.0
(SV)	13	81,740	1,149,984	346	397.9
	Total	108,026	1,512,845	352	532.9
Northern Central Valley	9	6,960	54,358	456	24.8
(NV)	11	69,667	573,758	564	323.6
	12	30,898	290,965	445	129.5
	17	19,963	108,805	580	63.1
	Total	127,488	1,027,886	526	541.0
Other California	10	6,575	17,331	1,143	19.8
(OC)	15	698	1,000	364	0.4
	16	1,257	3,391	1,209	4.1
	1	17,173	57,383	1,237	71.0
	2	8,347	34,004	1,186	40.3
	5	3,560	15,294	731	11.2
	6	6,817	21,948	999	21.9
	Total	44,427	150,351	1,122	168.7
California (CA)		480,311	3,346,940	725	2,425.4
Washington (WA)		43,850	142,000	987	140.2
Oregon (OR)		17,500	41,501	2,004	83.2
New York (NY)		31,803	188,000	373	70.1
Total United States (US)		573,464	3,718,441	731	2,718.8

Sources: Created by the authors using data from USDA NASS historical crush reports, available at http://www.nass.usda.gov/Statistics_by_State/California/Publications/Grape_Crush/index.asp, and USDA NASS historical acreage reports, available at http://www.nass.usda.gov/Statistics_by_State/California/Publications/Grape_Acreage/index.asp.

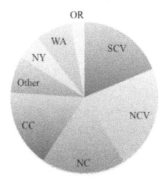

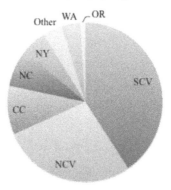

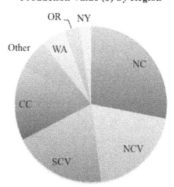

Figure 1. U.S. wine regions — Area, volume, and value of production, 2011

Sources: Created by the authors using data from USDA NASS historical crush reports, and USDA NASS historical acreage reports, 2011.

within regions in California). In 2011 in the Napa Valley the average yield was 2.7 tons/acre and the average crush price was $3,390/ton, almost ten times the average crush price in the Southern Central Valley where the average yield was over 14 tons/acre. The other regions were distributed between these extremes in a nonlinear fashion but with higher yields generally associated with lower prices per ton. Within regions, yields and prices are determined in part by the choice of varieties grown.

3. Varietal distinctiveness of U.S. wine regions

In what follows, we examine the patterns of varietal choice and quality as they vary among regions and over time. First, we examine the varietal distinctiveness of vineyard plantings in the United States vis-à-vis the rest of the world, the varietal differences among regions within the country and their changing varietal intensities.

3.1. Global and U.S. varietal distributions

As a starting point, consider the range of varieties grown. Anderson (2014, Figure 3.1) plots the shares of global bearing area for the world's top 35 wine varieties (by bearing area) in 2010, compared with 1990 and 2000. These 35 varieties accounted for 66 percent of the total bearing area in 2010. This figure (a variant of which is provided in the online supplementary Appendix Figure A-2) illustrates the enormous (but changing) diversity of global winegrape production while also showing the relative importance of the top 10 varieties, which accounted for 42 percent of the global total bearing area in 2010. Figure 3 is the U.S. counterpart: it plots the shares of U.S. bearing area for the top 30 U.S. wine varieties in 2010, compared with 1990 and 2000. The top 30 U.S. varieties accounted for 92.7 percent of the total U.S. bearing area in 2010, and the top 10 varieties accounted for 76.5 percent.

Figure 4 plots the evolving U.S. varietal mix over the past thirty years. The varietal mix has drifted toward red and away from white varieties (Panel a), and for both red and white varieties toward premium varieties (Panel b) — particularly Chardonnay, Cabernet Sauvignon, Merlot, Pinot

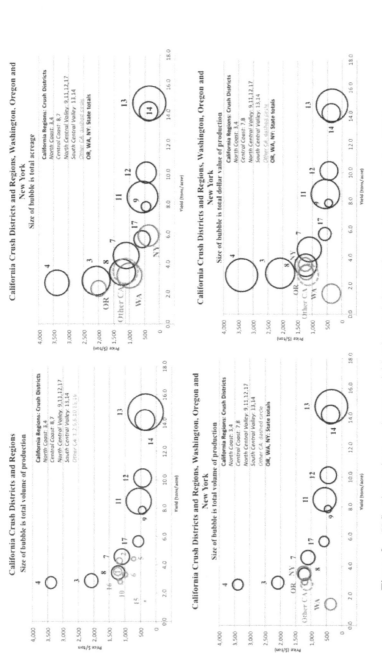

Figure 2. U.S. wine regions — Average yield, price, and shares of area, volume, and value, 2011

Sources: Created by the authors using data from USDA NASS historical crush reports, available at http://www.nass.usda.gov/Statistics_by_State/California/Publications/Grape_Crush/index.asp, and USDA NASS historical acreage reports, available at http://www.nass.usda.gov/Statistics_by_State/California/Publications/Grape_Acreage/index.asp.

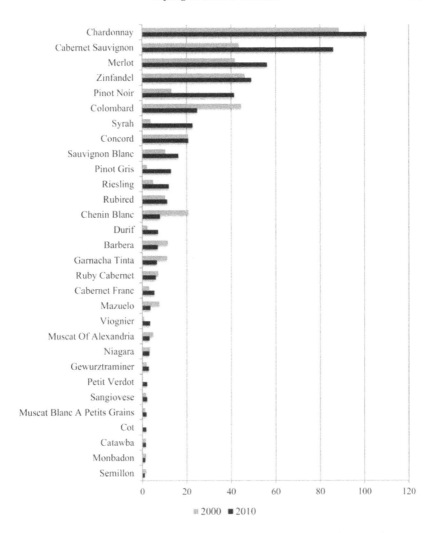

Figure 3. Top 30 U.S. winegrape varieties in 2010, compared with 2000 (bearing acres)
Source: Created by the authors using data from Anderson and Aryal (2013).

Noir, and Syrah (see online supplementary Appendix Figure A-3).[3] In the most recent decade or so, in particular, the picture is dominated by

---

[3] Online supplementary Appendix Table B-3 lists the varieties classified into premium and non-premium. This classification was somewhat subjective. The premium production areas, where these varieties are relatively favored, have also grown in relative importance.

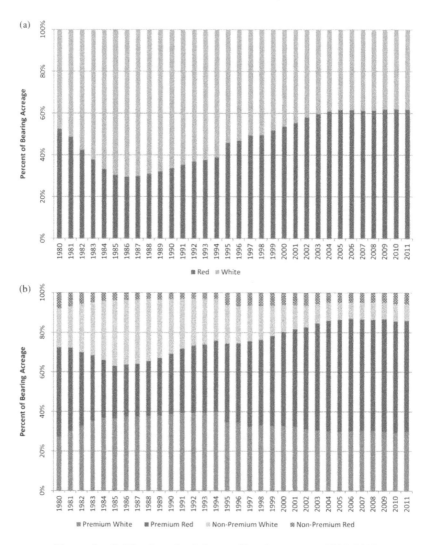

Figure 4. California varietal shares of bearing acreage, 1980–2011
Sources: Created by the authors using data from USDA NASS historical acreage reports, available at http://www.nass.usda.gov/Statistics_by_State/California/Publications/Grape_Acreage/index.asp.

increased plantings of popular premium red and white varieties (in rank order: Cabernet Sauvignon, Pinot Noir, Syrah, Merlot, Chardonnay, and Pinto Gris), at the expense of less-favored varieties (in rank order: French Colombard, Chenin Blanc, Barbera, and Grenache) (see online supplementary Appendix Figure A-4).

3.2. Regional differences within the United States

Within the United States, five varieties (Chardonnay, Cabernet Sauvignon, Merlot, Pinot Noir, and Zinfandel) accounted for 51.8 percent of the total volume and 65.6 percent of the total value of production in 2011.[4] These five varieties predominate in several of the main production regions — in particular in the premium price regions within California, as well as in Washington and Oregon — but the emphasis varies among the premium price regions and some regions are quite different. In particular, the hot Southern Central Valley (dominated by French Colombard and Rubired used to produce grape juice concentrate as well as bulk wine) and New York (dominated by non-*vinifera* American varieties, Concord and Niagara) are quite unlike the other regions climatically and in terms of their grape varietal mix (see online supplementary Appendix Figures A-5 and A-6).[5]

Chardonnay is the most important variety in terms of total bearing area nationally and is highly ranked throughout the premium regions, but the Napa-Sonoma region is especially known for its Cabernet Sauvignon, which is its most important variety and increasingly so, and likewise in Washington. The cooler coastal regions — in particular Oregon and the Central Coast of California — are relatively specialized in Chardonnay and Pinot Noir and other cool climate varieties. Zinfandel is more significant in the Northern Central Valley and other mid-price regions, and these patterns reflect this variety's dual roles in serving as both a premium red varietal wine and as a bulk "blush" (white zinfandel) wine.

Anderson (2010) defined the *Varietal Intensity Index*, VII_{im} for variety m in region i as:

$$VII_{im} = f_{im}/f_m. \qquad (1)$$

where f_m is the bearing area of grape variety m as a proportion of the total global bearing area of winegrapes, and f_{im} is the bearing area of grape

---

[4] While these are the largest varieties by acreage and value of production in 2011, they are not the five largest varieties by volume. The top five varieties by volume in 2011 are: Chardonnay, Cabernet Sauvignon, Zinfandel, French Colombard and Merlot.

[5] In addition to high-yielding, lower priced winegrapes, the Southern Central Valley region produces raisin grapes and table grapes (see Fuller, Alston, and Sambucci, 2014).

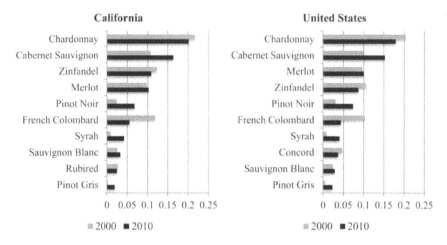

Figure 5. U.S. wine regions — Top 10 varieties, share of bearing acreage, 2000 and 2010
Sources: Created by the authors using data from USDA NASS historical acreage reports, available at http://www.nass.usda.gov/Statistics_by_State/California/Publications/Grape_Acreage/index.asp and data from Anderson and Aryal (2013).

variety m in region i, as a proportion of the total bearing area of winegrapes in that region, $0 \leq f_m, f_{im} \leq 1$ and $\Sigma f_m = \Sigma f_{im} = 1$. When region i is relatively specialized in production of variety m, compared with the world as a whole, $VII_{im} > 1$. Table 2 shows VIIs for the main varieties in the U.S. wine regions, the main states, the United States as a whole and, for comparison, Australia and France. The indexes in Panel a refer to 2010. Indexes greater than 3 are in bold face.

In some instances particular regions have very high VIIs for particular varieties. Whether these high VIIs are reflected in the state and national counterpart measures depends on the size of the regions and the extent to which they differ from other regions. The Southern Central Valley (SV) of California is a comparatively large producing region, with a distinctive varietal mix used for producing bulk wine and grape juice concentrate. In that region, the VII for Rubired is huge (VII_{sv} = 100.80), indicating that in that region the share of Rubired in winegrape area is over 100 times the share of Rubired in the global winegrape area. The counterpart index for California is over 25, and for the nation

Table 2a. U.S. wine regions: Varietal intensity indexes, 2000

	California Regions						U.S. States				Countries		
	NC	CC	NV	SV	OC	CA	WA	OR	NY	US	AU	FR
Chardonnay	4.92	7.00	5.35	1.81	4.26	4.63	3.88	1.03	0.63	4.12	4.21	1.25
Cabernet Sauvignon	4.70	2.47	2.24	1.05	3.01	2.62	3.71	0.19	0.13	2.43	2.73	1.04
Merlot	2.24	1.97	2.12	0.85	1.48	1.76	3.17	0.23	0.41	1.72	1.14	2.36
Zinfandel	9.34	5.25	29.79	10.58	20.84	15.27	0.13	0.00	0.00	12.21	0.14	0.00
Pinot Noir	6.25	6.37	0.93	0.01	3.32	3.14	0.67	30.10	0.46	3.42	1.44	1.67
French Colombard	0.04	0.00	2.22	30.53	0.32	7.80	0.00	0.00	0.00	6.22	2.05	1.38
Syrah	0.74	1.72	1.04	0.66	1.39	1.05	1.78	0.46	0.00	1.00	6.98	2.00
Sauvignon Blanc	2.00	1.11	1.59	0.09	3.02	1.37	1.03	0.00	0.14	1.19	1.76	1.38
Pinot Gris	0.71	2.94	3.92	0.48	1.86	2.03	3.34	16.55	0.32	2.41	2.28	0.34
Rubired	0.00	0.00	5.90	100.80	0.00	25.27	0.00	0.00	0.00	20.14	0.00	0.00
White Riesling	0.18	2.50	0.26	0.03	0.45	0.63	13.02	2.92	2.99	1.95	2.49	0.39

(*Continued*)

Table 2a. *(Continued)*

	California Regions						U.S. States				Countries		
	NC	CC	NV	SV	OC	CA	WA	OR	NY	US	AU	FR
Petite Sirah	15.67	23.07	29.91	1.12	47.95	20.34	0.00	0.00	0.00	16.22	3.55	0.00
Chenin Blanc	0.07	1.01	1.51	6.60	0.66	2.21	0.23	0.00	0.00	1.84	0.46	1.53
Barbera	0.13	0.20	0.38	10.95	1.75	2.90	0.16	0.00	0.00	2.33	0.15	0.00
Grenache	0.02	0.15	0.18	1.11	0.14	0.36	0.14	0.00	0.00	0.30	0.29	2.75
Ruby Cabernet	0.00	0.00	6.19	38.32	0.00	10.64	0.00	0.00	0.00	8.54	5.08	0.00
Cabernet Franc	1.53	0.67	0.25	0.05	1.16	0.65	1.82	0.00	1.35	0.84	0.34	3.76
Viognier	1.29	2.87	4.04	0.49	3.70	2.34	3.04	0.00	0.00	2.34	3.58	2.24
Carignane	0.12	0.01	0.66	0.91	0.79	0.49	0.00	0.00	0.00	0.39	0.00	3.51
Muscat of Alexandria	0.00	0.00	0.58	4.59	0.02	1.23	0.00	0.00	0.00	0.98	2.35	0.54
Gewurztraminer	0.42	3.88	0.27	0.00	3.21	1.20	5.22	2.79	1.57	1.60	1.76	1.21
Petit Verdot	4.65	2.92	2.02	0.00	2.86	2.37	4.22	0.00	0.00	2.37	5.11	0.68
Malbec	0.64	0.41	0.34	0.00	0.33	0.34	0.91	0.00	0.00	0.36	0.26	0.83
Sangiovese	0.39	0.25	0.10	0.14	0.57	0.24	0.24	0.00	0.00	0.22	0.23	0.11

Notes: Varieties are ranked in order of 2011 U.S. total acreage. California regions are North Coast (NC), Central Coast (CC), Northern Central Valley (NV), Southern Central Valley (SV), and Other California (OC). States are California (CA), Washington (WA), Oregon (OR) and New York (NY). VII is calculated using bearing acreage data from Anderson and Aryal (2013).

Table 2b. U.S. wine regions: Varietal intensity indexes, 2000

	California Regions							U.S. States				Countries		
	NC	CC	NV	SV	OC	CA	WA	OR	NY	US	AU	FR
Chardonnay	10.21	15.70	7.65	1.54	9.72	7.25	9.93	4.66	1.12	6.84	4.44	1.42
Cabernet Sauvignon	5.35	3.23	2.21	0.61	2.56	2.36	3.50	1.02	0.23	2.21	4.23	1.36
Merlot	3.87	2.44	2.59	1.14	2.18	2.24	5.47	1.22	0.47	2.21	1.35	2.70
Zinfandel	15.87	8.12	43.20	12.80	35.14	22.26	0.11	0.00	0.00	19.22	0.00	0.00
Pinot Noir	6.12	3.61	0.04	0.01	2.14	1.74	0.84	30.60	0.50	2.16	1.75	2.18
French Colombard	0.43	0.29	10.32	35.99	1.08	15.19	0.00	0.00	0.00	13.11	1.76	1.02
Syrah	0.36	0.58	0.50	0.29	0.73	0.43	0.82	0.40	0.00	0.41	10.78	2.82
Sauvignon Blanc	3.53	2.43	2.12	0.12	5.15	1.94	2.66	0.00	0.15	1.79	1.50	1.82
Pinot Gris	0.77	1.51	0.03	0.15	0.38	0.43	1.20	39.03	0.37	1.21	0.00	0.59
Rubired	0.00	0.00	5.63	89.92	0.00	32.17	0.00	0.00	0.00	27.77	0.00	0.00
White Riesling	0.33	2.78	0.13	0.03	0.73	0.55	11.83	7.97	1.58	1.26	2.71	0.45
Petite Sirah	34.01	26.92	31.85	4.72	67.53	24.80	0.00	0.00	0.00	21.41	5.65	0.00

(*Continued*)

Table 2b. (Continued)

	California Regions						U.S. States				Countries		
	NC	CC	NV	SV	OC	CA	WA	OR	NY	US	AU	FR
Chenin Blanc	0.52	2.50	5.40	11.32	1.17	5.81	2.51	0.00	0.00	5.11	0.69	1.21
Barbera	0.11	0.12	2.45	11.19	0.87	4.56	0.00	0.00	0.00	3.94	0.12	0.00
Grenache	0.01	0.06	0.51	1.50	0.28	0.68	0.00	0.00	0.00	0.59	0.37	2.52
Ruby Cabernet	0.08	0.00	12.35	27.16	0.39	12.55	0.00	0.00	0.00	10.83	12.20	0.00
Cabernet Franc	2.05	0.69	0.13	0.03	0.64	0.54	3.01	0.00	1.04	0.68	0.57	4.19
Viognier	5.88	3.66	1.25	1.25	10.81	3.11	1.80	0.00	0.00	2.76	1.38	4.21
Carignane	0.12	0.00	1.06	1.15	1.18	0.78	0.00	0.00	0.00	0.68	0.03	4.26
Muscat of Alexandria	0.01	0.00	0.02	6.42	0.01	2.20	0.00	0.00	0.00	1.90	3.17	0.58
Gewurztraminer	1.30	5.44	0.01	0.00	6.33	1.49	8.31	8.93	1.16	1.89	1.82	1.46
Petit Verdot	9.50	1.38	0.66	0.00	1.13	2.09	0.00	0.00	0.00	1.80	18.18	1.53
Malbec	0.47	0.06	0.12	0.00	0.02	0.12	0.12	0.00	0.00	0.11	0.66	1.42
Sangiovese	0.75	0.40	0.15	0.11	0.62	0.31	0.16	0.00	0.00	0.27	0.20	0.13

Notes: Varieties are ranked in order of 2011 U.S. total acreage. California regions are North Coast (NC), Central Coast (CC), Northern Central Valley (NV), Southern Central Valley (SV), and Other California (OC). States are California (CA), Washington (WA), Oregon (OR) and New York (NY). VII is calculated using bearing acreage data from Anderson and Aryal (2013).

Table 2c. U.S. wine regions: Varietal intensity indexes, ratio of 2010 VII to 2000 VII

	California Regions							U.S. States				Countries		
	NC	CC	NV	SV	OC	CA	WA	OR	NY	US	AU	FR
Chardonnay	0.48	0.45	0.70	1.18	0.44	0.64	0.39	0.22	0.56	0.60	0.95	0.88
Cabernet Sauvignon	0.88	0.76	1.01	1.72	1.18	1.11	1.06	0.19	0.57	1.10	0.65	0.76
Merlot	0.58	0.81	0.82	0.75	0.68	0.79	0.58	0.19	0.87	0.78	0.84	0.87
Zinfandel	0.59	0.65	0.69	0.83	0.59	0.69	1.18	0.00	0.00	0.64	0.00	0.00
Pinot Noir	1.02	1.76	23.25	1.00	1.55	1.80	0.80	0.98	0.92	1.58	0.82	0.77
French Colombard	0.09	0.00	0.22	0.85	0.30	0.51	0.00	0.00	0.00	0.47	1.16	1.35
Syrah	2.06	2.97	2.08	2.28	1.90	2.44	2.17	1.15	0.00	2.44	0.65	0.71
Sauvignon Blanc	0.57	0.46	0.75	0.75	0.59	0.71	0.39	0.00	0.93	0.66	1.17	0.76
Pinot Gris	0.92	1.95	130.67	3.20	4.89	4.72	2.78	0.42	0.86	1.99	0.00	0.58
Rubired	0.00	0.00	1.05	1.12	0.00	0.79	0.00	0.00	0.00	0.73	0.00	0.00
White Riesling	0.55	0.90	2.00	1.00	0.62	1.15	1.10	0.37	1.89	1.55	0.92	0.87

(*Continued*)

Table 2c. (Continued)

	California Regions						U.S. States				Countries		
	NC	CC	NV	SV	OC	CA	WA	OR	NY	US	AU	FR
Petite Sirah	0.46	0.86	0.94	0.24	0.71	0.82	0.00	0.00	0.00	0.76	0.63	0.00
Chenin Blanc	0.13	0.40	0.28	0.58	0.56	0.38	0.09	0.00	0.00	0.36	0.67	**1.26**
Barbera	**1.18**	**1.67**	0.16	0.98	2.01	0.64	0.00	0.00	0.00	0.59	**1.25**	0.00
Grenache	**2.00**	**2.50**	0.35	0.74	0.50	0.53	0.00	0.00	0.00	0.51	0.78	**1.09**
Ruby Cabernet	0.00	0.00	0.50	1.41	0.00	0.85	0.00	0.00	0.00	0.79	0.42	0.00
Cabernet Franc	0.75	0.97	**1.92**	**1.67**	**1.81**	**1.20**	0.60	0.00	**1.30**	**1.24**	0.60	0.90
Viognier	0.22	0.78	**3.23**	0.39	0.34	0.75	**1.69**	0.00	0.00	0.85	**2.59**	0.53
Carignane	**1.00**	0.00	0.62	0.79	0.67	0.63	0.00	0.00	0.00	0.57	0.00	0.82
Muscat of Alexandria	0.00	0.00	**29.00**	0.71	**2.00**	0.56	0.00	0.00	0.00	0.52	0.74	0.93
Gewurztraminer	0.32	0.71	**27.00**	0.00	0.51	0.81	0.63	0.31	**1.35**	0.85	0.97	0.83
Petit Verdot	0.49	**2.12**	**3.06**	0.00	**2.53**	**1.13**	0.00	0.00	0.00	**1.32**	0.28	0.44
Malbec	**1.36**	**6.83**	**2.83**	0.00	**16.50**	**2.83**	**7.58**	0.00	0.00	**3.27**	0.39	0.58
Sangiovese	0.52	0.63	0.67	**1.27**	0.92	0.77	**1.50**	0.00	0.00	0.81	**1.15**	0.85

Notes: Varieties are ranked in order of 2011 U.S. total acreage. California regions are North Coast (NC), Central Coast (CC), Northern Central Valley (NV), Southern Central Valley (SV), and Other California (OC). States are California (CA), Washington (WA), Oregon (OR) and New York (NY).

Source: Created by the authors using data from Anderson and Aryal (2013).

over 20, even though Rubired is not grown outside California's Central Valley. The Southern Central Valley is also comparatively highly specialized in French Colombard ($VII_{sv} = 30$) and Ruby Cabernet ($VII_{sv} = 38$), to an extent that makes the state and national VII_s large for these varieties, too. Every region of California is highly specialized in Zinfandel compared with the world as a whole ($VII_{US} > 12$). In the case of Petite Sirah, every California region except the Southern Central Valley has a large VII and consequently so do California and the nation as a whole. By global standards, the United States is comparatively specialized in Chardonnay ($VII_{US} > 4$) and Cabernet ($VII_{US} > 2$), and this is reflected in the VII_s in most regions (except New York, Oregon, and the Southern Central Valley). Washington is comparatively specialized in White Riesling while Oregon is comparatively specialized in Pinot Noir and Pinot Gris.

Comparing panels a and b of Table 2 reveals the shifts in varietal intensities between 2000 and 2010. In many instances, the bold entries in panel a (for 2010) are smaller than their counterparts in panel b (for 2000) indicating that the particular region has become less specialized, comparatively, in that variety. But in some cases the opposite is true. To clarify the comparison, in panel c each entry is the ratio of the *VII* for 2010 to its counterpart for 2000: that is, $VIIR_{im} = VII_{im(2010)}/VII_{im(2000)}$. If a ratio is greater than 1.0, it is shown in boldface. The majority of the entries are not bold but some are, indicating an increase over that decade in *VII*. The United States (in particular in the premium regions of California and Washington and Oregon, depending on the variety) has increased its relative specialization in production of some varieties in which it was already somewhat specialized — such as Cabernet Sauvignon and Pinot Noir — as well as some in which it was not, namely Syrah, Pinot Gris, Pinot Noir, Petit Verdot, Cabernet Franc, White Riesling, and Malbec. But France and Australia, by contrast, have tended to become less specialized in the varieties in which they were comparatively specialized.

3.3. National and regional varietal distinctiveness

Anderson (2010) defined a *Varietal Similarity Index (VSI)* as[6]:

$$VSI_{v,t} = \frac{\sum_{m=1}^{M} f_{i,m} f_{j,m}}{\left(\sum_{m=1}^{M} f_{i,m}^2\right)^{1/2} \left(\sum_{m=1}^{M} f_{j,m}^2\right)^{1/2}}. \quad (2)$$

This index can be used to measure the extent to which the winegrape varietal mix of one region or country, i matches that of another region or country (or the world), j. It can also be used to compare the varietal mix of a region or country over time. This index is conceptually similar to a correlation coefficient and, like a correlation coefficient, it is completely symmetric in that $VSI_{i,j} = VSI_{j,i}$ and $VSI_{i,i} = 1$.

The *VSI* between the United States and the world was 0.15 in 1990 but it rose to 0.42 in 2000 and 0.67 by 2010, indicating a very substantial drift in the U.S. varietal mix toward the world aggregate mix (Table 3, Panel a).

Table 3. Winegrape varietal similarity indexes: United States, Australia and the world

a. VSI of Australia and United States Relative to the World, 1990, 2000 and 2010

Year	Australia	United States
1990	0.31	0.15
2000	0.43	0.42
2010	0.62	0.67

b. VSI of Australia and the United States in 1990, 2000, and 2010

		Australia		
		1990	2000	2010
United States	1990	0.39		
	2000	0.46	0.60	
	2010	0.55	0.74	0.72

Source: Anderson and Aryal (2013), Anderson and Aryal (2014).

---

[6] In defining the index, Anderson (2010) borrows and adapts an approach introduced by Jaffe (1986) and Griliches (1979) that was used by Jaffe (1989) and others, including Alston *et al.* (2010, Ch. 4), to measure inter-firm or inter-industry or inter-regional technology spillover potential.

Over the same period, the *VSI* between Australia and the world rose from 0.31 in 1990 to 0.43 in 2000 and 0.62 by 2010 (Anderson, 2015). By this measure, in 1990 the mix of winegrape varieties in both the United States and Australia drifted toward the world aggregate mix, but the U.S. mix moved more: it was much less similar than the Australian mix to the world aggregate in 1990 (0.15 versus 0.31) but by 2010 it was more similar (0.67 versus 0.62). And the mixes in Australia and the United States today are much more similar than they were in 2000 and especially 1990 (Table 3, Panel b). These same developments are illustrated graphically by Anderson (2014, Figure 6 pp. 14–15; a variant of which is replicated as online supplementary Appendix Figure A-7. Since France is the country whose varietal mix is most similar to the world mix, this means in effect that the United States has become more like France.

Table 4 includes *VSI*s among U.S. regions relative to one another, and relative to U.S. states, as well as Australia and the United States. The upper

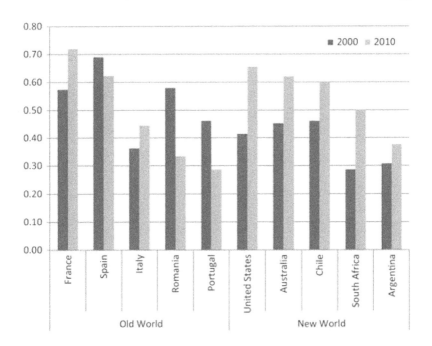

Figure 6. Index of varietal similarity between world and five largest Old World and New World wine-producing countries, 2000 and 2010

Source: Created by the authors using data from Anderson (2014).

Table 4. Varietal similarity indexes for U.S. regions, Australia, France, and the world

2010 VSIs	California Regions							U.S. States				Countries		
	NC	CC	NV	SV	OC	CA	WA	OR	NY	US	AU	FR
North Coast (NC)	1.00											
Central Coast (CC)	0.90	1.00										
N Central Valley (NV)	0.81	0.83	1.00									
S Central Valley (SV)	0.39	0.38	0.51	1.00								
Other California (OC)	0.93	0.88	0.94	0.46	1.00							
California (CA)	0.93	0.92	0.94	0.62	0.96	1.00						
Washington (WA)	0.84	0.80	0.71	0.37	0.77	0.80	1.00					
Oregon (OR)	0.37	0.42	0.13	0.04	0.27	0.28	0.13	1.00				
New York (NY)	0.05	0.06	0.05	0.03	0.05	0.06	0.07	0.03	1.00			
United States (US)	0.93	0.93	0.91	0.59	0.95	0.99	0.83	0.33	0.19	1.00		
Australia (AU)	0.69	0.75	0.62	0.36	0.71	0.71	0.74	0.16	0.04	0.72	1.00	
France (FR)	0.55	0.54	0.48	0.35	0.53	0.56	0.61	0.18	0.04	0.58	0.58	1.00
World (W)	0.64	0.61	0.55	0.40	0.63	0.65	0.68	0.20	0.07	0.67	0.62	0.73

2000 VSIs

North Coast (NC)	1.00											
Central Coast (CC)	0.91	1.00										
N Central Valley (NV)	0.80	0.76	1.00									
S Central Valley (SV)	0.24	0.21	0.52	1.00								
Other California (OC)	0.90	0.89	0.94	0.30	1.00							
California (CA)	0.86	0.83	0.94	0.66	0.90	1.00						
Washington (WA)	0.90	0.88	0.69	0.22	0.78	0.77	1.00					
Oregon (OR)	0.46	0.41	0.23	0.06	0.34	0.32	0.36	1.00				
New York (NY)	0.06	0.06	0.05	0.01	0.05	0.05	0.07	0.04	1.00			
United States (US)	0.86	0.84	0.92	0.62	0.86	0.90	0.79	0.36	0.04	1.00		
Australia (AU)	0.66	0.58	0.46	0.19	0.66	0.54	0.55	0.27	0.36	0.55	1.00	
France (FR)	0.47	0.35	0.38	0.27	0.47	0.40	0.44	0.23	0.23	0.45	0.48	1.00
World (W)	0.43	0.34	0.36	0.24	0.43	0.40	0.44	0.50	0.23	0.42	0.46	0.58

half of the table refers to *VSI*s in 2010 and the lower half refers to 2000. Between 2000 and 2010, the United States wine industry became more like the global wine industry: $VSI_{US,\,WORLD}$ increased from 0.42 to 0.67. This reflected a global trend — France and Australia also became more like the global wine industry, but did not adjust by as much as the United States did ($VSI_{FR,WORLD}$ increased from 0.58 to 0.73, reflecting in part the predominant role of France in the global total, and $VSI_{AU,\,WORLD}$ increased from 0.46 to 0.62). The U.S. adjustment reflected every U.S region becoming more like the global industry, in terms of its varietal mix, with two exceptions: Oregon (highly specialized in Pinot Noir) and New York (growing American varieties) became more dissimilar. Setting aside these two states, within the United States, the more premium regions (North Coast, Central Coast, Other California, and Washington) tend to have varietal mixes quite similar to one another (i.e., *VSI* > 0.8) and reasonably similar to the world as a whole (i.e., *VSI* > 0.6), whereas the regions specializing in bulk wines and grape juice concentrate are quite dissimilar to the other U.S. regions and to the world as a whole with *VSI*s < 0.5.

To highlight the changes between 2000 and 2010, the entries in Table 5 were computed by dividing each entry in the upper part of Table 4 (for 2010) by its counterpart in the lower part (for 2000): i.e., $VSIR_{ij} = VSI_{ij(2010)}/VSI_{ij(2000)}$. The resulting ratio of indexes will be greater than 1 if the index has increased (i.e., the varietal mixes have become more similar) over time. As can be seen in Table 5, the predominant pattern is for the indexes to increase — though not in every instance — and some of the increases are quite substantial. Figure 6 captures the key patterns for the five largest wine producing countries from the New World and the five largest from the Old World. The New World producers have become more like the world as a whole while the Old World producers have become less so, partly because the New World producers have become more important within the total.

4. Regional and varietal quality differences within the United States

That U.S. winegrape regions vary substantially in terms of average winegrape prices received by growers is apparent from the plots in Figure 1. Given that different varieties grow better in some regions than others, and

Table 5. Varietal similarity index ratios, 2010:2000 for U.S. regions, Australia, France, and the world

	California Regions							U.S. States				Countries		
	NC	CC	NV	SV	OC	CA	WA	OR	NY	US	AU	FR
North Coast (NC)	1.00											
Central Coast (CC)	0.99	1.00										
N Central Valley (NV)	1.01	1.09	1.00									
S Central Valley (SV)	1.64	1.82	0.98	1.00								
Other California (OC)	1.03	0.99	1.00	1.51	1.00							
California (CA)	1.08	1.11	1.00	0.95	1.07	1.00						
Washington (WA)	0.94	0.91	1.02	1.69	0.99	1.04	1.00					
Oregon (OR)	0.80	1.03	0.58	0.67	0.81	0.87	0.38	1.00				
New York (NY)	0.87	1.00	1.07	2.16	0.93	1.07	1.09	0.73	1.00			
United States (US)	1.08	1.10	0.99	0.95	1.06	1.00	1.05	0.92	0.88	1.00		
Australia (AU)	1.05	1.30	1.33	1.89	1.32	1.31	1.18	0.58	1.05	1.30	1.00	
France (FR)	1.17	1.55	1.26	1.27	1.33	1.27	1.22	0.77	1.37	1.28	1.22	1.00
World (W)	1.49	1.78	1.56	1.67	1.70	1.58	1.57	0.83	1.26	1.58	1.36	1.25

Source: Created by the authors using data from Anderson and Aryal (2013).

that consumer preferences differ across varieties and over time, it is not surprising to find considerable dispersion in the national average prices by variety. Figure 7 shows the U.S. average prices for the top 30 varieties in 2011, ranging from a little over $200 per ton for Burger to almost $1,600 per ton for Cabernet Sauvignon: an almost ten-fold difference across all varieties. These national average prices mask differences among regions and within regions — especially in the premium regions such as the North Coast, within which prices for a given variety can vary quite widely.

We use relative prices as an indicator of quality, comparing different varieties of winegrapes from different producing regions. Table 6 includes information on crush prices for winegrapes in 2010 by region for the top 25 varieties, for individual U.S. regions, states, and the nation as a whole. The last entry in each column of Table 6 is the *Regional Quality Index* (Anderson 2010), defined as the regional average winegrape price (across all varieties), P_i in region i, as a proportion of the national average winegrape (across all varieties and all regions), P:

$$RQI_i = P_i / P. \tag{3}$$

The last entry in each row of Table 6 is the *Varietal Quality Index*, VQI_m (Anderson 2010), defined as the ratio of the national average price for a particular variety across all regions, P_m for variety m, to the national average price of all wine-grape varieties:

$$VQI_m = P_m / P. \tag{4}$$

The entries in Table 6 are sorted according to this index, so they are ranked from highest to lowest average VQI.

As can be seen in Table 6, prices vary systematically among regions — the North Coast region has generally higher prices than other regions for all varieties and the Southern Central Valley has generally lower prices. In addition, prices vary systematically among varieties — among the higher-quality (higher-priced) varieties grown in significant quantity, Cabernet Sauvignon generally is ranked higher than Chardonnay, and Zinfandel generally is ranked lower. But the sizes of the premia, and even the rankings of varieties, vary among regions. For example, Pinot Noir ranks above Cabernet Sauvignon almost everywhere, but not in

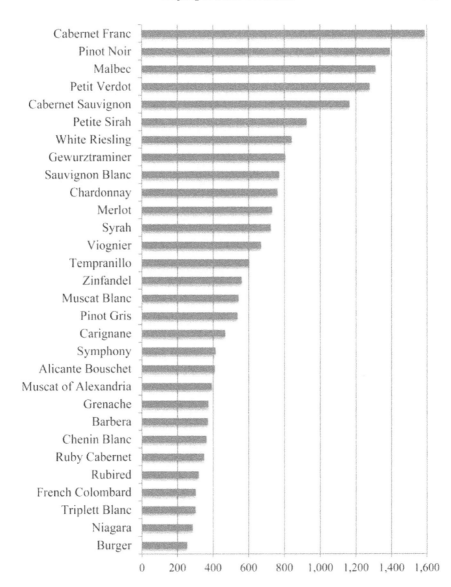

Figure 7. Average price of winegrapes, top 30 varieties, United States, 2011 in US$ per ton
Source: created by the authors using data from USDA NASS historical crush reports, available at http://www.nass.usda.gov/Statistics_by_State/California/Publications/Grape_Crush/index.asp

Table 6. U.S. regional and varietal winegrape prices and quality indexes, 2010

	California Regions					U.S. States				U.S	
	NC	CC	OC	NV	SV	CA	OR	WA	NY	Price	VQI
	$/t									$/t	Index
Cabernet Franc	4,147	1,150	1,257	487	350	1,663	2,240	1,342	1,378	1,589	2.35
Pinot Noir	2,837	1,924	1,858	591	481	1,272	2,270	868	1,378	1,392	2.06
Petit Verdot	4,162	1,296	1,474	665		1,279				1,279	1.89
Cabernet Sauvignon	3,655	1,054	1,318	598	484	1,154	2,370	1,312	1,378	1,167	1.72
Petite Sirah	2,776	1,146	1,187	679	471	925				925	1.37
White Riesling	2,581	960	1,336	543	398	827	880	784	1,378	842	1.24
Gewurztraminer	1,443	897	1,338	560	388	783	1,390	740	1,378	805	1.19
Sauvignon Blanc	1,594	965	905	464	347	765	1,660	824	1,378	772	1.14
Chardonnay	1,962	1,124	947	504	404	754	1,800	803	1,378	763	1.13
Merlot	2,009	919	943	519	435	693	1,870	1,117	1,378	732	1.08
Syrah	2,456	1,098	1,100	475	418	669	2,110	1,133		723	1.07
Zinfandel	2,468	1,160	1,154	577	343	560	1,630			561	0.83

Muscat Blanc	1,619	1,064	1,113	508	497	544				544	0.80
Pinot Gris	1,695	994	749	493	420	500	1,310	765	1,378	538	0.79
Carignane	2,048	1,638	945	395	350	468				468	0.69
Symphony	800		410	403	415	413				413	0.61
Muscat of Alexandria	1,333			363	395	393				393	0.58
Grenache	2,677	1,512	1,329	387	315	374				374	0.55
Barbera	2,796	1,337	1,228	471	340	371				371	0.55
Chenin Blanc	1,271	664	492	413	324	356		746		362	0.53
Ruby Cabernet				368	347	348				348	0.51
Rubired				329	319	319				319	0.47
French Colombard	519		818	314	301	302				302	0.45
Triplett Blanc				300	300	300				300	0.44
Burger				221	260	254				254	0.37
Average Regional Price	2,672	1,163	1,149	529	354	666	1,972	979	363	677	1.00
Regional Quality Index	3.95	1.72	1.70	0.78	0.52	0.98	2.91	1.45	0.54	1.00	1.00

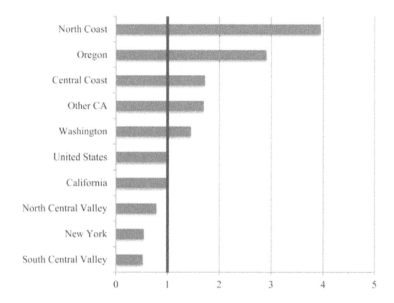

Figure 8. Regional quality index, United States, 2011

Source: Derived from Anderson and Aryal (2013), using data from USDA NASS historical crush reports (2011), available from http://www.nass.usda.gov/Statistics_by_State/California/Publications/Grape_Crush/index.asp

Oregon where Pinot is by far the dominant variety, nor in the North Coast region; Chardonnay is ranked above Cabernet Sauvignon in the Central Coast region.

The Regional Quality Indexes (*RQI*s) plotted in Figure 8 are all relative to the national average of 1. The Central Valley of California produces a large volume of lower quality grapes (*RQI*s of 0.52 and 0.78 in the southern and northern regions) and, as a result, the average quality for California is slightly below the national average even though California also produces most of the national volume of higher-quality winegrapes. Among other states, consequently, only New York ranks below California in this measure. But the North Coast region stands out from the rest, with an *RQI* of 3.95, followed by Oregon at 2.91.

Some insight into the region-by-variety interactions is gleaned by considering the variety-specific panels in online supplementary Appendix Figure A-8. For each of the top 12 U.S. varieties (ranked according to 2011 bearing acreage), we have plotted the Varietal Quality Index (*VQI*)

for each of our eight regions (i.e., five California regions, plus the three other states: Oregon, Washington, and New York), with the regions ranked according to the *VQI*. As one would expect, for many of the varieties the North Coast has the highest *VQI*, and it is often followed by Oregon for the premium varietals, but not always. The ranking and the size of the dispersion below the top varies considerably — compare Zinfandel and Pinot Noir.

5. Statistical analysis of the evolving varietal and quality mix

The changing patterns of production reflect producer investments and their other production decisions made in response to their perceptions of the evolving market for winegrapes, taking into account their expectations about regional-cum-varietal comparative advantage over the relevant planning horizon, which can amount to decades in the case of winegrapes. Modeling supply response of perennial crops is challenging, and in the case of winegrapes is made more difficult by the highly differentiated nature of the product both within and among regions (see, e.g., Volpe *et al.*, 2011 and Alston *et al.*, 2013). Here, while we do not propose a formal supply response model as such, we draw on the relevant literature to develop statistical models of the influences of readily observable economic variables on production patterns. The same ideas were implicit in our graphical analysis.

Our measure of regional comparative advantage, for a particular variety, v, is given by the average revenue per acre (i.e., average yield in tons per bearing acre times average price in dollars per ton) of that variety relative to the average revenue per acre of <u>all</u> varieties in the same region[7]:

$$\pi_{v,t} = \frac{P_{v,t} Y_{v,t}}{\overline{P}_t \overline{Y}_t}. \tag{5}$$

---

[7] If variable costs per acre were similar among varieties in a given location, then gross revenue per acre would be a good measure of net revenue per acre. Further, if planting materials and establishment costs and the life expectancy of the vineyard also were similar across varieties, then gross revenue per acre would be a good comparative indicator of profitability of investment in particular varieties.

Given the durable nature of vineyards, the current pattern of production might depend on expectations formed 10 or 20 years (or more) previously, and we should not expect to see large shifts in production, in a particular location, in response to contemporary or even recent changes in the values of this incentive variable. On the other hand, enduring differences in the varietal mix among locations ought to reflect enduring differences in these incentives, and significant shifts in production patterns over time should reflect changes in expectations that we would expect to be related to systematic changes in incentives.

We exploit variation in varietal production patterns, both over time and across regions of California, as they relate to this measure of incentives, with some allowance for lagged responses. The general form of the model we have in mind is one in which the "desired" variety-specific share of total vineyard area (including non-bearing area) in a particular region, R, is a function of expected relative profitability over the indefinite future, which we proxy using lagged values of the measure of comparative advantage given in equation (5), allowing for fixed effects of variety and year, as follows:

$$\ln\left(f_{v,t}^{*}\right) = \beta_{0}^{R} + \sum_{v=1}^{V}\beta_{v}^{R}D_{v} + \sum_{t=1}^{T}\beta_{t}^{R}D_{t} + \beta_{\pi}^{R}\ln\left(\pi_{v,t}^{e}\right) + \varepsilon_{v,t}. \tag{6}$$

In this model in region R, $f_{v,t}$ is the share of total acreage planted to variety v in year t, and the asterisk denotes the desired value that would maximize the producers' objective function; D_v and D_t are dichotomous (0–1) indicator variables to represent the effects of variety and year-specific fixed effects; and $\varepsilon_{v,t}$ is a random error term. The incentive variable, $\pi_{v,t}$, is a measure of the relative profitability (or regional comparative advantage) of variety v in year t, as given in (5), and the superscript e denotes the expected value of that incentive variable. Since the model is specified in natural logarithms, the parameters are elasticities.

We use a Nerlovian partial adjustment model to represent the link between actual and desired varietal shares, given that the costs of changing the varietal mix are relatively large unless the change takes place in the context of normal replacement of a vineyard (perhaps in a 25-year cycle), and increase with the rate of change. Specifically, we postulate the form in which the year-to-year proportional change in varietal share is equal to fixed fraction, λ of the proportional difference between the desired share and last year's actual share:

$$\ln(f_{v,t}) - \ln(f_{v,t-1}) = \lambda^R \left[\ln(f_{v,t}^*) - \ln(f_{v,t-1}) \right], \quad (7)$$

where $0 < \lambda^R \leq 1$ is the coefficient of adjustment of actual shares toward the desired share (in logarithms) in the region. In addition, we proxy expectations using a five-year moving average of lagged values of the measure of comparative advantage, consistent with previous studies of the supply response of perennial crops (e.g., Dorfman and Heien, 1989; Volpe et al., 2011; Alston et al., 2013):

$$\pi_{v,t}^e = \frac{1}{5} \sum_{k=1}^{5} \pi_{v,t-k}. \quad (8)$$

Combining (6), (7) and (8) yields:

$$\ln(f_{v,t}^*) = \alpha_0^R + \sum_{v=1}^{V} \alpha_v^R D_v + \sum_{t=1}^{T} \alpha_t^R D_t + \alpha_\pi^R \ln(\pi_{v,t}^e) + \alpha_f^R \ln(f_{v,t-1}) + \mu_{v,t}. \quad (9)$$

where $\alpha_0^R = \lambda^R \beta_0^R$, $\alpha_v^R = \lambda^R \beta_v^R$, $\alpha_t^R = \lambda^R \beta_t^R$, $\alpha_\pi^R = \lambda^R \beta_\pi^R$, and $\alpha_f^R = (1 - \lambda^R)$.

Of greatest interest are the region-specific short- and long-run elasticities (α_π and β_π, respectively) of varietal shares with respect to the measure of regional comparative advantage. We expect these to be positive: as the revenue per acre of a specific variety increases relative to the average revenue per acre for that region, that variety's share of acreage will also increase, and greater in the long run ($\alpha_\pi < \beta_\pi$).

We estimate the model in equation (10) separately for each of the five California regions defined in Table 1 (see online supplementary Appendix Table A-1) using the data for the nineteen years 1995–2013 on the top 12 varieties grown in the region — a total of 228 observations per region if we do not have any missing observations. Hence, a total of 20 different varieties were included for at least one region, reflecting the different varietal emphasis among the regions. In each region the top 12 varieties account for at least 82 percent of total acreage, but not all varieties are grown in all regions, and the shares are very unequal: a few varieties account for most of the planted area in each region, the share of acreage of even the tenth-ranked variety is usually around 1 or 2 percent.[8] We estimated the regional models using OLS with errors clustered by variety to correct for heterogeneity, given the systematically large differences in varietal shares. The results are summarized in Table 7.

The models all fit the data very well, accounting for a very high proportion of the variation in varietal shares in each region, as might be expected in a model that includes the lagged dependent variable and a great many fixed effects (one per variety and one per year in each regional model). Of primary interest is the coefficient on the incentive variable, representing the short-run elasticity of varietal shares with respect to the measure of varietal comparative advantage, an indicator of supply response. In four of the regions the estimate of this short-run elasticity is in the range of 0.08 to 0.17 and statistically significantly different from zero at the 10 percent level or better. The model fits less well overall and the elasticity coefficient is smaller and less statistically significant in the two Central Valley regions, especially in the South Central Valley region. On the whole the models are more satisfactory for the other three, predominantly coastal regions that produce generally higher-quality winegrapes.

Many of the coefficients measuring varietal fixed effects are statistically significant (lower half of Table 7) and mostly they are positive indicating, *ceteris paribus,* a higher share of that variety relative to the default, Grenache. These coefficients are particularly large and statistically significant, especially in the higher-quality regions, for the premium varieties, Cabernet Sauvignon, Chardonnay, Merlot, Pinot Noir, Zinfandel, Syrah, and to a lesser extent, Sauvignon Blanc, Petite Sirah, and Pinot Gris. Given the logarithmic form, a varietal indicator coefficient of 1.0

---

[8] Since inconsistency of OLS estimates is a potential concern in dynamic panel models with fixed effects (Nickell 1981), as a robustness check, we also estimated the model using a dynamic panel GMM (Arellano-Bond) estimator. The results (see Appendix Table A-2) are nearly identical to the OLS estimates, but do not allow for coefficients on individual varieties, so the OLS estimates are preferred. The results are also insensitive to alternative specifications of the model: without fixed effects, without the lagged dependent variable, and using multiple lags of the dependent variable.

Table 7. Regression results, models of varietal shares in California regions, 1995–2013

Coefficient	Dependent Variable is Varietal Share of Total Acres (LnShare) by Region				
	North Coast	Central Coast	South Valley	North Valley	Other California
$\ln(\pi^e_{v,t})$	0.174***	0.145***	0.033	0.0706*	0.128***
	(0.00)	(0.00)	(0.35)	(0.07)	(0.00)
Long-Run Elasticity	0.65	0.79	0.94	0.60	0.45
Lagged LnShare	0.733***	0.816***	0.965***	0.883***	0.715***
	(0.00)	(0.00)	(0.00)	0.00	(0.00)
Constant	−0.561***	−0.423***	−0.119	−0.221***	−0.728***
	(0.00)	(0.00)	(0.48)	(0.00)	(0.00)
Fixed Effects for Selected Varieties					
Cabernet Franc	−0.567***				−0.529***
Cabernet Sauvignon	0.183***	0.0755***	0.0332***	0.0285***	0.239***
Carignane			−0.0419	−0.306***	−0.482***
Chardonnay	0.144***	0.152***	0.0490**	0.0718***	0.238***
Chenin Blanc		−0.406***	−0.0354	−0.274***	
French Colombard			0.0602	−0.224***	
Gewurztraminer		−0.448***			−0.621***
Grenache			−0.0196	−0.287***	
Muscat of Alexandria			−0.0101		
Petite Sirah	−0.639***	−0.328***		−0.154***	−0.231***
Petite Verdot	−0.808***				
Pinot Gris		−0.217***			
Pinot Noir	0.0415***	0.0350***			−0.0556**
Rubired			0.0467		
Ruby Cabernet			0.00759		
Sangiovese	−0.760***				
Sauvignon Blanc	−0.250***	−0.261***		−0.135***	−0.0302**
Syrah	−0.408***	−0.0980***		−0.132***	−0.119***
Observations	154	168	168	154	154
R-squared	0.999	0.995	0.994	0.994	0.998

Notes: P-values in parentheses. Asterisks denote coefficients that are statistically significantly different from zero at 10% (*), 5% (**) and 1% (***) levels of significance.

implies scaling up the share by a factor of 2.72 (a coefficient of 0.5 implies scaling up the share by a factor of 1.65, and a coefficient of –0.2 implies scaling the share down by a factor of 0.82). These fixed effects account for a significant proportion of the variation in varietal shares, but some still is accounted for by variation in the comparative advantage measure.

Table 7 also reports the long-run elasticities implied by the models for the five regions. The long-run elasticity is inferred by dividing the short-run elasticity by the estimated adjustment coefficient: i.e., $\beta_\pi = \alpha_\pi/\lambda = \alpha_\pi/(1 - \alpha_f)$. With the exception of the South Central valley region, for which the point estimate is not statistically significant, the long-run elasticity estimates are all remarkably similar across the regions, in the range of 0.45 to 0.80. These estimates are plausible albeit small, suggestive of quite limited response of the varietal mix to changes in relative returns, even in the long run.

6. Summary and implications

The data and analysis here reveal five things about vineyards in the United States. First, even though wine and winegrapes are highly differentiated, and a great many diverse varieties are grown, a comparatively small number of varieties dominate the U.S. picture — in some regions just one or two varieties predominate, with the choice depending on climate and market segment targeted.

Second, broadly speaking, the mix of winegrape varieties in the United States is not very different from that in the rest of the world and, since 2000, it has become even less differentiated. The U.S. mix is now closer to that of France, since France is the closest to the global mix.

Third, U.S. regions vary considerably in the mix of varieties in which they specialize. The U.S. regions mostly have been changing like the national aggregate — each becoming more like France and the world as a whole — but some regions are more distinctive (i.e., New York, Oregon, and the Southern Central Valley), and one region (Oregon) has become more different and more specialized in particular varieties for which it appears to have a comparative advantage.

Fourth, U.S. regions vary considerably in the quality of grapes they produce of a given variety, and region-by-variety interactions have complex influences on the pattern of quality and production.

Fifth, we can account for some of the shifting varietal patterns in the U.S. vineyard and in winegrape production using measures of regional varietal comparative advantage, which reflect changes in both demand and supply and producer responses to them. But a significant share of the variation is not explained by our relatively simple model, in part because it only crudely represents the complexities of winegrape growers' long-run expectations, their intentions, the factors that influence them, and the constraints they face. A more-sophisticated representation of those complexities is not possible at present, however, given limitations on available data and other resources.

Supplementary material

For supplementary material accompanying this paper visit doi:10.1017/jwe.2015.29.

References

Alston, J.M., Andersen, M.A., James, S.J., and Pardey, P.G. (2010). *Persistence Pays: U.S. Agricultural Productivity Growth and the Benefits from Public R&D Spending*. New York: Springer.

Alston, J.M., Fuller, K.B., Kaplan, J.D., and Tumber, K.P. (2013). The economic consequences of Pierce's Disease and related policy in the California winegrape industry. *Journal of Agricultural and Resource Economics*, 38, 269–297.

Anderson, K. (2010). Varietal intensities and similarities of the world's wine regions. *Journal of Wine Economics*, 5(2), 270–309.

Anderson, K. (2013). *Which Winegrape Varieties are Grown Where? A Global Empirical Picture*. Adelaide: University of Adelaide Press. Available as a free ebook at www.adelaide.edu.au/press/winegrapes/.

Anderson, K. (2014). Changing varietal distinctiveness of the world's wine regions: Evidence from a new global database. *Journal of Wine Economics*, 9(3), 249–272.

Anderson, K. (2015). Evolving varietal and quality distinctiveness of Australia's wine regions. Working Paper 0115, Wine Economics Research Centre, University of Adelaide, March. Since published in *Journal of Wine Research*, 27(3), 173–192, September 2016.

Anderson, K., and Aryal, N.R. (2013). *Database of Regional, National and Global Winegrape Bearing Areas by Variety, 2000 and 2010.* Available at www.adelaide.edu.au/wine-econ/databases/.

Anderson, K., and Aryal, N.R. (2014). *Australian Grape Area and Wine Industry Database, 1843 to 2013.* Available at www.adelaide.edu.au/wine-econ/databases/.

Ashenfelter, O., and Storchmann, K. (2016). Climate change and wine: A review of the economic implications. *Journal of Wine Economics,* 11(1), forthcoming.

Dorfman, J.H., and Heien, D. (1989). The effects of uncertainty and adjustment costs on investment in the almond industry. *Review of Economics and Statistics,* 71(2), 263–274.

Eurostat (2013). Basic Vineyard Survey, Available at http://epp.eurostat.ec.europa.eu/portal/ page/portal/statistics/search_database/.

Fegan, P.W. (2003). *The Vineyard Handbook: Appellations, Maps and Statistics,* revised edition. Springfield IL: Phillips Brothers for the Chicago Wine School.

Fuller, K.B., Alston, J.M., and Sambucci, O.S. (2014). The value of Powdery Mildew resistance in grapes: Evidence from California. *Wine Economics and Policy,* 3(2), 90–107.

Gaeta, D., and Corsinovi, P. (2014). *Economics, Governance, and Politics in the Wine Market: European Union Developments.* London: Palgrave Macmillan.

Griliches, Z. (1979). Issues in assessing the contribution of R&D to productivity growth. *Bell Journal of Economics,* 10, 92–116.

Jaffe, A.B. (1986). Technological opportunity and spillovers of R&D: evidence from firms' patents profits and market value. *American Economic Review,* 76(5), 984–1001,

Jaffe, A.B. (1989). Real effects of academic research. *American Economic Review,* 79(5), 957–970.

Lapsley, J.T. (1996). *Bottled Poetry: Napa Winemaking from Prohibition to the Modern Era. Berkeley.* Berkeley, CA: University of California Press.

Nickell, S. (1981). Biases in Dynamic Models with Fixed Effects. *Econometrica,* 49(6), 1417–1426.

Olmstead, A.L., and Rhode, P.W. (2010). Quantitative indices of the early growth of the California wine industry. In José Luis García Ruiz, Juan Hernández Andreu, José Morilla Critz, José María Ortiz-Villajos (eds.), *Homenaje a Gabriel Tortella.* Madrid: Universidad de Alcala. 271–288.

Robinson, J., Harding, J., and Vouillamoz, J. (2012). *Wine Grapes: A Complete Guide to 1,368 Vine Varieties, Including their Origins and Flavours.* London: Allen Lane.

Sumner, D.A., Bombrun, H., Alston, J.M., and Heien, D.M. (2004). North America. In Kym Anderson (ed.), *Globalization of the World's Wine Markets,* London: Edward Elgar.

Volpe, R., Green, R., and Heien, D. (2011). Estimating the supply elasticity of California wine grapes using regional systems of equations. *Journal of Wine Economics* 5(2), 219–35.

USDA/NASS (2011). Historical Crush Reports. Available at: http://www.nass.usda.gov/Statistics_by_State/California/Publications/Grape_Crush/index.asp

USDA/NASS (2011). Historical Acreage Reports. Available at http://www.nass.usda.gov/Statistics_by_State/California/Publications/Grape_Acreage/index.asp

Chapter 24

Evolving Varietal and Quality Distinctiveness of Australia's Wine Regions*

Kym Anderson[†]

Abstract

In an ever-more-competitive global market, vignerons compete for the attention of consumers by differentiating their product while responding to technological advances, climate changes and evolving demand patterns. In doing so, they increasingly highlight their regional and varietal distinctiveness. This paper examines the extent to which the mix of winegrape varieties in Australia differs from the rest of the world and differs across wine regions within the country, and how that picture has altered over the first decade of this century. It reports varietal intensity indexes for different regions, indexes of similarity of varietal mix

---

*First published in *Journal of Wine Research* 27(3): 173–92, September 2016. The author is grateful for helpful comments from Brian Croser, Peter Dry and Terry Lee, for meticulous research assistance by Nanda Aryal in compiling the database and indicators, for helpful comments from referees and for financial assistance from the Australian Grape and Wine Authority (GWRDC Project Number UA 12/08). Views expressed are the author's alone.

[†]Wine Economics Research Centre, School of Economics, University of Adelaide, Adelaide, SA, Australia

between regions and over time, and quality indexes across regions and varieties within Australia. The study is based mainly on a new global database of vine bearing areas circa 2000 and 2010, supplemented by a more detailed database for Australia back to the 1950s. It reveals that the varietal distinctiveness of Australia vis-à-vis the rest of the world, and varietal differentiation between regions within the country, is far less than for most other countries — a pattern that has become even more pronounced since 2000. It concludes that there is much scope for Australia's winegrape plantings to become more diversified as producers respond to market and climate changes.

1. Introduction

Australia's vignerons have faced a multitude of challenges since their vineyard expansion ceased a decade ago. Meanwhile the globalization of the world's wine markets has encouraged wine consumers to seek new types of wines, and has generated many new wine consumers. Attracting and retaining consumer attention requires producers to be forever looking for new ways to differentiate their product. Traditionally, the Old World has emphasized regional differences and has restricted both the range of varieties grown in each region and the use of varietal labeling on bottles. In Australia and other New World countries, by contrast, product differentiation had been mainly through winegrape varietal labeling, although gradually more emphasis is being given also to regional and even single-vineyard labeling. Producers in both Old and New World countries are also differentiating by production technique. Some are emphasizing organic or biodynamic methods, for example, with the latter expanding rapidly in Australia in recent years, albeit from a very small base (Allen, 2010).

In addition to striving to differentiate their product, producers are also well aware of the impact climate changes, particularly higher temperatures and more extreme weather events, are having on their winegrapes (Jones, Reid, & Vilks, 2012; Moriondo et al., 2013). Adaptation strategies include switching to warmer climate or more resilient grape varieties, and sourcing more from regions with a higher latitude or altitude to retain the firm's current mix of grape varieties. In regions and sites whose varietal comparative advantages are still unclear — as in newly expanding regions of Australia and other New World countries — winegrowers are continually searching for potentially profitable alternative varieties that do well in climates similar to what they expect theirs to become in the future.

These marketing and climate/environment adaptation needs are generating a rapidly growing demand from vignerons for information on what winegrape varieties are grown where and how those patterns are changing over time. Consumers, too, are curious as to what winegrapes are grown where, and the more fashion-conscious are keen to know which are expanding or contracting (Robinson, 1986).

In Australia, well before the trebling of its vine area over the past two decades, it was noted that the varietal distinctiveness of Australia's vineyards relative to the rest of the world's, and the varietal differentiation between regions within the country, was far less than for other countries (Dry & Smart, 1980; Hickinbotham, 1947). That made the country's wines undistinguished, varietally, from those of the rest of the world. The purpose of this paper is to explore the extent to which that situation has changed in more recent decades, while leaving for future research the task of *explaining* the evolving pattern.

There are great books available on both the varieties and wine regions of major supplying countries, including the latest seminal ones by Robinson, Harding, and Vouillamoz (2012) and Johnson and Robinson (2013). Yet none of those resources provides enough empirical information to get a clear view of the relative importance of the various regions and their winegrape varieties in the global vineyard. To the best of this author's knowledge, the only other source of such global data is Fegan (2003), but it covers a relatively small number of regions and only for circa 2000. To respond to the need for more comprehensive empirical information, a global database for 2000 and 2010 has been compiled, based on national official or industry data on bearing area by winegrape variety (Anderson & Aryal, 2013). The 2010 database includes 639 regions in 44 countries, covering 99% of global wine production and more than 2000 varieties, of which 1542 are 'primes' and the rest are their synonyms (thanks to the painstaking scientific work that led to the 2012 book by Robinson, Harding and Vouillamoz, and the web-based resource at the Julius Kuhn-Institut, 2013). To make the data more digestible, various summary charts and tables have been published in a 700-page volume (Anderson, 2013).

This paper draws on that global database to generate several indicators that capture changes over the first decade of this century in the varietal mix in Australia and its wine regions relative to the rest of the world's. It also reports on a compilation of additional Australian data for prior decades and subsequent years that reveal major evolutionary changes in the varietal pattern of Australia's vineyards.

The indicators reveal that the varietal distinctiveness of Australia vis-à-vis the rest of the world, and the varietal differentiation between regions within the country, is still far less than for other countries. Moreover, this pattern — noted earlier by Hickinbotham (1947) and Dry and Smart (1980) — is one that has become even more pronounced since 2000. The key finding from the present analysis is that there remains much scope for Australia's winegrape plantings to become more diversified as producers learn more about the varietal potential of their vineyards and respond to perceived market, technological, governmental policy and climate changes.

The paper is structured as follows: the second section defines several indicators that are useful for analyzing the varietal and quality distinctiveness of wine regions/countries. The third section describes the global and Australian databases to be analyzed. A set of empirical pictures of the changing varietal distinctiveness of Australia's wine regions is presented in the fourth section, for the decade to 2010 and more recently in the case of emerging varieties. The changing varietal mix for Australia in aggregate is also shown back to 1956. The fifth section then analyzes regional and varietal quality differences within Australia, as reflected in winegrape prices paid by wineries. The final section discusses possible extensions of the analysis and implications for producers and consumers.

2. Methodology: Indicators of varietal and quality distinctiveness

To assist in digesting large databases, it is helpful to summarize these types of data through calculating various indexes. In addition to regional and varietal shares, we define here a Varietal Intensity Index and a Varietal

Similarity Index. We also define a Regional Quality Index and a Varietal Quality Index, using winegrape price as an indicator of quality.

2.1. Varietal Intensity Index

A Varietal Intensity Index (VII) is defined by Anderson (2010) as a variety's share of a region's winegrape area divided by that variety's share of the global winegrape bearing area. The Varietal Intensity Index is thus a complement to share information in that it indicates the importance of a variety in a region not relative to other varieties in that region but rather relative to that variety's importance in the world.

Specifically, define f_{im} as the proportion of bearing area of grape variety m in the total winegrape bearing area in region or country i such that the proportions fall between zero and one and sum to one (i.e. there is a total of M different grape varieties across the world, and $0 \leq f_{im} \leq 1$ and $\Sigma_m f_{im} = 1$). For the world as a whole, f_m is the bearing area of grape variety m as a proportion of the total global winegrape area, and $0 \leq f_m \leq 1$ and $\Sigma_m f_m = 1$. Then the Varietal Intensity Index, V_{im}, for variety m in region i, is

$$V_{im} = f_{im}/f_m. \qquad (1)$$

2.2. Varietal Similarity Index

To measure the extent to which the varietal mix of one region or country matches that of another region or country or the world, a Varietal Similarity Index (VSI) also has been defined by Anderson (2010). It can also be used to compare the varietal mix of a region or country over time. It borrows and adapts an approach used by Griliches (1979), Jaffe (1986, 1989) and Alston, Andersen, James, and Pardey (2010, Ch. 4), who used it to measure inter-firm, inter-industry or inter-regional technology spillover potential.

The mix of grape varieties is a form of revealed preference or judgment by vignerons about what is best to grow in their region. That judgment is affected by not only terroir but also past and present economic considerations, including current expectations about future price and technology trends plus the sunk cost that would be involved in grafting new varieties onto existing rootstocks or grubbing out and replacing existing varieties.

The vector of grape varietal shares defined above, $f_i = (f_{i1}, ..., f_{iM})$, locates region i in M-dimensional space. Noting that proximity is defined by the direction in which the f-vectors are pointing, but not necessarily their length, Jaffe (1989) proposes a measure called the angular separation of the vectors which is equal to the cosine of the angle between them. If there were just two varieties, m and n, and region i had 75% of its total vine area planted to variety m, whereas only 45% of region j was planted to variety m, then their index of regional similarity is the cosine of the arrowed angle between the two vectors. When there are M varieties, this measure is defined as

$$\omega_{ij} = \frac{\sum_{m=1}^{M} f_{im} f_{jm}}{\left(\sum_{m=1}^{M} f_{im}^2\right)^{1/2} \left(\sum_{m=1}^{M} f_{jm}^2\right)^{1/2}}, \qquad (2)$$

where again f_{im} is the area of plantings of grape variety m as a proportion of the total grape plantings in region i such that these proportions fall between zero and one and sum to one (i.e. there is a total of M different grape varieties across the world, and $0 \leq f_{im} \leq 1$ and $\sum_m f_{im} = 1$). This makes it possible to indicate the degree of varietal mix 'similarity' of any pair of regions. The index also can be generated for each region relative to the average of the world's N regions, call it ω. In short, ω_{ij} measures the degree of overlap of f_i and f_j. The numerator of Equation (2) will be large when i's and j's varietal mixes are very similar. The denominator normalizes the measure to be unity when f_i and f_j are identical. Hence, ω_{ij} will be zero for pairs of regions with no overlap in their grape varietal mix, and one for pairs of regions with an identical varietal mix. For cases in between those two extremes, $0 < \omega_{ij} < 1$. It is conceptually similar to a correlation coefficient. Like a correlation coefficient, it is completely symmetric in that $\omega_{ij} = \omega_{ji}$ and $\omega_{ii} = 1$. Thus the results can be summarized in a symmetric matrix with values of 1 on the diagonal, plus a vector that reports the index for each region relative to the global varietal mix.

The VSI, and the VII, could have been based on production rather than area data, but their comparisons over time would have been less reliable because of year-to-year seasonal variations in yield per hectare. In any case, production data by variety are less commonly available than data on vineyard bearing area.

2.3. *Regional and varietal quality indexes*

To capture differences in the quality of the grapes delivered, which reflect consumers' and thus winemakers' willingness to pay as well as growers' willingness to accept, we generate two price-based indexes on the assumption that prices indicate quality.

The overall quality of all winegrapes in region i, as perceived by wineries in the light of consumer willingness to pay, is indicated by the average winegrape price in that region, P_i, as a proportion of the national average winegrape price, P, across all varieties. We call that the Regional Quality Index, RQI_i, where

$$RQI_i = (P_i/P). \qquad (3)$$

The simplest index of quality of different varieties is the ratio of the national average price for variety m to the national average price of all winegrape varieties. We call that the Varietal Quality Index, VQI_m, where

$$VQI_m = (P_m/P). \qquad (4)$$

3. Data

Data on bearing area of winegrapes are available by variety and region for most key wine-producing countries. In the case of the European Union countries, plantings in several member countries are available from one source (Eurostat, 2013), while for other countries they are typically available online from a national wine industry body or national statistical agency. The United States and Canada are key exceptions, where data are collected at the state/provincial level by state-based industry bodies, and only for those states/provinces with significant wine production.

The years chosen correspond to the most recent decadal agricultural census periods of the European Union, which were 1999 or 2000 and 2009 or 2010. For the non-European Union countries, data have been sought for the earlier year in the Northern Hemisphere and the latter year in the Southern Hemisphere. Inevitably not all other countries or regions had data for exactly those vintages, but in most cases the data refer to vintages that were only six months apart.

The raw data have been compiled by Anderson and Aryal (2013), and various indicators from that database have been assembled in comprehensive tables and figures in Anderson (2013). As well, the global bearing area of the world's 50 most important varieties in 1990 has been estimated, using data in Fegan (2003).

The extent of varietal coverage varies by region within each country as well as by country and over time. For each region the residual 'Other varieties' category was sometimes specified as red or white winegrapes but, where it was not, we apportioned it to red or white according to the red/white ratio for that region's specified varieties. Globally the share of the winegrape bearing area that is not specified by variety is less than 6%.

In short, the global database on which this paper draws involves two years (2000 and 2010, plus some 1990 data), more than 600 regions (in 44 countries) and over 1500 prime varieties. Such a large three-dimensional database potentially has close to two billion numbers in its cells (many of which are zeros). It can be sliced in any of three ways: across regions/countries, years or varieties.

As well, supplementary data for Australia have been assembled by drawing on ABS (2012), www.wineaustralia.com and the Phylloxera Board (2013). Those data are as recent as 2012 and include production volume and average price by variety and region. Those price data are needed to calculate the Regional and Varietal Quality Indexes.

4. Results I: Australia's varietal distinctiveness

What insights for consumers and Australian producers can be drawn from these data? The following three sub-sections address that question in terms of the varietal distinctiveness of Australia's vineyard plantings compared with the rest of the world's, the varietal differences between regions within the country and their changing varietal intensities, and the emerging varieties that are adding to the diversity of Australia's vineyards.

4.1. National varietal distinctiveness

The Varietal Similarity Index or VSI between Australia and the world was 0.45 in 2000, but it rose to 0.62 by 2010, indicating a substantial drift in Australia's varietal mix toward the world aggregate mix. Meanwhile, the average of the VSIs for all other countries in the sample is much lower and hardly changed, at 0.35. In other words, Australia was much less distinct than the average country in its varietal mix in 2000, and its distinctiveness became even less so by 2010.[1] Since France is the country whose varietal mix is most similar to the world mix, this means in effect that Australia has become more like France: the two countries had a VSI of 0.47 in 2000 and 0.58 in 2010.

A key reason for Australia's varietal mix becoming more like the global mix has to do with syrah (most commonly known as shiraz in Australia). The popularity which Australia brought to syrah in the 1990s has led to many other countries expanding their plantings of this variety. In 1990 there were barely 35,000 bearing hectares, making it 35th in the area ranking of all winegrape varieties globally. But by 2000 there were 102,000 hectares, and by 2010 that had risen to 186,000, bringing syrah to the 6th position on that global ladder and less than one-third below the areas of the two now-most-widespread varieties, namely cabernet sauvignon and merlot. Over the decade to 2010, the syrah area grew more than either cabernet or merlot — in fact only tempranillo expanded faster globally. Certainly Australia contributed to that expanding area of syrah, but expansion was even greater in France and Spain. There were also large plantings in other key New World wine countries, and in Italy and

---

[1] The United States had a VSI with the world of 0.41 in 2000 and 0.65 in 2010, and so moved even closer than Australia to the global varietal mix over that decade (Alston, Anderson, & Sambucci, 2015). By contrast, New Zealand had a VSI with the world of 0.34 in 2000, which fell to 0.30 by 2010.

Portugal. As a result, Australia is no longer as globally dominant in this variety: its share of the global syrah area has dropped from 29% in 2000 to 23% in 2010 — even though syrah has increased its share of Australia's own vineyards over that decade, from 22% to 28% (the next-nearest countries being South Africa and France, with 10% and 8% of their vineyards under syrah, respectively).

A further reason Australia's varietal mix has become more like the world's has to do with the large declines in some of the main varieties traditionally used for producing non-premium wines in the Old World (airen, grasevina and mazuelo), the first two of which are not grown in Australia and mazuelo (locally known as carignan noir) has had only a tiny presence. Three other low-valued traditional varieties that have declined globally, garnacha tinta, sultaniye and trebbiano, have declined in Australia also, again contributing to Australia's lack of distinctiveness compared with the rest of the world.[2]

This is not to say that Australia is not highly ranked in terms of the global bearing area of certain varieties. On the contrary, in addition to some unique varieties developed in this country such as tarrango, Table 1 reveals that, among the varieties whose share of winegrape area in Australia exceeds that of the world (i.e. their Varietal Intensity Index, or VII, exceeds one), there are 10 in which Australia ranks 2nd, 5 in which it ranks 3rd, and 3 in which it ranks 4th globally. Australia also ranks in the top five for a further eight varieties whose VII is less than one.[3] But other key wine-producing countries also rank highly for handfuls of varieties, so Australia is not unusual in this respect either.

Australia's change in its varietal mix was even faster in earlier decades. Figure 1 reveals the expanded share of reds through the 1960s and 1970s before whites re-emerged with the take-off of chardonnay, and then the re-emergence of reds with the expansion of both cabernet sauvignon and syrah plus merlot.

---

[2] Two-thirds of what has disappeared as a winegrape in Australia since 2000 is Sultaniye, whose area globally fell by three-quarters over the 2000–2010 period.

[3] Dolcetto (second), nebbiolo and monastrell (third), touriga nacional and tribidrag (fourth), and chenin blanc, cot and tempranillo (fifth).

Table 1. Varietal Intensity Index and varietal area shares,[a] Australia, 2000 and 2010

	National Share, %, 2010	Global Share, %, 2010	Aust.'s Global Rank, 2010	VII 2010	VII 2000
Tarrango	0.0	100.0	1	30.3	37.4
Verdelho	1.0	76.6	1	23.2	29.5
Muscat a Petits Grains Rouge	0.2	37.5	2	11.4	28.4
Semillon	4.0	27.6	2	8.4	9.3
Syrah	28.1	23.0	2	7.0	10.4
Petit Verdot	0.8	17.0	2	5.1	18.2
Ruby Cabernet	0.6	16.8	3	5.1	12.2
Chardonnay	18.3	14.0	3	4.2	4.4
Marsanne	0.2	13.7	2	4.1	5.3
Arneis	0.1	13.6	2	4.1	n.a.
Crouchen	0.1	13.1	2	4.0	1.6
Sultaniye	0.3	12.6	3	3.8	26.8
Viognier	0.9	12.3	2	3.7	1.4
Durif	0.3	11.7	2	3.6	5.6
Cabernet Sauvignon	17.1	9.0	4	2.7	4.2
Riesling	2.7	8.2	3	2.5	2.7
Muscat of Alexandria	1.3	7.8	6	2.4	3.2
Pinot Gris	2.2	7.6	3	2.3	n.a.
Colombard	1.5	6.9	4	2.1	1.8
Sauvignon Blanc	4.3	5.9	7	1.8	1.5
Gewurztraminer	0.5	5.8	6	1.8	1.8
Pinot Noir	3.1	5.4	6	1.6	2.0
Savagnin Blanc	0.1	5.0	5	1.5	n.a.
Roussanne	0.1	4.8	4	1.4	n.a.
Muscadelle	0.0	4.1	2	1.2	3.4
Merlot	6.6	3.8	8	1.1	1.4
Other varieties	5.5	n.a.	n.a.	n.a.	n.a.
Total	100.0	3.3	8	n.a.	n.a.

[a] All varieties in Australia that had a Varietal Intensity Index (VII) above one in 2010.
Source: Anderson (2013).

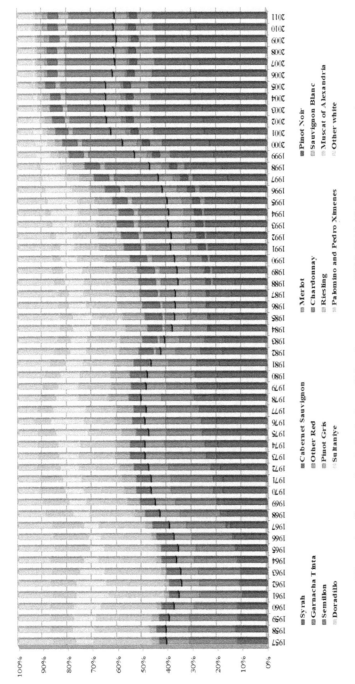

Figure 1. Shares of varieties in Australia's winegrape area, 1956–2012 (%, three-year averages)

Source: Anderson and Aryal (2015).

4.2. Regional differences within Australia

Varietal differences also are more muted between regions within Australia than is the case within other countries — notwithstanding the very large differences in growing conditions across Australia. Bear in mind that it is possible for the VSI for a country vis-à-vis the world to be high but the VSI of each region in that country to be low. In France, for example, where each region is required by law to grow only a small number of varieties that have been designated as most suitable for that region, the average of its regional VSIs of 0.29 is well below France's national VSI in 2010 of 0.72 when compared with the world's varietal mix (which is the highest in the world, because so many other countries have adopted varieties from France's various diverse regions). In Australia, however, the average of its regional VSIs in 2010 of 0.53 is not much below Australia's national VSI of 0.62, and it is almost double the average regional VSI of other countries in the sample (including New Zealand's, which is 0.37, and just below the United States' which is 0.65). Moreover, in 2010, of the 3 most similar regions in the world to each of Australia's 94 regions according to the VSI, less than 7% were non-Australian regions. In New Zealand, by contrast, more than two-thirds of the 3 most-similar regions to each of its 10 regions were in other countries.

It is true that some regions in Australia have managed to pull away from the pack and so are more differentiated from the national mix now than in 2000. However, a little over one-fifth of Australia's 74 regions in the database, comprising 40% of the national winegrape area in 2010, changed their varietal mix hardly at all (the VSI of their mix in 2010 vis-à-vis 2000 was 0.97 or higher). For another one-fifth of Australia's regions, accounting for 22% of the national area, their VSI was 0.95 or 0.96; and for yet another one-fifth (18% of the area) their VSI was between 0.91 and 0.94. Thus it was for just Australia's remaining regions (slightly less than one-fifth of the total number and the national area) that the VSI between their varietal mix in 2000 and 2010 was less than 0.91.

The Varietal Intensity Index or VII provides another way to check on the altered varietal distinctiveness of regions. That index is the ratio of the regional to global shares of the area under a particular variety. Figure 2 shows, for each of three red and three white varieties, the five Australian

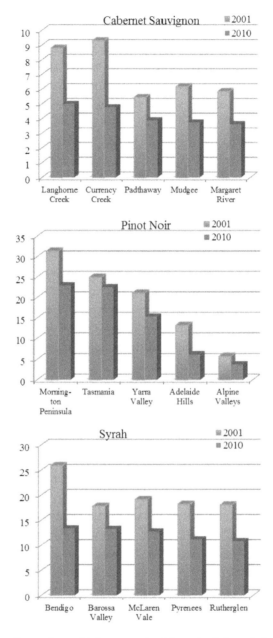

Figure 2. Australian regions with largest varietal intensity index relative to global average, selected varieties, 2001 and 2010

Source: Derived from Anderson (2013, Section VI).

Evolving Varietal and Quality Distinctiveness of Australia's Wine Regions

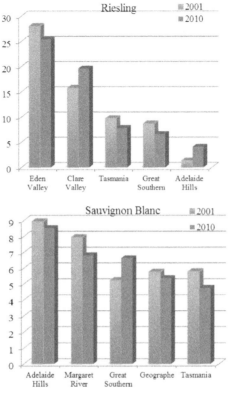

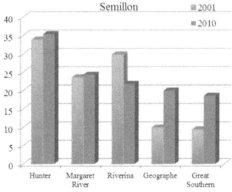

Figure 2. (*Continued*)

regions with the highest VIIs. In the case of red varieties, for example, the five most intense regions all have VIIs above three but they are all lower in 2010 than in 2000. In the case of whites there are a few regions where the VII has risen, but certainly not a majority. For Australia as a whole, for all the varieties that had a VII above one in 2010, as many as two-thirds of them had a higher VII in 2000 (Table 1).

4.3. Emerging varieties in Australia

What about the increased plantings of so-called emerging or alternative varieties that are diversifying Australia's vineyards? If we focus on those varieties not in the world's top 20 list, and which have expanded from less than 200 bearing hectares in Australia in 2000, there are 10 in the database whose areas have grown significantly since then. But in aggregate those 10 raised their share of Australia's total area by only 1.7% (Table 2). The eight varieties whose area in Australia expanded most over the first decade of this century (Figure 3(a)) are, apart from viognier, all in the top 20 globally. As for contracting varieties, sultaniye is by far the most dominant (Figure 3(b)).

Since there is a total of less than 50 varieties separately identified in the Australian official data, that list excludes many of the small emerging varieties that are collected in a residual 'Others' category. Even so, that 'Others' category accounted for just 5% of Australia's total area in 2000 and for only 1.6% by 2010, which means the main varieties have expanded much more than lesser alternative ones. As noted above, the share for syrah alone rose 6 percentage points over that decade, while chardonnay's rose 5 points and the shares of sauvignon blanc and pinot gris each rose 2 points.

Fortunately the Phylloxera and Grape Industry Board of South Australia has a much more detailed dataset for that state, and it reveals another dozen varieties that have shown some growth between 2006 and 2012. ABS (2012) also has provided some more varieties in its latest release, also for 2012. These data, shown on the right-hand side of Table 2, refer to planted area rather than bearing area, and so provide a better indicator of recent changes (because newly planted vines take

Table 2. Emerging winegrape varieties in Australia, 2001 to 2012[a]

	Bearing Area (hectares)		Total Area Including Newly Planted (hectares)		
	Australia		Australia	South Australia	
	2001	2010	2012	2006	2012
Arneis		153	81	12	18
Barbera	103	116	104	25	32
Dolcetto		154	124	20	18
Durif	181	417	500	17	37
Nebbiolo	50	98	122	39	47
Roussanne		83		18	27
Savagnin Blanc		94	140	13	56
Tempranillo	41	476	712	169	301
Tribidag (Zinfandel)		149	104	36	33
Viognier	117	1402	1197	506	521
Sub-total	**492+**	**3142**	**3081+**	**855**	**1090**
% of total	*0.4*	*2.1*	*2.1*	*1.2*	*1.4*
Aglianico				1	10
Alicante Henri Bouschet			12	15	
Alvarinho				4	15
Fiano			107	10	36
Graciano				7	15
Gruner Veltliner			18	0	15
Lagrain				16	19
Montepulciano			49	3	28
Nero d'Avola			33	1	25
Sagrantino				5	11
Saperavi				6	6
Vermentino			93	5	48
Sub-total			**300+**	**70**	**243**
% of total			*0.2*	*0.1*	*0.3*
Total	130,602	151,788	148,509	72,720	76,533

[a] Blank spaces mean data are unavailable, rather than zero. For a much longer list of emerging varieties, see Higgs (2010).
Source: Anderson and Aryal (2013, 2015), ABS (2012) and Phylloxera Board of SA (2013).

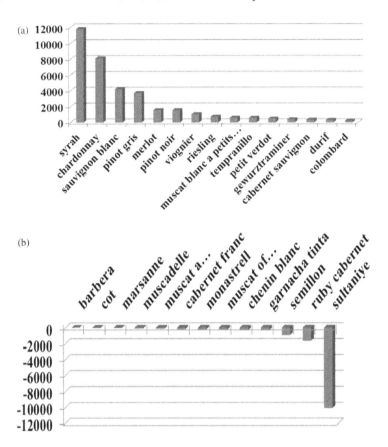

Figure 3. Change in bearing area for most expanded and most contracted varieties, Australia, 2001–2012. (a) Most expanded and (b) most contracted
Source: Derived from Anderson and Aryal (2015) and ABS (2012).

three years to bear). But even these data reveal that emerging varieties make up only a small fraction of 1% of the national area. The total number of varieties in South Australia with more than 0.5 hectares rose by only 20 between 2006 and 2012, from 91 to 111.[4]

---

[4] For more on these and other emerging varieties in Australia, and on which firms have planted them, see Higgs (2010) and his updates at www.vinodiversity.com. Winetitles (2013) also maintains a list of the varieties included on the labels of Australian wines: in 2013 it reported 144 varieties.

5. Results II: Regional and varietal quality differences within Australia

That Australian winegrape regions vary substantially in terms of average winegrape prices received by growers is evident from estimates of the Regional Quality Index, defined as the average winegrape price in a region (across all varieties) as a proportion of that average price nationally. Winegrapes from the hot inland irrigated regions of the Riverland, Riverina, Murray Darling and Swan Hill, which comprise nearly three-fifths of the national crush volume, received on average just 62% of the national average price in 2001, whereas regions with a warm (cool) climate received on average 42% (57%) above the national average price that vintage. Those differentials were muted at that time by the excess demand for winegrapes when wineries were rapidly expanding. By the time the global financial crisis hit in 2008, however, there were excess supplies of many types of winegrapes, and so those differentials widened as the national average price dropped. In 2010, the average winegrape prices in the hot, warm and cool regions were 57%, 154% and 191% of the national average, which had fallen in nominal AUD by two-fifths over that decade (from $941 to $557 per tonne — see Appendix Table A1). By 2013 that national average price was one-tenth lower again and price dispersion was even wider, ranging from $320 to $360 in the hot climate regions to more than seven times that (almost $2500) in cool Tasmania and Mornington Peninsula (Figure 4(a)). The dispersion is almost as wide even for just syrah winegrapes (Figure 4(b)). This increase in regional price dispersion between 2001 and 2013 is clearly visible in the histograms of Figure 5.

Given that different varieties grow better in some regions than others, and that consumer tastes differ across varieties and change over time, it is not surprising that there is also considerable dispersion in the national average prices by variety. In 2001 the difference between the lowest and highest varietal prices was more than six-fold, and it shrunk very little by 2010 despite the two-fifths fall in the nominal average price for all varieties. The ranking from lowest- to highest-priced varieties changed a lot over that decade though (Appendix Table A2). This reflects the fact that the mixes of varieties in all three climate zones in Australia have altered considerably. Figure 6 shows that the range in 2013 from lowest-priced to

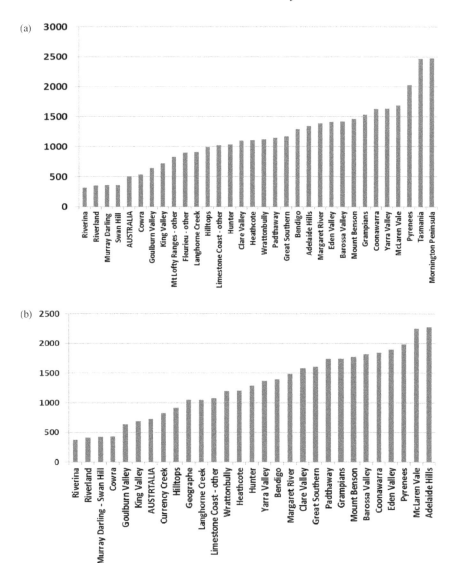

Figure 4. Average price of winegrapes, by region, Australia, 2013. (a) All varieties (AUD per tonne, after quality adjustments) and (b) syrah (AUD per tonne)

Source: Derived from Anderson and Aryal (2015), drawing on WINEFACTS data at www.wineaustralia.com, accessed 21 January 2014.

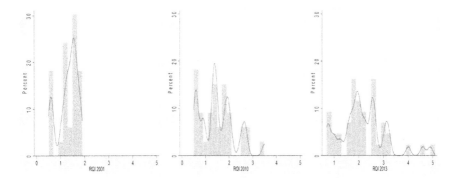

Figure 5. Dispersion in Australia's Regional Quality Index (the Regional Quality Index is defined as the ratio of the regional average price for all varieties to the national average price for all winegrapes), 2001, 2010 and 2013

Source: Derived from Anderson and Aryal (2015), drawing on WINEFACTS data at www.wineaustralia.com, accessed 21 January 2014.

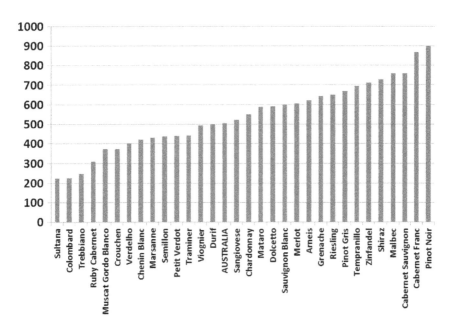

Figure 6. National average prices of main winegrape varieties [these are the varieties with the largest bearing area in Australia, using the varietal names most commonly used in Australia (as distinct from the prime varietal names used in Appendix Table A2)], Australia, 2013

Source: Derived from Anderson and Aryal (2015), drawing on WINEFACTS data at www.wineaustralia.com, accessed 21 January 2014.

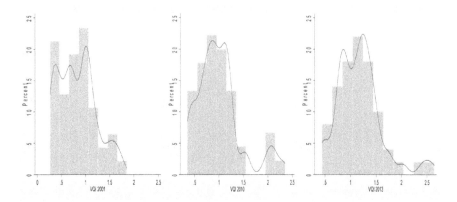

Figure 7. Dispersion in Australia's Varietal Quality Index (the Varietal Quality Index is defined as the ratio of the national average price for a variety to the national average price of all winegrape varieties), 2000, 2010 and 2013

Source: Derived from Anderson and Aryal (2015), drawing on WINEFACTS data at www.wineaustralia.com, accessed 21 January 2014.

highest-priced, even for just the main varieties, was four-fold, but it is six-fold if minor varieties such as pinot meunier are included. Moreover, for each variety there is a wide spectrum of prices across and even within regions. As Figure 4 reveals, the cross-regional range for syrah prices is almost as large as that for the all variety average regional prices, even though data are not available for including some of the highest-priced cool regions with emerging syrah vineyards. Notwithstanding that data limitation at the highest price levels, an increase in varietal price dispersion between 2001 and 2013 is clearly visible in the histograms for the Varietal Quality Index in Figure 7.

6. Conclusions

The above data reveal three things about Australia's viticulture. First, Australia's mix of winegrape varieties is not very different from the rest of the world's and, since 2000, it has become even less differentiated. One reason is that even though its signature variety, syrah, has expanded its share of Australia's vineyard, the variety's importance has expanded even faster in numerous other countries. Australia's mix is now closer to that of France, since France is the closest to the global mix.[5] Whether that is a good thing commercially is unclear, especially for Australia's hottest regions.[6] Perhaps Australian producers benefit enough by emulating France's varietal mix to offset any economic downsides, for example, from being less differentiated from the world mix, or from growing varieties that may be less than ideal for the terroir of Australia's various regions.

Second, even though there are very large differences in growing conditions and especially climates across Australia, cross-regional varietal differences within Australia are much less than is the case within other countries. Perhaps this is a consequence of producers finding it easier to market well-known 'international' (mostly French) varieties than trying to differentiate their offering and region with less familiar varieties. But it does suggest there is plenty of scope to explore alternative varieties in the various regions of Australia — which is something grapegrowers are doing in any case as they consider ways to adapt to climate changes.

And third, the global database, together with more recent and more detailed national data, reveal that Australia's various regions to date have made only a little headway in diversifying their vineyards — despite much discussion of alternative or emerging varieties in the media and at conferences.

This paper leaves open the question of *why* particular varieties have been produced at various times in Australia's various regions. To what extent is the varietal mix driven by what grows best in each location (the terroir explanation)? Gergaud and Ginsburgh (2008) argue that terroir has

---

[5] In 2000, Australia had a higher share (74%) of its winegrapes under varieties of French origin than any other country other than New Zealand and South Africa, and in 2010 its share was even higher at 88%, just below China, Chile and New Zealand. Between 2000 and 2010 the global winegrape area devoted to varieties of French origin rose from 26% to 36% (Anderson, 2013, Tables 21 and 22).

[6] Hickinbotham (1947) believed more than six decades ago that Australia's hot regions were too narrowly focused on varieties from France rather than from warmer parts of Europe. More specifically, McKay, Crittenden, Dry, and Hardie (1999) felt that varieties from the warmer parts of Italy were under-represented in Australia. Dry and Smart (1980) suggested that if acid addition had been outlawed in Australia, the hot regions would have been forced to at least add 'improver' varieties to their varietal mix.

not been the main explanation even in Bordeaux. Is the increasing concentration on major 'international' varieties partly a result of producers in newly expanding wine-producing regions finding it easier to market them because of France's strong reputation with those varieties? Might part of the explanation also be that those key varieties do well in a wide range of growing environments, or are more drought or salt tolerant, or have been found to be desirable for blending with other varieties that grow well in the same regions? These and other centripetal forces during the first decade of this century apparently have dominated possible centrifugal forces mentioned in the Introduction (intensifying competition from abroad, consumer demand for novel offerings). It will be interesting to see whether the latter are strong enough to dominate the former over the next decade so as to differentiate Australia's regions more and thereby reverse the trend of recent decades.

References

ABS. (2012, October). *Vineyards estimates, Australia, 2011–12.* Canberra: Australian Bureau of Statistics. Catalogue No. 1329.0.55.002.

Allen, M. (2010). *The future makers: Australian wines for the 21st century.* London: Hardie Grant Books.

Alston, J. M., Anderson, K., & Sambucci, O. (2015). Drifting towards Bordeaux? The evolving varietal emphasis of U.S. wine regions. *Journal of Wine Economics*, 10(3), 349–378.

Alston, J. M., Andersen, M. A., James, S. J., & Pardey, P. G. (2010). *Persistence pays: U.S. agricultural productivity growth and the benefits from Public R&D spending.* New York, NY: Springer.

Anderson, K. (2010). Varietal intensities and similarities of the world's wine regions. *Journal of Wine Economics*, 5(2), 270–309.

Anderson, K. (2013). *Which winegrape varieties are grown where? A global empirical picture.* Adelaide: University of Adelaide Press. Freely available as an e-book at www.adelaide.edu.au/press/ winegrapes

Anderson, K., & Aryal, N. R. (2013). *Database of regional, national and global winegrape bearing areas by variety, 2000 and 2010.* Freely available at the University of Adelaide's Wine Economics Research Centre, revised May 2014. Retrieved from www.adelaide.edu.au/wine-econ/databases

Anderson, K., & Aryal, N. R. (2015). *Australian grape and wine industry database, 1843 to 2013.* Adelaide: Wine Economics Research Centre. Posted at www.adelaide.edu.au/wine-econ/databases/winehistory. Also available in PDF form as a free e-book at www.adelaide.edu.au/press/titles/austwine

Dry, P. R., & Smart, R. E. (1980). The need to rationalize wine grape variety use in Australia. *Australian Grapegrower and Winemaker, 196*, 55–60.

Eurostat. (2013). Basic Vineyard Survey, accessible by navigating ['Agriculture, forestry and fisheries '→' Agriculture '→' Vineyard survey '→' Basic vineyard survey']. Retrieved from http://epp.eurostat.ec.europa.eu/portal/page/portal/statistics/search_database

Fegan, P. W. (2003). *The vineyard handbook: Appellations, maps and statistics* (revised ed.). Springfield, IL: Phillips Brothers for the Chicago Wine School.

Gergaud, O., & Ginsburgh, V. (2008). Endowments, production technologies and the quality of wines in Bordeaux: Does terroir matter? *The Economic Journal, 118:* F142–F157. Reprinted in *Journal of Wine Economics 5*, 3–21, 2010.

Griliches, Z. (1979). Issues in assessing the contribution of research and development to productivity growth. *Bell Journal of Economics, 10*, 92–116.

Hickinbotham, A. R. (1947). Problems of viticulture. *Australian Brewing and Wine Journal, 65*, 24–28, May 20 and 23–25, June 20.

Higgs, D. (2010). *Vinodiversity — the book: New grape varieties and wines in Australia.* Melbourne: Vinodiversity. For updates see www.vinodiversity.com

Jaffe, A. B. (1986). Technological opportunity and spillovers of R&D: Evidence from firms' patents profits and market value. *American Economic Review, 76*(5), 984–1001.

Jaffe, A. B. (1989). Real effects of academic research. *American Economic Review, 79*(5), 957–970.

Johnson, H. & Robinson, J. (2013). *World atlas of wine* (7th ed.). London: Mitchell Beasley.

Jones, G. V., Reid, R. & Vilks, A. (2012). Climate, grapes, and wine: Structure and suitability in a variable and changing climate. In P. Dougherty (Ed.), *The geography of wine: Regions, terrior, and techniques* (pp. 109–133). London: Springer Press.

Julius Kühn-Institut. (2013). *Vitis International Variety Catalogue.* Institute for Grapevine Breeding Geilweilerhof, Federal Research Centre for Cultivated Plants. Retrieved from www.vivc.de

McKay, A. D., Crittenden, G., Dry, P. R., & Hardie, J. (1999). *Italian winegrape varieties in Australia.* Adelaide: Winetitles.

Moriondo, M., Jones, G. V., Bois, B., Dibari, C., Ferrise, R., Trombi, G., & Bindi, M. (2013). Projected shifts of wine regions in response to climate change. *Climatic Change,* 119(3–4), 825–839. doi:10.1007/s10584-013-0739-y

Phylloxera Board. (2013). SA *Winegrape Crush Survey: State summary report 2013.* Adelaide: Phylloxera and Grape Industry Board of South Australia.

Robinson, J. (1986). *Vines, grapes and wines.* London: Mitchell Beazley.

Robinson, J., Harding, J., & Vouillamoz, J. (2012). *Wine grapes: A complete guide to 1,368 vine varieties, including their origins and flavours.* London: Allen Lane.

Winetitles. (2013). *The Australian and New Zealand Wine Industry Directory.* Adelaide: Author. Retrieved from www.winebiz.com.au

Appendix

Table A1. Price, yields, and regional quality indexes, Australian regions, 2001 and 2010

Region[a]		Price (AUD/t) 2001	Price (AUD/t) 2010	Yield (t/ha) 2001	Yield (t/ha) 2010	Area (%) 2001	Area (%) 2010	Production Volume (%) 2001	Production Volume (%) 2010	Production Value (%) 2001	Production Value (%) 2010	RQI 2001	RQI 2010
H	Riverland	658	301	16.8	16.6	14.0	13.2	22.1	21.7	15.5	11.7	0.7	0.5
H	Riverina	497	350	12.4	12.2	9.5	13.3	11.0	16.0	5.8	10.1	0.5	0.6
H	Murray Darling — VIC	562	310	12.5	16.1	12.0	5.5	14.1	8.8	8.4	4.9	0.6	0.6
H	Murray Darling — NSW	562	310	13.1	19.9	4.3	4.3	5.2	8.5	3.1	4.7	0.6	0.6
C	Limestone Coast — other	1474	962	11.4	8.1	5.8	6.5	6.1	5.3	9.6	9.1	1.6	1.7
W	Barossa Valley	1429	1057	8.3	7.0	5.9	6.4	4.6	4.4	7.0	8.4	1.5	1.9
H	Swan Hill (VIC)	562	310	8.1	17.0	2.9	2.5	2.2	4.3	1.3	2.4	0.6	0.6
W	Langhorne Creek	1429	742	12.7	8.9	2.9	3.9	3.4	3.5	5.2	4.6	1.5	1.3
W	Padthaway	1488	781	12.0	9.7	2.5	3.3	2.8	3.2	4.4	4.5	1.6	1.4
W	McLaren Vale	1681	1176	10.2	7.3	3.6	4.3	3.4	3.1	6.2	6.5	1.8	2.1
C	Adelaide Hills	1673	1100	8.7	8.7	1.4	2.5	1.1	2.2	2.0	4.3	1.8	2.0
W	Margaret River	1525	1426	7.2	6.4	2.6	3.2	1.7	2.0	2.8	5.2	1.6	2.6
W	Clare Valley	1424	1028	6.8	5.6	2.8	3.2	1.8	1.8	2.7	3.2	1.5	1.8
C	Yarra Valley	1654	1492	7.6	6.4	1.6	1.6	1.1	1.0	1.9	2.7	1.8	2.7
W	Hunter	1256	839	6.7	4.0	3.0	2.3	1.9	0.9	2.6	1.4	1.3	1.5
W	Eden Valley	1544	1106	7.7	6.5	0.9	1.3	0.7	0.8	1.1	1.6	1.6	2.0
W	Goulburn Valley	1268	813	9.0	7.2	0.8	1.1	0.7	0.8	1.0	1.1	1.3	1.5
W	Mudgee	1206	473	7.3	2.7	1.6	2.2	1.1	0.6	1.5	0.5	1.3	0.8

Evolving Varietal and Quality Distinctiveness of Australia's Wine Regions   625

	Region												
C	Mt. Lofty Ranges — other	1166	774	10.4	6.8	0.4	0.9	0.4	0.6	0.5	0.8	1.2	1.4
W	Currency Creek	1429	796	9.8	9.2	0.7	0.6	0.7	0.5	1.0	0.7	1.5	1.4
W	Orange	1408	702	9.0	3.6	0.8	1.0	0.6	0.4	1.0	0.5	1.5	1.3
W	Rutherglen	1307	748	6.2	6.3	0.6	0.6	0.4	0.4	0.5	0.5	1.4	1.3
W	Cowra	1114	527	10.5	3.6	1.2	0.9	1.2	0.3	1.4	0.3	1.2	0.9
C	Alpine Valleys	1058	779	10.5	6.0	0.6	0.5	0.6	0.3	0.7	0.4	1.1	1.4
C	Mornington Peninsula	1756	1928	6.7	5.1	0.3	0.5	0.2	0.2	0.4	0.9	1.9	3.5
H	Swan Hill (NSW)	562	310	7.4	12.0	0.4	0.2	0.3	0.2	0.2	0.1	0.6	0.6
W	Bendigo	1268	1054	5.3	4.1	0.5	0.5	0.2	0.2	0.3	0.4	1.3	1.9
W	Southern Fleurieu	1620	1380	6.0	7.6	0.3	0.3	0.1	0.2	0.2	0.5	1.7	2.5
C	Grampians	1346	1492	4.2	5.4	0.3	0.3	0.1	0.2	0.2	0.5	1.4	2.7
C	Hilltops	914	757	5.1	4.3	0.3	0.3	0.1	0.1	0.1	0.2	1.0	1.4
C	Mount Benson	1474	1045	11.4	7.3	0.2	0.2	0.2	0.1	0.4	0.2	1.6	1.9
W	Fleurieu — other	1620	582	8.7	8.2	0.4	0.1	0.3	0.1	0.5	0.1	1.7	1.0
W	Other regions	1073	526	6.6	5.9	15.1	12.4	9.4	7.3	10.7	6.9	1.1	0.9
	Total	**941**	**557**	**10.7**	**10.1**	**100**	**100**	**100**	**100**	**100**	**100**	**1.0**	**1.0**
	Sub-totals:												
C	Cool regions	1481	1065	9.7	7.5	11.8	14.6	10.7	10.9	16.9	20.7	1.57	1.91
W	Warm regions	1335	853	8.3	6.5	45.1	46.4	34.4	29.6	48.7	45.4	1.42	1.52
H	Hot regions	588	317	13.6	15.4	43.1	39.0	54.9	59.5	34.3	33.9	0.62	0.57

[a] Regions are designated climatically as either hot, warm or cool, according to their mean January temperature: H = hot (above 23.2°C); W = warm (between 20.0°C and 23.2°C); and C = cool (below 20.0°C).

Source: Anderson and Aryal (2015).

Table A2. Price, yield, production and varietal quality indexes, key varieties, 2001 and 2010

	Price (AUD/t)		Yield (t/ha)		Production Volume (%)		Area (%)		Production Value (%)		VQI	
	2001	2010	2001	2010	2001	2010	2001	2010	2001	2010	2001	2010
Syrah	1238	664	10.6	9.5	22.4	26.3	22.4	28.1	28.1	30.2	1.26	1.15
Chardonnay	987	520	14.2	10.7	17.6	19.4	13.2	18.3	17.7	17.5	1.00	0.90
Cabernet Sauvignon	1252	640	10.0	8.2	17.9	14.0	19.1	17.1	22.8	15.5	1.27	1.11
Merlot	1086	549	10.5	10.5	5.8	6.8	5.9	6.6	6.4	6.5	1.10	0.95
Semillon	732	447	13.5	12.5	6.4	5.0	5.0	4.0	4.7	3.9	0.74	0.77
Sauvignon Blanc	1063	690	9.7	11.1	1.8	4.7	2.0	4.3	2.0	5.6	1.08	1.19
Muscat of Alexandria	369	275	19.6	23.8	3.5	3.2	1.9	1.3	1.3	1.5	0.38	0.48
Colombard	380	204	21.7	20.8	2.8	3.0	1.4	1.5	1.1	1.1	0.39	0.35
Pinot Noir	1563	898	9.2	8.8	2.1	2.7	2.5	3.1	3.4	4.2	1.59	1.55
Pinot Gris	1426	709		11.9		2.6		2.2		3.1	1.45	1.23
Riesling	1001	721	8.6	8.2	1.9	2.2	2.4	2.7	2.0	2.7	1.02	1.25
Petit Verdot	988	351	8.5	15.5	0.4	1.2	0.6	0.8	0.4	0.8	1.00	0.61
Verdelho	874	408	10.1	9.3	0.9	0.9	1.0	1.0	0.8	0.7	0.89	0.71
Ruby Cabernet	651	251	12.8	13.9	2.2	0.9	1.9	0.6	1.5	0.4	0.66	0.43
Viognier	1451	561	5.3	8.8	0.0	0.8	0.1	0.9	0.1	0.8	1.47	0.97
Garnacha Tinta	883	629	10.5	6.5	1.6	0.7	1.6	1.2	1.5	0.8	0.90	1.09
Gewurztraminer	676	503	8.3	10.8	0.3	0.6	0.4	0.5	0.2	0.5	0.69	0.87
Chenin Blanc	519	425	16.5	12.5	1.0	0.4	0.6	0.4	0.5	0.3	0.53	0.74
Monastrell	693	484	12.3	7.9	0.8	0.4	0.7	0.5	0.6	0.3	0.70	0.84

Evolving Varietal and Quality Distinctiveness of Australia's Wine Regions

Variety											
Muscat Blanc a Petits Gr.	450	11.5	10.1	0.2	0.4	0.2	0.4	0.1	0.2	0.46	0.63
Sangiovese	978	8.9	8.5	0.2	0.3	0.3	0.4	0.2	0.3	0.99	0.96
Durif	680	8.3	10.5	0.1	0.3	0.1	0.3	0.1	0.2	0.69	0.74
Cabernet Franc	1110	8.3	5.2	0.4	0.2	0.6	0.4	0.5	0.2	1.13	1.09
Tempranillo	962	5.1	6.2	0.0	0.2	0.0	0.3	0.0	0.2	0.98	1.18
Sultaniye	312	7.2	6.1	5.3	0.2	7.9	0.3	1.7	0.1	0.32	0.37
Cot	1042	10.0	7.2	0.3	0.2	0.3	0.2	0.3	0.2	1.06	1.14
Crouchen	451	16.9	25.1	0.1	0.2	0.1	0.1	0.1	0.1	0.46	0.73
Dolcetto			11.6		0.1		0.1				
Muscat a Petits Gr. Rouge	922	4.2	7.2	0.1	0.1	0.3	0.2	0.1	0.1	0.94	0.78
Marsanne	819	10.5	6.8	0.2	0.1	0.2	0.2	0.1	0.1	0.83	1.07
Arneis			9.6		0.1		0.1				
Trebbiano	350	10.7	11.3	0.5	0.1	0.5	0.1	0.2	0.0	0.36	0.55
Tribidrag	1195		5.6		0.1		0.1		0.1	1.21	1.19
Savagnin Blanc	531	8.6		0.1		0.1		0.0			0.92
Barbera	605	7.8	6.7	0.1	0.1	0.1	0.1	0.0	0.0	0.61	0.38
Tarrango	653	22.2	9.3	0.2	0.0	0.1	0.0	0.1	0.0	0.66	0.47
Muscadelle	747	8.2	6.7	0.1	0.0	0.2	0.0	0.1	0.0	0.76	0.82
Roussanne	1600		4.8		0.0		0.1		0.1	1.63	1.97
Nebbiolo	1011	3.3	4.0	0.0	0.0	0.0	0.1	0.0	0.1	1.03	2.11
Touriga Nacional	1017	9.4	6.0	0.0	0.0	0.1	0.0	0.1	0.0	1.03	1.51
Doradillo	259	19.7		0.4		0.2		0.1		0.26	

(*Continued*)

Table A2. (Continued)

	Price (AUD/t) 2001	Price (AUD/t) 2010	Yield (t/ha) 2001	Yield (t/ha) 2010	Production Volume (%) 2001	Production Volume (%) 2010	Area (%) 2001	Area (%) 2010	Production Value (%) 2001	Production Value (%) 2010	VQI 2001	VQI 2010
Palomino Fino	272	358	13.3		0.1		0.1		0.0		0.28	0.62
Afus Ali	260		3.4		0.1		0.3		0.0		0.26	
Pedro Ximenez	302		10.1		0.1		0.1		0.0		0.31	
Canada Muscat	516		9.1		0.0		0.0		0.0		0.52	
Taminga	321		9.0		0.0		0.0		0.0		0.33	
Fiano		1337										2.31
Vermentino	614										1.06	
Korinthiaki			2.1		0.1		0.6					
Pinot Meunier	1715	1201	10.2		0.1		0.1		0.1		1.74	2.08
Mazuelo	428		5.2		0.0		0.1		0.0		0.43	
Tannat		505										0.87
Other reds	738	712	2.4	7.2	0.5	0.5	2.2	0.8	0.4	0.7	0.75	0.93
Other whites	587	535	3.8	12.2	1.0	1.0	2.8	0.8	0.6	0.9	0.60	1.23
Total	**984**	**578**	**10.7**	**10.1**	**100.0**	**100.0**	**100.0**	**100.0**	**100.0**	**100.0**	**1.0**	**1.0**
Sub-totals:												
All reds	1081	638	9.9	9.1	56	55	60	61	67	61	1.10	1.10
All whites	740	466	11.7	11.6	44	45	40	39	33	39	0.75	0.81

Source: Anderson and Aryal (2015).

F. Convergence in National Alcohol Consumption Patterns

Chapter 25

Convergence in National Alcohol Consumption Patterns: New Global Indicators*

Alexander J. Holmes[†] and Kym Anderson[‡]

Abstract

With increasing globalisation and interactions between cultures, countries are converging in many ways, including in their consumption patterns. The extent to which this has been the case in alcohol consumption has been the subject of previous studies, but those studies have been limited in scope to a specific region or group of high-income countries or to just one or two types of alcohol. The present study updates earlier findings, covers all countries of the world since 1961, and introduces two new summary indicators to capture additional dimensions of the

---

*First published in *Journal of Wine Economics* 12(2): 117–48, 2017. The authors are grateful for helpful journal reviewer comments and for financial support from the University of Adelaide's EU Centre for Global Affairs.

[†] Wine Economics Research Centre, School of Economics, University of Adelaide, Adelaide SA 5005, Australia; e-mail: alexander.holmes@student.adelaide.edu.au.

[‡] Wine Economics Research Centre, School of Economics, University of Adelaide, Adelaide SA 5005, Australia; and Arndt-Corden Department of Economics, Australian National University, Canberra ACT 2601; e-mail: kym.anderson@adelaide.edu.au (corresponding author).

extent of convergence in total alcohol consumption and in its mix of beverages. It also distinguishes countries according to whether their alcoholic focus was on wine, beer, or spirits in the early 1960s as well as their geographic regions and their real per-capita incomes. For recent years, we add expenditure data and compare alcohol with soft drink retail expenditure, and we show the difference it makes when unrecorded alcohol volumes are included as part of total alcohol consumption. The final section summarizes our findings and suggests that further research could provide new demand elasticity estimates and use econometrics to explain the varying extents of convergence over time, space, and beverage type.

1. Introduction

With increasing globalization and interactions between cultures, countries' behaviours are converging in many ways, including consumption patterns. This mimicry raises concerns when consumers in developing countries copy trends from high-income countries that are considered undesirable from such viewpoints as human health consequences. Tobacco and sugar are perhaps the most frequently mentioned items, as tobacco consumption globally has doubled since the early 1960s, and sugar use has increased by nearly half and is contributing to the spread of obesity. But the other item closely monitored by health authorities is the level of consumption of alcoholic and sweetened nonalcoholic drinks. Producers of beverages also seek to monitor consumer trends, focusing not only on overall levels of consumption but also on its composition or mix to ascertain changes in consumer preferences or behaviours. The wine, beer, and spirits industries, for example, are well aware that wine's share of global recorded alcohol consumption volume more than halved between 1961 and 2015, falling from 35% to 15%, while beer's increased from 29% to 42%, and the share of spirits rose from 36% to 43%.

The extent to which alcoholic beverage consumption patterns are converging across countries has been the subject of many previous studies. Examples since the new millennium include Smith and Solgaard (2000), Bentzen, Eriksson, and Smith (2001), Aizenman and Brooks (2008), and Colen and Swinnen (2016). However, those studies have limited the scope of their analysis to a specific region or group of high-income countries or to just one or two types of alcohol. The present study updates earlier findings, covers all countries of the world since 1961 and key high-income countries since 1888, and introduces new summary indicators to capture several dimensions of the extent of convergence in total alcohol consumption and its mix of beverages. It also distinguishes countries according to whether their alcoholic focus was on wine, beer, or spirits in the early 1960s as well as their geographic regions and their real per-capita incomes. For recent years, we also add expenditure data and compare alcohol with soft drink retail spending, and we show the difference it makes when unrecorded alcohol volumes are included as part of total alcohol consumption.

In exploring alcohol consumption trends in European countries from 1960 to 2000, Smith and Solgaard (2000) find that the market shares for traditional beverages declined. In the Nordic countries, for example, the dominance of spirits in 1960 diminished as beer and wine shares grew over those four decades. Bentzen, Eriksson, and Smith (2001) use time series techniques to study alcohol consumption convergence in a number of European countries. They conclude from their unit root tests that differences in total alcohol consumption levels are diminishing. Aizenman and Brooks (2008) study convergence during 1963 to 2000 across a larger sample of countries that included members of the Organisation for Economic Co-operation and Development (OECD) and middle-income countries, but only for beer and wine. Colen and Swinnen (2016) analyse mainly beer but also wine consumption across a large sample of high-income and developing countries. Echoing the conclusions of Smith and Solgaard (2000), they find that in many traditional beer- (wine-)drinking countries, the share of beer (wine) in total alcohol consumption is declining, and that of wine (beer) is increasing. They also show that beer consumption increased in developing countries with rising incomes but fell once higher levels of income were reached. However, spirits are omitted from their analysis.

The present paper first describes the data sources to be used. It then suggests several ways to indicate convergence over time in total recorded alcohol consumption and in the mix of beverages. The main section then presents findings based on annual data assembled for countries and regional residual country groups spanning the world from 1961 to 2014 and for some high-income countries dating to the late nineteenth century. The results from 1961 are shown also for groups of countries whose earlier focus was wine, beer, or spirits as well as for various regions of the world and by real per-capita income. Also shown is the relative importance of alcoholic versus various nonalcoholic drinks in total beverage consumption volumes and expenditures since 2001. Estimates of unrecorded alcohol consumption for the years 2000, 2005, and 2010 are then used to test the robustness of the convergence findings when these estimates are included as part of total alcohol consumption. The final section summarizes the findings and suggests that further research could provide new demand elasticity estimates, using econometrics to explain the varying extents of convergence over time, space, and beverage type.

2. Data sources

The wine, beer, and spirits consumption volume data in this study are sourced from two new annual databases: one that includes wine, beer, and spirits volumes and stretches from 2014 back to the 1880s for eleven high-income countries and back to 1961 for all other countries (Anderson and Pinilla, 2017); and another that includes wine, beer, and spirits average consumer expenditure data compiled for all countries back to 2001 and for some high-income countries back to the 1950s (Holmes and Anderson, 2017).

The longer time series on volumes consumed (in litres of alcohol, or LAL)[1] from 1961 includes 48 important wine-producing and/or wine-consuming countries plus 5 residual regions (treated here as 5 extra "countries") that together make up the world. That database has a full

---

[1]The average alcohol content by volume is assumed to be 4.5% for beer, 12% for wine, and 40% for spirits. Ready-to-drink spirits mixers are converted to spirits with the assumption that their alcohol content is 5%. Throughout, the term "wine" refers to grape wine. Wine from other fruits is a very small category in almost all countries. Rice "wine," which is made in many Asian countries but under different names (e.g., sake in Japan, mijiu in China, cheongju in Korea), is included in the spirits category: even though rice wine is fermented, it looks like a clear spirit, is brewed differently than beer, and is typically at least 15% alcohol.

matrix of data for the period 1961 to 2014, apart from information on Croatia, Georgia, Moldova, and Ukraine, data for which became available only after the breakup of the Soviet Union. The shorter time series (2001–2015) is available from Euromonitor International (2016) for 80 countries plus, again, 5 residual regions.

To estimate average prices for wine, beer, and spirits for each of the countries that have expenditure data, we simply divide expenditure by the consumption volume. The value data are expressed in current US dollars converted from local currencies using each country's annual average nominal exchange rate.

Euromonitor International (2016) also provides soft drink volume and expenditure data from 2001 and total expenditure on all products. Other key statistics used include figures compiled from the World Health Organization (2015) and, in the case of our proxy for real per-capita disposable income back to 1961, the Maddison gross domestic product (GDP) estimates in 1990 International Geary-Khamis dollars.[2]

All the consumption data mentioned above refer only to what has been recorded by national governments; an additional amount of alcohol produced and consumed each year is not recorded. WHO (2015) reports estimates of that unrecorded alcohol consumption volume for 98 countries for 2000, 2005, and 2010. In Section 5, these are used to test the robustness of our findings on convergence in recorded alcohol consumption levels and mixes.

3. Indicators of convergence

To study convergence across countries in national alcohol consumption volumes and beverage mixes, we employ a number of different indicators. One is simply the coefficient of variation (CoV) across countries each year. Then two indexes developed by Anderson (2014a) to study wine grape varietal patterns across countries and regions are adapted to

---

[2] The Maddison numbers, from www.ggdc.net/maddison/maddison-project/data.htm, have been updated to 2015 by taking the latest purchasing power parity (PPP) estimates in 2011 dollars from the World Bank's International Comparison Project at http://icp.worldbank.org and incorporating them into the Maddison series.

beverage consumption to measure convergence over time in national beverage consumption mixes toward the (changing) world average mix.

3.1. Coefficient of variation

CoV can be calculated across countries each year for total alcohol consumption volume and for the share of each of the three main beverage types in the total volume of recorded alcohol consumption. CoV measures the concentration of data around the mean value: If it declines over time, this serves as a simple indicator of cross-country convergence. It is calculated for each year by taking the level of consumption per capita across countries and dividing the standard deviation of the series, σ_t, by the mean value of the sample, $\bar{X}_t$:

$$CoV_t = \frac{\sigma_t}{\bar{X}_t}. \quad (1)$$

3.2. Beverage consumption intensity index

The beverage consumption intensity index indicates the importance in a particular year of one type of alcoholic beverage in a country's alcohol consumption relative to the average share of that beverage in alcohol consumption by all countries of the world. We thus define the consumption intensity index for country i as

$$V_{in} = \frac{f_{in}}{f_n}, \quad (2)$$

where there are $i = 1, ..., 53$ (or 85) countries, and $n = 1, 2, 3$ beverages corresponding to wine, beer, and spirits. We define f_{in} as the fraction of wine, beer, or spirits consumption in total national alcohol consumption volume or expenditure in country i, such that $0 \leq f_{in} \leq 1$ and $\sum_{n=1}^{3} f_{in} = 1$. This is divided by the fraction for that same beverage in world total alcohol consumption, f_n, with $0 \leq f_n \leq 1$ and $\sum_n f_n = 1$. For brevity, we tabulate weighted averages of intensity indexes for groups of countries, using as weights each country's consumption of that beverage as a fraction of the group's total consumption of that beverage.

3.3. *Alcohol consumption mix similarity index*

The similarity index is a variant of an index developed by Anderson (2014a) that in turn is adapted from indexes introduced by Griliches (1979) and Jaffe (1986). Anderson (2014a) uses it to measure the extent to which the wine grape varietal mix in the vineyards of one region or country matches that of another region or country or the world. Here, we adapt it for the purposes of comparing the beverage consumption mix of any one country with that of any other country or the average for the world.

The index uses vector representation to project combinations of variables, with lengths determined by the shares of wine, beer, and spirits in a country's total alcohol consumption volume or expenditure. The vector f_{im} is again the fraction of beer, wine, or spirits consumption in the national alcohol consumption volume or expenditure in country i, such that these fractions are between 0 and 1 and total 1. The index is defined as

$$\omega_{ij} = \frac{\sum_{m=1}^{M} f_{im} f_{jm}}{\left(\sum_{m=1}^{M} f_{im}^2\right)^{1/2} \left(\sum_{m=1}^{M} f_{jm}^2\right)^{1/2}}, \tag{3}$$

where $i = 1,..., 53$ (or 85) countries, $j = 1,..., 53$ (or 85) countries, and $m = 1, 2, 3$ beverages corresponding again to wine, beer, and spirits; therefore, $M = 3$. This makes it possible to indicate the degree of beverage mix "similarity" of any pair of countries. The index also can be generated for each country relative to the average of a sample of countries or of all the world's N countries. In short, ω_{ij} measures the degree of overlap between f_i and f_j. The numerator of Equation (3) is large when i's and j's beverage mixes are very similar. The denominator normalizes the measure to unity when f_i and f_j are identical. Hence, ω_{ij} is close to 0 for pairs of countries with little similarity in their beverage mix and 1 for pairs of countries with identical beverage consumption mixes. For cases between those two extremes, $0 < \omega_{ij} < 1$.

This index is conceptually similar to a correlation coefficient. Like a correlation coefficient, it is completely symmetrical in that $\omega_{ij} = \omega_{ji}$. Thus, the results can be summarized in a symmetrical matrix plus a vector that reports the index for each country relative to that for the world (as reported in Holmes and Anderson, 2017).

In a hypothetical two-beverage case, where country i has 50% of its alcohol consumption consisting of beer and country y has 30%, the index of consumption similarity is the cosine of the angle between the two vectors in Figure 1. Therefore, differences can be judged by the angular separation of the vectors f_i and f_j for the two countries (Jaffe 1986).

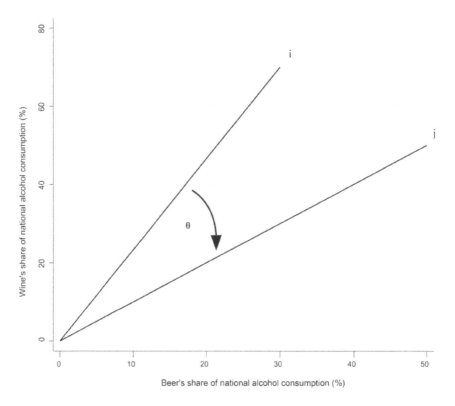

Figure 1. Angular separation between two countries (i and j), each consuming just two beverages (beer and wine)

Source: Authors' compilation.

It is possible to generate the similarity index for groups of countries by again using as weights each country's consumption of that beverage as a fraction of the group's total consumption of that beverage.

4. Findings

In this section, we examine two types of convergence across countries in their alcohol consumption patterns: (i) in the aggregate level of alcohol consumed per capita per year, and (ii) in the mix of wine, beer, and spirits. The volumes of consumption, measured in litres of alcohol, are compared where possible with values of consumption, because the latter also incorporate changes in prices paid by consumers (e.g., because of a desire for higher-quality beverages or a change in relative excise taxes).

Before examining our convergence indicators, it is worth reflecting on why consumption patterns might differ. If all products could be traded around the world without cost, and if there were no government interventions, such as consumption (excise) or trade taxes or differences in value-added tax rates across jurisdictions, then the retail prices of each type of beverage would be identical throughout the world. According to Stigler and Becker (1977), the key reason then for major differences in alcohol consumption patterns is differences in per-capita incomes. If all beverages were normal goods, we might then expect convergence in the level and mix of alcoholic (or indeed all) beverages consumed as convergence across countries occurs in national average per-capita incomes (which has been happening in recent decades — see, for example, Baldwin, 2016).

In reality, costs of trading beverages across national borders are not zero (even though they have declined greatly over the past 150 years), which means countries have tended in the past to concentrate their consumption on those alcoholic beverages that can be produced at the lowest cost locally — hence the dominance of spirits in cold countries, beer where malting barley can be easily grown, and wine in the 30° to 50° latitude range near maritime weather influences. Excise and import taxes on beverages are also dissimilar across countries, and they vary greatly across beverage types (Anderson, 2010, 2014b), in some cases to protect local producers and thereby reinforcing climate-induced differences. Value-added taxes also vary across countries. Moreover, temperance movements have had different effects on the social acceptability of alcohol consumption at different times in various places (see, for example, Briggs, 1985; Phillips, 2014; Pinney, 1989, 2005; Wilson 1940). So, too, have concerns about human health: as per-capita incomes rise, people can afford to spend more on alcohol consumption but also choose to limit its volume for health reasons (in some cases, switching to soft drinks, including bottled water); and some people are also substituting greater quantities of wine (especially still red) because of its perceived positive influence on health when drunk in moderation. Given all the above possible influences on beverage consumption patterns, it would not be surprising if convergence in those patterns were not evident in the data.

4.1. Alcohol consumption and income

One way to begin to look for convergence in alcohol consumption patterns is to plot consumption per capita against real income per capita. That is done in Figure 2 for 53 countries and residual regions spanning the world from 1961 to 2014, showing the volume of total alcohol consumption as well as of wine, beer, and spirits, respectively. As demonstrated by each beverage, the volume of consumption first tends to rise with per-capita incomes but then falls. The peak consumption occurs at a real per-capita income (in 1990 International Geary-Khamis dollars) of $16,900 in the case of all alcohol. That is just slightly above the average per-capita income of Western Europe in 1990. The peak consumption occurs at $15,100 for wine, $18,100 for beer, and $16,350 for spirits. These inverted U-shaped figures suggest that income convergence alone (the gradual catching up of developing countries to the per-capita incomes of high-income countries) does not necessarily lead to convergence in alcohol consumption patterns based on per-capita volumes.

4.2. Long-term trends in alcohol consumption per capita, total, and by type

Trends in the volume of total alcohol consumption per capita and in shares of overall alcohol consumption volume due to wine, beer, and spirits are shown in Tables 1 and 2 for a sample of high-income countries for which

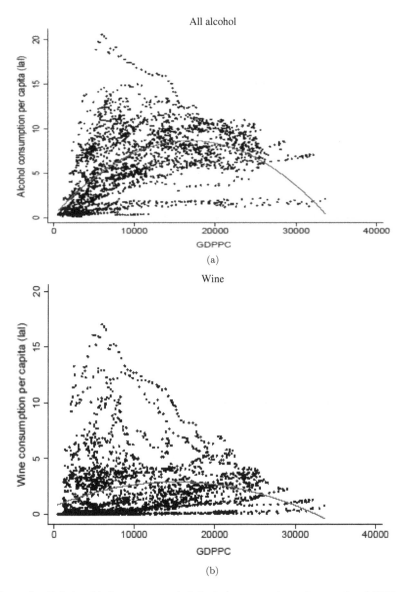

Figure 2. Relationship between recorded alcohol consumption volume and real GDP per capita, 53 countries/regions,[a] 1961–2014 (one dot per country-year)

[a]Real GDP per capita is in 1990 International Geary-Khamis dollars from www.ggdc.net/maddison/maddison-project/data.htm, updated to 2014 by taking the latest PPP estimates in 2011 dollars from the World Bank's International Comparison Project at http://icp.worldbank.org and splicing them to the Maddison series. The curved line is a fitted quadratic regression line.

Source: Compiled from data in Anderson and Pinilla (2017).

(c)

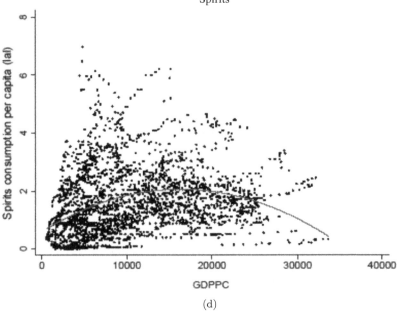

(d)

Figure 2. (*Continued*)

Table 1. Total alcohol consumption volume per capita,[a] high-income countries, 1888–2014 (litres of alcohol per year)

	1888–1892	1920s	1960s	1970s	1980s	1990s	2000s	2010–2014
Australia	5.9	3.8	7.1	9.5	9.7	8.1	8.1	7.3
Austria			8.7	10.8	11.1	11.0	10.3	10.4
Belgium	13.1	10.7	8.9	11.3	11.5	9.9	10.0	9.6
Canada			5.1	7.5	7.6	6.1	6.5	6.7
Denmark		5.0	5.6	8.3	9.8	9.9	9.1	8.0
Finland			1.9	4.3	5.1	5.9	7.0	6.9
France	16.3	22.1	17.7	15.9	13.3	11.2	10.3	9.2
Germany	9.8	4.4	10.3	12.9	12.7	11.3	10.2	9.6
Italy	11.8	14.5	14.3	14.0	10.8	8.4	7.5	6.1
Japan			4.3	5.6	6.5	7.2	5.8	5.6
Netherlands	5.7[b]	2.3[c]	3.8	7.5	8.6	8.1	7.9	7.4
New Zealand	3.8		6.7	8.9	9.1	7.6	6.5	6.4
Norway			4.0	5.5	5.2	5.0	6.2	6.3
Sweden			5.2	6.5	5.9	5.9	5.5	6.1
Switzerland	13.3	8.6	10.3	11.0	11.4	9.6	8.7	8.3
UK	8.7	4.5	5.7	7.7	8.0	7.5	8.8	8.0
United States	5.3		5.8	7.4	7.7	6.5	6.7	7.0
Unweighted average of above			7.7	9.4	9.3	8.3	8.0	7.6

[a]On average, the alcohol content by volume is assumed to be 4.5% for beer, 12% for wine, and 40% for spirits. Ready-to-drink spirits mixers are converted to spirits, assuming their alcohol content is 5%.
[b]1898–1902.
[c]1920–1923.
Source: Compiled from data in Anderson and Pinilla (2017).

we have data from the late 19th century and in Table 3 for the world's 53 countries/regions since 1961. For the larger set of countries, consumption-weighted averages are shown for seven regions and for the world as a whole in the final rows of Table 3.

For the majority of the 11 countries in Table 1 with data back to the 19th century, the alcohol consumption was greater in the 1960s than around 1890. For all but France and Italy, consumption rose even more by

Table 2. Shares of wine, beer, and spirits in total alcohol consumption volume, high-income countries, 1888–2014 (%, 5-year averages)

	Wine %					Beer %					Spirits %				
	1888–1892	1925–1929	1961–1964	1980–1984	2010–2014	1888–1892	1925–1929	1961–1964	1980–1984	2010–2014	1888–1892	1925–1929	1961–1964	1980–1984	2010–2014
Australia	10	19	12	24	40	47	62	75	64	46	43	20	13	12	14
Austria	na	na	30	37	35	na	na	55	49	51	na	na	15	14	14
Belgium	3	8	13	21	35	62	81	77	61	51	35	12	11	18	14
Canada	na	na	6	14	25	na	na	60	48	49	na	na	34	38	26
Denmark	na	4	8	19	47	na	55	77	65	38	na	42	15	16	16
Finland	na	na	13	12	21	na	na	21	42	53	na	na	66	46	26
France	68	82	78	69	59	6	6	10	16	19	26	12	13	16	23
Germany	7	na	18	51	53	49	na	57	56	53	44	na	24	20	19
Italy	95	95	87	80	65	0	1	3	8	23	5	4	10	12	11
Japan	na	na	2	4	5	na	na	20	29	21	na	na	78	67	74
Netherlands	4[a]	8[b]	9	22	35	25[a]	47[b]	48	49	48	na	45[b]	43	29	17
New Zealand	2	na	4	17	38	32	na	78	64	43	66	na	18	20	19
Norway	na	na	4	9	29	na	na	27	34	35	na	na	69	58	36
Sweden	na	na	9	20	48	na	na	39	39	37	na	na	52	41	15
Switzerland	63	49	42	49	47	17	25	38	31	34	20	27	20	20	19
UK	2	4	4	11	41	68	78	81	69	37	30	17	15	20	22
United States	4	na	8	13	18	47	na	48	51	49	49	na	44	36	34
WORLD av.	na	na	34	24	15	na	na	29	33	43	na	na	37	43	42

[a]1898–1902; [b]1920–1923

Source: Compiled from data in Anderson and Pinilla (2017).

Table 3. Alcohol per-capita consumption volume and shares of beer, wine, and spirits,[a] 53 countries, 5 regions, and the world, 1961–1964 and 2010–2014 (LAL and %)

	Consumption (LAL/capita)[a]		1961–1964 (%)[b]			2010–2014 (%)[b]		
	1961–1964	2010–2014	Wine	Beer	Spirits	Wine	Beer	Spirits
Algeria	0.9	0.4	**64**	28	8	**48**	39	13
Argentina	11.9	5.5	**84**	3	13	**50**	44	5
Australia	6.5	7.3	12	**75**	13	40	**46**	14
Austria	7.6	10.4	30	**55**	15	35	**51**	14
Bel-Lux	8.5	9.6	13	**77**	11	35	**51**	14
Brazil	1.1	5.6	22	37	**41**	5	**61**	34
Bulgaria	5.2	9.7	**48**	17	35	18	**37**	**44**
Canada	4.7	6.7	6	**60**	34	24	50	26
Chile	8.5	5.4	**85**	7	8	35	37	28
China	0.4	3.3	1	1	**98**	4	44	**52**
Croatia		9.9				**51**	39	11
Denmark	5.1	8.0	8	**77**	15	**47**	38	16
Finland	1.4	6.9	13	21	**66**	21	**53**	26
France	18.3	9.2	**78**	10	13	**59**	19	23
Georgia		5.8				**49**	21	31
Germany	9.7	9.6	18	**57**	24	28	**53**	19

(*Continued*)

Table 3. (Continued)

	Consumption (LAL/capita)[a]		1961–1964 (%)[b]			2010–2014 (%)[b]		
	1961–1964	2010–2014	Wine	Beear	Spirits	Wine	Beear	Spirits
Greece	7.1	6.8	**46**	23	31	**53**	27	20
Hong Kong	0.8	1.9	2	37	**62**	29	**53**	17
Hungary	7.1	9.5	**48**	28	24	30	**36**	34
India	0.3	0.9	0	2	98	0	15	**85**
Ireland	5.1	8.2	5	**76**	19	28	**52**	21
Italy	14.0	6.3	**87**	3	10	**65**	23	11
Japan	4.0	5.6	0	20	**78**	5	21	**77**
Korea	2.2	4.2	0	26	**74**	2	2	**96**
Malaysia	0.3	0.4	2	**65**	33	5	**74**	21
Mexico	1.5	3.7	4	**67**	29	3	**75**	22
Moldova		8.0				**43**	22	35
Morocco	0.7	0.4	**58**	21	21	**48**	36	15
Netherlands	3.2	7.4	9	**47**	43	35	**48**	17
New Zealand	6.2	6.4	4	**78**	18	38	**43**	19
Norway	6.4	7.9	3	27	**69**	29	35	36
Philippines	0.6	3.2	0	47	**53**	0	26	**74**

Portugal	12.1	9.2	96	2	2	65	27	8
Romania	4.8	7.9	64	13	23	31	53	16
Russia	4.2	8.9	16	15	69	11	39	**49**
Singapore	0.9	1.5	2	**70**	28	15	**71**	14
South Africa	2.6	4.4	43	13	**44**	21	**68**	11
Spain	10.1	8.0	**71**	9	21	22	**48**	29
Sweden	4.8	6.1	9	39	**52**	**49**	37	15
Switzerland	9.3	8.0	**42**	38	20	**47**	34	19
Taiwan	0.9	2.1	0	6	**94**	4	42	**54**
Thailand	0.4	5.1	0	5	**95**	0	26	**74**
Tunisia	0.8	1.0	68	26	5	29	**67**	**4**
Turkey	0.3	1.1	**39**	26	35	9	**58**	34
Ukraine		7.0				9	39	**52**
UK	5.6	8.0	4	**81**	15	**41**	37	22
US	5.4	7.0	8	**48**	44	18	**49**	34
Uruguay	5.4	4.6	**69**	25	9	**56**	33	11
O W Europe[c]	4.2	5.4	6	42	**52**	33	**45**	22
O E. Europe[c]	5.0	4.8	17	**43**	40	9	**52**	39
O L. America[c]	1.9	2.0	2	**84**	14	5	**59**	36

(Continued)

Table 3. (Continued)

	Consumption (LAL/capita)[a]		1961–1964(%)[b]			2010–2014 (%)[b]		
	1961–1964	2010–2014	Wine	Beer	Spirits	Wine	Beer	Spirits
Other Asia	0.2	0.2	2	5	**93**	3	13	**84**
O Africa/MEast[c]	0.4	0.4	12	**52**	36	9	**70**	22
Wted averages:								
W Europe	12.3	8.4	**55**	29	16	**42**	38	20
E. Europe	1.9	7.2	22	22	**56**	14	42	**44**
North America	5.4	7.0	8	**49**	43	18	**49**	33
Latin America	6.5	5.1	**48**	34	18	11	**60**	29
Aust. & NZ	6.5	7.1	10	**76**	14	39	**46**	15
Asia (incl. Pacific)	1.9	3.2	1	12	**87**	4	34	**62**
Africa & M East	1.0	1.7	27	**38**	35	14	**67**	19
WORLD	**2.5**	**2.7**	**34**	29	37	15	**43**	42

[a]These data are volume-based in litres of alcohol (LAL) per year, 4- or 5-year averages.
[b]The bold numbers indicate which beverage has the highest share in total alcohol consumption volume in the period shown.
[c]"O" refers to "Other" for the residual sub-group of countries for each of the five geographic regions that is not separately identified (each subgroup is treated like an extra country).

Sources: Compiled from data in Anderson and Pinilla (2017).

the 1980s, but then in all 11 countries, the total alcohol consumption per capita fell over the subsequent three decades to well below the unweighted average in the 1970s and 1980s. Even in the global database, which includes numerous developing and transition economies, the weighted average was almost the same in 2010–2014 as it was in 1961–1964 (last row of Table 3), despite having been higher than both of those period averages in each of the intervening decades. This is consistent with the inverted U-shaped trend of Figure 2(a).

Table 2 shows that the mix of alcohols was very different across the 11 high-income countries up to the 1960s, especially with respect to wine, which ranged from 2% to 87% of all national alcohol sales during 1961–1964, but also for beer (3%–81%) and spirits (10%–78%). By 2010–2014, the ranges had narrowed somewhat for beer (19%–53%) but less so for wine (5%–59%) and hardly at all for spirits (11%–74%).

The mix across the global database changed very substantially over the past 55 years: Wine's share more than halved from 34% to 15%; beer's rose by more than one-third, increasing from 29% to 42%; and spirits' rose only slightly, from 37% to 43% (final row of Table 3). For 11 countries, wine remained the main type of alcohol consumed; for 12 countries, beer continued to dominate; and for 10 countries, spirits retained the largest share (see the bold numbers in Table 3).

However, it is not possible to conclude from simply observing these per-capita volume trends whether alcohol consumption patterns are converging across countries — hence the need for better indicators, to which we now turn.

4.3. *Coefficient of variation*

Since 1961, CoV has fallen for all three beverage groups, which implies some convergence. This trend can be seen in Figure 3, where CoV across the full set of countries is shown for the per-capita total volume of alcohol consumption and for the shares of wine, beer, and spirits within that total for each country. The coefficient for the total volume of alcohol consumption has nearly halved over the last half century, declining steadily throughout the period. There has been very little decline in the coefficient for the share of spirits, but there has been a very steep

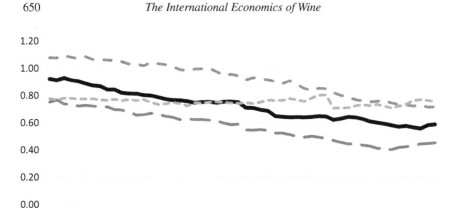

Figure 3. CoV in total alcohol consumption per capita and in shares of each beverage in that total consumption, across 53 countries/regions, 1961–2014

Sources: Compiled from data in Anderson and Pinilla (2017) and tabulated in Holmes and Anderson (2017).

decline for beer (falling from 0.8 to 0.4), while that for wine has fallen by more than one-quarter.

4.4. Beverage consumption intensity index

To examine trends in the beverage consumption intensity (and mix similarity) indexes, it is helpful to divide into groups our 48 countries plus one residual subgroup of countries for each of five geographic regions (also called "countries" hereafter, for simplicity), yielding a total of 53. Two groupings are used here. One is according to which of the three beverages has the highest share of the volume of alcohol consumption in 1961–1964. It turns out those three groups each have almost the same number of countries (19 wine-focused and 17 each for beer-focused and spirits-focused; see footnote b of Figure 4). The other grouping is according to geography, with six regions identified. Each region includes a varying number of countries, ranging from 17 in Western Europe to 11 in Asia, 9 in Eastern Europe and Central Asia, 6 in Latin America, 6 in Africa and the Middle East, and 2 in North America. One "country" in all but the last of those regions is the weighted average of all countries in the region that have not been separately identified. Australasia is omitted for space reasons.

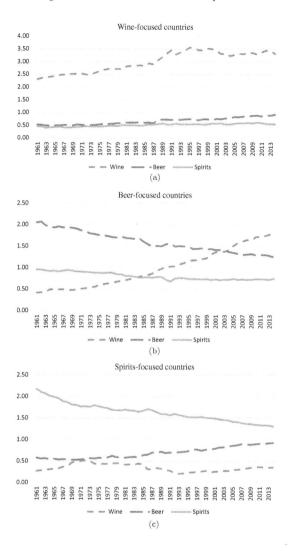

Figure 4. Wine, beer, and spirits consumption volume intensity indexes[a] for three subsets of 53 countries/regions, by main focus in 1961–1964,[b] 1961–2014

[a]The intensity index is defined as the fraction of wine, beer, or spirits consumption in total national alcohol consumption volume in country i divided by the fraction for that same beverage in world total alcohol consumption. [b]**Wine-focused**: Algeria, Argentina, Bulgaria, Chile, Croatia, France, Georgia, Greece, Hungary, Italy, Moldova, Morocco, Portugal, Romania, Spain, Switzerland, Tunisia, Turkey, Uruguay; **Beer-focused**: Australia, Austria, Belgium-Luxembourg, Canada, Denmark, Germany, Ireland, Malaysia, Mexico, Netherlands, New Zealand, Singapore, United Kingdom, United States, Other Eastern Europe, Other Latin America, Other African and Middle East; **Spirits-focused**: Brazil, China, Finland, Hong Kong, India, Japan, Korea, Norway, Philippines, Russia, South Africa, Sweden, Taiwan, Thailand, Ukraine, Other Western Europe, Other Asia.

Sources: Compiled from data in Anderson and Pinilla (2017) and tabulated in Holmes and Anderson (2017).

The decrease in the share of wine in the overall volume of global alcohol consumption has been faster than the decrease in wine's share of consumption in a number of wine-focused countries, so those countries' groups' wine consumption intensity index has risen over the past half century, from 2.2 to around 3.0. Those groups' spirits intensity index has not risen much (at around 0.5), but their beer intensity index has nearly doubled, from less than 0.4 to 0.75 (Figure 4(a)).

For the beer-focused countries, their beer intensity index has nearly halved, from close to 2.0 down to 1.2, while their wine intensity index has trebled and is now slightly above that for beer, and their spirits intensity index has fallen from just below to a little further below 1.0 (Figure 4(b)).

For the spirits-focused countries, their spirits intensity index has nearly halved in falling to 1.25, their beer intensity index has risen from 0.5 to 0.9, and their wine intensity index trend has remained flat at a little below 0.5 (Figure 4(c)).

Turning to the regions (Figure 5), the clearest convergence on intensity indexes of unity for the three beverages is found in Eastern Europe, and the next clearest region is North America. In Western Europe, by contrast, the beer and spirits intensity indexes have changed little from around 1.0 and 0.5, respectively, while the wine intensity index has risen from 1.6 to 2.7. The indexes for Africa and the Middle East also have diverged, with beer's rising further above 1.0 and spirits' falling further below 1.0, while wine's has remained just below 1.0. In Latin America, wine and spirits have converged to just below 1.0 (wine from above, spirits from below), while beer has risen from 1.0 to 1.5. And in Asia, beer's index has doubled to 0.8, the spirits index has fallen from 2.4 to 1.5, and the wine index has risen from just above zero to 0.2.

These volume indexes suggest there are still major differences across these regions in their consumers' beverage focus based on volume. But what do value-based indexes suggest, given that, as shown in Figure 6, tax-inclusive retail prices of alcoholic beverages vary enormously across these regions? We do not have expenditure data for all countries for the full period since 1961, but we do have them for recent years. Table 4 shows the differences by region between the consumption volume and value intensity indexes for the period 2013–2015. For three of the regions (Western Europe, Eastern Europe, and North America), all three value

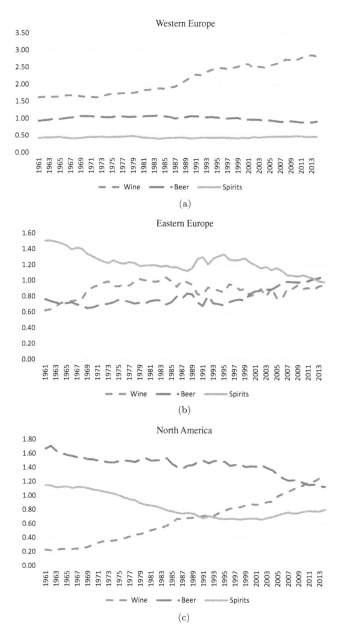

Figure 5. Wine, beer, and spirits consumption volume intensity indexes for three subsets of 53 countries, by region, 1961–2014

Sources: Compiled from data in Anderson and Pinilla (2017) and tabulated in Holmes and Anderson (2017).

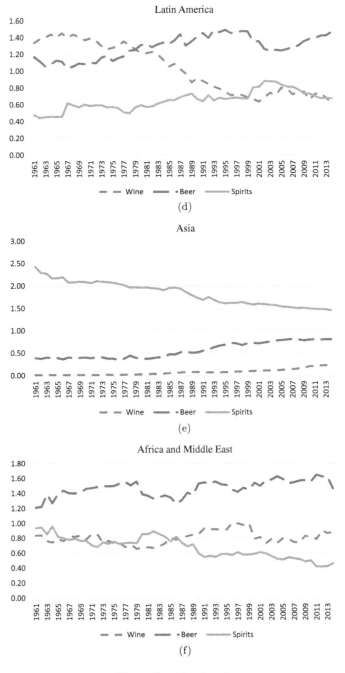

Figure 5. (*Continued*)

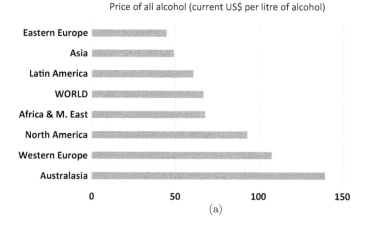

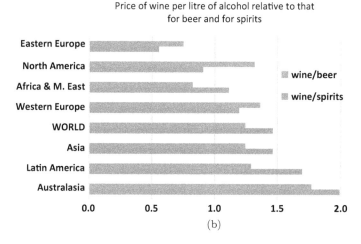

Figure 6. Weighted average tax-inclusive retail prices of alcoholic beverages, by region, 2013–2015

Source: Compiled from data in Holmes and Anderson (2017).

intensity indexes are closer to unity than are their volume indexes; for two regions (Australasia and Africa and the Middle East), two of the three value indexes are closer to unity than are their volume indexes; and for the other two regions, one of the three value indexes is closer to unity than their volume indexes. This comparison suggests that part of the reason for the cross-country variation in volume intensity indexes has to do with the variation in national average retail beverage prices.

Table 4. Wine, beer, and spirits consumption volume and value intensity indexes,[a] by region, 2013–2015

	Wine		Beer		Spirits	
	Volume	Value	Volume	Value	Volume	Value
Western Europe	2.51	1.62	0.85	0.90	0.53	0.75
Eastern Europe	0.90	0.93	1.01	1.01	1.03	1.02
Australasia	2.31	1.36	1.09	1.19	0.34	0.54
North America	1.07	1.01	1.16	1.08	0.79	0.89
Latin America	0.58	0.46	1.36	1.44	1.16	1.16
Africa & M. East	0.82	0.72	1.51	1.34	0.51	0.73
Asia	0.53	0.69	0.85	0.82	1.36	1.41
WORLD	1.00	1.00	1.00	1.00	1.00	1.00

[a]The intensity index is defined as the fraction of wine, beer, or spirits consumption in total national alcohol consumption volume in country i divided by the fraction for that same beverage in world total alcohol consumption.

Source: Compiled from data in Holmes and Anderson (2017).

4.5. *Alcohol consumption mix similarity index*

The alcohol consumption mix similarity indexes for various country groups are plotted in Figure 7. The beer- and spirits-focused countries converged rapidly toward the world average (that is, the indexes approached 1.0) from the early 1960s to the mid-1980s and then moved more slowly in the next two decades. By contrast, the consumption mix similarity index for the wine-focused countries has not converged over this period. This result again reflects the fact that many of the wine-focused countries have reduced the share of wine in their consumption mix less than in other areas of the world. This is the same conclusion that we reached above by inspecting the intensity index for wine-focused countries in Figure 4(a).

The same convergence toward unity in consumption mix similarity indexes is evident when countries are differentiated by geographic region, as in Figure 7(b). The convergence has been fastest for Asia and Latin America, albeit from a low base, but it is also evident for the other five regions, including North America and Eastern Europe, even though their indexes were already above 0.9 in the 1960s.

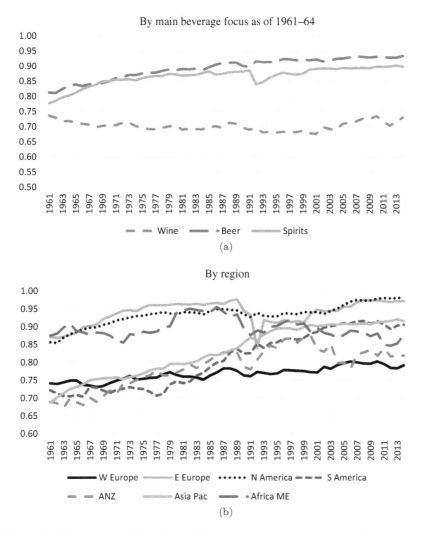

Figure 7. Consumption mix similarity index, volume-based, by sub-sets of 53 countries/regions, 1961–2014

Sources: Compiled from data in Anderson and Pinilla (2017) and tabulated in Holmes and Anderson (2017).

Even over the relatively short period of the 21st century for which we have data for 80 countries plus the 5 residual regions, as shown in Figure 8(a), the distribution of similarity indexes is becoming more skewed over time toward unity.

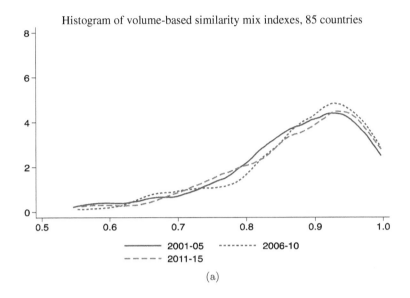

(a)

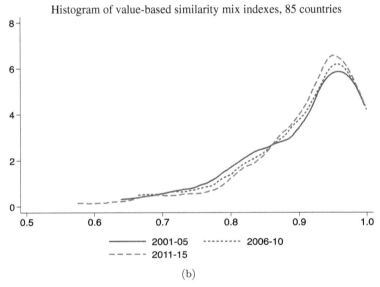

(b)

Figure 8. Convergence of volume- and value-based similarity mix indexes for all 85 countries/regions, 2001–2015

Source: Compiled from data tabulated in Holmes and Anderson (2017).

The volume-based distributions are comparable with those for value-based similarity indexes for the same three 5-year periods. The latter distributions are even more skewed toward unity than the volume-based similarity indexes (compare Figures 8(a) and 8(b)). Together, these findings indicate a general if not rapid global convergence in national beverage mixes.

4.6. *Alcohol consumption and aggregate expenditure*

The moderating impact on indicators of the differences across countries in retail prices of alcoholic beverages (both absolute and relative; see Figure 6) suggests the need to revisit the finding from Figure 2 of an inverted U-shaped relationship between national per-capita alcohol consumption volume and real GDP per capita. This is done for our larger sample of 85 countries for the years 2001–2015 in Figure 9 for volumes and values of total alcohol consumption per capita, which are plotted against aggregate expenditures per capita in 2015 US dollars. An inverted U-shape prevails for volume but not for value of alcohol consumption as national aggregate expenditure rises.

Also revealed in Figure 9 is the wide variance in per-capita alcohol expenditures across equally affluent countries. Partly that is due to differences across countries in value-added or goods-and-services taxes and in alcohol excise or consumption taxes (Table 5).

When the expenditure data are disaggregated into the three beverage types, Figures 10(a) and 10(b) reveal that wine and beer expenditures rise with aggregate expenditures. However, Figure 10(c) suggests that expenditures on spirits peak at an aggregate national expenditure level of US$27,800 per capita (in 2015 dollars) and decline thereafter.

4.7. *Alcoholic versus nonalcoholic beverages*

As of 2010–2014, alcohol made up nearly two-thirds of the world's recorded expenditures on beverages, with the rest being bottled water (8%), carbonated soft drinks (15%), and other soft drinks, such as fruit juices (13%). Those beverage shares varied widely across regions (Table 6), in part because retail prices varied between countries: For all

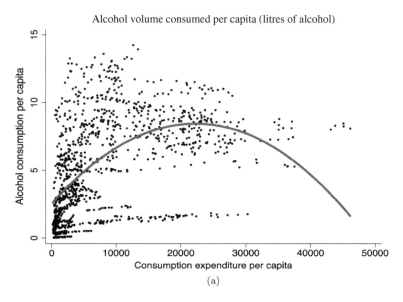

(a)

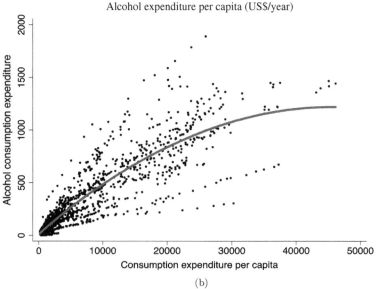

(b)

Figure 9. Relationship between per-capita aggregate expenditures and recorded alcohol consumption volume and value, 80 countries,[a] 2001–2015 (one dot per country-year)
[a]Excluding the five residual regions. Expenditures are inflated to 2015 dollars using the US CPI, 2015 = 1.00.
Source: Compiled from data tabulated in Holmes and Anderson (2017).

Table 5. Per-capita income, excise taxes on alcohol consumption by type, and VAT/GST, high-income countries, 2014 (% ad valorem equivalent)

	Per-Capita Income (US$'000)	Commercial Wine Excise Tax (%)	Beer Excise Tax (%)	Spirits Excise Tax (%)	VAT/GST (%)
Australia	26.6	29	117	211	10
Austria	24.8	2	18	46	20
Canada	26.1	8	75	30	5
Finland	22.8	65	116	176	24
France	22.5	1	27	66	20
Japan	22.7	14	35	14	8
New Zealand	20.2	34	66	127	15
Norway	34.8	114	179	292	25
Sweden	25.9	49	70	213	25
United Kingdom	25.2	66	87	136	20
United States	32.1	7	58	28	0
Unweighted average of above	*25.8*	*35*	*77*	*122*	*16*

Sources: Anderson and Pinilla (2017) and Anderson (2014b).

soft drinks, they ranged from an average for 2013–15 of 70 US cents per litre in Africa and the Middle East to 260 US cents in Australasia (Euromonitor International, 2016). The degree of substitutability between alcoholic and soft drink consumption may vary across countries; so too does the availability of low-cost reticulated potable water. These facts suggest further reasons to expect differences across countries in alcohol consumption volumes and mixes.

Globally, during 2001–2015, the world's volume of alcohol consumption increased by one-quarter while that of nonalcoholic beverages rose by two-thirds. However, global retail expenditures (including taxes) on those two product groups rose by similar current US dollar amounts: 81% for alcoholic and 90% for nonalcoholic beverages (Euromonitor International, 2016). That difference between the volume and value increases for alcohol consumption is not inconsistent with the findings of the previous subsection, in which the volume of alcohol consumption traces a much more-

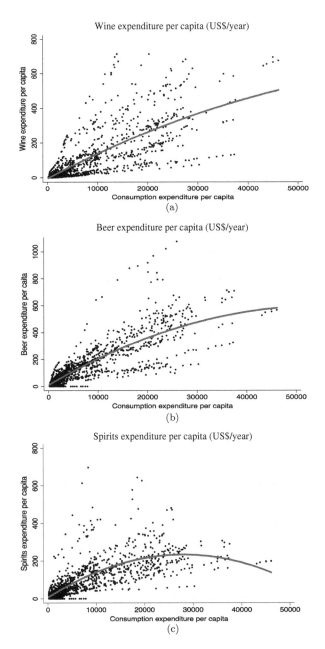

Figure 10. Relationship between per-capita aggregate expenditure and value of recorded alcohol consumption, 80 countries,[a] 2001–2015

[a]Excluding the five residual regions. Expenditures are inflated to 2015 dollars using the US CPI.
Source: Compiled from data in Holmes and Anderson (2017).

Table 6. Shares of beverage household expenditure by beverage type, seven regions spanning the world, 2010–2014 (%)

	Budget Shares of Alcohol Expenditures (%)			Beverage Shares of All Expenditures (%)				Alcohol as % of All Beverage Expenditures
	Beer	Wine	Spirits	All Alcohol	Bottled Water	Carbonates	Other Soft Drinks	
Western Europe	40	34	26	3.88	0.54	0.73	0.53	68
Eastern Europe	46	20	34	5.87	0.53	0.76	0.72	74
Australasia	53	28	19	3.49	0.17	0.77	0.51	71
North America	48	21	30	1.94	0.34	0.66	0.58	55
Latin America	64	10	26	4.22	0.61	2.01	0.76	56
Africa & M East	60	15	25	2.49	0.57	1.14	0.58	52
Asia	35	15	50	4.29	0.32	0.49	1.07	70
WORLD	**44**	**21**	**35**	**3.46**	**0.43**	**0.79**	**0.72**	**64**

Source: Holmes and Anderson (2017).

pronounced inverted U-shape as total expenditures rise than does the value of alcohol consumption.

5. Robustness test

All the consumption data reported above refer only to what have been recorded by national governments; an additional amount of alcohol produced and consumed each year is not recorded. WHO (2015) has compiled estimates of those amounts for 98 countries for 2000, 2005, and 2010.

Evidently, the share of unrecorded total alcohol consumption declines with real GDP per capita (Figure 11 and Table 7),[3] thus exposing another aspect of convergence across countries in alcohol consumption — namely,

---

[3] That share declined globally by one-eighth over the first decade of this century, and by 2010 was just under 25%.

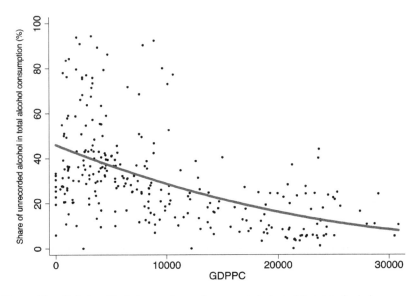

Figure 11. Relationship between share of unrecorded alcohol in total alcohol consumption volume and real GDP per capita,[a] 98 countries, 2000, 2005, and 2010 (one dot per country-year)

[a]Real GDP per capita is in 1990 International Geary-Khamis dollars from www.ggdc.net/maddison/maddison-project/data.htm. The dark line is a quadratic fitted regression line.

Source: Compiled from data in Anderson and Pinilla (2017).

in the share of national consumption that is unrecorded, which converges toward zero as per-capita income grows.

Another implication of this phenomenon is that the inverted U-shaped relationship between per-capita alcohol consumption and per-capita real GDP is flatter once unrecorded consumption is included, as shown by the quadratic fitted regression lines in Figure 12 for the 3 years and 98 countries for which estimates are available.

A more-specific implication is that the share of wine in total alcohol consumption globally is lower than its share of recorded alcohol consumption, because very little of that unrecorded alcohol is wine.[4] But as

---

[4]The exceptions are a dozen transition economies of Eastern Europe: Albania, Armenia, Azerbaijan, Bosnia & Herzegovina, Bulgaria, Croatia, Georgia, Hungary, Kazakhstan, Moldova, Romania, and Slovenia.

Table 7. Importance of unrecorded in total alcohol consumption volume, by region, 2000, 2005, and 2010 (litres of alcohol* per capita)

	Real GDP Per Capita[a]	Recorded Consumption (LAL per capita)	Unrecorded Consumption (LAL per capita)	Total Consumption (LAL per capita)	Unrecorded as % of Total Alcohol Consumption
2000					
Western Europe	19.3	9.4	1.3	10.7	12
Eastern Europe	6.0	8.3	4.3	12.6	34
Australasia	20.6	8.1	0.1	8.2	1
North America	28.1	8.0	1.1	9.1	12
Latin America	5.9	5.2	2.5	7.6	32
Africa & Middle East	2.3	2.2	1.4	3.6	37
Asia	3.8	1.7	1.4	3.1	38
WORLD	6.1	3.5	1.6	5.1	45
2005					
Western Europe	20.6	9.2	1.3	10.5	13
Eastern Europe	7.3	9.4	4.5	13.9	33
Australasia	22.9	7.8	0.2	8.0	2
North America	30.2	8.3	1.1	9.4	12
Latin America	6.3	4.6	2.6	7.2	36
Africa & Middle East	2.6	2.2	1.3	3.4	37
Asia	4.9	1.8	1.6	3.4	47
WORLD	7.0	3.4	1.7	5.2	33
2010					
Western Europe	20.9	8.4	0.8	9.2	9
Eastern Europe	8.7	9.5	3.2	12.7	25
Australasia	24.5	7.7	1.8	9.4	19
North America	29.9	8.4	0.7	9.0	7
Latin America	6.8	5.0	1.7	6.7	25
Africa & Middle East	3.0	2.3	1.1	3.4	33

(*Continued*)

Table 7. (*Continued*)

	Real GDP Per Capita[a]	Recorded Consumption (LAL per capita)	Unrecorded Consumption (LAL per capita)	Total Consumption (LAL per capita)	Unrecorded as % of Total Alcohol Consumption
Asia	6.3	2.1	1.7	3.8	44
WORLD	7.8	3.6	1.5	5.1	30

[a]Real GDP per capita is in thousands of 1990 International Geary-Khamis dollars from www.ggdc.net/maddison/maddison-project/data.htm, updated to 2010 by taking the latest PPP estimates in 2011 dollars from the World Bank's International Comparison Project at http://icp.worldbank.org and splicing them to the Maddison series.

*litres of alcohol = LAL

Source: Compiled from data in Holmes and Anderson (2017).

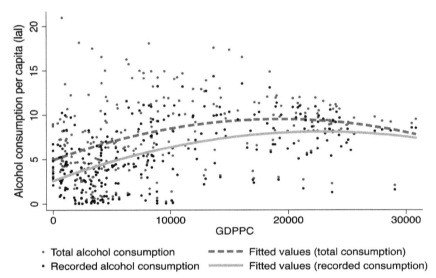

Figure 12. Relationships between alcohol consumption volume and real GDP per capita,[a] recorded and total (recorded plus unrecorded), 98 countries, 2000, 2005, and 2010 (one dot per country-year)

[a] Real GDP per capita is in 1990 International Geary-Khamis dollars from www.ggdc.net/maddison/maddison-project/data.htm.

Source: Compiled from data in Anderson and Pinilla (2017).

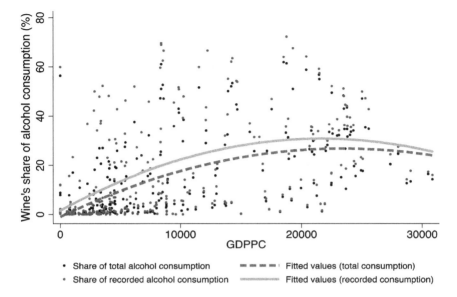

Figure 13. Relationships between wine's share of alcohol consumption volume and real GDP per capita, recorded and total (recorded plus unrecorded), 98 countries, 2000, 2005, and 2010 (one dot per country-year)[a]

[a] Assumes none of the unrecorded alcohol consumption is grape wine except in Albania, Armenia, Azerbaijan, Bosnia & Herzegovina, Bulgaria, Croatia, Georgia, Hungary, Kazakhstan, Moldova, Romania, and Slovenia.

Source: Compiled from data in Anderson and Pinilla (2017).

Figure 13 shows, when unrecorded consumption is included, the quadratic fitted regression line tracing wine's share of total alcohol consumption against real GDP per capita tends to plateau rather than turn down with higher per-capita income levels.

6. Conclusions

The above global data show big changes in national, regional, and global alcohol consumption patterns. At the global level, we note that during 1961–2014, wine's share of the total volume of alcohol consumption more than halved, from 34% to 15%; beer's rose by more than one-third, from

29% to 42%; and spirits' rose only a little, from 37% to 43%. These figures reveal a trend away from equal global shares of the three beverages. At the national level, the above analysis provides a number of indicators of convergence in alcohol consumption patterns toward that changing global average mix, but also some anomalies. Key findings include the following:

- The per-capita *volume* of total alcohol consumption first rises as per-capita income rises, but beyond a threshold income level, it falls.
  - However, that inverted U-shaped curve is flatter for per-capita *expenditures* on alcohol (at least for 2001–2015) and when unrecorded consumption is added to recorded consumption.
- Each of the three types of alcohol consumption per capita also traces out an inverted U-shaped curve over the per-capita income spectrum in *volume* terms, but that is true in *value* terms (at least for 2001–2015) only for spirits.
- CoV across countries in the total volume of alcohol consumption, and in the shares of each beverage in that total consumption, fell considerably over the 1961–2014 period (but least so for spirits).
- When countries are grouped by their main beverage focus as of 1961–1964, the share of that focus beverage in the total volume of alcohol consumption for that sub-group of countries fell over the next five decades.
  - However, the consumption intensity index *rose* rather than fell for wine in the wine-focused group of countries, due to the wine share's falling less for that group of countries than for the world as a whole.
- In beer-focused countries, wine's share grew rapidly, whereas in wine- and spirits-focused countries, beer rose in importance.
- When countries are grouped by geographic region, all three beverage consumption volume intensity indexes converged toward unity for North America and Eastern Europe, but they *diverged* for Western Europe and Africa and the Middle East.

- The consumption mix similarity indexes moved closer during 2001–2015 for most regional country groups and for beer- and spirits-focused countries — but not for wine-focused countries, and only barely for Western Europe.

In short, we find strong but not unequivocal indications of convergence in national alcohol consumption patterns across the world. It remains to draw out their implications for demand elasticity estimates and to explain these evolving patterns econometrically now that we have a comprehensive global database. A next step would be to build on and extend the seminal work by Selvanathan and Selvanathan (2007) to see to what extent income, own-price, and cross-price elasticities of demand for alcoholic and nonalcoholic beverages differ across countries and over time. Subsequent work could focus on explaining econometrically the cross-country differences in our two indexes in terms of such variables as beverage consumer tax rates, per-capita incomes, and trade costs.

References

Aizenman, J., and Brooks, E. L. (2008). Globalization and taste convergence: The cases of wine and beer. *Review of International Economics,* 16(2), 217–233.

Anderson, K. (2010). Excise and import taxes on wine versus beer and spirits: An international comparison. *Economic Papers,* 29(2), 215–228.

Anderson, K. (2014a). Changing varietal distinctiveness of the world's wine regions: Evidence from a new global database. *Journal of Wine Economics,* 9(3), 249–272.

Anderson, K. (2014b). Excise taxes on wines, beers and spirits: An updated international comparison. American Association of Wine Economists, Working Paper No. 170, October. Available from www.wine-economics.org/aawe/wp-content/uploads/2014/10/AAWE_WP170.pdf.

Anderson, K., and Pinilla, V. (with the assistance of A. J. Holmes) (2017). *Annual database of global wine markets, 1835 to 2016.* Wine Economics Research Centre, University of Adelaide. To be posted in October at www.adelaide.edu.au/wine-econ/databases/global-wine-history.

Baldwin, R. E. (2016). *The Great Convergence: Information Technology and the New Globalization.* Cambridge, MA: Belknap Press of Harvard University Press.

Bentzen, J., Eriksson, T., and Smith, V. (2001). Alcohol consumption in European countries. *Cahiers d'economie et sociologie rurales,* 60/61, 50–75.

Briggs, A. (1985). *Wine for Sale: Victoria Wine and the Liquor Trade, 1860–1984.* Chicago: University of Chicago Press.

Colen, L., and Swinnen, J. (2016). Economic growth, globalisation and beer consumption. *Journal of Agricultural Economics*, 67(1), 186–207.

Euromonitor International. (2016). *Passport.* Global market information database, http://www.euromonitor.com/.

Griliches, Z. (1979). Issues in assessing the contribution of research and development to productivity growth. *Bell Journal of Economics,* 10(1), 92–116.

Holmes, A. J., and Anderson, K. (2017). *Annual database of national beverage consumption volumes and expenditures, 1950 to 2015.* Wine Economics Research Centre, University of Adelaide, July, www.adelaide.edu.au/wine-econ/databases/alcohol-consumption.

Jaffe, A. B. (1986). Technological opportunity and spillovers of R&D: Evidence from firms' patents, profits, and market value. *American Economic Review,* 76(5), 984–1001.

Phillips, R. (2014). *Alcohol: A History* Chapel Hill: University of North Carolina Press.

Pinney, T. (1989). *A History of Wine in America: From the Beginnings to Prohibition.* Vol. 1. Berkeley: University of California Press.

Pinney, T. (2005). *A History of Wine in America: From Prohibition to the Present.* Vol. 2. Berkeley: University of California Press.

Selvanathan, S., and Selvanathan, E. A. (2007). Another look at the identical tastes hypothesis on the analysis of cross-country alcohol data. *Empirical Economics,* 32(1), 185–215.

Smith, D. E., and Solgaard, H. S. (2000). The dynamics of shifts in European alcoholic drinks consumption. *Journal of International Consumer Marketing,* 12(3), 85–109.

Stigler, G. J., and Becker, G. S. (1977). De gustibus non est disputandum. *American Economic Review,* 67(2), 76–90.

Wilson, G. B. (1940). *Alcohol and the Nation: A Contribution to the Study of the Liquor Problem in the United Kingdom from 1800 to 1935.* London: Nicholson and Watson.

World Health Organization. (2015). *Global health observatory data repository* Available at http://apps.who.int/gho/data/node.main.A1022?lang=en&showonly=GISAH.

Chapter 26

Global Alcohol Markets: Evolving Consumption Patterns, Regulations, and Industrial Organizations*

Kym Anderson,[†,‡,§] Giulia Meloni[¶,‖] and Johan Swinnen[¶,‖]

Abstract

For millennia, alcoholic drinks have played an important role in food security and health (both positive and negative), but consumption patterns of beer, wine, and spirits have altered substantially over the past two centuries. So too have their production technologies and industrial

---

* First published in *Annual Review of Resource Economics* 10: 105–32, October 2018. The authors are grateful for research funding by KU Leuven (Methusalem Funding). Views expressed are the authors' alone.

[†] School of Economics, University of Adelaide, Adelaide, South Australia 5005, Australia; email: kym.anderson@adelaide.edu.au

[‡] Arndt-Corden Department of Economics, Australian National University, Acton 2601, Australian Capital Territory, Australia

[§] Center for Economic and Policy Research, Washington, DC 20009, USA

[¶] LICOS Center for Institutions and Economic Performance and Department of Economics, KU Leuven, Leuven 3000, Belgium; email: giulia.meloni@kuleuven.be, jo.swinnen@kuleuven.be

[‖] Centre for European Policy Studies, Brussels 1000, Belgium organization. Globalization and economic growth have contributed to considerable convergence in national alcohol consumption patterns. The industrial revolution contributed to excess consumption by stimulating demand and lowering the cost of alcohol. It also led to concentration in some alcohol industries, especially brewing. In recent years, the emergence of craft producers has countered firm concentration and the homogenization of alcoholic beverages. Meanwhile, governments have intervened extensively in alcohol markets to reduce excessive consumption, raise taxes, protect domestic industries, and/or ensure competition. These regulations have contributed to, and been affected by, the evolving patterns of consumption and changing structures of alcohol industries.

1. Introduction

Throughout history, alcoholic drinks have played an important role in food security and health (both positive and negative), have been major sources of tax revenue for local and national governments, and in some countries, have been a major export item and thus subject to changes in foreign and trade policies. However, beverage consumption patterns have altered substantially during the first and latest globalization waves, as have production technologies and the industrial organization of beverage firms. Taxes and myriad other regulations have contributed to, and been affected by, those evolving patterns of consumption and production as well as firm concentration of alcohol industries. This review surveys the available evidence on and explanations for those developments and interactions. This topic is of interest both as a set of industry case studies of globalization and as a potential contribution to policy dialogs on the social and health consequences of alcohol consumption.

The review begins with a brief history of beverage consumption prior to the nineteenth century globalization wave. It summarizes evidence on the evolving patterns of national alcohol consumption across the world since then, focusing on both aggregate volumes and their mix of beer, wine, and spirits. Regulations affecting national alcoholic beverage consumption (and related production and international trade in beverages) are surveyed. Changes in the industrial organization of production for the three main alcohol groups (beer, wine, and spirits) are then reported. The final section summarizes what we know about the interactions between these markets and their regulation and suggests where subsequent economic research should be focused to further improve our understanding of the contribution of these markets and associated policies and institutions to global welfare.

2. A brief history of alcohol

Evidence of beer and wine production several thousand years ago has been found in distant places across the globe. Biomolecular archaeological evidence suggests that wine was produced at least 8,000 years ago in central Georgia (McGovern *et al.* 2017). There are indications that beer was produced and consumed more than 7,000 years ago in China, North Africa, and much of Europe — although the definition of beer included many types of brews (Nelson 2005, McGovern 2009).

The cultivation of *vintfera* vines and the making of grape wine gradually spread from the Caucasus region west to the Levant, Egypt, and Greece by 2,500 BCE. The Etruscans began vine cultivation in central Italy using native varieties in the eighth century BCE, which is also when the Greek colonists began to take cuttings to southern Italy and Sicily. Viticulture was introduced to southern France by the Romans around 600 BCE and was spread north in the second and first centuries BCE. Initially, these regions were mostly consumers of wine imported from Greece or Rome.[1] However, the settling armies soon started planting vineyards, and production spread in southern Europe. It took only until the fourth century AD for wine grapes to be well established in all areas of Europe suited to their cultivation and in North Africa (Nelson 2005).

---

[1] There is evidence that the Greeks exported wine to southern France, particularly via Massala (Marseille), from around 650 BCE, and that there was some local production around Massala at that time. However, for hundreds of years after that, wine was still a luxury item in Southern Gaul (today's France) and only consumed by the upper classes. According to Diodorus of Sicily, the price of wine was high: Gauls would exchange a slave for one jar of Italian wine (Nelson 2005, p. 49).

The Greeks and the Romans drank wine and only wine. They despised beer, whose drinkers they considered barbarians (Rabin & Forget 1998). Despite that, the cooler areas of northern Europe, under German rule, held out against the influence of wine (Poelmans & Swinnen 2011).

Distilled spirits are fermented liquids whose alcohol has been increased by distillation. The process involves heating the liquid to a temperature between 79°C (at which alcohol boils) and 99°C (after which water boils) and then cooling the vapor, which will then contain less water. The Chinese have distilled a beverage from rice beer since at least 800 BCE. Other regions making early use of this method include the East Indies, where arrack was made from sugarcane and rice, and Arab countries, using wine. Britain made spirits before the Roman conquest, as did people in other parts of Western Europe, but production was limited until the eighth century when contact with Arabs increased. Initially, spirits were used almost uniquely for medical purposes. Spirits based on starchy grains began to expand probably during the Middle Ages, and from the fifteenth and sixteenth centuries onward, distillation was increasingly used to produce not only whiskey, gin, and vodka from grains or potatoes but also brandy from grapes and rum from sugar. Certainly by the seventeenth century the production of spirits was sufficiently widespread as to attract the attention of government regulators. That was when the Dutch industrialized and commercialized brandy production and used it to lubricate its ever-enlarging navy. Spirits were considered ideal for long ocean voyages because their high alcohol content meant they took up little space, kept perfectly, and were saleable at the destination (Johnson 1989, chapter 17).

The intercontinental spread of beer, wine, and spirits consumption accompanied European conquests across the world. Trade costs and spoilage were proportionately lowest for higher-alcohol spirits, so beer and wine consumption in the settler economies of the New World had to wait until local production was commercialized.

Meanwhile, the industrial revolution got under way, first in Britain from the late 1700s and then in neighboring European countries. That totally transformed the production of consistent-quality beer and spirits, reduced their real prices, and contributed to both widespread alcoholism and a dramatic consolidation of producers in the brewing and distilling industries. It also led to the invention of new nonalcoholic drinks late in the eighteenth century, in particular, carbonated drinks. By the 1830s, there were 10 soft drink manufacturers in Britain and more than 50 by the 1840s.[2] These factors had a major impact on subsequent developments in alcohol consumption and production and on associated technologies and regulations, which we now consider in turn.

3. Alcohol consumption patterns

Alcohol consumption patterns have changed substantially over the past two centuries and are converging across countries with increasing globalization and associated interactions between cultures. At the same time, overall alcohol consumption has been affected by per capita income growth, the availability of alternatives, increased health concerns, and government regulations.

Several studies have analyzed these patterns, but most focus on a specific region or group of (high-income) countries and/or specific types of alcohol. For example, Smith & Solgaard (2000) explore alcohol consumption trends in European countries from 1960 to 2000. Bentzen *et al.* (2001) study alcohol consumption convergence in a number of European countries. Aizenman & Brooks (2008) study convergence from 1963 to 2000 across a larger sample of OECD and middle-income countries, but only for beer and wine. Colen & Swinnen (2016) analyze mainly beer consumption across a large sample of high-income and developing countries.

The most comprehensive study is by Holmes & Anderson (2017a,b), which covers all countries of the world since 1961 and key high-income countries since 1888. They look at aggregate consumption per capita of each of the three key beverages globally and nationally and differences between volume and expenditure (value). They also account for unrecorded alcohol consumption and compare alcohol with soft drink spending.

---

[2] Schweppes was the first, founded in Geneva in 1783 and relocated to London in 1792. Coca-Cola and Pepsi Cola were not born until 100 years later in the hot, humid US states of Georgia and North Carolina, respectively.

4. Determinants of alcohol consumption: Some conceptual issues

Several factors affect alcohol consumption patterns. Key determinants are trade costs, government taxes and regulations, consumer preferences, incomes, and the availability and cost of nonalcoholic beverages and other stimulants.

The costs of trading beverages across large distances were substantial in earlier times when transport infrastructure was less developed. This means countries in the past tended to concentrate their consumption on those alcoholic beverages that can be produced at the lowest cost locally. Hence the dominance of spirits in cold countries, beer where malting barley can be easily grown, and wine in countries in the 30° to 50° latitude range near maritime weather influences. Trade costs have declined greatly over the past 50 years, contributing to the price reduction and increase in consumption of imported alcoholic beverages. Cultural exchanges with increased travel and information transmission through global marketing campaigns and social media have been additional forces. The latter especially affect young people so that shifts in alcohol consumption have important demographic features (Deconinck & Swinnen 2015).

Excise and import taxes on beverages vary greatly across countries and across beverage types too (Anderson 2010, 2014). In some cases, those consumer tax differences are to protect local producers, thereby reinforcing climate-induced differences in the consumption mix. Generic value-added taxes as well as a variety of regulations that affect availability of alcoholic beverages also vary across countries (see next section).

In addition, temperance movements and religious groups have had different effects on the social acceptability of alcohol consumption at different times in various places (see, e.g., Eddy 1887; Wilson 1940; Briggs 1985; Pinney 1989, 2005; Phillips 2014). So too have personal concerns about human health: As per capita incomes rise, people can afford to spend more on alcohol consumption, but they also choose to limit its volume for health reasons (in some cases, switching to soft drinks including bottled water); and some people are also substituting with (especially still red) wine because of its perceived positive influence on health when drunk in moderation.

The degree of substitutability between alcoholic and soft drink consumption also may vary across countries because of differences in costs and availability of nonalcoholic drinks and other stimulants. For example, retail prices of soft drinks vary greatly between countries[3] and so too does the availability of low-cost reticulated potable water. Also influential are the availability and prices of (legal or illegal) recreational drugs (Clements *et al.* 2010). These facts suggest further reasons to expect differences across countries in alcohol consumption.

Given all of these possible influences on beverage consumption patterns, it would not be surprising if convergence in those patterns was not evident in the data, notwithstanding Stigler & Becker (1977).

4.1. Alcohol consumption and income

When total alcohol consumption per capita is plotted against real income per capita, for countries spanning the world from 1961 to 2014, the data suggest that the volume of consumption first tends to rise with per capita incomes but then falls (Figure 1). The peak consumption occurs at a real per capita income (in 1990 International Geary-Khamis dollars) of $16,900 in the case of all alcohol. That is just slightly above what the average per capita income of Western Europe was in 1990.[4]

Data on alcohol consumption suggest that it has nearly trebled globally over the past half century (Anderson *et al.* 2017a, table 151). However, those standard data refer only to what has been recorded by national governments and so overstate the rise because not all alcohol consumption is recorded: The poorer a country is, the larger is the share of alcohol consumption that is unrecorded. The World Health Organization (WHO 2015) reports survey estimates of the volume of unrecorded alcohol consumption in 98 countries for 2000, 2005, and 2010. When these are added to recorded alcohol consumption, an inverted U-shaped curve still

---

[3] Soft drink prices for 2013–2015 range from an average of 70 US cents per liter in Africa and the Middle East to 260 cents in Australasia (Euromonit. Int. 2016).
[4] Longer time-series data for 17 high-income countries back to 1888 add support to the inverted-U finding from Figure 1 (see Holmes & Anderson 2017a,b).

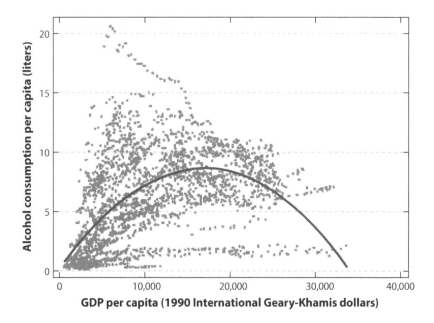

Figure 1. Relationship between recorded alcohol consumption volume and real GDP per capita, for 53 countries/ regions, from 1961 to 2014 (one dot per country-year). Real GDP per capita data points are in 1990 International Geary-Khamis dollars calculated from www.ggdc.net/maddison/maddison-project/data.htm. The curved line is a fitted quadratic regression line. Authors' compilation from the public database provided by Holmes & Anderson (2017b).

exists, although it is somewhat flatter than that just for recorded consumption (Figure 2).

If consumers switch from quantity to quality of consumption as their incomes rise, the inverted U-shaped curve would be flatter for alcohol expenditure. Holmes & Anderson (2017b) indeed find that expenditures on alcohol rise with income at low-income levels (as with volume) but do not decline with income growth at higher-income levels (Figure 3).

When alcohol expenditure data are disaggregated into the three key beverage types, they reveal that while both wine and beer expenditures rise with aggregate expenditure, spending on spirits peaks at an aggregate national expenditure level of $27,800 per capita (in 2015 US dollars) and declines thereafter (Holmes & Anderson 2017b).

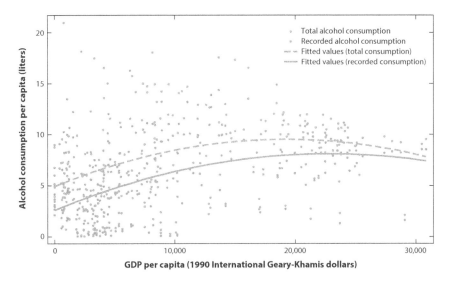

Figure 2. Relationships between alcohol consumption volume and real GDP per capita, recorded and total (recorded plus unrecorded), for 98 countries, in 2000, 2005, and 2010 (one dot per country-year). Real GDP per capita data points are in 1990 International Geary-Khamis dollars calculated from www.ggdc.net/maddison/maddison-project/data.htm. Authors' compilation from the public database provided by Holmes & Anderson (2017b).

4.2. Alcoholic versus nonalcoholic beverages

As of 2010–2014, alcohol composed nearly two-thirds of the world's recorded expenditure on beverages, with the rest being bottled water (8%), carbonated soft drinks (15%), and other soft drinks such as fruit juices (13%). Those beverage shares vary across regions (Table 1).

Globally, during 2001 to 2015 the world's volume of alcohol consumption increased by one-quarter while that of nonalcoholic beverages rose by two-thirds. However, global retail expenditure (including taxes) on those two product groups rose by similar current US dollar amounts: 81% for alcoholic and 90% for nonalcoholic beverages (Euromonit. Int. 2016, Holmes & Anderson 2017a). Assuming there is more scope to upgrade the quality of alcoholic beverages than there is for soft drinks, the fact that the difference between the volume and value increases for alcohol consumption is consistent with the above finding that the volume of alcohol

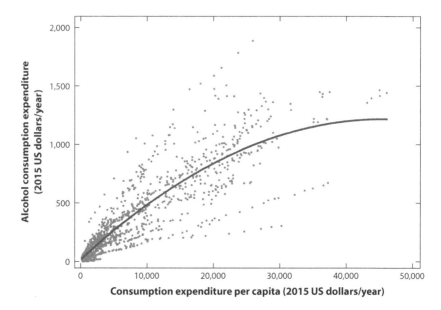

Figure 3. Relationship between per capita aggregate expenditure and recorded alcohol expenditure, for 80 countries, from 2001 to 2015 (US$/year in 2015 dollars, one dot per country-year). Authors' compilation from the public database provided by Holmes & Anderson (2017b).

Table 1. Shares of beverage household expenditure by beverage type from seven regions spanning the world, 2010–2014. Authors' compilation from the public database provided by Holmes & Anderson (2017a)

Region	Budget Shares of Alcohol Expenditure (%)			Beverage Shares of All Expenditure (%)				Alcohol as % of All Beverage Expenditure
	Beer	Wine	Spirits	All Alcohol	Bottled Water	Carbonates	Other Soft Drinks	
Western Europe	40	34	26	3.88	0.54	0.73	0.53	68
Eastern Europe	46	20	34	5.87	0.53	0.76	0.72	74
Australasia	53	28	19	3.49	0.17	0.77	0.51	71
North America	48	21	30	1.94	0.34	0.66	0.58	55
Latin America	64	10	26	4.22	0.61	2.01	0.76	56
Africa/Middle East	60	15	25	2.49	0.57	1.14	0.58	52
Asia	35	15	50	4.29	0.32	0.49	1.07	70
World	44	21	35	3.46	0.43	0.79	0.72	64

consumption traces a much more pronounced inverted U-shaped curve as total expenditure rises than does the value of alcohol consumption.

4.3. Trends in the mix of wine, beer, and spirits consumption

The global mix of recorded alcohol consumption has changed dramatically over the past half century: Wine's share of the volume of global alcohol consumption has fallen from 34% to 13% since the early 1960s, while beer's share has risen from 28% to 36%, and spirits' share has gone from 38% to 51%. In liters of alcohol per capita, global consumption of wine has halved, while that of beer and spirits has increased by 50% (Anderson et al. 2017b).

Several studies find a convergence in the consumption mix of alcoholic beverages. Smith & Solgaard (2000) and Bentzen et al. (2001) found that, in Europe, the market shares for traditional beverages declined. In the Nordic countries, for example, the traditional dominance of spirits diminished as beer and wine shares grew. Colen & Swinnen (2016) also find that, in many traditional beer- (wine-) drinking countries, the share of beer (wine) in total alcohol consumption is declining and that of wine (beer) is increasing.

To study convergence across all countries and all alcohols, Holmes & Anderson (2017b) define a consumption intensity index for country i as its fraction of beer, wine, or spirits consumption in total national alcohol consumption volume or value divided by the fraction of that same beverage in world total alcohol consumption. The indices in Table 2 reveal that, as of 2010–2014, there remain very wide differences across the regions of the world in their mix of alcoholic beverages consumed.

Nonetheless, there has been significant convergence, although convergence differs among regions and products. Figure 4 illustrates convergence for three different groups based on their traditional consumption patterns. According to which beverage had the highest volume share in 1961–1964, Holmes & Anderson (2017b) classify 19 countries as wine focused, 17 as beer focused, and 17 as spirits focused. On average, there is (a) no convergence in wine-focused countries; (b) convergence in the beer-focused countries not in terms of spirits but in beer and wine consumption [the intensity indices converge from 2.0 (beer) and 0.35 (wine) in the 1960s to

Table 2. Wine, beer, and spirits consumption volume and value intensity indexes, by region, 2013–2015. Authors' compilation from the public database provided by Holmes & Anderson (2017a)

Region	Wine		Beer		Spirits	
	Volume	Value	Volume	Value	Volume	Value
Western Europe	2.51	1.62	0.85	0.90	0.53	0.75
Eastern Europe	0.90	0.93	1.01	1.01	1.03	1.02
Australasia	2.31	1.36	1.09	1.19	0.34	0.54
North America	1.07	1.01	1.16	1.08	0.79	0.89
Latin America	0.58	0.46	1.36	1.44	1.16	1.16
Africa/Middle East	0.82	0.72	1.51	1.34	0.51	0.73
Asia	0.53	0.69	0.85	0.82	1.36	1.41
World	1.00	1.00	1.00	1.00	1.00	1.00

approximately 1.3 for both today]; and (c) convergence in the spirits-focused countries not in terms of wine but in spirits and beer [intensity indices converged from 2.2 (spirits) and 0.6 (beer) in the 1960s to between 1.3 and 0.9 today]. These volume indexes suggest there are still major differences in consumption patterns despite the convergence that has occurred in some regions for some beverages.

Holmes & Anderson (2017b) also analyze value-based indexes to account for the fact that tax-inclusive retail prices of alcoholic beverages vary enormously across regions (Table 2). For the period 2013–2015, all three value intensity indexes are closer to unity than are their volume indexes for three of the regions (Western Europe, Eastern Europe, and North America); two of the three value indexes are closer to unity than are their volume indexes for two regions (Australasia and Africa/Middle East); and for the other two regions, one of the three value indexes is closer to unity than their volume indexes. This comparison suggests that part of the reason for the cross-country variation in volume intensity indexes has to do with the variation in national average retail beverage prices. That, in turn, is partly due to wide differences in consumer taxation of the various beverages (Anderson 2010, 2014).

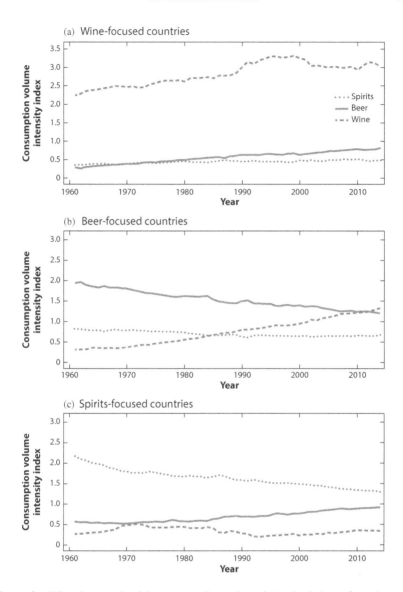

Figure 4. Wine, beer, and spirits consumption volume intensity indexes for subsets of 53 countries/regions, by main focus in 1961–1964, 1961, to 2014. (a) Wine-focused countries; (b) beer-focused countries; (c) spirits-focused countries. The consumption intensity index is defined as a country's fraction of beer, wine, or spirits consumption in total national alcohol consumption volume or value divided by the fraction of that same beverage in world total alcohol consumption. Authors' compilation from public database provided by Holmes & Anderson (2017b).

5. Alcohol regulations

Alcoholic products have been subject to many government regulations and for myriad reasons. Stated — and often conflicting — objectives include: to enhance government revenues through taxes, to protect consumer health, to lower health costs, to reduce violence from alcohol abuse, to raise producer product prices, to reduce the price of producers' inputs (grains), and to constrain market power of producers.

We consider four types of regulations in this review: health regulations, taxes and subsidies, quality and input regulations, and competition regulations.

5.1. Individual and social health regulations

> We are fighting Germany, Austria, and Drink, and as far as I can see, the greatest of these three deadly foes is Drink.
>
> — British Prime Minister, David Lloyd George, 1915[5]

In early history, wine and beer consumption was mostly positively perceived from health and food security perspectives. Both wine and beer were safe to drink in moderation because fermentation kills harmful bacteria. Where available at affordable prices, they were attractive substitutes for water in those settings in which people's access to potable water had deteriorated.[6] Beer was also a source of calories. For both reasons, beer was used to pay workers for their labor from Egyptian times to the Middle Ages. Wine too was part of some workers' remuneration and was included in army rations of some countries right up to World War II. Moreover, spirits such as rum and brandy were a standard part of the diet for those in European navies from the fifteenth century.

Most cultures and religions in ancient civilizations had alcohol deities. Examples are Osiris (Egyptian god of beer and wine), Dionysus/Bacchus (Greek and then Roman god of wine), or Tezcatzontecati

---

[5] Quoted in Hornsey (2003, p. 581).
[6] Potable water became available only from the nineteenth century, with the introduction of major public water projects and hydraulic engineering (Phillips 2014).

(the Aztec god of *pulque,* an alcoholic beverage made from the agave plant in Central America). For the Catholic Church, wine embodied a very strong symbol (the blood of Jesus Christ in communion), and wine was also integral to Jesus's first miracle, in which he turned water into wine at the wedding at Cana (Dion 1959, Johnson 1989, Unwin 1991, Kreglinger 2016). The Catholic Church often instigated winegrowing in New World countries, beginning in Latin America in the sixteenth century. At its beginning in the 1830s, even the Church of Jesus Christ of Latter-day Saints (Mormons) owned vineyards and used wine in their communion services, switching to water only in 1912 (Phillips 2014, p. 213).

In many societies, alcohol consumption was also seen as an aid to medicine. Hippocrates (460–377 BCE), the ancient Greek father of medicine, claimed that wine was a cure for a number of diseases (Hippocrates 1801, Hassan 1998, Phillips 2014). It was prescribed as a medicine by doctors and in hospitals until the nineteenth century (when drug therapy was introduced).[7] The welfare-enhancing use of wine was boosted after Pasteur's discoveries of yeast in the 1860s and the introduction of advanced refrigeration systems to control temperature during fermentation and prevent wine spoilage (Bohling 2012, Meloni & Swinnen 2014).

As for dealing with the welfare-reducing aspects of excessive alcohol consumption, the first major call to ban alcoholic drinks came from the Prophet Muhammad (c. 570–632 CE), founder of Islam.[8] This led to the first comprehensive prohibition policy that banned the production, distribution, and consumption of alcohol (Phillips 2014, p. 59). It is also the longest lasting prohibition, as 1,400 years later it is still in place in many countries with a Muslim majority.

---

[7] Until the mid-nineteenth century, only "natural remedies" such as plants, herbs, roots, and alcohol were used to relieve people's illnesses. This changed from 1869, when the first synthetic drug, chloral hydrate, was discovered (Jones 2011).

[8] Four verses in the Quran refer to wine, but there is consensus that the fourth verse enforces the alcohol prohibition: "Believers, wine and games of chance, idols and divining arrows, are abominations devised by Satan. Avoid them, so that you may prosper. Satan seeks to stir up enmity and hatred among you by means of wine and gambling, and to keep you from the remembrance of Allah and from your prayers. Will you not abstain from them?" (Sura 5, verse 90, in Unwin 1991, p. 150).

Other major regulations to reduce alcohol consumption came only several centuries later. The arrival of distilled spirits changed the general perception of alcohol and led to the introduction of a variety of regulations to limit the consumption of hard liquor in particular, and alcohol more generally. In many cases, these regulations were a combination of taxes and restrictions on the sales of alcohol. From the mid-fifteenth century onward, the Russian tsars imposed a state monopoly on sales of vodka (Pokhlebkin 1992). Around the same time, many German towns introduced regulations on where one could drink (citizens could not drink their brandy on the spot) and when (brandy sales were banned on feast days and during church services) (Forbes 1956, p. 144; Unwin 1991, p. 235). They also imposed taxes on spirits and were soon followed by the Dutch, the English (1643), and the Scots (1644). In France too, brandy was portrayed as a "bad beverage" (in contrast to "healthy" wine). In 1677, brandy sellers were forced to close their shops after 4 PM (Phillips 2014, p. 107).

Two major developments reinforced restrictions and regulations on alcohol use. The first was the industrial revolution, which (*a*) lowered the production cost and hence price of spirits and (*b*) created a class of industrial workers who became large consumers of spirits. Alcoholic drinks became more readily available, stronger, and cheaper. Consumption therefore grew — as did problems of abuse, especially in the industrializing regions (Gately 2008, Phillips 2014).

Britain, the most industrialized country, was the first to introduce a comprehensive anti-alcohol policy during the mid-eighteenth century. Following the "Gin Craze" period early that century, when the consumption of spirits increased massively, the British government implemented the so-called Gin Acts (in 1736 and 1751) to reduce spirits consumption by taxing retail sales and requiring sellers to be licensed (Nicholls 2009).

The second development was the growing availability of non-alcoholic safe drinks. Imports of tea, coffee, and cocoa were growing and, by the 1750s, were widely drunk in Western Europe and the United States (Wickizer 1951, Grigg 2002). Then scientific discoveries during the industrial revolution led to the invention of carbonated soft drinks.

The combination of these factors increased the demand by various groups for much wider restrictions on alcohol consumption, as alcoholic drinks were no longer needed for safe drinking, and the social and personal costs of excessive alcohol use had become much clearer. This translated into the temperance movement, which led to various restrictions on alcohol use.[9] That included total prohibitions in some countries, for example, in Russia from 1914 to 1933, the United States from 1920 to 1933,[10] and in various periods in Mexico, Canada, Finland, Norway, and India.

More recently, attempts have been made to estimate the social costs of excessive alcohol consumption, including as a risk factor for chronic disease and injury. Rehm *et al.* (2009), for example, quantify the burden of mortality and disease attributable to alcohol, both globally and for 10 large countries. An estimated 3.8% of all global deaths and 4.6% of global disability-adjusted life-years are attributable to alcohol. These costs amount to more than 1% of gross national product in high- and middle-income countries, with the costs of social harm constituting a major proportion in addition to health costs.

Current alcohol regulations[11] include restrictions on drinking age, advertising, drink-driving, and pub/liquor store opening hours (see Table 3).[12] Most governments have restricted the density of outlets and opening hours

---

[9] In some cases, restrictions prohibited certain types of alcoholic beverages (in 1916, Norway banned spirits and beer; in 1919, Finland banned all beverages with an alcohol level higher than 2%; and in 1918, Belgium banned distilled spirits), while in other cases, individual purchases of alcohol were limited, or alcohol sales were controlled by state monopolies (Phillips 2014).

[10] For an analysis of the political and economic factors driving the introduction and the repeal of Prohibition in the United States, see Okrent (2010), Malone & Stack (2017), and Poelmans *et al.* (2018).

[11] Several studies have developed comparative scales against which to rank national policies (see, e.g., Lehto 1997; Karlsson & Osterberg 2007; Babor *et al.* 2010, pp. 243–48; Giesbrecht *et al.* 2013; Nelson *et al.* 2013; Naimi *et al.* 2014). Other studies look at the relationship between restrictive policies and the level of consumption (Eisenbach-Stangl 2011, Karlsson *et al.* 2012, Allamani *et al.* 2014, Erickson *et al.* 2014).

[12] The WHO (2014) uses seven categories: (*a*) regulating the marketing of alcoholic beverages (in particular to younger people); (*b*) regulating and restricting availability of alcohol; (*c*) enacting appropriate drink-driving policies; (*d*) reducing demand through taxation and pricing mechanisms; (*e*) raising awareness of public health problems caused by harmful use of alcohol and ensuring support for effective alcohol policies; (*f*) providing accessible and affordable

Table 3. Health regulations on alcohol (beer, wine, and spirits) in China, France, and the United States, 2012. Data compiled from WHO (2014), Fed. Off. Public Health (2017)

Regulation	China	France	United States
Advertising restrictions			
On national TV	Partial restriction on time, place, content	Full ban	Voluntary, self-restricted
On national radio	Partial restriction on time, place, content	Partial restriction on time, place	Voluntary, self-restricted
Age limits			
Alcohol service/sales	No	18 (all three countries)	21 (all three countries)
Drink-driving			
Legal limit for blood alcohol (general/young/professional), in %[a]	0.02/0.02/0.02	0.05/0.05/0.05 (0.02 for public transport)	0.08/by state/0.04
Legally binding regulations on alcohol sponsorship/sales promotion	No/No	Yes/Yes	No/No
Legally required health warning labels on alcohol advertisements/containers	No/No	Yes/Yes	Yes/Yes
Licensing requirements			
Production	Yes	No	Yes
Retail sales	Yes	Yes	No
Restrictions for on-/off-premise sales			
Hours, days/places, density	No, no/no, no	No, no/yes, yes	By state
Specific events/intoxicated persons/petrol stations	No/yes/no	Yes/yes/yes	By state

[a]Definitions of categories: general, general population; young, novice drivers 17–24 years of age; professional, professional and/or commercial drivers with specific license.

of retailers selling alcohol. Canada, Finland, Norway, and Sweden have alcohol state monopolies, whereas Germany, Italy, Spain, and others have restrictions on places and hours of sale (Karlsson & Osterberg 2007, Butler et al. 2017). Other countries regulate the hours during which alcohol can

---

treatment for people with alcohol-use disorders; (g) and implementing in health services screening and brief interventions programs for hazardous and harmful drinking.

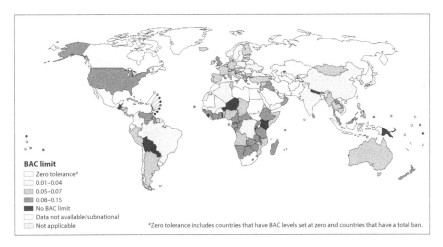

Figure 5. Blood alcohol concentration (BAC) limits for drivers in the general population, 2012. Adapted with permission from WHO (2014, p. 68).

be sold.[13] Most countries have a minimum age for alcohol purchase and consumption; in 115 countries, the age is 18 years (WHO 2014).[14]

The increase in automobile ownership in the twentieth century induced regulations to reduce the drink-driving problem. Most countries have blood alcohol concentration limits between 0.05% and 0.08% (Figure 5); others such as Brazil, Norway, Russia, and Sweden have a zero-tolerance regime (Room *et al.* 2005, Burns 2013).

Restrictions on alcohol advertising range from no restrictions to total bans, across all media types. Of the 158 WHO member states that reported on this in 2012, almost 40% (66 countries) had implemented at least a partial ban on product placement of beer advertisements on television (WHO 2014, pp. 77–78).

5.2. Taxes and subsidies

Alcoholic beverages have been a major source of government revenue through most of history. Unger (2001) documents how, in the Middle

---

[13] For instance, in Peru there is a local ban in Lima on the sale of alcohol during the week from Sundays to Wednesdays after midnight and from Thursdays to Sundays after 3 AM (WHO 2014, p. 71).

[14] In the United States, the National Minimum Drinking Age Act of 1984 required states to raise their minimum drinking age to 21 years (Phillips 2014, p. 305).

Ages and Renaissance, the main source of tax revenue in many towns in Western Europe was beer taxes, comprising up to 80% of revenue.[15] Nye (2007) argues that much of the British Royal Navy — and thus the growth of the British Empire — was financed by porter industry taxes, which could be sustained because of high tariffs on import-competing wine (see Ludington 2013, 2018). Deconinck *et al.* (2016) show that during the 80-year war between Dutch cities and the Spanish Empire in the sixteenth and seventeenth centuries (which led to the separation of the Netherlands), the military expenditures of the Dutch were largely financed by taxes on beer. Nor was it just the Protestants who used beer taxes to finance wars. Catholic Bavarian King Maximilian I used his monopoly on weissbier production and sales to finance the Catholic Counter-Reformation and its army to support the attacks on Protestant forces (Swinnen & Briski 2017).

The first revenue law introduced by the United States Congress was a liquor excise tax in order to finance the debt it had incurred during the American War of Independence in 1775–83 (Hu 1950, Natl. Res. Counc. 1981). Until Prohibition (in 1920), alcohol tax revenues represented up to 80% of all federal internal tax collections in the United States (Natl. Res. Counc. 1981).

With the spread of spirits and growing alcohol abuse, taxation of alcohol served the dual purpose of raising government revenue and reducing consumption (see previous section). However, taxes have also

---

[15] Tax policy also restricted the use of hops, the most important innovation in brewing that would ultimately transform the entire global beer economy. Its use spread only slowly over the beer-producing regions in Europe for several centuries before its use was widely accepted. The main reason for the slow diffusion of this innovation was its impact on the local tax base. Before hops were used, breweries were subjected to a so-called Grutrecht or flavoring license in many regions. This Grutrecht was named after the grut, a combination of herbs that was used to flavor beer (or to disguise faults in the brew) and to preserve it. The Grutrecht was determined by the local authorities and was used to tax breweries. All brewers were obliged to buy grut from the local rulers. To avoid tax evasion, the exact composition of grut was kept a secret (Mosher 2009). The innovation of hops threatened local rulers' revenue from the Grutrecht tax. Therefore, in many regions, including Britain and the Netherlands, the use of hops was prohibited for a long time (Unger 2001). It took several centuries and a reform of the tax system before the use of hops became commonplace in some European regions.

been used to protect domestic industries from foreign competition. For example, in the late-nineteenth and early-twentieth centuries, French import taxes protected domestic markets from imports of wine and raisins. That strongly affected not only trade in wine throughout the Mediterranean region (which at that point accounted for roughly 80% of global wine trade) but also the whole economies of the exporting countries of Spain, Italy, and Greece (Pinilla & Ayuda 2002, Meloni & Swinnen 2016, 2017). Likewise, wine import tariffs were used as a form of protection for vignerons in New World countries such as Argentina, Australia, Chile, and New Zealand (Anderson & Pinilla 2018, chapters 11–13).

Given the wide range of objectives that government policies seek to achieve and the large number of interventions adopted, it is a hazardous exercise to estimate an optimal set of taxes on national alcohol consumption. Attempts have been made (e.g., Kenkel 1996), but all such studies conclude that the optimal tax rates depend heavily on the other policy interventions by the government and on behavioral responses of consumers to those and alternative interventions.

5.3. *Quality and input regulations*

Quality concerns and asymmetric information on alcohol have existed as long as products have been produced and traded. The addition of water in wine, the use of cheap starches to produce beer, and home production of cheap spirits have been documented throughout history and across the globe. Authorities and producer organizations have tried to limit these problems through regulations (Swinnen 2016, 2017).[16] Regulations that refer to quality often relate to certain inputs that can(not) be used.

Over time, regulations have increased both geographically and in addressing new concerns. A crucial aspect of such regulations is that they may enhance aggregate welfare, e.g., by protecting consumers from

---

[16] The oldest written (literally, in stone) set of regulations come from Babylon, 2,000 BCE, and the Code of Hammurabi, King of Babylon, states that "If a wine-seller make the measure for drink smaller than the measure for corn, they shall ... throw her in the water" (Lyon 1904, Vincent 1904).

inferior (or unhealthy) products; but they can also be used to protect vested interests of producer groups at the expense of consumers. Alcohol regulations have done both.

In the case of beer standards, the German Reinheitsgebot is arguably the oldest still-active food law in the world. It demonstrates how beer standards, protection, and international integration interact. The Reinheitsgebot, or Purity Law, decrees that all beer be made from three ingredients: barley, water, and hops (yeast was added later when it was discovered). It was signed into law by Duke Wilhelm IV for Munich in 1487 and for all of Bavaria in 1516. It is generally argued that the Reinheitsgebot served first as a consumer protection policy — to ensure the quality and safety of beer (as brewers experimented with various additives) — and to protect consumers from rising bread prices if wheat was used for beer production. Later, however, brewers became the strongest lobby for it. Changes in the political constellations of Bavaria and Germany over the next five centuries were intertwined with discussions on the Reinheitsgebot because of the protection it provided to Bavarian and German brewers. After five centuries, the European Court of Justice (ECJ) ruled in 1987 that the Reinheitsgebot was a nontariff barrier and ordered it to be removed, at least for foreign beers.[17] The Reinheitsgebot transitioned to a private quality label as German breweries began advertising their adherence to the Reinheitsgebot on bottles.

Other input regulations in beer were introduced when grain was scarce. This was the case in the period 1915–1950, due to a combination of wars and economic declines. In both Europe and the United States, food and feed shortages meant that grains were expensive. The US government imposed grain rationing because of war-time emergencies, which induced the American brewers to brew beer with a lower alcohol content of 2.75% (Stack 2003). Government regulations on inputs of

---

[17] After the 1987 ECJ ruling, imports of foreign beer increased from 1% of German beer consumption to around 3% a decade later and around 8% three decades later. These numbers confirm the protectionist nature of the Reinheitsgebot but also suggest that other forces are at work. Van Tongeren (2011) argues that taste and consumer perception probably also played a big role in the slow change.

brewing continued during the Great Depression and the Dust Bowl, effectively changing the American consumers' tastes and preferences for lighter beer.

The case of wine standards is different in that several standards were introduced to protect producer interests from the beginning, although consumer benefits were often used to justify them. Most were introduced first in France, as a protectionist reaction to international trade; then with international integration, the standards expanded to much of Europe. By the mid-nineteenth century, France was the world's leading producer and exporter of wine. However, a dramatic invasion of the vine disease caused by the parasite *Phylloxera* destroyed many vineyards. French wine production fell by 70% between 1875 and 1889, and France became a net wine importer. Imports came initially mostly from Spain and Italy (Pinilla & Ayuda 2002) but later also from Algeria and Tunisia, France's North African colonies (Meloni & Swinnen 2013, 2014, 2018a).

When French vineyards recovered thanks to the use of resistant grape rootstocks from the United States, wine prices fell as expanding French production competed with imports. Under pressure from French producers, the government introduced several regulations. In addition to import tariffs, they included the following:

- Regulations explicitly linking the quality of the wine, its production location (the terroir), and the traditional way of producing wine: Between 1905 and 1912, regulations formally established the boundaries of Bordeaux, Cognac, Armagnac, and Champagne, called Appellations (Simpson 2011).
- Wine could no longer be produced from imported grapes, effectively destroying the raisin exports from Greece to France and today defining wine in the European Union (Meloni & Swinnen 2017).
- Restrictions on grape varieties and production methods included the prohibition of hybrid vines. The official argument was safety, as hybrid-based wines were argued to be harmful for human consumption. Later, these standards were integrated in the Appellations d'Origine Controlees (AOC), which restricted production to specific regions and grape varieties and imposed maximum vineyards yields, etc.

- Later regulations introduced minimum prices for wine producers, and planting rights were regulated (Gaeta & Corsinovi 2014, Deconinck & Swinnen 2015, Meloni & Swinnen 2018b).

Many French wine regulations were integrated into the official EU wine policy. These regulations thus expanded to a vast wine-producing region. As was initially the case in France, EU wine cannot be produced from imported grapes, hybrid vines are outlawed for quality wines, and vineyard planting is highly regulated.

EU winegrowers have been effectively subsidized through these regulations plus other support measures. It is difficult to estimate the extent of such assistance, but one recent attempt suggests in aggregate that they may have raised gross producer returns by as much as 20% (Anderson & Jensen 2016).

Regulations to protect the quality of spirits also abound, again with a mix of producer and consumer interests being served (Blue 2004). The large number of distilled beverages and the wide range of regulations in many countries make it impossible to provide a summary of them here.

5.4. *Competition regulations*

Competition issues have been especially important in the brewery sector because of its growing concentration after World War II. Regulations have addressed both horizontal and vertical competition concerns.

In horizontal terms, the main issue is the increasingly dominant power of a few brewers with increasing consolidation of breweries in the twentieth century, a process reinforced by global mergers and acquisitions (M&As) in the twenty-first century (see next section). In both the United States and the European Union, competition authorities have intervened several times to control anti-competitive behavior of large-scale breweries and have forced divestitures with M&As (Slade 1998, 2011; Tremblay & Tremblay 2005; Elzinga & Swisher 2011). Most recently, the takeover of SAB Miller by AB InBev, the world's two largest brewing multinationals, is inducing competition authorities worldwide to look into the competition implications for their local markets.

Vertical competition has often focused on vertical relationships, in particular "tied houses."[18] They have been an important feature of pubs in many countries.[19] In the United Kingdom, two-thirds of pubs are tied to regional breweries and so-called pub companies or pubcos (real estate companies specializing in pubs, for which they also act as exclusive beer distributors; see Gottfried & Muir 2011). It is estimated that approximately 60% of pubs in the Netherlands and Belgium have some form of contract (Van Passel & Wauters 2009, Pleijster et al. 2011). In addition, about 30% of Belgian pubs early this century had some form of exclusivity contract with one brewer, AB InBev (Eur. Comm. 2002).

The tied house system has received much criticism as an institution of market power. In the United States, tied houses have been illegal since 1933. After the repeal of Prohibition, a three-tier system was introduced with a strict separation between production, distribution, and retailing of alcohol (Adams 2006).[20] In the United Kingdom in the 1980s, complaints led the Thatcher government to force a divestiture of tied houses by breweries, in the hope of improving the situation of formerly tied publicans. In retrospect, however, it has become clear that the divestiture was a failure. It has merely caused a shift from pub ties with breweries to ties with real estate companies (Slade 1998, 2011).

Deconinck & Swinnen (2016) explain why tied houses are common and why they are charged high prices for their beer supplies. They do so with a model of rational agents who decide to join in a contractual

---

[18] Pubs with exclusivity contracts with breweries or drinks distributors are known as tied houses. Often, the building in which the pub is located is the property of the brewery or is being rented by the brewery from a third party on behalf of the publican. In other cases, the brewery has made financial or material investments in the pub, for example, by giving loans or providing furniture. In return, publicans agree to exclusively buy products from that brewery.

[19] See, for example, studies by Pleijster et al. (2011) on the Dutch market and a few studies on the UK market such as that by Gottfried & Muir (2011), Slade (1998, 2011) on competition policy and the divestiture of brewer-owned pubs, and Preece (2008) and his colleagues (Preece et al. 1999) on public house retailing in the United Kingdom.

[20] Interestingly, the prohibition of links between brewers and pubs in the United States created problems for craft brewers in recent years, as brew pubs were not allowed (Malone & Lusk 2016).

arrangement, taking into account important transaction costs, credit market imperfections, moral hazard, and differences in risk aversion. The widespread prevalence of tied houses (and the growth of pub companies with the forced divestiture of pubs in the United Kingdom) is driven by credit constraints on the part of publicans.

6. Industrial organization

The industrial organizations (IOs) of the beer, wine, and spirits industries differ substantially.[21] The beer industry is the most consolidated, whereas the wine industry is least so: The top five brewing companies have a global market share of more than 50%, whereas this is only 8% in the wine industry. The spirits industry is in between with 22% (Table 4). We discuss each in turn.

6.1. *Consolidation and a craft revolution in the brewing industry*

There have been major changes in the industrial organization of the brewing industry, equal to some of the most radical structural transformations of any industry (Elzinga *et al.* 2018). Throughout most of history, beer brewing was a household activity, often performed by women. Later, in the Early Middle Ages, monasteries became the centers of brewing in Europe. This lasted until the discovery of hops, as a way to preserve beer, allowed commercial brewing and the emergence of beer trade. Scale economies were fairly small and so were breweries until the scientific and industrial revolution transformed the brewing industry by yielding insights into the process of brewing and into creating scale economies.

The period of consolidation and homogenization in the beer industry started around 1900 in most countries. Breweries merged, were acquired,

---

[21] We focus on horizontal IO issues and ignore vertical relationships. Vertical IO issues relate to the downstream relations with wholesalers, retailers, and bars (as discussed in the previous section) and to the upstream relationships with suppliers of raw materials. The latter was particularly important in Eastern Europe in the 1990s when breweries were restructured, with significant foreign direct investment and upgrading of the entire vertical supply chain (see Swinnen & Van Herck 2011) — an issue that is highly relevant in today's brewery investments in Africa.

Table 4. Leading producer shares of global beer, wine, and spirits production, 2014. Data from Inst. Alcohol Stud. (2018)

Producer	Leading Producers (%)
Beer	
AB InBev	21
SABMiller	10
Heineken	9
Carlsberg	6
CR Snow Breweries	6
Total (top 5 producers)	52
Wine	
Constellation Brands	3
E & J Gallo	2
The Wine Group	2
Treasury Wine Estates	1
Total (top 4 producers)	8
Spirits	
Diageo	9
Pernod Ricard	5
Hite Jinro	3
Thai Beverage	3
Beam Suntory	2
Total (top 5 producers)	22

or went bankrupt. In the United States, the number of breweries fell from 421 in 1947 to fewer than 50 by 1980, with just a small number of beer styles dominating an increasingly homogenized market. In other traditional beer markets, the number of breweries fell by more than 90% over the same period (Table 5).

The reasons for this consolidation are well known (Tremblay & Tremblay 2005, Swinnen 2011). Technological progress — such as automation of beer production and packaging, lower distribution costs, and improved road networks — led to greater economies of scale (Gourvish 1994, Adams 2006). The introduction of bottom-fermented beers (lagers)

Table 5. Number of breweries and average brewery size in the United States, United Kingdom, and Belgium, 1900 to 1980 (index 1900 = 100). Adapted from Swinnen (2011, table 1.2)

Year	United States	United Kingdom	Belgium
Number of breweries			
1900	100	100	100
1920	Prohibition	45	62
1940	38	13	35
1960	13	6	13
1980	6	2	4
Average brewery size			
1900	100	100	100
1920	Prohibition	211	125
1940	376	544	225
1960	1,936	1,289	600
1980	8,764	5,344	2,900

led to higher fixed costs, as cooling is needed during fermentation and maturation. Large-scale advertising led to an escalation of sunk advertising costs, especially on commercial television (George 2009).

From the 1990s onward, consolidation went international. Cross-border M&As led to a few multinationals dominating the global market, notably AB InBev (21%), SABMiller (10%), and Heineken (9%). As of late 2017, AB InBev took over SABMiller, resulting in the world's two largest alcohol beverage companies and making it the third-biggest corporate takeover in history.

The consolidation and, even more, the homogenization of beers triggered the rise of craft brewing.[22] With the ascent of craft beer, the number of breweries increased again (Figure 6), and their share of the total beer market grew rapidly (Figure 7).

---

[22] Regulations have also affected the growth of craft brewing, either by restricting their growth (e.g., in Japan, and early on in the United States through the prohibition of home-brewing) or by stimulating it through tax advantages. Legalization of home brewing represented a key factor to facilitate entry of craft brewers.

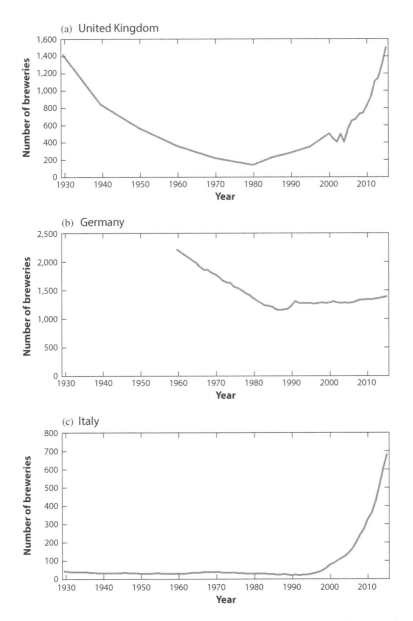

Figure 6. Number of breweries (a) the United Kingdom, (b) Germany, and (c) Italy, from 1930 to 2015. Adapted from Garavaglia & Swinnen (2017, 2018).

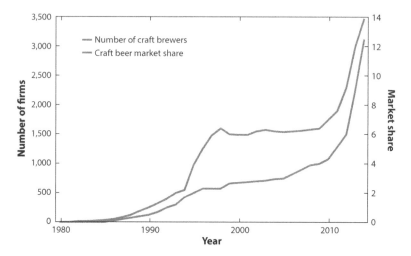

Figure 7. Number of craft brewers and craft beer market share in the United States (%), from 1980 to 2014. Adapted from Elzinga et al. (2018).

In countries where post-World War II consolidation was stronger and where craft brewers emerged earlier, the turnaround in the number of breweries occurred earlier.[23] For example, in the United States and the United Kingdom, the total number of breweries was at its lowest point around 1980. In the United States, the total number of breweries has since grown from fewer than 50 to more than 3,500, the vast majority of which are craft-type breweries. The growth of craft breweries started later and is less rapid in

---

[23] In some countries, it is relatively easy to identify the start of the craft revolution. Elzinga et al. (2018) point in the United States to when Fritz Maytag bought the Anchor Brewing Company of San Francisco in 1965. Similarly, van Dijk et al. (2018) identify the start in the Netherlands to when the first new brewery since World War II was launched in 1981. The first brew pub in Italy started in 1988 (Garavaglia 2018); in Australia craft brewing started around 1980 (Sammartino 2018). In the United Kingdom, the origin of the craft beer movement is typically associated with the emergence of the CAMRA association during the 1970s. In a way, Belgium has to some extent always been a craft beer nation (Swinnen & Briski 2017). In Germany, it is even more difficult to classify the beginning of craft beer given the continual historical presence of small and local producers (Depenbusch et al. 2018). However, in these countries, there is also a clear time period when new, mostly smaller, breweries started producing new specialty beers.

Table 6. Number of breweries per million inhabitants in key high-income countries, 1980 to 2015. Adapted from Garavaglia & Swinnen (2017, table 2)

Country	1980	1990	2000	2010	2015
Belgium	14.5	12.6	11.0	11.3	17.6
Germany	17.4	15.5	15.7	16.4	17.0
Italy	0.5	0.3	1.3	5.5	11.2
Netherlands	0.9	1.6	3.8	7.3	23.0
United Kingdom	2.5	4.9	8.5	13.1	23.0
United States	0.2	1.1	5.3	5.7	10.9

countries such as Belgium and Germany where more breweries survived the twentieth-century consolidation. They had (by far) the highest number of breweries per capita in the 1980s: 17.4 (Germany) and 14.5 (Belgium), respectively, per million people compared to less than 1 in the United Kingdom and the United States (Table 6). A third pattern is evident in countries with historically fewer breweries per capita because they consumed mostly other types of alcohol, such as wine in the case of Italy. In these countries, the recent growth of craft production has increased the number of breweries. As a result, the number of breweries per million people is converging across these different beer markets: In 2015, it was between 10 and 25 in all these countries. The emergence and growth of the craft breweries are thus strongly linked to the consolidation in the traditional brewing industry.

While the success of craft beer initially took the macrobrewers by surprise, they soon responded by a mixed strategy of (a) their own production of craft-style beer; (b) takeovers of successful craft breweries; and (c) using their control over bars and retailers to reduce access by craft breweries (Garavaglia & Swinnen 2017, 2018). As a result, a sizable share of the craft beer market is supplied now by multinational macrobreweries.

6.2. Firm concentration in the wine industry

The wine market is much more fragmented than that of beer, spirits, or soft drinks, with no single company holding a substantial share of the global market. The extent of concentration is far greater in the so-called

Table 7. Share (%) of national wine sales volume by the four largest firms, 2014. Adapted from Anderson et al. (2017a, Table 44)

Country	First	Second	Third	Fourth	Residual
Italy	8.1	7.8	1.2	1.1	81.8
Portugal	3.1	2.4	2.1	2.1	90.3
Spain	11.0	3.7	3.6	1.8	79.9
Austria	6.3	2.1	0.6	0.6	90.4
Germany	1.2	1.1	1.1	1.0	95.6
Greece	7.9	6.9	3.4	2.8	79.0
Switzerland	12.9	7.7	4.0	0.8	74.6
Bulgaria	12.2	11.1	9.5	6.9	60.3
Hungary	8.6	4.4	3.1	2.8	81.1
Romania	11.3	10.8	9.5	6.1	62.3
Russia	4.1	3.8	3.4	2.8	85.9
Ukraine	8.6	8.6	8.3	7.6	66.9
Australia	15.9	9.3	9.2	7.0	58.6
New Zealand	23.4	11.4	9.5	8.7	47.0
Canada	11.9	10.6	7.2	4.1	66.2
United States	22.9	14.5	12.9	5.6	44.1
Argentina	27.0	14.1	12.0	6.6	40.3
Chile	30.5	29.6	29.1	1.4	9.4
South Africa	30.5	2.5	1.6	1.4	64.0
China	3.2	2.8	1.0	0.9	92.1

New World than in Western Europe, however: The top four firms have domestic sales of less than 20% in total in most Western European countries (and less than 10% in Austria, Germany, and Portugal), whereas the top four firms have domestic sales of more than 40% of the total in Argentina, Australia, Chile, New Zealand, and the United States (Table 7). Nor is that difference between the Old and New Worlds just recent: Australian firms began to consolidate when exports took off in the first globalization wave (Anderson & Aryal 2015, pp. 21–23).

Constellation Brands, the world's largest wine company, represents less than 3% of the global wine market, despite its acquisitions of recent times.[24] The consolidations that have occurred have provided the opportunity to reap large economies of scale not only in winemaking but also in distribution and brand promotion, including through establishing their own sales offices abroad rather than relying on distributors. The large volumes of grapes grown and purchased by these firms from numerous regions in the Southern Hemisphere have enabled them to produce large volumes of consistent, popular wines for specific markets abroad. In particular, the production of large volumes of low-end premium wines that used grapes from several regions, so as to ensure little variation from year to year, suited perfectly the customers of large supermarkets in the United Kingdom. By the mid-1980s, those supermarkets, dominated by Sainsbury's, Marks & Spencer, Waitrose, and Tesco, accounted for more than half of all retail wine sales in the United Kingdom (Unwin 1991, p. 341).

6.3. *Firm concentration in the distilled spirits industry*

The global spirits market lies in between those of wine and beer in terms of industrial concentration. More than 70% of the market is still characterized by small local producers, but in recent decades, the spirits industry has experienced significant consolidation due to international M&As. Two leading producers — British Diageo (owner of Johnnie Walker, the world's top selling whiskey, and Smirnoff, the world's top selling vodka) and French Pernod Ricard (owner of Absolut, the number two vodka, and Chivas Regal, the number two whiskey) — together have 14% of the market (see Tables 4 and 8).

Diageo was formed in 1997 from the merger of Guinness and Grand Metropolitan. Between 2011 and 2012, Diageo acquired local spirits industries such as Mey Icki in Turkey, Ypioca in Brazil, and shares of China's Sichuan Shuijingfang and of India's United Spirits (the largest Indian spirits

---

[24] Among Constellation Brand's acquisitions are BRL Hardy (Australia) and Nobilo (New Zealand) in 2003, Robert Mondavi (United States) in 2004, Vincor International (Canada) in 2006, and Beam Wine Estates in 2008. Similar to the beer and spirits industries, Constellation also owns spirits and wine through the acquisitions of Spirits Marque One (owners of the SVEDKA vodka brand) in 2007, and of the Corona and Modelo beer brands (Constellation Brands 2016, Inst. Alcohol Stud. 2018). Constellation divested itself of its Australian wine assets in 2011 to a private equity firm, Accolade, which continued to operate on a similar scale.

Table 8. Leading global alcohol producers, 2014. Data from Inst. Alcohol Stud. (2018)

Company	Category	Headquarters	2014 Global Revenue (£)	Major Brands
AB InBev	Beer	Leuven	31 billion	Budweiser, Stella Artois, Corona, Skol, Brahma
SABMiller	Beer, cider	London	15 billion	Miller, Peroni, Pilsner Urquell, Grolsch, Aguila, Strongbow, Carling, Castle
Heineken	Beer, cider	Amsterdam	14 billion	Heineken, Amstel, Desperados, Sol, Strongbow
Carlsberg	Beer, cider	Copenhagen	6 billion	Carlsberg, Tuborg, Kronenbourg, Battika, Somersby
Diageo	Spirits, beer, wine	London	10 billion	Johnnie Walker, Smirnoff, Captain Morgan, Baileys, Guinness, Tanqueray
Pernod Ricard	Spirits, wine	Paris	6 billion	Jameson, Absolut, Malibu, Jacob's Creek, Chivas Regal
Constellation Brands	Wine, beer, spirits	Victor, New York	4 billion	Robert Mondavi, Clos du Bois, Blackstone, Modelo, Simi, Ruffino
E & J Gallo	Wine	Modesto, California	3 billion	Andre, Carlo Rossi, Boone's Farm, Barefoot

company). Pernod Ricard bought Allied Domecq in 2005 and the Swedish monopoly V&S Group in 2008 (Jones 2012, Inst. Alcohol Stud. 2018).[25]

The M&As were associated with a global shift in sales. From 2000 to 2015, Diageo's traditional markets in Europe and North America dropped from 83% to 42% of all sales, whereas its sales in fast-growing economies such as Brazil, China, India, and Turkey increased from 10% to 40% in the same period (Inst. Alcohol Stud. 2018).

Along these consolidation trends, the spirits industry is recently also experiencing a craft revolution.[26] In less than two decades, the number of

---

[25] Note that the larger spirits companies also own beer and wine (see Table 8). For instance, Diageo also owns famous beer brands (such as Guinness) and Cognac and Champagne brands (34% of Motet Hennessy). Similarly, in 2010, Pernod Ricard launched its wine company Pernod Ricard Winemakers, which owns, among others, Jacob's Creek, the Australian wine brand.

[26] In the last decade in Norway, the production of artisan Akvavit or aquavit, a spirit that has been produced in Scandinavia since the fifteenth century in various flavors, has grown again (Lascelles 2017).

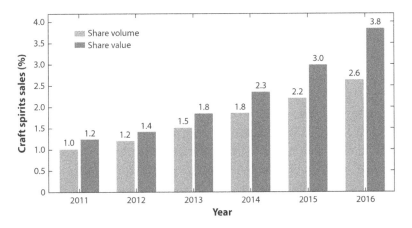

Figure 8. Craft spirits sales as a share of total US spirits volume and value, from 2011 to 2016. Adapted with permission from the Am. Craft Spirits Assoc. (2017).

distilleries increased from 50 to 1,589 in the United States. The market share of US craft spirits increased from 1.2% to 3.8% in value between 2011 and 2015 (Figure 8), confirming very rapid growth (Am. Craft Spirits Assoc. 2017).

7. Conclusions

The past decade has witnessed a rapidly growing literature on the economic aspects of alcoholic beverage production, consumption, trade, and regulation. This article is the first broad review of how alcohol markets have evolved in terms of consumption and industrial organization and how these have interacted with a variety of regulations. It is clear that throughout history, alcoholic drinks have played an important role in food security and health (both positive and negative). Consumption patterns have altered substantially over the past two centuries, as have production technologies and the industrial organization of beverage firms. Governments have intervened in many ways in alcohol markets: They have (a) imposed taxes to raise revenue and to protect domestic industries, (b) introduced regulations to protect individuals' and social health, (c) determined which ingredients can be used in alcohol production, and (d) tried to prevent excessive concentration in vertical and horizontal organizations of the alcohol industry.

Although much has been learned through recent research, there is room for more economic research to further improve our understanding of the contribution of these markets and associated policies and institutions to global welfare. The availability of more data (see also Anderson & Pinilla 2018) allows an update of global demand elasticity estimates to be made, along the lines of those in Selvanathan & Selvanathan (2007) and Srivastava *et al.* (2015), and allows more precise convergence estimates as well. It should also allow us to better disentangle the forces that cause differences in consumer demand across countries and generations, such as differences in quality, taxes, availability of alternatives, etc. This review has pointed to the different relationship of volume versus value with income growth. As with tobacco consumption, the volume of alcohol consumption declines with health concerns rising as income rises; but the value of alcohol consumption does not seem to decline, probably because of a shift to higher-quality products. If so, this shift may benefit consumer health and industry profits simultaneously. These relationships are likely to be affected in the future by the emergence of new products that may influence alcohol consumption, and emerging issues such as the legalization of marijuana or the new attempt by multinational firms to promote alcohol-free beer and low-alcohol wine.

There is also much to learn from further analysis of the changes in alcohol industry structures, and in particular, the quasi-simultaneous process of consolidation and growth of niche products — changes that have already occurred in a dramatic way in the brewing industry over recent decades and that may be developing in other alcohol markets as well.

References

Adams WJ. 2006. Markets: beer in Germany and the United States. *J. Econ. Perspect.* 20(1):189–205

Aizenman J, Brooks E. 2008. Globalization and taste convergence: the cases of wine and beer. *Rev. Int. Econ.* 16(2):217–33

Allamani A, Pepe P, Baccini M, Massini G, Voller F. 2014. Europe. An analysis of changes in the consumption of alcoholic beverages: the interaction among consumption, related harms, contextual factors and alcoholic beverage control policies. *Subst. Use Misuse* 49:1692–715

Am. Craft Spirits Assoc. 2017. *The Craft Spirits Data Project.* Econ. Brief., Oct., Louisville KY. http://americancraftspirits.org/wp-content/uploads/2017/02/2017-Craft-Spirits- Data-Project.pdf

Anderson K. 2010. Excise and import taxes on wine versus beer and spirits: an international comparison. *Econ. Pap.* 29(2):215–28

Anderson K. 2014. Excise taxes on wines, beers and spirits: an updated international comparison. *Wine Vitic. J.* 29(6):66–71

Anderson K. (with the assistance of Aryal NR) 2015. *Growth and Cycles in Australia's Wine Industry: A Statistical Compendium, 1843 to 2013.* Adelaide: Univ. Adelaide Press. https://www.adelaide.edu.au/press/titles/austwine

Anderson K, Jensen HG. 2016. How much government assistance do European wine producers receive? *J. Wine Econ.* 11(2):289–305

Anderson K, Nelgen S, Pinilla V. 2017a. *Global Wine Markets, 1860 to 2016: A Statistical Compendium.* Adelaide: Univ. Adelaide Press. https://www.adelaide.edu.au/press/titles/global-wine-markets

Anderson K, Pinilla V, eds. 2018. *Wine Globalization: A New Comparative History.* Cambridge, UK: Cambridge Univ. Press

Anderson K, Pinilla V. 2017. *Annual database of global wine markets, 1835 to 2016.* Wine Econ. Res. Cent., Univ. Adelaide. https://www.adelaide.edu.au/wine-econ/databases/global-wine-history

Babor T, Caetano R, Casswell S, Edwards G, Giesbrecht N, et al. 2010. *Alcohol, No Ordinary Commodity: Research and Public Policy.* Oxford, UK: Oxford Univ. Press. 2nd ed.

Bentzen J, Eriksson T, Smith V. 2001. Alcohol consumption in European countries. *Cah. d. Econ. Soc. Rur.* (60–61):50–75

Blue AD. 2004. *The Complete Book of Spirits: A Guide to Their History, Production, and Enjoyment.* New York: Harper Collins

Bohling JE. 2012. *The sober revolution: the political and moral economy of alcohol in modern France, 1954–1976.* PhD Thesis, Univ. Calif., Berkeley

Briggs A. 1985. *Wine for Sale: Victoria Wine and the Liquor Trade, 1860–1984.* London: B.T. Batsford

Burns H. 2013. Towards a global alcohol policy: current directions. In *Alcohol: Science, Policy and Public Health*, ed. P Boyle, P Boffetta, A Lowenfels, H Burns, O Brawley, et al., pp. 395–406. Oxford, UK: Oxford Univ. Press

Butler S, Elmeland K, Thom B, Nicholls J. 2017. *Alcohol, Power and Public Health: A Comparative Study of Alcohol Policy.* London: Routledge

Clements K, Lan Y, Zhao X. 2010. The demand for marijuana, tobacco and alcohol: intercommodity interactions with uncertainty. *Empir. Econ.* 39(1):203–39

Colen L, Swinnen J. 2016. Economic growth, globalisation and beer consumption. *J. Agric. Econ.* 67(1):186–207

Constellation Brands. 2016. *2016 summary annual report.* Rep., Constellation Brands, Victor, NY. http://www.cbrands.com/investors/reporting

Deconinck K, Poelmans E, Swinnen J. 2016. How beer created Belgium (and the Netherlands): the contribution of beer taxes to war finance during the Dutch Revolt. *Bus. Hist.* 58(5):694–724

Deconinck K, Swinnen J. 2015. The economics of planting rights in wine production. *Eur. Rev. Agric. Econ.* 42(3):419–40

Deconinck K, Swinnen J. 2016. Tied houses: why they are so common and why breweries charge them high prices for their beer. In *Brewing, Beer and Pubs,* ed. I Cabras, D Higgins, D Preece, pp. 231–46. London: Palgrave Macmillan

Depenbusch L, Ehrich M, Pfizenmaier U. 2018. Craft beer in Germany: new entries in a challenging beer market. In Garavaglia & Swinnen 2018, pp. 183–210

Dion R. 1959. *Histoire de la Vigne et du Vin en France des Origines au XIXe Siecle.* Paris: CNRS

Eddy R. 1887. *Alcohol in History: An Account of Intemperance in AH Ages; Together with a History of the Various Methods Employed for Its Removal.* New York: Natl. Temper. Soc. Pub. House

Eisenbach-Stangl I. 2011. *Comparing European alcohol polices: What to compare?* Policy Brief, June, Eur. Cent. Soc. Welf. Policy Res., Vienna. http://observgo.uquebec.ca/observgo/fichiers/94238_1308130015_ 25850.pdf

Elzinga KG, Swisher AW. 2011. Development in US merger policy: the beer industry as lens. In Swinnen 2011, pp. 173–95

Elzinga KG, Tremblay CH, Tremblay VJ. 2018. Craft beer in the United States: strategic connections to macro and European brewers. In Garavaglia & Swinnen 2018, pp. 55–88

Erickson D, Lenk K, Toomey T, Nelson T, Jones-Webb R, Mosher J. 2014. Measuring the strength of state-level alcohol control policies. *World Med. Health Policy* 6:171–86

Eur. Comm. 2002. Notice published pursuant to article 19(3) of Regulation No. 17 concerning notification COMP/A37.904/F3 — Interbrew. *Off.J. Eur. Comm.* 283(14). https://publications.europa.eu/en/publication-detail/-/publication/a6fdf622-48dd-4248-95b7-f3c57b4e205e/language-en

Euromonit. Int. 2016. *Passport global market information database,* London. http://go.euromonitor.com/passport.html

Fed. Off. Public Health. 2017. *Alcohol regulations in Europe database.* Fed. Off. Public Health, Bern, Switz. http://www.suchtschweiz.ch/index.php?id=808&L=8

Forbes RJ. 1956. Food and drink. In *A History of Technology, Vol. 2: The Mediterranean Civilization and the Middle Ages c. 700 BC to c. AD 1500,* ed. C Singer, EJ Holmyard, AR Hall, TI Williams, pp. 103–46. Oxford, UK: Clarendon

Gaeta D, Corsinovi P. 2014. *Economics, Governance, and Politics in the Wine Market: European Union Developments.* London: Palgrave Macmillan

Garavaglia C. 2018. Birth and diffusion of craft breweries in Italy. In Garavaglia & Swinnen 2018, pp. 229–58

Garavaglia C, Swinnen J. 2017. The craft beer revolution: an international perspective. *Choices* 32(3):1–8

Garavaglia C, Swinnen J, eds. 2018. *Economic Perspectives on Craft Beer: A Revolution in the Global Beer Industry.* London: Palgrave MacMillan

Gately I. 2008. *Drink: A Cultural History of Alcohol.* New York: Gotham

George LM. 2009. National television and the market for local products: the case of beer. *J. Ind. Econ.* 57(1):85–111

Giesbrecht N, Wettlaufer A, April N, Asbridge M, Cukier S, et al. 2013. *Strategies to Reduce Alcohol-Related Harms and Costs in Canada: A Comparison of Provincial Policies.* Toronto: Cent. Addict. Ment. Health

Gottfried G, Muir R. 2011. *Tied down: the beer tie and its impact on British pubs.* Work. Pap., Inst. Public Policy Res., London

Gourvish TR. 1994. Economics of brewing, theory and practice: concentration and technological change in the USA, UK and West Germany since 1945. *Bus. Econ. Hist.* 23(1):253–61

Grigg D. 2002. The worlds of tea and coffee: patterns of consumption. *GeoJournal* 57(4):283–94

Hassan J. 1998. *A History of Water in Modern England and Wales.* Manchester, UK: Manchester Univ. Press

Hippocrates. 1801. *Traduction des Oeuvres Médicales d'Hippocrate, sur le Texte Grec, d'Après l'Édition de Foës.* Toulouse: Maison Broulhiet

Holmes AJ, Anderson K. 2017a. *Annual Database of National Beverage Consumption Volumes and Expenditures, 1950 to 2015.* Wine Econ. Res. Cent., Univ. Adelaide. https://www.adelaide.edu.au/wine-econ/databases/alcohol-consumption

Holmes AJ, Anderson K. 2017b. Convergence in national alcohol consumption patterns: new global indicators. *J. Wine Econ.* 12(2):117–48

Hornsey IS. 2003. *A History of Beer and Brewing.* Cambridge, UK: R. Soc. Chem.

Hu T-Y. 1950. *The Liquor Tax in the United States, 1791–1947.* New York: Columbia Univ. Press Inst.

Alcohol Stud. 2018. *The alcohol industry.* Factsheet, Inst. Alcohol Stud., London. http://www.ias.org.uk/Alcohol-knowledge-centre/The-alcohol-industry.aspx

Johnson H. 1989. *The Story of Wine.* New York: Simon & Schuster

Jones AW. 2011. Early drug discovery and the rise of pharmaceutical chemistry. *Drug Test. Anal.* 3(6):337–44

Jones D. 2012. Diageo leads Pernod in race into emerging markets. *Reuters,* June 10. https://www.reuters.com/article/us-diageo-emergingmarkets/diageo-leads-pernod-in-race-into-emerging-markets-idUSBRE85908720120610

Karlsson T, Lindeman M, Osterberg E. 2012. Does alcohol policy make any difference? Scale and consumption. In *Alcohol Policy in Europe: Evidence from AMPHORA,* ed. P Anderson, F Braddick, J Reynolds, A Gual, pp. 15–23. Brussels: Eur. Comm. http://www.drugs.ie/resourcesfiles/ResearchDocs/Europe/Research/2012/Alco_Policy_Euro_Evidence_From_Amphora_2012.pdf

Karlsson T, Österberg E. 2007. Scaling alcohol control policies across Europe. *Drugs Educ. Prev. Policy* 14(6):499–511

Kenkel DS. 1996. New estimates of the optimal tax on alcohol. *Econ. Inq.* 34(2):296–319

Kreglinger GH. 2016. *The Spirituality of Wine*. Grand Rapids, MI: Eardmans

Lascelles A. 2017. Norway's craft spirit revolution. *Financial Times*, July 21. https://howtospendit.ft.com/food-drink/201315-norway-s-craft-spirit-revolution

Lehto J. 1997. The economics of alcohol. *Addiction* 92(Suppl. 1):S55–59

Ludington CC. 2013. *The Politics of Wine in Britain: A New Cultural History*. London: Palgrave Macmillan

Ludington CC. 2018. United Kingdom. In *Wine Globalization: A New Comparative History*, ed. K Anderson, V Pinilla, pp. 239–71. Cambridge, UK: Cambridge Univ. Press

Lyon DG. 1904. The structure of the Hammurabi Code. *J. Am. Orient. Soc.* 25:248–65

Malone T, Lusk JL. 2016. Brewing up entrepreneurship: government intervention in beer. *J. Entrep. Public Policy* 5(3):325–42

Malone T, Stack M. 2017. What do beer laws mean for economic growth? *Choices* 32(3):1–7

McGovern PE. 2009. *Uncorking the Past: The Quest for Wine, Beer and Other Alcoholic Beverages*. Berkeley, CA: Univ. Calif. Press

McGovern PE, Jalabadze M, Batiuk S, Callahan MP, Smith KE, et al. 2017. Early Neolithic wine of Georgia in the South Caucasus. *PNAS* 114(48):E10309–18

Meloni G, Swinnen J. 2013. The political economy of European wine regulations. *J. Wine Econ.* 8(3):244–84

Meloni G, Swinnen J. 2014. The rise and fall of the world's largest wine exporter — and its institutional legacy. *J. Wine Econ.* 9(1):3–33

Meloni G, Swinnen J. 2016. The political and economic history of vineyard planting rights in Europe: from Montesquieu to the European Union. *J. Wine Econ.* 11(3):379–413

Meloni G, Swinnen J. 2017. Standards, tariffs and trade: the rise and fall of the raisin trade between Greece and France in the late nineteenth century. *J. World Trade* 51(4):711–40

Meloni G, Swinnen J. 2018a. Algeria, Morocco and Tunisia. In *Wine Globalization: A New Comparative History*, ed. K Anderson, V Pinilla, pp. 441–65. Cambridge, UK: Cambridge Univ. Press

Meloni G, Swinnen J. 2018b. The political economy of regulations and trade: wine trade 1860–1970. *World Econ.* 41:1567–95

Mosher R. 2009. *Tasting Beer: An Insider's Guide to the World's Greatest Drink*. North Adams, MA: Storey Publ.

Naimi TS, Blanchette J, Nelson TF, Nguyen T, Oussayef N, et al. 2014. A new scale of the US alcohol policy environment and its relationship to binge drinking. *Am. J. Prev. Med.* 46:10–16

Natl. Res. Counc. 1981. Regulating the supply of alcoholic beverages. In *Alcohol and Public Policy: Beyond the Shadow of Prohibition,* ed. MH Moore, DR Gerstein, pp. 61–78. Washington, DC: Natl. Acad. Press. https://www.ncbi.nlm.nih.gov/books/NBK216427/

Nelson M. 2005. *The Barbarian's Beverage: A History of Beer in Ancient Europe*. London: Routledge

Nelson TF, Xuan Z, Babor TF, Brewer RD, Chaloupka FJ, et al. 2013. Efficacy and strength of evidence of U.S. alcohol control policies. *Am. J. Prev. Med.* 45:19–28

Nicholls J. 2009. *The Politics of Alcohol: A History of the Drink Question in England.* Manchester, UK: Manchester Univ. Press

Nye JVC. 2007. *War, Wine, and Taxes: The Political Economy of Anglo-French Trade, 1689–1900.* Princeton, NJ: Princeton Univ. Press

Okrent D. 2010. *Last Call: The Rise and Fall of Prohibition.* New York: Scribner

Phillips R. 2014. *Alcohol: A History.* Chapel Hill: Univ. N.C. Press

Pinilla V, Ayuda MI. 2002. The political economy of the wine trade: Spanish exports and the international market, 1890–1935. *Eur. Rev. Econ. Hist.* 6:51–85

Pinney T. 1989. *A History of Wine in America: From Beginning to Prohibition*, Vol. 1. Berkeley: Univ. Calif. Press

Pinney T. 2005. *A History of Wine in America: From Prohibition to the Present*, Vol. 2. Berkeley: Univ. Calif. Press

Pleijster F, Van der Zeijden P, Ruis A, Overweel M. 2011. *Rendement en Relatie: Een Onderzoek naar Rendementsverklarende Factoren voorDrankverstrekkende Bedrijven in de Horeca.* Zoetermeer, Neth.: Panteia/EIM

Poelmans E, Dove JA, Taylor JE. 2018. The politics of beer: analysis of the Congressional votes on the Beer Bill of 1933. *Public Choice* 174(1–2):81–106

Poelmans E, Swinnen J. 2011. From monasteries to multinationals (and back): a historical review of the beer economy. *J. Wine Econ.* 6(2):196–216

Pokhlebkin W. 1992. *A History of Vodka.* London: Verso

Preece D. 2008. Change and continuity in UK public house retailing. *Serv. Ind. J.* 28(8):1107–24

Preece D, Steven G, Steven V. 1999. *Work, Change and Competition: Managing for Bass.* London: Routledge

Rabin D, Forget C. 1998. *The Dictionary of Beer and Brewing.* Abingdon, UK: Taylor & Francis. 2nd ed.

Rehm J, Mathers C, Popova S, Thavorncharoensap M, Teerawattananon Y, Patra J. 2009. Global burden of disease and injury and economic cost attributable to alcohol use and alcohol-use disorders. *Lancet* 373(9682):2223–33

Room R, Babor T, Rehm J. 2005. Alcohol and public health. *Lancet* 365(9458):519–30

Sammartino A. 2018. Craft brewing in Australia, 1979–2015. In Garavaglia & Swinnen 2018, pp. 397–423

Selvanathan S, Selvanathan EA. 2007. Another look at the identical tastes hypothesis on the analysis of cross-country alcohol data. *Empir. Econ.* 32(1):185–215

Simpson J. 2011. *Creating Wine: The Emergence of a World Industry, 1840–1914.* Princeton, NJ: Princeton Univ. Press

Slade M. 1998. Beer and the tie: did divestiture of brewer-owned public houses lead to higher beer prices? *Econ. J.* 108:565–602

Slade M. 2011. Competition policy towards brewing: Rational response to market power or unwarranted interference in efficient markets? In Swinnen 2011, pp. 173–95

Smith DE, Solgaard HS. 2000. The dynamics of shifts in European alcoholic drinks consumption. *J. Int. Consum. Mark.* 12(3):85–109

Srivastava PD, McLaren KR, Wohlgenant MK, Zhao X. 2015. Disaggregated econometric estimation of consumer demand response by alcoholic beverage types. *Aust. J. Agric. Resour. Econ.* 59(3):412–32

Stack M. 2003. A concise history of America's brewing industry. In *Economic History Net Encyclopedia of Economic and Business History*, ed. R Whaples. https://eh.net/encyclopedia/a-concise-history-of-americas-brewing-industry/

Stigler GJ, Becker GS. 1977. De gustibus non est disputandum. *Am. Econ. Rev.* 67(2):76–90

Swinnen J, ed. 2011. *The Economics of Beer*. Oxford, UK: Oxford Univ. Press

Swinnen J. 2016. Economics and politics of food standards, trade, and development. *Agric. Econ.* 47(Suppl. 1):7–19

Swinnen J. 2017. Some dynamic aspects of food standards. *Am.J. Agric. Econ.* 99(2):321–38

Swinnen J, Briski D. 2017. *Beeronomics: How Beer Explains the World*. Oxford, UK: Oxford Univ. Press

Swinnen J, Van Herck K. 2011. How the East was won: the foreign takeover of the Eastern European brewing industry. In Swinnen 2011, pp. 247–66

Tremblay V, Tremblay C. 2005. *The U.S. Brewing Industry: Data and Economic Analysis*. Cambridge, MA: MIT Press

Unger RW. 2001. *A History of Brewing in Holland, 900–1900: Economy, Technology, and the State*. Leiden, Neth.: Brill Acad.

Unwin T. 1991. *Wine and the Vine: An Historical Geography of Viticulture and the Wine Trade*. London: Routledge

van Dijk M, Kroezen J, Slob B. 2018. From pilsner desert to craft beer oasis: the rise of craft brewing in the Netherlands. In Garavaglia & Swinnen 2018, pp. 259–93

Van Passel S, Wauters E. 2009. *Vertical agreements: an empirical price analysis of beer*. Paper presented at the Beeronomics Conference, Leuven, Belgium, May 27–30

Van Tongeren F. 2011. Standards and international trade integration: a historical review of the German 'Reinheitsgebot'. In Swinnen 2011, pp. 51–61

Vincent GE. 1904. The laws of Hammurabi. *Am.J. Sociol.* 9(6):737–54

WHO (World Health. Organ.). 2014. *Global Status Report on Alcohol and Health*. Geneva: WHO

WHO (World Health. Organ.). 2015. *Global Health Observatory data repository: levels of consumption*. Accessed December 15. http://apps.who.int/gho/data/node.main.A1022?lang=en&showonly=GISAH

Wickizer VD. 1951. *Coffee, Tea and Cocoa: An Economic and Political Analysis*. Stanford, CA: Stanford Univ. Press

Wilson GB. 1940. *Alcohol and the Nation: A Contribution to the Study of the Liquor Problem in the United Kingdom from 1800 to 1935*. London: Nicholson & Watson

CPSIA information can be obtained
at www.ICGtesting.com
Printed in the USA
JSHW021132141119
2436JS00001B/2